Moral Issues
in Global Perspective

Moral Issues
in Global Perspective

second edition

Volume II: Human Diversity and Equality

edited by

Christine M. Koggel

broadview press

Library and Archives Canada Cataloguing in Publication

Moral issues in global perspective / edited by Christine M. Koggel. — 2nd ed.

Includes bibliographical references.
Contents: v. 1. Moral and political theory — v. 2. Human diversity and equality — v. 3. Moral issues.
ISBN 1-55111-747-9 (v. 1).—ISBN 1-55111-748-7 (v. 2).—ISBN 1-55111-749-5 (v. 3)

1. Social ethics—Textbooks.   I. Koggel, Christine M.

HM665.M67 2006   170   C2005-907079-X

Broadview Press is an independent, international publishing house, incorporated in 1985. Broadview believes in shared ownership, both with its employees and with the general public; since the year 2000 Broadview shares have traded publicly on the Toronto Venture Exchange under the symbol BDP.

We welcome comments and suggestions regarding any aspect of our publications—
please feel free to contact us at the addresses below or at broadview@broadviewpress.com.

North America
Post Office Box 1243, Peterborough, Ontario, Canada K9J 7H5
Post Office Box 1015, 3576 California Road, Orchard Park, NY, USA 14127
Tel: (705) 743-8990; Fax: (705) 743-8353;
email: customerservice@broadviewpress.com

UK, Ireland, and continental Europe
NBN International, Estover Road, Plymouth PL6 7PY UK
Tel: 44 (0) 1752 202300   Fax: 44 (0) 1752 202330
email: enquiries@nbninternational.com

Australia and New Zealand
UNIREPS, University of New South Wales
Sydney, NSW, 2052 Australia
Tel: 61 2 9664 0999; Fax: 61 2 9664 5420
email: info.press@unsw.edu.au

www.broadviewpress.com

Broadview Press gratefully acknowledges the financial support of the Government of Canada through the Book Publishing Industry Development Program for our publishing activities.

Copy-edited by Betsy Struthers.

Typesetting and assembly: True to Type Inc., Mississauga, Canada.

PRINTED IN CANADA

For Locrin

Contents

CHAPTER FOUR: SEXUAL ORIENTATION

CHAPTER FIVE: DISABILITY

CHAPTER SIX: POVERTY AND WELFARE

PREFACE

A central question in ethics is: how should we live our lives and interact with others? Exploring answers to this question in the context of the international community or "global village" in which we live was the prime motivation for putting out the First Edition of this anthology. This motivation persists into the production of this Second Edition, now expanded into three volumes.

The collection works with the idea that we live in an increasingly interdependent world, one in which features and factors of globalization shape the lives and experiences of people no matter who they are or where they live. "Globalization" is a concept used increasingly in a variety of contexts and in ways that are both positive and negative: in discussions of markets, international relations, economic development, human rights, education, health care, the environment, labor, media, and information technology. Globalization can be characterized as increased flows — of people, information, technology, consumer goods, and trade — across ever more permeable borders. Globalization in the form of increased flows of information, for example, has broadened our exposure to beliefs and values very different from our own and allowed us to communicate instantaneously with people from faraway places. The almost limitless access to information through television and the Internet not only makes it possible for us to learn about others, but it also makes it easy to praise or condemn people, policies, practices, values, beliefs, and political structures in other places. Globalization has universalized human rights discourse from its roots in liberal theory and has given a prominent place to international organizations that monitor human rights violations. An important effect of globalization has been to intensify our awareness of the devastating ways in which policies and practices in one area may affect not only the livelihood and choices of people in other areas, but the world as a whole.

Increased globalization not only means that no community is isolated from the world's gaze and influence, but also that virtually no communities remain unaffected by the influx of people from other places. The latter describes the phenomenon of multiculturalism: difference and diversity within a community of people who have various beliefs. Multiculturalism means that we need not look across borders to find instances of discrimination against and unequal treatment of people identified as different. It calls on us to examine the ways in which our embeddedness in particular contexts and practices shapes our perceptions of and interactions with those different from ourselves. Multiculturalism opens the door to examining relationships and to thinking critically about our interactions with others. In making it possible to scrutinize beliefs and practices different from our own, globalization and multiculturalism ask us to critically examine the judgments we render about others both across and within borders.

These facts and effects of globalization and the related phenomenon of multiculturalism raise questions that have become increasingly pressing to moral inquiry. This anthology assumes that these questions are relevant to the central question of how we live our lives and interact with others. Does our situatedness in a Western liberal democratic society generate problematic assumptions about what human beings are like; what we need to flourish; and what rights and responsibilities we hold? Might our commitment to the notion of the primacy of individual liberty rights change if we learned about commitments to rights different from these in contexts, including liberal societies, outside the U.S.? Would our understanding of what constitutes just social and political structures change if we became aware of theories that defend alternative structures, particularly by authors from societies with structures different from our own? Can social relations and policies in other contexts give us insights into ways to approach moral issues of inequality and discrimination in our own context? Does our understanding of the right way to live and of how to determine morally right action reflect the biases of Western liberal beliefs and values? Does the impact of policies in one society on the welfare and well-being of members of another society hinder us from acquiring an adequate understanding of moral, social, and political issues and of how to resolve them? In general, does our view of moral issues change when we turn our attention to the global context?

Most contemporary collections on moral issues make it difficult to raise these questions. They tend to feature the narrow band of agreements and disagreements within Western liberal theory and practice. As with the First Edition, this Second Edition of *Moral Issues in Global Perspective* seeks to challenge our thinking about morality and moral issues as it has been shaped by the Western liberal tradition and to extend the inquiry beyond the context of North America and specifically that of the U.S. It includes analyses of moral issues by both liberal and non-liberal theorists from around the world, many of whom question predominant understandings of human rights, justice, democracy, social welfare, and development. It includes critiques of traditional accounts of moral theory, rights, justice, and democracy, critiques that examine whether these accounts ignore or fail to address the discriminatory treatment of disadvantaged groups inside and outside the borders of countries. It incorporates work by race, class, feminist, and disability theorists that challenges traditional moral and political theory and opens up new perspectives on issues such as reproduction, euthanasia, censorship, animal rights, and environmental ethics.

This collection incorporates these kinds of perspectives into each chapter, more so than is the case with many of the textbooks on practical ethics that are currently available in North America. So, for example, we are asked to confront challenges by non-Western writers that liberal beliefs about the importance of individual rights to free speech and property may reflect a discourse about rights that has little or no application in places with traditions that uphold community values, or with pasts they want to change, or in countries struggling to achieve stability, let alone economic viability. We may need to question our assumptions about gender when we examine the role and activities of women in places like Indonesia. We are asked to think about how issues of reproductive health may be shaped differently in a context like Argentina where a strong tradition of Catholicism pulls against the interests and aspirations of women. This expanded Second Edition gives testimony to the importance of these issues and to the approach to ethics that it adopts.

Even greater efforts were made with this new edition than with the previous to represent the range of theories and the work of theorists from around the world. In its current three volumes, this anthology collects the work of more than 80 authors, thus presenting a broad range of views from all over the world. In doing so, it attempts to show the complexity of moral issues when examined in a global context and the richness and diversity of writing on these issues by authors outside American and Western thought more generally. Of course, one cannot move in new directions without a base in the familiar. Many of the readings are intended to reflect not only the wide spectrum of views among liberal theorists, but also the discussion of moral issues as it takes place in North America. With this background, we can then take up the two challenges of globalization and multiculturalism. A global context of increased awareness of the impact of globalization on the environment, levels of poverty, prospects for human flourishing, and indigenous cultures challenges the notion that answers to complex moral issues can be found by focusing only on Western liberal values in a North American context. *Moral Issues in Global Perspective* stands as an illustration of how the field of moral inquiry is greatly enriched when we turn our attention to disenfranchised voices within particular societies and to contexts outside North America.

This expanded Second Edition is divided into three separate volumes, each of which corresponds roughly with the three parts of the single volume First Edition. Volume I covers kinds of moral and political theory and topics related to these. The first four chapters in Volume I present traditional and contemporary theories of morality and of concepts such as human rights, justice, and democracy. These concepts have been central to Western liberal theory. The fundamental teaching of classical liberal theory that each human being has equal moral value and deserves equal concern and respect has become the foundation for theories about how societies ought to be structured to ensure equal treatment, for accounts of what human beings need in order to flourish, and for attempts to formulate universal human rights. Yet, liberal theory has been criticized for its excessive individualism, an individualism that critics take to be apparent in the policies, structures, and kinds of human rights that liberals tend to defend. This criticism moves to center stage when we turn to a global context and examine theorists who challenge the very framework of individual freedom that dominates accounts of human rights and theories of justice and democracy in Western liberal societies. The final two chapters in Volume I apply insights from these theories to concrete contexts, ones in which awareness of histories and social conditions in specific parts of the world sometimes support and sometimes challenge understandings of justice, human rights, and democracy. Chapter Six applies these insights to the specific and timely issue of war and terrorism.

Volume II continues the exploration of the relevance of globalization and multiculturalism to moral inquiry by zeroing in on accounts of human nature and the moral questions raised by issues of diversity and difference among human beings. Are we all the same? Can we provide a list of essential human functions and capabilities that generates moral imperatives for what it is for human beings to flourish no matter who they are or where they live? Do we operate with a set of assumptions about human beings that result in stereotypes about difference and critical judgments about other people's beliefs and practices? Do facts of discrimination and inequality both across and within borders shape perceptions, self-perceptions, and opportunities in ways that call for international policies to eliminate the resulting injustices? Is it possible to understand the perspectives and life experiences of members of disadvantaged groups from a vantage point of privilege or to speak for them when making judgments about them? Answers to these sorts of questions in the theory chapter that opens Volume II are then followed by several chapters in which discrimination on the grounds of race and ethnicity, gender, sexual orientation, disability, and poverty are examined. These chapters explore moral issues raised by relationships that are shaped by the different histories, identities, and levels of power of people within and across societies. The issues in this volume cut to the heart of the central question of how to interact with others in morally responsible ways.

The relationship of the individual to society tends to be central to most collections about moral issues. Volume III explores the relationship between the individual and society by surveying some of the practical issues that have acquired particular prominence in Western liberal contexts: individual choice and social responsibility at the beginning and end of human life, the value of liberty and its connection to pornography and hate speech, and how we live and interact with animals and the environment. Liberal theory has tended to examine these issues in terms of the conflict between the individual and society: what, if any, restrictions to individual freedom are permissible and what sorts of moral justifications can be provided for using the power of the state to limit individual freedom? The readings in the chapters of Volume III represent both defenses and critiques of this characterization of how practical moral issues need to be resolved, and they open up inquiry into how moral issues are impacted by a global context. Do debates about issues such as reproduction, euthanasia, health care, pornography, hate speech, animals, and the environment change when we learn about concrete practices in non-Western contexts or in places outside North America? Do the policies in place for dealing with these issues in particular contexts have a differential impact on members of traditionally disadvantaged groups?

The three volumes can be used separately or as a whole. Various threads related to globalization and multiculturalism weave their way through all the volumes and allow issues to cross over from one volume to the next. For example, issues of discrimination on the basis of gender and race are covered explicitly in Volume II but can be found in the examination of reproductive issues, pornography, and hate speech in Volume III. Tendencies of ethnocentrism that result in judgments by developed countries about practices and beliefs in developing countries are explored in the conceptions of human rights, justice, and democracy discussed in Volume I and also in the discussions of health care, the environment, and pornography in Volume III. Discussions in Volume I of the significance of historical and cultural contexts in the shaping of beliefs, practices, and values are revisited in Volume II in the examination of discrimination and unequal relations of power between peoples within a country and across the borders of countries. And arguments by theorists in Volume I that defend particular accounts of morally right action or conceptions of justice are applied to specific moral issues in Volume III. While the volumes may have distinctive topics and titles, the issues and themes intersect and are interconnected.

The revision and expansion of the First Edition would not have been possible without the help and support of many people along the way. I want to begin by thanking all the authors who granted permission to print their work in the collection, including both the authors who were first time contributors to the First Edition and whose work reappears in this Second Edition and the authors whose work appears for the first time in this Second Edition. Don LePan, the long time President of Broadview Press who stepped down in 2004, was committed to the project from its earliest stages and has provided encouragement and support throughout and into the preparation of this Second Edition. The torch has been passed to Michael Harrison, someone as committed to supporting authors and their work. Broadview people are wonderful to work with and their competence and care are greatly appreciated. The Production Editors, Barbara Conolly, Jennifer Bingham, and Judith Earnshaw handled this large and complex project with professionalism and enthusiasm throughout. Tania Terrien, Jennifer Findlay, Tammy Roberts, and Joelle Dunne dealt with the many details of permissions and my questions of process and procedures along the way. Betsy Struthers edited each of the volumes in a way that made my job easier and the production process smoother. I would like to thank several anonymous reviewers of early versions of the Second Edition for their helpful suggestions concerning the organization, topics, and readings. A special thanks goes to Keith Burgess-Jackson, whose advice and impressive knowledge of the extensive literature in moral theory and practical issues was as important to the Second Edition as it was to the First.

Countless people took an interest in this project and discussions with them sometimes provided valuable advice and sometimes unearthed readings that have turned out to be key pieces in both the First and Second Editions. In this respect, I would like to thank Susan Babbitt, Nathan Brett, Cheshire Calhoun, David Crocker, Jay Drydyk, Marvin Glass, Jennifer Llewellyn, and Janice Newberry. In doing revisions for the Second Edition, I was fortunate to be in the right places at the right times to discover important and innovative work being done at conferences and colloquia. Working with these people on their contributions to the Second Edition has been a pleasure. In particular, I would like to thank Frank Cunningham, Sally Haslanger, Alison Minea, Roland Pierik, Ingrid Robeyns, Asuncion Lera St. Clair, and Kok-Chor Tan.

I could not have completed the painstaking work of preparing the manuscript if it were not for the competence and dedication of two fabulous Bryn Mawr students: Valori Jankowski and Risa Rice. I cannot say enough about how important they were to the completion of this project. Jessica Moss, Erin McCartney, Erin LaFarge, and Lilian Bürgler are just some of the many students who offered valuable advice as I worked my way through the structure of and selections for the Second Edition. Sue Campbell, Lorraine Code, Lorraine Kirschner, Michael Krausz, Ralph Kuncl, Christine Overall, and Susan Sherwin influenced the project and ensured its completion in ways that only they can know. This is not the first project that Andrew Brook has been there to help me through. His help was, as always, matched by his unwavering confidence in my work and his encouragement and support throughout. Finally, I would like to express my gratitude to the many students with inquiring minds and diverse backgrounds who made this exploration possible and to the young people in my life, to whom I dedicate these volumes. It is they who keep me optimistic about the future.

CHAPTER ONE: THEORIES AND CRITICAL ANALYSIS

INTRODUCTION

Volume I began with theoretical accounts of morality, human rights, justice, and democracy and then moved to examinations of particular contexts and issues that give substance to and raise questions about various understandings of these concepts in moral and political theory. We have learned thus far that there is virtual universal agreement about the principle of equality, the foundational idea that all people are equal and ought to be treated equally. However, there is a great deal of disagreement about the basis for equality and about how the principle should be applied. People are very different one from another. They differ with respect to physical features, capacities, needs, interests, and levels of ability. Differences of these sorts have been and continue to be the basis for determining the distribution of rights and privileges and of social goods such as food, education, and employment. There is now widespread consensus, exemplified in international human rights documents as well as the human rights codes and constitutions of many countries, that specific differences such as race, ethnicity, gender, sexual orientation, and levels of ability and wealth should not be grounds for justifying unequal treatment. However, these very same differences continue to be significant with respect to the inequalities experienced by members of these groups. This is so not only all over the world, but in liberal societies where the belief in the inherent worth of all people is a central tenet and enshrined in many constitutions.

Two main conceptions of equality are prominent in the liberal tradition: formal and substantive equality. They begin with similar accounts of the human capacity to make choices and the value of allowing people the freedom to make their own choices in pursuit of their interests, projects, and goals. However, they arrive at different conclusions about the structures and policies needed to promote freedom and human flourishing. Formal equality theorists argue that people are treated equally when formal and legal barriers barring people from participating in society and from having the opportunities enjoyed by all are removed. Examples of these barriers are laws that once barred African Americans and women, for example, from entering particular establishments, enrolling in professional schools, or having certain jobs. Substantive equality theorists argue that the removal of barriers is necessary but not sufficient — sometimes equality demands that special measures be implemented so that those whose differences have been and continue to be sources of disadvantage can begin to undo the effects of a history of entrenched discrimination. "Leveling the playing field" is a phrase that describes what these programs attempt to achieve. Welfare measures and affirmative action programs are examples of special treatment or positive measures designed to make it possible for members of traditionally disadvantaged groups to achieve genuine or substantive equality.

Discrimination is morally wrong when irrelevant differences are taken to be grounds for justifying unequal treatment. Discrimination is a moral issue when inequalities and disadvantages are generated merely by one's membership in a group and so affect one's life prospects and opportunities. Discrimination is also a moral issue because it represents the breakdown of relationships, sometimes with those in one's community and sometimes with citizens of other countries. A fundamental part of living a good life is to be able to interact with and respond to others in morally appropriate ways. Questions about human diversity and equality raise issues about our responsibility for acquiring a proper understanding of discrimination and its effects on people and for attending to these relations in morally appropriate ways in our daily lives.

This first chapter of Volume II opens with theories of human diversity and the concept of equality. This is then followed by chapters that discuss kinds of discrimination in the form of race and ethnicity, gender, sexual orientation, disability, and poverty. The first three readings of this current chapter on theory outline broad questions about human diversity and sameness, including the question of whether an *essentialist* account of human beings can be formulated. They then explore issues of *ethnocentrism* and *universalism* that often influence assessments by one country of the lives of citizens in other countries and the inequalities they suffer. First, an explanation of these terms, which are also defined in the Introduction to Chapter Two of Volume I. *Essentialism* is the tendency to characterize all human beings as having the same features, capacities, and needs irrespective of social conditions, political contexts, and the particular circumstances of people's lives. *Ethnocentrism* is the disposition to judge foreign peoples or groups by the standards and practices of one's own culture or ethnic group. The term *Eurocentrism* is reserved for the particular bias in favor of the culture and values of Western liberal thinking. *Universalism* is the tendency to view concepts such as human rights and justice ahistorically and in isolation from their social, political, and economic habitat. Often this tendency emerges from generalizing from one's own social context of specific values and political structures to all contexts and all people.

In the first reading, Martha Nussbaum is critical of relativists who argue that there is no vantage point from which judgments about beliefs, practices, and values different from one's own can be rendered. She argues that in the face of the very diverse range of conditions, contexts, beliefs, and practices in the world, we can provide a list of essential human capabilities and needs that generates moral imperatives for what is required to promote human flourishing no matter who the people are or where they live. She defends a version of essentialism that she takes to be sensitive to historical and cultural differences, inclusive with respect to members of various oppressed groups, and open to debate and reformulation. Her account has come to be known as the *capabilities*

approach. This essentialist account of what it is to be human, argues Nussbaum, gives us the tools for criticizing practices in other cultures that disadvantage certain members or treat them unequally.

In the second reading, David Crocker returns us to a discussion of the dangers of ethnocentrism. Assessments about people and policies in other places, biased as they are by a strong tendency to judge others by our own standards and practices, can be particularly pernicious in relationships between Western and non-Western countries. Assumptions about the superiority of values and of models of economic development in rich and powerful North/Western and developed countries have shaped international development policies in poor South/non-Western and developing countries. Crocker attempts to avoid some of the perplexing and difficult questions raised by debates about ethnocentrism and relativism by employing what he refers to as an insider-outsider framework.

Crocker develops an account of insiders and outsiders that captures the roles and knowledge that people have by virtue of being members of particular groups. Insiders are recognized or accepted by a group because the members share such things as beliefs, desires, memories, and hopes. Outsiders are not recognized or accepted as members of a group because they lack shared beliefs, desires, memories, and hopes. Crocker argues that we are all insiders and outsiders in multiple ways and with respect to a variety of groups both within and across cultures. He uses this model of insider and outsider identities and roles to survey the advantages and disadvantages of each in cross-cultural dialogue and in assessments of practices in countries different from our own. He believes that this dialogue can further a global community and global ethic.

The third reading by Philomena Essed and David Goldberg raises questions about essentialism by connecting the contemporary biological discourse about cloning with a cultural discourse that promotes sameness. With the cloning of human beings comes the possibility for erasing difference by reproducing preferred types of human beings: white, male, able-bodied, heterosexual, highly intelligent, and living in economically privileged places. Cloning, they argue, is not merely a biological and scientific issue, but a cultural one that reflects an unspoken tendency to comply with normative standards by reproducing imagined perfections of the same type and profile as those already in positions of power. They argue that a preference for sameness is also evident in a global context that reflects the mass production of Western culture and consumerism in ways that flatten, erase, and undermine difference and diversity.

The last three readings in this chapter turn to questions of diversity and discrimination within countries by focusing on the North American context. Shelby Steele discusses discrimination in the context of defending what he takes to be central to liberal democracy in the U.S.: an emphasis on the freedom and equality of individuals. He applauds the strategies and goals of the early civil rights movements to achieve the integration of women and African Americans into mainstream American society. He argues, however, that the democratic goal of integration has been abandoned in current movements that focus on collective or group entitlements rather than individual rights. According to Steele, the shift in these movements from integration to collective entitlements is evident in separatist strategies such as affirmative action and the creation of African American and women's studies programs. He argues that group entitlements violate the principles upon which American democracy is founded by using the arbitrary characteristics of race, ethnicity, gender, and sexual preference as the basis for identity and claims to entitlement. He defends an account of American democracy that is based on integration, which represents the absence of arbitrary barriers to freedom and the inclusion of all citizens into the sphere of rights it espouses and the range of opportunities it promotes.

Iris Young challenges Steele's depiction of current social movements in the U.S. She agrees that there has been a shift in strategy on the part of members of disadvantaged groups from removing formal barriers to freedom so that all individuals have the same rights and opportunities (formal equality) to affirming group difference and championing special treatment for disadvantaged groups (substantive equality). However, she disagrees with Steele's rejection of substantive equality.

Young grants that the goal of integration has been enormously important in improving the opportunities and lives of individual members of disadvantaged groups. However, she argues that it has had little effect in unsettling the balance of economic and political power, changing the structural patterns of group privilege, or making differences irrelevant to a person's life prospects. She supports strategies of affirming group difference evident in the recovery and promotion of the language, culture, organizations, and experiences of various social groups. A politics of difference promotes group solidarity, provides perspectives from which to criticize prevailing institutions and norms, and unsettles entrenched stereotypes and self-perceptions of difference as inferiority or liability. Young defends a relational understanding of difference, one in which difference is contextual, ambiguous, shifting, and non-essentialist.

Young's analysis undermines the idea that there is a neutral and universal vantage point from which to understand difference and the life experiences of people. Laurence Thomas explores this argument further by asking what is required of us in our relations with those who are disadvantaged or have been wronged. He argues that people who are members of well-defined social categories suffer a kind of pain and misfortune that is distinguishable from that suffered by people who are victims of robberies or car accidents, for example. Being a member of a socially diminished category makes it likely that one's life will be affected by oppressive and prevailing negative attitudes and by the hostile misfortunes specific to that category. Thomas argues that because people are socially constituted by the categories to which they belong and are emotionally configured by the hostile misfortunes they experience as members of a particular category, their lives and experiences cannot be understood from the outside simply through reasoning about oppressive experiences or sympathizing with those who have them. People in socially diminished categories are owed moral deference by those who are not members of these categories. Moral deference is a mode of moral learning owed to those who are oppressed as a way of working toward the elimination of oppression in its various forms and manifestations.

HUMAN FUNCTIONING AND SOCIAL JUSTICE:
IN DEFENSE OF ARISTOTELIAN ESSENTIALISM[1]

Martha C. Nussbaum

Martha Nussbaum is Ernst Freund Distinguished Service Professor of Law and Ethics at the Law School, University of Chicago. She is the author of numerous books, some of the most recent of which include Sex and Social Justice *(1999),* Women and Human Development *(2000), and* Upheavals of Thought: The Intelligence of Emotions *(2001). She is also co-editor of* Women, Culture, and Development: A Study of Human Capabilities *(1995, with Jonathan Glover) and of* The Quality of Life *(1993, with Amartya Sen).*

Nussbaum defends an essentialist account of the human being by providing a list of the most important functions that define human life. She calls her account of human functions and capabilities the "thick vague theory of the good." She argues that this account avoids the problems of a too rigid and universalist metaphysical realism by being sensitive to historical and cultural differences, inclusive with respect to members of various oppressed groups, and open to debate and reformulation.

It will be seen how in place of the *wealth* and *poverty* of political economy come the *rich human being* and rich human need. The *rich* human being is simultaneously the human being *in need of* totality of human life-activities — the man in whom his own realization exists as an inner necessity, as *need.*
— *Marx, Economic and Philosophical Manuscripts of 1844*

Svetaketu abstained from food for fifteen days. Then he came to his father and said, "What shall I say?" The father said: "Repeat the Rik, Yagus and Saman verses." He replied, "They do not occur to me, Sir." The father said to him ... "Go and eat! Then wilt thou understand me." Svetaketu ate, and afterwards approached his father. And whatever his father asked him, he knew it all by heart ... After that, he understood what his father meant when he said: "Mind my son, comes from food, breath from water, speech from fire." He understood what he said, yea, he understood it.
— *Chandogya-Upanishad, VI Prapathaka, 7 Kanda*

When you love a man, you want him to live and when you hate him you want him to die. If, having wanted him to live, you then want him to die, this is a misguided judgment. "If you did not do so for the sake of riches, you must have done so for the sake of novelty."
— *Confucius, Analects, Book 12.10*

Antiessentialist Conversations

I begin with three conversations, taken from my experience working in Helsinki as a research advisor at an international institute affiliated with the United Nations, which brings people from many disciplines together to work on problems connected with development economics.[2] Contemporary assaults on "essentialism" and on nonrelative accounts of human functioning have recently made a dramatic appearance there, with potential implications for public policy that I view with alarm. I have in some cases conflated two separate conversations into one, but otherwise, things happened as I describe them.[3]

1. At a conference on value and technology, an American economist who has long been consid-

ered a radical delivers a paper urging the preservation of traditional ways of life in a rural area of India, now under threat of contamination from Western values. As evidence of the excellence of this rural way of life, he points to the fact that, whereas we Westerners experience a sharp split between the values that prevail in the workplace and the values that prevail in the home, here, by contrast, there exists what the economist calls "the embedded way of life." His example: just as in the home a menstruating woman is thought to pollute the kitchen and so may not enter it, so too in the workplace a menstruating woman is taken to pollute the loom and may not enter the room where looms are kept. An economist from India objects that this example is repellent rather than admirable, for surely such practices both degrade the women in question and inhibit their freedom. The first economist's collaborator, an elegant French anthropologist (who would, I suspect, object violently to a purity check at the seminar room door) addresses the objector in contemptuous tones. Doesn't he realize that there is, in these matters, no privileged place to stand? Doesn't he know that he is neglecting the radical otherness of these village people by bringing his Western essentialist values into the picture?

2. The same French anthropologist now delivers her paper. She expresses regret that the introduction of smallpox vaccination to India by the British eradicated the cult of Sittala Devi, the goddess to whom one used to pray in order to avert smallpox. Here, she says, is another example of Western neglect of difference. Someone (it might have been me) objects that it is surely better to be healthy rather than ill, to live rather than to die. The frosty answer comes back: Western essentialist medicine conceives of things in terms of binary oppositions: life is opposed to death, health to disease. But if we cast away this blinkered way of seeing things, we will comprehend the radical otherness of Indian traditions. At this point, Eric Hobsbawm, who has been listening to the proceedings in increasingly uneasy silence, rises to deliver a blistering indictment of the traditionalism and relativism that prevail in this group. He lists examples of how the appeal to tradition has been used in history to defend various types

of oppression and violence. His final example is that of National Socialism. In the chaos that ensues, most of the traditionalist social scientists (above all the ones from abroad, who do not know who Hobsbawm is) demand that Hobsbawm be asked to leave the conference room. The radical American economist, covered with embarrassment at this evidence of a split between his relativism and his left-wing affiliations, convinces them, with much difficulty, to let Hobsbawm remain.

3. We shift now to another conference,[4] a philosophical conference organized by me and by the objector of my first story, the economist from India who objected to the degradation of women by menstruation taboos. (He also holds the unsophisticated view that life is opposed to death.) His paper contains much "essentialist" talk of human functioning and human capability; he begins to speak of freedom of choice as a basic human good. At this point he is interrupted by the radical economist, who points out, with the air of one in the know, that contemporary anthropology has shown that non-Western people are not especially attached to freedom of choice. His example: a new book on Japan has shown that Japanese males, when they get home from work, do not wish to choose what to eat for dinner, what to wear, and so on. They wish all these choices to be taken out of their hands by their wives.[5] A heated exchange follows about what this example really shows. I leave it to your imagination to reconstruct it; it did have some humorous dimensions. But in the end, the confidence of the radical economist is unshaken: we are both victims of bad essentialist thinking, who fail to recognize the beauty of otherness.

These examples are not unusual; I could cite many more. What we see in such cases is an odd phenomenon indeed. Highly intelligent people, people deeply committed to the good of women and men in developing countries, people who think of themselves as progressive and feminist and antiracist, are taking up positions that converge, as Hobsbawm correctly saw, with the positions of reaction, oppression, and sexism. Under the banner of their radical and politically correct "antiessentialism" march ancient religious taboos, the luxury of pampered husband, ill health, ignorance, and death. (And in my own essentialist way, I say it at the outset. I do hold that death is opposed to life in the most binary way imaginable, and slavery to freedom, and hunger to adequate nutrition, and ignorance to knowledge.)

Essentialism is becoming a dirty word in the academy and in those parts of human life that are influenced by it. Essentialism — which for these purposes I shall understand as the view that human life has certain central defining features — is linked by its opponents with an ignorance of history, with lack of sensitivity to the voices of women and minorities.[6] It is taken, usually without extended argument, to be in league with racism and sexism, with "patriarchal" thinking generally, whereas extreme relativism is taken to be a recipe for social progress. In this essay, I question these connections. I grant that some criticisms of some forms of essentialism have been fruitful and important: They have established the ethical debate on a more defensible metaphysical foundation and have redirected our gaze from unexamined abstract assumptions to the world and its actual history. But I argue that those who would throw out all appeals to a determinate account of the human being, human functioning, and human flourishing are throwing away far too much — in terms even, and especially, of their own compassionate ends.

I argue, first, that the legitimate criticisms of essentialism still leave room for essentialism of a kind: for a historically sensitive account of the most basic human needs and human functions. I then sketch such an account, which I have developed at length elsewhere, showing how it can meet the legitimate objections. I then argue that without such an account, we do not have an adequate basis for an account of social justice and the ends of social distribution. With it, on the other hand, we have — what we urgently need at this time — the basis for a global ethic and a fully international account of distributive justice....

The Assault on Essentialism

The contemporary assault on universal accounts of the human being and human functioning is not always accompanied by clear and explicit philosophical arguments. All too often, as in my examples, the opponents of essentialism use the word polemically as a term of abuse and with a certain air of superiority, as if they were in the know about some new and decisive discovery that removes the need for argument.[7] So, the first task for anyone who wishes to defend a position in this debate must be, it seems to me, to introduce some clarity into the picture by sorting out the varieties of antiessentialist argument and describing the train of thought that has led to the extreme relativist traditionalism exemplified in my Helsinki conversations. The attacks can, I believe, be divided into two groups: attacks that depend on a general attack on metaphysical realism and attacks that are independent of the attack on realism and might be pressed, therefore, against versions of essentialism that do not depend on realism.

Attacks on Metaphysical-Realist Essentialism

Metaphysical realism claims that there is some determinate way that the world is apart from the interpretive workings of the cognitive faculties of living beings. A description of the world is true just in case it corresponds to that independently existing structure, false insofar as it does not so correspond. Unless the metaphysical realist is also a skeptic — a combination rarely found, since it is hard to sustain confidence in realism without the belief that someone can adequately grasp reality — realism is accompanied by some related account of knowledge. Some mind or other — whether God's alone or certain human minds also — is said to be able to grasp this real structure as it is in itself; knowledge is defined in terms of this grasp. In thinking about this position, it is useful to consider the myth in Plato's *Phaedrus*. The gods, who have no internal impediments to understanding, march out to the rim of the heavens, and here, as the heavens turn, they see going past them the true forms or structures of the world, independent, eternal, and unchanging. Other souls, whose internal structure is more turbulent and conflicted, fail to stand serenely on the rim of heaven, and so fail to know the whole of reality. Some souls see bits and pieces of reality as they struggle upwards: these are the ones that will be human beings. Others grasp nothing of the truth — and these will be animals.

On such a view, the way the human being essentially is will be a part of the independent furniture of the universe, something the gods can see and study independently of any experience of human life and human history. The paradigms that yield knowledge of what we in our nature are, are radically independent of our actual choices, our self-understandings, our hopes and loves and fears. They are there to be discovered by experts — whether philosophical, biological, or religious — and delivered to us by those figures or intermediaries as a correct account of the way things are. This account is usually understood to have normative force: the heavenly account of what we are constrains what we may legitimately seek to be.

The common objection to this sort of realism is that this sort of metaphysical truth is not in fact available. Sometimes this is put skeptically: the independent structure may still exist, but we can know nothing of it. More often, today, doubt is cast on the coherence of the whole realist idea that there is some one determinate structure to the way things are, independent of all human interpretation. This is the objection the nonphilosophers tend to associate with Jacques Derrida's assault on the "metaphysics of presence," which he takes to have dominated the entirety of the Western philosophical tradition.[8] But it actually has a much longer and more complicated history. It begins in the Western tradition at least as early as Kant's assault on transcendent metaphysics — and perhaps far earlier, since some scholars have found a version of it in Aristotle's anti-Platonist arguments.[9] Its contemporary versions are themselves many and complex — involving, frequently, technical issues in the philosophy of science and the philosophy of language. In this sophisticated literature — whose major contributors include such outstanding philosophers as Ludwig Wittgenstein, W.V.O. Quine, Donald Davidson, Hilary Putnam, and Nelson Goodman — the arguments of Derrida are relatively minor contributions, which do not even

confront a great many of the pressing questions that are at issue.

The attack on metaphysical realism is far too complex to be summarized here, but its implications for essentialism are clear. If the only available (or perhaps even coherent) picture of reality is one in the derivation of which human interpretations play a part, if the only defensible conceptions of truth and knowledge hold truth and knowledge to be in certain ways dependent on human cognitive activity within history, the hope for a pure unmediated account of our human essence as it is in itself, apart from history and interpretation, is no hope at all but a deep confusion. To cling to it as a goal is to pretend that it is possible for us to be told from outside what to be and what to do, when in reality the only answers we can ever hope to have must come, in some manner, from ourselves.

Attacks on Internalist Essentialism

But one might accept these conclusions and still be an essentialist. One might, that is, believe that the deepest examination of human history and human cognition *from within* still reveals a more or less determinate account of the human being, one that divides its essential from its accidental properties. Such an account would say: take away properties X, Y, and Z (a suntan, let us say, or a knowledge of Chinese, or an income of $40,000 a year) and we will still have what we count as a human being on our hands. On the other hand, take away properties A, B, and C (the ability to think about the future say, or the ability to respond to the claims of others, or the ability to choose and act) and we no longer have a human life at all. Separating these two groups of properties requires an evaluative inquiry: for we must ask, which things are so important that we will not count a life as a human life without them? Such an evaluative inquiry into what is deepest and most indispensable in our lives need not presuppose an external metaphysical foundation, clearly: it can be a way of looking at ourselves, asking what we really think about ourselves and what holds our history together. Later on, I shall propose one version of such a historically grounded empirical essentialism — which, since it takes its stand within human experience, I shall now call "internalist" essentialism.[10] Such internalist conceptions of the human being are still vulnerable to some, if not all, of the charges brought against essentialism generally. So even though the opposition rarely makes the externalist/internalist distinction, I shall myself introduce it, mentioning three charges that I think any good internalist account will need to answer.

1. *Neglect of Historical and Cultural Differences*
The opposition charges that any attempt to pick out some elements of human life as more fundamental than others, even without appeal to a transhistorical reality, is bound to be insufficiently respectful of actual historical and cultural differences. People, it is claimed, understand human life and humanness in widely different ways, and any attempt to produce a list of "essential properties" is bound to enshrine certain understandings of the human and to demote others. Usually, the objector continues, this takes the form of enshrining the understanding of a dominant group at the expense of minority understandings. Such objectors usually also suggest that only an actual unanimous agreement would be sufficient to justify an essentialist conclusion. But in practice, such agreements are not forthcoming, so essentialism is bound to consist of the imposition of someone's authority on someone else.

2. *Neglect of Autonomy*
A different objection is pressed by liberal opponents of essentialism; usually these opponents are themselves willing to be essentialist about the central importance of human freedom and autonomy.[11] The objection is that by determining in advance what elements of human life have most importance, the essentialist is failing to respect the right of people to choose a plan of life according to their own lights, determining what is most central and what is not. Such evaluative choices must be left to each citizen. For this reason, politics must refuse itself a determinate theory of the human being and the human good.

3. *Prejudicial Application*
If we operate with a determinate conception of the human being that is meant to have some normative moral and political weight, we must also, in applying it, ask which beings we take to fall under the concept. Here, the objector notes that all too easily the powerless can be excluded. Aristotle himself, it is pointed out, held that women and slaves were not full-fledged human beings; and since his politics was based on his essentialism, the failure of these beings (in his view) to exhibit the desired essence led to their political exclusion and oppression. The suggestion is that renouncing the use of such a determinate conception of the human will make it easier for such people to be heard and included.

The Collapse into Subjectivism

Each of these objections has some force. Later on in the essay, I ask how much force each of them has and whether there is a version of essentialism that can survive them. But what is alarming about the current debate in a variety of fields — literary theory, some parts of legal theory, and much of economic theory and development studies — is that this further inquiry has not taken place. Very often, as in my Helsinki examples, the collapse of metaphysical realism is taken to entail not only the collapse of essentialism about the human being but a retreat into an extreme relativism, or even subjectivism, about all questions of evaluation.[12]....

Confronting the Objections

...When we get rid of the hope of a transcendent metaphysical grounding for our evaluative judgments — about the human being as about anything else — we are not left with the abyss. We have everything that we always had all along: the exchange of reasons and arguments by human beings within history, in which, for reasons that are historical and human but not the worse for that, we hold some things to be good and others bad, some arguments to be sound and others not sound. Why, indeed, should the relativist conclude that the absence of a transcendent basis for judgment — a basis that, according to them, was never there anyway — should make us despair of doing as we have done all along, distinguishing persuasion from manipulation?

In fact, the collapse into extreme relativism or subjectivism seems to me to betray a deep attachment to metaphysical realism itself. For it is only to one who has pinned everything to that hope that its collapse will seem to entail the collapse of all evaluation — just as it is only to a deeply believing religious person, as Nietzsche saw, that the news of the death of God brings the threat of nihilism. What we see here, I think, is a reaction of *shame* — a turning away of the eyes from our poor humanity, which looks so mean and bare — by contrast to a dream of another sort. What do we have here, these critics seem to say? Only our poor old human conversations, our human bodies that interpret things so imperfectly? Well, if that is all there is, we do not really want to study it too closely, to look into the distinctions it exhibits. We will just say that they are all alike, for, really, they do look pretty similar when compared to the heavenly standard we were seeking. It is like the moment reported by Aristotle when some students arrived at the home of Heraclitus, eager to see the great sage and cosmologist. They found him — not on a hilltop gazing at the heavens but sitting in his kitchen or, perhaps, on the toilet (for there is a philological dispute at this point!). He looked at their disappointed faces, saw that they were about to turn away their eyes, and said, "Come in, don't be afraid. There are gods here too." Aristotle uses this story to nudge his reluctant students out of the shame that is preventing them from looking closely at the parts of animals. When you get rid of your shame, he says, you will notice that there is order and structure *in* the animal world.[13]

So too, I think, with realism: the failure to take an interest in studying our practices of analyzing and reasoning, human and historical as they are, the insistence that we would have good arguments only if they came from heaven — all this betrays a shame before the human. On the other hand, if we really think of the hope of a transcendent ground for value as uninteresting and irrelevant, as we should, then the news of its collapse will not

change the way we do things: it will just let us get on with the business of reasoning in which we were already engaged.

And as Hilary Putnam argues,[14] the demise of realism may even boost the status of ethical evaluation. For the metaphysical realist frequently made a sharp distinction between fact and value, believing that truth of the sort the realist is after was available in the scientific realm but not in the realm of value. Bringing science inside human history makes what was already believed to be in there look better, not worse — because its claims are no longer contrasted sharply with claims that look "harder" and more "factual." Thus the polarity between scientific fact and subjective ethical value on which much of neoclassical economics rests is called into question by the collapse of realism — from the side of science, to be sure, but this reopens the whole question of the relationship between ethics and science and makes it possible to argue, as does Putnam, that ethics is no worse off than any science.

As for the objections to internalist essentialism, each of them has some force. Many essentialist conceptions have been insular in an arrogant way and neglectful of choice and autonomy. And some have been prejudicially applied — sometimes even by their inventors (as in the cases of Aristotle and Rousseau). But none of this, it seems to me, shows that all essentialism *must* fail in one or more of these ways. And if one feels that there are urgent reasons why we need such an account of human functioning, one will be motivated to try to construct one that will in fact meet the objections. I now propose such an account and then return to the area of development policy, offering my reasons for thinking that we do in fact urgently need such an account.

An Essentialist Proposal: The Basic Human Functions

Here, then, is a sketch of an internal-essentialist proposal, an account of the most important functions of the human being, in terms of which human life is defined.[15] The idea is that once we identify a group of especially important functions in human life, we are then in a position to ask what social and political institutions are doing about them. Are the giving people what they need in order to be capable of functioning in all these human ways? And are they doing this in a minimal way, or are they making it possible for citizens to function *well*? I will consider the political implications of the account in the next section; now I must describe the account itself.

I call this account of the human functions the "thick vague theory of the good."[16] The point of this name is to insist, first of all, on the normative character of the list. We are not pretending to discover some value-neutral facts about ourselves, independently of all evaluation; instead, we are conducting an especially probing and basic sort of evaluative inquiry. The name is also chosen to contrast the account with John Rawls's "thin theory of the good," which insists on confining the list of the "primary goods" that will be used by the members of the Original Position to a group of allegedly all-purpose means that have a role in any conception of the human good whatever. By contrast, my Aristotelian conception is concerned with *ends* and with the overall shape and content of the human form of life.[17] Finally the list is "vague," and this deliberately so and in a good sense, for, as we shall see, it admits of much multiple specification in accordance with varied local and personal conceptions. The idea is that it is better to be vaguely right than precisely wrong; I claim that without the guidance offered by such a list, what we often get in public policy is precise wrongness.

This conception is emphatically *not* metaphysical; that is, it does not claim to derive from any source external to the actual self-interpretations and self-evaluations of human beings in history.[18] Nor is it peculiar to a single metaphysical or religious tradition. It aims to be as universal as possible, and its guiding intuition, in fact, directs it to cross religious, cultural, and metaphysical gulfs. For it begins from two facts: first, that we do recognize others as human across many divisions of time and place. Whatever the differences we encounter, we are rarely in doubt, as to when we are dealing with a human being and when we are not. The essentialist account attempts to describe

the bases for these recognitions, by mapping out the general shape of the human form of life, those features that constituted a life as human wherever it is. Second, we do have a broadly shared general consensus about the features whose absence means the end of a human form of life. We have in medicine and mythology alike an idea that some traditions or changes just are not compatible with the continued existence of that being as a member of the human kind (and thus as the same individual, since species identity seems to be necessary for personal identity). This is really just another way of coming at the first question, of asking what the most central features of our common humanity are, without which no individual can be counted (or counted any longer) as human.[19]

This evaluative inquiry proceeds by examining a wide variety of self-understandings of people in many times and places. Especially valuable are myths and stories that situate the human being in some way in the universe: between the beasts, on one hand, and the gods, on the other; stories that ask what it is to live as a being with certain abilities that set it apart from the rest of the living beings in the world of nature, and with, on the other hand, certain limits that derive from our membership in the world of nature. The idea is that we do share at least a very general outline of such a conception. Frequently, we find such ideas elucidated in stories of beings who look like humans but are not recognized as human. When we ask ourselves, "Why, if these creatures resemble human beings, don't we count them as human?" we learn something about ourselves....

The list of features that we get if we reflect in this way is, and should be, open-ended. For we want to allow the possibility that we will learn from our encounters with other human societies to recognize things about ourselves that we had not seen before, or even to change in certain ways, according more importance to something we had considered more peripheral. The list is an intuitive approximation, whose purpose is not to cut off discussion but to direct attention to certain features of importance. The list, moreover, is heterogeneous, for it contains both limits against which we press and capabilities through which we aspire. This is not surprising, since we begin from the idea of a creature who is both capable and needy. We shall return to this point, showing how it affects the political use of the list.

Here, then as a first approximation, is a story about what seems to be part of any life that we will count as a human life.

Level 1 of the Thick Vague Conception:
The Shape of the Human Form of Life

Mortality. All human beings face death and, after a certain age, know that they face it. This fact shapes more or less every other element of human life. Moreover, all human beings have an aversion to death. Although in many circumstances death will be preferred to the available alternatives, the death of a loved one or the prospect of one's own death is an occasion for grief and/or fear. If we encountered an immortal anthropomorphic being *or* a mortal being that showed no aversion to death and no tendency to avoid death, we would judge, in both these cases, that the form of life was so different from our own that the being could not be acknowledged as human.

The human body. We live all our lives in bodies of a certain sort, whose possibilities and vulnerabilities do not as such belong to one human society rather than another. These bodies, similar far more than dissimilar (given the enormous range of possibilities), are our homes, so to speak, opening certain options and denying others, giving us certain needs and also certain possibilities for excellence. The fact that any given human being might have lived anywhere and belonged to any culture is a great part of what grounds our mutual recognitions; this fact, in turn, has a great deal to do with the general humanness of the body, its great distinctness from other bodies. The experience of the body is, to be sure, culturally shaped, but the body itself, not culturally variant in its nutritional and other related requirements, sets limits on what can be experienced, ensuring a great deal of overlap.

There is much disagreement, of course, about *how much* of human experience is rooted in the body. Here, religion and metaphysics enter the

picture in a nontrivial way. Therefore, in keeping with the nonmetaphysical character of the list, I shall include at this point only those features that would be agreed to be bodily even by determined dualists. The more controversial features, such as thinking, perceiving, and emotion, I shall discuss separately, taking no stand on the question of dualism.[20]

1. *Hunger and thirst; the need for food and drink.* All human beings need food and drink in order to live; all have comparable, though varying, nutritional requirements. Being in one culture rather than another does not make one metabolize food differently. Furthermore, all human beings have appetites that are indices of need. Appetitive experience is to some extent culturally shaped, but we are not surprised to discover much similarity and overlap. Moreover, human beings in general do not wish to be hungry or thirsty (though, of course, they might choose to fast for some reason). If we discovered someone who really did not experience hunger or thirst at all, or, experiencing them, really did not care about eating and drinking, we would judge that this creature was (in Aristotle's words) "far from being a human being."

2. *Need for shelter.* A recurrent theme in myths of humanness is the nakedness of the human being, its relative susceptibility to heat, cold, and the ravages of the elements. Stories that explore the difference between our needs and those of furry or scaly or otherwise protected creatures remind us how far our life is constituted by the need to find refuge from the cold, the withering heat of the sun, from rain, wind, snow, and frost.

3. *Sexual desire.* Though less urgent as a need than the needs for food, drink, and shelter (in the sense that one can live without its satisfaction), sexual need and desire are features of more of less every human life. It is, and has been all along, a most important basis for the recognition of others different from us as human beings.

4. *Mobility.* Human beings are, as the old definition goes, featherless bipeds — that is, creatures whose form of life is in part constituted by the ability to move from place to place in a certain characteristic way, not only through the aid of tools

that we have made but with our very own bodies. Human beings like moving about and dislike being deprived of mobility. An anthropomorphic being who, without disability, chose never to move from birth to death would be hard to view as human.

Capacity for pleasure and pain. Experiences of pain and pleasure are common to all human life (though once again both their expression and, to some extent, the experience itself may be culturally shaped). Moreover, the aversion to pain as a fundamental evil is a primitive and, it appears, unlearned part of being a human animal. A society whose members altogether lacked that aversion would surely be judged to be beyond the bounds of humanness.

Cognitive capability: perceiving, imagining, thinking. All human beings have sense perception, the ability to imagine, and the ability to think, making distinctions and "reaching out for understanding,"[21] and these abilities are regarded as of central importance. It is an open question what sorts of accidents or impediments to individuals in these areas will be sufficient for us to judge that the life in question is not really human any longer. But it is safe to say that if we imagine a tribe whose members totally lack sense perception or totally lack imagination or totally lack reasoning and thinking, we are not in any of these cases imagining a tribe of human beings, no matter what they look like.

Early infant development. All human beings begin as hungry babies, aware of their own helplessness, experiencing their alternating closeness to and distance from that, and those, on whom they depend. This common structure to early life — which clearly is shaped in many different ways by different social arrangements — gives rise to a great deal of overlapping experience that is central in the formation of desires and of complex emotions such as grief, love, and anger. This, in turn, is a major source of our ability to recognize ourselves in the emotional experiences of those whose lives are very different in other respects from our own. If we encountered a tribe of apparent humans and then discovered that they never had been babies and had never, in consequence, had those experi-

ences of extreme dependency, need, and affection, we would, I think, have to conclude that their form of life was sufficiently different from our own that they could not be considered part of the same kind.

Practical reason. All human beings participate (or try to) in the planning and managing of their own lives, asking and answering questions about what is good and how one should live. Moreover, they wish to enact their thought in their lives — to be able to choose and evaluate and to function accordingly. This general capability has many concrete forms and is related in complex ways to the other capabilities, emotional, imaginative, and intellectual. But a being who altogether lacks this would not be regarded as fully human in any society.

Affiliation with other human beings. All human beings recognize and feel some sense of affiliation and concern for other human beings. Moreover, we value the form of life that is constituted by these recognitions and affiliations. We live for and with others and regard a life not lived in affiliation with others to be a life not worth living. (Here, I would really wish, along with Aristotle, to spell things out further. We define ourselves in terms of at least two sorts of affiliation: intimate family and/or personal relations and social or civic relations.)

Relatedness to other species and to nature. Human beings recognize that they are not the only living things in their world, that they are animals living alongside other animals and also alongside plants in a universe that, as a complex interlocking order, both supports and limits them. We are dependent on that order in countless ways, and we also sense that we owe that order some respect and concern, however much we may differ about exactly what we owe, to whom, and on what basis. Again, a creature who treated animals exactly like stones and could not be brought to see any difference would probably be regarded as too strange to be human. So, too, would a creature who did not in any way respond to the beauty and wonder of the natural world.

Humor and play. Human life, wherever it is lived, makes room for recreation and laughter. The forms that play takes are enormously varied; yet we recognize other humans, across cultural barriers, as the animals who laugh. Laughter and play are frequently among the deepest and also the first modes of our mutual recognition. Inability to play or laugh is taken, correctly, as a sign of deep disturbance in an individual child; if it proves permanent, we will doubt whether the child is capable of leading a fully human life. An entire society that lacked this ability would seem to us both terribly strange and terribly frightening.

Separateness. However much we live with and for others, we are, each of us, "one in number," proceeding on a separate path through the world from birth to death. Each person feels only his or her own pain and not anyone else's. Each person dies without entailing logically the death of anyone else. When one person walks across the room, no other person follows automatically. When we count the number of human beings in a room, we have no difficulty figuring out where one begins and the other ends. These obvious facts need stating because they might have been otherwise. We should bear them in mind when we hear talk of the absence of individualism in certain societies. Even the most intense forms of human interaction, for example, sexual experience, are experiences of responsiveness, not of fusion. If fusion is made the goal, the result is bound to be bitter disappointment.

Because of separateness, each human life has, so to speak, its own peculiar context and surroundings — objects, places, a history, particular friendships, locations, sexual ties — that are not exactly the same as those of anyone else, and in terms of which the person to some extent identifies oneself. Although societies vary a great deal in the degree and type of strong separateness that they permit and foster, there is no life yet known that really does (as Plato wished) fail to use the words "mine" and "not mine" in some personal and nonshared way. What I use, touch, love, and respond to, I touch, use, love, and respond to from my own separate existence. And on the whole, human beings recognize one another as beings who wish to have at least some separateness of context, a little space to move around in, some special items to love or use.

As already said, the list is composed of two different sorts of items: limits and capabilities. As far as capabilities go, to call them part of humanness is to make a very basic sort of evaluation. It is to say that a life without this item would be too lacking, too impoverished, to be human at all. Obviously, then, it could not be a *good* human life. So, this list of capabilities is a ground-floor, or minimal, conception of the good. With the limits, things are more complicated. For we have said that humans do not wish to be hungry, to feel pain to die. (Separateness is highly complex — both a limit and a capability.) Yet we cannot assume that the correct evaluative conclusion to draw is that we should try as hard as possible to get rid of the limit altogether. It is characteristic of human life to prefer recurrent hunger plus eating to a life with neither hunger nor eating, to prefer sexual desire and its satisfaction to a life with neither desire nor satisfaction. Even where death is concerned, the desire for immortality, which human beings certainly seem to have, is a peculiar desire. For it is not clear that the wish to lose one's finitude completely is a desire that one can coherently wish for oneself or for someone whom one loves. That would seem to be a wish for a transition to a way of life so wholly different, with such different values and ends, that it is not clear that the identity of the individual could be preserved. So the evaluative conclusion needs to be expressed with much caution, clearly, in terms of what would be a humanly good way of countering the limitation.[22]

Things now get complicated, for we want to describe two distinct thresholds: a threshold of capability to function, beneath which a life will be so impoverished that it will not be human at all, and a somewhat higher threshold, beneath which those characteristic functions are available in such a reduced way that although we may judge the form of life a human one, we will not think it a *good* human life. The latter threshold is the one that will eventually concern us most when we turn to public policy, for we do not want societies to make their citizens capable of the bare minimum. These are clearly, in many areas, two distinct thresholds, requiring distinct levels of resource and capability. Yet there is need for caution here. For, in many cases the move from human life to good human life is supplied by the citizens' own powers of choice and self-definition, in such a way that once society places them above the first threshold, moving above the second is more or less up to them. This is especially likely to be so, I think, in areas such as affiliation and practical reasoning, where what we want from society and from other associations within it, such as the family, is a development of the child so that it passes the first threshold. On the other hand, it is clear that where bodily health and nutrition, for example, are concerned, there is a considerable difference between the two thresholds, a difference made by resources over which individuals do not have full control. Clearly, there is a continuum here, and it is always going to be difficult to say where the upper threshold, especially, should be located.

Here, then, as the next level of the conception of the human being, I now specify certain basic functional capabilities at which societies should aim for their citizens (in accordance with the political idea more fully investigated in the next section). In other words, this will be an account of the second threshold — although in some areas, it seems to me to coincide with the first. I shall actually introduce the list as one of related capabilities rather than of actual functioning, since I shall argue that capability to function, not actual functioning, should be the goal of legislation and public planning.

Level 2 of the Thick Vague Conception:
Basic Human Functional Capabilities

1. Being able to live to the end of complete human life, as far as is possible; not dying prematurely, or before one's life is so reduced as to be not worth living.
2. Being able to have good health; to be adequately nourished; to have adequate shelter; having opportunities for sexual satisfaction; being able to move from place to place.
3. Being able to avoid unnecessary and nonbeneficial pain and to have pleasurable experiences.
4. Being able to use the five senses; being able to imagine, to think, and to reason.
5. Being able to have attachments to things and persons outside ourselves; to love those who love and care for us, to grieve at their absence,

in general, to love, grieve, to feel longing and gratitude.
6. Being able to form a conception of the good and to engage in critical reflection about the planning of one's own life.
7. Being able to live for and with others, to recognize and show concern for other human beings, to engage in various forms of familial and social interaction.
8. Being able to live with concern for and in relation to animals, plants, and the world of nature.
9. Being able to laugh, to play, to enjoy recreational activities.
10. Being able to live one's own life and nobody else's; being able to live one's own life in one's very own surroundings and context.

The Aristotelian essentialist claims that a life that lacks any one of these, no matter what else it has, will be lacking in humanness. So it would be reasonable to take these things as a focus for concern, in asking how public policy can promote the good of human beings. The list is, emphatically, a list of separate components. We cannot satisfy the need for one of them by giving a larger amount of another one. All are of central importance, and all are distinct in quality. This limits the trade-offs that it will be reasonable to make and thus limits the applicability of quantitative cost-benefit analysis. At the same time, the items on the list are related to one another in many complex ways. For example, our characteristic mode of nutrition, unlike that of sponges, requires moving from here to there. And we do whatever we do as separate beings, tracing distinct paths through space and time.

Among the capabilities, two — practical reason and affiliation — play a special role as architectonic, holding the whole enterprise together and making it human. All animals nourish themselves, use their senses, move about, and so forth; what is distinctive and distinctively valuable to us about the human way of doing all this is that each and every one of these functions is, first of all, planned and organized by practical reason and, second, done with and to others. Human nourishing is not like animal nourishing, nor human sex like animal sex, because human beings can choose to regulate their nutrition and their sexual activity by their very own practical reason; also because they do so not as solitary Cyclops (who would eat anything at all, even their own guests) but as beings who are bound to other human beings by ties of mutual attention and concern.[23]

Answering the Objections

I must now try to show how the thick vague theory of the good can answer the objections most commonly made against essentialism. First of all, it should be clear by now that the list does not derive from any extra historical metaphysical conception, or rely on the truth of any form of metaphysical realism. As I have said, its guiding intuition is that we do recognize as human, people who do not share our own metaphysical and religious ideas; it aims to get at the root of those recognitions. It does so by conducting an inquiry that is, frankly, both evaluative and internal to human history. Furthermore, the conception does not even demand universal actual agreement among human beings in order to play the moral and political role that we want it to play, I have tried to arrive at a list that will command a very wide consensus, and a consensus that is fully international. Its very close resemblance to other similar lists worked out independently in parts of the world as divergent as Finland and Sri Lanka[24] gives some reason for optimism about consensus. On the other hand, unanimity is not required; for people who have not been willing to engage in the cross-cultural study and the probing evaluation that is behind the list may well refuse assent for varied reasons. Even among those who do engage in the inquiry, there may be differences of opinion. With regard to some components of the list, the very act of entering a disagreement seems to be an acknowledgment of the importance of the component: this seems true, for example, of both practical reasoning and affiliation. But with regard to others, there will be room for ongoing debate and reformulation. The aim is, simply, to achieve enough of a working consensus that we can use the list as a basis for the kind of political reflection that I

describe in the next section. (We may usefully compare, at this point, John Rawls's idea of an "overlapping consensus" that is political and not metaphysical.[25]) So, the objections to essentialism that assume its dependence on realism seem to fail, in this particular case.

As for the three objections to "internalist" essentialism, each one of them is, and should remain, a central concern of the Aristotelian essentialist. For the list will command the sort of broad consensus she wishes only if these objections can be successfully met.

Concerning *neglect of historical and cultural difference,* the Aristotelian begins by insisting that the thick vague conception is vague for precisely this reason. The list claims to have identified in a very general way components that are fundamental to any human life. But it allows in its very design for the possibility of multiple specifications of each of the components. This is so in several different ways. First, the constitutive circumstances of human life, while broadly shared, are themselves realized in different forms in different societies. The fear of death, the love of play, relationships of friendship and affiliation with others, even the experience of the bodily appetites — these never turn up in simply the vague and general form in which they have been introduced here but always in some specific and historically rich cultural realization, which can profoundly shape not only the conceptions used by the citizens in these areas but their experiences themselves. Nonetheless, we do have in these areas of our common humanity sufficient overlap to sustain a general conversation, focusing on our common problems and prospects. Sometimes, the common conversation will permit us to criticize some conceptions of the grounding experiences themselves, as at odds with other things that human beings want to do and to be.[26]

When we are choosing a conception of *good* functioning with respect to these circumstances, we can expect an even greater degree of plurality to become evident. Here, the Aristotelian essentialist wants to retain plurality in two significantly different ways: what we may call the way of *plural specification* and the way of *local specification.*[27]

Plural specification means what its name implies. The political plan, while using a determinate conception of the good at a high level of generality, leaves a great deal of latitude for citizens to specify each of the components more concretely and with much variety, in accordance with local traditions or individual tastes.

As for local specification, Aristotelian practical reasoning is always done, when well done, with a rich sensitivity to the concrete context, to the characters of the agents and their social situation. This means that in addition to the pluralism I have just described, the Aristotelian needs to consider a different sort of plural specification of the good. For sometimes what is a good way of promoting education in one part of the world will be completely ineffectual in another. Forms of affiliation that flourish in one community may prove impossible to sustain in another. In such cases, the Aristotelian must aim at some concrete specification of the general list that suits and develops out of the local conditions. This will always most reasonably be done in a participatory dialogue with those who are most deeply immersed in those conditions. For although Aristotelianism does not hesitate to criticize tradition where tradition perpetrates injustice or oppression, it does not believe in saying anything at all without rich and full information, gathered not so much from detached study as from the voices of those who live the ways of life in question. Later, when I discuss efforts made to enhance female literacy in rural Bangladesh, I shall give a concrete example of this sort of participatory dialogue and draw some further conclusions about this problem.

The liberal charges the Aristotelian with *neglect of autonomy,* arguing that any such determinate conception removes from the citizens the chance to make their own choices about the good life. This is a complicated issue; four points can be stressed.[28] First, the list is a list of capabilities, and not actual functions, precisely because the conception is designed to leave room for choice. Government is not directed to push citizens into acting in certain valued ways; instead, it is directed to make sure that all human beings have the necessary resources and conditions for acting in those ways. It leaves

the choice up to them. A person with plenty of food can always choose to fast; a person who has access to subsidized university education can always decide to do something else instead. By making opportunities available, government enhances, and does not remove, choice.[29] Second, this respect for choice is built deeply into the list itself in the architectonic role it gives to practical reasoning. One of the most central capabilities promoted by the conception will be the capability of choosing itself, which is made among the most fundamental elements of the human essence.[30] Third, we should note that the major liberal view in this area, the view of John Rawls, does not shrink from essentialism of our internal sort in just this area. Rawls insists that satisfactions that are not the outgrowths of one's very own choices have no moral worth, and he conceives of the "two moral powers" (analogous to our practical reasoning) and of sociability (corresponding to our affiliation) as built into the definition of the parties in the original position and thus as necessary constraints on any outcome they will select.[31] In this way, the liberal view and the Aristotelian view converge more than one might initially suppose. Finally, the Aristotelian insists that choice is not pure spontaneity, flourishing independently of material and social conditions. If one cares about autonomy, then one must care about the rest of the form of life that supports it and the material conditions that enable one to live that form of life. Thus the Aristotelian claims that her own comprehensive concern with flourishing across all areas of life is a better way of promoting choice than is the liberal's narrower concern with spontaneity alone, which sometimes tolerates situations in which individuals are in other ways cut off from the fully human use of their faculties.

The Aristotelian conception can indeed by *prejudicially applied.* It is possible to say all the right things about humanness and then to deny that women or blacks or other minorities fall under the concept. How should the essentialist deal with this problem? First of all, it should be stressed that the fact that a conception can be withheld for reasons of prejudice or lack love undermines not the conception itself but the person who withholds it. One may, looking at a minority whom one hates, speak of them as beetles or ants, and one may carry this refusal of humanity into the sphere of law and public action. Does this undermine our idea that a conception of the human being is a good basis for moral obligation? It seems to me that it does not. For what such cases reveal is the great power of the conception of the human. Acknowledging this other person as a member of the very same kind would have generated a sense of affiliation and responsibility; this was why the self-deceptive stratagem of splitting the other off from one's own species seemed so urgent and so seductive. And the stratagem of denying humanness to beings with whom one lives in conversation and some form of human interaction is a fragile sort of self-deceptive tactic, vulnerable to sustained and consistent reflection and also to experiences that cut through self-deceptive rationalization.[32]

Raul Hilberg, for example, has amassed an impressive amount of evidence concerning the psychology of such denials.[33] He argues that whenever circumstances arose that made it possible for the Nazi functionaries, whose actions depended on the denial of humanness to Jews, to sustain this denial in a particular case, what ensued was an emotional "breakthrough," in which action was indeed, at least temporarily, transformed. What were these occasions? Times, above all, when it became impossible to avoid the fact that one was interacting with a Jewish prisoner in a human manner: occasions of personal conversation or emotional connection that eluded the watchful protective mechanisms of denial. Thus one can say, I think, that focusing on the importance of the shared human functions makes it harder for prejudicial applications of the conception to take place: if we get clearer about what we are looking for in calling a being human, we will hardly avoid noticing the extent to which we acknowledge such functions, implicitly, in our dealings with others.

Any moral conception may be withheld, out of ambition or hatred or shame. But the conception of the human being seems so much more difficult to withhold than other conceptions that have been put forward as the basis for ethical obligation. The notion of the "person," for example, has sometimes been preferred to the notion of the human

being as a basis for ethics, on the grounds that it is clearly a normative conception, whose connection with certain sorts of ethical obligations is especially evident. I have argued that the conception of the human being is itself, in a certain way, a normative conception, in that it involves singling out certain functions as more basic than others. And there is no getting around the fact that correct application of the concept will involve answering evaluative questions that will sometimes be difficult to answer: for a creature falls under the concept only if it possesses some basic, though perhaps altogether undeveloped, capability to perform the functions in question. It will sometimes be very difficult to say whether a certain patient with senile dementia or a certain extremely damaged infant has enough of those basic capabilities to fall under the concept. On the other hand, we have far less flexibility in the application of the concept than we do with "person," which has in history been applied and withheld extremely capriciously, more or less as the lawgiver decides to favor one group over another…With "person," the defender of equality is on uncertain ground, ground that the opponent can at any moment shift under her feet. With "human being," on the other hand, it is always open to her to say to the opponent, "Look at these beings: you cannot fail to grant that they use their senses, that they think about the future, that they engage in ethical conversation, that they have needs and vulnerabilities similar to your own. Grant this, and you grant that they are human. Grant that they are human, and you grant that they have needs for flourishing that exert a moral pull on anyone who would deny them." As I have said, it is always possible to deny such an appeal, even when looking into the face of a woman with whom one lives and bears children. On the other hand, it is impossible to do so with full and honest and consistent reflection, that is to say, at the conclusion of a fully human process of deliberation.

So far, I have focused on the higher-level (developed) human capabilities that make a life a good human life but have not spoken at length about the empirical basis for the application of the concept "human being" to a creature before us. The basis cannot, of course, be the presence of the higher-level capabilities on my list, for one of the main points of the list is to enable us to say, of some being before us, that this being might possibly come to have these higher-level capabilities but does not now have them. It is that gap between basic (potential) humanness and its full realization that exerts a claim on society and government. What, then, is to be the basis for a determination that this being is one of the human beings, one of the ones whose functioning concerns us? I claim that it is the presence of a lower-level (undeveloped) capability to perform the functions in question, such that with the provision of suitable support and education, the being would be capable of choosing these functions.[34]

There is, of course, enormous potential for abuse in determining who has these basic capabilities. The history of IQ testing is just one chapter in an inglorious saga of prejudiced capability testing that goes back at least to the Noble Lie of Plato's *Republic.* Therefore we should, I think, proceed as if every offspring of two human parents has the basic capabilities, unless and until long experience *with the individual* has convinced us that damage to that individual's condition is so great that it could never in any way, through however great an expenditure of resources, arrive at the higher capability level. (Certain patients with irreversible senile dementia or a permanent vegetative condition would fall into this category, as would certain very severely damaged infants. It would then fall to other moral arguments to decide what treatment we owe to such individuals, who are unable ever to reach the higher capabilities to function humanly. It certainly does not follow that we would be licensed to treat such individuals harshly; we simply would not aim at making them fully capable of the various functions on our list.)

Concerning individuals who can profit from education, care, and resources — and I emphasize that in practice this is to be taken to include all individuals, with the very rare exceptions just noted — the Aristotelian view observes that these basic human capabilities exert a claim on society that they should be developed. Human beings are creatures such that, provided with the right educa-

tional and material support, they can become capable of the major human functions. When their basic capabilities are deprived of the nourishment that would transform them into the higher-level capabilities that figure on my list, they are fruitless, cut off, in some way but a shadow of themselves. They are like actors who never get to go on the stage or a musical score that is never performed. The very being of these basic capabilities makes forward reference to functioning; thus if functioning never arrives on the scene, they are hardly even what they are. This basic intuition underlies the recommendations that the Aristotelian view will make for public action: certain basic and central human powers have a claim to be developed and will exert that claim on others — and especially, as Aristotle held, on government.[35]

Our Need for Essentialism in Public Policy

I have said that we urgently need a version of essentialism in public life. If we reject it, we reject guidance that is crucial if we are to construct an adequate account of distributive justice to guide public policy in many areas. It is time for me to substantiate these claims. I shall focus on the area with which I began: the assessment of the "quality of life" in developing countries, with a view to formulating policy, both within each separate country and between one country and another. The general direction of my argument should by now be clear: we cannot tell how a country is doing unless we know how the people in it are able to function in the central human ways. And without an account of the good, however vague, that we take to be *shared,* we have no adequate basis for saying what is *missing* from the lives of the poor or marginalized or excluded, no adequate way of justifying the claim that any deeply embedded tradition that we encounter is unjust.

Public policy analyses of the quality of life in developing countries often use measures that are extremely crude.[36] It is still common to find countries ranked in accordance with their gross national product per capita, even though this measure does not even concern itself with the distribution of resources and thus can give good marks to a country with enormous inequalities. Such an approach, furthermore, does not look at all at other human goods that are not reliably correlated with the presence of resources: infant mortality, for example, or access to education, or the quality of racial and gender relations, or the presence or absence of political freedoms. Such an approach might fail to arouse the ire of the antiessentialist because it appears to take no stand on questions of value. But, first of all, it really does take a stand, albeit a perverse one, for it assumes that the presence of more money and resources is the one important determinant of life quality. And second, insofar as it fails to take a stand on other components of the human good, such as freedom, or health, or education, it fails to offer useful guidance to the social scientist seeking to understand how countries are doing or to the policy maker seeking to make things better.

One step up in level of sophistication is an approach that measures the quality of life in terms of utility. This would be done, for example, by polling people about whether they are satisfied with their current health status or their current level of education. This approach at least has the merit of focusing on people and viewing resources as valuable because of what they do in human lives. But its narrow focus on subjective expressions of satisfaction brings with it a number of serious problems. First of all, desires and subjective preference are not always reliable indices of what a person really needs, of what would really be required to make that life a flourishing one. Desires and satisfactions are highly malleable. The rich and pampered easily become accustomed to their luxury and view with pain and frustration a life in which they are treated just like everyone else. The poor and deprived frequently adjust their expectations and aspirations to the low level of life they have known; thus their failure to express dissatisfaction can often be a sign that they really do have enough. This is all the more true when the deprivations in question include deprivation of education and other information about alternative ways of life. Circumstances confine the imagination.[37]

Thus, if we rely on utility as our measure of life quality, we most often will get results that support the status quo and oppose radical change. A poll of widowers and widows in India showed that the widowers were full of complaint about their health status; the widows, on the other hand, in most cases ranked their health status as "good." On the other hand, a medical examination showed that the widows were actually suffering far more than the males from diseases associated with nutritional deficiency. The point was that they had lived all their lives expecting that women will eat less, and the weakened health status produced in this way was second nature to them. Some years later, after a period of political "consciousness raising," the study was repeated. The utility of the women had gone down, in the sense that they expressed far more dissatisfaction with their health. (Their objective medical situation was pretty much unchanged.[38]) On the other hand, to the Aristotelian, this is progress, for their desires and expectations are now more in tune with information about what a flourishing life could be. They know what functioning they are missing. Similar results obtain in the educational sphere — where, once again, polls of women in India asking whether they are satisfied with their educational status usually produce affirmative results, so deep are the cultural forces militating against any change in this area and so little information is there concerning how education has transformed and could transform female lives....

Finally, utilitarianism, neglecting as it does the inalienability of certain elements of the self, neglects also the ethical salience of the boundaries between persons. As a theory of public measurement, utilitarianism is committed to the aggregation of satisfactions. Individuals are treated as centers of pleasure or pain satisfaction or dissatisfaction, and the fact of their separateness one from another is not given special weight in the theory, which proceeds by summing. But in the world we actually inhabit, it is a highly relevant fact that my pain is not yours, nor yours mine. If trade-offs between functions are problematic where a single life is concerned, they are all the more problematic when they cross the boundaries of lives, purchasing one person's satisfaction at the price of another's misery. It is easy to see what consequences this can have for policy. For the utilitarian is frequently willing to tolerate huge inequalities for the sake of a larger total or average sum. The Aristotelian's fundamental commitment, by contrast, is to bring each and every person across the threshold into capability for good functioning. This means devoting resources to getting everyone across before any more is given to those who are already capable of functioning at some basic level. If all cannot be brought across the threshold, to this extent the ends of public policy have not been met.

The local tradition relativism endorsed in my Helsinki examples claims to be different from prevailing economic-utilitarian views, on account of its close attention to the fabric of daily life in traditional societies. But it actually shares many of the defects of the utilitarian view, for it refuses to subject preferences, as formed in traditional societies, to any sort of critical scrutiny. It seems to assume that all criticism must be a form of imperialism, the imposition of an outsider's power on local ways. Nor does it simply claim to avoid normative judgments altogether, for it actually endorses the locally formed norms as good and even romanticizes them in no small degree. It confers a bogus air of legitimacy on these deeply embedded preferences by refusing to subject them to ethical scrutiny. So far as my other objections to utilitarianism go, it does not really avoid them either, for if some local traditions wishes to treat all values as commensurable or to commodify parts of the self (or even as often happens, whole women), the "embedded" view (associated with writers like S.A. and F.A. Marglin) must accept this result and accept it as good. The concrete consequences of this emerge clearly from the conclusions of their volume, for they end by rejecting most of what is usually called "development" — that is, most agricultural, technological, and economic change and most educational change as well — and supporting as good ways of life in which it is unlikely that they would themselves wish to dwell for more than a brief period of time, especially as a woman. One may sympathize with some of the Marglins' goals — respect for diversity, desire to protect from exploitation ways of life that seem to be rich in spiritual and artistic value — without agreeing that

extreme relativism of the sort they defend is the best way to articulate and pursue these goals.

One more antiessentialist approach to questions of distributive justice must now be considered. It is by far the most powerful alternative to the Aristotelian approach, and its differences from it are subtle and complex. This is the liberal idea, defended in different forms by John Rawls and Ronald Dworkin, that distribution should aim at an equal allotment of certain basic resources (or, in the case of Rawls, should tolerate inequalities only where this would improve the situation of the worst off).[39]

The Rawlsian liberal insists on distributing basic resources without taking a stand on the human good, even in the vague way in which the "thick vague theory" has done so. The aim is to leave to each citizen a choice of the conception of the good by which he or she will live. As we have said, Rawls does take a stand on some of the components of our conception. For sociability and practical reason are treated as essential to any conception of human flourishing that can be entertained; liberty is on the list of "primary goods" as are the "social conditions of self-respect"; and in argument against utilitarianism, Rawls commits himself very strongly to the centrality of the separateness of persons.[40] On the other hand, as we have seen, the Aristotelian conception does itself insist on the fundamental role of choice and autonomy. But there are still significant differences between the two conceptions, for the Rawlsian view treats income and wealth as "primary goods" of which more is always better, independently of the concrete conception of the good. And he does define the "better off" and "worse off" in terms of quantities of these basic resources rather than in terms of functioning or capability.

To this, the Aristotelian has three replies. First, as we have said, wealth and income are not good in their own right; they are good only insofar as they promote human functioning. Rawls's view, which appears to treat them as having independent significance, obscures the role that they actually play in human life.

Second, human beings have variable needs for resources, and any adequate definition of the better off and worse off must reflect that fact. A pregnant woman has nutritional needs that are different from those of a nonpregnant woman and a child from those of an adult. The child who has exactly the same amount of protein in her diet as an adult is less well off, given her greater needs. A person whose mobility is impaired will need a significantly greater amount of resources than will a person of average mobility in order to achieve the same level of capability to move about. These are not just rare exceptions; they are pervasive facts of life. Thus the failure of the liberal theory to deal with them is a serious defect. And yet, to deal with then, we need a general conception of what functions we are trying to support.[41]

Third, the liberal, by defining being well-off in terms of possessions alone, fails to go deep enough in imagining the impediments to functioning that are actually present in many human lives. Marx argued, for example, that workers who lack control over their own activity and its products lead lives less than fully human, even if they do get adequate wages. In general, the structure of labor relations, of class relations, and of race and gender relations in a society can alienate its members from the fully human use of their faculties even when their material needs are met. It is possible to hold that a pampered middle-class housewife is well off, despite the barriers that prevent her from expressing herself fully in employment and education. What is very unclear is whether Rawls — who does indeed decide to postpone consideration of structures of power within the household — should allow himself to be in this position, given his commitment to the realization of the two moral powers for each and every citizen. At the very least, there is a tension internal to the view, which can be dispelled only by a more explicit consideration of the relationship between the two moral powers and various other human functions and their material and institutional necessary conditions.[42] With political liberty, Rawls fully seizes this problem; therefore he places liberty among the primary goods. My claim is that he needs to go further in this direction, making the list of primary goods not a list of resources and commodities at all but a list of basic capabilities of the person.

The political and economic alternative to these various antiessentialist views does exist and is in use in a variety of areas. In development economics, a position strikingly similar to the Aristotelian position has been developed by economist-philosopher Amartya Sen. Arguing that the focus of development analysis should be on human capabilities rather than on opulence or utility or resources, he has proposed ways of assessing the quality of life in developing countries that begin from a list of interrelated capabilities. His arguments for this approach and against others are closely related to the arguments of this essay. Other related approaches have been worked out by Scandinavian social scientists, by doctors measuring patients' quality of life, by teachers in a troubled society interested in laying a foundation for the peaceful resolution of conflict.[43]

Now I return to the antiessentialist stories with which I began, showing how the Aristotelian view would handle them. The case of smallpox vaccination is relatively clear-cut. The Aristotelian, while not wishing to interfere with the capability of citizens to use their imaginations and their senses for the purposes of religious expression should they choose to do so, would certainly make bodily health a top priority and would not be deterred in a program of smallpox vaccination by the likelihood that it would eradicate the cult of Sittlala Devi. The Aristotelian would introduce the vaccination scheme and then leave it to the citizens to see whether they wished to continue their relationship with that goddess. Nothing would prevent them from doing so, but if they ceased to see the point in the observances, once the disease had been eradicated, the Aristotelian would weep no nostalgic tears.

As for freedom and the Japanese husband, the Aristotelian will simply remind the objector of what she means by freedom, which is the power to form a conception of the good and to select action toward its realization. She will point out that in that sense of freedom, the Japanese husband in the example has (and no doubt values) freedom; his freedom, indeed, is enhanced by having someone who will look after boring details of life. But if the freedom of one person requires pushing someone else below the threshold of capability to exercise practical reason, the Aristotelian will call this injustice and exploitation, and will not rest content until a searching examination of gender relations in this case has shown to what extent the capabilities of women are in fact being undercut in the name of male leisure.

As for menstruation taboos, they look like a clear restriction on women's power to execute a plan of life that they have chosen. This is so even if, as is sometimes claimed, such taboos end up giving women more rest and a little more pleasure than they would have had if they were working; for some tradeoffs that diminish the power of choice, even when they result in greater comfort, are not supported by the Aristotelian view.

To conclude this part of my argument, I would now like to examine a case that is more complicated and problematic than the ones I have just related rather briefly. This case will dramatize the difference between the Aristotelian approach and its rivals in the development sphere, and will also indicate how the Aristotelian proposes to balance sensitivity to local tradition against her commitment to a theory of the human being. The case concerns a literacy campaign directed at women in rural Bangladesh. It is described in Marty Chen's excellent book, *A Quiet Revolution: Women in Transition in Rural Bangladesh.*[44]

The women in the village in which Chen worked had low status in every area, in terms of our account of human functioning. They were less well nourished than males, less educated, less free, and less respected. Let us now consider their situation with respect to just one question: the question of literacy. As I have said, polls based on the idea of utility typically show, in this and related cases, that women have no desire for a higher rate of literacy. The poll is taken; women express satisfaction; no action follows. This, of course, is not surprising, given the weight of the cultural forces pressing these women not to demand more education (and also not to feel that they want more) given, as well, the absence in their daily lives of paradigms of what education could do and be in lives similar to theirs.

The development agency with which Chen was working went into the village holding firmly to the conviction that literacy was an important basic good. At first, they tried a liberal approach, based on the distribution of resources: in cooperation with the local government, they handed out to the women of the village ample adult literacy materials, taking no stand on whether they should choose to use them. (Notice that already this approach is not really a liberal approach, in that it takes a stand on the importance of education, giving these women literacy materials rather than cash. It is also not a pure liberal approach because it singled out the women of the village, recognizing their special impediments to functioning as giving them a greater claim on resources.) The distribution had little impact on women's functioning. This was so because the development people made no attempt to perceive the women's lives in a broad or deep way or to ask what role literacy might play in those lives and what strategies of education were most suited for their particular case. Perhaps even more important, they did not ask the women to tell their own story.

The liberal project had failed. Yet the development workers did not simply drop their general conception of the good, concluding that local traditions should in each case be the arbiter of value and that belief in their own way was bound to be paternalistic. Instead, they made a transition to a more Aristotelian approach. Over a period of several years, they set up women's cooperatives in which members of the development agency joined with the local women in a searching participatory dialogue concerning the whole form of life in the village. They discussed with the women the role that literacy was currently playing in the lives of women elsewhere, showing concrete examples of transformations in empowerment and self-respect. The women, in turn, told them their own story of the special impediments to education that their traditions had given them. The result, over time, was a gradual but deep transformation in the entire shape of the women's lives. Once literacy was perceived not as a separate and highly general thing but as a skill that might be deployed in particular ways in their particular context, it became of enormous interest and led to many changes in women's lives. For example, women were able to take over the tailoring industry in the village as well as other similar functions. In this way, they began to earn wages outside the home, a circumstance that has been shown to give women a stronger claim to food and medical care when resources are scarce. On the other hand, none of these concrete transformations could have happened had the women of the development agency not held fast to their general conception, showing the women its many other concrete realizations, and proceeding with confidence that it did have some concrete realization in these particular lives. Essentialism and particular perception were not opposed: they were complementary aspects of a single process of deliberation. Had the women not been seen as human beings who shared with the other women a common humanity, the local women could not have told their story in the way they did, nor could the development workers have brought their own experiences of feminism to the participatory dialogue as if they had some relevance for the local women. The very structure of the dialogue presupposed the recognition of common humanity, and it was only with this basis securely established that they could fruitfully explore the concrete circumstances in which they were trying, in the one case, to live and in the other case, to promote flourishing human lives. ...

Author's Note

A version of this essay was presented at the Institute for the Humanities at the University of Chicago in May 1991; I am grateful to Norma Field for arranging the invitation and to the participants, especially David Gitomer and Chris Bobonich, for their helpful comments. I also owe thanks to Amartya Sen for many discussions, to Frédérique and Steve Marglin for challenging and provoking me, to David Crocker and Henry Richardson for valuable comments on earlier related work, and to Tracy Strong and Cass Sunstein for comments on an earlier draft.

NOTES

1. The argument of this essay is closely related to that of several others, to which I shall refer frequently in what follows: "Nature, Function, and Capability," *Oxford Studies in Ancient Philosophy,* suppl. vol. 1 (1988): 145-84 (hereafter NFC); "Non-relative virtues: An Aristotelian Approach," *Midwest Studies in Philosophy* 13 (1988): 32-53, and, in an expanded version, in *The Quality of Life,* edited by M. Nussbaum and A. Sen (Oxford: Clarendon, 1992) (hereafter NRV); "Aristotelian Social Democracy," in *Liberalism and the Good*, edited by R.B. Douglas et al. (New York: Routledge, 1990) 203-52 (hereafter ASD); "Aristotle on Human Nature and the Foundations of Ethics," in a volume on the philosophy of Bernard Williams, edited by R. Harrison and J. Altham (Cambridge: Cambridge University Press, 1992) (hereafter HN); "Human Capabilities, Female Human Beings," in *Women, Culture and Development: a Study of Human Capabilities*, ed. M. Nussbaum and J. Glover (Oxford: Clarendon, [1995]) (hereafter HC).

2. For relevant publications of the United Nations University/World Institute for Development Economics Research (WIDER), see Nussbaum and Sen, eds., *The Quality of life*, and Nussbaum and Glover, eds., *Women, Culture and Development*.

3. Much of the material described in the examples is now published in *Dominating Knowledge: Development, Culture, and Resistance*, edited by Frédérique Apffel Marglin and Stephen A. Marglin (Oxford: Clarendon, 1990). The issue of "embeddedness" and menstruation taboos is discussed in S.A. Marglin, "Losing Touch: The Culture Conditions of Worker Accommodation and Resistance," 217-82, and related general issues are developed in S.A. Marglin, "Toward the Decolonization of the Mind," I-28. On Sittala Devi, see S.A. Marglin, "Smallpox in Two Systems of Knowledge," 102-44; and for related arguments, see Ashis Nandy and Shiv Visvanathan, "Modern Medicine and Its Non-Modern Critics," 144-84.

4. The proceedings of this conference are published as Nussbaum and Sen, *The Quality of Life.*

5. This point is now made in S.A. Marglin, "Toward the Decolonization"; his reference is to Takeo Doi, *The Anatomy of Dependence* (Tokyo: Kedansho, 1971)

6. Because of such pervasive assumptions, in general I have not used the vocabulary of "essentialism" in

describing my own (historically embedded and historically sensitive) account of the central human functions. I do so here, somewhat polemically, in order to reclaim the word for reasoned debate, and I assume that the reader will look closely at my account of what the "essentialism" I recommend, in fact, entails. For further comments on this, see HN, ASC, and HC.

7. Much of the same has been true of at least some of the opponents of relativist "antiessentialism," who speak of relativism as the source of all modern evil, without saying how they themselves would answer relativist arguments. See, for example, my criticisms of Allan Bloom's *The Closing of the American Mind* (New York: Simon and Schuster, 1987) in "Undemocratic Vistas," *The New York Review of Books*, November 5, 1987.

8. Jacques Derrida, *Of Grammatology*, translated By G.C. Spivak (Baltimore: Johns Hopkins University Press, 1977).

9. For my account of Aristotle's position, see *The Fragility of Goodness: Luck and Ethics in Greek Tragedy and Philosophy* (Cambridge: Cambridge University Press, 1986), chap.8. Related debates in Indian philosophy are given a most illuminating discussion in B.K. Matilal, *Perception* (Oxford: Clarendon, 1985).

10. In this category, as close relatives of my view, I would place the "internal-realist" conception of Hilary Putnam, *Reason, Truth and History* (Cambridge: Cambridge University Press, 1981), *The Many Faces of Realism* (La Salle: Open Court, 1987) and *Realism With a Human Face* (Cambridge, MA: Harvard University Press, 1990); and also Charles Taylor *Sources of the Self: The Making of Modern Identity* Cambridge, MA: Harvard University Press 1989). For my discussion of Taylor's arguments, see *New Republic*, April 1990.

11. See esp. John Rawls, *A Theory of Justice* (Cambridge, MA: Harvard University Press 1971.) Rawls's position and its relationship to the Aristotelian view is discussed in NFC, in HC and especially in ASD, with references to other later articles in which Rawls has further developed his position concerning the role of a conception on the good in his theory.

12. By relativism I mean the view that the only available standard to value is some local group or individual; by subjectivism I mean the view that the only available standard to value is some local group or individual; by subjectivism I mean the view that the standard is given by each individual's subjective preferences; thus relativism, as I understand it here, is a genus of which subjectivism is one extreme species.

13. Aristotle, *Parts of Animals* 1.5, 645 a5-37. Aristotle notes that anyone who has this shame about looking at the animal world is bound to take up the same attitude to himself, since an animal is what he is.

14. See esp. *Reason, Truth and History* and also Putnam's chapter in Nussbaum and Sen, eds., *The Quality of Life*.

15. For further elaboration, see HN, ASD, and HC.

16. See ASD; for detailed argument concerning the normative character of such an inquiry into "essence," see HN.

17. For a detailed account of this contrast, see ASD and NFC.

18. For a closely related idea, see Charles Taylor, *Sources of the Self*.

19. HN discusses the relation of this idea to some debates about the end of life in contemporary medical ethics.

20. On the question of cultural variation in the construction of these basic experiences, see NRV and ASD.

21. See Aristotle, *Metaphysics 1.1*.

22. This problem is confronted in "Transcending Humanity," in Nussbaum, *Love's Knowledge: Essays on Philosophy and Literature* (New York: Oxford University Press, 1990).

23. For the relationship of these ideas to Marx's account of truly human functioning in the *Economic and Philosophical Manuscripts of 1844*, see NFC.

24. For Scandinavian conceptions, see the chapters by E. Allardt and R. Erikson in Nussbaum and Sen, eds., *The Quality of Life*. On capabilities in Sri Lanka, see Carlos Fonseka, *Toward a Peaceful Sri Lanka*, WIDER Research for Action series, World Institute for Developments Economics Research, Helsinki, 1990.

25. John Rawls, "The Idea of an Overlapping Consensus," *Oxford Journal of Legal Studies* 7 (1987).

26. For some examples, see NRV.

27. This is developed more fully in ASD.

28. See the longer treatment of this issue in ASD.

29. This distinction is central in the political theory of Amartya Sen. See, among others "Equality of What?" in Sen, *Choice, Welfare, and Measurement* (Oxford: Blackwell, 1982) 353-69, and *Commodities and Capabilities* (Amsterdam: North-Holland, 1985.)

30. See also Sen, *Commodities and Capabilities.*

31. See esp. Rawls, "The Priority of the Right and Ideas of the Good," *Philosophy and Public Affairs* 17 (1988); for further references and discussions, see ASD.

32. Compare the remarks on slaves in Stanley Cavell, *The Claim of Reason* (New York: Oxford University Press, 1979).

33. Raul Hilberg, *The Destruction of the European Jews* (New York: Holmes and Meier, 1985).

34. This idea is developed more fully in NFC and HC.

35. For more on this, see NFC and HC.

36. See Nussbaum and Sen, "Introduction," *The Quality of Life.*

37. For these objections, see also Sen, "Equality of What?" and *Commodities and Capabilities.* Recent utilitarian work in philosophy has to some extent addressed these objections, introducing many corrections to actual preferences, but the practice of development economists has not been much altered.

38. See Sen, *Commodities and Capabilities*; also J. Kynch and A. Sen, "Indian Women: Well-Being and Survival," *Cambridge Journal of Economics* 7 (1983).

39. For a longer account of these criticisms, see ASD.

40. Rawls, *A Theory of Justice* (Cambridge, MA: Harvard University Press, 1922) 189-92.

41. See Sen, "Equality of What?"

42. On this point, see Okin, *Justice, Gender and the Family*, and my review of her in *New York Review of Books,* [October 1992].

43. See the chapters by Allardt, Erikson, and Brock in Nussbaum and Sen, eds., *The Quality of Life*; also Fonseka, *Towards a Peaceful Sri Lanka.*

44. Cambridge, MA: Schenkman, 1983. See also Chen, "A Matter of Survival: Women's Right to Work in India and Bangladesh," in Nussbaum and Glover, eds., *Women, Culture and Development.*

INSIDERS AND OUTSIDERS
IN INTERNATIONAL DEVELOPMENT

David A. Crocker

David A. Crocker is a Senior Research Scholar at the Institute for Philosophy and Public Policy and teaches in the School of Public Affairs at the University of Maryland, College Park. He is the author of Praxis and Democratic Socialism *(1983) and co-editor of* Ethics of Consumption: The Good Life, Justice, and Global Stewardship *(1998, with Toby Linden). Crocker is the founder and former President of the International Development Ethics Association (IDEA).*

Crocker discusses the question of who should engage in the moral evaluation of a country's development goals and strategies. Answers to this question have tended to be framed in terms of the debates about ethnocentrism/anti-ethnocentrism and particularism/universalism. Instead of defending a position within this framework, Crocker attempts to recast the debate by developing an account of insiders and outsiders and of the advantages and disadvantages each bring to moral inquiry about issues of development. He argues that we are all insiders and outsiders to various groups, associations, and countries and that we can become more complete persons and better developmental ethicists by exploring and utilizing insider and outsider insights.

International development ethics is moral reflection on the ends and means of societal and global change.[1] Who should engage in this activity and how should it be done? We can make headway on this large question by answering some more specific questions. Should only citizens of a given nation reflect on that country's development goals and strategies? Should only a society's members morally evaluate that society's present development models, policies, and practices or advocate alternatives? Or do foreigners have a contribution to make as well?[2] Who should conduct ethical research with respect to regional and, especially, global development when regional identity is comparatively shallow and global citizenship is arguably utopian or non-existent?

I try to answer these questions in four steps. First, I briefly discuss and criticize the context in which the questions are usually framed and debated, namely the ethnocentrism/anti-ethnocentrism and particularism/universalism controver-

sies. Second, I explain the distinction between social insiders and outsiders and argue that it is a more fruitful angle from which to address the topic of who should engage in development ethics. Foreigners can become partial insiders in an initially alien society just as citizens can be outsiders in their own societies. Third, I argue that in development ethics, as in other cross cultural activities such as sports and business, there are both advantages and disadvantages to being social insiders as well as social outsiders. In development ethics both insiders and outsiders have positive roles to play and temptations to avoid. Finally, I urge development ethicists to cultivate a mixture of insiderness/outsiderness with respect to both their own and other societies. Moreover, there are good reasons for strengthening a global community in which ethicists, among others, are partial insiders. As world citizens, as well as partial insiders in other communities, ethicists can evaluate present international institutions, hammer out global norms, and forge improved international structures and relations. International norms and structures are not insignificant; they can hinder or help good national and regional development just as national and regional progress can contribute to global improvement.

I

It is widely believed, especially by those living in rich and powerful countries, that appropriate Third World and global development models, policies, and projects should reflect Northern/Western development experience. Increasingly this belief is seen, especially by those living in the Third World, as ethnocentrism. Here "ethnocentrism" means two things. First, Northern/Western ethnocentrics employ their own cultural norms in evaluating foreign practices. In this first sense, ethnocentrism is "a habitual disposition to judge foreign peoples or groups by the standards and practices of one's own culture or ethnic group." Second, these ethnocentrics employ their standards to make *invidious* comparisons. Foreign standards and practices are judged to be inferior to those of the evaluator. In this second sense, ethnocentrism is "a tendency toward viewing alien cultures with disfavor and a resulting sense of (one's own) inherent superiority."[3] Ethnocentrism is not limited to but is especially prevalent in the United States. As Ofelia Schutte remarks, "One basic difficulty with our attitude toward the rest of the world is the implicit belief that our way of life in the United States is superior to any other ... and deserves to be exported to others."[4]

Given this definition, ethnocentrism might arguably occur if a development ethicist from one culture evaluates development in another culture. The likelihood is increased when the ethicist comes from the rich North or West to assess development ends and means in the poor South or East. The ethicist is likely to judge Third World development in terms of his or her own societal norms and propose development goals and strategies to help "them" become like "us." There are three main responses to this likelihood of ethnocentrism: (1) particularist anti-ethnocentrism, (2) universal-ist anti-ethnocentrism, and (3) particularist anti anti-ethnocentrism.

First, particularist anti-ethnocentrism rejects the exporting of foreign development models and practices and sometimes repudiates the very idea of development.[5] Each "developing" society or region should define desirable social change according to its own "lights" (stock of ideas) and its own traditions. The particularist enjoins: "Cast your buckets where you are!"[6] Every society should be loyal to its own moral traditions and development ethic. A foreign development ethicist would have a role in an alien culture's development only if there were some overlap in the moral traditions of the two countries. The foreigner's "lights" would be shared, at least partially, by indigenous ethicists. Sometimes this kind of anti-ethnocentrism is supported on nationalistic and even ethnocentric grounds. Sometimes it is argued for on universal moral grounds: each society has the right or the duty to determine its own path and develop itself in its own way — free from foreign influence, let alone economic domination or military intervention. Schutte nicely captures (and endorses) particularist (anti-U.S.) anti-ethnocentrism:

We should recognize that issues of national sovereignty, autonomy, and self-determination in Latin America take precedence for its inhabitants over issues related to the notion of "progress" as determined by U.S. standards of what ought to occur in the region. In philosophy, this means that there is a strong desire to preserve the legacy of Latin American thought over and against the constant incursion of U.S. — backed ideas.... Latin American intellectuals tend to agree that Latin American problems need and ought to be resolved by Latin Americans and by no one else.[7]

As Schutte indicates, the more extreme versions of this position are explicitly separatist: foreigners are not welcome in a region's or a nation's development debate. Less extreme positions leave open the possibility of some general cross-cultural dialogue, but see no value and much danger in foreigners engaging in the development dialogue in and for another society.

Much of this view deserves acceptance. National and regional self-determination should be respected. It does not follow, however, that foreigners, even from North America, cannot play a positive role in a Third World development dialogue. For as Schutte herself recognizes, this dialogue can and should take place "on no less than a perfectly equal basis."[8] But more needs to be said about the assumptions and implications of this conversational equality. Moreover, the issue is not that of foreigner versus native; for some foreigners are more a part of the "alien" society than some of that society's own members and, as we shall see, there are morally significant insider/outsider distinctions among the society's own members.

Universalist anti-ethnocentrism, a second response to ethnocentrism, seeks to get beyond all cultural bias, whether of First, Second or third World varieties, by ascending to an ahistorical, transcendent Archimedean point.[9] From this standpoint, the timeless Truth about desirable social change can be discerned (or constructed) and then applied to societies at different stages of the one development path. Ethnocentrism is objectionable, and it should be reduced if not eliminated by replacing cultural bias with Reason.

Universalism has stronger and weaker versions depending on differences concerning how far Reason can go in reducing the plurality of development perspectives to one perspective. The weaker versions elevate national or regional self-determination and mutual tolerance to super-ethical principles and then prescribe that each society determine its own development path and be tolerant of the like effort of others. The stronger versions propose more determinate fundamental ends and basic means for *all* countries.

Common to these universalist approaches is the belief that the Truth about development can be grounded in some noncontingent source above history or deeply rooted in human nature. Rational investigators can get outside all development vocabularies, compare them with (or construct) the Truth, and rationally select the vocabulary that matches or at least best approximates the universal,

transcultural Truth about what development should be. Foreigners are on an equal footing with compatriots if and when they equally transcend their cultural identity. Truth is nation-blind and region-blind, equally open to culture-transcending and knowing minds in touch with the Truth "out there" or "in here."

The trouble with the universalist critique of and alternative to ethnocentrism is that universalism (1) cannot, except by begging the question, establish itself or any non-vacuous truth; (2) provides no conclusive means of deciding among candidates for the True development model; and (3) opens the door to domination of others by those who think they have the Truth.

Finally, anti anti-ethnocentrism bites the bullet and both rejects universalism's pretensions and affirms that ethnocentrism is desirable as well as unavoidable. We cannot but evaluate by our "lights" and make invidious comparisons of our society with others. And even if we could do so, we shouldn't. Foreign development ethicists can not get outside their cultural skin and should be loyal to their own communities and moral tradition. Richard Rorty, in a passage whose length is outweighed by its verve, expresses anti anti-ethnocentrism when he characterizes pragmatism as the "accepting of the contingency of starting points" rather than "attempting to evade this contingency":

To accept the contingency of starting-points is to accept our inheritance from, and our conversation with, our fellow humans as our only source of guidance. To attempt to evade this contingency is to hope to become a properly-programmed machine. This was the hope which Plato thought might be fulfilled at the top of the divided line, when we passed beyond hypotheses. Christians have hoped it might be attained by becoming attuned to the voice of God in the heart, and Cartesians that it might be fulfilled by emptying the mind and seeking the indubitable. Since Kant, philosophers have hoped that it might be fulfilled by finding the a priori structure of any possible inquiry, or language, or form of social life. If we give up this hope, we shall lose what Nietzsche called "metaphysical comfort," but we may gain a renewed sense of community. Our identification with our community — our society, our political tradition, our intellectual heritage — is heightened when we see this community as *ours* rather than *nature's, shaped* rather than *found,* one among many which men have made. In the end, the pragmatists tell us, what matters is our loyalty to other human beings clinging together against the dark, not our hope of getting things right.[10]

A more ambitious form of anti anti-ethnocentrism affirms that "our" ethics — where "our" refers to "we relatively rich, liberal North Americans and Europeans" — is an ethic with global pretensions. Loyalty to our historical community (rather than to ahistorical Reason) requires that this society's development ethic be spread to — if not imposed on — other cultures. Thus, so the argument goes, we Northern Liberals have a duty to spread our liberal development ethics to societies other than our own — even if the execution of this duty clashes with what Hegel called the other society's own "moral substance." The liberal ethic requires, however, that the clash be resolved by freedom-respecting argument rather than by coercion.

This sophisticated endorsement of ethnocentrism has much to recommend it. It rightly gives up on ahistorical grounding and recognizes that we cannot avoid evaluating by our own cultural lights. It goes too far (or in the wrong direction), however, in making these lights impervious to change and in assuming the inevitability of invidious comparison in favor of one's own society. Moreover, the ambitious forms of anti anti-ethnocentrism presume too much when they uncritically assume that what is good for one, "our development ethic," is good and relevant for all.

An approach to international development ethics is needed whereby an ethicist from a "developed" society can become convinced that a "developing" society offers some progressive ideas for the ethicist's *own* society. This better idea need not be merely a better employment of a shared ideal; it could be something new and different that substantially alters the foreigner's ethical assumptions.

Each ethicist starts from but need not end with the ethics inherited from his or her society. Genuine dialogue involves a "continual reweaving" of the web of the desires and beliefs of all those involved.[11] North American and European development ethicists need to understand their activity in such a way that one upshot of international dialogue is that their own group's standards and practices might come to be seen as "bad" development or "anti-development."

Each of the three responses to ethnocentrism in development ethics has merits and deficiencies. However, instead of trying to devise a position that retains each position's strengths while avoiding its weaknesses, let us make a new start on the question.

II

Instead of focusing on the role of foreigners in a country's development debate, let us first make a distinction between the roles of social insiders and social outsiders in development ethics. What should we mean by "insider" and "outsider"? Both terms refer to persons in relation to groups rather than to persons in and of themselves. An insider is one who is counted, recognized, or accepted, by himself/herself and the other group members, as belonging to the group. One is so identified on the basis of such things as shared beliefs, desires, memories, and hopes.[12] Accordingly, one is an outsider with respect to a group just in case he or she is not counted, recognized or accepted by himself/herself and/or the group members — as belonging to the group, due to lack of these shared beliefs, desires, memories, hopes, and so forth. This insider/outsider distinction also applies to a situation as well as to a group. Some people, for example, feel "at home" in Mexican villages but alien to the streets of Mexico City.

My recognition of myself and the recognition by other group members that I too am a group member are conditions that are individually necessary and together sufficient for insiderness. If I count myself as a member of a team, and my teammates do not, I may feel like an insider but not really be one. Moreover, if my teammates recognize me as one of the team, but I do not so accept myself, my sense of myself as an outsider *makes* me an outsider.

It is important to underscore that the insider/outsider distinction does not coincide with the distinction of native/foreigner or citizen/foreigner. On the one hand, one can be outside the group formally but really be an insider. Someone can become (more or less) an insider to Mexican culture and not have been born in Mexico, reared there, or be a Mexican citizen; for example, the Guatemalan refugees' children quickly can become insiders to the Mexican culture to which their parents remain outsiders. On the other hand, one can be formally a member of a group and not (yet) be an insider, for example, a new player on the team, an adopted child, a spouse whose heart is elsewhere. Like many a Yucatecan Indian, one can be a Mexican citizen, born and reared in Mexico, and not be viewed or view oneself as a Mexican.

We are all insiders and outsiders in a multitude of ways. I am an insider in my family but an outsider in yours. I am at home in small cities but an outsider in huge metropoles, small towns, and the country. A poor Yucatecan fisherman may be an insider on the piers of Puerto Progreso yet an outsider in the nearby condos of Cancun. A Costa Rican Professor of philosophy is an insider in the University of Costa Rica but an outsider among the *vaqueros* of the Costa Rican Province of Guanacaste.

Even with respect to the same group we can be both insiders and outsiders. I identify with some of my country's values and practices and not with others. A person can be an insider in his or her family in some respects and an outsider in others. As Ruth Hubbard and Margaret Randall tell us, "Insider and outsider are not mutually exclusive. We are usually both at the same time and in the same place."[13] There may be ambiguity even with regard to one and the same plan, belief, hope or memory. Hubbard suggests the "ambiguities and continuities of insider/outsiderness"[14] by the symbol of a Möbius strip:

If you travel along it, starting at any point, say on the outside, you are shortly inside, then outside again, then inside, on and on as you go round and round. There is no demarcation or point of transition between inside and outside.[15]

So with respect to the same group we can be "quasi-insiders" and "quasi-outsiders."[16]

It follows that the insider/outsider distinction is better understood as a continuum or spectrum rather than a rigid dichotomy whose categories are mutually exclusive. Insiderness and outsiderness are differences on a continuum. You, My Costa Rican friend, are not totally an outsider or totally an insider in our family; you rightly call us your "second family." Time spent in another country can make one less an outsider to the "adopted" country and, sometimes, more an outsider to one's own country; for one can take on some of the commitments of the former and weaken or extinguish some of the latter. The result is often an exotic collage of insiderness/outsiderness, as evidenced in cities that are becoming more like (pre-Desert Storm) "Kuwaiti bazaars" than "English gentlemen's clubs."[17] Salmon Rushdie, the beleaguered Indian novelist who has lived for many years in London, observes such polychromatic mixtures in Indian immigrants living in London's Brick Lane:

The thing you have to understand about a neighborhood like this ... is that when people board an Air India jet and come halfway across the planet, they don't just bring their suitcases. They bring everything and even as they reinvent themselves in the new city — which is what they do — there remain these old selves, old traditions erased in part but not fully. So what you get are these fragmented, multifaceted, multicultural selves.

And this can lead to such strange things.... You will find teen-age girls in this neighborhood who in so many ways are London kids: Levi 502s, Madonna T-shirts, spiky hair. They never think at all of going back to India or Pakistan, even for a visit. They might actually have been born here in London. And yet you may find among them a willingness, an eagerness in some cases, to have an arranged marriage. An *arranged marriage*.

Or this story: In this very neighborhood, it was early in the 1980s. A Pakistani father stabbed and murdered his daughter, his only child, because he heard she had made love to a white boy. Which turned out not to be true, but that is not my point: My point is that he had brought with him this idea of honor and shame. And when I wrote about this later, I said that although I was obviously appalled — I mean, what can be more awful than murdering your own child? — I understood what had motivated him. I am a first-generation immigrant from that part of the world. I know how you can be here, and, in a way, still be there.[18]

Being a pure insider or a pure outsider would be difficult if not impossible. One would have to consider oneself (and be considered by others) as in *total* agreement, disagreement or indifference in relation to a group. One reason that pure cases of insiderness would be best construed as only a hypothetical limit is that the groups with which we identify have diverse and often antagonistic factions. And even if Alasdair MacIntyre is correct when he says that premodern societies were marked by homogeneity, he also sees that — from the point of view of its own standards — every tradition must "view itself as to some degree inadequate."[19] Another reason that pure insiderness is a conceptual limit is that we are members of different groups that pull us in different directions. Finally, in becoming *aware* of our insider status, we become something of an outsider to it. Similarly, the case of a pure outsider would be a hypothetical limit; for we find it difficult and undesirable to be completely outside human bonds. One is reminded of Sartre's dictum that "human reality ... [is] a being which is what it is not and which is not what it is."[20]

Changes occur in one's insider or outsider relations. These changes can have various reasons and causes. I just may find myself thinking more like (one type of) Costa Rican and less like a gringo. The refugee from Chilean repression found it impossible to continue identifying with a nation that had descended into barbarism. Costa Ricans and Mexicans often unthinkingly make Central American refugees into a "Them." Choice, however, is sometimes possible. There are several options here. Sometimes, the immigrant or exile, in Rushdie's words, "reinvents" himself or herself, consciously deciding to take on some of the values of the new homeland without giving up insider status in the old country. Sometimes outsiders, trying to gain acceptance as insiders, single-mindedly strive to transform themselves into fanatic representations of their new life.[21] Refugees and immigrants, however, can resist identification with the "host" country in order to keep alive insiderness with respect to the homeland. Costa Ricans decide to extend *pura vida* (the good life, Costa Rican style) to select others, such as rich gringo *pensionados* (retirees), but not others, such as refugees from Nicaraguan turmoil, Guatemalan repression, or Atlantic coast poverty.

We have seen the multiplicity of groups in relation to which one can have insider or outsider status. Are there any limits? On one extreme, one can talk — at least by metaphorical extension of oneself as a group with one member. Moral integrity is a form of insiderness. I become an outsider to myself when I violate my core values. Margaret Randall puts it well:

I became at one and the same time more of an outsider vis-à-vis the mainstream beliefs and values of my country and more of an insider, if by that term one means someone closer to the core of her own authentic identity.[22]

What about extensions of insiderness in the other direction? In particular, can one be an insider to the biotic community or global humanity? Remember that the primary use of the insider/outsider distinction concerns human groups. Yet we find it useful to extend insiderness to non-human groups and non-groups. Suppose morality has to do with what Rorty, following Wilfred Sellars, calls "we-intentions" — with purposes that we share with others and obligations to help those who are part of the "we." Then, although the purposes I can share with non-humans may be limited, I can view myself as grateful and obligated to that biotic-natural community of which I am a part if not a member. Although "humanity" refers to an abstract class rather than to a concrete group or a common essence that binds us together, I can pledge to extend the "we" of my communities to include all persons, however distant in space and time. And just as expanding the "we" beyond the family to the tribe need not extinguish the family, so too extending our we-intentions regionally and globally need not erase — it may even nurture — our narrower group loyalties.[23]

How should we evaluate insiderness and outsiderness? There are distinctive goods and bads, opportunities and temptations, advantages and disadvantages in being outsiders as well as insiders. By virtue of one's insider and outsider status, respectively, one has different sorts of possibilities for both good and evil. The particular valuational balance will change with respect to several variables, such as the moral character and relative power of the groups from which one comes and to which one goes. Opportunities for good and temptations for evil vary with respect to the nature of the groups in relation to which one is insider and outsider. To be outside a despicable group and inside an admirable group is morally desirable.

Let us now apply this analysis of the insider/outsider distinction to our original question concerning international development ethics.

III

Suppose that a development ethicist is a member of a group and critically reflects on that group's present and future development. That group, as we have seen, may be of different kinds. In today's world, nation-states, and to a lesser extent regions, have a certain priority as development units. But the groups in which the ethicist functions range geographically from local neighborhoods, through cities/areas, to huge regions such as Central America, Latin America, the Western Hemisphere, the Third World, and the planet. Beyond political-geographical communities, the groups in which the ethicist functions can be social classes or ethnic groups as well as local, national, regional, or international enterprises. With respect to any of these

groups, what opportunities and dangers does an insider-ethicist face *by virtue of being an insider?*

The advantages are at least three in number. First, by virtue of being an insider, the insider-ethicist knows what things mean to the community, for the ethicist shares in the community's practices, vocabulary, memories, hopes, and fears. This capacity is particularly important insofar as the ethicist is committed to an Aristotelian "internalist" ethics that takes into account and contributes to the community's aspirations and beliefs. Martha Nussbaum and Amartya Sen make the point well:

> Ethical inquiry, he [Aristotle] insists, must be what we might call "value-relative." That is, they are not "pure" inquiries conducted in a void; they are questions about living asked by communities of human beings who are actually engaged in living and valuing. What will count as an appropriate, and even a *true*, outcome of such inquiry is constrained, and appropriately constrained; by what human beings antecedently value and need.[24]

As part of the "we," the insider-ethicist also has the capacity not only to understand but to make himself/herself understood as a conversation partner in the group's dialogue about its identity. The insider is "one of us," literally and figuratively speaks our language; and, we presume, knows whereof he or she speaks. Development ethics should be done in a contextually sensitive way, in relation to actual facts, interpreted meanings, and shared values. As Rorty puts it, "To imagine great things is to imagine a great future *for a particular community*, a community one knows well, identifies with, can make plausible predictions about."[25] An outsider-ethicist may miss altogether the real meaning of a past event, present policy, or future option, and, hence, be in no position ethically to evaluate them.

Second, in addition to knowing the "interpreted" facts, the insider-ethicist's moral judgments about the community's past, present, and future will be in terms *accessible* to the community in question. This is not to say it will always be clear which norm to appeal to or that there will not be two communal norms in tension or conflict. But it is to say that the insider-ethicist has an advantage over the outsider in that the former can more easily appeal to an understood and presumed set of moral assumptions, even when that set involves ambiguity and inconsistency.

Third, having insider standing gives the ethicist a prima facie right to criticize the group's development path, identify costs and benefits of current development strategy, and recommend what he or she considers better alternatives for the future. By virtue of being part of the group's cooperative activity, the insider has a generally acknowledged right and responsibility to contribute to the weaving and reweaving of the group's identity. Where the relatively pure outsider's assessments may be met with, "What right have you to stick your nose into *our* business," the insider is accorded that right by virtue of being a member of the community. Or, I would argue, *should be* so accorded. This "right to evaluate" is based not only on the insider's contribution to the group but also on the likelihood that the insider knows the facts, as interpreted by the group, the values that inform the group, and the desires that its members express.

The advantages of insider development ethics have a flip-side; definite disadvantages and dangers also exist for insiders in development ethics. First, an insider may be oblivious to constitutive meanings in his or her community precisely because they are so omnipresent. Like a fish unaware of the water in which it continually swims, the insider-ethicist may not be cognizant of certain features of his or her tradition and community. The community may be too close to get things into the focus requisite for ethical assessment.

Second, depending on the purity and exclusivity of their insiderness, insider ethicists are more or less limited to the vocabularies and valuational resources of their group. To become more of an insider in a group, particularly when the group is a "melting pot," may require the foregoing of alternative perspectives and becoming more of an outsider to one's former allegiances. This has costs both for the group and the ethicist. The group may desperately need new ideas to replace stale ones that have been dogmatically preserved. The ethicist may find himself or herself confined to and even trapped in familiar and conventional concepts — unable to expand the horizons of the possible and desirable. The insider-ethicist may purchase "relevance" at the price of needed novelty. The danger is that the insider will give the community comforting reassurances about past achievements rather than imaginative challenges for future greatness.

Insiders in development ethics face a third limitation and related risk. To be an insider is to live in the midst of loyalties, debts, favors, obligation, promises — things which one owes to others and which one is owed. These "debts" may be owed to the group's co-members or subgroups or to other groups to which one belongs. Such debts may be compromising or corrupting. Although group membership might give one the right to criticize and propose alternatives, loyalties to co-members and debts to others may inhibit the exercise of responsibilities. In such cases the temptation may be too great; it may be too much to expect insiders to be sufficiently and properly impartial. In contrast, the outsider may be able to say what the group needs to hear, but none of the members dare say. For this reason, each university graduate committee has an "outside" member, World Cup referees come from nations different from those of the competing teams, labor arbitrators are supposedly neutral in relation to both union and management, and Costa Rican elections are monitored by an institution independent of the contending parties.

IV

Like insider-ethicists, outsider-ethicists have certain liabilities and temptations as well as advantages and opportunities. Let us first consider the negative side.

Outsiders often are ignorant about what is going on in the group, what things mean, and what the group's normative resources are. The Third World is littered with development models, policies, and projects invented by societal outsiders and properly abandoned by societal insiders. For outsiders often ignorantly assume that "what is good for us, is good for them." More specifically, outsider ethi-cists are often closed off from the facts, meaning, and communal values relevant for progressive social change.

Second, while the insider-ethicist is usually accorded the right to evaluate present structures and future options, doors are often closed to the outsider-ethicist, especially when this outsider comes from a "developed" and powerful group. If the group's development debate is about its own identity, only members of the group may be viewed as having a right to participate — espe-cially if outsiders come from a dominating group. Recall, for example, Ofelia Schutte's endorsement cited earlier of particularist anti-ethnocentrism when discussing Latin America's condemnation of standards imposed by U.S. outsiders.

Supposing an invitation has been extended to an outsider-ethicist, we assume that to be effective the outsider would become "immersed," in Nuss-baum's and Sen's sense, in the "alien" society:

[Evaluation and criticism of the society] must be *immersed rather than detached* (i.e., the norm of objectivity should not be one that involves the detachment of the judging subject from the prac-tices, the perceptions, even the emotions, of the culture), stressing, instead, that objective value judgments can be made from the point of view of experienced immersion in the way of life of a culture.[26]

Still, the outsider's temptations and liabilities are not yet eliminated. Outside-ethicists who come from the more powerful and exploitative "center" and go to the more vulnerable and dependent "periphery" tend to accord their own ideas more weight than they deserve.[27] Even more, the pow-erful, "developed," and "modern" outsider is tempted to *assume* that his or her ideas are more worthy than those of the weak, "underdeveloped," or traditional insider. Similarly, the ethicist inside a peripheral group might tend to respond to the outsider's ethics by according them more weight than they merit and even by assuming they are correct. These dangers are all the more pro-nounced when outsider proposals go hand-in-hand

with economic inducements or when there exist strong traditions of host hospitality. The converse is also true: outsider-ethicists who go from the periphery to the center may not trust their own intuitions or principles when they clash with those of someone from the capital city, the aristocratic or educational elite, the "mother country," or the "colossus of the North." We don't have to buy the transcendental scaffolding of Habermas's theory of ideal communication to be well aware that undistorted communication and reasonable con-sensus require relative equality among dialogue partners. To the extent that this equality is missing, the outsider-ethicist from the "devel-oped" center runs serious risk of having undue influence and exerting subtle coercion; the out-sider-ethicist from the "less developed" periphery runs the contrary risk of being insufficiently self-reliant and bold.

Opposite dangers exist as well for both types of outsider-ethicists. Outsider-ethicists from the center and their insider hosts may practice a form of "reverse discrimination." The outsider-ethicist, aware of his or her own nation's history of cultural imperialism, may refrain from negative evalua-tions in favor of fawning approval of the host group's norms and practices. It is tempting to slide from an affirmation of the insider's right of self-determination to the view that the insider can't make mistakes. Similarly, the insider's justified anti-imperialism may become a dogmatic trap. Assuming a priori that nothing can be learned from an outsider, especially from the center, the insider-ethicist may close himself or herself off from new and potentially useful ideas.[28]

It must be conceded that a long-term danger of outsiders in development ethics is that peripheral communities become willingly but unfortunately dependent on outsider help, thereby failing to nurture and institutionalize their indigenous capacity for ethical reflection. Indeed, since the 1940s such Latin American philosophers as Leopoldo Zea have argued, with good reason, that Latin American thought is too imitative of and dependent upon European and North American thought.[29] The opposite consequence, however, is also a danger: peripheral groups can promote their capacity for development ethics in such a way that they overlook potential benefits of cross-cultural dialogue.

These dangers can be reduced, if not eliminated, by (1) the achievement of more equality between the various centers and their corresponding peripheries, (2) the recognition of dangers peculiar to insiders and outsiders, respectively, and (3) the promotion of appropriate kinds of insider/outsider combinations in development ethicists. Even under present, all too unequal, social circumstances, dialogue can occur that reduces the extent to which outsiders as well as insiders are either acquiescent or presumptuous.

Let us now turn to the positive contributions that outsiders can make when they reflect on an alien group's development goals and strategies. Here, outsider-ethicist strengths are the mirror image of insider-ethicist weaknesses. First, an outsider-ethicist may see and reveal things that an insider misses; we know *what-is* by contrast with *what-is-not*, and the outsider's very different experience may highlight what is hidden or obscure to the insider. Charles Taylor calls this "the language of perspicuous contrast."[30]

One way for the outsider to accomplish this is to *clarify* the debate over social identity that is taking place within that alien group. The outsider can be a sort of mirror — not a mirror to gain access to transcendental Truth but a mirror to reflect back to the group its own internal dialogue. A group is always in process. It perpetually crystallizes itself in and through dialogue about its past and future. The participants in this communal process are subgroups and individuals with more or less differing outlooks and development vocabularies. The outsider-ethicist can compare and contrast these insider traditions and perspectives. In this way, by "playing vocabularies and cultures off against each other," the insiders may see more clearly what they share with, and where they diverge from, others in their society.[31] Outsider Constantino Láscaris did this when he contrasted the everyday morality of the inhabitants of Costa Rica's four main cities, Alajuela, Cartago, Heredia, and San José, thereby helping Costa Ricans understand their differences as well as their similarities.[32] Denis Goulet's and

Kwan S. Kim's recent book compares and contrasts four competing Mexican development models: growth, growth-with-redistribution, basic human needs, and development from tradition.[33]

Second, by drawing on his or her own quite different tradition, vocabulary, and experience, the outsider can inject new and sometimes needed ideas into an alien group's development deliberations. Novelty here takes several different forms and is often a matter of degree. The outsider may provide a new way of integrating prevailing commitment. Goulet and Kim for instance, have clarified and argued for a novel way of combining the best Mexican development perspectives into a mode of "plural, federated development."[34] Perhaps more frequently, the outsider-ethicist will identify — on the basis of his or her own lights — beliefs already implicit in some insider practices and (partially) explicit in some insider theory. Nussbaum and Sen emphasize that outsiders, after immersion in an alien culture, can appeal to one part of the culture or tradition in order to criticize another part. Nussbaum and Sen illustrate this practice — what is sometimes called "building on the best" — when they draw on the (Asian) Indian rationalist tradition as a basis for their own affirmation of the potential importance of modern science and technology of Asian development.[35] Sometimes the progressive insider-beliefs that the outsider appeals to will have solely indigenous roots. Often, however, they will have had external origins and have been internalized at an earlier time by the culture in question.

Although Nussbaum and Sen helpfully widen the "reach" of internal critique to appeal to ideas that a culture has internalized from external sources, we also want to urge that the outsider ethicist can play a role in contributing moral ideas that are novel in two stronger senses. Drawing on the resources of his or her own tradition, the outsider ethicist can introduce moral ideas unanticipated in that society. Alternatively, outsiders and insider, in and through cross-cultural dialogue, together can create or invent novel ideas.[36]...

Rorty puts the general point well in describing what he calls the "pragmatist." Such a thinker, says Rorty, does not believe that one can get beyond or beneath vocabularies to get to the Truth "against which to test vocabularies and cultures." Rather, the pragmatist "does think that in the process of playing vocabularies and cultures off against each other, we produce new and better ways of talking and acting — not better by reference to a previously known standard, but just better in the sense that they come to *seem* clearly better than their predecessors."[37]

To come to grips with outsider ideas — be they initially unheard of or seemingly crazy or irrelevant — may prompt a beneficial reweaving of the group's beliefs and desires. The truth of particularism is that this reweaving will take place at the outset according to the group's prior stock of ideas. The truth of universalism is that the reevaluation can issue in new and better conceptions. But here the better is not measured by some historically transcendent and culturally independent standard but merely by the new lights of the community in question. ...

Outsiders, whether from the periphery or the center, both can criticize the status quo and propose new alternatives in and for alien social contexts. Drawing out the flip side of an earlier point, we can identify a third advantage that outsider development ethicists can have over their insider counterparts. And outsider-ethicist can be free from the insider's prior commitments and loyalties. This freedom can enhance the outsider's ability and willingness to say what needs to be said in the comparison and assessment of development options. Sometimes, of course, such outsider activity is foolish. ("Fools rush in where wise men fear to tread.") For such "contributions" often are unwelcome or uninformed. Sometimes, however, the outsider's work is more acceptable to some subgroups than to others. In the judgment of the subgroups that agree, the outsider may have "said some things that needed saying." This positive role played by the outsider can be dramatically important when it enables a weak or repressed group to gain a voice in relation to a hegemonic and oppressive group. Exiled Chilean novelist Ariel Dorfman, a national outsider to Argentina and a cultural outsider to indigenous cultures, spent time with the marginalized and threatened Matacos Indians in

Argentina's inhospitable Gran Chaco. We expect that one result of Dorfman's visit with and writing about the Matacos plight, will be that the Argentinean government, with some "encouragement" from foreign development agencies, will be more helpful to the Matacos as this small tribe tries to survive both economically and culturally.[38] Paula Palmer offers another such example. Initially a *gringa* outsider, for fifteen years she has immersed herself in Costa Rica's Talamanca coast and has helped the region's poor and vulnerable blacks and Indians articulate their traditions and protect their threatened way of life.[39] Ofelia Schutte formulates the general point:

The idea ... is to open up dialogue with the repressed, silent, or excluded Other who is such relative to the power that controls the discourse in which she, he, or it is framed. ... If philosophy is the love of wisdom, then its function cannot be merely to reproduce the discourse and assumptions of the established powers. On the contrary, its function is to penetrate through to the other side and create favorable conditions for the Other to come forward and express concerns, cares, disquietudes, and aspirations. In this process of recognizing and respecting the oppressed Other, the legitimacy of the Other's discourse must first be established.[40]

How different this outsider stance is from what Bimal Krishna Matilal calls "liberal colonialism." The 19th century liberal colonialist would tolerantly but ethnocentrically accept "primitive" or "backward" societies, "barbaric" practices and all, because that was something *those* curious (and inferior) savages were wont to do. The 20th century version, often in the interest of Northern tourism, keeps the "culture of a subdued group completely separated in a protected area as a museum piece or an 'endangered' zoological species."[41] Development ethicists, whether or not from dominating nations, not only can criticize the neo-colonialist societies, but, as outsiders in the "subdued" society, they also can "open up dialogue" with those subgroups that are "repressed, silent, or excluded."

V

Let us draw out a few of the implications of the above considerations for the kinds of persons we as development ethicists should be and the kind of ethics we should practice. Although I address these remarks to development ethicists, I believe they are relevant for those involved in other forms of cross-cultural and global ethics. We development ethicists should be insider-outsider mixes in relation to the "alien" groups whose development goals and strategies become the focus of our moral reflection. We should combine insiderness and outsiderness in such a way as to accentuate the positives and reduce if not eliminate the negatives of both postures. We should be sufficiently inside so as to immerse ourselves in this different form of life, to grasp some of what is going on, and to be accepted as dialogue partners. But we should not fall into the bad faith of believing that we have become completely "one of them." We should retain and take advantage of our outsiderness so as to be able to reflect an alien culture back to its insiders, call attention to the omnipresent obvious by contrasting it with our different experience, bring in new ideas, mediate between various factions, help the vulnerable gain a voice, and speak the truth made elusive by group loyalties. Yet we should not mislead ourselves or others by pretending to ascend to what is an impossible standpoint: a view of the inside from an ahistorical, transcendent, objective outside. No such "view from nowhere"[42] exists. To assume it does breeds both dominance on the part of those who think they have the Truth and servility on the part of those who long for it.

We should also cultivate a certain kind of insider-outsider mix in relation to our own groups. We must aspire to sufficient outsiderness to be able to learn from other groups. They can teach us, through the "language of perspicuous contrast," of the limitations and defects in our ways of doing things, as well as suggest better ideas that we can choose to weave into our beliefs and actions. But this outsiderness supplements an abiding insiderness which prima facie requires

loyalty. Alexandrians especially are tempted to escape from the "grey in grey"[43] of their own group to the creative instability of exotic places. Our insider status not only provides a starting point for moral reflection; it also gives us the responsibility to return to our own society's ongoing debate about what it should be and how it should relate to other groups. Moreover, one does not have to be an outsider in one's own culture as long as avenues exist for social transformation with which one can identify. One can remain or become again an insider to one's self and one's group by working for desirable change in one's self and society.

We insider-outsiders in development ethics have responsibilities beyond doing moral reflection in and both our own and other groups. Without abandoning our own cultural substance, we need to help further a global community and a global ethic. We need to extend our national, ethnic, class, and gender identities to a global "we." Insofar as such a world community does not exist, we need to build it. Insofar as it does, we need to strengthen it. To guide us in these tasks as well as to help us when we cross boundaries and interact cross-culturally, we need a global ethic.

This global ethic would not be a total ethic for a *Gemeinschaft* but a "moral minimum," a basic moral charter to which most people of good will could agree, for a global *Gesellschaft*. It would be what Rawls calls an "overlapping consensus," a public and publicly-forged moral vision to which persons and groups with a variety of moral, metaphysical, and religious views could have allegiance.[44] It would provide protection for the vulnerable wherever they exist as well as enjoin respect for each group's prima facie right to hammer out its own ethics. It would give all people a common vocabulary for coping with global problems that refuse to respect national or other boundaries as well as for resolving problems among and within nations and regions. It would guide us as we wrestle with the issue of what sort of international institutions would be good to have. These global norms and institutions are important because not only do they contribute to and partially constitute global progress, but they can promote useful development in nations and regions as well.

Although to develop the idea here is beyond the scope of this essay, I suspect that this global ethic will converge on some general cross-cultural ethical categories related in some way to certain general cross-cultural human traits and experiences that take specific forms in particular cultures. It remains to be determined whether this ethical convergence will emphasize basic human needs, capabilities, and/or rights.[45]

Like most good things, such a global community and global ethic could go bad; for rich and powerful centers could (self-deceptively) extend their domination precisely by packaging their own self-serving ethic as the new global ethic. To guard against this continual danger, we need to expand our "we intentions" beyond our groups of origin and check particularist self-serving intentions. We need to forge a global community and international ethic that celebrate regional and national differences and self-determination, and yet refuse to accept misery, oppression, and environmental degradation. We need to explore what sort of international institutions, agencies, and linkages support and are supported by such an ethic. If we are to save ourselves from global economic, ecological, and cultural disaster, our answers will need to be a good deal more robust than Rorty's model of a global Kuwaiti bazaar surrounded by exclusive national private clubs.

Such a global ethic neither eliminates nor always trumps the ethics of our narrower groups, any more than our emerging global community extinguishes or overrides groups of narrower scope. Rather, a transnational ethic requires, and is required by, the ethics of national and regional groups. Each can and should be a seed bed for and corrective of the other. The international moral minimum can both be inspired by and nurtured from good and exportable ideas invented by particular groups. In turn the global ethic can be a basis for criticizing and improving the outlooks and practices of particular traditions. Slavery as institution and ideal is a thing of the past; gender inequality is under attack throughout the world; respect for basic needs or rights and the environ-

ment are rapidly emerging as part of a global vision of "just, participatory eco-development." National development models, informed by national ethics, must be forged in relation to regional and global development models informed by international ethics. Regardless of where good ideals originated, they can move us as world citizens; and we can apply them as members of particular groups.

This is not to say that there will not be clashes between global and parochial loyalties. Unfortunately, or perhaps fortunately, we have no algorithm to adjudicate these conflicts. One of our hopes rests in the increasing number of insider-outsiders (in relation to groups of various scope) engaged in ongoing moral dialogue about good local, national, regional, and global development.

VI

Ethnocentrics and particularists begin and end inside their own groups. Universalists yearn to attain an impossible standpoint beyond all particularity. Like so many traditional philosophical problems, the particularist/universalist debate is so designed as to remain unsolved. Rather than attempting to resolve the controversy, I have elected to recast it. With the insider/outsider distinction, the theoretical problem has been transformed into a practical task. First, in doing development ethics, we must seize the opportunities and avoid the dangers of being outsiders as well as insiders in relation to various groups. Second, we development ethicists must strive to become optimal insider-outsider combinations in relation to existing groups. Third, we must promote the emergence of a world community which contributes to and is guided by a global development ethics. We must not just "think globally and act locally." As insider-outsiders we must think and act globally, regionally, nationally, and locally. We begin in our groups and return to our groups. In between, we can learn from and benefit other groups. As insider-outsiders, we can become more complete persons and better development ethicists and, thereby, help build a more desirable world.

Author's Note

The present essay is a revised and expanded English version of David A. Crocker. "Participantes internos y externos en la ética del desarrollo internacional," *Revista de la Universidad Autonoma de Yucatán*, special edition (February 1990), pp. 57-71. Earlier versions of the paper were given at the V Congreso Centroamericano de Filosofía, San José, Costa Rica, May 8-12, 1989; the Second International Conference on Ethics and Development, Universidad Autónoma de Yucatán. July 3-8, 1989; and the Departments of Philosophy of the University of Florida and Colorado State University in March 1990. I have benefited from comments by Jann Benson, Cynthia Botteron, David Freeman, Lyanda Haupt, Michael Losonsky, Ofelia Schutte, and Jerome M. Segal.

NOTES

1. For the nature, tasks, and methods of international development ethics, see David A. Crocker, "Hacia una ética del desarollo," *Revista de Filosofía de la Universidad de Costa Rica*, Vol. *25,* No. 62 (December 1987) pp.129-41; "La naturaleza y la practica de una ética del desarrollo," *Revista de Filosofía de la Universidad de Costa Rica* Vol 26, No. 63-64 (December 1988), pp. 49-56: "Toward Development Ethics." *World Development*; "Cuatro modelos de desarrollo costarricense: Un analisis y evaluación ética," *Revista de Filosofía de la Universidad de Costa Rica*, Vol. 27, No. 66 (1989), pp. 317-32: "The Hope for Just, Participatory Ecodevelopment in Costa Rica," in J. Ronald Engel and Joan Gibb Engel, eds., *Ethics of Environment and Development: Global Challenge and International Response* (Tucson: University of Arizona Press, 1990), pp. 150-63; Denis Goulet, "Tasks and Methods in Development Ethics," *Cross Currents*, Vol. 38, No. 2 (1988), pp. 146-64, 172.

2. One finds many examples of foreigners evaluating another nation's practices and norms. Constantino Láscaris, A Spanish philosopher, wrote *El Costarricense*, 5th ed. (San José, Costa Rica: Educa, 1985), an important study of Costa Rican identity. The U.S. development ethicist Denis Goulet has evaluated development strategies in several countries, most recently those of Mexico. See Denis Goulet and Kwan S. Kim, *Estratégias de Desarrollo Para el Futuro de México* (Guadalajara: ITESCO, 1989). Jerome M. Segal, a U.S. philosopher, offers moral and prudential arguments for a "two state" solution to the Middle-Eastern conflict. As a Jew, Segal is an outsider in relation to the PLO; as a *U.S.* Jew and an advocate of a Palestinian state, Segal is an outsider in relation to Israel. See Segal, *Creating the Palestinian State: A Strategy for Peace* (Chicago: Lawrence Hill Books, 1989). V.S. Naipaul, born in Trinidad of Hindu parents, is only the most recent of a series of foreigners who have analyzed and evaluated U.S. life and institutions. See Naipaul's *A Turn in the South* (New York: Knopf, 1989). Other foreign commentators on the United States include two important European writers: The Frenchman, Alexis de Tocqueville, *Democracy in America*, trans. George Lawrence, J.P. Mayer, ed. (New York: Doubleday, Anchor Books, 1969); and the Swede, Gunnar Myrdal, *An American Dilemma: The Negro Problem and Modern Democracy* (New York and London: Harper, 1944).

3. *Webster's Third New International Dictionary*, Vol. I (Chicago: Encyclopedia Britannica, Inc. 1976), p. 781.

4. Ofelia Schutte, "Overcoming Ethnocentrism in the Philosophy Classroom," *Teaching Philosophy*, Vol. 8, No. 2 (April 1985), pp. 139-40.

5. See Howard J. Wiarda, "Toward a Nonethnocentric Theory of Development: Alternative Conceptions from the Third World," in Charles K. Wilber, ed., *The Political Economy of Development and Underdevelopment* (New York: Random House, 1984), pp. 59-82.

6. In 1895 in his "Atlanta Exposition Address," Booker T. Washington employed this metaphor to enjoin blacks to take advantage of economic and other opportunities in the U.S. South and to urge whites to have confidence in the economic productivity and loyalty of the South's blacks. See Booker T. Washington, *Up From Slavery: An Autobiography* (Williamstown, MA: Corner House Publishers, 1978). H. Odera Oruka, a Kenyan philosopher, gives the metaphor a particularist spin as he

applauds a recent book by Johnny Washington, a black U.S. philosopher (H. Odera Oruka, "Forward," in Johnny Washington, *Alain Locke and Philosophy: A Quest for Cultural Pluralism* (New York: Greenwood Press, 1986), p. xiii.

7. Ofelia Schutte, "Notes on the Issue of Cultural Imperialism," *Proceedings and Addresses of the American Philosophical Association*, Vol. 59, No. 5 (June 1986), pp. 758-59. For an important statement of Latin American particularism, see Leopoldo Zea, "Identity: A Latin American Philosophical Problem," *Philosophical Forum*, Vol. 20, Nos. 1-2 (1988-89), pp. 33-42.

8. *Ibid.*, p. 759.

9. See, for example, Risiri Frondisi, "Is There an Ibero-American Philosophy?" *Philosophy and Phenomenological Research*, Vol. 9 (1948-49), pp. 345-55; Onora O'Neill, "Ethical Reasoning and Ideological Pluralism," *Ethics*, Vol. 98, No. 4 (July 1988), pp. 705-22.

10. Richard Rorty, *Consequences of Pragmatism* (Minneapolis: University of Minnesota Press, 1982), p. 166. Rorty has called himself both an "Ethnocentrist" and an "anti anti-ethnocentrist." In my view Rorty has either misdescribed himself, employs a different concept, or is inconsistent. For, as we shall see, Rorty recognizes — at least in his article on Roberto Unger — the way in which cross-cultural dialogue can result in the modification and even abandonment of the norms with which one starts. See Richard Rorty, "Unger, Castoriadis, and the Romance of a National Future," *Northwestern University Law Review*, Vol. 82, No. 2 (1988), pp. 335-51; "Solidarity or Objectivity," in Michael Krausz, ed., *Relativism; Interpretation and Confrontation* (Notre Dame: University of Notre Dame Press, 1989), pp. 12-13; "On Ethnocentrism: A Reply to Clifford Geertz." *Michigan Quarterly Review*, Vol. 25, No. 3 (Summer 1986), pp. 525-34. Compare with Clifford Geertz "Anti Anti-Relativism," reprinted in Krausz, ed., *Relativism*, pp. 12-34; "The Uses of Diversity," *Michigan Quarterly Review*, Vol. 25, No. 1 (1986), pp. 105-23.

11. For a description of "human life by the metaphor of a continual reweaving of a web of beliefs and desires." see Rorty. "On Ethnocentrism" p. 531.

12. Compare with Rorty's definition of a societal member: "To be part of a society is, in the relevant sense, to be taken as a possible conversational partner by those who shape that society's self-image" ("On Ethnocentrism," p. 529). The emphasis on "subjective" states should not be taken to exclude "objective" structures or public realities such as inherited vocabularies or "canonical texts," for a person's intentional states may be shaped by or have these realities as objects. Alasdair MacIntyre emphasizes the role of "canonical texts" such as the Bible or *Don Quixote* in defining a social identity; see MacIntyre, "Relativism, Power, and Philosophy," reprinted in Krausz, ed., *Relativism*, pp. 182-204.

13. Ruth Hubbard and Margaret Randall, *The Shape of Red: Outsider/Insider Reflections* (San Francisco: Cleis Press, 1988), p. 12.

14. *Ibid*, p. 26.

15. *Ibid*, p. 26.

16. *Ibid*, p. 22.

17. Clifford Geertz uses these metaphors descriptively in, "The Uses of Diversity," *Michigan Quarterly Review*, Vol. 25, No. 1 (Winter 1986), p. 121. Rorty employs the metaphors normatively: "We can urge the construction of a world order whose model is a bazaar surrounded by lots and lots of exclusive private clubs" ("On Ethnocentrism." p. 533).

18. Quoted Gerald Marzorati, "Salman Rushdie: Fiction's Embattled Infidel," *New York Times Magazine*, January 29, 1989, pp.27, 44.

19. MacIntyre, "Relativism," p. 201.

20. Jean-Paul Sartre, *Being and Nothingness: An Essay in Phenomenological Ontology*, trans. Hazel E. Barnes (New York; Philosophical Library, 1956). p. 58.

21. Rodolfo Stavenhagen reminded me of this important point.

22. Hubbard and Randall, *The Shape of Red*, p. 17.

23. See J. Baird Callicott, "Toward an Environmental Ethic," in Tom Regan, ed., *Matters of Life and Death*, 2nd ed. (New York: Random House, 1986), pp. 381-424, esp. pp. 403-17.

24. Martha C. Nussbaum and Amartya Sen, "Internal Criticism and Indian Rationalist Traditions," in Krausz, ed., *Relativism*, p. 310. See also, Martha C. Nussbaum, *The Fragility of Goodness: Luck and*

Ethics in Greek Tragedy and Philosophy (Cambridge: Cambridge University Press, 1986), esp. Part III: "Non-Relative Virtues: An Aristotelian Approach," *Mid-West Studies in Philosophy*, Vol. 13 (1988), pp. 32-53; "Aristotelian Social Democracy," in R. Bruce Douglass, Gerald M. Mara, and Henry S. Richardson, eds., *Liberalism and the Good* (New York: Routledge, 1990), pp. 203-52.

25. Rorty, "Unger," p. 343.

26. Nussbaum and Sen, "Internal Criticism," p. 308.

27. I use "center" to include the industrialized northern nations as well as Third world national or provincial capitals. Similarly, "peripheries" include "developing" nations as well as areas — especially rural areas — remote from Third world capitals, whether national or provincial. I assume that "center/periphery" is more than a merely economic distinction and can be characterized as a relation of unequal power as well as unequal resource flows. The center dominates the periphery, and the periphery is dependent on the center.

28. In his pronouncements, if not in his actual practice, Enrique Dussel, the Argentinean "philosopher of liberation," veers close to this geographical genetic fallacy: any idea originating from the North is thereby both incorrect and a tool of Northern domination of the South. This tendency in Dussel is sharply criticized by his fellow countryman Horacio Cerutti Guldberg in *Filosofía de la liberación latinoamericana* (México: fondo de Cultura Económica, 1983).

29. See Schutte, "Notes on the Issue of Cultural Imperialism," and Zea, "Identity: A Latin American Philosophical Problem."

30. Charles Taylor, "Understanding and Ethnocentricity," in *Philosophy and the Human Sciences*, Vol. 2 of *Philosophical Papers* (Cambridge: Cambridge University Press, 1985), p. 129.

31. Rorty, *Consequences*, p. xxxvii.

32. Láscaris, *El Costarricense,* pp. 65-74.

33. See Goulet and Kim, *Estratégias de Desarrollo*, chaps., I-III.

34. See *Ibid.*, chaps. IV, V. See also, David Barkin, *Distorted Development: Mexico in the World Economy* (Boulder, CO.: Westview Press, 1990). For similar efforts in relation to Costa Rican development, see Crocker, "Cuatro Modelos: The Hope for Just, Participatory Ecodevelopment"; Sheldon Annis, "Debt and Wrong Way Resource Flows in Costa Rica," *Ethics & International Affairs*, Vol. 4 (1990), pp. 107-21.

35. Nussbaum and Sen, "Internal Criticism," esp. pp. 317-21.

36. Clifford Geertz emphasized this in "Outsider Knowledge and Insider Criticism: What Can We Do for One Another?" (An unpublished response to Nussbaum and Sen, "Internal Criticism.")

37. Richard Rorty, *Consequences*, p. xxxvii.

38. Ariel Dorfman, "Into Another Jungle: The Final Journey of the Matacos?" *Grassroots Development Journal of the Inter-American Foundation*, Vol. 12, No. 2 (1988), pp. 2-15.

39. See Paula Palmer, *"What Happen": A Folk-History of Costa Rica's Talamanca Coast* (San Jose, Costa Rica: Ecodesarrollos, 1977). For an important Latin American study that appreciatively evaluates Palmer's work, see Ariel Dorfman, "Bread and Burnt Rice: Culture and Economic Survival in Latin America." *Grassroots Development: Journal of the Inter-American Foundation*, Vol. 8, No. 2 (1984), pp. 3-5.

40. Schutte, "Overcoming Ethnocentrism," p. 143.

41. Bimal Krishna Matilal, "Ethical Relativism and Confrontation of Cultures," in Krausz, ed., *Relativism*. p. 358.

42. See Thomas Nagel, *The View from Nowhere* (New York: Oxford University Press, 1986).

43. *Hegel's Philosophy of Right,* trans. R.M. Knox (Oxford: Oxford University Press, 1952), pp. 12-13. We "Alexandrian" ethicists must guard against the temptation of believing that it is only the "exemplary instability" of the Third World (and of, at long last, the Second World) that permits and activist and socially responsible role for ethics, the "cut and dried" First World, too, has a need to be "rejuvenated."

44. John Rawls, "Justice as Fairness: Political not Metaphysical," *Philosophy and Public Affairs*, Vol. 14, no. 3 (1985), pp. 223-51; and "The Idea of an Overlapping Consensus," *Oxford Journal of Legal Studies*, Vol 7 (1987), pp. 1-25. For the possibility of a "partial convergence ... through proper confrontation and clash between culture[s], a convergence not necessarily of local moral norms, but ...

of basic ethical normal," see Matilal, "Ethical Relativism," p. 358. See also Charles R. Beitz, *Political Theory and International Affairs* (Princeton: Princeton University Press, 1979); Terry Nardin, *Law, Morality and the Relations of States* (Princeton: Princeton University Press, 1983); Thomas Donaldson, "Moral Minimums for Multinationals," *Ethics & International Affairs*, Vol. 3 (1989), pp. 163-82.

45. See David Braybrooke, *Meeting Needs* (Princeton University Press, 1987); Nussbaum "Aristotelian Social Democracy"; Amartya Sen, *Resources, Values and Development* (Cambridge, MA: Harvard University Press, 1984): Henry Shue, *Basic Rights: Subsistence, Affluence, and U.S. Foreign Policy* (Princeton: Princeton University Press, 1980); David Braybrooke, "Meeting Needs: Toward a New Needs-Based Ethic"; David A. Crocker, "Functioning and Capability: the Foundations of Sen's Development Ethic"; James W. Nickel, "Rights and Development"; and G. Peter Penz, "The Priority of Basic Needs: Toward a Consensus in Development Ethics for Political Engagement." The last four papers were presented at the IDEA Montclair Workshop, entitled "Ethical Principles for Development: Needs, Capabilities, or Rights?" Montclair State College, January 24-27, 1991. The Workshop was sponsored by the Institute for Critical Thinking of Montclair State College and the International Development Ethics Association (IDEA).

CLONING CULTURES:
THE SOCIAL INJUSTICES OF SAMENESS

Philomena Essed and David Theo Goldberg

Philomena Essed is Senior Researcher at the Amsterdam Institute for Global Issues and Development Studies at the University of Amsterdam and Visiting Professor of Women's Studies at the University of California, Irvine. She is the author of Diversity: Gender, Color and Culture *(1996) and co-editor with David Theo Goldberg of* Race Critical Theories: Text and Context *(2002).*

David Theo Goldberg is the Director of the University of California Humanities Research Institute and Professor in African American Studies and Criminology in Law and Society at the University of California, Irvine. He is the author of Racist Culture *(1993) and* The Racial State *(2002).*

Essed and Goldberg connect the contemporary biological discourse about cloning with a cultural discourse that promotes sameness within and across cultures. Cloning, they argue, is not merely a biological and scientific issue, but a cultural one that reflects an unspoken tendency to comply with normative standards by reproducing imagined perfections of the same type and profile as those already in positions of power. With the cloning of human beings comes the possibility for erasing difference by reproducing preferred types of human beings: white, male, able-bodied, heterosexual, highly intelligent, and living in economically privileged places. They argue that a preference for sameness is also evident in a global context that manifests the mass production of Western culture and consumerism in ways that flatten, erase, and undermine difference and diversity.

Cloning is a troubling notion, the suggestion of which triggers images of cold laboratories and gruesome Nazi experiments. But human cloning does not have to be horrible, its advocates claim. In an article (February 2001) about the "cloning mission" the *New York Times* journalist, Margaret Talbot, comments that individuals and couples eager to serve as guinea pigs for cloning purposes

> will tell you that they realize cloning does not produce a copy of the original person, but something more than a later-born identical twin, and yet say that they would want to do it anyway. They'd want to do it so that they could know in advance about their unborn children, so that they wouldn't have to take their chances of sexual reproduction, so they could perpetuate their own

genes or so they could hope against hope to get somebody very, very much like somebody they had lost (p. 43).

Putting aside our own moral objections against cloning, for the sake of the argument, let us listen seriously to these wishes. These voices express a desire for ultimate control of nature, most notably, regarding self-determination with respect to the genetic composition of offspring. The desire to subject nature to the hands of human beings is not new. It has been central to the project of modernization, granting to human beings virtually limitless dominion over "things," including animals. In that process, human bodies too have been objectified and increasingly subjected to manipulation in order to fit images of perfection, cosmetic surgery being a case in point.

Here we find an overriding concern with human bodies made to order. The Platonic possibility of a baby just like us, no unexpected surprises, no physical or character traits hidden from view, yet to be discovered. Indeed, no procreation. Perfect reproductive efficiency and sterile social reproducibility. The dream of simply ordering exactly the type of child — and by extension social order — deemed desirable, and more of the same if pleased with the result. This dream, not that far from what is being made technically possible, says something not only about the cloning of human beings but also about the social context in which a fantasy like this could emerge in the first place. We wish in this discussion piece to draw attention to the socio-cultural fabric enabling the desire to clone.

Who would be cloned, one might rightfully ask, if bio-medical factories were to take over from sexual reproduction? Thinking about cloning is saturated with references to the biological. For example, web searches reference only the biological or ethical issues emerging out of the biological considerations. Cloning thus is widely considered to be no more than a biological discourse. Radical biological cloning, the cloning of human beings, has been awaited anxiously now for some time, the technological inevitability prompting the tension between socio-scientific celebration and ethico-religious palpitation. The almost exclusive fixation on the biotechnology of cloning around the world concerns the ethics of human cloning followed distantly by concerns over the propriety of genetically engineered food products. Broadly, the ethical objections to human cloning concern intervention in nature; aiming for perfect bodies (implications of imperfect sameness: racism, eugenics, sexism, able-ism, ageism, hetero-normativity); and the danger for the sustainability of human kind (biodiversity).

While the discursive focus has been on the biological side of cloning, few have paid attention to the social and cultural contexts that make cloning possible, that have rendered it thinkable. By cloning in this broader sense we understand the systemic reproduction of sameness. This is a phenomenon deeply engrained in the organization of contemporary culture, in social life generally, and in the racial, gendered class structures of society, in particular.

In the light of this, one can imagine "who" will be cloned. It seems not unlikely that the *biological* cloning of human beings will inevitably implicate the cloning of preferred *types* of human beings: male, white, able-bodied, heterosexual, highly intelligent, to be placed in economically privileged habitats. One can also imagine the cloning of nonwhite, able-bodied, good-natured, caring, docile, moderately smart but not too intelligent bodies to do the service work that those more privileged seem to demand more and more. Whereas biological cloning is still for the most part a fiction waiting to be realized, the *cultural cloning* of preferred types to inhabit segregated spaces is everyday practice, especially among social elites. The notion of *cultural cloning*, initially used to problematize the systemic reproduction of white, masculine homogeneity in high status positions (Essed 2002), brings into focus another side of exclusion. Yet, same-kind preference reproducing white (Euro) masculine privileges in terms of race, ethnicity, gender, or profession is not countered with the same force of indignation as we find in the case of the suggestion of biological cloning.

Longing for a clone of a loved one is not simply or indeed principally a desire for a biological clone. In picturing cloned duplicates of loved ones, those contemplating cloning must necessarily also imagine same-kind personality traits, identities, life histories, in short, a socio-cultural context for the would-be-clone to inhabit. One might more properly think of biological cloning as instrumental to — making materially possible — the deeper desire for these forms of social sameness. While public conscience, national governments and international NGOs are denouncing the biological cloning of human beings, we want to insist here that cloning as a practice is not a new phenomenon, and not even a phenomenon that is generally rejected. Quite the contrary. The very context prompting the desire to clone human beings biologically is framed in historically rooted systems of preference for real or imagined replica and homogeneities. Cloning, in this sense, is properly *bio-social* reproduction, and not simply or strictly or primarily a biological phenomenon. We intend to elaborate on this theme below. In doing this we are taking a risk, because our thoughts are far from fully developed. We are offering here a discussion piece, eliciting responses to a set of concerns long passed over largely in silence. We shall draw substantially from decades of insightful and important critical research on difference, discrimination and the struggles for equality. At the same time, we seek to offer something innovative. We believe that critical research can gain from exploring the function and manifestations of normative preference for sameness and how these are instrumental in reproducing systems of social injustice.

There are good reasons to problematize normative preference for sameness, whether the "normative" is the result of explicit choice or of hegemonic consensus. The glass ceiling phenomenon is a case in point. The number of critical publications on (intertwined) processes of exclusion along racial, ethnic, gender, sexual, class, and other structural demarcations is abundant. As a result, we have come to a much better understanding of the relation between inequality and difference. In focusing on sameness our aim is not to discount or disqualify established models of difference and social exclusion, but to build on their critical modes (Essed and Goldberg 2002). We have also witnessed decades of policies regarding an inclusive work place, ranging across affirmative action in the US, equity policies in Canada, equal opportunity in the UK, and positive action in some European countries. But according to the weekly magazine *Newsweek*, problematizing the exclusive whiteness of the highest European echelons remains silenced (see special report on Race in the Boardroom, 18 February 2002). Thirty years of feminism and race critical literature notwithstanding, the (culturally contextualized) privileging of white men and the social delimitation and denigration of women and people of colour in the world have not been erased. Furthermore, in spite of improvements of facilities for people with physical challenges, disabilities are generally perceived as indicative of a less than full human life.

A New Paradigm?

Converging discriminations *against* particular groups are also indicative of normative preferences *for* clones of imagined perfections of the same type and profile. We are concerned to problematize the *context* that makes it so "evident" that certain criteria will be taken into and "others" kept out of consideration in the cloning process, just as we are concerned to place a critical spotlight on the forms of inequality resulting from privileging those, or those criteria marking one as same.

In speaking about context, we are raising questions concerning the cultural assumptions about humanity, humanness, and humaneness, but also concerning preference for a certain kind of human The deeper concern therefore is to engage in questioning what it means to be human, and implicitly what the normative commitment to humanism effects. This engagement reveals that the preference for one's own kind, whether at the micro level of the family or at the macro level of the nation, implies to varying degrees the dehumanizing of all others who are then seen as less deserving of human dignity and respect. By drawing attention to the socio-cultural fabric enabling cloning cultures, we wish in this discussion piece to re-direct focus from identity and difference to the social injustices and inequalities embedded silently in the reproduction of sameness. Ultimately, we see that the work focusing on identity and difference would be complemented by that focused on sameness. Here, we are concerned to raise the question.

The effects of preference for sameness, whether intended or unintended, have been shown to be manifestations of all kinds of debilitating exclusions: racism, genderism, able-bodiedness, and so on. What we are claiming is new, because newly revealing, is the sustained critical focus on sameness for which we are calling. It follows from this shift that the cloning debate, with its focus on biological cloning of the human race, is only a symptom of a whole set of other social malaises, of which we should be critically aware. For instance, the drive to insist on difference that we have witnessed in social theorizing and some aspects of popular culture over the past two decades is predicated on the underlying assumption that the values of sameness represent the prevailing social norm. Questioning the normativity of sameness (equal-ness) implies that the need to exaggerate the right to be different (the difference debate) is problematized by the same token. Commitments to discourses of difference are dialectically tied to the (embedded or underlying) socio-cultural investment in sameness.

Cultural cloning is predicated on the taken-for-granted desirability of certain types, the often-unconscious tendency to comply with normative standards, the easiness with the familiar and the subsequent rejection of those who are perceived as deviant. In this sense, cultural cloning is enormously widespread if not a universal phenomenon, descriptively considered. It is neither confined to Western cultures nor to dominant groups. Non-dominant groups or communities too can be essentialist in choosing for their own kind, whether or not as a reaction against exclusion. We are mostly interested in cultural cloning as reproducing gender and racial inequalities. Preferences for sameness, whether gendered or racially indexed, are historically part and parcel of the social fabric of our societies. Race as an ordering principle has been interwoven in the very nature of and in the making of modernity (Goldberg 2002). The same holds true for gender, where modern manhood required the construction of dominant rational, emotionally suppressed identities and the imitation of these images of manhood over generations (Seidler 1997). At the same time, a critique of cultural cloning goes much beyond the injustices of reproducing homogenous circles of privilege along lines of race and gender. Preference for sameness is embedded in our allegiance to copy cultures, mass productions, consumerism and the promise of eternal growth (Schwarz 1996, Klein 1999). Moreover, the issue is not only cultural cloning but wider domains of the cloning of cultures and the cultures of cloning.

The Scope of Cloning Cultures

Cloning culture in this broader sense accordingly has come to saturate politics (profiles of acceptable political figures), law (flattened notions of equal-

ity), education (profiled standards of merit and ability), management (normative embodied profiles of organizational orderings), aesthetics (somatic norm images; cosmetic surgery), the military (uniforms, depersonalization), and processes of production and reproduction (advertising, mass production). However, not all standardizations, copies, replications, mass productions or equations can or ought to be treated in the same way. They serve different purposes, and have different implications.

We are seeking here accordingly to link three socio-political debates: the first concerns a relatively new problem, at least in the bio technological sense — the biological cloning of human beings. The second concerns the phenomenon of reproducing sameness. We believe that a critical account of systems of preference for sameness — from kinship to nation, from aesthetics to production and consuming — can be revealed as contributing to the reproduction of systems of social distinction and privilege. This introduces the third debate, which has to do with an old, yet unresolved, global problem: (attributed) social differences and systemic inequalities. Social distinctions refer here to those of "race," ethnicity, gender, and other ordering processes. The related concepts of "cloning of cultures" and "cultures of cloning," when considered critically in their relation, shed a different light on issues of injustice and inequality. We believe that a focus on what we call "cloning cultures" (as uniting both concerns) has the potential to shift the debates on social injustices and inequalities. This will open up dimensions of social injustice that for the most part have remained hidden from view or under-emphasized. In addressing how the hegemony of normative models and systems of sameness disadvantage groups, this critical focus calls attention to new and overlooked grounds and highlights (relatively) unexplored processes of injustice.

We agree that there is no question that people's experiences and identities are multidimensional, not reducible to only one interest or category (Goldberg 1993; Essed 1996). At the same time the range of literature on categorizing and standardizing suggests that people tend to seek a certain degree of sameness, in the sense of familiarity, similarity, identicality in their surroundings so as more easily to cope socially. In getting to know new situations and new people we search for what looks and sounds familiar in order to establish a common ground from which to proceed. Sameness, repetition, predictability renders social circumstance more manageable, more comfortable, more readily negotiable.

There is no clarity as to the nature of sameness we seek out and what establishes a minimum basis of comfort when entering new situations. Is it the architecture, food, ways of dressing, or shared values, whether assumed or real? Is it the assumption of shared experience or reference, revealed by what, exactly? The relation of skin colour and gender to clothing and accent, hair style and smell? Under what circumstances are others induced or even forced to ensure familiarity and comfort through behaviour that suggests sameness, social habits that guarantee belonging, customs that conjure identity? Is conformity, then, a process by which group members demand from each other that no one disturb the equilibrium of familiarity and sameness? What does it say about (dominant) groups when they insist upon sameness enforced upon others? How do deep-seated normative assumptions of social and cultural preference and aesthetic sameness express themselves?

Crucial Concerns of Cloning Cultures

Human histories have been replete with violations of nature and of health in the name of progress, and the projection of normative models for bodies in the name of civilization. In other words, in the course of history, economic, social, and cultural preferences have paved the way for human cloning to emerge as a pressing set of social commitments. The ease with which biological cloning has been taken up in contemporary thinking has been made possible by the widespread acceptance of the normative assumption of cultural sameness throughout much of mainstream modern thinking. In short, it is not that the interest in cloning has belatedly given rise to the preference for sameness. Rather, the longstanding drives and demands for sameness have made possible the very conceivability of

cloning as a supposed ideal worthy of pursuit. The ethical concerns about biological cloning, by extension, arise only in the context of broader contexts of social reproducibility and propriety. It is these broad social(ly manifest) dispositions to reproduce sameness that we reference as *cloning cultures*.

Familiarity, shared taste and style, common values, and recognizable surroundings provide a certain degree of comfort, which we probably need as social beings. In one sense, at least, any cultural reproduction can be seen as a form of cloning. We are careful, however, not to equate reproduction as such with cloning culture. To speak of "cloning culture" presupposes a society where productivity and efficiency occupy a prized position on the list of values (little time and energy wasted on the tensions and trials of difference and distinction), where one can expect a consumptive demand for certain types of children (think, for instance, of the ethno-national fantasies and fashions around adoption) as well as for other products, according to what, aesthetically, is considered the fashion of the day. These societal dimensions are best referenced, we want to suggest, in terms of the principal concepts constitutive of cloning culture, which we delineate as *kinhood, productivism, consumerism,* and *aestheticism*. Each of these dimensions manifests through gender, racial, ethno-national and socio-economic dynamics. These dimensions factor also into understanding globalization for it is through the standardization of each dimension in their interactive relation with the others that global penetration is exercised.

Kinhood: This notion we use to refer to any form of (imagined) connectedness on the basis of sameness — from kinship, usually reserved for family, clans, and tribes, to "own kind," often the basis of a sense of shared community, nation, race, and gender. The urge to belong, to share a sense of familiarity and similarity with others, is among the stronger forces of social arrangement and order. Familiarity connects conceptually to kinship via the symbolics of "the" family, as though the assumptions of singularity naturalize the connectivity. Social upheavals follow from disturbances in the balance of emotions of pride and shame that go together with the social longing to be part of, or to identify with, same kinds on the basis of a (perceived) common ground (Scheff 1994, p. 277). The smallest and most immediate (though hardly unmediated) unit of social belonging is the family, whatever format "family" takes in a particular historical-cultural context; the largest units are ordered imaginaries of community, nation or humankind itself. In most cultures, love for close family is not based for the most part on the quality of its character but on the sheer fact of kinship, acceptance of bonding because of shared "blood" or lineage or natal connectivity.

Analogies abound between the defence of the family and the defence of "the race." The assimilation of "race feeling" to "family feeling" and to "people with whom we are connected" through sameness makes the idea of "fraternity" one that is all too easily applied in nationalist discourse (Appiah 1990). The Christian doctrine of fraternity, that "all men (sic) are my brothers," has slid too easily in the direction of privileging kin and same kind while dehumanizing all "others" — non-Christians, non-nationals, non-men (sic), non-members of the same "race" or ethnicity or kinship group. Kinship and connectivity tend to be extended outwards from the narrower circle of "organic" or "nuclear" family to wider circles of claimed community, ultimately to embrace the metaphorics of "national family," "family of nations," or indeed to some idealized, naturalized, and stereotypically streamlined "human family." The universalist doctrine of brotherhood "interacts with institutional issues involving affinities such as adoption, (...) authochtony, baptism, blood brotherhood, brotherhood-in-arms, carnal contagion, catenary lineage, class groupings, (...), consanguinity, conversion, Eucharist bonding, (...) foster relationships, fratriarchy, friendship, (...). All these mark societal articulations of universal with particular" (Shell 1993, p. 197).

Kinhood and associated familial identifications are relevant in a study of cloning cultures because of the tendency to prioritize larger collective identifications (notably, race, gender, nationality) while reducing those perceived as "other" to one-dimensional and so static prototypical images of identity.

In the revolutionary period of US history, the prevailing politics of identity reinforced the preferred state of human life — whiteness, heteronormative masculinity, and ruling classes — in and through centring on those human variations perceived as problematic in their distinctiveness, primarily race, gender, and social class (Wiley 1994). Today, so-called colourblindness proclaims homogeneity (only one race, the human race), but in practice the "race" of "others" is as visible as it is disturbing in the eyes of the dominant group (Goldberg 2002). In Europe, a growing sense of "we-Europeans" goes hand in hand with the resurgence of Neo-Nazi groups, the increasing respectability of ultra-nationalist parties, and the more and more openly expressed assertion that immigrants are a threat to the cultural heritage of established residents. While problematizing others, in particular Muslims, for their "backward" or "threatening" cultures, the implicit message is a preference for cultural homogenization. Stereotypical in-group and out-group conceptions essentialistically defined and refined, and grounded in normative preference for traits of the dominant group are reinforced through the very denial of preference for sameness of a certain kind when racial equality is the formal ideology. Cases in point are the unnamed preference for the comfort, safety, familiarity, and privilege associated with whiteness (Roediger 2001). Conversely, black nationalism and ethnic fundamentalisms are implicated in cultural cloning, as these discursive formations express preference for those seen as the same "race," religion or culture, in reaction and conflicted resistance to racism and globalization.

Fitting the group norm by displaying prototypical behaviour is at once a way of being accepted into a certain race, class, or community and a mechanism of cloning through culture. At the same time, the normative principle of merit regulates access to resources. The industrial and, more recently, information revolutions have increased competitive pressures to reward according to efficiency and systems of fashioned merit, inevitably to be measured by the use of standardized tests (Zwick 2002). The idea that merit (for the most part technically defined as IQ) plus effort can be measured in a culturally neutral way has come under attack. It has repeatedly been shown that the myth of merit has served the cloned reproducibility of masculine-dominated, elite cultures. Becoming and succeeding as a business leader in Europe is largely a function of a prestigious education, wealthy families, and sustained networks. This seems strongly counter to what one would be tempted to believe in the wake of a century of women's emancipation, transformative social movements and structural change. Nevertheless, business elites remain resiliently homogeneous (masculine, middle to higher social classes) even while women have democratized higher education along gender lines. Critiques of prevailing ideas of rewarded credit according to certain prototypes of merit, the inherent privileging of cognitive intelligence and competence established on fixed terms, and the principle that only the "most deserving" can gain admission or promotion have had little substantive impact on eroding their effects.

The concept of family has been commercialized to fit the needs of global productivism and consumerism and the cloning of taste and behaviour according to class and spending power. In the age of mass production and consumption, the McDonalds "family restaurant" exemplifies the global cloning of a US prototype of family nourished by a certain culture of eating. This fast food franchise, quintessentially a product of late modernity, represents "all that is efficient, calculated, predictable and over which we can exercise control" (Gabriel 1994, p. 100). But it also reproduces a profile of desired (if far from healthily desirable) nutrition, of body types, and of "spending" fun time with a narrowly idealized sense of the family.

If we disaggregate the analytic elements concerning cloning cultures in these examples, then, we focus accordingly on three interactive constitutive considerations: productivism, consumerism, and aestheticism.

a. Productivism concerns the widespread cultural commitment being productive and efficient, in material or non-material ways, as a goal in itself. The production of goods in factories has overflooded the market with uniform mass-products

virtually indistinguishable from one another. The introduction of brand marks and logos distinguish privileged circles signified by a particular highly priced brand family from the anonymous masses. But imitations, theft of brand names, and literal cloning of brand products have emerged as a prevailing trend, expanding circles of consumption as they throw in question while at once mimicking systems of prevailing privilege. IMB clones are a well-known example (Klein 1999). In terms of quality or design, it is often difficult even to distinguish the original from the many inexpensive clones. Productivism sustains the focus on quantity, time management, and cost-benefit analysis. And it involves the profiling of the perfect worker in terms of productivity and notions of competence for different kinds of occupation. Those who do not fit the productivity profile along lines of gender, race, first-third world situatedness, or educated-illiterate are likely to be marginalized, for example, by way of surveillance and disciplining through the criminal justice system. Architecture and urban design are often predicated on these assumptions (consider, for instance, Bauhaus buildings, ghettoes and suburbanization, and more recently gated communities). Plagiarism, understood as the cloning of someone else's work, is fuelled by the drive to get ahead on these terms.

b. Consumerism concerns the age of homogenizing shopping malls and shared products revealing as they reproduce assumptions of shared identity and belonging along lines of class, ethnoracial formations, and gender. Examples include the likes of The Body Shop, IKEA furniture, warehouse shopping at US mega stores such as Costco or Circuit City, and food consumption at family restaurants like McDonald's or Pizza Hut or indeed Mövenpick, Hard Rock Café, Starbucks coffee, or the Four Seasons. These modes of consumptive recreation and recreational consumption fashion identity formation: you belong to the class or peers of what and where you eat (Bell and Valentine 1997), or how and where you exercise, whether and where, for instance, you play basketball or golf. As many have pointed out, consumerism has implications for exploitation of nature for the purpose of mass production with disastrous consequences for the environment, health, the gap between rich and poor. It presupposes the creation of markets by creating needs: from dishwashers to brands of shampoo, from mobile phones to cosmetics for men. Consumerism dominates other less consumptive-friendly social values and social values are increasingly expressed in market terms. So shopping in malls is promoted as an intrinsically rewarding family experience, heavily financed sports events that serve as media for advertising have become daily forms of mass entertainment, and so on. Other instances of cultural cloning as/through consumption include the universalizing of cultural taste through the mass consumption of media products such as the domination of world cinema markets by Hollywood films or turning to CNN for breaking news and political analysis, as well as the global proliferation of technological products such as Microsoft.

c. Aestheticism: Tastes are shaped by and reproduced (cloned) through the impress of the tastes of others in one's own group and by the advertising power of mass media. Around the globe cosmetic surgery has become a medico-cultural fixture (Gilman 1999). Ideals of perfect bodies are rationalized in terms of universal standards of beauty (for instance, the cosmetic industry, the exercise industry, fashion, health fads). Disciplined, docile bodies and emphasis on an "ethics of the self" are founded upon basic concerns with how one looks and acts as reflections of one's projection of how others do and would have one look (a)like in the culture about one. Perception and personal profile reflect and are reflected in the cultures in which "agents" are embedded. The reduction of ethics to the aesthetics of the care for the already raced and gendered self reveals some of the complex processes at work in cloning cultures.

We conceive of these dimensions not as static but as general place-holders for complex and interactive processes. We regard consumerism accordingly not as basic but as the intersection point of the mutually constitutive and overlapping relationships between all three of the dimensions. For example, uniforms pertain to consumerism as well

as to aesthetics and labour and productive practices, revealing features of each. Uniforms are about certain modes of fashion, of what people choose to wear or through which to express themselves. But they also mark one kind of productive activity or class from another, such as who occupies what position in the stratification of a society while perhaps denying that such stratification exists or persists (consider, for instance, school uniforms). And they represent standards of beauty and acceptability, normative dispositions to regard what is acceptable in a society and what not.

Towards a Definition

We are conceiving of cloning cultures, then as the reproduction of systems of preference for sameness shaped by real or imagined kinhood in dynamic relation to modes of productivism, consumerism and aestheticism. Cloning through cultures is producing *more of the same at the same time* as well as *more of the same across time.*

Cloning is the copying of a model with the intended result of potentially limitless copies of the same item. Such copying does not, of course, preclude variations on the theme. Indeed, often such variations are deemed desirable, but the logic of variation is both that it is predicated on an original model and serves to replicate and so reproduce identifiable qualities of the original in its variation. Referring to sameness, nevertheless, does not imply that it is a transparent notion. Crosscutting and shaping the tendency to create sameness through cloning is that the original clone should be worked upon and improved to a status of perfection. Cloning accordingly presupposes the initial fashioning of a supermodel. The idea of a supermodel is clearly visible in the fashion industry and in cosmetic surgery, thus embedding Platonic ideals of beauty and perfection. But it is a notion with considerably wider resonance. Consider, for instance, the role of prototypes in product design, or more pressing (because closer to what we are driving at) of "role models" especially with respect to children's socialization. Sameness according to a model of perfection reinstates the underlying hierarchy of humanity, revealing that its definition is always contrasted with the different and excluded, the deviant and excommunicated.

By cloning (as a quality *of*) culture we mean the reproduction of these cultures through the processes of kinhood, productivism, consumerism, and aestheticism. These processes in turn embed those of socialization, education, mass media, and mass production. The debates on multi-culturalism amounted to a critique of exclusion, a plea to reproduce other cultures rather than only the dominant one, but not a questioning of the assumption that cultures (of sameness) need to be maintained or reproduced. What for, and why? The mere fact of a culture is not reason sufficient for its maintenance or reproduction. Besides the reproduction *of* cultures there is also the reproduction *through* cultures of models, procedures, modes of thought, and ways of being, from generation to generation.

The Culture of Cloning

Horizontal Cloning: More of the Same at the Same Time

As we have moved in the name of individualism increasingly to privilege preference-based social schemas, the assumption is that we supposedly avoid the pitfalls of group-based exclusions and practices. If individuals' actions and their outcomes are the products of individual preferences and rational choices, group-based determinations seemingly become moot. Individuals can claim to avoid discrimination because they are not intending any exclusion or harm to or denigration of groups or individuals as group members. But do these interests amount to anything more than face-keeping and an image of non-discriminatory commitment behind which preferences and choices embed discrimination as usual (Goldberg 2002, pp. 227)? What remain hidden are the mechanisms of preferences for cultural and embodied similarity and sameness. Choices are made in virtue of these embedded assumptions. Whereas "choice against" — choice to exclude — has been problematized as everyday discrimination, "preference for" — choice for one's own, those like one, the similar and the same — is taken for granted as an affirmative

value in dominant (and non-dominant) cultures. Our focus here has been on calling into question *dominant* forms of cloning cultures. Nevertheless, it should be noticed that preference for sameness occurs as well in marginalized cultures. In the latter cases, the necessary resistance against assimilation into the dominant model has resulted sometimes in the uncritical embrace of tradition, or even radical fundamentalism, without questioning whether all elements of that culture acknowledge the equal standing of all members of and in that community. The reproduction of gender inequality in the name of cultural autonomy has been a repeated case in point. A central aim of this project, then, would be to explore critically the varied agendas of the politics of preference in the reproduction of sameness.

If the politics of preference have been predicated so heavily, as we claim, on the presumptive desirability of sameness and excludability of the different, the ideal is undercut by the inevitable failure of the ensuing pursuit to effect or institute the perfect clone. The ideal turns out to be the Holy Grail. Imperfect clones are the order of the day, producing at once dismissive discourses of the monstrous, the grotesque, the queer, the crippled, in short, the inherently imperfect. The impossibility of perfection becomes at once the possibility of imperfection, the impossibility of the perfect same, of the clone. All we have are degrees of imperfection. Degrees of imperfection, of course, presuppose the artifice of the ideal against which the measure is taken. Pursuit of perfection thus inevitably involves social transgression at the expense of those deemed less perfect than others. We are raising questions at the heart of thinking about cultures of inequality and their reproduction when one takes seriously as a critical project the dissolution of ideals of perfection and normative sameness.

The Cloning of Cultures

Vertical Cloning: More of the Same Across Time

While we are arguing that the culture of cloning as well as cloning within culture has grown out of deep-seated assumptions about the value of sameness, the cloning *of* cultures, in turn, perhaps quite obviously, is sustained and promoted, often without notice, by the cultures of cloning.

This complex picture has potential for opening up and shifting critical debate across and between a broad range of issues, disciplines and perspectives concerning matters of social structure, organization, reproduction and representation. Themes for critical focus may include:

- Family: preference for blood lines over adopted family or friends
- Preferred body images: able-bodiedness, cosmetic surgery, obsession with perfection of the body in certain cultures
- Education: the idea that smartness is reproduced by the same set of traits
- Professions: the higher the status and power, the stronger the preference for the (embodied) profile as white, masculine, heterosexual, middle class, married (managers, leaders)
- Fashion: dress codes and models
- Uniforms generally: whether in school, military, sports, employment
- Mass production and consumption: the phenomenon of brand names as well as Veblen's bandwagon effect and snob effects predicated on taking one's distance from sameness
- Ideologies: dominant — nationalism, whiteness — as well as co-optation of counter ideologies — antiracism, feminism
- Perceptions of justice: based in presuppositions of equality as sameness, standard conceptions of justice focus the debate on a right to be different. Critiquing sameness calls into question the claim to the right to difference as the latter is predicated on the assumption of, as a reaction to, the former.
- Disciplines in academia: dominant — the institutional privileging of disciplinary units, as modes of normative sameness — as well as the cooptation and copying of models of interdisciplinarity.

The critical project we are proposing thus offers the potential to develop a comprehensive, critical, vocabulary and grammar for addressing the pressing and emerging socio-cultural (including biolog-

ical), concerns of our times. The lexicon of cloning culture includes the conceptual likes of replication and familiarity, networking and regularity, simulation and regulation, typification and stereotyping, copying and facsimiles (Schwartz 1996), emulation and adaptation (Tilly 1998).

In terms of logic, sameness requires for its very conception, its identification, the delineation of difference, the different, as its principal and principled mode of contrast through the processes of productivism, consumerism and aestheticism delineated above. And out of these interactive processes are prompted and promoted the entire panoply of technologies of differentiation and exclusion, from ostensive identification (body search) to identity (identity papers), profiling, statistical generalizations and metrics of variable treatment, to the various social determinations of death.

**Transforming Interdisciplinarities:
More Relevant Than Ever**

To summarize, we return to the opening paragraph of this essay. What do those who volunteer as guinea pigs for cloning want? They talk about control, when outcomes are otherwise uncertain or perceived as unsafe. They seek familiarity, they express self-love, desire for the same-kind. They express difficulty to cope with loss, they want their deceased loved ones back. If biological cloning is a microcosm, cloning culture is a macrocosm, likewise locked (in) between the logics and contradictions of individuality and belonging, choice and conformity, consensus and tolerance, security and limitless growth, social inequality and safety, punishing bodies in pursuit of eternal lives, manipulating nature while fabricating natural ties in making more of the same. Ironically, the extreme implications of an unqualified culture of cloning reproduce the very prospects of stasis and death to which it considers itself threatened by the proliferation and incorporation of the different.

What, do we want, then, with the concept of cloning cultures?

Preliminary collection of ideas about cloning cultures suggests that we are dealing with a systemic and complex problem. Once we employ the critical notion that societies have reproduced themselves through taking for granted the preference for sameness, examples can be found everywhere, as are counter-moves, for example, the insistence on being, or on the right to be, different and preferences for counter-standard expressions and articulations. The concept of cloning cultures problematizes the preference for sameness, including the pursuit of unique perfection both across and within difference, which then is invoked as a model for cloning. This is a genuinely novel way of approaching the question of the systemic reproduction of systems of inequality and injustice. We are suggesting that the concept of cloning cultures exhibits considerable potential for pulling together a range of compelling issues in thinking about contemporary social problems.

By way of conclusion, a word on the imperative of a research agenda that reflects in its nature as well as in its institutional arrangements the limits of emulating preference for trodden patterns and hierarchies of sameness. The fact that the culture of cloning broadly construed embeds both social and biological dynamics, indeed, in mutually constitutive fashion, automatically conjures the possibility of productive exchanges between genetic engineers, genome scientists, and critical geographers working on agribusiness, as well as anthropologists, sociologists, and humanists concerned with the socio-cultural assumptions, implications, and representations of these bodies of work. Interdisciplinarity and joint productions demand viable institutional arrangements to promote these inter- and transdisciplinary discussions and research programmes and the products they are most likely to generate. We suggest therefore that disciplinarity and disciplinarization are both product and replicative of cloning culture, and that the kind of critical analysis of the range of phenomena falling under its conceptual and logical domains demand a vigorous and vibrant but also self-critical commitment to interdisciplinary practices.

Initial circulation of the idea of cloning cultures has triggered a snowball of enthusiastic response from colleagues adding ideas and suggestions. This is encouraging, but the conceptual underpin-

nings — the concepts and assumptions, range of issues and logics of analysis — need to be coherently focused from scratch. It is to these critical needs that we are here drawing attention and to which we hope readers will respond.

References

Appiah, Kwame A. 1990. "Racisms," in David T. Goldberg (ed.), *Anatomy of Racism.* Minneapolis: University of Minneapolis Press, pp. 3-17

Bell, David and Valentine, Gill. 1997. *Consuming Geographies: We Are What We Eat.* London: Routledge

Essed, Philomena. 1996. *Diversity: Gender, Color and Culture.* Amherst: University of Massachusetts Press

— 2002. "Cloning Cultural Homogeneity While Talking Diversity: Old Wine in New Bottles in Dutch Work Organizations?" *Transforming Anthropology.* Volume 11. Nr 1. (in Press)

Essed, Philomena and Goldberg, David Theo (eds.). 2002. *Race Critical Theories. Text and Context.* Oxford: Blackwell

Gabriel, John. 1994. *Racism, Culture, Markets.* London and New York: Routledge

Gilman, Sander. 1999. *Making the Body Beautiful.* Princeton and Oxford: Princeton UP

Goldberg, David Theo. 1993. *Racist Culture.* Oxford: Blackwell

— 2002 *The Racial State.* Oxford: Blackwell

Klein, Naomi. 1999. *No Logo.* New York: Picador

Roediger, David. 2001. "Whiteness and Ethnicity in the History of "White Ethnics" in the United States," in Philomena Essed and David Theo Goldberg (eds). *Race Critical Theories.* Oxford: Basil Blackwell, pp. 325-44

Scheff, Thomas. 1994. "Emotions and Identity: A Theory of Ethnic Nationalism," in Craig Calhoun (ed.). *Social Theory and the Politics of Identity.* Oxford, UK: Blackwell, pp. 277-303

Schwartz, Hillel. 1996. *The Culture of Copy. Striking Likeness, Unreasonable Facsimiles.* New York: Zone Books

Seidler, Victor J. 1997. *Not Man Enough. Embodying Masculinities.* London: Sage.

Shell, Marc. 1993. *Children of the Earth. Literature, Politics, and Nationhood.* New York, Oxford: Oxford University Press

Talbot, Margaret. 2001. "A Desire to Duplicate." The New York Times Magazine, February 4, 2001

Tilly, Charles. 1998. *Durable Inequality*. Berkeley, Los Angeles, London: University of California Press

Wiley, Norman. 1994. "The Politics of Identity in American History," Craig Calhoun (ed.). *Social Theory and the Politics of Identity*. Oxford, UK: Blackwell, pp. 130-149

Zwick, Rebecca. 2002. *Fair Game? The Use of Standardized Admissions Tests in Higher Education*. New York and London: Routledge Falmer

THE NEW SOVEREIGNTY

Shelby Steele

Shelby Steele is a Senior Research Fellow at the Hoover Institution. He is the author of The Content of Our Character: A New Vision of Race in America *(1990) and an Emmy Award winner for his work on "Seven Days in Bensonhurst" (1990), a PBS* Frontline *documentary examining the racially motivated killing of Yusef Hawkins in Brooklyn, New York.*

Steele defends the early American civil rights movements on the basis of their goals of "democracy, integration, and developmental uplift," goals that were achieved through the removal of laws barring certain people from having the rights and opportunities espoused in the American ideal of democracy. He claims, however, that current social movements, angered by a perceived lack of progress toward equality, have rejected these goals in favor of demanding group or collective entitlements. In Steele's view, collective entitlements based on race, gender, ethnicity, and other group grievances are not justified, and the affirmative action measures and separatist strategies that are thereby endorsed violate the democratic ideal of integration and harmony.

In *The True Believer,* Eric Hoffer wrote presciently of this phenomenon I have come to call the New Sovereignty:

> When a mass movement begins to attract people who are interested in their individual careers, it is a sign that it has passed its vigorous state; that it is no longer engaged in molding a new world but in possessing and preserving the present. It ceases then to be a movement and becomes an enterprise.

If it is true that great mass movements begin as spontaneous eruptions of long-smoldering discontent, it is also true that after significant reform is achieved they do not like to pass away or even modify their grievance posture. The redressing of the movement's grievances wins legitimacy for the movement. Reform, in this way, also means recognition for those who struggled for it. The movement's leaders are quoted in the papers, appear on TV, meet with elected officials, write books — they come to embody the movement.

Over time, they and they alone speak for the aggrieved; and, of course, they continue to speak *of* the aggrieved, adding fresh grievances to the original complaint. It is their vocation now, and their means to status and power. The idealistic reformers thus become professional spokespersons for the seemingly permanently aggrieved. In the civil rights movement, suits and briefcases replaced the sharecropper's denim of the early years, and $500-a-plate fund-raisers for the National Association for the Advancement of Colored People replaced volunteers and picket signs. The raucous bra burning of late Sixties feminism gave way to women's studies departments and direct-mail campaigns by the National Organization of Women.

This sort of evolution, however natural it may appear, is not without problems for the new grievance-group executive class. The winning of reform will have dissipated much of the explosive urgency that started the movement; yet the new institutionalized movement cannot justify its existence without this urgency. The problem becomes one of maintaining a reformist organization after considerable reforms have been won.

To keep alive the urgency needed to justify itself, the grievance organization will do three things. First, it will work to inspire a perpetual sense of grievance in its constituency so that grievance becomes the very centerpiece of the group itself. To be black, or a women, or gay, is, in the eyes of the NAACP, NOW, or Act Up, to be essentially threatened, victimized, apart from the rest of America. Second, these organizations will up the ante on what constitutes a grievance by making support of sovereignty itself the new test of grievance. If the women's studies program has not been made autonomous, this constitutes a grievance. If the national Council of La Raza hasn't been consulted, Hispanics have been ignored. The third strategy of grievance organizations is to arrange their priorities in a way that will maximize their grievance profile. Often their agendas will be established more for their grievance potential. Often their agendas will be established more for their grievance potential than for the actual betterment of the group. Those points at which there is resistance in the larger society to the group's entitlement demands will usually be made into top-priority issues, thereby emphasizing the status of victim and outsider necessary to sustain the sovereign organization.

Thus, at its 1989 convention, the NAACP put affirmative action at the very top of its agenda. Never mind the fact that studies conducted by both proponents and opponents of affirmative action indicate the practice has very little real impact on the employment and advancement of blacks. Never mind, too, that surveys show most black Americans do not consider racial preferences *their* priority. In its wisdom the NAACP thought (and continues to think) that the national mood against affirmative-action programs is a bigger problem for black men and women than teen pregnancy, or the disintegrating black family, or black-on-black crime. Why? Because the very resistance affirmative action meets from the larger society makes it an issue of high grievance potential. Affirmative action can generate the urgency that justifies black sovereignty far more than issues like teen preg-

nancy of high dropout rates, which carry no load of collective entitlement and which the *entire* society sees as serious problems....

How did America evolve its now rather formalized notion that groups of its citizens would be entitled collectively? I think it goes back to the most fundamental contradiction in American life. From the beginning America has been a pluralistic society, and one drawn to a radical form of democracy — emphasizing the freedom and equality of *individuals* — that could meld such diversity into a coherent nation. In this new nation no group would lord it over any other. But, of course, beneath this America of its ideals there was from the start a much meaner reality, one whose very existence mocked the notion of a nation made singular by the equality of its individuals. By limiting democracy to their own kind — white, male landowners — the Founding Fathers collectively entitled themselves and banished all others to the edges and underside of American life. There, individual entitlement was either curtailed or — in the case of slavery — extinguished.

The genius of the civil rights movement that changed the fabric of American life in the late 1950s and early 1960s was its profound understanding that the enemy of black Americans was not the ideal America but the unspoken principle of collective entitlement that had always put the lie to true democracy. This movement, which came to center stage from America's underside and Margins, had as its single, overriding goal the eradication of white entitlement. And correspondingly, it exhibited a belief in democratic principles at least as strong as that of the Founding Fathers, who themselves had emerged from the (less harsh) margins of English society. In this sense the civil rights movement re-enacted the American Revolution, and its paramount leader, Martin Luther King, spoke as twentieth-century America's greatest democratic voice.

All of this was made clear to me for the umpteenth time by my father on a very cold Saturday afternoon in 1959. There was a national campaign under way to integrate the lunch counters at Woolworth stores, and my father, who was more a persuader than an intimidator, had made it a point of honor that I join him on the picket line, civil rights being nothing less than the religion of our household. By this time, age twelve or so, I was sick of it. I'd had enough of watching my parents heading off to still another meeting or march; I'd heard too many tedious discussions on everything from the philosophy of passive resistance to the symbolism of going to jail. Added to this, my own experience of picket lines and peace marches had impressed upon me what so many people who've partaken of these activities know: that in themselves they can be crushingly boring — around and around and around holding a sign, watching one's own feet fall, feeling the minutes like hours. All that Saturday morning I hid from my father and tried to convince myself of what I longed for — that he would get so busy that if he didn't forget the march he would at least forget me.

He forgot nothing. I did my time on the picket line, but not without building up enough resentment to start a fight on the way home. What was so important about integration? We had never even wanted to eat at Woolworth's. I told him the truth, that he never took us to *any* restaurants anyway, claiming always that they charged too much money for bad food. But he said calmly that he was proud of me for marching and that he knew *I* knew food wasn't the point.

My father — forty years a truck driver, with the urges of an intellectual — went on to use my little rebellion as the occasion for a discourse, in this case on the concept of integration. Integration had little to do with merely rubbing shoulders with white people, eating bad food beside them. It was about the right to go absolutely anywhere white people could go being the test of freedom and equality. To be anywhere they could be and do anything they could do was the point. Like it or not, white people defined the horizon of freedom in America, and if you couldn't touch their shoulder you weren't free. For him integration was the *evidence* of freedom and equality.

My father was a product of America's margins, as were all the blacks in the early civil rights movement, leaders and foot soldiers alike. For them integration was a way of moving from the margins into the mainstream. Today there is considerable

ambivalence about integration, but in that day it was nothing less than democracy itself. Integration is also certainly about racial harmony, but it is more fundamentally about the ultimate extension of democracy — beyond the racial entitlements that contradict it. The idea of racial integration is quite simply the most democratic principle America has evolved, since all other such principles depend on its reality and are diminished by its absence.

But the civil rights movement did not account for one thing: the tremendous release of black anger that would follow its victories. The 1964 Civil Rights Act and the 1965 Voting Rights Act were, on one level, admissions of guilt by American society that it had practice white entitlement at the expense of all others. When the oppressors admit their crimes, the oppressed can give full vent to their long repressed rage because now there is a moral consensus between oppressor and oppressed that a wrong was done. This consensus gave blacks the license to release a rage that was three centuries deep, a rage that is still today everywhere visible, a rage that — in the wake of the Rodney King Verdict, a verdict a vast majority of all Americans thought unfair — fuelled the worst rioting in recent American history.

By the mid-Sixties, the democratic goal of integration was no longer enough to appease black anger. Suddenly for blacks there was a sense that far more was owed, that a huge bill was due. And for many whites there was also the feeling that some kind of repayment was truly in order. This was the moral logic that followed inevitably from the new consensus. But it led to an even simpler logic: if blacks had been oppressed collectively that oppression would now be redressed by entitling them collectively. So here we were again, in the name of a thousand good intentions, falling away from the hard challenge of a democracy of individuals and embracing the principle of collective entitlement that had so corrupted the American ideal in the first place. Now this old sin would be applied in the name of uplift. And this made an easy sort of sense. If it was good enough for whites for three hundred years, why not let blacks have a little of it to get ahead? In the context of the Sixties — black outrage and white guilt — a principle we had just decided was evil for whites was redefined as a social good for blacks. And once the formula was in place for blacks, it could be applied to other groups with similar grievances. By the 1970s more than 60 percent of the American population — not only blacks but Hispanics, women, Asians — would come under the collective entitlement of affirmative action.

In the early days of the civil rights movement, the concept of solidarity was essentially a moral one. That is, all people who believed in human freedom, fairness, and equality were asked to form a solid front against white entitlement. But after the collaboration of black rage and white guilt made collective entitlement a social remedy, the nature of solidarity changed. It was no longer the rallying of diverse peoples to breach an oppressive group entitlement. It was the very opposite: a rallying of people within a grievance group to pursue their own group entitlement. As early as the mid-Sixties, whites were made unwelcome in the civil rights movement, just as, by the mid-Seventies, men were no longer welcome in the women's movement. Eventually, collective entitlement *always* requires separation. And the irony is obvious: those who once had been the victims of separatism, who had sacrificed so dearly to overcome their being at the margins, would later create an ethos of their own separatism. After the Sixties, solidarity became essentially a separatist concept, and exclusionary principle. One no longer heard words like "integration" or "harmony"; one heard about "anger" and "power." Integration is anathema to grievance groups for precisely the same reason it was anathema to racist whites in the civil rights era: because it threatens their collective entitlement by insisting that no group be entitled over another. Power is where it's at today — power to set up the organization, attract the following, run the fiefdom.

But it must also be said that this could not have come to pass without the cooperation of the society at large and its institutions. Why did the government, the public and private institutions, the corporations and foundations, end up supporting principles that had the effect of turning causes into

sovereign fiefdoms? I think the answer is that those in charge of America's institutions saw the institutionalization and bureaucratization of the protest movements as ultimately desirable, at least in the short term, and the funding of group entitlements as ultimately a less costly way to redress grievances. The leaders of the newly sovereign fiefdoms were backing off from earlier demands that America live up to its ideals. Gone was the moral indictment. Gone was the call for difficult, soulful transformation. The language of entitlements is essentially the old, comforting language of power politics, and in the halls of power it went down easily enough.

With regard to civil rights, the moral voice of Dr. King gave way to the demands and cajolings of poverty-program moguls, class-action lawyers, and community organizers. The compromise that satisfied both political parties was to shift the focus from democracy, integration, and developmental uplift to collective entitlements. This satisfied the institutions because entitlements were cheaper in every way than real change. Better to set up black studies and women's studies departments than to have wrenching debates within existing departments. Better to fund these new institutions clamoring for money because who knows what kind of fuss they'll make if we turn down their proposals. Better to pass laws permitting Hispanic students to get preferred treatment in college admission — it costs less than improving kindergartens in East Los Angeles.

And this way to uplift satisfied the grievance-group "experts" because it laid the ground for their sovereignty and permanency: You negotiated with *us*. You funded *us*. You shared power, at least a bit of it, with *us*.

This negotiation was carried out in a kind of quasi-secrecy. Quotas, set-asides, and other entitlements were not debated in congress or on the campaign trail. They were implemented by executive orders and Equal Employment Opportunity Commission guidelines without much public scrutiny. Also the courts played a quiet but persistent role in supporting these orders and guidelines and in further spelling out their application. Universities, corporations, and foundations implemented their own grievance entitlements, the workings of which are often kept from the public.

Now it should surprise no one that all this entitlement has most helped those who least need it — white middle-class women and the black middle class. Poor blacks do not guide the black grievance groups. Working-class women do not set NOW's agenda. Poor Hispanics do not clamor for bilingualism. Perhaps there is nothing wrong with middle class people being helped but their demands for entitlements are most often in the names of those less well off than themselves. The negotiations that settled on entitlements as the primary form of redress after the Sixties have generated a legalistic grievance industry that argues the interstices of entitlements and does very little to help those truly in need.

In a liberal democracy, collective entitlements based upon race, gender, ethnicity, or some other group grievance are always undemocratic expedients. Integration, on the other hand, is the most difficult and inexpedient expansion of the democratic ideal; for in opting for integration, a citizen denies his or her impulse to use our most arbitrary characteristics — race, ethnicity, gender, sexual preference — as the basis for identity, as a key to status, or for claims to entitlement. Integration is twentieth-century America's elaboration of democracy. It eliminates such things as race and gender as oppressive barriers to freedom, as democrats of an earlier epoch eliminated religion and property. Our mistake has been to think of integration only as utopian vision of perfect racial harmony. I think it is better to see integration as the inclusion of all citizens into the same sphere of rights, the same range of opportunities and possibilities that our Founding Fathers themselves enjoyed. Integration is not social engineering or group entitlements; it is a fundamental *absence* of arbitrary barriers to freedom.

If we can understand integration as an absence of barriers that has the effect of integrating all citizens into the same sphere of rights, then it can serve as a principle of democratic conduct. Anything that pushes anybody out of this sphere is undemocratic and must be checked, no matter the good intentions that seem to justify it. Understood in this light, collective entitlements are as undemocratic as racial and gender discrimination, and a group grievance is no more a justification for entitlement than the notion of white supremacy was at an earlier time. We are wrong to think of democracy as a gift of freedom; it is really a kind of discipline that avails freedom. Sometimes its enemy is racism and sexism; other times the enemy is our expedient attempts to correct these ills.

I think it is time for those who seek identity and power through grievance groups to fashion identities apart from grievance, to grant themselves the widest range of freedom, and to assume responsibility for that freedom. Victimhood lasts only as long as it is accepted, and to exploit it for an empty sovereignty is to accept it. The New Sovereignty is ultimately about vanity. It is the narcissism of victims, and it brings only a negligible power at the exorbitant price of continued victimhood. And all the while integration remains the real work.

SOCIAL MOVEMENTS AND THE POLITICS OF DIFFERENCE

Iris Marion Young

Iris Marion Young is Professor of Political Science at the University of Chicago. She is affiliated with the Gender Studies Center and the Human Rights program. Her books include Throwing Like a Girl and Other Essays in Feminist Philosophy and Social Theory *(1990),* Intersecting Voices: Dilemmas of Gender, Political Philosophy, and Policy *(1997), and* Inclusion and Democracy *(2000). She is also a co-editor of* A Companion to Feminist Philosophy *(1998, with Alison M. Jaggar).*

While Young applauds the progress toward equality gained through the ideal of equality as equal treatment for all people, she is critical of the goal of assimilation that is assumed in this conception of equality. She defends the positive self-definition of group difference that is evident in current social movements of oppressed groups and endorses a politics of difference as a way of reconceiving the meaning of equality. Sometimes the elimination of oppression and the inclusion of members of all groups requires not the equal treatment goal of the assimilationist model, but special or different treatment for members of disadvantaged groups.

The idea that I think we need today in order to make decisions in political matters cannot be the idea of a totality, or of the unity, of a body. It can only be the idea of a multiplicity or a diversity. ... To state that one must draw a critique of political judgment means today to do a politics of opinions that at the same time is a politics of Ideas ... in which justice in not placed under a rule of convergence but rather a rule of divergence. I believe that this is the theme that one finds constantly in present day writing under the name "minority."
— Jean-François Lyotard

There was once a time of caste and class, when tradition decreed that each group had its place, and that some were born to rule and others to serve. In this time of darkness, law and social norms defined rights, privileges, and obligations differently for different groups, distinguished by characteristics of sex, race, religion, class, or occupation. Social inequality was justified by church and state on the grounds that people have different natures, and some natures are better than others.

Then one day Enlightenment dawned, heralding a revolutionary conception of humanity and society. All people are equal, the revolutionaries declared, inasmuch as all have a capacity for reason and moral sense. Law and politics should therefore grant to everyone equal political and civil rights. With these bold ideas the battle lines of modern political struggle were drawn.

For over two hundred years since those voices of reason first rang out, the forces of light have struggled for liberty and political equality against the dark forces of irrational prejudice, arbitrary metaphysics, and the crumbling towers of patriarchal church, state, and family. In the New World we had a head start in this fight, since the American War of Independence was fought on these Enlightenment principles, and our Constitution stood for liberty and equality. So we did not have to throw off the yokes of class and religious privilege, as did our Old World comrades. Yet the United States had its own oligarchic horrors in the form of slavery and the exclusion of women from public life. In protracted and bitter struggles these bastions of privilege based on group difference began to give way, finally to topple in the 1960s.

Today in our society a few vestiges of prejudice and discrimination remain, but we are working on them, and have nearly realized the dream those Enlightenment fathers dared to propound. The state and law should express right only in universal terms applied equally to all, and differences among persons and groups should be a purely accidental and private matter. We seek a society in which differences of race, sex, religion, and ethnicity no longer make a difference to people's rights and opportunities. People should be treated as individuals, not as members of groups; their life options and rewards should be based solely on their individual achievement. All persons should have the liberty to be and do anything they want, to choose their own lives and not be hampered by traditional expectations and stereotypes.

We tell each other this story and make our children perform it for our sacred holidays — Thanksgiving Day, the Fourth of July, Memorial Day, Lincoln's Birthday. We have constructed Martin Luther King, Jr., Day to fit the narrative so well that we have already forgotten that it took a fight to get it included in the canon year. There is much truth to this story. Enlightenment ideals of liberty and political equality did and do inspire movements against oppression and domination, whose success has created social values and institutions we would not want to lose. A people could do worse than tell this story after big meals and occasionally call upon one another to live up to it.

The very worthiness of the narrative, however, and the achievement of political equality that it recounts, now inspires new heretics. In recent years the ideal of liberation as the elimination of group difference has been challenged by movement of the oppressed. The very success of political movements against differential privilege and for political equality has generated moments of group specificity and cultural pride.

In this chapter I criticize an ideal of justice that defines liberation as the transcendence of group difference, which I refer to as an ideal of assimilation. This ideal usually promotes equal treatment as a primary principle of justice. Recent social movements of oppressed groups challenge this ideal. Many in these movements argue that a positive self-definition of group difference is in fact more liberatory.

I endorse this politics of difference, and argue that at stake is the meaning of social difference itself. Traditional politics that excludes or devalues some persons on account of their group attributes assumes an essentialist meaning of difference; it defines groups as having different natures. An egalitarian politics of difference, on the other hand, defines difference more fluidly and relationally as the product of social processes. An emancipatory politics that affirms group difference involves a reconception of the meaning of equality. The assimilationist ideal assumes that equal social status for all persons requires treating everyone according to the same principles, rules, and standards. A politics of difference argues, on the other hand, that equality as the participation and inclusion of all groups sometimes requires different treatment for the oppressed or disadvantaged groups....

Competing Paradigms of Liberation

In "On Racism and Sexism" [in *Philosophy and Social Issues*, 1980], Richard Wasserstrom develops a classic statement of the ideal of liberation from group-based oppression as involving the elimination of group-based difference itself. A truly nonracist, nonsexist society, he suggests, would be one in which the race or sex of an individual would be the functional equivalent of eye color in our society today. While physiological differences in skin color or genitals would remain, they would have no significance for a person's sense of identity or how others regard him or her. No political rights or obligations would be connected to race or sex, and no important institutional benefits would be associated with either. People would see no reason to consider race or gender in policy or everyday interactions. In such a society, social group differences would have ceased to exist.

Wasserstrom contrasts this ideal of assimilation with an ideal of diversity much like the one I will argue for, which he agrees is compelling. He offers three primary reasons, however, for choosing the assimilationist ideal of liberation over the ideal of diversity. First, the assimilationist ideal exposes the arbitrariness of group-based social distinctions which are thought natural and necessary sees more clearly how pervasively these group categories unnecessarily limit possibilities for some in existing society. Second, the assimilationist ideal presents a clear and unambiguous standard of equality and justice. According to such a standard, any group-related differentiation or discrimination is suspect. Whenever laws or rules, the division of labor, or other social practices allocate benefits differently according to group membership, this is a sign of injustice. The principle of justice is simple: treat everyone according to the same principles, rules, and standards. Third, the assimilationist ideal maximizes choice. In a society where differences make no social difference people can develop themselves as individuals, unconstrained by group norms and expectations.

There is no question that the ideal of liberation as the elimination of group difference has been enormously important in the history of emancipatory politics. The ideal of universal humanity that denies natural differences has been a crucial historical development in the struggle against exclusion and status differentiation. It has made possible the assertion of the equal moral worth of all persons, and thus the right of all to participate and be included in all institutions and positions of power and privilege. The assimilationist ideal retains significant rhetorical power in the face of continued beliefs in the essentially different and inferior natures of women, blacks, and other groups.

The power of this assimilationist ideal has inspired the struggle of oppressed groups and the supporters against the exclusion and denigration of these groups, and continues to inspire many. Periodically in American history, however, movements of the oppressed have questioned and rejected this "path to belonging." Instead they have seen self-organization and the assertion of a positive group cultural identity as a better strategy for achieving power and participation in dominant institutions.

Recent decades have witnessed a resurgence of this "politics of difference" not only among racial and ethnic groups, but also among women, gay men and lesbians, old people, and the disabled.

Not long after the passage of the Civil Rights Act and the Voting Rights Act, many white and black supporters of the black civil rights movement were surprised, confused, and angered by the emergence of the Black Power movement. Black Power advocates criticized the integrationist goal and reliance on the support of white liberals that characterized the civil right movement. They encouraged blacks to break their alliance with whites and assert the specificity of their own culture, political organization, and goals. Instead of integration, they encouraged blacks to seek economic institutions at least as much as they have lessened black-white animosity and opened doors of opportunity. While some individual blacks may be better off than they would have been if these changes had not occurred, as a group, blacks are not better off and may be worse off, because the blacks who have succeeded in assimilating into the American middle class no longer associate as closely with lower-class blacks.

While much black politics has questioned the ideal of assimilation in economic and political terms, the past twenty years have also seen the assertion and celebration by blacks of a distinct Afro-American culture, both as a recovery and revaluation of an Afro-American history and in the creation of new cultural forms. The slogan "black is beautiful" pierced American consciousness, deeply unsettling the received body aesthetic which I [have] argued . . . continues to be a powerful reproducer of racism. Afro-American hairstyles pronounced themselves differently stylish, not less stylish. Linguistic theorists asserted that black English is English differently constructed, not bad English, and black poets and novelists exploited and explored its particular nuances.

In the late 1960s Red Power came fast on the hells of Black Power. The American Indian Movement and other radical organization of American Indians rejected perhaps even more vehemently than blacks the goal of assimilation which has dominated white-Indian relations for most of the twentieth century. They asserted a right to self-government on Indian lands and fought to gain and maintain a dominant Indian voice in the Bureau of Indian Affairs. American Indians have sought to recover and preserve their language, rituals, and crafts, and this renewal of pride in traditional culture has also fostered a separatist political movement. The desire to pursue land rights claims and to fight for control over resources on reservations arises from what has become a fierce commitment to tribal self-determination, the desire to develop and maintain Indian political and economic bases in but not of white society.

These are but two examples of a widespread tendency in the politics of the 1970s and 1980s for oppressed, disadvantaged, or specially marked groups to organize autonomously and assert a positive sense of their cultural and experiential specificity. Many Spanish-speaking Americans have rejected the traditional assumption that full participation in American society requires linguistic and cultural assimilation. In the last twenty years many have developed a renewed interest and pride in their Puerto Rican, Chicano, Mexican, or other Latin American heritage. They have asserted the right to maintain their specific culture and speak their language and still receive the benefits of citizenship, such as voting right, decent education, and job opportunities. Many Jewish Americans have similarly rejected the ideal of assimilation, instead asserting the specificity and positive meaning of Jewish identity, often insisting publicly that Christian culture cease to be taken as the norm.

Since the late 1960s the blossoming of gay cultural expression, gay organizations, and the public presence of gays in marches and other forums have radically altered the environment in which young people come to sexual identity, and changed many people's perceptions of homosexuality. Early gay rights advocacy had a distinctly assimilationist and universalist orientation. The goal was to remove the stigma of being homosexual, to prevent institutional discrimination, and to achieve societal recognition that gay people are "no different" from anyone else. The very process of political organization against discrimination and police harass-

ment and for the achievement of civil rights, however, fostered the development of gay and lesbian communities and cultural expression, which by the mid-1970s flowered in meeting places, organizations, literature, music, and massive street celebrations.

Today most gay and lesbian liberation advocates seek not merely civil right, but the affirmation of gay men and lesbians as social groups with specific experiences and perspectives. Refusing to accept the dominant culture's definition of healthy sexuality and respectable family life and social practices, gay and lesbian liberation movements have proudly created and displayed a distinctive self-definition and culture. For gay men and lesbians the analogue to racial integration is the typical liberal approach to sexuality, which tolerates any behavior as long as it is kept private. Gay pride asserts that sexual identity is a matter of culture and politics, and not merely "behavior" to be tolerated or forbidden.

The women's movement has also generated its own versions of a politics of difference. Humanist feminism, which predominated in the nineteenth century and in the contemporary women's movement until the late 1970s, finds in any assertion of difference between women and men only a legacy of female oppression and an ideology to legitimate continued exclusion of women from socially valued human activity. Humanist feminism is thus analogous to an ideal of assimilation in identifying sexual equality with gender blindness, with measuring women and men according to the same standards and treating them in the same way. Indeed, for many feminists, androgyny names the ideal of sexual liberation — a society in which gender difference it would be eliminated. Given the strength and plausibility of this vision of sexual equality, it was confusing when feminists too began taking the turn to difference, asserting the positivity and specificity of female experience and values.

Feminist separatism was the earliest expression of such gynocentric feminism. Feminist separatism rejected wholly or partly the goal of entering the male-dominated world, because it requires playing according to rules that men have made and that have been used against women, and because trying to measure up to male-defined standards inevitably involves accommodating or pleasing the men who continue to dominate socially valued institutions and activities. Separatism promoted the empowerment of women through self-organization, the creation of separate and safe spaces where women could share and analyze their experiences, voice their anger, play with and create bonds with one another, and develop new and better institutions and practices.

Most elements of the contemporary women's movement have been separatist to some degree. Separatists seeking to live as much of their lives as possible in women-only institutions were largely responsible for the creation of the women's culture that burst forth all over the United States by the mid-1970s, and continues to claim the loyalty of millions of women — in the form of music, poetry, spirituality, literature, celebrations, festivals, and dances. Whether drawing on images of Amazonian grandeur, recovering and revaluing traditional women's arts, like quilting and weaving, or inventing new rituals based on medieval witchcraft, the development of such expressions of women's culture gave many feminists images of a female-centered beauty and strength entirely outside capitalist patriarchal definitions of feminine pulchritude. The separatist impulse also fostered the development of the many autonomous women's institutions and services that have concretely improved the lives of many women, whether feminists or not — such as health clinics, battered women's shelters, rape crisis centers, and women's coffeehouses and bookstores.

Beginning in the late 1970s much feminist theory and political analysis also took a turn away from humanist feminism, to question the assumption that traditional female activity expresses primarily the victimization of women and the distortion of their human potential and that the goal of women's liberation is the participation of women as equals in public institutions now dominated by men. Instead of understanding the activities and values associated with traditional femininity as largely distortions and inhibitions of women's truly human potentialities, this gynocentric analysis sought to revalue the caring, nurturing, and

cooperative approach to social relations they found associated with feminine socialization, and sought in women's specific experiences the bases for an attitude toward the body and nature healthier than that predominant in male dominated Western capitalist culture.

None of the social movements asserting positive group specificity is in fact a unity. All have group differences within them. The black movement, for example, includes middle-class blacks and working-class blacks, gays and straight people, men and women, and so it is with any other group. The implications of group differences within a social group have been most systematically discussed in the women's movement. Feminist conferences and publications have generated particularly fruitful, though often emotionally wrenching discussions of the oppression of racial and ethnic blindness and the importance of attending to group differences among women. From such discussions emerged principled efforts to provide autonomously organized forums for black women, Latinas, Jewish women, lesbians, differently abled women, old women, and any other women who see reason for claiming that they have as a group a distinctive voice that might be silenced in a general feminist discourse. Those discussions, along with the practices feminists instituted to structure discussion and interaction among differently identifying groups of women, offer some beginning models for the development of a heterogeneous public. Each of the other social movements has also generated discussion of group differences that cut across their identities, leading to other possibilities of coalition and alliance.

Emancipation through the Politics of Difference

Implicit in emancipatory movements asserting a positive sense of group difference is a different ideal of liberation, which might be called democratic cultural pluralism. In this vision the good society does not eliminate or transcend group difference. Rather, there is equality among socially and culturally differentiated groups, who mutually respect one another and affirm one another in their differences. What are the reasons for rejecting the assimilationist ideal and promoting a politics of difference?

Some deny the reality of social groups. For them, group difference is an invidious fiction produced and perpetuated in order to preserve the privilege of the few. Others, such as Wasserstrom, may agree that social groups do now exist and have real social consequences for the way people identify themselves and one another, but assert that such social group differences are undesirable. The assimilationist ideal involves denying either the reality or the desirability of social groups.

Those promoting a politics of difference doubt that a society without group differences is either possible or desirable. Contrary to the assumption of modernization theory, increased urbanization and the extension of equal formal rights to all groups has not led to a decline in particularist affiliations. If anything, the urban concentration and interactions among groups that modernizing social processes introduce tend to reinforce group solidarity and differentiation. Attachment to specific traditions, practices, language, and other culturally specific forms is a crucial aspect of social existence. People do not usually give up their social group identifications, even when they are oppressed.

Whether eliminating social group difference is possible or desirable in the long run, however, is an academic issue. Today and for the foreseeable future societies are certainly structured by groups, and some are privileged while others are oppressed. New social movements of group specificity do not deny the official story's claim that the ideal of liberation as eliminating difference and treating everyone the same has brought significant improvement in the status of excluded groups. Its main quarrel is with the story's conclusion, namely, that since we have achieved formal equality, only vestiges and holdovers of differential privilege remain, which will die out with the continued persistent assertion of an ideal of social relations that make differences irrelevant to a person's life prospects. The achievement of formal equality does not eliminate social differences, and rhetorical commitment to the sameness of persons makes it impossible even to

name how those differences presently structure privilege and oppression.

Though in many respects the law is now blind to group differences, some groups continue to be marked as deviant, as the Other. In everyday interactions, images, and decisions, assumptions about women, blacks, Hispanics, gay men and lesbians, old people, and other marked groups continue to justify exclusion, avoidance, paternalism, and authoritarian treatment. Continued racist, sexist, homophobic, ageist, and ableist institutions and behavior create particular circumstances for these groups, usually disadvantaging them in their opportunity to develop their capacities. Finally, in part because they have been segregated from one another, and in part because they have particular histories and traditions, there are cultural differences among social groups — differences in language, style of living, body comportment and gestures, values, and perspectives on society.

Today in American society, as in many other societies, there is widespread agreement that no person should be excluded from political and economic activities because of ascribed characteristics. Group differences nevertheless continue to exist, and certain groups continue to be privileged. Under these circumstances, insisting that equality and liberation entail ignoring difference has progressive consequences in three respects.

First, blindness to difference disadvantages groups whose experience, culture, and socialized capacities differ from those of privileged groups. The strategy of assimilation always implies coming into the game after it is already begun, after the rules and standards have already been set, and having to prove oneself according to those rules and standards. In the assimilationist strategy, the privileged groups implicitly define the standards according to which all will be measured. Because their privilege involves not recognizing these standards as culturally and experientially specific, the ideal of a common humanity in which all can participate without regard to race, gender, religion, or sexuality poses as neutral and universal. The real differences between oppressed groups and the dominant norm, however, tend to put them at a disadvantage in measuring up to these standards, and for that reason assimilationist policies perpetuate their disadvantage. Later in this chapter, I shall give examples of facially neutral standards that operate to disadvantage or exclude those already disadvantaged.

Second, the ideal of a universal humanity without social group differences allows privileged groups to ignore their own group specificity. Blindness to difference perpetuates cultural imperialism by allowing norms expressing the point of view and experience of privileged groups to appear neutral and universal. The assimilationist ideal presumes that there is a humanity in general, and instituted group-neutral human capacity for self-making that left to itself would make individuality flower, thus guaranteeing that each individual will be different. Because there is no such instituted group-neutral point of view, the situation and experience of dominant groups tend to define the norms of such a humanity in general. Against such a supposedly neutral humanist ideal, only the oppressed groups come to be marked with particularity; they, and not the privileged groups, are marked, objectified as the Others.

Thus, third, this denigration of groups that deviate from an allegedly neutral standard often produces an internalized devaluation by members of those groups themselves. When there is an ideal of general human standards according to which everyone should be evaluated equally, then Puerto Ricans or Chinese Americans are ashamed of their accents or their parents, black children despise the female-dominated kith and kin networks of their neighborhoods, and feminists seek to root out their tendency to cry, or to feel compassion for a frustrated stranger. The aspiration to assimilate helps produce the self-loathing and double consciousness characteristic of oppression. The goal of assimilation holds up to people a demand that they "fit," be like the mainstream, in behavior, values and goals. At the same time, as long as group differences exist, group members will be marked as different — as black, Jewish, gay — and thus as unable simply to fit. When participation is taken to imply assimilation the oppressed person is caught in an irresolvable dilemma: to participate means to accept and adopt an identity one is not, and to try

to participate means to be reminded by oneself and others of the identity one is.

A more subtle analysis of the assimilationist ideal might distinguish between a conformist and a transformational ideal of assimilation. In the conformist ideal, status quo institutions and norms are assumed as give, and disadvantaged groups who differ from those norms are expected to conform to them. A transformational ideal of assimilation, on the other hand, recognized that institutions as given express the interests and perspective of the dominant groups. Achieving assimilation therefore requires altering many institutions and practices in accordance with neutral rules that truly do not disadvantage or stigmatize any person, so that group membership really is irrelevant to how persons are treated. Wasserstrom's ideal fits a transformational assimilation, as does the group-neutral ideal advocated by some feminists. Unlike the conformist assimilationist, the transformational assimilationist may allow that group-specific policies, such as affirmative action, are necessary and appropriate means for transforming institutions to fit the assimilationist ideal. Whether conformist or transformational, however, the assimilationist ideal still denies that group difference can be positive and desirable; thus any form of the ideal of assimilation constructs group difference as a liability or disadvantage.

Under these circumstances, a politics that asserts the positivity of group difference is liberating and empowering. In the act of reclaiming the identity the dominant culture has taught them to despise, and affirming it as an identity to celebrate, the oppressed remove double consciousness. I am just what they say I am — a Jewboy, a colored girl, a fag, a dyke, or a hag — and proud of it. No longer does one have the impossible project of trying to become something one is not under circumstances where the very trying reminds one of who one is. This politics asserts that oppressed groups have distinct cultures, experiences, and perspectives on social life with humanly positive meaning, some of which may even be superior to the culture and perspectives of mainstream society. The rejection and devaluation of one's culture and perspective should not be a condition of full participation in social life.

Asserting the value and specificity of the culture and attributes of oppressed groups, moreover, results in a relativizing of the dominant culture. When feminists assert the validity of feminine sensitivity and the positive value of nurturing behavior, when gays describe the prejudice of heterosexuals as homophobic and their own sexuality as positive and self-developing, when blacks affirm a distinct Afro-American tradition, then the dominant culture is forced to discover itself for the first time as specific: as Anglo, European, Christian, masculine, straight. In a political struggle where oppressed groups insist on the positive value of their specific culture and experience, it becomes increasingly difficult for dominant groups to parade their norms as neutral and universal, and to construct the values and behavior of the oppressed as deviant, perverted, or inferior. By puncturing the universalist claim to unity that expels some groups and turns them into the Other, the assertion of positive group specificity introduces the possibility of understanding the relation between groups as merely difference, instead of exclusion, opposition, or dominance.

The politics of difference also promotes a notion of group solidarity against the individualism of liberal humanism. Liberal humanism treats each person as an individual, ignoring differences of race, sex, religion, and ethnicity. Each person should be evaluated only according to her or his individual efforts and achievements. With the institutionalization of formal equality some members of formerly excluded groups have indeed succeeded by mainstream standards. Structural patterns of group privilege and oppression nevertheless remain. When political leaders of oppressed groups reject assimilation they are often affirming group solidarity. Where the dominant culture refuses to see anything but the achievement of autonomous individuals, the oppressed assert that we shall not separate from the people with whom we identify in order to "make it" in a white Anglo male world. The politics of difference insists on liberation of the whole group of blacks, women, American Indians, and that this can be accomplished only through basic institutional changes.

These changes must include group representation in policy-making and an elimination of the hierarchy of rewards that forces everyone to compete for scarce positions at the top.

Thus the assertion of a positive sense of group difference provides a standpoint from which to criticize prevailing institutions and norm. Black Americans find in their traditional communities, which refer to their members as "brother" and "sister," a sense of solidarity absent from the calculating individualism of white professional capitalist society. Feminists find in the traditional female values of nurturing a challenge to a militarist worldview, and lesbians find in their relationships a confrontation with the assumption of complementary gender roles in sexual relationships. From their experience of a culture tied to the land American Indians formulate a critique of the instrumental rationality of European culture that results in pollution and ecological destruction. Having revealed the specificity of the dominant norms which claim universality and neutrality, social movements of the oppressed are in a position to inquire how the dominant institutions must be changed so that they will no longer reproduce the patterns of privilege and oppression.

From the assertion of positive difference the self-organization of oppressed groups follows. Both liberal humanist and leftist political organizations and movements have found it difficult to accept this principle of group autonomy. In a humanist emancipatory politics, if a group is subject to injustice, then all those interested in a just society should unite to combat the powers that perpetuate that injustice. If many groups are subject to injustice, moreover, then they should unite to work for a just society. The politics of difference is certainly not against coalition, nor does it hold that, for example, whites should not work against racial injustice or men against sexist injustice. This politics of group assertion, however, takes as a basic principle that members of oppressed groups need separate organizations that exclude others, especially those from more privileged groups. Separate organization is probably necessary in order for these groups to discover and reinforce the positivity of their specific experience, to collapse and eliminate double consciousness. In discussions within autonomous organizations, group members can determine their specific needs and interests. Separation and self-organization risk creating pressures toward homogenization of the groups themselves, creating new privileges and exclusions. But contemporary emancipatory social movements have found group autonomy an important vehicle for empowerment and the development of a group-specific voice and perspective.

Integration into the full life of the society should not have to imply assimilation to dominant norms and abandonment of group affiliation and culture. If the only alternative to the oppressive exclusion of some groups defined as Other by dominant ideologies is the assertion that they are the same as everybody else, then they will continue to be excluded because they are not the same.

Some might object to the way I have drawn the distinction between as assimilationist ideal of liberation and a radical democratic pluralism. They might claim that I have not painted the ideal of a society that transcends group differences fairly, representing it as homogeneous and conformist. The free society envisaged by liberalism, they might say, is certainly pluralistic. In it persons can affiliate with whomever they choose; liberty encourages a proliferation of life-styles, activities, and associations. While I have no quarrel with social diversity in this sense, this vision of liberal pluralism does not touch on the primary issues that give rise to the politics of difference. The vision of liberation as the transcendence of group difference seeks to abolish the public and political significance of group difference while retaining and promoting both individual and group diversity in private, or nonpolitical, social contexts. This way of distinguishing public and private spheres, where the public represents universal citizenship and the private individual differences, tends to result in group exclusion from the public. Radical democratic pluralism acknowledges and affirms the public and political significance of social group differences as a means of ensuring the participation and inclusion of everyone in social and political institutions.

Reclaiming the Meaning of Difference

Many people inside and outside the movements I have discussed find the rejection of the liberal humanist ideal and the assertion of a positive sense of group difference both confusing and controversial. They fear that any admission by oppressed groups that they are different from the dominant groups risks justifying anew the subordination, special marking, and exclusion of those groups. Since calls for a return of women to the kitchen, blacks to servant roles and separate schools, and disabled people to nursing homes are not absent from contemporary politics, the danger is real. It may be true that the assimilationist ideal that treats everyone the same and applies the same standards to all perpetuates disadvantage because real group differences remain that make it unfair to compare the unequals. But this is far preferable to a reestablishment of separate and unequal spheres for different groups justified on the basis of group difference.

Since those asserting group specificity certainly wish to affirm the liberal humanist principle that all persons are of equal moral worth, they appear to be faced with a dilemma. Analyzing W.E.B. du Bois's arguments for cultural pluralism, Bernard Boxill poses the dilemma this way: "On the one hand, we must overcome segregation because it denies the idea of human brotherhood; on the other hand, to overcome segregation we must self-segregate and therefore also deny the idea of human brotherhood." Martha Minow finds a dilemma of difference facing any who seek to promote justice for currently oppressed or disadvantaged groups. Formally neutral rules and policies that ignore group differences often perpetuate the disadvantage of those whose difference is defined as deviant; but focusing on difference risks recreating the stigma that difference has carried in the past.

The dilemmas are genuine, and exhibit the risks of collective live, where the consequences of one's claims, actions, and policies may not turn out as one intended because others have understood them differently or turned them to different ends. Since ignoring group differences in public policy does not mean that people ignore them in everyday life and interaction, however, oppression continues even when law and policy declare that all are equal. Thus, I think for many groups and in many circumstances it is more empowering to affirm and acknowledge in political life the group differences that already exist in social life. One is more likely to avoid the dilemma of difference in doing this if the meaning of difference itself becomes a terrain of political struggle. Social movements asserting the positivity of group difference have established this terrain, offering an emancipatory meaning of difference to replace the old exclusionary meaning.

The oppressive meaning of group difference defines it as absolute otherness, mutual exclusion, categorical opposition. This essentialist meaning of difference submits to the logic of identity. One group occupies the position of a norm, against which all others are measured. The attempt to reduce all persons to the unity of a common measure constructs as deviant those whose attributes differ from the group-specific attributes implicitly presumed in the norm. The drive to unify the particularity and multiplicity of practices, cultural symbols, and ways of relating in clear and distinct categories turns difference into exclusion. Thus the appropriation of a universal subject position by socially privileged groups forces those they define as different outside the definition of full humanity and citizenship. The attempt to measure all against some universal standard generates a logic of difference as hierarchical dichotomy — masculine/feminine, civilized/salvage, and so on. The second term is defined negatively as a lack of the truly human qualities; at the same time it is defined as the complement to the valued term, the object correlating with its subject, that which brings it to completion, wholeness, and identity. By loving and affirming him, a woman serves as a mirror to a man, holding up his virtues for him to see. By carrying the white man's burden to tame and educate the savage peoples, the civilized will realize universal humanity. The exotic orientals are there to know and master, to be the completion of reason's progress in history, which seeks the unity of the world. In every case the valued term achieves its value by its determinately negative relation to the Other.

In the objectifying ideologies of racism, sexism, anti-Semitism, and homophobia, only the oppressed and excluded groups are defined as different. Whereas the privileged groups are neutral and exhibit free and malleable subjectivity, the excluded groups are marked with an essence, imprisoned in a given set of possibilities. By virtue of the characteristics the group is alleged to have by nature, the ideologies allege that group members have specific dispositions that suit them for some activities and not others. Difference in these ideologies always means exclusionary opposition to a norm. There are rational men, and then there are women; there are civilized men, and then there are wild and savage peoples. The marking of difference always implies a good/bad opposition; it is always a devaluation, the naming of an inferiority in relation to a superior standard of humanity.

Difference here always means absolute otherness; the group marked as different has no common nature with the normal or neutral ones. The categorical opposition of groups essentializes them, repressing the differences within groups. In this way the definition of difference as exclusion and opposition actually denies difference. This essentializing categorization also denies difference in that its universalizing norms preclude recognizing and affirming a group's specificity in its own terms.

Essentializing difference expresses a fear of specificity, and a fear of making permeable the categorical border between oneself and the others. This fear is not merely intellectual and does not derive only from the instrumental desire to defend privilege, though that may be a large element. It wells from the depths of the Western subject's sense of identity, especially, but not only in the subjectivity of privileged groups. The fear may increase, moreover, as a clear essentialism of difference wanes, as belief in a specifically female, black, or homosexual nature becomes less tenable.

The politics of difference confronts this fear, and aims for an understanding of group difference as indeed ambiguous, relational, shifting, without clear borders that keep people straight — as entailing neither amorphous unity nor pure individuality. By asserting a positive meaning for their own identity, oppressed groups seek to seize the power of naming difference itself, and explode the implicit definition of difference as deviance in relation to a norm, which freezes some groups into a self-enclosed nature. Difference now comes to mean not otherness, exclusive opposition, but specifically, variation, heterogeneity. Difference names relations of similarity and dissimilarity that can be reduced to neither coextensive identity nor overlapping otherness.

The alternative to an essentializing, stigmatizing meaning of difference as opposition is an understanding of difference as specificity, variation. In this logic, as Martha Minow suggests, group differences should be conceived as relational rather than defined by substantive categories and attributes. A relational understanding of difference relativizes the previously universal position of privileged groups, which allows only the oppressed to be marked as different. When group difference appears as a function of comparison between groups, whites are just as specific as black or Latinos, men just as specific as women, able-bodied people just as specific as disabled people. Difference thus emerges not as a description of the attributes of a group, but as a function of the relations between groups and the interaction of groups with institutions.

In this relational understanding, the meaning of difference also becomes contextualized. Group differences will be more or less salient depending on the groups compared, the purposes of the comparison, and the point of view of the comparers. Such contextualized understandings of difference undermine essentialist assumptions. For example in the context of athletics, health care, social service support, and so on, wheelchair-bound people are different from others, but they are not different in many other respects. Traditional treatment of the disabled entailed exclusion and segregation because the differences between the disabled and the able-bodied were conceptualized as extending to all or most capacities.

In general, then, a relational understanding of group difference rejects exclusion. Difference no longer implies that groups lie outside one another. To say that there are differences among groups does not imply that there are not overlapping experiences, or that two groups have nothing in common. The assumption that real differences in affinity, culture, or privilege imply oppositional categorization must be challenged. Different groups are always similar in some respects, and always potentially share some attributes, experiences, and goals.

Such a relational understanding of difference entails revising the meaning of group identity as well. In asserting the positive difference of their experience, culture, and social perspective, social movements of groups that have experienced cultural imperialism deny that they have a common identity, a set of fixed attributes that clearly mark who belongs and who doesn't. Rather, what makes a group a group is a social process of interaction and differentiation in which some people come to have a particular affinity for others. My "affinity group" in a given social situation comprises those people with whom I feel the most comfortable, who are more familiar. Affinity names the manner of sharing assumptions, affective bonding, and networking that recognizably differentiates groups from one another, but not according to some common nature. The salience of a particular person's group affinities may shift according to the social situation or according to changes in her or his life. Membership in a social group is a function not of satisfying some objective criteria, but of a subjective affirmation of affinity with that group, the affirmation of that affinity by others members of the group, and the attribution of membership in that group by persons identifying with other groups. Group identity is constructed from a flowing process in which individuals identify themselves and others in terms of groups, and thus group identity itself flows and shifts with changes in social process.

Groups experiencing cultural imperialism have found themselves objectified and marked with a devalued essence from the outside, by a dominant culture they are excluded from making. The assertion of a positive sense of group difference by these groups is emancipatory because it reclaims the definition of the group by the group, as a creation and construction, rather than a given essence. To be sure, it is difficult to articulate positive elements of group affinity without essentializing them, and these movements do not always succeed in doing so. But they are developing a language to describe their similar social situation and relations to one another, and their similar perceptions and perspectives on social life. These movements engage in the project of cultural revolution I recommended in chapter [5 of *Justice and the Politics of Difference*], insofar as they take culture as in part a matter of collective choice. While their ideas of women's culture, Afro-American culture, and American Indian culture rely on past cultural expressions, to a significant degree these movements have self-consciously constructed the culture that they claim defines the distinctiveness of their groups.

Contextualizing both the meaning of difference and identity thus allows the acknowledgment of difference within affinity groups. In our complex, plural society, every social group has group differences cutting across it, which are potential sources of wisdom, excitement, conflict, and oppression. Gay men, for example, may be black, rich, homeless, or old, and these differences produce different identifications and potential conflicts among gay men as well as affinities with some straight men. ...

MORAL DEFERENCE

Laurence Thomas

Laurence Thomas teaches in the Department of Philosophy and the Department of Political Science at Syracuse University. He is the author of Living Morally: A Psychology of Moral Character *(1989),* Vessels of Evil: American Slavery and the Holocaust *(1993), and* Sexual Rights and Human Orientation *(1999).*

   Thomas rejects the idea that there is an impartial vantage point from which any person can understand the morally significant experiences of others. He formulates the notion of moral deference as the kind of stance that allows one to respond in the morally appropriate way to someone who has been wronged. Moral deference is about listening to another's moral pain as a way of gaining insight into the character of the pain and how that person has been emotionally configured by it. Moral deference is owed to members of disadvantaged groups because it opens the way to understanding the social injustices they have experienced and responding in a morally appropriate way to particular injustices.

Why is this peach-tree said to be better than that other; but because it produces more or better fruit? ... In morals, too, is not *the tree known by the fruit?*
— David Hume, *Enquiry Concerning the Principles of Morals* (V, IIn 1)

In "What Is It Like To Be a Bat?," Thomas Nagel tells us that we hardly come to know what it is like to be a bat by hanging upside down with our eyes closed.[1] That experience simply tells us what it is like to be a human behaving or attempting to behave like a bat. If bats were intelligent creatures possessing a natural language, which we could translate, surely we would have to take their word for what it is like to be a bat. If, in batese, bats — including the most intelligent and articulate ones — generally maintained that "Hanging upside down is extraordinarily like experiencing death through colors," we human beings would probably not know how to get a handle on what was being claimed, since the notion of experiencing death already strains the imagination. Just so, we would be in no position to dismiss their claim as so much

nonsense because we cannot get a handle on it — because, after all, we humans experience no such thing when we engage in bat-like behavior. On this matter, bats would be owed deference.

   Some people are owed deference — moral deference, that is. Moral deference is meant to stand in opposition to the idea that there is a vantage point from which any and every person can rationally grasp whatever morally significant experiences a person might have. A fundamentally important part of living morally is being able to respond in the morally appropriate way to those who have been wronged. And this ability we cannot have in the absence of a measure of moral deference. David Hume's position on the human sentiments gives us insight regarding the matter. Or so I claim in Section III. The full account of moral deference is offered in Section IV, the final section. I maintain that the attitude of moral deference is, as it were, a prelude to bearing witness to another's pain, with that person's authorization — the person's blessings, if you will.

   On my view, moral deference is the bridge between individuals with different emotional category configurations owing to the injustices of society. I do not claim that moral deference will serve as a bridge between intelligent creatures who differ radically in their biological constitution from one another, though moral deference may nonetheless be owed. Moral deference, as I conceive of it is not about whether individuals are innocent with respect to those who have been treated unjustly; rather, it is simply about the appropriate moral attitude to take when it comes to understanding the ways in which another has been a victim of social injustice. A person's innocence or lack thereof is irrelevant.

Social Categories

If one encounters a holocaust survivor, it would be moral hubris of the worst sort — unless one is also such a survivor — to assume that by way of rational imaginative role-taking, à la Kohlberg,[2] one could even begin to grasp the depth of that person's experiences — the hurts, pains, and anxieties of that individual's life. There is not enough good will in the world to make it possible for persons (who are not Holocaust survivors) to put themselves imaginatively in the mind of a Holocaust survivor, to do so simply as an act of ratiocination.

The slaveowners who lived among slaves and, in fact, ruled the very lives of slaves knew a great deal about slaves. In many cases, slaveowners knew more about the intimate lives of slaves than a person has the right to know about another's intimate life (unless such information is freely and voluntarily offered in a noncoercive context). Yet, for all that white slaveowners knew about black slaves, the owners did not know what it was like to be a slave. Naturally, there were slave uprisings; but no slaveowner knew what it was like to be a slave on account of being a victim of such uprisings.

If a woman has been raped, it is clear that the last thing in the world that a heterosexual man should say is, "I can imagine how you feel." A great many men can barely imagine or grasp the fear of rape that, to varying degrees, permeates the lives of women, let alone the profoundly violent act of rape itself. Few actions could be more insensitive to victims of rape than a man's supposition that via a feat of imagination he can get a grip on the pain that a victim of rape has experienced.

I am, of course, aware that heterosexual men can be raped. But given the assumption of heterosexuality, male victims of rape, unlike female victims of rape, do not in general have the awkwardness of seeking to be personally fulfilled romantically by forming a relationship with a person who belongs to the very same social category as does the person who has harmed them. Nor, in any case, do males have to contend with social attitudes — some subtle, some ever so explicit — that make them the target of sexual violence or that minimize the significance of their consent as an appropriate condition of sexual intercourse. Lesbians do not escape this latter injustice; gay men who have been raped do. Given the assumption of heterosexuality, while both a woman and a man have to recover from the mental anguish of having been violated, complete recovery of a man does not involve being able to have sex with a man again. Thus, a fortiori, complete recovery is not a matter of his being able to do so without that act conjuring up the pain of rape. By contrast, complete recovery for a woman is generally seen along precisely these lines. Hence, recovery for a heterosexual man involves nothing like the phenomenal ambivalence that it involves for a woman.

Why is it that we cannot simply imaginatively put ourselves in the shoes of a Holocaust survivor or, in the case of a man, in the shoes of a rape victim? The answer is painfully obvious: even if we had a complete description of the person's experiences, we would nonetheless not be the subject of those experiences. Nor would we have the painful memory of being the subject of those experiences. So a description, no matter how full and complete, would fail on two counts to capture the subjective element of an experience. The latter count — namely, the memories — is far from trivial, because part of the way in which experiences shape our lives is through the memories of them impressing themselves upon our lives. In fact, there are times when the impact of a bad experience upon our lives would be virtually nugatory but for the way in which our lives are affected by the memories of it.

Suppose that one has been robbed at gunpoint. The actual loss may not amount to much at all, say $20 or $30. Suppose one has not suffered any physical or mental abuse, since two police officers came on the scene just in time. Yet, the event may alter the way in which one lives for years to come. Of course, one will realize how lucky one was. It is just that one cannot help thinking about what might have happened but for a fluke of luck — a mode of thought that very nearly cripples one emotionally. Rehearsing an experience in one's mind can frighteningly reveal just how lucky one was. A woman who has been raped can be having sex with her male partner, which has been ever so explicitly consensual, only to find that she can no longer continue the act because she has suddenly been assailed by the painful memories of being raped.

No amount of imagination in the world can make it the case that one has the subjective imprimatur of the experiences and memories of another. And an individual's subjective imprimatur makes a very real difference. Let me tie some things together.

There can be appropriate and inappropriate responses to the moral pain of another. When a person has suffered a grave misfortune the type of moral response that will serve to help that person to recover must be sensitive to the adverse ways in which the person will be haunted by painful memories, the person's feelings of emotional and social vulnerability, and so one. For as I have noted, the bodily damage can, itself, be negligible. It is not in the damage done to the body that the horror of armed robbery necessarily lies — since there might be none — but in the damage done to the victim's sense of self. Again, while rape can certainly be physically violent, it need not be, as the idea gaining acceptance of acquaintance rape reveals.[3]

Now to be sure, there are many misfortunes, at the hands of others, which any human being can experience, and so which are independent of social categories. We may think of these as generalized misfortunes. Anyone can be robbed, or be the victim of a car accident caused by an intoxicated driver, or be hit by a stray bullet. Anyone can lose a loved one owing to a flagrant disregard for human rights. These misfortunes do not know the boundaries of social categories. And though there can be difficulties, perhaps insuperable ones in some instances, with how to individuate (events that are) misfortunes, when people have experienced generalized misfortunes of the same type, then they have considerable insight into one another's suffering. The experience of losing a leg as a teenager is perhaps qualitatively different from that of losing a leg as an adult of 50, but no doubt the two experiences are far closer qualitatively than is either to the experience of losing a parent as a teenager or as an adult of 50. And between two teenagers both of whom lose a leg, it perhaps matters if one is an athlete and one is not.[4]

To be contrasted with generalized misfortunes are misfortunes that are quite tied to diminished social categories — misfortunes owing to oppressive, if not prevailing, negative attitudes about the members of well-defined diminished social categories. As it happens, the diminished social category may be coextensive with a natural category, as may be the case with gender.[5] I shall use the euphemism "hostile misfortunes" to refer to these misfortunes, where "hostile" is intended to capture both that the misfortune is owing to agency and that the agency, with respect to the relevant set of acts, is owing to morally objectionable attitudes regarding the diminished social category. I shall often refer to a person in such a category as a category person.

Not everyone in a diminished social category experiences all, and to the same extent, the hostile misfortunes specific to that category, but being in a diminished social category makes it exceedingly likely that one's life will be tinged with some of the hostile misfortunes specific to that diminished social category. More over, is one is not in that diminished social category, the likelihood of one's experiencing any of the hostile misfortunes will be virtually nil. I regard gender, ethnicity, and race as obviously involving diminished social categories of this kind, though there need not be hostile misfortunes specific to every ethnic and racial group. Although people of the same diminished social category do not all endure the same hostile experiences, the relevant experiential psychological distances between their lives will be less than such distances between their lives and the lives of those who do not belong to any diminished social category or to a very different one. Interestingly, there can be subgroups within a diminished social category, and hostile misfortunes tied to those subgroups. For instance, there are very light-complexioned blacks (some of whom are phenotypically indistinguishable from whites) and there are darker-complexioned blacks; and each subgroup has its own hostile misfortunes, in addition to those associated simply with being black. Finally, it is possible for the hostile misfortunes of two different diminished social categories to parallel one another to a considerable degree. Such may be the case with the hostile misfortunes of African-American and Hispanic-American peoples. Individuals from these groups do not experience exactly the same hostile misfortunes. But there appears to be considerable overlap. The hostile misfortunes of a diminished social category group need not be fixed. Hence, there could be less overlap between two groups at one time than at another time.

As with generalized misfortunes, though, I shall assume that when two people of the same diminished social category experience the same type of hostile misfortune, then they have considerable insight into one another's experiencing of that misfortune. Of course, the problem of individuating types of events does not disappear here. Numerous refinements are possible. However, I shall leave such matters aside. Furthermore, there is the very thorny issue of when the hostile misfortunes of two diminished social category groups are similar enough to one another that each group has some insight into the moral pains of the other. There is certainly no reason to rule this out of court on conceptual grounds; on the other hand, one of the worst mistakes that can be made is for one diminished social category group to assume, without having attended to the matter, that its suffering gives it insight into the suffering of another diminished social category group. But this issue, too, I shall leave aside.

Now, the knowledge that someone belongs to a diminished social category group does not, in and of itself, give one insight into the subjective imprimatur of that individual's experiences of and memories stemming from the hostile misfortunes tied to the category to which the person belongs. If so, then a very pressing question is: how is it possible to be morally responsive in the appropriate way to those belonging to a diminished social category if one does not belong to that category? Here is where moral deference enters into the picture, though first more needs to be said about being a member of a diminished social category.

Being Socially Constituted

David Hume observed that "Human nature cannot by any means subsist, without the association of individuals ..."[6] His point can be rendered in a contemporary vein as follows: we are constituted through others, by which I mean that the way in which we conceive of ourselves is, at least in part, owing to how others conceive of us, and necessarily so, the way in which we think of us. In a fully just world, all would be constituted so as to see her or himself in this way. By contrast, in an oppressive society, the victims of oppression — diminished social category persons, I mean — are constituted, in both masterfully subtle ways and in ever so explicit ways, so as not to see themselves as full and equal members of society. I shall refer to this as downward social constitution. Each group of diminished social category persons in society experiences different forms of downward social constitution, although I have allowed that there may be overlap. Painfully, social groups that are themselves victims of downward social constitution may engage in downward social constitution of one another. Victims of sexism can be antisemitic; victims of racism can be sexist. And so on for each diminished social category group. Even worse, perhaps, there can be downward social constitution by members within a group. In an oppressive society, downward social constitution is an ongoing and pervasive phenomenon, which is not to deny that there can be pockets of relief to varying degrees. Needless to say, a society with diminished social categories will have one or more privileged social categories, the members of which are favored and have full access to the goods of society.

One of the most important ways in which downward social constitution occurs pertains to expectations. It is just assumed, often without awareness of what is being done, that this or that category person cannot measure up in an important way. The reality that we do not expect much of a person on account of her category can be communicated in a thousand and one ways. One may listen inattentively, or interrupt ever so frequently, or not directly respond to what the person actually says, or not respond with the seriousness that is appropriate to the persons concerned. Most significantly, owing to meager expectations, one may fail to give the benefit of the doubt to the diminished social category person. We often do not realize that we are participating in the downward constitution of others because communicating favorable and negative expectations with regard to others is a natural part of life. Further, behavior that contributes to the downward constitution of another may manifest itself in other contexts that have nothing to do with downward constitution. After all, one can listen inattentively simply because one is preoccupied. Or, one can fail to respond directly because one misunderstood what the person said. Accordingly, negative expectations toward a member of a diminished social category need not feel any different from negative expectations toward any other member of society, nor need the behavior bear a special mark. Except for the blatant bigot or sexist, participating in the downward social constitution of another rarely has any special phenomenological feel to it.

Thus, it is interesting that for most people the evidence that they do not engage in downwardly constituting behavior is that they do not have the appropriate feelings. It is true that if one has and sustains the appropriate feelings, then one is an X-ist (racist, sexist, and so forth), or one has acted in an X-ist way if such feelings fuel one's behavior; on the other hand, it is manifestly false that if one lacks such feelings, the X-ism is not a part of one's life.

I have said that in an oppressive society downward social constitution is an ongoing and pervasive phenomenon despite pockets of relief. Such constitution may show up in advertisements, in the casting of characters for a film (play or television program), in the assumptions about the interests (as well as professional aims and hobbies) that a person has or what such a person should be satisfied with. The list goes on. Further, an expression of downward constitution may manifest itself at almost any time in almost any context. An expression of downward constitution may come from those who are so eager to put up an appearance of caring that they deceive themselves in believing that they actually care. Such an expression may even come from those who in fact care.[7]

To be a member of a diminished social category group is invariably to have to contend with what I shall call the problem of social category ambiguity. Often enough the question will be: was that remark or piece of behavior a manifestation of downward social constitution or something else or both? It may not have been, but the very nature of the context and one's social reality as a diminished social category person does not allow one to rule out that possibility with the desired confidence. On the one hand, one does not want to accuse someone falsely; on the other, one may not want to put up with an affront owing to being a member of a diminished social category. Yet, there may be no way to inquire about the matter without giving the appearance of doing the former. Finally, there is the painful reality that one may not be able to share one's own feelings about one's social category status with those who do not belong to that category, without giving the impression of being overly concerned with such matters — even with those who regard themselves as friends. It is a reality that sometimes requires a kind of profound disassociation from one's own experiences, at least momentarily.

Together, these things all speak to a profound sense of vulnerability that comes with being a member of a diminished social category. Part of that vulnerability is owing not just to being a subject of downward social constitution, but to the memories of such experiences. Invariably, the diminished social category person will be haunted by some of these memories to varying degrees. Then there is the fact that a memory (sometimes painful, sometimes not) of an experience of downward social constitution can be triggered by any number of things, including the witnessing of another's experience of downward social constitution, or another such experience of one's own. There is a sense in which one can be assailed by the memories of past undesirable experiences. A diminished social category person is vulnerable in this way. People who are downwardly constituted socially are victims of a social claim about them — not just any old claim but the claim that they lack the wherewithal to measure up in an important social dimension. In this regard, diminished social category persons are vulnerable on several counts. First, there is the vulnerability owing to being weary of always feeling the need to prove that this social claim is a lie — if not to themselves then to others. Second, there is the vulnerability owing to the reality that there is almost nothing that diminished social category persons can do which will decisively establish the falsity of the social claim. Third, there is the vulnerability owing to the weariness of it all that stems from the feeling that one must speak up because no one else will, although one is concerned that continually speaking up will diminish one's effectiveness. Obviously, diminished social category persons cope with these vulnerabilities in a variety of different ways and with varying degrees of success. But successfully coping with a vulnerability is hardly tantamount to not being vulnerable, any more than not showing anger is tantamount to not being angry.

The remarks in the preceding two paragraphs are meant to bring out the sense of *otherness* that inescapably comes with being a person belonging to a diminished social category, the sense of what it means to be socially constituted as such a person. This sense of otherness is not something that a person who does not belong to one's particular diminished social category can grasp simply by an act of ratiocination. In particular, it is not something to which people belonging to privileged social categories can grasp. People who belong to a privileged social category can, of course, experience insults and affronts to their person, even at the hands of those belonging to a diminished social category. Indeed, privileged social category

persons can experience these things precisely because they belong to a privileged social category. But, clearly, just as a person does not know what it is like to be a bat by hanging upside down with closed eyes, a person does not know what it is like to be a member of a diminished social category merely on account of having been affronted and insulted by diminished social category persons for being a privileged social category person. For the hallmark of a diminished social category person is that of being a person whose life has been downwardly constituted socially, with all that this implies in terms of vulnerability as noted above. A privileged social category person who has experienced affronts at the hands of diminished social category persons has no more had a downwardly constituted life on that account, with all that this implies in terms of vulnerability, than has a seventy-year-old person led a life marred by sickness for having had to spend three weeks at twenty in the hospital of exposure to meningitis and again at fifty for exposure to hepatitis.

Emotional Configuration

Hume seems to have held that if our natural capacity for sympathy and benevolence were sufficiently cultivated, we would have adequate insight into the weal and woe of others.[8] I disagree, although I think that his heart was in the right place. In a world without hostile misfortunes and diminished social category groups, and so without privileged social category groups, I think that Hume's position would, indeed, be correct or very nearly that. I hesitate only because it might be that even in a perfectly just world some differences might be impassable despite unqualified good will on all accounts. Hume's point holds given two assumptions: (a) the emotional capacities of people are essentially the same; (b) the configuration of these emotional capacities of people are essentially the same, the primary difference with respect to the latter being in their development. Thus, for Hume, Nero is simply one whose capacity for benevolence and sympathy virtually went uncultivated. By contrast, Hume thought it obvious that anyone who had benefited from some cultivation of these sentiments could not help but see that Nero's actions were criminal.

Such social phenomena as downward social constitution and diminished social categories would not have occurred to Hume. Specifically, and more pointedly, it would not have occurred to him that a person's emotions could be configured along a dimension other than the extent of their cultivation, the case of gender aside.[9] So, given Hume's moral psychology, anyone whose capacity for sympathy and benevolence was properly cultivated was in a position to understand sufficiently the moral experiences of all others. I am suggesting that Hume's moral psychology must be adjusted to take into account the reality that the emotional makeup of persons can be configured along dimensions other than cultivation. There is what I shall call emotional category configuration.

In a sexist society, a politically correct male who abhors violence against females, and understands ever so well why a victim of rape would rather be comforted by a female rather than a male nonetheless does not have the emotional configuration of a female. This is because the kind of fears that he experiences when he walks alone at night do not have as their source a concern about sexual violence; whereas they do for a woman whether or not she has been raped.[10] In a sexist society, at any rate, the emotional category configuration of women and men are different. This follows from women and men being socially constituted differently.

Likewise, a white can be attacked by blacks, and that attack can be brutal and absolutely inexcusable. As a result, the person may be emotionally crippled in terms of his fear of interacting with blacks. This is painfully sad. All the same, this suffering experience does not parallel the suffering of blacks. His fear of blacks may very well be a reminder of the random brutality of some blacks and of the moral squalor in which some wallow. The experience may seal his conviction that blacks lack the wherewithal to live morally decent lives.

But for all of that, the experience will not be a reminder that he is a second-class citizen. It will not make him vulnerable to that pain. He will not have the pain of being scarred by those who in fact have power over so very much of his life. By and large, the white will not really have to concern himself with having to trust blacks who have power over him, as with a little effort and creativity the white can avoid situations of this kind; whereas for the black, having to trust whites who have power over him is a real possibility. So, whereas some physical distance from blacks, coupled with time, might serve to heal the wounds of the white, this healing route is not a genuine possibility for a black. This is yet another dimension along which the black will live with his pain in a quite different manner than the white. Certainly no innocent white should be a victim of black anger and hostility; certainly no innocent black should either. The moral wrong may be equal in either case. My point is that because the black and the white have different emotional category configurations, each will experience their respective pain in a radically different manner. While economic differences could be factored in here, I did not develop the point with such differences in mind. The force of the point is not diminished in the least if both the white and the black are quite upper middle-class people enjoying equal salaries.

A fortiori, we have a difference in emotional category configuration here rather than a difference in the cultivation of the emotions if we suppose that the black and the white went to the very same kind of schools, read many of the same books, and have overlapping interests and musical tastes. We can imagine that they have similar personalities, and have had similar maturation experiences and wrestled with many of the same issues. Nonetheless, it is most likely they will be socially constituted in different ways. In the case of the black, strangers might be surprised that he was not born poor, or wonder where he learned to speak so well. The police at the university where he has just joined the faculty might regard him with suspicion. Or, at the checkout desk at the university library, the staff person might ask him for a piece of photo-identification to confirm that he is actually the owner of the university library card (which does not have a photograph on it) that he presented. These experiences will not be a part of the white person's life.

The cumulative effect of these experiences contributes to the significant difference in the emotional category configuration of which I have been speaking. Time and time again, a well-off black must steel himself against such experiences in settings of equality, while a white need not. Ironically, some of the experiences of downward social constitution — some of the insults — that a black will encounter, the person could only encounter if she were well-off, since a black in the throes of poverty would be too far removed from such social situations in the first place.[11] A black American in the throes of poverty is not apt to experience racism in a Middle Eastern or European hotel by a white American.

Nothing that I have experienced in my entire life had prepared me for the shock of being taken as a would-be purse snatcher in a Middle Eastern hotel by a white American who saw me enter the hotel lobby from the guest rooms. The person leapt for her pocketbook on the counter as if she had springs on her feet, although people had been sitting in the lobby all along. Worse still, she and I had been sitting in the lobby opposite one another only two days earlier. As I play back the experience in my mind, it seems so incredibly surrealistic to me that I continually find myself stunned. Even granting racism, and that she had been robbed by a black man while she was in Harlem, just how reasonable under the circumstances could it have been for her to suppose that *I* was a poor black out to steal her purse? After all, it takes more than cab fare to get from New York, New York, to any place in the Middle East.[12] I have been called a "nigger" to my face three times in my life. One of them was in Harvard Yard between Widner and Emerson. If I were to walk around with a fear that whites might call me "nigger," I would surely be taken as mad by most of my friends and acquaintances. Or, I would be seen as having enormous and unjustified hostility against whites.

Hume's moral psychology cannot account for the emotional vulnerability that comes with the above experience. This is because it would not have occurred to him that a person would be treated as anything other than a full citizen of the world on a par with all others — at least among other equally cultivated individuals — *if* the individual displayed the refinements of education and culture. It would not have occurred to him that persons displaying such refinements could be the object of hostile misfortunes. For on his view, the display of these things should suffice to elicit admiration.[13]

The Idea of Moral Deference

Moral deference is owed to persons of good will when they speak in an informed way regarding experiences specific to their diminished social category from the standpoint of an emotional category configuration to which others do not have access. The idea behind moral deference is not that a diminished social category person can never be wrong about the character of his own experiences. Surely he can, since anyone can. Nor is it that silence is the only appropriate response to what another says when one lacks that individual's emotional category configuration. Rather, the idea is that there should be a presumption in the favor of the person's account of her experiences. This presumption is warranted because the individual is speaking from a vantage point to which someone not belonging to her diminished social category group does not have access. It is possible to play a major role in helping a person to get clearer about the character of an experience delivered from the vantage point of an emotional category configuration. But helping someone get clearer is qualitatively different from being dismissive. Indeed, how a person feels about a matter can be of the utmost importance even if the individual's feelings are inappropriate, since inappropriate feelings can shed considerable light on the very appearances of things in themselves.

While I do not think that moral deference is owed only to persons of good will who are members of diminished social categories, my account begins with such persons. The assumption here is that in characterizing their feelings and experiences as diminished social category persons, those of good will do not tell an account that is mired and fueled by feelings of rancor and bitterness. This is not to suggest that persons of good will never experience tremendous anger and rage on account of experiences of downward social constitution. They sometimes do, and rightly so. Occasionally experiencing anger and rage, though, is by no means the same thing as becoming consumed by these feelings. A complete account of moral deference would have to be extended to include those who, understandably or not, have come to be full of bitterness and rancor owing to the ways in which they have been downwardly constituted socially. It becomes especially important to extend the account in this direction if one considers that oppression, itself, can render its victims so full of rancor and bitterness that the manifestation of these sentiments can blind us to their underlying cause, namely oppression itself.

Moral deference is meant to reflect the insight that it is wrong to discount the feelings and experiences of persons in diminished social category groups simply because their articulation of matters does not resonate with one's imaginative take on their experiences. Moral deference acknowledges a vast difference between the ideal moral world and the present one. In the ideal moral world there would be only one category of emotional configuration, namely the human one — or at most two, allowing for differences in the sexes. So, given adequate cultivation of emotions and feelings, everyone would be able to get an imaginative take on the experiences of others. Interestingly, this way of understanding the role of emotions in the ideal world might point to a reason for making them irrelevant entirely; for if rightly cultivated emotions would result in everyone's making the same moral judgments on the basis of them, then the emotions do not make for a morally relevant difference between people, at least not among those with rightly cultivated emotions. On this view, the emotions can only make a morally relevant difference if they are seen as constitutive feature of what it means to be a person, and so of moral personhood. But, alas, philosophers often seem anxious to deny that the emotions have any moral relevance, in and of themselves, at the foundational conception of moral personhood.[14]

In a far from ideal moral world, such as the one we live in, which privileges some social categories

and diminishes others, it stands to reason that there will be emotional boundaries between people, owing to what I have called emotional category configuration. This is one of the bitter fruits of immorality. Recall Hume's question: "In morals, too, is not the tree known by its fruits?" The idea of moral deference is true to the moral reality that the mark of an immoral society is the erection of emotional walls between persons. It is true to the reality that social immorality cannot be eliminated in the absence of a firm grasp of how it has affected its victims. It is not enough to be confident that social immorality harms. One must also be sensitive to the way in which it harms. Thus, the idea of moral deference speaks to an attitude that a morally decent person should have in an immoral society.

We can best get at what moral deference involves, and its importance, by thinking of what it means to bear witness to another's moral pain with that person's authorization. To bear witness to the moral pain of another, say, Leslie, with Leslie's authorization, is to have won her confidence that one can speak informedly and with conviction on her behalf to another about the moral pain she has endured. It is to have won her confidence that one will tell her story with her voice, and not with one's own voice. Hence, it is to have won her trust that one will render salient what was salient for her in the way that it was salient for her; that one will represent her struggle to cope in the ways that she has been in getting on with her life; that one will convey desperation where desperation was felt, and hurt where hurt was felt. And so on.

To bear witness to Leslie's pain is not to tell Leslie's story of pain as a means to explicating how her pain has affected one's own life. Accordingly, to be authorized by Leslie to bear witness to her pain is to have won her confidence that her story of pain will not take a back seat to telling one's own story of pain as caused by her story. Not that it will always be impossible for people to make reasonable inferences about how one has been affected. It stands to reason that how one has been affected will surely be obvious in some cases. Rather, whatever inferences reasonable people might be able to draw, the point of bearing witness to the moral pain of another will not be so that others can see how one has been affected by the other person's pain. Thus, to be authorized to bear witness for another is to have won her confidence that one will tell her story with a certain motivational structure.

Now, it may be tempting to think that bearing witness to the moral pain of others requires something amounting to a complete diminution of the self, to becoming a mere mouthpiece for another. But this is to think of bearing witness to the moral pain of others as something that happens to one — a state that one falls into or whatever. Perhaps there are such cases of bearing witness. I do not write with them in mind, however. Instead, as I conceive of the idea, bearing witness to the moral pain of another is very much an act of agency and, as such, it can be an extremely courageous thing to do. During the time of slavery, whites who endeavored to bear witness to the moral pain of blacks were sometimes called "nigger lovers." In Nazi Germany, some who endeavored to bear witness to the moral pain of the Jews were killed. Nowadays, those who endeavor to bear witness to the moral pain of lesbians and homosexuals are often branded as such themselves. Far from being an activity only for the faint of heart, bearing witness to the moral pain of others can require extraordinary courage and resoluteness of will.

Well, needless to say, there can be no bearing witness, as I have explicated it, to the moral pain of another without having heard his story and heard it well. One will have had to have heard the glosses on the story and the nuances to the story. One will have had to have been sensitive to the emotions that manifested themselves as the story was told, and to the vast array of nonverbal behavior with which the story was told. One will have to have heard his story well enough to have insight into how his life has been emotionally configured by his experiences. One rightly authorizes a person to bear witness to his moral pain only if these things are true.

To have such insight into another's moral pain will not be tantamount to having that person's fears or being haunted by his memories, but it will entail having a sense of the kinds of things and circum-

stances that will trigger his fears and memories. It will not entail being vulnerable when he is downwardly constituted on account of his diminished social category, but it will entail a sense of the kinds of social circumstances that will give rise to such vulnerability. Moreover, it will entail being appropriately moved on account of these things. To have such insight is to be in as good a position as one can be to understand while yet lacking a complete grasp of another's moral pain.

Moral deference, then, is the act of listening that is preliminary to bearing witness to another's moral pain, but without bearing witness to it. I do not see the step from moral deference to bearing witness as an easy one. A person may lack the fortitude or courage to bear witness, however well he might listen. Moral deference is not about bearing witness. It is about listening, in the ways characterized above, until one has insight into the character of the other's moral pain, and so how he has been emotionally configured by it. In any case, moral deference may be appropriate on occasions when bearing witness is not. You may not want me to bear witness to your moral pain; yet, you may be deeply gratified that I have listened well enough that I could in the ever so unlikely event that you should want me to.

Moral deference, too, is not an activity for the faint of heart. For it is a matter of rendering oneself open to another's concern, and to letting another's pain reconstitute one so much that one comes to have a new set of sensibilities — a new set of moral lenses if you will. Moral deference is rather like the moral equivalent of being nearsighted, putting on a pair of glasses for the first time, and discovering just how much out there one had been missing. Of course, one had always seen trucks, and sayings on shirts, and facial expressions that people displayed, and minute movements that people made, and slight variances in colors — none of which one could see at a distance. With moral deference one acquires sensibility to the way in which a self-respecting oppressed person lives in the world. Hence, to engage in moral deference is to allow oneself to become affected in a direct interpersonal way by the injustices of this world. While not the only way in which to do this, it is a very important way in which to do this. Thus, it is a fundamentally important mode of moral learning. It is a mode of moral learning which those who have been oppressed are owed in the name of eliminating the very state of their oppression. In the absence of such learning, oppression cannot but continue to be a part of the fabric of the moral life. Indeed, the absence of such learning, the studied refusal to engage in such learning, is one of the very ways in which oppression manifests itself. Worse, such studied refusal to learn adds insult to injury.

Significantly, moral deference involves earning the trust of another — in particular, the trust of one who has been oppressed. And earning the trust of another, especially someone who is weary of trusting anyone from a different social category (diminished or privileged), is an act of great moral responsibility — something not to be taken lightly in the least. It would be morally egregious in the very worst of ways to earn such a person's trust, and then abuse it or merely withdraw from the person. If the struggle for equality is ever to be won, we must be strong enough to be vulnerable. That is, we must be strong enough to prove ourselves worthy of the trust of those whom we have oppressed. This is well-nigh impossible in the absence of moral deference given to those whom we have oppressed. Moral deference is by no means a weakness. It is quite a matter of courage, instead.

In an important essay entitled "The Need for More than Justice," Annette Baier explains the significance of departing from John Rawls's claim that justice is the first virtue of social justice.[15] One thing that is needed is the appropriate moral posture toward those who have been oppressed. Without it, we often blithely trample upon those whom we mean to help. The notion of moral deference is meant to give expression to one aspect of what that posture calls for. It is impossible to responsively help those who have been hurt if one does not understand the nature of their pain. And while it may be true that we can know what is right and wrong behavior for others without consulting them, it is simply false that, in the absence of similar experiences, we can know how others are affected by wrongdoing without consulting them.

Let me repeat a point made at the outset: the idea of moral deference helps us to understand the inadequacy of the response that one has not contributed to another's oppression. To the extent that it is true, the response does not entail that one understands another's downward social constitution. Moral innocence does not entail understanding. Neither, for that matter, does good will. Nor does either entail that one has earned the trust of one who has been downwardly constituted by society. It goes without saying that the innocence of others should never be discounted; neither should it be trumpeted for what it is not, namely understanding and the earned trust of others.

A final comment: the account of moral deference offered suggests why both those who have been downwardly constituted by society and those who have not been should think differently of one another. If, as I have argued, those who have not been should be willing to earn the trust of the downwardly constituted, then the downwardly constituted must not insist that, as a matter of principle this is impossible. Understandably, it may be difficult to earn the trust of those who have been downwardly constituted by society. And it may, in fact, not be possible for some outside of the social category in question actually to do so. But what has to be false is that, as a matter of principle, it is impossible for anyone outside of that social category to do so.

Apart from the context of the loves of friendship and romance, there is no greater affirmation that we can want from another than that which comes in earning her or his trust. If we should be willing to accept moral affirmation from others, then surely we are more likely to treat them justly. Moral deference embodies this idea.

Author's Note

This paper owes its inspiration to my 1991 winter quarter class on the Gilligan-Kohlberg debate (which I taught while visiting at the University of Chicago); Alison M. Jaggar's, "Love and Knowledge: Emotion in Feminist Epistemology," in eds. Alison M. Jaggar and Susan R. Bordo, *Gender/Body/Knowledge: Feminist Reconstruction of Being and Knowing* (New

Brunswick: Rutgers University Press, 1989); and Seyla Benhabib's "The Generalized and the Concrete Other: The Kohlberg-Gilligan Controversy and Moral Theory," in eds. Eva Feder Kittay and Diana T. Meyers, *Women and Moral Theory* (Rowman and Littlefield, 1978). I see moral deference as a way of responding to the moral significance of the concreteness of other. I received instructive comments from Norma Field, John Pittman, and Julian Wuerth. At various times, conversations with Linda Alcoff, Alan J. Richard, Michael Stocker (always a present help), and Thomas Nagel (over the penultimate draft) were very helpful. A special debt of gratitude is owed to writer Jamie Kalven whose life reveals the richness that moral deference can yield.

Some recent works on the subject of racism have been most illuminating: David Theo Goldberg, "Racism and Rationality: The Need for a New Critique," *Philosophy of the Social sciences*, Vol. 20 (1990); Adrian M.S. Piper's paper "Higher-Order Discrimination," in Owen Flanagan and Amelie Oksenberg Rorty, *Identity, Character, and Morality: Essays in Moral Psychology* (Cambridge: Massachusetts Institute of Technology Press, 1990); Elizabeth V. Spelman, *Inessential Women: Problems of Exclusion in Feminist Thought* (Beacon Press, 1988). My essay has very nearly turned out to be something of a companion piece to Michael Stocker's wonderful essay "How Emotions Reveal Value" (unpublished).

NOTES

1. In *Mortal Questions* (Cambridge University Press, 1979).
2. *The Philosophy of Moral Development* (New York: Harper & Row, 1981). See especially the essay entitled "From Is to Ought: How to Commit the Naturalistic Fallacy and Get Away with It."
3. See, for instance, "Tougher Laws Mean More Cases are Called Rape," *The New York Times*, 27 May 1991: p. 9.
4. For a very important discussion of events, and their individuation, see Judith Jarvis Thomson, *Acts and Other Events* (Cornell University Press, 1977).
5. That gender is both a biological and a social category is developed at length in my essay "Sexism

and Racism: Some Conceptual Differences," *Ethics* (1980).
6. *Enquiries Concerning the Principles of Morals*, IV, par. 165.
7. For an absolutely masterful discussion of these matters, see Adrian Piper, "Higher-Order Discrimination."
8. *Enquiries Concerning the Principles of Morals*: V, pt. II, pars. 183, 189; IX, pt. 1, par. 220.
9. For an important discussion of Hume regarding gender, see Annette Baier, *A Progress of Sentiments* (Cambridge: Harvard University Press, 1991), pp. 273-75. Hume thought that women who desired to become wives and to bear children should be held to stricter standards of chastity than men. Cf. David Hume, *Enquiries concerning the Principles of Morals*, Section V, Section VIII, par. 215 and, especially, Section VI, part I, par. 195.
10. Perhaps male child victims of male rape can approximate such fears in their own lives. Still the adult life of such males will be qualitatively different from the adult life of females, owing to great differences in the way in which society portrays women and men as sex objects. See the discussion in Section I above. This, of course, hardly diminishes the pain of having been a male victim of child rape.
11. Bernard Boxill, in a very powerful essay, "Dignity, Slavery, and the 13th Amendment," has demonstrated the deep and profound way in which slavery was insulting. His essay appears in Michael J. Meyer and William A. Parent (eds.) *Human Dignity, the Bill of Rights and Constitutional Values* (Cornell University Press, 1992).
12. I was so enraged by the experience that it was clear to me that I had better channel my rage lest I do something that I would regret. Fortunately, I had a micro-cassette recorder with me. I walked the streets of Tel Aviv and taped the essay "Next Life, I'll Be White," *The New York Times Op-Ed* page (13 August 1990), an expanded version of which appeared in *Ebony Magazine* (December, 1990). It is, among other things, profoundly insulting when the obvious is discounted at one's own expense.
13. *Enquires Concerning the Principles of Morals*: V, pt. II-180; VIII.

14. Cf. my "Rationality and Affectivity: The Metaphysics of the Moral Self," *Social Philosophy and Policy* 5 (1988): 154-72.

15. "Morality and Feminist Theory," *Canadian Journal of Philosophy*, Supp. Vol. 13 (1987). Rawls's first sentence is "Justice is the first virtue of social institutions as truth is of systems of thought," *A Theory of Justice* (Cambridge: Harvard University Press, 1971), p. 3.
    As I was typing the final draft of this essay, Martha Minow's book, *Making all the Difference: Inclusion, Exclusion, and American Law* (Ithaca: Cornell University Press), was brought to my attention. But I did read the Afterword in which she writes: "Claiming that we are impartial is insufficient if we do not consider changing how we think. Impartiality is the guise that partiality takes to seal bias against exposure" (p. 376). This essay points to a way in which that change must go.

STUDY QUESTIONS

1 In an initial reaction to the examples that open Martha Nussbaum's paper, whose views would you defend: Nussbaum's or those of the people at the conference she is critical of? What is Nussbaum's version of essentialism and does it avoid charges commonly leveled against essentialism? Provide reasons for your answers.

2 Do you think that Nussbaum's list of "essential properties" or human functions — what she refers to as the "thick vague theory of the good" — captures what it is to be a human being? What would you add to or remove from the list? Provide reasons for your answers.

3 Does Nussbaum's application of her essentialist account to the examples that opened the paper strengthen her approach? Does it answer the objections to essentialist accounts that she identifies? Provide reasons for your answers.

4 How does David Crocker define international development ethics and what sorts of questions does it raise about who can engage in this inquiry? What are the three main responses to ethnocentrism as outlined by Crocker? Do you find any of them satisfactory? Why or why not?

5 Outline Crocker's account of insiders and outsiders and his analysis of the advantages and disadvantages of each. Does his account answer some of the concerns raised by ethnocentrism?

6 Does Crocker's account of insiders and outsiders answer concerns that may have been raised by Nussbaum's essentialist account of human beings? Can Crocker's account of insiders and outsiders "further a global community and a global ethic"? Provide reasons for your answers.

7 What concerns do Philomena Essed and David Goldberg raise with respect to accounts or defenses of sameness? What are the connections they make between contemporary biological discourse about cloning and a cultural discourse that promotes sameness?

8 In your view, do Essed and Goldberg provide a convincing account of how the cloning of human beings raises possibilities for erasing difference by reproducing preferred types of human beings: white, male, able-bodied, heterosexual, highly intelligent, and living in economically privileged places? Defend your answer.

9 Do you agree with the Essed and Goldberg claim that difference and diversity is undermined in a global context that reflects the mass production of Western culture and consumerism? What, if any, implications does their skepticism about sameness have for policies with respect to biotechnology or preserving cultural differences?

10 What does Shelby Steele mean by "the new sovereignty"? In your view, is this a fair depiction of the current social movements for change in the U.S.? Why or why not?

11 Explain and evaluate Steele's claim that "in a liberal democracy, collective entitlements based upon race, gender, ethnicity, or some other group grievance are always undemocratic expedients. ... for in opting for integration, a citizen denies his or her impulse to use our most arbitrary characteristics — race, ethnicity, gender, sexual preference — as the basis for identity, as a key to status, or for claims to entitlement."

12 While Iris Young's description of the two stages in the struggle of oppressed groups to achieve equality is similar to Steele's account, she draws conclusions quite different from his about the goal of integration and what is needed to achieve equality. How do the arguments differ? Whose account do you favor and why?

13 What does Young mean by a "politics of difference"? How does Young defend the view that a strategy of affirming group difference involves a "reconception of the meaning of equality" and a better way for achieving equality?

14 Compare and contrast Young's account of a politics of difference with Nussbaum's account of "essential properties" and Crocker's account of insiders and outsiders. Which underlying account of "human nature" do you favor and why?

15 What does Laurence Thomas mean by the term "moral deference"? Who is owed moral deference and why?

16 What implications does moral deference have for the ability to speak for others, that is, to be able to understand and represent the experiences of those in a "diminished social category group" different from one's own? What implications does Thomas's account of moral deference have for the project of articulating a universal account of human nature?

SUGGESTED READINGS

Alcoff, Linda Martin. "The Problem of Speaking for Others." In *Overcoming Racism and Sexism*, edited by Linda Bell and David Blumenfeld. Lanham, MD: Rowman & Littlefield, 1995.

Appiah, Kwame Anthony. "Cosmopolitan Patriots." *Critical Inquiry*, v. 23 (Spring 1997): 617-39.

Benhabib, Seyla. *The Claims of Culture: Equality and Diversity in the Global Era*. Princeton, NJ: Princeton University Press, 2002.

— . "Cultural Complexity, Moral Interdependence, and the Global Dialogical Community." In *Women, Culture and Development: A Study of Human Capabilities*, edited by Martha Nussbaum and Jonathan Glover. Oxford: Clarendon Press, 1995.

Cohen, G.A. "Equality of What? On Welfare, Goods, and Capabilities." In *Quality of Life*, edited by Martha C. Nussbaum and Amartya Sen. Oxford: Clarendon Press, 1993.

Crocker, David A. "Cross-Cultural Criticism and Development Ethics." *Philosophy & Public Policy Quarterly*, v. 24, no. 3 (Summer 2004): 2-8.

— . "Functioning and Capability: The Foundation of Sen's and Nussbaum's Development Ethic." *Political Theory*, v. 20, no. 4 (November 1992): 584-612.

Dillon, Robin S. "Self-Respect: Moral, Emotional, and Political." *Ethics*, v. 107 (January 1997): 226-49.

Frye, Marilyn. "Oppression." In *The Politics of Reality*. Freedom, CA: Crossing Press, 1982.

Gasper, Des. "Is Sen's Capability Approach an Adequate Basis for Considering Human Development?" *Review of Political Economy*, v. 14, no. 4 (2002): 435-61.

Glover, Jonathan. "The Research Programme of Development Ethics." In *Women, Culture and Development: A Study of Human Capabilities*, edited by Martha Nussbaum and Jonathan Glover. Oxford: Clarendon Press, 1995.

Koggel, Christine M. *Perspectives on Equality: Constructing a Relational Theory*. Lanham, MD: Rowman & Littlefield, 1998.

Nussbaum, Martha. "Capabilities and Social Justice." *International Studies Review*, v. 4, no. 2 (2002): 123-35.

— . "Capabilities as Fundamental Entitlements: Sen and Social Justice." *Feminist Economics*, v. 9, nos. 2-3 (2003): 33-59.

O'Neill, Onora. "Justice, Capabilities, and Vulnerabilities." In *Women, Culture and Development: A Study of Human Capabilities*, edited by Martha Nussbaum and Jonathan Glover. Oxford: Clarendon Press, 1995.

Phillips, Anne. "Dealing with Difference: A Politics of Ideas or a Politics of Presence?" *Constellations*, v. 1, no. 1 (1994): 74-91.

Sen, Amartya. "Capability and Well-Being." In *Quality of Life*, edited by Martha C. Nussbaum and Amartya Sen. Oxford: Clarendon Press, 1993.

— . "Equality of What?" In *The Tanner Lectures on Human Values*, edited by S.M. McMurrin. Cambridge: Cambridge University Press, 1980: 195-220.

Shweder, Richard, Martha Minow, and Hazel Markus (editors). *Engaging Cultural Differences: The Multicultural Challenge in Liberal Democracies*. New York, NY: Russell Sage, 2002.

Young, Iris Marion. "Five Faces of Oppression." *Philosophical Forum*, v. 19, no. 4 (1988): 270-90.

— . *Justice and the Politics of Difference*. Princeton: Princeton University Press, 1990.

— . "Polity and Group Difference: A Critique of the Ideal of Universal Citizenship." *Ethics* 99 (January 1989): 250-74.

INTRODUCTION

One of the threads running through the readings in the first chapter of this volume is that difference and discrimination are highly complex concepts. We may agree that discrimination is wrong when morally irrelevant differences determine how one is treated and thereby shape one's life prospects, but there is a great deal of disagreement about what constitutes discrimination and how to eliminate it. In this and the four chapters of Volume II that follow, this complexity is highlighted in separate discussions of the forms of discrimination that continue to be relevant and prevalent within and across cultures: race and ethnicity, gender, sexual orientation, disability, and poverty. Most of the chapters in Volume II include discussions of these forms of discrimination in contexts outside of North America. Many of the readings in these chapters explore discrimination across borders and by North/Western countries and people against South/non-Western countries and people. They also provide analyses that move the focus from individuals as such to the structures, practices, and political contexts that support conditions of disadvantage and inequality for people who are members of disadvantaged groups. Contributions by feminist, race, class, and disability theorists are vital to the examination of the difference that difference makes both across and within countries and are well represented here.

This chapter examines how race and ethnicity continue to be relevant to the perception and treatment of people even in the face of quite widespread agreement that racism is morally reprehensible. It opens with a reading by Kwame Anthony Appiah, who provides a conceptual clarification of racism as a way of exposing underlying presuppositions to show how racism works and how it can be entrenched. Appiah distinguishes three doctrines that fall under racism. He uses the term "racialism" to refer to the view that distinct char-

acteristics — such as morphological differences of skin color, hair type, and facial features as well as differences in moral and intellectual capacities — divide people into a set of races. While Appiah holds that racialism is false, he maintains that it need not be pernicious. One could hold, for example, that positive moral qualities are distributed in ways that make races separate but equal. However, racialism is a presupposition of two other doctrines that have been the basis for a great deal of moral error and immoral acts.

Extrinsic racists believe that racial essence entails certain morally relevant qualities that warrant differential treatment for members of some races. Some extrinsic racists can be led out of their racism if presented with evidence, for example, that blacks are not less intelligent than whites. For an intrinsic racist, however, no amount of evidence that a member of another race is capable of great moral, intellectual, or cultural achievements offers any ground for treating that person as he or she treats someone of their own race. Appiah takes beliefs that are held about others despite overwhelming evidence to the contrary to be indicative of a cognitive incapacity, a deformation of rationality in judgment that results in racial prejudice for which training and treatment rather than reasoning may be appropriate. Appiah is concerned mainly with racists who can be persuaded by reason to give up their racist beliefs. Racism violates the universal moral imperative of using only morally relevant grounds in making moral distinctions.

In the second reading, Sally Haslanger analyzes race and the concept of "future races" by comparing race to gender and exploring similarities and differences. She employs the feminist distinction between "sex" and "gender" to describe a corresponding distinction between "color" and "race." "Color" describes the physical markers of race such as skin tone; eye, nose, and lip shape; hair texture; and physique. "Race" describes the social implications that these markers have. While sex marks a difference of a biological capacity to bear children that a just society must address, Haslanger argues that color is not and should not be a physical fact that a just society must address. She acknowledges that we still need an account of race that does the work of identifying those affected by discrimination and remedying its harms, but she envisions a future in which we are rid of race and instead have a rich array of cultural practices and ethnicities. Because race continues to function in ways that order human groups both scientifically and socio-politically, an interim strategy on the road to the elimination of race is to challenge and reconstruct these groupings through the common culture, commitment to shared identity, and positive group solidarity of "ethnoraces."

Marilyn Frye is also concerned with eliminating the socially divisive forms and consequences of racism, but focuses on what those engaged in racist attitudes and behavior can do. Frye recounts her own experiences of frustration and despair as a white, privileged woman trying to change attitudes. The solution, as she came to realize, was not to change her attitudes to people of color but to change what it meant for her to be white. She argues that being white is not a biological condition but a social/political category, one that holds itself together by rituals of unity and exclusion, that develops styles and attitudes of exploiting others, and that defines itself as the paradigm of humanity. Frye argues that just as masculinity and femininity are tied to certain conceptions and perceptions of what it is to be male or female, "whiteliness" is a deeply ingrained way of being in the world that is tied to being white-skinned. Whiteliness, Frye argues, is a way of being that is a monotonous similarity extending across ethnic, cultural, and class categories, one in which variations approximate or blend toward a norm set by elite groups of whitely people. However, whiteliness is not the same thing in the lives of women as it is in the lives of men. While whiteliness buys some respectability for women, it undermines feminist goals of women

organizing to eliminate their oppression by encouraging alliances and solidarity with men.

As a social construct shaped by historical events and circumstances, whiteliness is entrenched and well-established, but Frye believes that it can be unlearned and deconstructed by practicing new ways of being in environments that nurture different habits of feeling, perception, and thought. In commenting on Frye's analysis of racism, Victoria Davion agrees that promoting white supremacy is not a matter of genetic coding but of social training and that ceasing to be racist requires more than simply believing in racial equality and consciously trying to promote it. She raises questions, however, about aspects of Frye's account of the monotonous similarity of whiteliness. Davion recognizes the characteristics of whiteliness in herself, but as a white Jew she has also learned that white skin alone does not guarantee privileges. For some people, being whitely requires the erasure of one's ethnicity, which in turn confirms rather than challenges aspects of whiteliness that connect with other forms of racism such as anti-Semitism.

In the fifth and final reading, Mitsuye Yamada continues the exploration of ethnicity in the examination of issues of race and racism. She describes her experiences in the classroom to challenge prevalent beliefs that Asian Americans are not oppressed and that their expressions of anger are unjustified. Yamada explains that stereotypes of Asian Americans, particularly of Asian American women, as quiet, obedient, passive, and polite, contribute to these beliefs and result in a specific sort of oppression — the invisibility of Asian Americans. Invisibility, argues Yamada, has its source for Japanese Americans in their experiences of the internment camps in the U.S. during World War II, where conditioning shaped an attitude of resigned acceptance and beliefs that "natural disasters" such as internment camps were to be endured as inevitable and out of one's control. Invisibility, she argues, continues to be a feature in the lives of Asian American women, whose protests and involvement in social movements fighting oppression are not heard or taken seriously.

RACISMS

Kwame Anthony Appiah

Kwame Anthony Appiah is Laurance S. Rockefeller University Professor of Philosophy, University Center for Human Values, Princeton University. He is the author of In my Father's House: Africa and the Philosophy of Culture *(1992) and* Thinking It Through: An Introduction to Contemporary Philosophy *(2003), and co-author with Amy Gutmann of* Color Conscious: The Political Morality of Race *(1996).*

Appiah argues that while it is now commonplace to express abhorrence for racism, we lack an explicit definition and understanding of what it is. He discusses our ordinary ways of thinking about race and racism and exposes the underlying presuppositions. He defines "racialism" as the view that there are essential characteristics that allow us to classify people into distinct races, each of which shares certain traits and tendencies. He rejects this view as false, but explains that it is a presupposition for two distinct kinds of racism. Extrinsic racists take racial essence to entail that members of particular races possess certain morally relevant qualities that thereby justify discrimination and differential treatment. Intrinsic racism is the view that the moral differentiation of races is justified irrespective of racial essence or moral characteristics. Appiah argues that both kinds of racism are theoretically and morally wrong.

If the people I talk to and the newspapers I read are representative and reliable, there is a good deal of racism about. People and policies in the United States, Eastern and Western Europe, in Asia and Africa and Latin America are regularly described as "racist." Australia had, until recently, a racist immigration policy; Britain still has one; racism is on the rise in France; many Israelis support Meir Kahane, an anti-Arab racist; many Arabs, according to a leading authority, are anti-Semitic racists;[1] and the movement to establish English as the "official language" of the United States is motivated by racism. Or, at least, so many of the people I talk to and many of the journalists with the newspapers I read believe.

But visitors from Mars — or from Malawi — unfamiliar with the Western concept of racism could be excused if they had some difficulty in identifying what racism was. We see it everywhere, but rarely does anyone stop to say what it is, or to explain what is wrong with it. Our visitors from Mars would soon grasp that it had become at least conventional in recent years to express abhorrence for racism. They might even notice that those most often accused of it — members of the South African nationalist party, for example — may officially abhor it also. But if they sought in the popular media of our day — in newspapers and magazines, on television or radio, in novels or films — for an explicit definition of this thing "we" abhor, they would very likely be disappointed.

Now, of course, this would be true of many of our most familiar concepts. *Sister, chair, tomato* — none of these gets defined in the course of our daily business. But the concept of racism is in worse shape than these. For much of what we say about it is, on the face of it, inconsistent.

It is, for example, held by may to be racist to refuse entry to a university to an otherwise qualified "Negro" candidate, but not to be so to refuse entry to an equally qualified "Caucasian" one. But "Negro" and "Caucasian" are both alleged to be names of races, and invidious discrimination on the basis of race is usually held to be a paradigm case of racism. Or, to take another example, it is widely believed to be evidence of an unacceptable racism to exclude people from clubs on the basis of race; yet most people, even those who think of "Jewish" as a racial term, seem to think that there is nothing wrong with Jewish clubs, whose members do not share any particular religious beliefs, or Afro-American societies, whose members share the juridical characteristic of American citizenship and the "racial" characteristic of being black.

I say that these are inconsistencies "on the face of it," because, for example, affirmative action in university admissions is importantly different from the earlier refusal to admit blacks or Jews (or other "Others") that it is meant, in part, to correct. Deep enough analysis may reveal it to be quite consistent with the abhorrence of racism; even a shallow analysis suggests that it is intended to be so. Similarly, justifications can be offered for "racial" associations in a plural society that are not available for the racial exclusivism of the country club. But if we take racism seriously we ought to be concerned about the adequacy of these justifications.

In this essay, then, I propose to take our ordinary ways of thinking about race and racism and point up some of their presuppositions. And since popular concepts are, of course, usually fairly fuzzily and untheoretically conceived, much of what I have to say will seem to be both more theoretically and more precisely committed than the talk of racism and racists in our newspapers and on television. My claim is that these theoretical claims are required to make sense of racism as the practice of reasoning human beings. If anyone were to suggest that much, perhaps most, of what goes under the name "racism" in our world cannot be given such a rationalized foundation, I should not disagree: but to the extent that a practice cannot be rationally reconstructed it ought, surely, to be given up by reasonable people. The right tactic with racism, if you really want to oppose it, is to object to it rationally in the form in which it stands the best chance of meeting objections. The doctrines I want to discuss can be rationally articulated: and they are

worth articulating rationally in order that we can rationally say what we object to in them.

Racist Propositions

There are at least three distinct doctrines that might be held to express the theoretical content of what we call "racism." One is the view — which I shall call *racialism*[2] — that there are heritable characteristics, possessed by members of our species, that allow us to divide them into a small set of races, in such a way that all the members of these races share certain traits and tendencies with each other that they do not share with members of any other race. These traits and tendencies characteristic of a race constitute, on the racialist view, a sort of racial essence; and it is part of the content of racialism that the essential heritable characteristics of what the nineteenth century called the "Races of Man" account for more than the visible morphological characteristics — skin color, hair type, facial features — on the basis of which we make our informal classifications. Racialism is at the heart of nineteenth-century Western attempts to develop a science of racial difference; but it appears to have been believed by others — for example, Hegel, before then, and many in other parts of the non-Western world since — who have had no interest in developing scientific theories.

Racialism is not, in itself, a doctrine that must be dangerous, even if the racial essence is thought to entail moral and intellectual dispositions. Provided positive moral qualities are distributed across the races, each can be respected, can have its "separate but equal" place. Unlike most Western-educated people, I believe — and I have argued elsewhere[3] — that racialism is false; but by itself, it seems to be a cognitive rather than a moral problem. The issue is how the world is, not how we would want it to be.

Racialism is, however, a presupposition of other doctrines that have been called "racism," and these other doctrines have been, in the last few centuries the basis of a great deal of human suffering and the source of a great deal of moral error.

One such doctrine we might call "extrinsic racism": extrinsic racists make moral distinctions between members of different races because they believe that the racial essence entails certain morally relevant qualities. The basis for the extrinsic racists discrimination between people is their belief that members of different races differ in respects that *warrant* the differential treatment, respects — such as honesty or courage or intelligence — that are uncontroversially held (at least in most contemporary cultures) to be acceptable as a basis for treating people differently. Evidence that there are no such differences in morally relevant characteristics — that Negroes do not necessarily lack intellectual capacities, that Jews are not especially avaricious — should thus lead people out of their racism if it is purely extrinsic. As we know, such evidence often fails to change an extrinsic racist's attitudes substantially, for some of the extrinsic racist's best friends have always been Jewish. But at this point — if the racist is sincere — what we have is no longer a false doctrine but a cognitive incapacity, one whose significance I shall discuss later in this essay.

I say that the *sincere* extrinsic racist may suffer from a cognitive incapacity. But some who espouse extrinsic racist doctrines are simply insincere intrinsic racists. For *intrinsic racists,* on my definition, are people who differentiate morally between members of different races because they believe that each race has a different moral status, quite independent of the moral characteristics entailed by its racial essence. Just as, for example, many people assume that the fact that they are biologically related to another person — a brother, an aunt, a cousin — gives them a moral interest in that person,[4] so an intrinsic racist holds that the bare fact of being of the same race is a reason for preferring one person to another. (I shall return to this parallel later as well.)

For an intrinsic racist, no amount of evidence that a member of another race is capable of great moral, intellectual, or cultural achievements, or has characteristics that, in members of one's own race, would make them admirable or attractive, offers any ground for treating that person as he or she would treat similarly endowed members of his or her own race. Just so, some sexists are "intrinsic sexists," holding that the bare fact that someone is a woman (or man) is a reason for treating her (or him) in certain ways.

There are interesting possibilities for complicating these distinctions: some racists, for example, claim, as the Mormons once did, that they discriminate between people because they believe that God requires them to do so. Is this an extrinsic racism, predicated on the combination of God's being an intrinsic racist and the belief that it is right to do what God wills? Or is it intrinsic racism because it is based on the belief that God requires these discriminations because they are right? (Is an act pious because the gods love it, or do they love it because it is pious?) Nevertheless, the distinctions between racialism and racism and between two potentially overlapping kinds of racism provide us with the skeleton of an anatomy of the propositional contents of racial attitudes.

Racist Dispositions

Most people will want to object already that this discussion of the propositional content of racist moral and factual beliefs misses something absolutely crucial to the character of the psychological and sociological reality of racism, something I touched on when I mentioned that extrinsic racist utterances are often made by people who suffer from what I called a "cognitive incapacity." Part of the standard force of accusations of racism is that their objects are in some way *irrational.* The objection to Professor Shockley's claims about the intelligence of blacks is not just that they are false; it is rather that Professor Shockley seems, like many people we call "racist," to be unable to see that the evidence does not support his factual claims and that the connection between his factual claims and his policy prescriptions involves a series of non sequiturs.

What makes these cognitive incapacities especially troubling — something we should respond to with more than a recommendation that the individual, Professor Shockley, be offered psychotherapy — is that they conform to a certain pattern: namely, that it is especially where beliefs and policies that are to the disadvantage of nonwhite people that he shows the sorts of disturbing failure that have made his views both notorious and noto-riously unreliable. Indeed, Professor Shockley's reasoning works extremely well in some other areas: that he is a Noble Laureate in physics is part of what makes him so interesting an example.

This cognitive incapacity is not, of course, a rare one. Many of us are unable to give up beliefs that play a part in justifying the special advantages we gain (or hope to gain) from our positions in the social order — in particular, beliefs about the pos-itive characters of the class of people who share that position. Many people who express extrinsic racist beliefs — many white South Africans, for example — are beneficiaries of social orders that deliver advantages to them by virtue of their "race," so that their disinclination to accept evi-dence that would deprive them of a justification for those advantages is just an instance of this general phenomenon.

So too, evidence that access to higher education is as largely determined by the quality of our earlier educations as by our own innate talents, does not, on the whole, undermine the confidence of college entrants from private schools in England or the United States or Ghana. Many of them con-tinue to believe in the face of this evidence that their acceptance at "good" universities shows them to be intellectually better endowed (and not just better prepared) than those who are rejected. It is facts such as these that give sense to the notion of false consciousness, the idea that an ideology can prevent us from acknowledging facts that would threaten our position.

The most interesting cases of this sort of ideo-logical resistance to the truth are not, perhaps, the ones I have just mentioned. On the whole, it is less surprising, once we accept the admittedly prob-lematic notion of self-deception, that people who think that certain attitudes or beliefs advantage them or those they care about should be able, as we say, to "persuade" themselves to ignore evidence that undermines those beliefs or attitudes. What is more interesting is the existence of people who resist the truth of a proposition while thinking that its wider acceptance would in no way disadvantage them or those individuals about whom they care — this might be thought to describe Professor Shock-

ley; or who resist the truth when they recognize that its acceptance would actually advantage them — this might be the case with some black people who have internalized negative racist stereotypes; or who fail, by virtue of their ideological attach-ments, to recognize what is in their own best inter-ests at all.

My business here is not with the psychological or social processes by which these forms of ideo-logical resistance operate, but it is important, I think, to see the refusal on the part of some extrin-sic racists to accept evidence against the beliefs as an instance of a widespread phenomenon in human affairs. It is a plain fact, to which theories of ideol-ogy must address themselves, that our species is prone both morally and intellectually to such dis-tortions of judgment, in particular to distortions of judgment that reflect partiality. An inability to change your mind in the face of appropriate[5] evi-dence is a cognitive incapacity but it is one that all of us surely suffer from in some areas of belief; especially in areas where our own interests or self-images are (or seem to be) at stake.

It is not, however, as some have held, a ten-dency that we are powerless to resist. No one, no doubt, can be impartial about everything — even about everything to which the notion of partiality applies; but there is no subject matter about which most sane people cannot, in the end, be persuaded to avoid partiality in judgment. And it may help to shake the convictions of those whose incapacity derives from this sort of ideological defense if we show them how their reaction fits into this general pattern. It is, indeed, because it generally *does* fit this pattern that we call such views "racism" — the suffix "-ism" indicating that what we have in mind is not simply a theory but an ideology. It would be odd to call someone brought up in a remote corner of the world with base and demean-ing views about white people a "racist" if that person gave up these beliefs quite easily in the face of appropriate evidence.

Real live racists, then, exhibit a systematically distorted rationality, the kind of systematically distorted rationality that we are likely to call "ide-ological." And it is a distortion that is especially striking in the cognitive domain: extrinsic racists, as I said earlier, however intelligent or otherwise well informed, often fail to treat evidence against the theoretical propositions of extrinsic racism dispassionately. Like extrinsic racism, intrinsic racism can also often be seen as ideological; but since scientific evidence is not going to settle the issue, a failure to see that it is wrong represents a cognitive incapacity only on controversially realist views about morality. What makes intrinsic racism similarly ideological is not so much the failure of inductive or deductive rationality that is so striking in someone like Professor Shockley but rather the connection that it, like extrinsic racism, has with the interest — real or perceived — of the dominant group.[6] Shockley's racism is in a certain sense directed *against* nonwhite people: many believe that his views would, if accepted, operate against their objective interest, and he certainly presents the black "race" in a less than flattering light.

I propose to use the old-fashioned term "racial prejudice" in the rest of this essay to refer to the deformation of rationality in judgment that characterizes those whose racism is more than a theoretical attachment to certain propositions about race.

Racial Prejudice

It is hardly necessary to raise objections to what I am calling "racial prejudice"; someone who exhibits such deformations of rationality is plainly in trouble. But it is important to remember that propositional racists in a racist culture have false moral beliefs but may not suffer from racial prejudice. Once we show them how society has enforced extrinsic racist stereotypes, once we ask them whether they really believe that race in itself, independently of those extrinsic racist beliefs, justifies differential treatment, many will come to give up racist propositions, although we must remember how powerful a weight of authority our arguments have to overcome. Reasonable people may insist on substantial evidence if they are to give up beliefs that are central to their cultures.

Still, in the end, many will resist such reasoning; and to the extent that their prejudices are really not

subject to any kind of rational control, we may wonder whether it is right to treat such people as morally responsible for the acts their racial prejudice motivate, or morally reprehensible for holding the views to which their prejudice leads them. It is a bad thing that such people exist; they are, in a certain sense, bad people. But it is not clear to me that they are responsible for the fact that they are bad. Racial prejudice, like prejudice generally, may threaten an agent's autonomy, making it appropriate to treat or train rather than to reason with them.

But once someone has been offered evidence both (1) that their reasoning in a certain domain is distorted by prejudice, and (2) that the distortions conform to a pattern that suggests a lack of impartiality, they ought to take special care in articulating views and proposing policies in that domain. They ought to do so because, as I have already said, the phenomenon of partiality in judgment is well attested in human affairs. Even if you are not immediately persuaded that you are yourself a victim of such a distorted rationality in a certain domain, you should keep in mind always that this is the usual position of those who suffer from such prejudices. To the extent that this line of thought is not one that itself falls within the domain in question, one can be held responsible for not subjecting judgments that *are* within that domain to an especially extended scrutiny; and this is a fortiori true if the policies one is recommending are plainly of enormous consequence.

If it is clear that racial prejudice is regrettable, it is also clear in the nature of the case that providing even a superabundance of reasons and evidence will often not be a successful way of removing it. Nevertheless, the racist's prejudice will be articulated through the sorts of theoretical propositions I dubbed extrinsic and intrinsic racism. And we should certainly be able to say something reasonable about why these theoretical propositions should be rejected.

Part of the reason that this is worth doing is precisely the fact that many of those who assent to the propositional content of racism do not suffer from racial prejudice. In a country like the United States, where racist propositions were once part of the national ideology, there will be many who assent to racist propositions simply because they were raised to do so. Rational objection to racist propositions has a fair chance of changing such people's beliefs.

Extrinsic and Intrinsic Racism

It is not always clear whether someone's theoretical racism is intrinsic or extrinsic, and there is certainly no reason why we should expect to be able to settle the question. Since the issue probably never occurs to most people in these terms, we cannot suppose that they must have an answer. In fact, given the definition of the terms I offered, there is nothing barring someone from being both an intrinsic and an extrinsic racist, holding both that the bare fact of race provides a basis for treating members of his or her own race differently from others and that there are morally relevant characteristics that are differentially distributed among the races. Indeed, for reasons I shall discuss in a moment, *most* intrinsic racists are likely to express extrinsic racist beliefs, so that we should not be surprised that many people seem, in fact, to be committed to both forms of racism.

The Holocaust made unreservedly clear the threat that racism poses to human decency. But it also blurred our thinking because in focusing our attention on the racist character of the Nazi atrocities, it obscured their character as atrocities. What is appalling about Nazi racism is not just that it presupposes, as all racism does, false (racialist) beliefs — not simply that it involves a moral incapacity (the inability to extend our moral sentiments to all our fellow creatures) and a moral failing (the making of moral distinctions without moral differences) — but that it leads, first, to oppression and then to mass slaughter. In recent years, South African racism has had a similar distorting effect. For although South African racism has not led to killings on the scale of the Holocaust — even if it has both left South Africa judicially executing more (mostly black) people per head of population than most other countries and led to massive differences between the life chances of white and nonwhite South Africans —

it *has* led to the systematic oppression and economic exploitation of people who are not classified as "white," and to the infliction of suffering on citizens of all racial classifications, not least by the police state that is required to maintain that exploitation and oppression.

Part of our resistance, therefore, to calling the racist ideas of those, such as the Black Nationalists of the 1960s, who advocate racial solidarity, by the same term that we use to describe the attitudes of Nazis or of members of the South African Nationalist party, surely resides in the fact that they largely did not contemplate using race as a basis for inflicting harm. Indeed, it seems to me that there is a significant pattern in the modern rhetoric of race, such that the discourse of racial solidarity is usually expressed through the language of *intrinsic* racism, while those who have used race as the basis for oppression and hatred have appealed to *extrinsic* racist ideas. This point is important for understanding the character of contemporary racial attitudes.

The two major uses of race as a basis for moral solidarity that are most familiar in the West are varieties of Pan-Africanism and Zionism. In each case it is presupposed that a "people," Negroes or Jews, has the basis for shared political life in the fact of being of the same race. There are varieties of each form of "nationalism" that make the basis lie in shared traditions; but however plausible this may be in the case of Zionism, which has in Judaism, the religion, a realistic candidate for a common and nonracial focus for nationality, the peoples of Africa have a good deal less in common culturally than is usually assumed. I discuss this issue at length in *My Father's House: Essays in the Philosophy of African Culture,* but let me say here that I believe the central fact is this: what blacks in the West, like secularized Jews, have mostly in common is that they are perceived — both by themselves and by others — as belonging to the same race, and that this common race is used by others as the basis for discriminating against them. "If you ever forget you're a Jew, a goy will remind you." The Black Nationalists, like some Zionists, responded to their experience of racial discrimination by accepting the racialism it presupposed.[7]

Although race is indeed at the heart of Black Nationalism, however, it seems that it is the fact of a shared race, not the fact of a shared racial character, that provides the basis for solidarity. Where racism is implicated in the basis for national solidarity, it is intrinsic, not (or not only) extrinsic. It is this that makes the idea of fraternity one that is naturally applied in nationalist discourse. For, as I have already observed, the moral status of close family members is not normally thought of in most cultures as depending on qualities of character; we are supposed to love our brothers and sisters in spite of their faults and not because of their virtues. Alexander Crummell, one of the founding fathers of Black Nationalism, literalizes the metaphor of family in these startling words:

Races, like families, are the organisms and ordinances of God; and race feeling, like family feeling, is of divine origin. The extinction of race feeling is just as possible as the extinction of family feeling. Indeed, a race *is* a family.[8]

It is the assimilation of "race feeling" to "family feeling" that makes intrinsic racism seem so much less objectionable than extrinsic racism. For this metaphorical identification reflects the fact that, in the modern world (unlike the nineteenth century), intrinsic racism is acknowledged almost exclusively as the basis of feelings of community. We can surely, then, share a sense of what Crummell's friend and co-worker Edward Blyden called "the poetry of politics," that is, "the feeling of race," the feeling of "people with whom we are connected."[9] The racism here is the basis of acts of supererogation, the treatment of others better than we otherwise might, better than moral duty demands of us.

This is a contingent fact. There is no logical impossibility in the idea of racialists whose moral beliefs lead them to feelings of hatred for other races while leaving no room for love of members of their own. Nevertheless most racial hatred is in fact expressed through extrinsic racism: most people who have used race as the basis for causing harm to others have felt the need to see the others as independently morally flawed. It is one thing to espouse fraternity without claiming that your brothers and sisters have any special qualities that deserve recognition, and another to espouse hatred of others who have done nothing to deserve it.[10]

Many Afrikaners — like many in the American South until recently — have a long list of extrinsic racist answers to the question why blacks should not have full civil rights. Extrinsic racism has usually been the basis for treating people worse than we otherwise might, for giving them less than their humanity entitles them to. But this too is a contingent fact. Indeed, Crummell's guarded respect for white people derived from a belief in the superior moral qualities of the Anglo-Saxon race.

Intrinsic racism is, in my view, a moral error. Even if racialism were correct, the bare fact that someone was of another race would be no reason to treat them worse — or better — than someone of my race. In our public lives, people are owed treatment independently of their biological characters: if they are to be differently treated there must be some morally relevant difference between them. In our private lives, we are morally free to have aesthetic preferences between people, but once our treatment of people raises moral issues, we may not make arbitrary distinctions. Using race in itself as a morally relevant distinction strikes most of us as obviously arbitrary. Without associated moral characteristics, why should race provide a better basis than hair color or height or timbre of voice? And if two people share all the properties morally relevant to some action we ought to do, it will be an error — a failure to apply the Kantian injunction to universalize our moral judgment — to use the bare facts of race as the basis for treating them differently. No one should deny that a common ancestry might, in particular cases, account for similarities in moral character. But then it would be the moral similarities that justified the different treatment.

It is presumably because most people — outside the South African Nationalist party and the Ku Klux Klan — share the sense that intrinsic racism requires arbitrary distinctions that they are largely unwilling to express it in situations that invite moral criticism. But I do not know how I would argue with someone who was willing to announce an intrinsic racism as a basic moral idea; the best one can do, perhaps, is to provide objections to possible lines of defense of it.

De Gustibus

It might be thought that intrinsic racism should be regarded not so much as an adherence to a (moral) proposition as the expression of a taste, analogous say, to the food prejudice that makes most English people unwilling to eat horse meat, and most Westerners unwilling to eat the insect grubs that the !Kung people find so appetizing. The analogy does at least this much for us namely, to provide a model of the way that *extrinsic* racist propositions can be a reflection of an underlying prejudice. For, of course, in most culture food prejudices are rationalized: we say insects are unhygienic and cats taste horrible. Yet a cooked insect is no more health-threatening than a cooked carrot, and the unpleasant taste of cat meat, far from justifying our prejudice against it, probably derives from that prejudice.

But there the usefulness of the analogy ends. For intrinsic racism, as I have defined it, is not simply a taste for the company of one's "own kind," but moral doctrine, one that is supposed to underlie differences in the treatment of people in contexts where moral evaluation is appropriate. And for moral distinctions we cannot accept that "de gustibus non est disputandum." We do not need the full apparatus of Kantian ethics to require that public morality be constrained by reason.

A proper analogy would be with someone who thought that we could continue to kill cattle for beef, even if cattle exercised all the complex cultural skills of human beings. I think it is obvious that creatures that share our capacity for understanding as well as our capacity for pain should not be treated the way we actually treat cattle — that "intrinsic speciesism" would be as wrong as racism. And the fact that most people think it is worse to be cruel to chimpanzees than to frogs suggests that they may agree with me. The distinction in attitudes surely reflects a belief in the greater richness of the mental life of chimps. Still, I do not know how I would *argue* against someone who

could not see this; someone who continued to act on the contrary belief might, in the end, simply have to be locked up.

The Family Model

I have suggested that intrinsic racism is, at least sometimes, a metaphorical extension of the moral priority of one's family; it might, therefore, be suggested that a defense of intrinsic racism could proceed along the same lines as a defense of the family as a center of moral interest. The possibility of a defense of family relations as morally relevant — or, more precisely, of the claim that one may be morally entitled (or even obliged) to make distinctions between two otherwise morally indistinguishable people because one is related to one and not to the other — is theoretically important for the prospects of a philosophical defense of intrinsic racism. This is because such a defense of the family involves — like intrinsic racism — a denial of the basic claim, expressed so clearly by Kant, that from the perspective of morality, it is as rational agents *simpliciter* that we are to assess and be assessed. For anyone who follows Kant in this, what matters, as we might say, is not who you are but how you try to live. Intrinsic racism denies this fundamental claim also. And, in so doing, as I have argued elsewhere, it runs against the mainstream of the history of Western moral theory.[11]

The importance of drawing attention to the similarities between the defense of the family and the defense of the race, then, is not merely that the metaphor of family is often invoked by racism; it is that each of them offers the same general challenge to the Kantian stream of our moral thought. And the parallel with the defense of the family should be especially appealing to an intrinsic racist, since many of us who have little time for racism would hope that the family is susceptible to some such defense.

The problem in generalizing the defense of the family, however, is that such defenses standardly begin at a point that makes the argument for intrinsic racism immediately implausible: namely, with the family as the unit through which we live what is most intimate, as the center of private life. If we distinguish, with Bernard Williams, between ethical thought, which takes seriously "the demands, needs, claims, desires, and generally, the lives of other people,"[12] and morality, which focuses more narrowly on obligation, it may well be that private life matters to us precisely because it is altogether unsuited to the universalizing tendencies of morality.

The functioning family unit has contracted substantially with industrialization, the disappearance of the family as the unit of production, and the increasing mobility of labor, but there remains that irreducible minimum: the parent or parents with the child or children. In this "nuclear" family, there is, of course, a substantial body of shared experience, shared attitudes, shared knowledge and beliefs; and the mutual psychological investment that exists within this group is, for most of us, one of the things that gives meaning to our lives. It is a natural enough confusion — which we find again and again in discussions of adoption in the popular media — that identifies the relevant group with the biological unit of *genitor, genetrix,* and *offspring* rather than with the social unit of those who share a common domestic life.

The relations of parents and their biological children are of moral importance, of course, in part because children are standardly the product of behavior voluntarily undertaken by their biological parents. But the moral relations between biological siblings and half-siblings cannot, as I have already pointed out, be accounted for in such terms. A rational defense of the family ought to appeal to the causal responsibility of the biological parent and the common life of the domestic unit, and not to the brute fact of biological relatedness, even if the former pair of considerations defines groups that are often coextensive with the groups generated by the latter. For brute biological relatedness bears no necessary connection to the sorts of human purposes that seem likely to be relevant at the most basic level of ethical thought.

An argument that such a central group is bound to be crucially important in the lives of most human beings in societies like ours is not, of course, an argument for any specific mode of organization of the "family": feminism and the gay liberation movement have offered candidate groups that could (and sometimes do) occupy the same sort of role in the lives of those whose sexualities or whose dispositions otherwise make the nuclear family uncongenial; and these candidates have been offered specifically in the course of defenses of a move toward societies that are agreeably beyond patriarchy and homophobia. The central thought of these feminist and gay critiques of the nuclear family is that we cannot continue to view any one organization of private life as "natural," once we have seen even the broadest outlines of the archaeology of the family concept.

If that is right, then the argument for the family must be an argument for a mode of organization of life and feeling that subserves certain positive functions; and however the details of such an argument would proceed it is highly unlikely that the same functions could be served by groups on the scale of races, simply because, as I say, the family is attractive in part exactly for reasons of its personal scale.

I need hardly say that rational defenses of intrinsic racism along the lines I have been considering are not easily found. In the absence of detailed defenses to consider, I can only offer these general reasons for doubting that they can succeed; the generally Kantian tenor of much of our moral thought threatens the project from the start; and the essentially unintimate nature of relations within "races" suggests that there is little prospect that the defense of the family — which seems an attractive and plausible project that extends ethical life beyond the narrow range of a universalizing morality — can be applied to a defense of races.

Conclusions

I have suggested that what we call "racism" involves both propositions and dispositions.

The propositions were, first, that there are races (this was *racialism*) and, second, that these races are morally significant either (a) because they are contingently correlated with morally relevant properties (this was *extrinsic racism*) or (b) because they are intrinsically morally significant (this was *intrinsic racism*).

The disposition was a tendency to assent to false propositions, both moral and theoretical, about races — propositions that support policies or beliefs that are to the disadvantage of some race (or races) as opposed to others, and to do so even in the face of evidence and argument that should appropriately lead to giving those propositions up. This disposition I called "racial prejudice."

I suggested that intrinsic racism had tended in our own time to be the natural expression of feelings of community, and this is, of course, one of the reasons why we are not inclined to call it racist. For, to the extent that a theoretical position is not associated with irrationally held beliefs that tend to the *dis*advantage of some group, it fails to display the *directedness* of the distortions of rationality characteristic of racial prejudice. Intrinsic racism may be as irrationally held as any other view, but it does not *have* to be directed *against* anyone.

So far as theory is concerned I believe racialism to be false: since theoretical racism of both kinds presupposes racialism, I could not logically support racism of either variety. But even if racialism were true, both forms of theoretical racism would be incorrect. Extrinsic racism is false because the genes that account for the gross morphological differences that underlie our standard racial categories are not linked to those genes that determine, to whatever degree such matters are determined genetically, our moral and intellectual characters. Intrinsic racism is mistaken because it breaches the Kantian imperative to make moral distinctions only on morally relevant grounds — granted that there is no reason to believe that race, *in se,* is morally relevant, and also no reason to suppose that races are like families in providing a sphere of ethical life that legitimately escapes the demands of a universalizing morality.

NOTES

1. Bernard Lewis, *Semites and Anti-Semites* (New York: Norton, 1986).
2. I shall be using the words "racism" and "racialism" with the meanings I stipulate: in some dialects of English they are synonyms, and in most dialects their definition is less than precise. For discussion

of recent biological evidence see M. Nei and A.K. Roychoudhury, "Genetic Relationship and Evolution of Human Race." *Evolutionary Biology*, vol. 14 (New York: Plenum, 1983), pp. 1-59; for useful background see also M. Nei and A.K. Roychoudhury, "Gene Differences between Caucasian, Negro, and Japanese Populations," *Science*, 177 (August 1972), pp. 434-35.

3. See my "The Uncompleted Argument: Du Bois and the Illusion of Race," *Critical Inquiry*, 12 (Autumn 1985); reprinted in Henry Louis Gates (eds.), *"Race," Writing, and Difference* (Chicago: University of Chicago Press, 1986), pp. 21-37.

4. This fact shows up most obviously in the assumption that adopted children intelligibly make claims against their natural siblings: natural parents are, of course, causally responsible for their child's existence and that could be the basis of moral claims, without any sense that biological relatedness entailed rights or responsibilities. But no such basis exists for an interest in natural *siblings*, my sisters are not causally responsible for my existence. See "The Family Model," later in this essay.

5. Obviously what evidence should *appropriately* change your beliefs is not independent of your social or historical situation. In mid-nineteenth-century America, in New England quite as much as in the heart of Dixie, the pervasiveness of the institutional support for the prevailing system of racist belief — the fact that it was reinforced by religious and state, and defended by people in the universities and colleges, who had the greatest cognitive authority — meant that it would have been appropriate to insist on a substantial body of evidence and argument before giving up assent to racist propositions. In California in the 1980s, of course, matters stand rather differently. To acknowledge this is not to admit to a cognitive relativism; rather, it is to hold that, at least in some domains, the fact that a belief is widely held — and especially by people in positions of cognitive authority — may be a good prima facie reason for believing it.

6. Ideologies, as most theorists of ideology have admitted, standardly outlive the period in which they conform to the objective interests of the dominant group in a society; so even someone who thinks that the dominant group in our society no

longer needs racism to buttress its position can see racism as the persisting ideology of an earlier phase of society. (I say "group" to keep the claim appropriately general; it seems to me a substantial further claim that the dominant group whose interest an ideology serves is always a class.) I have argued, however, in "The Conservation of 'Race'" that racism continues to serve the interests of the ruling classes in the West; in *Black American Literature Forum*, 23 (Spring 1989), pp. 37-60.

7. As I argued in "The Uncompleted Argument: Du Bois and the Illusion of Race." The reactive (or dialectical) character of this move explains why Sartre calls it manifestations in Négritude an "antiracist racism"; see "Orphée Noir," his preface to Senghor's *Anthologie de la nouvelle poésie nègre et malagache de langue française* (Paris: PUF, 1948). Sartre believed, of course, that the synthesis of this dialectic would be the transcendence of racism; and it was his view of it as a stage — the antithesis — in that process that allowed him to see it as a positive advance over the original "thesis" of European racism. I suspect that the reactive character of antiracist racism accounts for the tolerance that is regularly extended to it in liberal circles; but this tolerance is surely hard to justify unless one shares Sartre's optimistic interpretation of it as a stage in a process that leads to the end of all racisms. (And unless your view of this dialectic is deterministic, you should in any case want to play an argumentative role in moving to this next stage.)

For a similar Zionist response see Horace Kallen's "The Ethics of Zionism," *Maccabaeau*, August 1906.

8. "The Race Problem in America." in Brotz's *Negro Social and Political Thought* (New York: Basic Books, 1966), p. 184.

9. *Christianity, Islam and the Negro Race* (1887; reprinted Edinburgh: Edinburgh University Press, 1967), p. 197.

10. This is in part a reflection of an important asymmetry: loathing, unlike love, needs justifying; and this, I would argue, is because loathing usually leads to acts that are *in se* undesirable, whereas love leads to acts that are largely *in se* desirable — indeed, supererogatorily so.

11. See my "Racism and Moral Pollution," *Philosophical Forum* 18, (Winter-Spring 1986-87), pp. 185-202.

12. *Ethics and the Limits of Philosophy* (Cambridge, Mass.: Harvard University Press, 1985,) p. 12. I do not, as is obvious, share Williams's skepticism about morality.

FUTURE GENDERS? FUTURE RACES?

Sally Haslanger

Sally Haslanger is a Professor in the Department of Linguistics and Philosophy at MIT. She is co-editor of Adoption Matters: Philosophical and Feminist Essays *(2004, with Charlotte Witt) and is completing a monograph tentatively titled* The Social Embodiment of Gender and Race.

    Haslanger employs the distinction between "sex" and "gender" to describe a corresponding distinction between "color" and "race." "Color" describes the physical markers of race, and "race" describes the social implications that these markers have. While sex marks a difference of a biological capacity to bear children that a just society must address, Haslanger argues that color is not and should not be a physical fact that a just society must address. She acknowledges that we still need an account of race that does the work of identifying those affected by discrimination and remedying its harms, but envisions a future in which we are rid of race and instead have a rich array of cultural practices and ethnicities. She proposes an interim strategy of challenging and reconstructing these groupings through the common culture, commitment to shared identity, and positive group solidarity that "ethnoraces" offer.

1. Background

In the social world as we know it, two of the most salient dimensions of human difference are race and gender. If I mention that I met an interesting person while waiting for the subway last week, a first step to understanding the nature of our contact would be to identify whether the person was a man or a woman, and what race they were. (Also especially useful would be their relative age.) To describe someone by their race and gender is not simply to describe their appearance, but to situate them in a framework of meaning and indicate the social norms that govern our interactions.

Drawing on the insight that one's sex has quite well-defined and systematic social implications, feminists have argued that it is helpful to distinguish sex and gender. Very roughly, as the slogan goes, gender is the social meaning of sex. The idea is that gender is not a classification scheme based simply on anatomical or biological differences, but marks social differences between individuals. Sex differences are about testicles and ovaries, the penis and the uterus (and on some theories, quite a bit more),[1] gender, in contrast, is a classification of individuals in terms of their social position as determined by interpretations of their sex.

To help understand this, consider, for example, the category of landlords. To be a landlord one must be located within a broad system of social and economic relations which includes tenants, private property, and the like. It might have been that all and only landlords had only four toes on their left foot. But even if this were the case, having this physical mark is not what it is to be a landlord. Being nine-toed is an anatomical kind; being a landlord is a social kind. Similarly, we can draw a distinction between sex and gender: *sex* is an anatomical distinction based on locally salient sexual/reproductive differences, and *gender* is a distinction between the social/political positions of those with bodies marked as of different sexes.

To be clear, I'll use the terms "male" and "female" to designate sexes, "man" and "woman" to designate genders.[2] Because one is a female by virtue of some (variable) set of anatomical features, and one is a woman by virtue of one's position within a social and economic system, we should allow, at least in principle, that some males are women and some females are men. Although it is clear enough for our purposes here what distinguishes males and females, the question of what it is to be a man or woman is not at all clear. And this has been a major site of controversy amongst feminists.

I'll return to how we might define gender. In the meantime, it is interesting to note that there is a parallel to the sex/gender distinction in the case of race. Just as one's primary and secondary sex characteristics are socially meaningful, so are the color of one's skin, shape of one's eyelids, color and texture of one's hair, and so on. So we can distinguish the physical markers of race from the social implications that these markers have. To register this terminologically, let's distinguish "color" and "race" as parallel to sex and gender. I will use the term "color" to refer to the (contextually variable) physical "markers" of race, just as I use the term "sex" to refer to the (contextually variable) physical "markers" of gender. I mean to include in "color" more than just skin tone: common markers also include eye, nose, and lip shape; hair texture; physique; and so on. And in principle I want to allow that virtually any cluster of physical traits that are assumed to be inherited from those who occupy a specific geographical region or regions can count as "color." (Although the term "people of color" is used to refer to non-Whites, I want to allow that the markers of "Whiteness" count as "color.") Borrowing the slogan we used before, we can say then that race is the social meaning of "color."

So far I've characterized race and gender very vaguely. It is one thing to say that race and gender are social categories that capture the social implications of certain bodily traits, but can we give them more content? For example, what are the specific social implications of sex in terms of which we should define gender?

Among feminist theorists there are two problems that have generated pessimism about providing any unified account of women; I'll call them the *commonality problem* and the *normativity problem*. Very briefly, the commonality problem

questions whether there is anything social that females have in common that could count as their "gender." If we consider *all* females — females of different times, places, and cultures — there are reasons to doubt that there is anything beyond body type (if even that) that they all share. The normativity problem raises the concern that any definition of "what woman is," because it must select amongst the broad variation in women's traits, cannot help but be value-laden and so will marginalize certain females, privilege others, and reinforce current gender norms (Butler 1990, Ch. 1).

A primary concern of feminist and antiracist theorizing is to give an account of the social world that will assist us in the struggle for justice. Given this goal, I take the primary motivation for distinguishing sex from gender to arise in the recognition that societies, on the whole, privilege individuals with male bodies. Although the particular forms of oppression vary from culture to culture, societies have found many ways — some ingenious, some crude — to control and exploit the sexual and reproductive capacities of females. So one important strategy for defining gender has been to analyze it in terms of women's subordinate position in systems of male dominance. Recognizing the legitimate goals of feminist and antiracist theory, we can allow, then, that certain values guide our inquiry. Pursuing this line of thought, here is a (rough) proposal for specifying what it is to be a man or a woman:[3]

S *is a woman* iff$_{df}$[4] S is systematically subordinated along some dimension (economic, political, legal, social, etc.), and S is "marked" as a target for this treatment by observed or imagined bodily features presumed to be evidence of a female's biological role in reproduction.

S *is a man* iff$_{df}$ S is systematically privileged along some dimension (economic, political, legal, social, etc.), and S is "marked" as a target for this treatment by observed or imagined bodily features presumed to be evidence of a male's biological role in reproduction.

It is a virtue, I believe, of these accounts, that depending on context, one's sex may have a very different meaning and may position one in very different kinds of hierarchies. The variation will clearly occur from culture to culture (and sub-culture to sub-culture): to be a Chinese woman of the 1790s, a Brazilian woman of the 1890s, or an American woman of the 1990s may involve very different social relations and very different kinds of oppression. Yet on the analysis suggested, these groups count as women insofar as their subordinate positions are marked and justified by reference to female sex.

With this strategy of defining gender in mind, we can now consider whether it will help in giving some content to the social category of race. The feminist approach recommends the following: consider how members of the group are *socially positioned* and what *physical markers* serve as a supposed basis for such treatment. Elaborating the earlier slogan, we might say that race is the social meaning of the geographically marked "colored" body. To develop this, consider the following account.[5]

> A group is *racialized* (in context C) iff$_{df}$ its members are socially positioned as subordinate or privileged along some dimension (economic, political, legal, social, etc.) (in C), and the group is "marked" as a target for this treatment by observed or imagined bodily features presumed to be evidence of ancestral links to a certain geographical region.

In other words, races are those groups demarcated by the geographical associations accompanying perceived body type, when those associations take on evaluative significance concerning how members of the group should be viewed and treated. Given this definition, we can say that S is of the White (Black, Asian...) race [in C] iff Whites (Blacks, Asians...) are a racialized group [in C], and S is a member.[6]

Note that on this view, whether a group is racialized, and so how and whether an individual is raced, is not an absolute fact, but will depend on context. For example, Blacks, Whites, Asians, and Native Americans, are currently racialized in the U.S. insofar as these are all groups defined in terms of physical features associated with places of origin and insofar as membership in the group functions socially as a basis for evaluation. However, some groups are not currently racialized in the U.S., but have been so in the past and possibly could be again (and in other contexts are); the Italians, the Germans, and the Irish are examples.

Given these accounts, a primary task in the quest for social justice is to eliminate those social structures that constitute races (or racialized groups) and eliminate men and women. Of course this is not to say that we should eliminate males and females or impose a "khaki" appearance on everyone. Rather, it is to say that we should work for a day when sex and "color" markers do not have hierarchical implications.

2. Alternatives

At this stage one might reasonably ask, however: Why build hierarchy into the definitions? Why not define gender and race as those social positions motivated and justified by cultural responses to the body, without requiring that the social positions are hierarchical? Wouldn't that provide what we need without implying (implausibly) that women are, by definition, subordinate; that men, by definition, are privileged; and that races, by definition, are hierarchically positioned?

Even allowing that gender is the social meaning of sex and race is the social meaning of "color," one could maintain that the social implications of sex and "color" are, *as we know them*, hierarchical, but insist that sex and "color" can nonetheless remain meaningful under conditions of justice. If so, then in envisioning a just future we should include the option of preserving race and gender while working towards race and gender *equality*.

Pursuing this strategy, we could use the definitions of *man* and *woman* offered above: it is clear that these dominant nodes of our current gender structures are hierarchical. But *gender* could serve as a broader genus allowing both hierarchical and non-hierarchical cases. For example (roughly),

> A group G is *a gender* (in context C) iff$_{df}$ its members are similarly positioned as along some

social dimension (economic, political, legal, social, etc.) (in C), and the members are "marked" as appropriately in this position by observed or imagined bodily features presumed to be evidence of reproductive capacities or function.

A similar approach to race would yield the following:

A group G is *racialized* (in context C) iff$_{df}$ its members are similarly positioned as along some social dimension (economic, political, legal, social, etc.) (in C), and the members are "marked" as appropriately in this position by observed or imagined bodily features presumed to be evidence of ancestral links to a certain geographical region.

As in the case of gender, we could retain the hierarchical analysis for existing races: Black, White, Latina/o, and so on are hierarchical groups. But we might envision a new egalitarian structure of races, new races, to take their place.

In what follows, I will argue that there are interesting and important differences between race and gender that count *against* treating them as parallel. Because sex is, from a political point of view, inevitably meaningful, we need to envision new egalitarian genders, but race is different. Rather than creating new egalitarian races, we should aim for the elimination of race altogether.

3. "Sex," "Color," and Biology

Start with gender. I am sympathetic to radical rethinkings of sex and gender. In particular, I believe that we should refuse to use anatomy as a primary basis for classifying individuals and that any distinctions between kinds of sexual and reproductive bodies are importantly political and open to contest. Some authors have argued that we should acknowledge the continuum of anatomical differences and recognize at least five sexes (Fausto-Sterling 1993). And if sexual distinctions become more complex, we would also need to rethink sexuality, given that sexual desire would not fit neatly within existing homosexual/heterosexual paradigms.

However, one can encourage the proliferation of sexual and reproductive options without thinking that we can or should eliminate *all* social implications of anatomical sex and reproduction. Given that as a species there are substantial differences in what human bodies contribute to reproduction and what sorts of bodies bear the main physical burdens of reproduction, and given further that reproduction cannot really help but be a socially significant fact (it does, after all, produce children), it is difficult to imagine a functioning society — more specifically, a functioning *feminist* society — that doesn't acknowledge in some way the difference between those kinds of bodies that are likely able to bear children and those that are not. On this issue I am sympathetic to Beauvoir's argument that females, on the whole, bear a greater physical burden for the species than males and that it is the responsibility of society to address this in order to achieve justice (Beauvoir 1989/1949, Ch. 2).

The argument just sketched (more is certainly needed to flesh it out) asserts that sexual differences would be in some way meaningful in any society of people with bodies like ours, at least in any society in which humans are sexual beings and reproduce biologically,[7] so eliminating social categories that take sexual difference into account would not be an effective way to create a just future. Instead of attempting to eliminate gender, we should try to envision new non-oppressive ways of being gendered *without* being a man or a woman, and we should eventually incorporate these new gender concepts as parts (possibly very small parts) of our self-understandings (Frye 1996). Consequently, it is an important project within a feminist antiracism to construct alternative social positions and identities (hopefully many of them!) for people of different sexes.

It is worth emphasizing that although justice requires that we radically rethink the structure of relationships that constitute our societies, this does not mean that "anything goes." There are some limits to what alternatives are viable: there may be things necessary for the society to function at all, or for it to be just, or that are especially desirable in some way. Sexual reproduction, I submit, imposes some limits in forming a just society, though it is not clear what those limits are. Given that sex needs to be meaningful in order to achieve justice, a conception of gender that allows new non-hierarchical cases will be valuable in our efforts.

The question arises, however, whether there is something about race that should also constrain us. What condition for justice might we miss, should we pursue the elimination of race?[8] One quick reply would be to point out that the quest for *racial equality* presupposes that there are races. However, racial equality should be our goal — as opposed to the *elimination* of race — only if we have reason to view "color" as a justifiable way for societies to differentiate groups of people. Although it appears that there are reasons for *any* functioning society to take sex and reproduction seriously, there is no comparable reason for thinking that functional societies must acknowledge those physical differences that distinguish "colors." Classifications based on "color" vary tremendously depending on the socio-historical-legal context and are not grounded in meaningful biological categories (Appiah 1992, Ch. 2; Appiah 1996; Root 2000; Zack 2002; Lewontin 1982; cf. Kitcher 1999; Andreason 1998; Andreason 2000). For example, the markers of "Blackness" differ when considering the contemporary U.S. or Brazil or South Africa, and the rules for racial marking change over time (Davis 1991). Moreover, "color" classification is not just an informal practice, but is often legally imposed and based on biological myths of "blood": think of the "one drop" rule, enforced under Jim Crow (Lopez 1996). It is not plausible to explain the variation and development of "color" distinctions in terms of increased understanding of biology or genetics. Rather, the best explanations point to their social and political implications (Fields 1982; Mills 1997).

These facts indicate an important difference between race and gender. Although gender as we know it is a site of social injustice, just societies should be concerned with those functions of human bodies that matter for reproduction. But "color" — those clusters of real or imagined anatomical differences used to mark races — does not seem to correlate with any feature that carries sufficient biological weight that it must be socially addressed.

Of course, "color" currently carries significant social weight. So it is important to note that even if society should not be structured to recognize "color" distinctions, this does not entail a politics of "race blindness." Race, as I've argued, is more than just "color"; it concerns the systematic subordination of groups of people marked by "color." The effort to end racism must recognize racialized groups in order to understand the processes by which they are formed and sustained and to remedy the ongoing injustice done to their members. Recognizing racialized groups is not only compatible with justice but essential to achieving it. On this account, affirmative action programs designed to remedy a history of racial oppression are entirely warranted. One might put the point by saying that we should be attentive to race, but not to "color." Or, that we should be attentive to "color" only insofar as it is a marker of racialization.

In the contemporary U.S., there are many groups that define themselves by reference to race and racial injustice: some form on the basis of a common history of racial oppression or in solidarity against such oppression, others on the basis of cultural practices that have evolved within racialized groups. What is required for membership in these groups is a common history, a moral stand against injustice, or the enjoyment of a celebratory practice. These groups, or at least many of them, do not define themselves by reference to "color," even if in the context of racial oppression some of them correspond in their membership roughly to groups that are marked by "color." Groups based on history, politics, and other social commonalities avoid false assumptions about biology and geography in constructing group solidarity and also avoid the entrenchment of social divisions along existing racial lines; at least in principle and often in practice, the membership of such groups is "multiracial" by the dominant standards of racialization.

The Medical Necessity of "Color" Coding

But perhaps this is too fast. What about racial patterns in susceptibility to disease? Shouldn't societies be prepared, as a matter of justice, to address disadvantages that some suffer due to genetic risk factors? And don't some of these correlate with "color"? The weight of current research suggests not (Root 2001). Although there are significant generalizations linking race/"color" with disease in the U.S., the basis for these generalizations is social, not biological:

> Blacks are seven times more likely to die of tuberculosis than whites, three times more likely to die of H.I.V.-A.I.D.S. and twice as likely to die of diabetes. The diseases are biological but the racial differences are not; How is this possible? ... No mystery. Race affects income, housing, and healthcare, and these, in turn, affect health. Stress suppresses the immune system and being black in the U.S. today is stressful. (Root 2000, S629)

Given the contextual variability of "color" classifications, it is not surprising that generalizations linking "color" with disease are only local and do not support a biological basis for race. For example,

> An individual with sickle-cell disease can be black in the U.S., but white in Brazil, for the category of black or white is defined differently here and there. As a result, rates of sickle-cell disease for blacks differ from place to place, in part because race does. (Root 2000)

Thus, it seems that although there are reasons for a society to take "color" seriously as an indicator of risk under conditions where groups are racialized (or are suffering the long-term effects of racialization), this only shows that prior injustice imposes constraints on the construction of a just society; it does not show that "color," or a biological fact correlating with "color," imposes such a constraint. Again, it may be appropriate for societies to be structured so that there are social implications of having suffered injustice — implications that attempt to redress the injustice or prevent recurring injustice — but history rather than biology is what requires our response.

One might insist, however, that although we currently think of "color" as something that is easily observable in everyday interaction, perhaps instead it should be genetically defined. If so, then in keeping with the terminology I've introduced, the genetic traits in question would count as "color." And, to be more explicit, we might adjust our slogan for race: race is the social meaning of certain (to be specified) genetic traits.

In pursuing this approach, we cannot assume that such genetically defined groups will correspond with the groups we currently count as races, that the external appearance of the groups will correspond to the "color" divisions we make now, or even that the external appearance of members of a single group will be similar. But that's just to say, on this view, that our current racial classifications are misguided. Moreover, one might argue, we need to treat such genetic groups as socially relevant because they correlate with socially meaningful traits, for example, susceptibility to disease. Because medical care is something that a just society must be concerned to provide, "color," like sex, must be taken into account even under conditions of justice. As a result, we should treat *race* like *gender* as a category that currently has hierarchical forms, but need not.

The question of whether there are genetically defined groups that are medically significant and should count as races is a large issue in contemporary genomics and biomedical ethics. I will not be in a position to address fully the literature on this topic here. However, there are three points that count against revising my account of race to include non-hierarchical groups defined by reference to genetic traits.

First, according to my definition, racial divisions are marked by *observed or imagined clusters of physical traits that are assumed to be inherited from those who occupy a specific geographical region or regions*. Consequently, not just any medically relevant genetic division amongst humans will count as a basis for race: the genetic traits must be interpreted as being a marker of geographical origins. The connection between race and geography is, I believe, a key factor in distinguishing race from other social categories that are marked on the body and assumed to be natural, for example, gender, certain forms of disability and disease, (sometimes) sexual orientation, and (sometimes) caste. The link with geography also helps explain the role of racial concepts in the context of imperialism and the process of nation-building (Mills 1997). So there are good reasons to maintain the geographical element in the definition of race.

Second, although my definition of "color" does not require that the physical traits in question be easily observable in ordinary interaction, the marking of racialized bodies involves appearance. For example, at certain times and places, Jews have been racialized. The specifics of the racialization process vary, but on one scenario Jews are imagined to have some physical feature inherited from populations originating in what is now the Middle East. In some cases, however, it is recognized that there is no reliably observable physical feature that distinguishes Jews from non-Jews, so other devices, such as yellow stars, have been introduced to make sure that their race is identifiable in casual encounters. So even if geneticists can find ways of dividing humans into groups based on genetic features that are assumed to be inherited from populations originating in a particular region, as I see it, those groups are racialized in a context only if in that context it is thought that there are observable markers, either anatomical or artificial, that — at least in paradigm cases — distinguish members of the group. Such observable marking is important to the process of racialization, for a key factor in racializing a group is the invocation of social norms that differentiate "appropriate" behavior towards the members of the group (normally) before any interaction is possible. You experience the "color," behave in accordance with the norms for individuals of that kind, and ask questions later, if ever (Alcoff 2000a, Alcoff 2000b).

Granting these two points, one can still construct cases that would seem to satisfy my definition of race, given certain social responses to genetic facts. For example, suppose that a group from a particular region is susceptible to a specific genetically based disease, and those susceptible are marked as such and marginalized or otherwise oppressed. Should we count this as racial oppression, as oppression imposed according to one's "color"?

I would argue that a group originating in a specific region who are (genetically or otherwise) susceptible to disease should be taken into account in the distribution of resources. Medical conditions are relevant in considering what justice requires, and it may be that medical conditions sometimes correlate with geographical origins. The basis for the differential treatment in these cases is the medical condition; any real or imagined links with geography is, from the medical point of view, accidental. Presumably, an individual born in or with ancestors from a very different area with the same susceptibility should be grouped with them for medical purposes. So these groups should not be considered races, and their oppression, although objectionable, should not be considered racial oppression.

As I see it, the main issue is how we draw distinctions between humans for the purposes of justice. I've argued that it is important to distinguish existing races and genders because of historical and contemporary forms of oppression. I've argued that we should distinguish new forms of gender in order to accommodate the special burdens some humans carry in the process of reproduction. I have also suggested that we should distinguish groups with respect to medical conditions in order to provide adequate care and support. These different categories of concern require different strategies of response. Although there are cases where the genetics, geography, and marking relevant to medicine can trigger racialization, I submit that this occurs when hierarchy is imposed. In effect, there will be cases in which racism and ableism overlap and in which antiracists and antiableists are confronting structurally similar injustice. However, for the most part, the challenges facing those who have suffered racial injustice and those who have suffered medical/ableist injustice are very different; race and disability require different responses in order to achieve justice. This provides good reason for not expanding the definition of race to include non-hierarchical genetic divisions between us as racial divisions.

Evolution, Populations, and Life-worlds

But perhaps there are other biological explanations of the persistence of race. Lucius Outlaw provides further reason to pause before we reject "color" as a legitimate, perhaps even inevitable, source of social meaning. He asks, concerning the number and persistence of differently "colored" populations,

> Might these populations not be the result of bio-cultural group attachments and practices that are conducive to human survival and well-being, and hence must be understood, appreciated, and provided for in the principles and practices of, say, a liberal democratic society? (Outlaw 1996, 13)

He seems to answer that populations defined at least in part by "color" are valuable and virtually inevitable, because humans on the whole desire "to achieve relative immortality" by having offspring "who look and carry on somewhat like ourselves" (Outlaw 1996, 17); because we have reason to be fearful of "significantly different and objectionable strangers" (Outlaw 1996, 17); and finally, because the "valorization of descent" increases our chances of survival by motivating cooperation (Outlaw 1996, 18). Thus, our communities develop into "self-reproducing populations that share distinguishing physical and cultural features that set the demographic boundaries of a life-world" (Outlaw 1996, 17). On his view, when such a population is defined to a significant degree by physiological factors, it is a race; when it is thus defined to a lesser degree, it is an ethnicity (Outlaw 1996, 136). Races are, then, enduring, if not inevitable, facts of social life, and because they promote cooperation, security, and so survival of a community's life-world, they are valuable.

Although I am sympathetic to Outlaw's interest in the embodiment of social norms and the development of an aesthetic of "color" (see, for example, Haslanger 2004), this narrative is worrisome. There are two possible connections with biology in Outlaw's account: on the one hand, individual choices for "same-color" mates are being cast as natural, although shaped by cultural cues; and on the other hand, the model of natural selection is being applied to the society: the societies that are "color"-conscious in their choices are more "fit" than others, and so survive.

To begin, employing an evolutionary model and the notion of "fitness" to societies is highly problematic. But even setting that aside, there are other serious concerns. Considering the course of human history, societies have not uniformly granted individuals the option of "choosing" their mates; in particular, fathers or tribal elders commonly control the reproductive options for women and girls. Moreover, women have been used in the context of gift-exchange between "foreign," even hostile, groups as a means of increasing the chance of friendly relations (Rubin 1975), not to mention as a way of expanding the gene pool. So Outlaw's suggestion that individuals naturally choose mates who are marked as being the same "color" is not well-supported; the alleged "choice" of mates is plausibly accounted for by a broad range of social facts rather than any biological predisposition on the part of individuals. Moreover, given the potential value of out-group mating (as evidenced by the practices of gift-exchange), more is needed to support the claim that in-group mating is the most successful strategy.

A further concern is whether, even if the choice of a same-"color" mate is common, and even if to some extent "natural," this is good. Outlaw suggests that it is valuable because it promotes the survival of the "life-world." But of course, not all "life-worlds" should be preserved, even within a "liberal democratic society." For example, Outlaw maintains that the "valorization of descent" contributes to the uniformity of "color" in a population and serves as a means of promoting cooperation between members of the population. Setting aside the issue of cooperation, valorizing descent surely results in an unjust hierarchy of family forms. The history of adoption provides a rather gruesome tale of its effects: orphaned and "illegitimate" children are systematically abandoned; women who give birth to "illegitimate" children are cast out, even murdered, if discovered; and parentless and adopted children through history have been mistreated, denied legal protections, and severely stigmatized. Families that are formed through (either formal or informal) adoption are very often not regarded as "real" with the implication (among many others) that individuals and couples who want children nevertheless remain childless rather than face the stigma of adoption. This suggests that the "valorization of descent" should be rejected in a "liberal democratic society," not preserved.

In summary, it appears that "color" may in some hypothetical contexts and by accident be morally significant. But this is not sufficient reason to treat race like gender as a response to a physical fact that even a just society must address. Although both "color" and sex as we know them are socially significant, "color" need not, and in most cases, should not be. However, thus far I've supposed that if "color" does impose constraints on what can be just, it would be due to the biological basis of "color." Are there other aspects of "color" that might legitimately constrain us?

4. "Color" and Culture

It is hard to imagine any function essential to a society that could only be served by distinguishing people along the lines of "color," so we don't yet have an argument for treating "race" as a genus of social categories that includes both hierarchical and non-hierarchal forms, analogous to the argument offered for gender. But an engaged feminist antiracism should ask not only what sorts of idealized societies there might be, but what a just society would look like that could plausibly evolve as a successor to ours. One might argue, for example, that racial groups, although originating as offshoots of racist practices and policies, develop cultural forms and self-understandings that are valuable. It might seem, more specifically, that a society without race couldn't plausibly evolve from ours without cutting itself off from its own history and doing damage to meaningful communities. Linda Alcoff argues in her paper "Mestizo Identity":

within the context of racially based and organized systems of oppression, racial identity will continue to be a salient internal and external component of identity. Systems of oppression, segregated communities, and practices of discrimination create a collective experience and a shared history for a racialized grouping. It is that shared experience and history, more than any physiological or morphological features, that cements the community and creates connections with others along racial lines. And that history cannot be deconstructed by new scientific accounts that dispute the characterization of race as a natural kind. Accounts of race as a social and historical identity, though this brings in elements that are temporally contingent and mutable, will probably prove to have more persistence than accounts of race that tie it to biology. Ironically history will probably have more permanence than biology. (Alcoff 1995, 272)

Here Alcoff suggests that race might be best understood as "a social and historical identity," and that race is more meaningfully centered on "shared experience and history" than on body type.

The idea of grounding racial unity in shared experience and history is especially significant as we move away from the "Black-White binary" and think more carefully about the racialization of Latina/os and Asians. For example, Latinas/os do not fit many of the assumptions typically made about races. Latin America is highly diverse in the "color" of its populations and the cultures it includes:

By U.S. categories, there are black, brown, white, Asian and Native American Latinas/os. There are many Latinas/os from the southern cone whose families are of recent European origin, a large number of Latinas/os from the western coastal areas whose families came from Asia, and of course a large number of Latinas/os whose lineage is entirely indigenous to the Americas or entirely African. (Alcoff 2000b, 31)

Moreover, the cultures of Cuba, Brazil, Panama, Mexico, Chile, Columbia, and Costa Rica (to name a few) vary widely in their dominant (and regional) languages, cuisine, holidays, political structures, and virtually every other dimension of culture. Comparable diversity can be found in Asia. (And it should not be forgotten that there is tremendous cultural diversity in all of major groups racialized in the U.S. The cultures of sub-Saharan Africa and the African Diaspora are by no means homogeneous.) This is, of course, compatible with Latinas/os and Asians being racialized in the U.S.

If not appearance or culture, what unifies Latina/os and Asians other than being racialized? Although racial identity has been imposed by systems of oppression, there are and have been movements within the groups to construct positive identities (pan-Latina/o, pan-Asian) to counter stigmatized identities and fight against the injustices inherent in the process of racialization.[9] Do these count as "racial" identities? Should we reconceive the notion of racial group in their terms? Should a feminist antiracism support the formation of racial identities and racial groups in this sense?

History, Experience, and Self-interpretation

One goal of this inquiry is to provide an account of race and racial identity that will be useful in the quest for social justice. As Alcoff suggests, this will be to a significant extent a constructive project requiring us to look back to history and also forward towards a better future. In developing accounts of race and gender, we should not ignore the fact that the oppressed are not passive victims, but are agents engaged in the construction of their own meanings. Racial affiliation — as it has been constructed *from within* a racialized group — is often not only a source of pride and value, but provides resources to combat racial oppression. So if we are thinking about the possible future of race, one option is to build on these positive racial reconstructions, rather than the damaging structures of oppression.

For example, amongst those working on reconstructions of "Blackness," one theme emphasized is *shared history* as opposed to "color" and cultural *inter-connections* as opposed to common culture (Gilroy 1993; Gooding-Williams 1998). This option is also considered by those working on Latina/o and Asian identity (Gracia 2000; Alcoff

2000; LeEspiritu 1992), though as suggested above, the prospects of finding a plausible way to characterize the historical and cultural connections are diminished as the group becomes more diverse. Moreover, insofar as a reconstruction of race in terms of history and experience will have to provide an interpretation of that history and experience, and so select what aspects to highlight, we re-encounter the problem of normativity.

For example, in determining what history and experiences should count as definitive of Blackness, or of Asianness, there is a danger that the narrative would privilege men, heterosexuals, the economically advantaged, the educated, and so on. Even if we insist that a reconstructed race would be defined by its members through some highly democratic process (Gooding-Williams, 1988), democracy doesn't guarantee equitable inclusion. Although such a project may be workable, we should be alert to the challenge of simultaneously accommodating the broad diversity of people who count as members of a race and the selectivity involved in constructing a basis for group membership. Because the effects of such efforts have substantial ramifications in law and politics, there is reason to be extremely cautious.

I agree with Alcoff that there are a variety of groups unified by social/historical background and/or culture and that these are valuable and are likely to persist. If we build on the positive reconstructions of race to envision the future of race, then we might pursue Alcoff's suggestion that the future of race lies in panethnicities, or what she calls (following David Goldberg) *ethnoraces*, that are unified around the history of being racialized as a group and the positive cultural forms that have evolved in response.

Ethnorace

Alcoff introduces the notion of ethnorace because so much of social and historical reality is poorly captured using the notions of either race or ethnicity. But many of those who grant that race is a problematic category have embraced ethnic classification in its place. What is the argument against viewing races as ethnicities?

Ethnicities, as Alcoff is using the term, concern "cultural practices, customs, language, sometimes religion, and so on" (Alcoff 2000, 25). Some ethnicities, in this sense, are sub-groups of existing races (all of the standard races include various ethnic groups) and some ethnicities cross racial lines. She recommends that we think of currently racialized groups (perhaps especially groups such as "Latina/os") in terms of ethnoraces rather than ethnicities for three main reasons:

(1) Culture, especially the cultures of racialized groups, tends to be naturalized and to entail membership in a race. For example, as soon as one reveals information about one's *culture* of origin, one is immediately racialized. If one has grown up in Mexico and is culturally Mexican, then regardless of how one physically appears, one is assumed to be Latina/o (Alcoff 2000, 37-8).
(2) The racial coding of the body trumps cultural identification (Alcolff 2000, 38). Because current social perception is conditioned to interpret "color" as culturally meaningful, classifications of individuals into ethnic groups will continue to rely on the physical markers of race.
(3) Positive group solidarity amongst currently racialized groups in the U.S. is likely to provoke anxiety and resistance because the long history of their subordination is a threat to the dominant American self-image. Insofar as the U.S. identifies with and takes pride in its commitment to equality and freedom for all, the affirmation of Otherness is a reminder of a shameful history that many long to erase (Alcoff 2000, 39). Because racialization has been rhetorically crucial to the legitimizing narratives of white supremacy, deracialization will be resisted.

So because race and racialization are intimately bound up with culture and so ethnicity, Alcoff recommends *ethnorace*:

Unlike race, ethnorace does not imply a common descent, which is precisely what tends to embroil race in notions of biological determinism and natural and heritable characteristics. Ethnorace might have the advantage of bringing into play the elements of both human agency and subjectivity involved in ethnicity — that is, an identity that is the product of self-creation — at the same time that it acknowledges the uncontrolled racializing aspects associated with the visible body. (Alcoff 2000, 42)

Although intriguing and suggestive, I'm not sure I have a firm grasp on the notion. My best guess is that an ethnorace is a group of people who have been "marked" as of the same race (this is the uncontrolled racializing aspect), who share some common cultural elements, and who are collectively involved in the constitution of their shared identity. Ethnorace differs from race, as I've defined race, in including the conditions of common culture and agency in the construction of identity. Races, as I've characterized them, do not require any commonality in culture, commitment, or identity. They only require that members are similarly positioned structurally in society, whether they want to be or not, whether they even notice this or not. Races are more ascribed than embraced. Plausibly Alcoff's ethnoraces count as a subset of races in my sense: if races are groups whose "color" affects their social position, ethnoraces are those among them who have developed a common culture and a commitment to shared identity. Some, but not all, races are ethnoraces.

Alcoff offers the notion of ethnorace not as a vision of the groups that should be part of a utopian future, but as a reconstruction of the notion of race that applies to (some of) us now and an exploration of what the next step in the elimination of race might look like. I would assume that in a context where racialization is long past, ethnorace could be replaced by ethnicity. In effect, not only the condition of common descent, but also the practice of "color" marking would disappear.

Are ethnoraces a valuable interim category? This is controversial. I take it that Alcoff (and others) encourage the formation of ethnoraces because they highlight and encourage agency in group formation and acknowledge some degree of common subjectivity amongst those who are similarly racialized. Others, however, will urge us to resist racism by rejecting membership in "color"-

defined groups, and resisting identities formed around "color." I prefer not to take a stand on this normative issue. In any case, we have reason to be theoretically attentive to the formation of such groups as we trace the workings of racializing practices and active resistance to them.

However, I believe that we also need to maintain a conception of *race* or *racialized group* that is not as concerned with culture or agency. For example, internationally adopted children of color who are brought up in the U.S. are ethnically American; if they are adopted transracially, they often are not involved in the self-creation of an ethnic identity associated with their birth country or even a panethnic identity. And yet they are raced; they don't become the race or ethnorace of their adoptive parents (see also Corlett 2000, 227). At least we need some way of including such adoptees within the racialized group they are taken to belong to in order to understand some of the injustices they face in the U.S.

Moreover, although it is clear that ethnicity is racialized, race is also "ethnicized" in problematic ways. Alcoff herself points out that because she is Latina, she is assumed to enjoy spicy food, even though in Panama (her ancestral home) the food is mild (Alcoff 2000, 33). Racial stereotypes that allegedly capture "cultural" differences abound (Blacks enjoy basketball, Asians value education). In the context of adoption, a link between race and culture has been a site of controversy for decades. In the 1950s, internationally adopted children were forced to assimilate and were allowed to have little, if anything, to do with the culture of their birth country. By the early 1970s, transracial adoption (both domestic and international) was challenged for, among other things, denying a child "her" culture. By the 1990s when international adoption boomed and domestic transracial adoption began to significantly increase, the pressure on adoptive parents to become educated in the child's culture and to provide "cultural competence" in this culture to the child, remained very strong (in some cases being written into policies determining who could adopt). There is a way of seeing this as an enforcement of ethnorace (see also Allen 1993). Such practices are, I believe, at odds with Alcoff's recommendations. However, they alert us both to concerns about the normative import of the category of ethnorace and to the need for a category that allows us to keep race and ethnicity apart.

V. Conclusion

I recommend that we opt for the account of race that I've proposed as useful for doing the work of identifying those affected by racialization and remedying its harms. I further propose that we employ the notions of culture, ethnicity, panethnicity, and ethnorace for understanding the more constructive efforts to form new identities that do justice to our histories and our experiences. This proposal leaves open the possibility that currently racialized groups will either form more encompassing identities describable in terms of shared history and experience (a pan-Latina/o identity) or will retain a variety of more local identities (Puerto-Rican, Brazilian, Cuban-American, Chicana/o).

I have argued (though the argument is far from conclusive) that in the long run, social justice does not require the formation or maintenance of groups defined by "color," though "color"-based groups may be valuable as part of an interim strategy. Race, as I've proposed we understand it, is something to be rid of. Ethnicity or ethnorace, if understood as involving both "color" and culture, may be helpful in the short term, but I believe that an ongoing social investment in "color" is harmful. In short, "after the revolution" we should anticipate that there will be no men and women, but there will be males and females (and other sexes to accommodate, among others, intersexed people), and these sexual differences will have distinct but egalitarian implications. And although, we should hope, people will come in the broad variety of skin tones, shapes, and appearances they do now and will organize themselves around a rich array of cultural practices, there will be no races. Although from the point of view of justice, it would be irresponsible not to accord some social meaning to the differences between our bodies, it would also be irresponsible not to overturn the meanings we now assume to be natural and right.

Author's Note

A longer version of this paper can be found in *Philosophic Exchange* 34 (2004). The material in this first background section is developed more fully in Haslanger (2000).

NOTES

1. The everyday distinction between males and females leaves out the intersexed population. Under conditions of justice it may be appropriate to introduce terms for different or additional sexes. Anne Fausto-Sterling has suggested "merms," "ferms," and "herms" (Fausto-Sterling 1993). However the intersex movement does not endorse this vocabulary. Thanks to Lori Gruen for bringing to my attention the rejection of Fausto-Sterling's terminology. For more information, see <http://www.intersexinitiative.org/index.html>.

2. Some have argued that there are as many as ten indicators of sex, not all of which are anatomical. However, as I will be using the term, sex distinctions are anatomical.

3. This is a simplified version of the account I offer in Haslanger (2000).

4. "iff$_{df}$" is short for "if and only if, by definition." In joining two statements using "iff" one is claiming that the statement on the left of the "iff" is true in all and only those cases in which the statement on the right of the "iff" is true. By adding the phrase (or abbreviation for) "by definition" one is further maintaining that the result is a good definition of the term or terms italicized in the statement to the left of the "iff."

5. On this I am deeply indebted to Stevens (1999, Ch. 4), and Omi and Winant (1994, esp. 53-61). I develop this definition more fully in Haslanger (2000).

6. I recommend that we view membership in a racial/ethnic group in terms of how one is viewed and treated *regularly and for the most part in the context in question*; one can also distinguish *being* a member of a given race from *functioning as* one by considering the degree of one's entrenchment in the racialized social position (not on the basis of biology or ancestry). The same holds true for gender.

7. Would gender be eliminable if reproductive technology advanced so far that pregnancy and childbirth were no longer necessary to produce children? Only when the process for egg retrieval becomes as simple and pleasurable as the process for sperm retrieval. Would it be eliminable if males, females, and other sexes were equally good candidates for pregnancy and childbirth? It depends on what biological differences remain.

8. Note that there are several different questions at issue. Considering a just future when the effects of contemporary racialization have been remedied: (1) Must the state, in its laws and policies, be "color-blind" or is attention to "color" differences required for justice? (2) Must we eliminate "color" categories in our social practices and our self-understandings in order to achieve justice? (3) Is there something socially valuable in "color" classification, and would its elimination destroy something valuable? (4) Even if not required for justice, would the elimination of "color" as a way of organizing ourselves socially be better overall? In what follows I gloss over the important differences between these questions.

9. For example, Simón Bolívar, José Martí, and Che Guevara have promoted a pan-Latina/o solidarity (Alcoff 2000b, 27). There have also been moves, especially amongst feminists of color, to embrace mixed identity (Anzaldúa 1987, Zack 1995).

REFERENCES

Alcoff, Linda M. 1995. "Mestizo Identity." In *American Mixed Race: The Culture of Microdiversity*, edited by N. Zack. Lanham, MD: Rowman & Littlefield.

— . 2000a. "Habits of Hostility: On Seeing Race." *Philosophy Today*, v. 44 (Supp.): 30-40.

— . 2000b. "Is Latina/o Identity a Racial Identity?" In *Hispanics/Latinos in the United States: Ethnicity, Race, and Rights*, edited by Jorge J.E. Gracia and Pablo De Greiff. (New York, NY: Routledge).

Allen, A. 1993. "Does a Child Have A Right To A Certain Identity?" *Rechtstheorie*, v. 15, Supplement 15: 109-19.

Andreasen, R.O. 1998. "A New Perspective on the Race Debate." *British Journal of the Philosophy of Science*, v. 49, no. 2: 199-225.

— . 2000. "Race: Biological Reality or Social Construct?" *Philosophy of Social Science*, v. 67 (Proceedings): S653-S666.

Anzaldúa, Gloria. 1987. *Borderlands/La Frontera: The New Mestiza*. San Francisco, CA: Aunt Lute Books.

Appiah, Kwame Anthony. 1992. "Illusions of Race." In *In My Father's House: Africa in the Philosophy of Culture*. New York, NY: Oxford University Press.

— . 1996. "Race, Culture, Identity: Misunderstood Connections." In *Color Conscious: The Political Morality of Race,* edited by K.A. Appiah and A. Gutmann. Princeton, NJ: Princeton University Press.

Beauvoir, Simone de. 1989/1949. *The Second Sex*, translated by H.M. Parshley. New York, NY: Vintage Books.

Butler, Judith. 1990. *Gender Trouble*. New York, NY: Routledge.

Corlett, J. Angelo. 2000. "Latino Identity and Affirmative Action." In *Hispanic/Latino Identity in the United States: Ethnicity, Race, and Rights*, edited by J.J.E. Gracia. New York, NY: Routledge.

Davis, F. James. 1991. *Who is Black? One Nation's Definition*. University Park, PA: Pennsylvania State University Press.

Espiritu, Yen Le. 1992. *Asian American Panethnicity*. Philadelphia, PA: Temple University Press.

Fausto-Sterling, Anne. 1993. "The Five Sexes: Why Male and Female Are Not Enough." *The Sciences*, v. 33, no. 2: 20-24.

Fields, Barbara. 1982. "Ideology and Race in American History." In *Region, Race and Reconstruction: Essays in Honor of C. Vann Woodward*, edited by J.M. Kousser and J.M. McPherson. Oxford: Oxford University Press.

Frye, Marilyn. 1996. "The Necessity of Differences: Constructing a Positive Category of Woman." *Signs*, v. 21, no. 4: 991-1010.

Gilroy, Paul. 1993. *The Black Atlantic: Modernity and Double Consciousness*. Cambridge, MA: Harvard University Press.

Gooding-Williams, Robert. 1988. "Race, Multiculturalism and Democracy." *Constellations*, v. 5, no. 1: 18-41.

Gracia, Jorge J.E. 2000. *Hispanic/Latino Identity*. Oxford: Blackwell Publishers.

Haslanger, Sally. 2000. "Gender and Race: (What) Are They? (What) Do We Want Them To Be?" *Noûs*, v. 34, no. 1: 31-55.

— . 2003. "Social Construction: The 'Debunking' Project." In *Socializing Metaphysics*, edited by Frederick F. Schmitt. Lanham, MD: Rowman & Littlefield.

— . 2004. "You Mixed? Racial Identity without Racial Biology." In *Adoption Matters*, edited by Sally Haslanger and Charlotte Witt. Ithaca, NY: Cornell University Press.

Kitcher, Philip. 1999. "Race, Ethnicity, Biology, Culture." In *Racism,* edited by L. Harris. Amherst, NY: Humanity Books.

Lewontin, Richard C. 1982. *Human Diversity*. New York, NY: Scientific American Press.

Lopez, Ian F. Haney. 1996. *White By Law: The Legal Construction of Race*. New York, NY: New York University Press.

Mills, Charles. 1997. *The Racial Contract*. Ithaca, NY: Cornell University Press.

Omi, Michael, and Howard Winant. 1994. *Racial Formation in the United States*. New York, NY: Routledge.

Outlaw, Lucius T., Jr. 1996. *On Race and Philosophy*. New York, NY: Routledge.

Root, Michael. 2000. "How We Divide the World." *Philosophy of Social Science*, v. 67 (Proceedings): 628-39.

— . 2001. "The Problem of Race in Medicine." *Philosophy of the Social Sciences*, v. 31, no. 1: 20-39.

Rubin, Gayle. 1975. "The Traffic in Women: Notes on the 'Political Economy' of Sex." In *Toward an Anthropology of Women*, edited by R.R. Reiter. New York, NY: Monthly Review Press.

Stevens, Jacqueline. 1999. *Reproducing the State*. Princeton, NJ: Princeton University Press.

Zack, Naomi. ed. 1995. *American Mixed Race*. Lanham, MD: Rowman & Littlefield.

— . 2002. *Philosophy of Science and Race*. New York, NY: Routledge.

WHITE WOMAN FEMINIST

Marilyn Frye

Marilyn Frye teaches philosophy at Michigan State University. She is the author of The Politics of Reality: Essays in Feminist Theory *(1983) and* Willful Virgin: Essays in Feminism, 1976-1992 *(1992).*

Frye describes her own struggles to understand racism as a way of conceptualizing why being white makes combating racism confounding and difficult. She begins by defending the notion that race is socially constructed and argues that like "masculine" and "masculinity," "whitely" and "whiteliness" are ways of being in the world that are learned and deeply ingrained. Frye articulates an account of whiteliness and its connections to class and gender that is designed to elucidate features of racism that make it difficult to eradicate. She calls for the unlearning of whiteliness as a way of becoming less well assimilated members of the racial group called "white."

This essay is the latest version of something I have been (re-) writing ever since my essay "On Being White" was published in *The Politics of Reality*. In a way, this *is* that first essay, emerging after several metamorphoses.

"On Being White" grew out of experiences I had in my home lesbian community in which I was discovering some of what it means for a woman, a feminist, to be white. These were very frustrating experiences: they played out and revealed the ways in which the fact that I am white gave unbidden and unwanted meanings to my thought and my actions and poisoned them all with privilege.

An intermediate version of this work, delivered at various colleges and universities around 1984-86, began with the following account of my attempts to come to grips with the fact of being white in a white-supremacist racist state, and with some of the criticism my first effort had drawn.[1]

Many white feminists, myself included, have tried to identify and change the attitudes and behaviors that blocked our friendly and effective comradeship with women of color and limited our ability to act against institutional racism. I assumed at first that these revisions would begin with analysis and decision: I had to understand the problems and then do whatever would effect the changes dictated by this understanding. But as I entered this work, I almost immediately learned that my competence to do it was questionable.

The idea was put to me by several women of color (and was stated in writings by women of color) that a white woman is not in a good position to analyze institutional or personal racism and a white woman's decisions about what to do about racism cannot be authentic. About consciousness-raising groups for white women, Sharon Keller said to me in a letter,

> I think that there are things which white women working together can accomplish but I do not think that white women are in the best positions usually to know what those things are or when it is the right time to do them. It would go a long way ... for white women to take seriously their [relative] helplessness in the matter.

White women's analysis of their own racism has also often been heard by women of color as "mere psychologizing." To be rid of racism, a white woman may indeed have to do some introspecting, remembering, and verbalizing feelings, but the self-knowledge that she might achieve by this work would necessarily produce profound change, and there are many reasons why many white women may not want to change. White women's efforts to gain self-knowledge are easily undermined by the desire not to live out the consequences of getting it; their/our projects of consciousness raising and self-analysis are very susceptible to the slide from "working on yourself" to "playing with yourself." Apparently the white women herself is ill-situated for telling which is which.

All of my ways of knowing seemed to have failed me — my perception, my common sense, my goodwill, my anger, honor, and affection, my intelligence and insight. Just as walking requires something fairly sturdy and firm underfoot, so being an actor in the world requires a foundation of ordinary moral and intellectual confidence. Without that, we don't know how to be or how to act; we become strangely stupid; the commitment against racism becomes itself immobilizing. Even obvious and easy acts either do not occur to us or threaten to be racist by presumptuous assumptions or misjudged timing, wording, or circumstances. Simple things like courtesy or giving money, attending a trial, working on a project initiated by women of color, or dissenting from racist views expressed in white company become fraught with possibilities of error and offense. If you want to do good, and you don't know good from bad, you can't move.[2] Thus stranded, we also learned that it was exploitive and oppressive to ask for the help of women of color in extricating ourselves from this ignorance, confusion, incompetence, and moral failure. Our racism is our problem, not theirs.[3]

Some white women report that the great enemy of their efforts to combat their own racism is their feelings of guilt. That is not my own experience, or that is not my word for it. The great enemies in my heart have been the despair and the resentment that come with being required (by others and by my own integrity) to repair something apparently irreparable, to take responsibility for something apparently beyond my powers to effect. Both confounded and angry, my own temptation is to collapse — to admit defeat and retire from the field.

What counteracts that temptation, for me, seems to be little more than willfulness and lust: I *will* not be broken, and my appetite for woman's touch is not, thank goodness, thoroughly civilized to the established categories. But if I cannot give up and I cannot act, what do Will and Lust recommend? The obvious way out of the relentless logic of my situation is to cease being white.

The Contingency of Racedness

I was brought up with a concept of race according to which you cannot stop being the race you are: your race is an irreversible physical, indeed, ontological fact about you. But when the criteria for membership in a race came up as an issue among white people I knew, considerations of skin color and biological lineage were not definitive or decisive, or rather, they were so only when white people decided they should be, and were not when white people wanted them not to be.[4] As I argued in "On Being White,"[5] white people actively legislate matters of race membership, and if asserting their right to do so requires making decisions that override physical criteria, they ignore physical criteria (without, of course, ever abandoning the ideological strategy of insisting that the categories are given in nature). This sort of behavior clearly demonstrates that people construct race actively, and that people who think they are unquestionably white generally think the criteria of what it is to be of this race or that are theirs to manipulate.[6]

Being white is not a biological condition. It is being a member of a certain social/political category, a category that is persistently maintained by those people who are, in their own and each other's perception, unquestionably in it. It is like being a member of a political party or a club or a fraternity — or being a Methodist or a Mormon. If one is white, one is a member of a continuously and politically constituted group that holds itself together by rituals of unity and exclusion, that develops in its members certain styles and attitudes useful in the exploitation of others, that demands and rewards fraternal loyalty, that defines itself as the paradigm of humanity, and that rationalizes (and naturalizes) its existence and its practices of exclusion, colonization, slavery, and genocide (when it bothers to) in terms of a mythology of blood and skin. If you were born to people who are members of that club, you are socialized and inducted into that club. Your membership in it is, in a way or to a degree, compulsory — nobody gave you any choice in the matter — but it is contingent and, in the Aristotelian sense, accidental. If you don't like being a member of that club, you might think of resigning your membership or of figuring out how to get yourself kicked out of the club, how to get yourself excommunicated.

But this strategy of "separation" is vulnerable to a variety of criticisms. A white woman cannot cease having the history she has by some sort of divorce ritual. Furthermore, the renunciation of whiteness may be an act of self-loathing rather than an act of liberation.[7] And disassociation from the race-group one was born into might seem to be an option for white folks, but it seems either not possible or not politically desirable to most members of the other groups from which whites set themselves off.[8] This criticism suggests that my thinking of disassociating from membership in the white fraternity is just another exercise (hence, another reinforcement) of that white privilege that I was finding so onerous and attempting to escape. All these criticisms sound right (and I will circle back to them at the end of the essay), but there is something very wrong here. This closure has the distinctive finality of a trap.

In academic circles where I now circulate, it has become a commonplace that race is a "social construction" and not a naturally given and naturally maintained grouping of human individuals with naturally determined sets of traits. And the recognition of race as nonnatural is presumed, in those circles, to be liberatory. Pursuing the idea of disassociating from the race category in which I am placed and from the perquisites attached to it is a way of pursuing the question of what freedom can be made of this, and for whom. But it seems to me that race (together with racism and race privilege) is *constructed as* something inescapable. And it makes sense that it would be, since such a construction would best serve those served by race and racism. *Of course* race and racism are impossible to escape; of course a white person is always in a

sticky web of privilege that permits only acts that reinforce ("reinscribe") racism. This just means that some exit must be forced. That will require conceptual creativity, and perhaps conceptual violence.

The "being white" that has presented itself to me as a burden and an insuperable block to my growth out of racism is not essentially about the color of my skin or any other inherited bodily trait, even though doctrines of color are bound up with this status in some ways. The problem, then, is to find a way to think clearly about some kind of whiteness that is *not essentially* tied to color and yet has some significant relation to color. The distinction feminists have made between maleness and masculinity provides a clue and an analogy. Maleness we have construed as something a human animal can be born with; masculinity we have construed as something a human animal can be trained to — and it is an empirical fact that most male human animals are trained to it in one or another of its cultural varieties.[9] Masculinity is not a blossoming consequence of genetic constitution, as lush growths of facial hair seem to be in the males of many human groups. But the masculinity of an adult male is far from superficial or incidental, and we know it is not something an individual could shuck off like a coat or snap out of like an actor stepping out of his character. The masculinity of an adult male human in any particular culture is also profoundly connected with the local perceptions and conceptions of maleness (as "biological"), its causes and its consequences. So it may be with being white, but we need some revision of our vocabulary to say it rightly. We need a term in the realm of race and racism whose grammar is analogous to the grammar of the term "masculinity." I am tempted to recommend the neologism "albosity" for this honor, but I am afraid it is too strange to catch on. So I will introduce "whitely" and "whiteliness" as terms whose grammar is analogous to that of "masculine" and "masculinity." Being white-skinned (like being male) is a matter of physical traits presumed to be physically determined; being whitely (like being masculine) I conceive as a deeply ingrained way of being in the world. Following the analogy with masculinity, I assume that the connection between whiteliness and light-colored skin is a *contingent* connection: whiteliness can be manifested by persons who are *not* "white"; it can be absent in persons who *are*.

In the next section, I talk about whiteliness in a free and speculative way, exploring what it may be. This work is raw preliminary sketching; it moves against no such background of research and attentive observation as there is to guide accounts of masculinity. There is of course a large literature on racism, but I think that what I am after here is not one and the same thing as racism, either institutional or personal. Whiteliness is connected to institutional racism (as this discussion will show) by the fact that individuals with this sort of character are well suited to the social roles of agents of institutional racism, but it is a character of persons, not of institutions. Whiteliness is also related to individual or personal racism, but I think it is not one and the same thing as racism, at least in the sense where "racism" means bigotry/hate/ignorance/indifference. As I understand masculinity, it is not the same thing as misogyny; similarly, whiteliness is not the same thing as race hatred. One can be whitely even if one's beliefs and feelings are relatively well informed, humane, and goodwilled. So I approach whiteliness freshly, as itself, as something which is both familiar and unknown.

Whiteliness

To begin to get a picture of what whiteliness is, we need to invoke a certain candid and thoughtful reflection on the part of white people, who of course in some ways know themselves best; we also need to consider how people of color perceive white people, since in some ways they know white people best. For purposes of this preliminary exploration, I draw on material from three books for documentation of how white people are, as presented in the experience of people of color. The three are *This Bridge Called My Back*,[10] which is a collection or writings by radical women of color, *Feminist Theory: From Margin to Center*,[11] by black theorist bell hooks, and *Drylongso*,[12] which is a collection of narratives of members of what its editor calls the "core black community."[13] For

white voices, I draw on my own and those I have heard as a participant/observer of white culture, and on Minnie Bruce Pratt.

Minnie Bruce Pratt, a feminist and a white southerner, has spelled out some of what I call the whitely way of dealing with issues of morality and change.[14] She said she had been taught to be a *judge* — a judge of responsibility and of punishment, according to an ethical system that countenances no rival; she had been taught to be a *preacher* — to point out wrongs and tell others what to do; she had been taught to be a *martyr* — to take all responsibility and all glory; and she had been taught to be a *peacemaker* — because she could see all sides and see how it all ought to be. I too was taught something like this, growing up in a small town south of the Mason-Dixon line, in a self-consciously Christian and white family. I learned that I, and "we," knew right from wrong and had the responsibility to see to it that right was done, that there were others who did not know right from wrong and should be advised, instructed, helped, and directed by us. I was taught that *because* one knows what is right, it is morally appropriate to have and exercise what I now call race privilege and class privilege. Not "might is right," but "right is might," as Carolyn Shafer puts the point.[15] In any matter in which we did not know what is right, through youth or inexpertise of some sort, we would await the judgment or instruction of another (white) person who did.

Drylongso: White people are bolder because they think they are supposed to know everything anyhow. (97)

White men look up to their leaders more than we do and they are not much good without their leaders. (99)

White people don't really know how they feel about anything until they consult their leaders or a book or other things outside themselves. (99)

White people are not supposed to be stupid, so they tend to think they are intelligent, no matter how stupidly they are behaving. (96)

Margin: The possibility [they] were not the best spokespeople for all women made [them] fear for [their] self-worth. (13)

Whitely people generally consider themselves to be benevolent and good willed, fair, honest, and ethical. The judge, preacher, peace-maker, martyr, socialist, professional, moral majority, liberal, radical, conservative, working men and women — nobody admits to being prejudiced, everybody has earned every cent they ever had, doesn't take sides, doesn't hate anybody, and always votes for the person they think best qualified for the job, regardless of the candidate's race, sex, religion, or national origin, maybe even regardless of their sexual preferences. The professional version of this person is always profoundly insulted by the suggestion that s/he might have permitted some personal feeling about a client to affect the quality of services rendered. S/he believes with perfect confidence that s/he is not prejudiced, not a bigot, not spiteful, jealous, or rude, does not engage in favoritism or discrimination. When there is a serious and legitimate challenge, a negotiator has to find a resolution that enables the professional person to save face, to avoid simply agreeing that s/he made an unfair or unjust judgment, discriminated against someone, or otherwise behaved badly. Whitely people have a staggering faith in their own rightness and goodness, and that of other whitely people. We are not crooks.

Drylongso: Every reasonable black person thinks that most white people do not mean him well. (7)

They figure, if nobody blows the whistle, then Nothing wrong has gone down. (21)

White people are very interested in seeming to be of service. ... (4)

Whitefolks *can't* do right, even if there was one who wanted to. ... They are so damn greedy and cheap that it even hurts them to *try* to do right. (59)

Bridge: A child is trick-or-treating with her friends. At one house the woman, after realizing the child was an Indian, "quite crudely told me so, refusing to give me treats my friends had received." (47)

Drylongso: I used to be a waitress, and I can still remember how white people would leave a tip and then someone at the table, generally some white woman, would take some of the money. (8)

Bridge: The lies, pretensions, the snobbery and cliquishness. (69)

We experience white feminists and their organizations as elitist crudely insensitive, and condescending. (86)

White people are so rarely loyal. (59)

Whitely people do have a sense of right and wrong, and are ethical. Their ethics in great part an ethics of forms, procedures, and due process. As Minnie Bruce Pratt said, their morality is a matter of "ought to," not "want to" or "passionately desire to." And the "oughts" tend to factor out into propriety or good manners and abiding by the rules. Change cannot be initiated unless the moves are made in appropriate ways. The rules are often-rehearsed. I have participated in whitely women's affirming to each other that some uncomfortable disruption caused by someone objecting to some injustice or offense could have been avoided: had she brought "her" problem forth in the correct way, it could have been correctly processed. We say:

She should have brought it up in the business meeting.

She should have just taken the other woman aside and explained that the remark had offended her.

She should not have personally attacked me; she should have just told me that my behavior made her uncomfortable, and I would have stopped doing it.

She should take this through the grievance procedure.

By believing in rules, by being arbiters of rules, by understanding agency in terms of the applications of principles to particular situations, whitely people think they preserve their detachment from prejudice, bias, meanness, and so on. Whitely people tend to believe that one preserves one's goodness by being principled, by acting according to rules instead of according to feeling.

Drylongso: We think white people are the most unprincipled folks in the world. ...(8)

White people are some writing folks! They will write! They write everything. Now they do that because they don't trust each other. Also, they are the kind of people who think that you can think about everything, about whether you are going to do, before you do that thing. Now, that's bad for them because you can't do that without wings. ... All you can do is do what you know has got to be done as right as you know how to do that thing. White people don't seem to know that. (88)

... he keeps changing the rules. ... Now, Chahlie will rule you to death. (16)

Authority seems to be central to whiteliness, as you might expect from a people who are raised to run things, or to aspire to that: belief in one's authority in matters practical, moral, and intellectual exists in tension with the insecurity and hypocrisy that are essentially connected with the pretense of infallibility. This pretentiousness makes a whitely person simultaneously rude, condescending, overbearing, and patronizing on the one hand, and on the other, weak, helpless, insecure, and seeking validation of their goodness.

Drylongso: White people have got to bluff it out as rulers ... [they] are always unsure of themselves. (99)

No matter what Chahlie do, he want his mama to pat him on the head and tell him how cute he is. (19)

[I]n a very real sense white men never grow up. (100)

Hard on the outside, soft on the inside. (99)

Bridge: Socially ... juvenile and tasteless. (99)

No responsibility to others. (70)

The dogmatic belief in whitely authority and rightness is also at odds with any commitment to truth.

Drylongso: They won't tell each other the truth, and the lies they tell each other sound better to them than the truth from our mouths. (29)

As long as they can make someone say rough is smooth, they are happy. ... Like I told you, white folks don't care about what the truth is. ... It's like when you lie but so much, you don't know what the truth is. (21)

You simply cannot be honest with white people. (45)

Bridge: White feminists have a serious problem with truth and "accountability." (85)

And finally, whitely people make it clear to people of other races that the last thing those people are supposed to do is to challenge whitely people's authority.

Bridge: [W]e are expected [by white women] to move, charm or entertain, but not to educate in ways that are threatening to our audiences. (71)

Margin: Though they expected us to provide first hand accounts of black experience, they felt it was their role to decide if these experiences were authentic. (11)

Often in situations where white feminists aggressively attacked individual black women, they saw themselves as the ones who were under attack, who were the victims. (13)

Drylongso: Most white people — anyways all the white people I know — are people you wouldn't want to explain Anything to. (67)

No wonder whitely people have so much trouble learning, so much trouble receiving, understanding, and acting on moral or political criticism and demands for change. How can you be a preacher who does not know right from wrong, a judge who is an incompetent observer, a martyr who victimizes others, a peacemaker who is the problem, an authority without authority, a grownup who is a child? How can those who are supposed to be running the world acknowledge their relative powerlessness in some matters in any politically constructive way? Any serious moral or political challenge to a whitely person must be a direct threat to her or his very being.

Whiteliness and Class

What I have been exploring here, and calling whiteliness, may sound to some like it is a character of middle-class white people or perhaps of middle-class people whatever their race; it may sound like class phenomenon, not a race phenomenon. Before addressing this question more deeply, I should register that it is my impression, just looking around at the world, that white self-righteousness is not exclusive to the middle class. Many poor and working-class white people are perfectly confident that they are more intelligent, know more, have better judgment, and are more moral than black people or Chicanos or Puerto Ricans of Indians or anyone else they view as not white, and believe that they would be perfectly competent to run the country and to rule others justly and righteously if given the opportunity.

But this issue of the relationship of whiteliness to class deserves future attention.

Though I think that what I am talking about *is* a phenomenon of race, I want to acknowledge a close interweaving and double determination of manifestations and outcomes of race and of class, and to consider some of the things that give rise to the impression that what I am calling whiteliness may really be just "middle-classliness." One thing that has happened here is that the person who contributed to the observations assembled in the preceding section as a "participant observer" among white people (that is, the author of this analysis) is herself a lifelong member of the middle class. The whiteliness in which she has participated and about which she can write most vividly and authentically is that of her own kin, associates, and larger social group. This might, to a certain extent, bias that description of whiteliness toward a middle-class version of it.

Another reason that what I am calling whiteliness might appear to be a class character rather than a race one is that even if it is not peculiar to whites of the middle classes, it is nonetheless peculiarly suitable to them: it suits them to their jobs and social roles of managing, policing, training, disciplining, legislating, and administering, in a capitalist bureaucratic social order.

Another interesting point in this connection is that the definition of a dominant race tends to fasten on and project an image of a dominant group within that race as paradigmatic of the race.[16] The ways in which individual members of that elite group enact and manifest their racedness and dominance would constitute a sort of norm of enacting and manifesting this racedness to which nonelite members of the race would generally tend to assimilate themselves. Those ways of enacting and manifesting racedness would also carry marks of the class position of the paradigmatic elite within the race, and these marks too would appear in the enactments of race by the nonelite. In short, the ways in which members of the race generally enact and stylistically manifest membership in the race would tend to bear marks of the class status of the elite paradigmatic members of the race.

I do not think whiteliness is just middle-class-liness misnamed. I think of whiteliness as a way of being that extends across ethnic, cultural, and class categories and occurs in ethnic, cultural, and class varieties — varieties that may tend to blend toward a norm set by the elite groups within the race. Whatever class and ethnic variety there is among white people, though, such niceties seem often to have no particular salience in the experience that people of other races have with white people. It is very significant that the people of color from whose writings and narratives I have quoted in the preceding section often characterize the white people they talk about in part by class status, but they do not make anything of it. They do not generally indicate that class differences among white people make much difference to how people of color experience white people.

Speaking of the oppression of women, Gayle Rubin noted its "endless variety and monotonous similarity."[17] There is great variety among the men of all the nationalities, races, religions, and positions in various economies and polities, and women do take into account the particulars of the men they must deal with. But when our understanding of the world is conditioned by consciousness of sexism and misogyny, we see *also*, very clearly, the impressive and monotonous *lack* of variety among "masculinities." With my notion of whiteliness, I am reaching for the monotonous similarity, not the endless variety, in white folk's ways of being in the world. For various reasons, that monotonous similarity may have a middle-class cast to it, or my own perception of it may give it a middle class cast, but I think that what I am calling "whiteliness" is a phenomenon of race. It is integral to what constructs and what is constructed by race, and only indirectly related to class.

Feminism and Whiteliness

Being whitely, like being anything else in a sexist culture, is not the same thing in the lives of white women as it is in the lives of white men. The political significance of one's whiteliness interacts with the political significance of one's status as female

or male in a male-supremacist culture. For white men, a whitely way of being in the world is very harmonious with masculinity and their social and political situation. For white women it is, of course, much more complicated.

Femininity in white women is praised and encouraged but is nonetheless contemptible as weakness, dependence, featherbrainedness, vulnerability, and so on, but whiteliness in white women is unambivalently taken among white people as an appropriate enactment of a positive status. Because of this, for white women whiteliness works more consistently than femininity does to disguise and conceal their negative value and low status as women, and at the same time to appear to compensate for it or to offset it.

Those of us who are born female and white are born into the status created by white men's hatred and contempt for women, but white girls aspire to Being and integrity, like anyone else. Racism translates this into an aspiration to whiteliness. The white girl learns that whiteliness is dignity and respectability; she learns that whiteliness is her aptitude for partnership with white men; she learns that partnership with white men is her salvation from the original position of Woman in patriarchy. Adopting and cultivating whiteliness as an individual character seems to put it in the woman's own power to lever herself up out of a kind of nonbeing (the status of woman in a male-supremacist social order) over into a kind of Being (the status of white in white-supremacist social order). But whiteliness does not save white women from the condition of *woman*. Quite the contrary. A white woman's whiteliness is deeply involved in her oppression as a woman and works against her liberation.

White women are deceived, deceive ourselves, and will deceive others about ourselves, if we believe that by being whitely we can escape the fate of being the women of the white men. Being rational, righteous, and ruly (rule-abiding and rule-enforcing) does for some of us some of the time buy a ticket to a higher level of material well-being than we might otherwise be permitted (though it is not dependable). But the reason, right, and rules are not of our own making. White men may welcome our whiteliness as endorsement of their own values and as an expression of our loyalty to them (that is, as proof of their power over us) and because it makes us good helpmates to them. But if our whiteliness commands any respect, it is only in the sense that a woman who is chaste and obedient is called (by classic patriarchal reversal) "respectable."

It is commonly claimed that the women's movement in the United States, during the past couple of decades, is a white women's movement. This claim is grossly disrespectful to the many feminists whom the label "white" does not fit. But it is indeed the case that millions of white women have been drawn to and engaged in feminist action and theorizing, and this creative engagement did *not* arise from those women's being respected for their nice whitely ways by white men: it arose from the rape, battery, powerlessness, poverty or material dependence, spiritual depletion, degradation, harassment, servitude, insanity, drug addiction, botched abortions, and murder of those very women, those women who are white.[18]

As doris davenport put it in her analysis of white feminists' racism:

A few of us [third world women] ... see beyond the so-called privilege of being white, and perceive white wimmin as very oppressed, and ironically, invisible. ... [I]t would seem that some white feminists could [see this] too. Instead, they cling to their myth of being privileged, powerful, and less oppressed ... then black wimmin. .... Somewhere deep down (denied and almost killed) in the psyche of racist white feminists there is some perception of their real position: powerless, spineless, and invisible. Rather than examine it, they run from it. Rather than seek solidarity with wimmin of color, they pull rank within themselves.[19]

For many reasons it is difficult for women (of any intersection of demographic groups) to grasp the enormity, the full depth and breadth, of their oppression and of men's hatred and contempt for them. One reason is simply that the facts are so ugly and the image of that oppressed, despised, and degraded woman so horrible that recognizing

her as oneself seems to be accepting utter defeat. Some women, at some times, I am sure, must deny it to survive. But in the larger picture, denial (at least deep and sustained denial) of one's own oppression cuts one off from the appreciation of the oppression of others that is necessary for the alliances one needs. This is what I think Cherríe Moraga is pointing out when she says: "Without an emotional, heartfelt grappling with the source of our own oppression, without naming the enemy within ourselves and outside of us, no authentic, non-hierarchical connection among oppressed groups can take place."[20] If white women are not able to ally with women of other races in the construction of another world, we will indeed remain defeated, in this one.

White women's whiteliness does not deliver the deliverance we were taught it would. Our whiteliness interferes with our ability to form necessary alliances both by inhibiting and muddling our understanding of our own oppression as women and by making us personally obnoxious and insufferable to many other women much of the time; it also is directly opposed to our liberation because it joins and binds us to our oppressors. By our whitely ways of being we enact partnership and racial solidarity with white men, we animate a social (if not also sexual) heterosexual union with white men, and we embody and express our possession by white men.

A feminism that boldly names the oppression and degraded condition of white women and recognizes white men as its primary agents and primary beneficiaries — such a feminism can make it obvious to white women that the various forms of mating and racial bonding with white men do not and will not ever save us from that condition. Such a feminist understanding might free us from the awful confusion of thinking that our whiteliness is dignity, and might make it possible for us to know that it is a dreadful mistake to think that our whiteliness earns us our personhood. Such knowledge can open up the possibility of practical understanding of whiteliness as a learned character (as we have already understood masculinity and femininity), a character by which we facilitate our own containment under the "protection" of white men, a character that interferes constantly and often conclusively with our ability to be friends with women of other races, a character by which we station ourselves as lieutenants and stenographers of white male power, a character that is not desirable in itself and neither manifests nor merits the full Being to which we aspire. A character by which, in fact, we both participate in and cover up our own defeat. We might then include among our strategies for change a practice of unlearning whiteliness, and as we proceed in this, we can only become less and less well-assimilated members of the racial group called "white." (I must state as clearly as possible that I do not claim that unbecoming whitely is the only thing white women need to do to combat racism. I have said that whiteliness is not the same thing as racism. I have no thought whatever that I am offering a panacea for the eradication of racism. I *do* think that *being* whitely interferes enormously with white women's attempts in general to be antiracist.)

Disaffiliation, Deconstruction, Demolition

To deconstruct a concept is to analyze it in a way that reveals its construction — both in the temporal sense of its birth and development over time and in a certain cultural and political matrix, and in the sense of its own present structure, its meaning, and its relation to other concepts.[21] One of the most impressive aspects of such an analysis is the revelation of the "contingency" of the concept, that is, the fact that it is only the accidental collaboration of various historical events and circumstances that brought that concept into being, and the fact that there could be a world of sense without that concept in it. The other impressive thing about such analyses is what they reveal of the complex and intense interplay of construction of concepts and construction of concrete realities. This interplay is what I take to be that phenomenon called the "social construction of reality."

In combination, the revelation of the historical contingency of a concept and the revelation of the intricacy of interplay between concept and concrete lived reality gives rise to a strong sense that "deconstruction" of a concept simultaneously dis-

mantles the reality in whose social construction the evolution of the concept is so closely involved. But things do not work that way. In the first place, analyzing a concept and circulating the analysis among a few interested colleagues does not make the concept go away, does not dislodge it from the matrix of concepts in the active conceptual repertoire even of those few people, much less of people in general. In the second place, even if the deconstructive analysis so drains the concept of power for those few individuals that they can no longer use it, and perhaps their participation in the social constructions of which that concept is a part becomes awkward and halting (like tying your shoelaces while thinking directly about what you are doing), it still leaves those social constructions fully intact. Once constructed and assimilated, a social construct may be a fairly sturdy thing, not very vulnerable to erosion, decay, or demolition.[22] It is one thing to "deconstruct" a concept, another to dismantle a well-established, well-entrenched social construct. For example, Foucault's revelations about the arbitrariness and coerciveness of classifications of sexualities did not put an end to queer bashing or to the fears lesbians and gay men have of being victims of a witch-hunt.

I am interested, as I suggested earlier, in the matter of how to translate the recognition of the social-constructedness of races into some practice of the freedom these contingencies seem to promise, some way to proceed by which people can be liberated from the concrete reality of races as determined by racism. But the social-constructedness of race and races in the racist state has very different meanings for groups differently placed with respect to these categories. The ontological freedom of categorical reconstruction may be generic, but what is politically possible differs for those differently positioned, and not all the political possibilities for every group are desirable. Attempts by any group to act in this ontological freedom need to be informed by an understanding of how the action is related to the possibilities and needs of the others.

I have some hope that if I can manage to refuse to enact, embody, animate this category — the white race — as I am supposed to, I can free my energies and actions from a range of disabling confinements and burdens, and align my will with the forces that eventually will dissolve or dismantle that race as such. If it is objected that it is an exercise of white privilege to dissociate myself from the white race this way, I would say that in fact this project is strictly forbidden by the rules of white solidarity and white supremacy, and is *not* one of the privileges of white power. It may also be objected that my adoption or recommendation of this strategy implies that the right thing to do, in general, for everyone, is to dissolve, dismantle, and bring an end to races; and if this indeed is the implication, it can sound very threatening to some of the people whose races are thus to be erased. This point is well made by Franz Fanon in a response to Jean-Paul Sartre, described by Henry Louis Gates, Jr., "Reading Sartre's account of Négritude (as an antithesis preparatory to a 'society without races,' hence 'a transition and not a conclusion'), Fanon reports: 'I felt I had been robbed of my last chance ... Sartre, in this work, has destroyed black zeal. ...'"[23] The dynamic creative claiming of racial identities (and gender identity), identities that were first imposed as devices of people's oppression, has been a politically powerful and life-enhancing response of oppressed people in modern and contemporary times. For members of oppressor groups to suddenly turn around and decide to abolish races would be, it seems, genocide, not liberation. (I have a parallel unease about the project of dismantling the category of women, which some feminists seem to favor.)

But I am not suggesting that if white women should try to abandon the white race and contribute to its demolition, then women of other races should take that same approach to their racial categorization and their races. Quite the contrary. Approaches to the matter of dismantling a dominance-subordinance structure surely should be asymmetrical — they should differ according to whether one has been molded into its category of dominance or its category of subordination. My hope is that it may contribute to the demise of *racism* if we upset the logical symmetry of race — if black women, for instance, cultivate a racial

identity and a distinctive (sexually egalitarian) black community (and other women of racialized groups, likewise), while white women are undermining white racial identity and cultivating communities and agency among women along lines of affinity not defined by race. Such an approach would work toward a genuine redistribution of power.

Growing Room

The experiences of feminists' unlearning femininity and our readiness to require men to unlearn masculinity show that it is thinkable to unlearn whiteliness. If I am right about all this, then, indeed, we even know a good deal about how to do it.

We know we have to inform ourselves exhaustively of its politics. We know we have to avoid, or be extremely alert in, environments in which whiteliness is particularly required or rewarded (for example, academia). We know we have to *practice* new ways of being in environments that nurture different habits of feeling, perception, and thought, and that we will have to make these environments for ourselves since the world will not offer them to us. We know that the process will be collective and that this collectivity does not mean we will blend seamlessly with the others in to a colorless mass; women unlearning femininity together have not become clones of each other or of those who have been valuable models. As feminists we have learned that we have to resist the temptation to encourage femininity in other women when, in moments of exhaustion and need, we longed for another's sacrificial mothering or wifing. Similarly, white women have to resist the temptation to encourage whiteliness in each other when, in moments of cowardice or insecurity, we long for the comfort of "solidarity in superiority," or when we wish someone would relieve our painful uncertainty with a timely application of judgments and rules.

Seasoned feminists (white feminists along with feminists of other races) know how to transform consciousness. The first breakthrough is in the moment of knowing that another way of being is possible. In the matter of a white women's racedness, the possibility in question is the possibility of disengaging (on some levels, at least) one's own energies and wits from the continuing project of the social creation and maintenance of the white race, the possibility of being disloyal to that project by stopping constantly making oneself whitely. And this project should be very attractive to white women once we grasp that it is the possibility of *not being whitely*, rather than the possibility of *being whitely,* that holds some promise of our rescuing ourselves from the degraded condition of women in a white men's world.

NOTES

1. The working title during that period was "Ritual Libations and Points of Explosion," which referred to a remark made by Helen Wenzel in a review of my *Politics of Reality* which appeared in *The Women's Review of Books,* 1, no. 1 (October 1983). Wenzel said, "Even when white women call third world women our friends, and they us, we still agonize over 'the issue.' The result is that when we write or teach about race, racism and feminism we tend either to condense everything we have to say to the point of explosion, or, fearing just that explosion, we sprinkle our material with ritual libations which evaporate without altering our own, or anyone else's consciousness." And, coming down to cases, she continued, "Frye has fallen into both of these traps."

2. For critical reflection on "wanting to do good" and on "not knowing how to act," See "A Response to Lesbian Ethics: Why Ethics?" in *Willful Virgin: Essays in Feminism*, ed. Marilyn Frye (Freedom, Calif.: The Crossing Press, 1992),138-46.

3. Actually, what I think women of color have communicated in this matter is not so harsh as that. The point is that no one can do someone else's growing for her, that white women must not expect women of color to be *on call* to help, and that there is a great deal of knowledge to be gained by reading, interacting, and paying attention, which white women need not ask women of color to supply. Some women of color have helped me a great deal (sometimes in spite of me).

4. Tamara Buffalo, mixed-race Chippewa, writes: "My white husband said, 'Don't think that you

have any Indian-ness, that was taken from you years ago. You speak English don't you? The way you think is white, how you dress, your ambitions, how you raise your daughter, all this is white. I know what is white and what is not white!' I told the group word for word, everything he said. Repeating it in the same flat tone he used, I was bearing witness. I was testifying against him." Tamara Buffalo, "Adopted Daughter," in *Hurricane Alice: A Feminist Quarterly* 10, no. 2 (Spring 1994). Thanks to Carolyn Shafer for bringing this statement to my attention.

5. Marilyn Frye, *The Politics of Reality* (Freedom, Calif.: The Crossing Press, 1983), 115-16.

6. It is easy for a white person who is trying to understand white privilege and white power in white supremacist states to make the mistake of (self-servingly) exaggerating that power and privilege, assuming it is total. In this case, I was making the mistake earlier of thinking that white domination means that white people totally control the definition of race and the races. Reading bell hooks's *Yearning* (Boston: South End Press, 1990), I awoke to the fact that Afro-Americans (and other racialized people) are also engaged in the definition of black (and other "race" categories); white people have the power to enforce their own definitions in many (but not all) situations, but they are not the only people determining the meanings of race categories and race words, and what they determine for themselves (and enforce) is not necessarily congruent with what others are determining for *them*selves.

7. I want to thank María Lugones, whose palpably loving anger on this point made me take it seriously. See María Lugones, "Hablando cara a cara/ Speaking Face to Face: An Exploration of Ethnocentric Racism," in *Making Face, Making Soul: Haciendo Caras: Critical and Creative Perspectives by Women of Color*, ed. Gloria Anzaldúa (San Francisco: aunt lute foundation press, 1990).

8. Carrie Jane Singleton, "Race and Gender in Feminist Theory," *Sage* VI, no. 1 (Summer 1989):15.

9. I am not unmindful here of the anxiety some readers may have about my reliance on a distinction between that which is physically given and that which is socially acquired. I could complicate

this passage immensely by shifting from the material mode of talking about maleness and skin colors to the formal mode of talking about conceptions or constructions of maleness and skin colors. But it would not make anything clearer. It is perfectly meaningful to use the term "male" and the term "white" (as a pigment word), while understanding that sex categories and color categories are "constructed" as the kinds of categories they are, that is, physical categories as opposed to social categories like "lawyer" or arithmetic categories like "ordinals."

10. Cherríe Moraga and Gloria Anzaldúa, eds., *This Bridge Called My Back: Writing By Radical Women of Color* (Brooklyn, N.Y.: Kitchen Table: Women of Color Press, 1981). I quote from writings by Barbara Cameron, Chrystos, doris davenport, and Mitsuye Yamada.

11. bell hooks, *Feminist Theory: From Margin to Center* (Boston: South End Press, 1985).

12. John Langston Gewaltney, *Drylongso: A Self-Portrait of Black America* (New York: Random House, 1983). I quote from statements by Jackson Jordan, Jr., Hannah Nelson, John Oliver, Howard Roundtree, Rosa Wakefield, and Mabel Lincoln.

13. The people speaking in *Drylongso* were responding to questions put by an interviewer. The narratives as published do not include the questions. But the people clearly were asked in some manner to say something about how they see white people or what they think white people generally are like. Most of them, but not every one, prefaced or appended their comments with remarks to the effect that they did not think white people were "like that" by birth or blood, but by being brought up a certain way in certain circumstances.

14. Minnie Bruce Pratt, "Identity: Skin Blood Heart," in *Yours in Struggle*, ed. Elly Bulkin, Minnie Bruce Pratt, and Barbara Smith (Brooklyn: Long Haul Press, 1984).

15. For more exploration of some of the meanings of this, see Frye, "A Response to Lesbian Ethics: Why Ethics?"

16. Cf. Etienne Balibar, "Paradoxes of Universality," trans. Michael Edwards, in *Anatomy of Racism*, ed. David Theo Goldberg (Minneapolis: University of Minnesota Press, 1990), 284-85, extracted from "Racisme et nationalism," in *Race, Nation, Classe*, Etienne Balibar and Immanuel Wallerstein (Paris: Editions La Decouverte, 1988).

17. Gayle Rubin, "The Traffic in Women," in *Toward An Anthropology of Women*, ed. Rayna R. Reiter (New York: Monthly Review Press, 1975), 160.

18. Carolyn Shafer is the one who brought to my attention the fact that there is a certain contradiction in claiming *both* that this stage of the women's movement was created by and belongs to white women *and* (on the grounds of the generally better material welfare of white women, compared to women of other races in the United States) that white women are not all that badly off and don't really know what suffering is about. If white women were as generally comfortable, secure, and healthy as they might appear to some observers, they would not have participated as they have in an enormous movement the first and most enduring issues of which are bodily integrity and economic self-sufficiency.

19. doris davenport, "The Pathology of Racism: A Conversation with Third Work Wimmin," in *This Bridge Called My Back*, ed. Moraga and Anzaldda, 89-90.

20. Moraga, *This Bridge Called My Back*, 21.

21. It will be clear to those who learned the word "deconstruction" from the writings of Jacques Derrida that I have wandered off with it in pursuit of interests other than his. They will agree, though, that he gave it up the moment he first wrote it down or uttered it.

22. My lover Carolyn was explaining what I do for a living to our coheart Keyosha, and included an account of "deconstruction." Keyosha, a welder and pipefitter in the construction trades, said that it wasn't a real word and offered "demolition" as the real word for this. Carolyn then had to admit (on my behalf) that all this deconstructing did not add up to any demolition, and a made-up abstract word was probably suitable to this abstract activity.

23. Henry Louis Gates, Jr., "Critical Remarks," in *Anatomy of Racism*, ed. David Theo Goldberg (Minneapolis: University of Minnesota Press, 1990), 325.

REFLECTIONS ON THE MEANING OF WHITE

Victoria Davion

Victoria Davion teaches philosophy at the University of Georgia, Athens. She is the founder and current editor of the journal Ethics and the Environment. *Her areas of interest are ethics, feminist philosophy, and political theory.*

    Davion supports Frye's argument that being white is the result of social training that can be unlearned. However, she questions Frye's tendency to think of whiteness in universal terms and explores the ways in which ethnic differences further complicate an account of whiteness. While Davion recognizes correspondences between being whitely and being Jewish, she also identifies some of the characteristics of being Jewish in a primarily Christian society that fail to fit Frye's account of whiteness. She argues that ceasing to be whitely means unlearning whiteliness, but not necessarily getting rid of one's ethnicity.

Marilyn Frye is right to insist that the link between promoting white supremacy and being white skinned is contingent. Certainly white people do not have to act in ways that promote white supremacy. Acting in these ways is not a matter of genetic coding; it is a matter of social training. Frye is also right to point out that although there is only a contingent link between promoting a system based on white supremacy and having white skin, ceasing to promote white supremacy requires more than simply believing in racial equality. It requires close examination of and changes in behaviors that may not appear on the surface to promote white supremacy but in fact keep a white supremist system in place. Frye's strategy of searching for these behaviors and attitudes in both her own experiences and experiences that people of color have of white people is a good one. Thus, I want to add to this project by looking at how ethnic differences fit into this kind of analysis.

Frye's description of whiteliness is very familiar to me. It also seems very Protestant, and I am Jewish. I don't deny that white Jews and other ethnic groups engage in the kinds of behaviors she describes, but I want to make clear that many different worldviews can produce these behaviors.

Whiteliness is not a particular worldview. Frye focuses on the monotonous similarity of whitely oppression, and I think she is right to do this. If, however, her analysis implies that in order to stop being whitely we must disaffiliate from our ethnic backgrounds, as a Jew I cannot accept it. I don't in fact think that ceasing to be whitely requires this, and I think it is important that this be made clear.

Frye states that whitely people trust each other. One of the quotations she cites from *Drylongso* claims just the opposite: "White people are some writing folks! They will write. They write everything. Now they do that because they don't trust each other."[1] Interestingly, I think both perceptions are right. My upbringing as a white Jew in America included education about anti-Semitism. I was raised not to trust non-Jews because they can turn on you at any time. I will return to this point shortly.

As Frye characterizes some of the other values and beliefs involved in whiteliness, these are not the values I was taught. She states: "I learned that I, and 'we,' knew right from wrong and had the responsibility to see to it right was done, that there were others who did not know what is right and wrong and should be advised, instructed, helped, and directed by us. ... Not 'might is right,' but 'right is might.'"[2] As a Jew, I was taught that being right doesn't insure one any power whatsoever, and that the majority doesn't know right from wrong. Yet, because might makes right in reality, I was taught to leave the Christian majority alone to do its own thing. I was certainly not encouraged at all to spread the truth of Judaism. Rather, I was warned to shut up about all of this if I wanted to be safe.

It is in the ways that I learned how to be careful around non-Jews that I recognized much of what Frye calls whitely behavior in myself. I learned how to tone down behaviors that might be considered stereotypical Jewish around those who might find me too loud or pushy. Although I was taught to trust and favor Jews and to hate certain groups of whites, I know how to behave as if I hate no one, trust other white people, and don't discriminate.

Why do I know how to behave in these ways? I was taught this as a survival mechanism. Although this was never stated explicitly, I now realize that I was given the message that white skin alone wouldn't guarantee me certain privileges. In addition to having white skin, I needed to be or pretend to be Christian. Often, passing for a white Christian doesn't involve doing anything. However, I learned to be sure not to call attention to the fact that I wasn't really Christian. The message was that insofar as I am white, it is safe to trust other whites in seeking white privileges. However, insofar as I am Jewish in a primarily Christian society, this isn't the case.

What does this imply about whiteliness in general and about me as a white Jew? Whiteliness is not, in my opinion, a particular worldview. Whitely behavior can be the result of a variety of worldviews. The motivation for being whitely, and also for stopping being whitely, will therefore come from a variety of sources depending on who one is. I have come to realize that in my own case, to promote the particular white-supremacist system in which we now live is at the same time to promote a system that is antisemitic to its roots. This is why it is so important to learn the dominant behaviors and practices and to avoid acting too Jewish in public. In supporting the myth that all white people are basically the same in certain respects, which is what a white-supremacist

system must do, I contribute to the fracturing of my being by being whitely. I cannot be whole in such a system.

I want to make a few things clear before going any further. I am not saying that white Jews are any less whitely or even any less racist than other whites. In fact, we may be more whitely in that the behaviors are learned as a survival mechanism. Nor am I saying that white Jews should be excused for being whitely while others should not. Supporting a white-supremacist system is wrong no matter who does it. I don't want to try to rank blame for whitely behavior. What I am saying is that as a white Jew, I have a particular motive for ceasing to be whitely. In being whitely I contribute to the erasure of myself as Jewish, and the fracturing of my identity.

If whitely behaviors are behaviors that whites from various backgrounds engage in, then getting rid of them need not mean getting rid of one's ethnicity. Rather, it will mean looking at behaviors and attitudes and rooting out the whitely ones, the ones that promote white supremacy. This brings me to a final point with regard to Frye's analysis of whiteliness. Many of the characteristics Frye names seem as if they might not be bad in themselves, but only in certain contexts. If this is true, then nobody's ethnic background is polluted to the point where it must be discarded. Instead, the strategy will be to look at the way one engages in various behaviors. Following rules is one example. Rule-following has its place. However, it is oppressive to insist that everyone follow the rules when not everyone thinks rules are appropriate for that situation to begin with, or not everyone has had the opportunity to help construct the rules. Voting for the person one thinks is best qualified for the job doesn't seem like a bad behavior in itself. It depends on what is meant by most qualified. Therefore, it is not the behaviors themselves that are the problem; it is the way that we engage in them.

Some of the other attitudes and behaviors Frye mentions are always unfortunate regardless of the context. She says:

Many poor and working class white people are perfectly confident that they are more intelligent, know more, have better judgment, and are more moral than Black people or Chicanos or Puerto Ricans or Indians or anyone else they view as not white, and believe that they would be perfectly competent to run the country and to rule others justly and righteously if given the opportunity.[3]

The version of whiteliness described above sounds like racism. One of the things I find very important in Frye's project is her insistence that whitely behaviors can be manifested in people who believe in racial equality. That is, even those of us who do not think that whites are more intelligent, know more, and so on, can act in ways that promote white supremacy. This description does not seem to capture that.

I conclude that Frye is exactly right to seek something analogous to masculinity that white people are socialized into but that we can learn to stop being and doing. She is also right to listen to people of color describe the endless monotony and similarity in their experiences of race oppression. I think it is a mistake, however, to conclude that this monotony is due to any common worldview in those who behave in whitely ways (I am not saying that she does this). Many systems are at work. In addition, while I think Frye is right to look for whiteliness as she describes it abstractly, I am still not sure exactly what it is. I am not sure because some of the behaviors she mentions do not seem necessarily bad in themselves, and others seem blatantly racist. Nevertheless, her analysis has started me thinking about when and why I behave in whitely ways. It has helped me to realize that acting whitely involves affirming a framework in which behavior stereotyped as ethnically Jewish is looked down upon. Thus, in acting whitely I erase my ethnicity. Perhaps if more white people celebrated our differences publicly, the myth that whites are basically the same, a myth that is necessary for upholding a white-supremacist system, would be impossible to maintain. Thus, I regard this essay as a call for the celebration of ethnic diversity as well as a call for whites to stop acting whitely. I hope I have shown that these projects are compatible.

NOTES

1. John Langston Gewaltney, *Drylongso: A Self-Portrait of Black America* (New York: Random House, 1983), 88.
2. Marilyn Frye, "White Woman Feminist," in *Overcoming Racism & Sexism* (Rowman and Littlefield, 1995).
3. Ibid.

INVISIBILITY IS AN UNNATURAL DISASTER:
REFLECTIONS OF AN ASIAN AMERICAN WOMAN

Mitsuye Yamada

Mitsuye Yamada has been Visiting Associate Professor of English and Asian American Studies at the University of California, Irvine. She is the author of Sowing Ti Leaves: Anthology *(1991),* Camp Notes and Other Poems *(1992, second edition), and* Teaching Human Rights Awareness Through Poetry *(1999). Her work has been included in anthologies such as* Women Poets of the World *(1983) and* This Bridge Called My Back *(1983). The film* Mitsuye and Nellie: Asian American Poets *was produced by Light-Saraf Film in 1981.*

Yamada describes her experiences in academic settings of having students and administrators fail to understand anger expressed by Asian Americans because they do not think Asian Americans constitute an oppressed group. She uses the concept of invisibility to elucidate the kind of oppression experienced by Asian Americans and, in particular, by Japanese Americans. Some effects of the evacuations of Japanese Americans during World War II were the shaping of prevalent stereotypes of Asian Americans as polite, passive, and accepting and the internalization of these stereotypes by Asian Americans.

Last year for the Asian segment of the Ethnic American Literature course I was teaching, I selected a new anthology entitled *Aiiieeeee!* compiled by a group of outspoken Asian American writers. During the discussion of the long but thought-provoking introduction to this anthology, one of my students blurted out that she was offended by its militant tone and that as a white person she was tired of always being blamed for the oppression of all the minorities. I noticed several of the classmates' eyes nodding in tacit agreement. A discussion of the "militant" voices in some of the other writings we had read in the course ensued. Surely, I pointed out, some of these other writings have been just as, if not more, militant as the words in this introduction? Had they been offended by those also but failed to express their feelings about them? To my surprise, they said they were not offended by any of the Black American, Chicano or American Indian writings, but were hard-pressed to explain why when I asked for an explanation. A little further discussion revealed that they "understood" the anger expressed by the Black and Chicanos and they "emphasized" with the frustrations and sorrow expressed by the American Indian. But the Asian Americans?

Then finally, one student said it for all of them: "It made me angry. *Their* anger made *me* angry, because I didn't even know the Asian Americans felt oppressed. I didn't expect their anger."

At this time I was involved in an academic due process procedure begun as a result of a grievance I had filed the previous semester for violation of my rights as a teacher who had worked in the district for almost eleven years. My student's remark "Their anger made me angry ... I didn't expect their anger," explained for me the reactions of some of my own colleagues as well as the reactions of the administrators during those previous months. The grievance procedure was a time-consuming and emotionally draining process, but the basic principle was too important for me to ignore. That basic principle was that I, an individual teacher, do have certain rights which are given and my superiors cannot, should not, violate them with impunity. When this was pointed out to them, however, they responded with shocked surprise that I, of all people, would take them to task for violation of what was clearly written policy in our college district. They all seemed to exclaim, "We don't understand this; this is so uncharacteristic of her; she seemed such a nice person, so polite, so obedient, so non-trouble making." What was even more surprising was once they were forced to acknowledge that I was determined to start the due process action, they assumed I was not doing it on my own. One of the administrators suggested someone must have pushed me into this, undoubtedly some of "those feminists" on our campus, he said wryly.

In this age when women are clearly making themselves visible on all fronts, I, an Asian American woman, am still functioning as a "front for those feminists" and therefore invisible. The realization of this sinks in slowly. Asian Americans as a whole are finally coming to claim their own, demanding that they be included in the multicultural history of our country. I like to think, in spite of my administrator's myopia, that the most stereotyped minority of them all, the Asian American woman, is just now emerging to become part of that group. It took forever. Perhaps it is important to ask ourselves why it took so long. We should ask ourselves this question just when we think we are emerging as a viable minority in the fabric of our society. I should add to my student's works, "because I didn't even know they felt oppressed," that it took this long because we Asian American women have not admitted to ourselves that we *were* oppressed. We, the visible minority that is invisible.

I say this because until a few years ago I have been an Asian American woman working among non-Asians in an educational institution where most of the decision-makers were men;[1] an Asian American woman thriving under the smug illusion that I was *not* the stereotypic image of the Asian woman because I had a career teaching English in a community college. I did not think anything assertive was necessary to make my point. People who know me, I reasoned, the ones who count, know who I am and what I think. Thus, even when what I considered a veiled racist remark was made in a casual social setting, I would "let it go" because it was pointless to argue with people who didn't even know their remark was racist. I had supposed that I was practicing passive resistance while being stereotyped, but it was so passive no one noticed I was resisting; it was so much my expected role that it ultimately rendered me invisible.

My experience leads me to believe that contrary to what I thought, I had actually been contributing to my own stereotyping. Like the hero in Ralph Ellison's novel *The Invisible Man*, I had become invisible to white Americans, and it clung to me like a bad habit. Like most bad habits, this one crept up on me because I took it in minute doses like Mithradates' poison and my mind and body adapted so well to it I hardly noticed it was there.

For the past eleven years I have busied myself with the usual chores of an English teacher, a wife of a research chemist, and a mother of four rapidly growing children. I hadn't even done much to shatter this particular stereotype: the middle class woman happy to be bringing home the extra income and quietly fitting into the man's world of work. When the Asian American woman is lulled into believing that people perceive her as being different from other Asian women (the submissive, subservient, ready-to-please, easy-to-get-along-with Asian woman), she is kept comfortably content with the state of things. She becomes ineffectual in the milieu in which she moves. The seemingly apolitical middle class woman and the apolitical Asian woman constituted a double invisibility.

I had created an underground culture of survival for myself and had become in the eyes of others the person I was trying not to be. Because I was permitted to go to college, permitted to take a stab at a career or two along the way, given "free choice" to marry and have a family, given a "choice" to eventually do both, I had assumed I was more or less free, not realizing that those who are free make and take choices; they do not choose from options proffered by "those out there."

I, personally, had not "emerged" until I was almost fifty years old. Apparently through a long conditioning process, I had learned how *not* to be seen for what I am. A long history of ineffectual activities had been, I realize now, initiation rites toward my eventual invisibility. The training begins in childhood; and for women and minorities whatever is started in childhood is continued throughout their adult lives. I first recognized just how invisible I was in my first real confrontation with my parents a few years after the outbreak of World War II.

During the early years of the war, my older brother, Mike, and I left the concentration camp in Idaho to work and study at the University of Cincinnati. My parents came to Cincinnati soon after my father's release from Internment Camp (these were POW camps to which many of the Issei[2] men, leaders in their communities, were sent by the FBI), and worked as domestics in the suburbs. I did not see them too often because by this time I had met and was much influenced by a pacifist who was out on a "furlough" from a con-scientious objectors' camp in Trenton, North Dakota. When my parents learned about my "boy friend" they were appalled and frightened. After all, this was the period when everyone in the country was expected to be one-hundred percent behind the war effort, and the Nisei[3] boys who had volunteered for the Armed Forces were out there fighting and dying to prove how American we really were. However, during interminable argu-ments with my father and overheard arguments between my parents, I was devastated to learn they were not so much concerned about my having become a pacifist, but they were more concerned about the possibility of my marrying one. They were understandably frightened (my father's prison years of course were still fresh on his mind) about repercussions on the rest of the family. In an attempt to make my father understand me, I argued that even if I didn't marry him, I'd still be a paci-fist; but my father reassured me that it was "all right" for me to be a pacifist because as a Japanese national and a "girl" *it didn't make any difference to anyone.* In frustration I remember shouting, "But can't you see, *I'm* philosophically committed to the pacifist cause," but he dismissed this with "In my college days we used to call philosophy,

foolosophy," and that was the end of that. When they were finally convinced I was not going to marry "my pacifist," the subject was dropped and we never discussed it again.

As if to confirm my father's assessment of the harmlessness of my opinions, my brother Mike, an American citizen, was suddenly expelled from the University of Cincinnati while I, "an enemy alien," was permitted to stay. We assumed that his stand as a pacifist, although he was classified a 4-F because of his health, contributed to his expulsion. We were told the Air Force was conducting sensitive wartime research on campus and requested his removal, but they apparently felt my presence on campus was not as threatening.

I left Cincinnati in 1945, hoping to leave behind this and other unpleasant memories gathered there during the war years, and plunged right into the politically active atmosphere at New York Univer-sity where students, many of them returning veter-ans, were continuously promoting one cause or other by making speeches in Washington Square, passing out petitions, or staging demonstrations. On one occasion, I tagged along with a group of students who took a train to Albany to demonstrate on the steps of the State Capitol I think I was the only Asian in this group of predominantly Jewish students from NYU. People who passed us were amused and shouted "Go home and grow up." I suppose Governor Dewey, who refused to see us, assumed we were a group of adolescents without a cause as most college students were considered to be during those days. It appears they weren't expecting any results from our demonstration. There were no newspersons, no security persons, no police. No one tried to stop us from doing what we were doing. We simply did "our thing" and went back to our studies until next time, and my father's words were again confirmed: it made no difference to anyone, being a young student demonstrator in peacetime, 1947.

Not only the young, but those who feel power-less over their own lives know what it is like not to make a difference on anyone or anything. The poor know it only too well, and we women have known it since we were little girls. The most insidious part of this conditioning process, I realize now, was that we have been trained not to expect a response in ways that mattered. We may be listened to and responded to with placating words and gestures, but our psychological mind set has already told us time and again that we were born into a ready-made world into which we must fit ourselves, and that many of us do it very well.

This mind set is the result of not believing that the political and social forces affecting our lives are determined by some person, or a group of persons, probably sitting behind a desk or around a conference table.

Just recently I read an article about "the remarkable track record of success" of the Nisei in the United States. One Nisei was quoted as saying he attributed our stamina and endurance to our ancestors whose characters had been shaped, he said, by their living in a country which has been constantly besieged by all manner of natural disasters, such as earthquakes and hurricanes. He said the Nisei has inherited a steely will, a will to endure and hence, to survive.

This evolutionary explanation disturbs me, because it equates the "act of God" (i.e. natural disasters) to the "act of man" (i.e., the war, the evacuation). The former is not within our power to alter, but the latter, I should think, is. By putting the "acts of God" on par with the acts of man, we shrug off personal responsibilities.

I have, for too long a period of time accepted the opinion of others (even though they were directly affecting my life) as if they were objective events totally out of my control. Because I separated such opinions from the persons who were making them, I accepted them the way I accepted natural disasters; and I endured them as inevitable. I have tried to cope with people whose points of view alarmed me in the same way that I had adjusted to natural phenomena, such as hurricanes, which plowed into my life from time to time. I would readjust my dismantled feelings in the same way that we repaired the broken shutters after the storm. The Japanese have an all purpose expression in their language for this attitude of resigned acceptance: "Shikata-ganai." "It can't be helped." "There's nothing I can do about it." It is said with the shrug of the shoulders and tone of finality, perhaps not unlike the "those-were-my-orders" tone that was used at the Nuremberg trials. With all the sociological studies that have been made about the causes of the evacuations of the Japanese Americans during World War II, we should know by now that "they" knew that the West Coast Japanese Americans would go without too much protest, and of course, "they" were right, for most of us (with the exception of those notable few), resigned to our fate, albeit bewildered and not willingly. WE were not perceived by our government as responsive Americans; we were objects that happened to be standing in the path of the storm.

Perhaps this kind of acceptance is a way of coping with the "real" world. One stands against the wind for a time, and then succumbs eventually because there is no point to being stubborn against all odds. The wind will not respond to entreaties anyway, one reasons; one should have senses enough to know that. I'm not ready to accept this evolutionary reasoning. It is too rigid for me; I would like to think that my new awareness is going to make me more visible than ever, and to allow me to make some changes in the "man made disaster" I live in at the present time. Part of being visible is refusing to separate the actors from their actions, and demanding that they be responsible for them.

By now, riding along with the minorities' and women's movements, I think we are making a wedge into the main body of American life, but people are still looking right through and around us, assuming we are simply tagging along. Asian American women still remain in the background and we are heard but not really listened to. Like Musak, they think we are piped into the airwaves by someone else. We must remember that one of the most insidious ways of keeping women and minorities powerless is to let them only talk about harmless and inconsequential subjects, or let them speak freely and not listen to them with serious intent.

We need to raise our voices a little more, even as they say to us "This is so uncharacteristic of you." To finally recognize our own invisibility is to finally be on the path toward visibility. Invisibility is not a natural state for anyone.

NOTES

1. It is hoped this will change now that a black woman is Chancellor of our college district.
2. Issei — Immigrant Japanese, living in the U.S.
3. Nisei — Second generation Japanese, born in the U.S.

STUDY QUESTIONS

1. What does Anthony Appiah mean by racialism? What is the distinction between "extrinsic" and "intrinsic" racism meant to capture and what is the connection of each to racialism?

2. What does Appiah mean by the claim that intrinsic racism has tended to be "the natural expression of feelings of community"? Do Black Nationalists of the 1960s fit the description of intrinsic racists? Why or why not? What objections does Appiah raise against intrinsic racism?

3. Do you agree with Appiah that the right tactic for opposing racism "is to object to it rationally in the form in which it stands the best chance of meeting objections"? Do you agree with Appiah that those who hold on to their prejudices even when confronted with incontrovertible evidence that their prejudices are based on false beliefs are perhaps not morally responsible? Provide reasons for your answers.

4. What are the parallels that Sally Haslanger draws between "sex" and "gender" and "color" and "race"? Why does she think that sex is different from color? Do you agree? Why or why not?

5. According to Haslanger, will there be races in the future? What is captured by the concept "ethnorace" and what role can it play now and into the future?

6. Beginning with the idea of the social construction of race, Marilyn Frye invents the terms "whitely" and "whiteliness" on analogy with masculine and masculinity. What does she mean by these terms? Does Frye's account of parallels between sexism and racism differ from Haslanger's? Defend your answer.

7. Do you recognize whiteliness in white people? Is this account of a way of being in the world relevant to an analysis of racism? Defend your answers.

8. According to Frye, how do factors such as class and gender affect the account of whiteliness? Do you think that the unlearning of femininity, masculinity, or whiteliness is an effective strategy for eliminating sexism or racism? Why or why not?

9. What are some of the concerns raised by Victoria Davion about Frye's account of whiteliness? What does Davion mean by her claim that getting rid of whiteliness does not mean getting rid of one's ethnicity?

10. How does Mitsuye Yamada's account of student reactions to "outspoken Asian American writers" illuminate the kind of oppression experienced by Asian Americans? What does she mean by invisibility and what strategies does she propose for changing it?

SUGGESTED READINGS

Alcoff, Linda Martin. "Philosophy and Racial Identity." *Radical Philosophy*, v. 75 (Jan/Feb 1996): 5-14.

Babbitt, Susan, and Sue Campbell. *Racism and Philosophy*. Ithaca, NY: Cornell University Press, 1999.

Bowen, William G., and Derek Bok. *The Shape of the River: Long-Term Consequences of Considering Race in College and University Admission*. Princeton, NJ: Princeton University Press, 1998.

Brittan, Arthur, and Mary Maynard. "Primary and Secondary Oppression." In *Sexism, Racism and Oppression*. Oxford: Blackwell, 1984.

Card, Claudia. "On Race, Racism, and Ethnicity." In *Overcoming Racism and Sexism*, edited by Linda Bell and David Blumenfeld. Lanham, MD: Rowman & Littlefield, 1995.

Collins, Patricia Hill. *Black Feminist Thought: Knowledge, Consciousness and the Politics of Empowerment*. Boston, MA: Unwin Hyman, 1990.

Corlett, Angelo J. "Analyzing Racism." *Public Affairs Quarterly*, v. 12, no. 1 (January 1998): 23-50.

Du Bois, W.E.B. "The Concept of Race." In *Dusk of Dawn*. New York, NY: Harcourt, Brace and World, 1940.

Dworkin, Ronald. "Affirming Affirmative Action." *New York Review of Books* (22 October 1998): 91-102.

— . "Is Affirmative Action Doomed?" *New York Review of Books* (5 November 1998): 56-60.

Garcia, J.L.A. "Current Conceptions of Racism: A Critical Examination of Some Recent Social Philosophy." *Journal of Social Philosophy*, v. 28, no. 2 (Fall 1997): 5-42.

— ."Philosophical Analysis and the Moral Concept of Racism." *Philosophy & Social Criticism*, v. 25, no. 5 (1999): 1-32.

Goldberg, David Theo. "Racist Exclusions." *Philosophical Forum (Boston)*, v. 26, no. 1 (Fall 1994): 1-32.

— . "The Social Formation of Racist Discourse." In *Anatomy of Racism*, edited by David Theo Goldberg. Minneapolis, MN: University of Minnesota Press, 1990.

Haslanger, Sally. "Gender and Race: (What) Are They? (What) Do We Want Them to Be?" *Nous*, v. 34, no. 1 (March 2000): 31-55.

— . "Oppression: Racial and Other." In *Racism, Philosophy and Mind: Philosophical Explanations of Racism and its Implications*, edited by Michael Levine and Tamas Pataki. Ithaca, NY: Cornell University Press, 2005.

Lichtenberg, Judith. "Racism in the Head, Racism in the World." *Report from the Institute for Philosophy & Public Policy*, v. 12, no. 1 (Spring/Summer 1992): 3-5.

Lorde, Audre. "Age, Race, Class, and Sex: Women Redefining Difference." In *Sister Outsider*. Freedom, CA: Crossing Press, 1984: 114-23.

May, Larry. "Shared Responsibility for Racism." In *Sharing Responsibility*. Chicago, IL: University of Chicago Press, 1992.

Narayan, Uma. "Colonialism and its Others: Considerations on Rights and Care Discourses." *Hypatia*, v. 10, no. 2 (1995): 133-40.

Outlaw, Lucius (Jr.). *On Race and Philosophy*. New York, NY: Routledge, 1996.

— . "Philosophy, Ethnicity, and Race." The Alfred P. Stiernotte Lectures in Philosophy. Hamden, CT: Quinnipiac College, 1989.

Scheman, Naomi. "Jewish Lesbian Writing: A Review Essay." *Hypatia*, v. 7, no. 4 (Fall 1992): 186-94.

Schmid, W. Thomas. "The Definition of Racism." *Journal of Applied Philosophy*, v. 13, no. 1 (1996): 31-40.

Shelby, Tommie. "Is Racism in the 'Heart'?" *Journal of Social Philosophy*, v. 33, no. 3 (Fall 2002): 411-20.

Singer, Peter. "Is Racial Discrimination Arbitrary?" *Philosophia*, v. 8, nos. 2-3 (1978): 185-205.

Thomas, Laurence. "Power, Trust, and Evil." In *Overcoming Racism and Sexism*, edited by Linda Bell and David Blumenfeld. Lanham, MD: Rowman & Littlefield, 1995.

— . "What Good Am I?" In *Affirmative Action and the University: A Philosophical Inquiry*, edited by Steven M. Cahn. Philadelphia, PA: Temple University Press, 1993: 125-31.

Wasserstrom, Richard. "Racism, Sexism, and Preferential Treatment: An Approach to the Topics." *UCLA Law Review*, v. 24 (1977): 581-622.

Waters, Anne (editor). *American Indian Thought: Philosophical Essays*. Oxford: Blackwell Publishing, 2004.

West, Cornel. "The Black Underclass and Black Philosophers." In *Prophetic Thought in Postmodern Times*. Monroe, ME: Common Courage Press, 1993: 143-57.

CHAPTER THREE: GENDER

INTRODUCTION

In the previous chapter, Sally Haslanger identifies a place where racism and sexism are similar: an entrenched belief in the inherent biological differences marked by "color" or by "sex" shapes the social, economic, and political positions of those with bodies marked as different. In this chapter, we examine what having a female body, marked as different, means with respect to differences in treatment and the kinds of inequalities women continue to suffer. We will also examine the question of whether these meanings and socioeconomic effects vary within and across cultures. Does gender have the same meaning across cultures? Do women experience similar kinds of oppression no matter what their experiences are or where they live?

It will be useful, however, to first stop and explain the concept "feminism" already mentioned in several of the readings in Volumes I and II. Feminism is generally associated with the social movement to achieve equality for women. It also represents an ever expanding body of theory, which makes it increasingly difficult to define it in a way that captures the diversity of feminist activists and the range of feminist theories. There are at least two elements common to feminism: a recognition that women are oppressed and a commitment to ending that oppression. This definition leaves room for a wide variety of explanations for women's oppression and strategies advocated for eliminating that oppression. It also leaves room for the important realization that there is no examination of women as such because there are women of different races, ethnicities, sexual orientations, and levels of ability and wealth.

The chapter opens with an examination of one kind of difference that has resulted in different treatment, perceptions, and self-perceptions: women's bodies as different from men's and the resulting manipulation, sculpting, and changing of them to fit an ideal of the perfect female body. Elayne Saltzberg and Joan Chrisler argue that this ideal of female beauty varies across cultures and changes over time, but is always that which is difficult to achieve and "unnatural" in some sense. Because it is a fluctuating ideal that women strive for and few are able to attain, failure and disappointment are inevitable. By providing examples from history, such as Chinese foot binding, tight and constraining corsets, and surgical enhancement of breast size, Saltzberg and Chrisler highlight the toil on women of striving for that ideal in terms of physical pain, health problems, medical procedures, costs of beauty products, time and effort, and damaging psychological effects. Psychological effects that social conceptions of beauty have on women include unhappiness, confusion, misery, insecurity, high stress, chronic anxiety, and negative body images. Moreover, an obsessive concern with body shape and weight in the form of the North American ideal of thinness has resulted in increasing incidences of anorexia and bulimia among women.

Saltzberg and Chrisler also provide evidence that beauty ideals are affected by racism, class prejudice, and the rejection of disabled bodies in ways that make it difficult for those in these groups to approach the ideal. They end by describing some of the detrimental consequences for women who fail to reach the ideal: punishment for social transgressions, losing one's job for being too old or unattractive, and discrimination in hiring and promotion. Saltzberg and Chrisler take these effects to be aspects of what it means to be a woman and suffer oppression and disempowerment. They end by advocating that women become aware of the effects on their bodies and their lives of pursuing the ideal of the perfect female body.

The second reading examines another aspect of what it means to be a woman in North America: the prevalence of sexual violence that leads to women being disproportionately more fearful than men. Keith Burgess-Jackson observes that accounts of distribution in justice theory tend to focus on benefits such as opportunities, income, wealth, health care services, and rights to property rather than on burdens such as the payment of taxes, military service, and criminal punishment. He argues for extending the analysis of burdens by analyzing fear, a burden that the social-scientific literature shows to be unevenly distributed between men and women in identifiable and insidious patterns. While the fear of being a victim of criminal behavior is prevalent in the lives of many Americans, particularly the elderly, non-whites, those with low incomes, and those who live in urban areas, the most powerful predictor of fear of crime is gender. Data shows that fear of rape is a core fear for women, one that is more prevalent than fear of murder and that underlies fears of being robbed, for example.

Fear, argues Burgess-Jackson, disrupts, debilitates, and places restrictions on women's freedom. It also leads to chronic anxiety, dependence on men, and a loss of self-confidence and self-respect. Fear is an issue for distributive justice because women are disproportionately burdened and because the fears they have are generated by social life itself. Burgess-Jackson argues that justice demands collective action to reduce the overall level of fear in society and redistribute it so that women no longer bear the brunt of it. He offers several policy suggestions: taking steps to prevent rape through the criminal justice system, reducing or eliminating women's sense of vulnerability through self-defense training courses, increasing the number of police officers on the street, improving street lighting, and funding programs such as consciousness raising groups for men.

In the readings so far, the idea that women share commonalities that make their experiences of discrimination and oppression similar has been, to some extent at least, assumed. Susan Moller Okin explores this question of shared features and experiences by discussing women in countries and cultures outside North America. Her specific worry is that emphasizing differences will undermine

attempts to formulate a theory of justice that can address injustices for women in developing countries. She admits the force of the charge of essentialism, which, within feminism, has resulted in taking the lives and experiences of white middle- and upper-class women to be representative of all women and in ignoring the effects of race, class, ethnicity, and other differences on women's lives. Okin claims, however, that contemporary anti-essentialist critics lack empirical evidence to support their claims that there are no experiences shared by all women. By providing an account of shared experiences, she defends the position that Western feminist accounts of justice can be applied to the situations of poor women in poor countries.

Okin outlines several aspects of a "generalizable, identifiable and collectively shared experience of womanhood," which she extracts through critiques of current theories of justice and development. Both kinds of theories assume a dichotomy between a public/political sphere, to which theories of justice and development apply, and a private/domestic sphere, to which theories of justice and development do not apply. In both, it is assumed that women are caretakers of families in the private sphere, where work is invisible in data about economic development. The devaluation of women's work results in their economic dependence on men and their being subjected to physical and psychological abuse by men. Attention to gender, argues Okin, highlights inequalities in opportunity, access to jobs, and pay for women in the U.S. These inequalities can be fatal for poor women in poor countries where power differentials between men and women are magnified and where laws and cultural norms bar women from the workforce. According to Okin, the similar situation of women in different parts of the world calls for similar strategies and solutions: challenging the dichotomization of public and private spheres and treating women as individuals with equal rights to full economic participation.

Like Okin, Chandra Mohanty focuses on Western feminist discourse about women in developing countries. However, she rejects Okin's account of a generalizable, collectively shared experience of womanhood by claiming that the monolithic "Third World Woman" in recent Western feminist texts fails to capture the differences that characterize the lives of women in the Third World. Mohanty challenges Western feminists to examine their role in producing scholarship that stands as authoritative, yet dismisses the differences in the lives and experiences of women in various developing countries. She also urges that portrayals of Third World women as a homogeneous group characterized by common dependencies, powerlessness, and victim status need to be understood in the context of relations of power between Western and developing countries.

Rather than focus on mothering, marriage, or a sexual division of labor as such, Mohanty argues that we need to understand the relationships and structures within which these practices are given the meaning and value that they have in particular historical contexts. A monolithic notion of gender ignores the effects of social class, ethnic identities, and cultural practices on the meaning of gender and results in a serious failure to understand the kinds of oppression experienced by women and to effectively organize to eliminate it. Mohanty does not reject generalization as such, but calls for careful historically specific generalizations that are responsive to complex realities. To erase the relevance of gender differences, argues Mohanty, is to rob Third World women of their historical and political agency and to subject them to judgments about their lack of development and their susceptibility to false consciousness about their oppression.

In the final reading, Janice Newberry applies the lessons learned from Mohanty's attention to the particular contexts within which women are located. Newberry examines political structures in Indonesia from the perspectives, lives, and experiences of Indonesian women who are affected by them. Specifically, she describes the Indonesian government program known as PKK, a national housewives' organization institutionalized in 1973 and responsible for monitoring and promoting health, literacy, skills training in cooking, and small business endeavors in households and communities. PKK, as Newberry explains it, is a form of state-sponsored domesticity, a structure imposed by the Indonesian government to mobilize women as unpaid community development workers responsible for improving the standards of living of families and communities. The rhetoric of PKK upholds the nuclear family organized around a single couple with the woman staying at home as the model of good households and communities. This model has its source in Indonesia's history of Dutch colonialism, both in its struggles against it and its appropriation of Western notions of good mother and housewife that it brought.

Newberry uses the term "good terrorist" to argue that the very roles taken to be constitutive of what it is to be a good mother and housewife can be and are used by Indonesian women to generate social change. Within the confines of PKK, women contest the moral order promulgated by the state. The concept of the "good terrorist" captures the paradoxical idea that maintaining a social order can actually be subversive as women make use of the contradictions in the practices and values endorsed by the state to challenge and change the social order. Women in Indonesia, argues Newberry, are good terrorists to the extent that they comply with government directives on proper homes and domesticity, but only insofar as it serves their own ends and the needs of their communities. In the process, they open up spaces for changing not only their own lives but the very picture of what counts as a good mother and citizen.

BEAUTY IS THE BEAST: PSYCHOLOGICAL EFFECTS OF THE PURSUIT OF THE PERFECT FEMALE BODY

Elayne A. Saltzberg and Joan C. Chrisler

Elayne Saltzberg (Daniels) was a postdoctoral clinical psychology fellow at Yale University School of Medicine. Her major interests include body image and eating disorders. She is an eating disorder specialist with a practice in Massachusetts.

Joan C. Chrisler is Professor of Psychology at Connecticut College. She is the author of From Menarche to Menopause: The Female Body in Feminist Therapy *(2004) and co-editor of* Arming Athena: Career Strategies for Women in Academe *(with 1998, Lynn H. Collins and Kathryn Quina) and* Charting a New Course for Feminist Psychology *(2002, with Michelle R. Dunlap).*

Saltzberg and Chrisler discuss the ideal of the perfect female body, one that varies across cultures; changes over time; and is impacted by racism, class prejudice, and ableism. Because it is a fluctuating ideal that women strive for and few are able to attain, failure and disappointment are inevitable. Striving to attain the ideal takes its toil on women in the form of physical pain, health problems, medical procedures, costs of beauty products, time and effort, and damaging psychological effects. They argue that there are detrimental consequences for women who fail to reach the ideal: being punished for social transgressions, fired from jobs for being too old and unattractive, and discrimination in hiring and promotion. Saltzberg and Chrisler advocate that women become more aware of the effects on their bodies and their lives of pursuing ideals of the perfect female body.

Ambrose Bierce (1958) once wrote, "To men a man is but a mind. Who cares what face he carries or what he wears? But woman's body is the woman." Despite the societal changes achieved since Bierce's time, his statement remains true. Since the height of the feminist movement in the early 1970s, women have spent more money than ever before on products and treatments designed to make them beautiful. Cosmetic sales have increased annually to reach $18 billion in 1987 ("Ignoring the economy...," 1989), sales of women's clothing averaged $103 billion per month in 1990 (personal communication, U.S. Bureau of Economic Analysis, 1992), dieting has become a $30-billion-per-year industry (Stoffel, 1989), and women spent $1.2 billion on cosmetic surgery in 1990 (personal communication, American Society of Plastic and Reconstructive Surgeons, 1992). The importance of beauty has apparently increased even as women are reaching for personal freedoms and economic rights undreamed of by our grandmothers. The emphasis on beauty may be a way to hold onto a feminine image while shedding feminine roles.

Attractiveness is prerequisite for femininity but not for masculinity (Freedman, 1986). The word *beauty* always refers to the female body. Attractive male bodies are described as "handsome," a word derived from "hand" that refers as much to action as appearance (Freedman, 1986). Qualities of achievement and strength accompany the term *handsome*; such attributes are rarely employed in the description of attractive women and certainly do not accompany the term *beauty*, which refers only to a decorative quality. Men are instrumental; women are ornamental.

Beauty is a most elusive commodity. Ideas of what is beautiful vary across cultures and change over time (Fallon, 1990). Beauty cannot be quantified or objectively measured; it is the result of the judgments of others. The concept is difficult to define, as it is equated with different, sometimes contradictory, ideas. When people are asked to define beauty, they tend to mention abstract, personal qualities rather than external, quantifiable ones (Freedman, 1986; Hatfield & Sprecher, 1986). The beholder's perceptions and cognitions influence the degree of attractiveness at least as much as do the qualities of the beheld.

Because beauty is an ideal, an absolute, such as truth and goodness, the pursuit of it does not require justification (Herman & Polivy, 1983). An ideal, by definition, can be met by only a minority of those who strive for it. If too many women are able to meet the beauty standards of a particular time and place, then those standards must change in order to maintain their extraordinary nature. The value of beauty standards depends on their being special and unusual and is one of the reasons why the ideal changes over time. When images of beauty change, female bodies are expected to change, too. Different aspects of the female body and varying images of each body part are modified to meet the constantly fluctuating ideal (Freedman, 1986). The ideal is always that which is most difficult to achieve and most unnatural in a given time period. Because these ideals are nearly impossible to achieve, failure and disappointment are inevitable (Freedman, 1988).

Although people have been decorating their bodies since prehistoric times, the Chinese may have been the first to develop the concept that the female body can and should be altered from its natural state. The practice of foot binding clearly illustrates the objectification of parts of the female body as well as the demands placed on women to conform to beauty ideals. The custom called for the binding of the feet of five-year-old girls so that as they grew, their toes became permanently twisted under their arches and would actually shrink in size. The big toe remained untouched. The more tightly bound the feet, the more petite they became and the more attractive they were

considered to be (Freedman, 1986; Hatfield & Sprecher, 1986; Lakoff & Scherr, 1984). The painful custom of foot binding finally ended in the twentieth century after women had endured over one thousand years of torture for beauty's sake (Brain, 1979).

In the sixteenth century, European women bound themselves into corsets of whalebone and hardened canvas. A piece of metal or wood ran down the front to flatten the breasts and abdomen. This garment made it impossible to bend at the waist and difficult to breathe. A farthingale, which was typically worn over the corset, held women's skirts out from their bodies. It consisted of bent wood held together with tapes and made such simple activities as sitting nearly impossible. Queen Catherine of France introduced waist binding with a tortuous invention consisting of iron bands that minimized the size of the waist to the ideal measurement of thirteen inches (Baker, 1984). In the seventeenth century, the waist was still laced, but breasts were once again stylish, and fashions were designed to enhance them. Ample breasts, hips, and buttocks became the beauty ideal, perhaps paralleling a generally warmer attitude toward family life (Rosenblatt & Stencel, 1982). A white pallor was also popular at that time, probably as an indication that the woman was so affluent that she did not need to work outdoors, where the sun might darken her skin. Ceruse, a white lead-based paint now known to be toxic, was used to accentuate the pallor.

Tight corsets came back into vogue in Europe and North America in the mid-nineteenth century, and many women were willing to run the risk of developing serious health problems in order to wear them. The tight lacing often led to pulmonary disease and internal organ damage. American women disregarded the advice of their physicians, who spoke against the use of corsets because of their potential to displace internal organs. Fainting, or "the vapors," was the result of wearing such tightly laced clothing that normal breathing became impossible. Even the clergy sermonized against corsets; miscarriages were known to result in pregnant women who insisted on lacing themselves up too tightly. In the late nineteenth century, the beauty ideal required a tiny waist and full hips and bustline. Paradoxically, women would go on diets to gain weight while, at the same time, trying to achieve a smaller waistline. Some women were reported to have had their lower ribs removed so that their waists could be more tightly laced (Brain, 1979).

In the twentieth century, the ideal female body has changed several times, and American women have struggled to change along with it. In the 1920s, the ideal had slender legs and hips, small breasts, and bobbed hair and was physically and socially active. Women removed the stuffing from their bodices and bound their breasts[1] to appear young and boyish. In the 1940s and 1950s, the ideal returned to the hourglass shape. Marilyn Monroe was considered the epitome of the voluptuous and fleshy yet naive and childlike ideal. In the 1960s, the ideal had a youthful, thin, lean body and long, straight hair. American women dieted relentlessly in an attempt to emulate the tall, thin, teenage model Twiggy, who personified the 1960s' beauty ideal. Even pregnant women were on diets in response to their doctors' orders not to gain more than twenty pounds, advice physicians later rejected as unsafe (Fallon, 1990). Menopausal women begged their physicians to prescribe hormone replacement therapy, which was rumored to prevent wrinkles and keep the body youthful, and were willing to run any health risk to preserve their appearance (Chrisler, Torrey, & Matthes, 1989). In the 1970s, a thin, tan, sensuous look was "in." The 1980s' beauty ideal remained slim but required a more muscular, toned, and physically fit body. In recent decades the beauty ideal has combined such opposite traits as erotic sophistication with naive innocence, delicate grace with muscular athleticism (Freedman, 1988), and thin bodies with large breasts. The pressure to cope with such conflicting demands and to keep up with the continual changes in the ideal female body is highly stressful (Freedman, 1988) and has resulted in a large majority of American women with negative body images (Dworkin & Kerr, 1987; Rosen, Saltzberg, & Srebnik, 1989). Women's insecurity about their looks has made it easy to convince them that small breasts are a "disease" that require surgical inter-vention. The sophisticated woman of the 1990s who is willing to accept the significant health risks of breast implants in order to mold her body to fit the beauty ideal has not progressed far beyond her sisters who bound their feet and waists.

The value of beauty depends in part on the high costs of achieving it. Such costs may be physical, temporal, economic, or psychological. Physical costs include the pain of ancient beauty rituals such as foot binding, tatooing, and nose and ear piercing as well as more modern rituals such as wearing pointy-toed, high-heeled shoes, tight jeans, and sleeping with one's hair in curlers. Side effects of beauty rituals have often been disastrous for women's health. Tatooing and ear piercing with unsanitary instruments have led to serious, sometimes fatal, infections. Many women have been poisoned by toxic chemicals in cosmetics (e.g., ceruse, arsenic, benzene, and petroleum) and have died from the use of unsafe diet products such as rainbow pills and liquid protein (Schwartz, 1986). The beauty-related disorders anorexia nervosa and bulimia have multiple negative health effects, and side effects of plastic surgery include hemorrhages, scars, and nerve damage. Silicone implants have resulted in breast cancer, autoimmune disease, and the formation of thick scar tissue.

Physical costs of dieting include a constant feeling of hunger that leads to emotional changes, such as irritability; in cases of very low caloric intake, dieters can experience difficulty concentrating, confusion, and even reduced cognitive capacity. The only growing group of smokers in the United States are young women, many of whom report that they smoke to curb their appetites (Sorensen & Pechacek, 1987). High heels cause lower back pain and lead to a variety of podiatric disorders. Furthermore, fashion trends have increased women's vulnerability in a variety of ways; long hair and dangling earrings have gotten caught in machinery and entangled in clothing and led to injury. High heels and tight skirts prevent women from running from danger. The *New York Times* fashion reporter Bernadine Morris was alarmed to see in Pierre Cardin's 1988 summer fashion show tight wraps that prevented the models from moving their arms (Morris, 1988).

Attaining the beauty ideal requires a lot of money. Expensive cosmetics (e.g., makeup, moisturizers, and hair dyes and straighteners) are among the most popular and are thought to be the most effective, even though their ingredients cost the same (and sometimes are the same) as those in less expensive products (Lakoff & Scherr, 1984). Health spas have become fashionable again as vacation spots for the rich and famous, and everyone wants to wear expensive clothing with designer labels. Plastic surgery has become so accepted and so common that, although it's quite expensive, surgeons advertise their services on television. Surgery is currently performed that can reduce the size of lips, ear lobes, noses, buttocks, thighs, abdomens, and breasts; rebuild a face; remove wrinkles; and add "padding" to almost any body part. Not surprisingly, most plastic surgery patients are women (Hamburger, 1988).

Beauty rituals are time-consuming activities. Jokes about how long women take to get ready for a date are based on the additional tasks women do when getting dressed. It takes time to pluck eyebrows, shave legs, manicure nails, apply makeup, and arrange hair. Women's clothing is more complicated than men's, and many more accessories are used. Although all women know that the "transformation from female to feminine is artificial" (Chapkis, 1986, p. 5), we conspire to hide the amount of time and effort it takes, perhaps out of fear that other women don't need as much time as we do to appear beautiful. A lot of work goes into looking like a "natural" beauty, but that work is not acknowledged by popular culture, and the tools of the trade are kept out of view. Men's grooming rituals are fewer, take less time, and need not be hidden away. Scenes of men shaving have often been seen on television and in movies and have even been painted by Norman Rockwell. Wendy Chapkis (1986) challenges her readers to "imagine a similar cultural celebration of a woman plucking her eyebrows, shaving her armpits, or waxing her upper lip" (p. 6). Such a scene would be shocking and would remove the aura of mystery that surrounds beautiful women.

Psychological effects of the pursuit of the perfect female body include unhappiness, confusion, misery, and insecurity. Women often believe that if only they had perfect looks, their lives would be perfectly happy; they blame their unhappiness on their bodies. American women have the most negative body image of any culture studied by the Kinsey Institute (Faludi, 1991). Dissatisfaction with their bodies is very common among adolescent girls (Adams & Crossman, 1978; Clifford, 1971; Freedman, 1984), and older women believe that the only way to remain attractive is to prevent the development of any signs of aging. Obsessive concern about body shape and weight have become so common among American women of all ages that they now constitute the norm (Rodin, Silberstein, & Streigel-Moore, 1985). The majority of women in the United States are dieting at any given time. For them, being female means feeling fat and inadequate and living with chronic low self-esteem (Rodin, et al, 1985). Ask any woman what she would like to change about her body and she'll answer immediately. Ask her what she likes about her body and she'll have difficulty responding.

Those women who do succeed in matching the ideal thinness expected by modern beauty standards usually do so by exercising frenetically and compulsively, implementing severely restrictive and nutritionally deficient diets, developing bizarre eating habits, and using continuous self-degradation and self-denial. Dieting has become a "cultural requirement" for women (Herman & Polivy, 1983) because the ideal female body has become progressively thinner at the same time that the average female body has become progressively heavier. This cultural requirement remains in place despite the fact that physiology works against weight loss to such an extent that 98 percent of diets fail (Chrisler, 1989; Fitzgerald, 1981). In fact, it is more likely for someone to fully recover from cancer than for an obese person to lose a significant amount of weight and maintain that loss for five years (Brownell, 1982). Yet a recent study (Davies & Furnham, 1986) found that young women rate borderline anorexic bodies as very attractive. Thus, even the thinnest women find it nearly impossible to meet and maintain the beauty ideal.

The social pressure for thinness can be directly linked to the increasing incidence of anorexia nervosa and bulimia among women (Brumberg, 1988; Caskey, 1986). There are presently at least one million Americans with anorexia nervosa, and 95 percent of them are women. Between sixty thousand and 150,000 of them will die as a result of their obsession (Schwartz, 1986). Although cases of anorexia nervosa have been reported in the medical literature for hundreds of years (Bell, 1985), it was considered to be a rare disorder until the 1970s. Today's anorexics are also thinner than they were in the past (Brumberg, 1988). It is estimated that at least seven million American women will experience symptoms of bulimia at some point in their lives (Hatfield & Sprecher, 1986). A recent study (Hall & Cohn, 1988) found that 25 to 33 percent of female first-year college students were using vomiting after meals as a method of weight control. An accurate estimate of the number of women who are caught in the binge-purge cycle is difficult because women with bulimia are generally secretive about their behavior and the physical signs of bulimia are not nearly as obvious as those of anorexia nervosa.

Exercise has become for many women another manifestation of their body dissatisfaction. Studies have found that most men who exercise regularly do so to build body mass and to increase cardiovascular fitness; most women who exercise do so to lose weight and to change the shape of their bodies in order to increase their attractiveness (Garner, Rockert, Olmstead, Johnson, & Coscina, 1985; Saltzberg, 1990). Exercise has lost its status as a pleasurable activity and become yet another way for women to manipulate their bodies, another vehicle for narcissistic self-torture. Reports of the number of women exercising compulsively are increasing and may become as widespread as compulsive calorie counting and the compulsive eating habits of anorexics and bulimics.

Beauty ideals are created and maintained by society's elite. Racism, class prejudice, and rejection of the disabled are clearly reflected (Chapkis, 1986) in current American beauty standards. For example, women from lower socioeconomic groups typically weigh more than women in higher

socioeconomic groups (Moore, Stunkard, & Srole, 1962); they are thus excluded by popular agreement from being considered beautiful. The high costs of chic clothing, cosmetics, tanning salons, skin and hair treatments, weight loss programs, and plastic surgery prevent most American women from access to the tools necessary to approach the ideal. Furthermore, the beauty standard idealizes Caucasian features and devalues those of other races (Lewis, 1977; Miller, 1969). In recent years, Asian American and African-American women have sought facial surgery in order to come closer to the beauty ideal (Faludi, 1991), and psychotherapists have noted increased reports from their black women clients of guilt, shame, anger, and resentment about skin color, hair texture, facial features, and body size and shape (Greene, 1992; Neal & Wilson, 1989; Okazawa-Rey, Robinson, & Ward, 1987). Obviously, women with visible disabilities will never be judged to have achieved "perfection." Whoopi Goldberg's routine about the black teenager who wrapped a towel around her head to pretend it was long, blonde hair and Alice Walker's (1990) essay about her psychological adjustment after the eye injury that resulted in the development of "hideous" scar tissue provide poignant examples of the pain women experience when they cannot meet beauty standards.

The inordinate emphasis on women's external selves makes it difficult for us to appreciate our own internal selves (Kano, 1985). The constant struggle to meet the beauty ideal leads to high stress and chronic anxiety. Failure to meet the beauty ideal leads to feelings of frustration, low self-worth, and inadequacy in women whose sense of self is based on their physical appearance. The intensity of the drive to increase attractiveness may also contribute to the high rate of depression among women.[2]

Insecurity is common even among beautiful women, and studies show that they are as likely as their plain sisters to be unhappy about their looks (Freedman, 1988). Beautiful women are all too aware of the fleeting nature of their beauty; the effects of aging must be constantly monitored, and these women worry that the beauty ideal they've tried so hard to match may change without warning. When such women lose their beauty due to illness or accidents, they often become depressed and are likely to have difficulty functioning in society and to believe that their entire identity has been threatened.

Given the high costs of striving to be beautiful, why do women attempt it? Attractiveness greatly affects first impressions and later interpersonal relationships. In a classic study titled "What Is Beautiful Is Good," psychologists Kenneth Dion, Ellen Berscheid, and Elaine Hatfield (Dion, Berscheid, & Walster, 1972) asked college students to rate photographs of strangers on a variety of personal characteristics. Those who were judged to be attractive were also more likely to be rated intelligent, kind, happy, flexible, interesting, confident, sexy, assertive, strong, outgoing, friendly, poised, modest, candid, and successful than those judged unattractive. Teachers rate attractive children more highly on a variety of positive characteristics including IQ and sociability, and attractive babies are cuddled and kissed more often than unattractive babies (Berscheid & Walster, 1974). Attractive people receive more lenient punishment for social transgressions (Dion, 1972; Landy & Aronson, 1969), and attractive women are more often sought out in social situations (Walster, Aronson, Abrahams, & Rottman, 1966; Reis, Nezlek, & Wheeler, 1980).

Furthermore, because unattractive people are more harshly punished for social transgressions and are less often sought after social partners, failure to work toward the beauty ideal can result in real consequences. Television newswoman Christine Craft made the news herself when she was fired for being too old and too unattractive. Street harassers put women "in their place" by commenting loudly on their beauty or lack of it. Beauty norms limit the opportunities of women who can't or won't meet them. Obese women, for example, have experienced discrimination in a number of instances including hiring and promotion (Larkin & Pines, 1979; Rothblum, Miller, & Gorbutt, 1988) and college admissions (Canning & Mayer, 1966). Obese people even have a harder time finding a place to live; Lambros Karris (1977) found that landlords are less likely to rent to obese

people. Even physicians view their obese patients negatively (Maddox & Liederman, 1969).

There is considerable evidence that women's attractiveness is judged more harshly than men's. Christine Craft was fired, yet David Brinkley and Willard Scott continue to work on major television news shows; their abilities are not thought to be affected by age or attractiveness. Several studies (Adams & Huston, 1975; Berman, O'Nan, & Floyd, 1981; Deutsch, Zalenski, & Clark, 1986; Wernick & Manaster, 1984) that asked participants to rate the attractiveness of photographs of people of varying ages found that although attractiveness ratings of both men and women decline with age, the rate of decline for women was greater. In one study (Deutsch, Zalenski, & Clark, 1986), participants were asked to rate the photographs for femininity and masculinity as well as attractiveness. The researchers found that both the attractiveness and femininity ratings of the female photographs diminished with age; the masculinity ratings were unaffected by the age or attractiveness of the photographs. Women are acutely aware of the double standard of attractiveness. At all ages women are more concerned than men about weight and physical appearance and have lower appearance self-esteem; women who define themselves as feminine are the most concerned about their appearance and have the lowest self-esteem (Pliner, Chaiken, & Flett, 1990). In fact, women are so concerned about their body size that they typically overestimate it. Women who overestimate their size feel worse about themselves, whereas men's self-esteem is unrelated to their body size estimates (Thompson, 1986). In a review of research on the stigma of obesity, Esther Rothblum (1992) concluded that the dieting industry, combined with Western attitudes toward weight and attractiveness, causes more pain and problems for women than for men.

Thus, the emphasis on beauty has political as well as psychological consequences for women, as it results in oppression and disempowerment. It is important for women to examine the effects that the pursuit of the perfect female body has had on their lives, challenge their beliefs, and take a stand against continued enslavement to the elusive beauty ideal. Women would then be able to live life more freely and experience the world more genuinely. Each woman must decide for herself what beauty really is and the extent to which she is willing to go to look attractive. Only a more diverse view of beauty and a widespread rebellion against fashion extremes will save us from further physical and psychological tolls.

Imagine an American society where the quality and meaning of life for women are not dependent on the silence of bodily shame. Imagine a society where bodies are decorated for fun and to express creativity rather than for self-control and self-worth. Imagine what would happen if the world's women released and liberated all of the energy that had been absorbed in the beautification process. The result might be the positive, affirming, healthy version of a nuclear explosion!

Author's Note

The authors thank Jo Freeman, Sue Wilkinson, and Paulette Leonard for their helpful comments on an earlier version of this paper and Barbara Weber for locating the business and industry statistics.

NOTES

1. Bras were originally designed to hide breasts.
2. Statistics indicate that women are far more likely than men to be diagnosed as depressed. The ratio is at least 3:1 (Williams, 1985).

REFERENCES

Adams, Gerald R., & Crossman, Sharyn M. (1978). *Physical attractiveness: A cultural imperative.* New York: Libra.

Adams, Gerald R., & Huston, Ted L. (1975). Social perception of middle-aged persons varying in physical attractiveness. *Developmental Psychology*, 11, 657-58.

Baker, Nancy C. (1984). *The beauty trap: Exploring woman's greatest obsession.* New York: Franklin Watts.

Bell, Rudolph M. (1985). *Holy anorexia.* Chicago: University of Chicago Press.

Berman, Phyllis W., O'Nan, Barbara A., & Floyd, Wayne. (1981). The double standard of aging and the social situation: Judgments of attractiveness of the middle-aged woman. *Sex Roles*, 7, 87-96.

Berscheid, Ellen, & Walster, Elaine. (1974). Physical attractiveness. *Advances in Experimental Social Psychology*, 7, 158-215.

Bierce, Ambrose. (1958). *The devil's dictionary.* New York: Dover.

Brain, R. (1979). *The decorated body.* New York: Harper & Row,

Brownell, Kelly. (1982). Obesity: Understanding and treating a serious, prevalent, and refractory disorder. *Journal of Consulting and Clinical Psychology*, 55, 889-97.

Brumberg, Joan J. (1988). *Fasting girls.* Cambridge, MA: Harvard University Press.

Canning, H., & Mayer, J. (1966). Obesity: An influence on high school performance. *Journal of Clinical Nutrition*, 20, 352-54.

Caskey, Noelle. (1986). Interpreting anorexia nervosa. In Susan R. Suleiman (Ed.), *The female body in western culture* (pp. 175-89). Cambridge, MA: Harvard University Press.

Chapkis, Wendy. (1986). *Beauty secrets: Women and the politics of appearance.* Boston: South End Press.

Chrisler, Joan C. (1989). Should feminist therapists do weight loss counseling? *Women & Therapy*, 8(3), 31-37.

Chrisler, Joan C.,Torrey, Jane W., & Matthes, Michelle. (1989, June). *Brittle bones and sagging breasts, loss of femininity and loss of sanity: The media describe the menopause.* Paper presented at the meeting of the Society for Menstrual Cycle Research, Salt Lake City, UT.

Clifford, Edward. (1971). Body satisfaction in adolescence. *Perceptual and Motor Skills*, 33, 119-25.

Davies, Elizabeth, & Furnham, Adrian. (1986). The dieting and body shape concerns of adolescent females. *Child Psychology and Psychiatry*, 21, 417-28.

Deutsch, Francine M., Zalenski, Carla M., & Clark, Mary E. (1986). Is there a double standard of aging? *Journal of Applied Social Psychology*, 16, 771-85.

Dion, Kenneth K. (1972). Physical attractiveness and evaluation of children's transgressions. *Journal of Personality and Social Psychology*, 24, 285-90.

Dion, Kenneth, Berscheid, Ellen, & Walster [Hatfield], Elaine. (1972). What is beautiful is good. *Journal of Personality and Social Psychology*, 24, 285-90.

Dworkin, Sari H., & Kerr, Barbara A. (1987). Comparison of interventions for women experiencing body image problems. *Journal of Consulting and Clinical Psychology*, 34, 136-40.

Fallon, April. (1990). Culture in the mirror: Sociocultural determinants of body image. In Thomas Cash & Thomas Pruzinsky (Eds.), *Body images: Development, deviance, and change* (pp. 80-109). New York: Guilford Press.

Faludi, Susan. (1991). *Backlash: The undeclared war against American women*. New York: Crown Publishers.

Fitzgerald, Faith T. (1981). The problem of obesity. *Annual Review of Medicine*, 32, 221-31.

Freedman, Rita. (1984). Reflections on beauty as it relates to health in adolescent females. In Sharon Golub (Ed.), *Health care of the female adolescent* (pp. 29-45). New York: Haworth Press.

Freedman, Rita. (1986). *Beauty bound*. Lexington, MA: D.C. Heath.

Freedman, Rita. (1988). *Bodylove: Learning to like our looks — and ourselves*. New York: Harper & Row.

Garner, David M., Rockert, Wendy, Olmstead, Marion P., Johnson, C, & Coscina, D. V. (1985). Psychoeducational principles in the treatment of bulimia and anorexia nervosa. In David M. Garner & Paul E. Garfinkel (Eds.), *Handbook of psychotherapy for anorexia nervosa and bulimia* (pp. 513-62). New York: Guilford.

Greene, Beverly. (1992). Still here: A perspective on psychotherapy with African American women. In Joan C. Chrisler & Doris Howard (Eds.), New *directions in feminist psychology: Practice, theory, and research* (pp. 13-25). New York: Springer.

Hall, L., & Cohn, L. (1988). *Bulimia: A guide to recovery*. Carlsbad, CA: Gurze Books.

Hamburger, A.C. (1988, May). Beauty quest. *Psychology Today*, 22, 28-32. Hatfield, Elaine, & Sprecher, Susan. (1986). *Mirror, mirror: The importance of looks in everyday life*. Albany: State University of New York Press.

Herman, Peter, & Polivy, Janet. (1983). *Breaking the diet habit*. New York: Basic Books.

Ignoring the economy, cosmetic firms look to growth. (1989, July 13). *Standard and Poor's Industry Surveys*, 1, 37-38.

Kano, Susan. (1985). *Making peace with food: A step-by-step guide to freedom from diet/weight conflict*. Danbury, CT: Amity.

Karris, Lambros. (1977). Prejudice against obese renters. *Journal of Social Psychology*, 101, 159-60.

Lakoff, Robin T., & Scherr, Raquel L. (1984). *Face value: The politics of beauty*. Boston: Routledge & Kegan Paul.

Landy, David, & Aronson, Elliot. (1969). The influence of the character of the criminal and his victim on the decisions of simulated jurors. *Journal of Experimental Social Psychology*, 5, 141-52.

Larkin, Judith, & Pines, Harvey. (1979). No fat person need apply. *Sociology of Work and Occupations*, 6, 312-27.

Lewis, Diane K. (1977). A response to inequality: Black women, racism, and sexism. *Signs*, 3(2), 339-61.

Maddox, G., & Liederman, V. (1969). Overweight as a social disability with medical implications. *Journal of Medical Education*, 44, 214-20.

Miller, E. (1969). Body image, physical beauty, and color among Jamaican adolescents. *Social and Economic Studies*, 18(1), 72-89.

Moore, M.E., Stunkard, Albert, & Srole, L. (1962). Obesity, social class, and mental illness. *Journal of the American Medical Association*, 181, 138-42.

Morris, Bernardine. (1988, July 26). Paris couture: Opulence lights a serious mood. *New York Times*, p. B8.

Neal, Angela, & Wilson, Midge. (1989). The role of skin color and features in the black community: Implications for black women and therapy. *Clinical Psychology Review*, 9, 323-33.

Okazawa-Rey, Margo, Robinson, Tracy, & Ward, Janie V. (1987). Black women and the politics of skin color and hair. *Women & Therapy*, 6(1/2), 89-102.

Pliner, Patricia, Chaiken, Shelly, & Flett, Gordon L. (1990). Gender differences in concern with body weight and physical appearance over the life span. *Personality and Social Psychology Bulletin*, 16, 263-73.

Reis, Harry T., Nezlek, John, & Wheeler, Ladd. (1980). Physical attractiveness in social interaction. *Journal of Personality and Social Psychology*, 38, 604-17.

Rodin, Judith, Silberstein, Lisa, & Streigel-Moore, Ruth. (1985). Women and weight: A normative discontent. In Theo B. Sonderegger (Ed.), *Nebraska symposium on motivation: Psychology and gender* (pp. 267-307). Lincoln: University of Nebraska Press.

Rosen, James C, Saltzberg, Elayne A., & Srebnik, Debra. (1989). Cognitive behavior therapy for negative body image. *Behavior Therapy*, 20, 393-404.

Rosenblatt, J., & Stencel, S. (1982). *Weight control: A national obsession*. Washington, DC: Congressional Quarterly.

Rothblum, Esther D. (1992). The stigma of women's weight: Social and economic realities. *Feminism & Psychology*, 2(1), 61-73.

Rothblum, Esther D., Miller, Carol, & Gorbutt, Barbara. (1988). Stereotypes of obese female job applicants. *International Journal of Eating Disorders*, 7, 277-83.

Saltzberg, Elayne A. (1990). *Exercise participation and its correlates to body awareness and self-esteem.* Unpublished master's thesis, Connecticut College, New London, CT.

Schwartz, Hillel. (1986). *Never satisfied: A cultural history of diets, fantasies, and fat.* New York: Free Press.

Sorensen, Gloria, & Pechacek, Terry F. (1987). Attitudes toward smoking cessation among men and women. *Journal of Behavioral Medicine*, 10, 129-38.

Stoffel, Jennifer. (1989, November 26). What's new in weight control: A market mushrooms as motivations change. *New York Times*, p. C17.

Thompson, J. Kevin. (1986, April). Larger than life. *Psychology Today*, pp. 41-44.

Walker, Alice. (1990). Beauty: When the other dancer is the self. In Evelyn C. White (Ed.), *The black women's health book: Speaking for ourselves* (pp. 280-87). Seattle: Seal Press.

Walster, Elaine, Aronson, Vera, Abrahams, Darcy, & Rottman, Leon. (1966). Importance of physical attractiveness in dating behavior. *Journal of Personality and Social Psychology*, 4, 508-16.

Wernick, Mark, & Manaster, Guy J. (1984). Age and the perception of age and attractiveness. *Gerontologist*, 24, 408-14.

Williams, Juanita H. (1985). *Psychology of women: Behavior in a biosocial context.* New York: Norton.

JUSTICE AND THE DISTRIBUTION OF FEAR

Keith Burgess-Jackson

Keith Burgess-Jackson is Associate Professor of Philosophy at the University of Texas at Arlington, where he teaches courses in logic, philosophy of law, moral philosophy, philosophy of religion, and feminism. He is the author of Rape: A Philosophical Investigation *(1996) and co-author, with Irving M. Copi, of* Informal Logic, *third edition (1996). He is also the editor of, and a multiple contributor to,* A Most Detestable Crime: New Philosophical Essays on Rape *(1999).*

Burgess-Jackson believes that philosophers have unduly neglected the distribution of socially created burdens, focusing instead on benefits (such as health care). He tries to rectify this omission by addressing the distribution of a particular burden, fearfulness. Social-scientific literature shows that fear of crime is distributed in patterns, not haphazardly. Women, for example, are significantly more fearful than men, in large part because women, but not men, are victimized by rape. Burgess-Jackson argues that this state of affairs is unjust and that, since the distribution of fear can be rectified by collective action, it must be. He considers and dismisses several objections to this argument.

Rape operates as a social control mechanism to keep women in their "place" or put them there. The fear of rape, common to most women, socially controls them as it limits their ability to move about freely. As such, it establishes and maintains the woman in a position of subordination.[1]

Introduction

By default or by design, philosophical discussions of distributive justice concern the distribution of benefits rather than burdens. One influential philosopher, Stanley Benn, has gone so far as to say that "the problem [of distributive justice] is to allocate benefits."[2] The benefits in question are variable, taking the form of material objects (such as heart-lung machines), services (the provision of health care), opportunities (for example, to employment and education), rights (to property), income, wealth, offices, rewards, and other goods. Each benefit is supposed to be made possible by communal living and is, in the economist's sense,

scarce — meaning that its supply is exceeded by aggregate demand. The problem of distributive justice, so conceived, is to state the principle(s) by which these benefits are to be allocated among individuals who desire or need them. The work of Rawls, Nozick, Walzer, and Ronald Dworkin exemplifies this class of normative theory.

But distributive justice is concerned with the burdens as well as the benefits of social living, Benn's characterization notwithstanding. These burdens take the form of unpleasant or undesirable things, obligations, and experiences,[3] such as labor, the payment of taxes, military service, and criminal punishment. By analogy to the case of benefits, we can say that each burden is made *necessary* by communal living. Each arises from the fact that human beings live in communities and have only partially overlapping interests and objectives....

My aim in this essay is to address an item on the neglected "burden" side of the ledger. What I want to explore are the normative implications of the distribution of a particular socially created burden:

fearfulness (hereafter "fear"). I begin by reciting facts drawn from the social-scientific literature on fear, which has become quite sophisticated. This literature shows unequivocally that fear of crime, far from being distributed uniformly or randomly throughout the population, is distributed in identifiable and insidious patterns.[4] Women, for example, are more fearful of crime then men. Why this is so is a matter of disagreement among social scientists, and since the answer to the explanatory question bears on the argument I go on to make as well as on some of the objections I consider, I state the most widely proffered explanations of why these patterns exist.

Having set out the facts and some explanations, I proceed to argue that while fear, or a certain amount and kind of fear, may be useful in keeping individuals safe from harm, it is, as a mental state, burdensome to those who experience it. Fear of crime in particular is a socially created burden. It follows that women bear a disproportionate share of this burden, a state of affairs that I argue in Part III is unjust in principle and, given its remediability through collective action (which I address in Part IV), unacceptable in practice. Justice, I maintain, requires that the state employing institutions such as law and education and using the power of the purse, both reduce the overall level of fear in society and, more particularly, redistribute fear so that women no longer bear the brunt of it....

I. The Distribution of Fear

Let us begin with the facts. Any person, nonhuman animal, physical object, event, or state of affairs can, logically, be the object of fear, but one state of affairs that nearly everyone fears at one time or another in his or her life (albeit to different degrees), and one that nearly half of adult Americans have altered their lifestyle in some way to accommodate,[5] is victimization — being a victim of criminal behavior. But this fact, taken alone, is apt to mislead, for studies routinely show that fear of crime is distributed in patterns throughout society. For example, the elderly are more likely than the nonelderly to fear victimization. The same is true of nonwhites, those with low incomes, the

comparatively uneducated, and those who live in urban areas, each of whom, as a class, is more fearful than its counterpart.[6] But the "most powerful predictor of fear of personal crimes" turns out to be not age, income, race, or class, but sex.[7] "[F]emales," a researcher writes, "exhibit higher fear than males for every offense,"[8] from being threatened with a knife, club, or gun to being murdered, having one's car stolen, or receiving an obscene telephone call.[9]

In one study men and women were asked "How safe do you feel being out alone in your neighborhood at night: very safe, reasonably safe, somewhat unsafe or very unsafe?"[10] More than 43 percent of the female respondents reported being either somewhat or very unsafe; but only 17.9 percent of the male respondents gave that answer. The disparity is even greater with respect to the response "very unsafe," with 22.8 percent of the women and 6.4 percent of the men giving that answer.[11] As for how often men and women reflect on their safety (or lack thereof), it has been found that "48 percent of the women, compared with 25 percent of the men, reported 'thinking of their own safety all or most of the time' or 'fairly often.'"[12] It appears from these and other studies that women, as compared to men, fear more different crimes, fear them to a greater degree, and fear them a greater proportion of the time.

That much is clear. What puzzles researchers is that, for most crime categories, "there are substantially lower victimization rates for women" than for men.[13] In other words, fear of crime does not track reality. If fear were a function solely of the likelihood of being victimized, then men, not women, should experience greater fear, for men are more often victimized. So why are women more fearful? One obvious explanation is that some or much of women's fear is unfounded.[14] But this explanation is implausible on its face and to this point at least lacks experimental confirmation. I address it in Part V.

Another hypothesis is that men and women assign different degrees of seriousness to the various crimes, so that even if they agree on the *likelihood* of being victimized, they respond differently to the risk. As one researcher put it, men and women have "differential sensitivity to risk."[15] This hypothesis, unlike the first, *has* been experimentally confirmed; "[f]emales," it has been discovered, "typically view each offence as more serious than males."[16] Yet another hypothesis concerns differential vulnerability, the suggestion being that women, the elderly, and other fearful individuals are, and take themselves to be, more vulnerable to crime (in the sense of being less able to defend themselves in case of attack), which gives rise to greater fear. Unfortunately, this hypothesis has not been rigorously tested and so has not been confirmed.

A fourth hypothesis, which *has* been confirmed, maintains that women are more fearful than men because only women are targets of sexual assault, "an especially terrifying form of personal violation."[17] Not only is rape particularly frightening to women, for obvious reasons, it is often accompanied by other crimes against person and property. "[A] high perceived probability of residential burglary," for example, "may provoke intense fear among many women because assault, rape, and even homicide are viewed as likely contemporaneous offenses."[18] One empirical study found that "fear of rape is significantly correlated ... with fear of all other offenses measured,"[19] which included threats, robbery, burglary while home, assault, murder, and loitering. The differential fear of crime experienced by women is explicable, at least in part, in terms of their fear of rape, which women as a class view as one of the most serious of offenses; if not *the* most serious. "Among women in each age group," sociologist Mark Warr writes, "the perceived seriousness of rape is approximately equal to the perceived seriousness of murder."[20]

Rape (or sexual assault, I use the terms interchangeably) is a crime that almost all women but no men fear. For women between the ages of nineteen and thirty-five rape is the *most-feared* crime, more feared even than murder.[21] A team of researchers concludes that "virtually all adult women live at some level of consciousness with the fear and threat of sexual assault."[22] These researchers discovered that "67 percent of the women interviewed, when asked a direct question, said they were worried about sexual assault, while

only 7 percent of the men interviewed said the same."[23]

The disparity between fear of rape and fear of other crimes has led social scientists to view rape as a "core" fear, a fear that "underlies" others, and as a "master offense."[24] Indeed, for younger women, "fear of crime *is* fear of rape."[25] While fear of sexual assault is not universal among women, all or most women "experience a period of routine or habitual fear at some point in their lives."[26] Warr concludes that "it is difficult to imagine many other social problems [besides rape] that affect so many people in such a direct way."[27]

II. The Burden of Fear

I use the word "burden" in the ordinary way, to refer to "something carried, a heavy load,"[28] the implication being that one would prefer not to have to carry the load. It is in this normatively loaded sense — the sense in which a benefit, by contrast, is *desired* — that fear is burdensome. But the burdens of fear are of different types as well as degrees. First, fear — the condition of being afraid — is an intrinsically unpleasant mental state.[29] This is true even when the mental state itself leads one to take self-protective action. We would not say in such a case that the fear was *pleasant,* or even affectively neutral, but that its *unpleasantness* served a useful purpose and was for that reason tolerable. Fear, in other words, can be functional. Moreover, like any strong emotion, fear can distract one's attention, disrupt otherwise operative mental processes, and displace or inhibit pleasant mental states. To be preoccupied with or overcome by fear is to be incapable of attending to other matters. At the extreme, fear can paralyze.

Second, fear debilitates. It can, and very often does, cause one to be feeble, weak, and vulnerable, with obvious detrimental effects on one's life plan. This is certainly true with respect to the fear of crime. Researchers have learned that fear of crime is correlated with limitations on liberty in general and mobility in particular. Since, as we have seen, women experience greater fear than men, especially in connection with rape, women suffer most from these debilitating effects. According to one research team, "78 percent of the men, compared with 32 percent of the women, reported they never avoid doing things they need to for fear of crime."[30]

To give some idea of the extent to which and ways in which women limit their behavior as a result of fear, consider that 25.3 percent of women, but only 2.9 percent of men, never walk alone in their neighborhood after dark. More than 68 percent of women, but only 5.4 percent of men, say they never go alone to bars or clubs after dark. Comparable differences exist with respect to going alone to movies after dark, going downtown alone after dark, and walking by parks or lots alone after dark.[31] As one group of researchers put it, "Our data suggest that women may have developed lifestyles that include restrictions on their freedom and behavior and that may keep them safe by limiting their chances of becoming victims."[32] Unfortunately, the lifestyles women adopt as a means of keeping them safe are not always successful; but even if they were, it would not make the costs of fear disappear and would not eliminate what I shall argue is the injustice of women's having to develop such lifestyles.

The costs of women's fear of rape, calculated both quantitatively and qualitatively, are enormous. They include the limitations on liberty just described[33] as well as the many reverberations from that constraint. One such reverberation is the reluctance of many women to assume positions of authority and public responsibility that might place them in dangerous situations or places. This consequence has immediate and obvious implications for distributive justice, for, as one feminist scholar has put it, "we cannot function as a true democracy as long as women's well-founded fear of rape inhibits our full participation in society."[34] A fearful woman is a woman drawn inward and kept on the defensive, not a woman focused on the sports arena, the economic marketplace, the laboratory, or the legislative chamber.

Other costs, some tangible and some not (although no less real for that), include: loss of self-confidence, self-respect, and self-esteem; nightmares and other sleep disorders; distrust and suspicion of strangers and acquaintances; chronic anxiety, stress,[35] and depression; inability to live alone (when that is desired);[36] and increased dependence on men for protection, which in turn undermines self-respect and self-confidence, Susan Sontag was not far off the mark, if at all, when she wrote many years ago that "Basically, a woman is only safe at 'home' or when protected by a man."[37] The fear of crime generally, and of rape in particular, may, according to Margaret Gordon and Stephanie Riger, "lead [women] to experience their whole environment as a dangerous place to be."[38] No criminal conspiracy, no organized patriarchal religion, no oppressive political regime could be as effective a means of social control.

I take it as established for purposes of this essay that fear is an unwelcome burden to be carried, however useful it may be (when properly focused and limited) in promoting personal safety. Fear is intrinsically unpleasant, distracting, disruptive, and debilitating; it is — and is universally experienced as — a cost to those who are in its grip. Nobody would voluntarily undertake to carry such a load without the prospect of a greater good. But the burdensomeness of fear alone, however great, does not implicate distributive justice. Distributive justice is implicated only when one *conjoins* to the burdensomeness of fear that fact that women, as a class, are significantly more fearful than men as a class — that women are *disproportionately* burdened. The questions then become (1) whether anything can be done about this state of affairs, and (2) if so, what justice requires to be done. It is to these and other normative matters that I now turn.

III. The Injustice of the Existing Distribution of Fear

There is no question that fear, as an unpleasant mental state, can and does have value. Its main value, as I have suggested, lies in the fact that it motivates individuals to take precautions against risks of harm to themselves and others. To that extent fear has instrumental value. But as I have shown, fear can also interfere with one's plan of life in drastic and deleterious ways. To that extent fear is a significant burden. Other things being equal, the less fear one experiences, the better off one is. Ideally, there would be only enough fear at any given time and place to motivate individuals to take precautions against harm. But what if certain fears, such as the fear of crime, are generated by social life itself; what if those fears fall disproportionately on certain individuals as defined by their membership is a class; and what if the class-defining characteristic is beyond individual control? Then we are in the realm of justice.

Some burdens of social living can be reduced or eliminated only by creating or increasing burdens on other individuals. There is in such a case, as economists are wont to say, no Pareto superior move — no move that makes some individuals better off without making at least one other individual worse off. Fear appears to be of this type. The newly imposed burdens can be of the same type as, or of a different type than, the existing burdens. For example, it may be that in order to reduce the burden of military service on one group of individuals (say, the poor), it is necessary to increase the burden of military service on another (the nonpoor). This would be the case if a certain level of military service must be maintained. But the burden of fear is not of this type. Nobody, least of all I, seriously suggests that in order to reduce the burden of fear on women, the elderly, and others, society should increase the burden on their counterparts. First, it's not clear how this could be done; but second, even if it could, it's not clear that it would be justified. What point would be served by increasing the fear of one group of individuals without decreasing the fear of anyone else?...

Some burdens can be reduced or eliminated only by increasing or creating different types of burdens on others. The burden of fear is of this type. While it would be nice if women's fear of crime could be reduced without imposing costs on them or on anyone else, this is not likely to be the case. More likely, such measures which reduce women's fear will be costly in the economist's sense; to achieve the desired results, other goods will have to be forgone. Since those who forgo these goods are not necessarily the same as those who benefit from the reduction or elimination of fear on the part of women, considerations of distributive justice come to the fore. The main question is one of principle

— namely, whether justice requires that the existing distribution of fear be altered. I maintain that it does. Specifically, as I go on to argue, steps must be taken to reduce women's fear of crime, a significant part of which is women's fear of rape. A subsidiary question concerns who — that is, which class of individuals — ought to bear the cost of redistribution. In Part IV, I argue that since women's fear of crime is caused overwhelmingly by men as a class, men should bear all or most of the cost.

My argument is as follows. I assume that it is incompatible with justice for major benefits and burdens of social living to be distributed on the basis of irrelevant personal characteristics, by which I understand characteristics that are beyond a person's capacity to control or alter. This premise does not say which characteristics are *relevant*; it says only that if a particular characteristic is *irrelevant,* it cannot, consistently with justice, be the basis of distribution. Nor does the premise presuppose that we know or can specify in advance all of the characteristics that are relevant to each distribution. We can know that something is *irrelevant* to a distribution without knowing all the things that are relevant.[39] The second premise of the argument is the normative claim, defended above, that fear is a major burden of social living. Since sex, by hypothesis, is irrelevant to whether one should bear a particular benefit or burden — or rather, since sex is irrelevant to whether one should bear the burden of *fear* — fear may not be distributed on the basis of sex.[40] Unfortunately, as we have seen, it *is* distributed in just that way, so the existing distribution of fear is unjust.

I take it as uncontroversial that the state, as the instrument of the collective will, has an affirmative obligation to rectify injustice of all types, distributive and retributive, so it follows that the state has an affirmative obligation to reduce women's fear — even if the reduction comes at the expense of others, such as men, who do not stand to benefit, or do not stand to benefit to the same extent, from its actions. Like Rawls, I view justice as "the first virtue of social institutions,"[41] one that may not be subjugated to other virtues or values. But whereas Rawls explicitly limits justice to "laws and institutions," I include states of affairs that constitute, exemplify, or result from social interaction. To paraphrase Rawls, however "efficient and well-arranged" the existing distribution of fear, and however haphazardly it may have come into existence, it "must be reformed or abolished" if unjust.[42] The state, therefore, as the instrument of social justice, must use whatever means it has at its disposal to achieve this end.

IV. Rectifying the Injustice

I assume, then, that justice requires the redistribution of fear. But this claim is intolerably abstract. What concrete measures can be taken to reduce women's fear of crime, the bulk of which, as we have seen, consists in fear of sexual assault? First and foremost, the state can, through the criminal-justice system, take steps to prevent rape. We have seen that rape is fear-provoking in its own right and also that it is the source of much ancillary fear. If the incidence of rape is decreased, it stands to reason that a significant amount of women's fear will decrease as well.

But how can that be achieved? One way, which assumes that rape is a deterrable offense (there is no reason to think it is not),[43] is to increase the cost of rape to the prospective rapist. There are different ways to do this. The first and most obvious is to increase the magnitude of punishment for those convicted of rape. But this strategy, given prevailing attitudes, may have the perverse effect of *decreasing* the number of rape convictions, and thus lowering the expected punishment of the crime.[44] The problem is that jurors may be reluctant to convict men whom they believe to be guilty but who aren't seen as "deserving" of "severe" punishment.

A second and potentially more fruitful strategy is to increase the likelihood of apprehension, trial, and conviction of rapists while either leaving punishment as it is or reducing its magnitude. This would increase the expected punishment for the prospective rapist without encouraging or tempting jurors to ignore the law, and since we are assuming that rapists are rational and self-interested, it would have the salutary effect of deterring, and hence preventing, rape. It will take empirical research to

discover which combination of punishment and likelihood of apprehension has the greatest deterrent effect. But in principle that is one action the state can take to reduce women's fear.

Apprehension, conviction, and punishment of rapists, while important components of an overall strategy to reduce women's fear of crime, are not the only components and may in the long run not be the most effective. It has been suggested that fear of crime is directly related to one's sense of vulnerability. This would explain why the elderly, for example, are more fearful than the nonelderly, for the elderly tend to experience themselves as weak and helpless. If that is so, then one way to reduce women's fear is to reduce or eliminate their sense of vulnerability. This can be done in many ways, foremost among which is to encourage women to learn self-defense techniques.[45] Studies show that "women who perceive themselves as less physically able are more likely to say they are afraid. However, after taking self-defense training courses, women reported feeling stronger, braver, more active, more in control, bigger, more efficacious in a variety of arenas — and less afraid."[46]

Related to this is a general sense of competence and control. Women traditionally have not been encouraged to participate — indeed, have been actively discouraged from participating — in athletic competition at either the individual or team level. Women have been "systematically instructed in the feminine virtues of ladylike behavior, particularly to be submissive to men."[47] As a result, many women reach adulthood without the most rudimentary of physical skills, such as running, jumping, kicking, striking a target, and fending off an attack. Criminologists Kurt Weis and Sandra Borges say that "Fearfulness and inhibition are core components of conventional femininity."[48] If they are right about this, and if fear of crime is to be reduced or eliminated, then conventional femininity must be supplanted or modified. The state can promote this objective by providing, subsidizing, or offering tax breaks for self-defense courses; insuring that women's athletics receive adequate funding at every age, grade, and skill level; and by altering or destroying socialization processes that cause girls and women to internalize a sense of inferiority, dependency, and vulnerability.[49] The state, using its power of the purse, club, and lectern, must break the cycle of socialized vulnerability and victimhood. This will go a long way toward alleviating women's fear of crime.

Two obvious but underestimated fear-reducing measures are increasing the number of police officers on the street and improving street lighting in neighborhoods and other public places, such as parks. Gordon and Riger write that "Many of the women we interviewed indicated that improved lighting is streets, alleys, and parks and/or more police on the streets would help to prevent rape, or at least make them feel less frightened."[50] Environmental psychologist Yvonne Bernard has found that "A well-lit place creates a warm, friendly atmosphere and reduces anxiety in people,"[51] particularly those, such as women, who are most afraid of crime. Yet another means is for the state to sponsor research on the etiology, nature, and consequences of sexual assault. The National Institute of Mental Health, for example, now includes a National Center for the Prevention and Control of Rape, which, among other things, funded the research by Gordon and Riger that culminated in the book *The Female Fear.*[52] Perhaps there should be a "war on fear" along lines of the recent "war on drugs" (although one hopes with greater success)....

This list of fear reducing measures is not meant to be (and is not) exhaustive. It is suggestive. Anything that reduces the incidence of rape is likely to reduce women's fear of rape, not only for the obvious reason that a given woman's chances of being raped are thereby reduced, but because statistically speaking, fewer rape victims means fewer women who *know* a rape victim. Gordon and Riger discovered that one "major factor" in a woman's fear of rape is whether she knows someone who has been raped.[53] Women who know a rape victim, other things being equal, are more fearful than those who don't. The fear appears to be cyclical. Rape causes fear, which breeds more fear, which makes women draw inward for self-protection or to men for protection, which increases women's sense of vulnerability, which makes them better targets for rapists, which increases the likelihood

of rape. This fear, I have argued, is an unjust burden for women to bear. I have tried to show, moreover, that there is much that can be done to lighten or eliminate the load. What exactly *should* be done, all things considered, is a matter of policy rather than principle.

There is one other matter of principle to be addressed, and that concerns who should bear the costs of fear-reducing measures. Ideally, since the overwhelming majority of rapes are by men of women, men should bear the cost. Men — not just rapists, but men as a class — are the source of women's fear of rape and of those crimes associated with rape, Male college students, for example, can be made to pay a surcharge while attending universities, the revenues to be used for self-defense classes for women, improved lighting, greater campus security, and other fear reducing measures. Men's athletic programs and scholarships might be slashed or restructured, or additional tax monies collected, in order to create comparable programs and scholarships for women. All men can be required to participate in study groups or consciousness-raising sessions as a condition of receiving certain privileges, such as drinking alcoholic beverages or driving a motor vehicle, or to visit rape-crisis centers and hospitals to see the effects of rape on women. In areas with particularly high incidences of rape, there might be curfews for men. Men should pay higher taxes. Admittedly, these and other measures create practical and theoretical problems that must be solved. Precisely which measures should be adopted, and how their costs should be distributed, remains to be worked out. My philosophical point is that, for reasons of justice, the costs of fear-reducing measures should fall solely, or at least disproportionately, on men.

V. Objections and Replies

I have argued that the existing distribution of fear, in which women are disproportionately fearful, is unjust — and that the state, as the instrument of justice, has an affirmative obligation to rectify it. It might be objected that this claim is nonsensical, for no person or group of persons has *distributed* fear, either consciously or unconsciously. But if no person or group has distributed fear, then (so the objection goes) there is no obligation on the part of the state or anyone else to *re*distribute it. This objection has been made by F.A. Hayek in connection with the distribution of wealth in a market economy.[54] Hayek's argument is that since, strictly speaking, wealth is not *distributed,* and since distributive justice by definition concerns only *distributions,* distributive justice has nothing to say about wealth or any other good allocated in a market by market mechanisms.[55] An analogous objection might be made with respect to fear.

But as Tom Campbell has pointed out, Hayek "fails to make the important distinction between states of affairs which are consciously and deliberately brought about and those which *can* be intentionally altered, whatever their origin."[56] Why should justice concern only the former? As long as a particular "distribution" can be altered, it is an open question whether it should be. How the state of affairs came into existence may be relevant to the question of responsibility and to who should pay the cost of the alteration (see the discussion in Part IV), but it is irrelevant to whether alteration should be undertaken at all. If this is correct, and I believe it is, then *even if* fear is neither deliberately nor consciously distributed, its distribution — the patterns in which one finds it — can be unjust and rectifiable.[57]

This, however, may be to concede too much to the critic. Can it be said that women's fear of rape and other crimes *is* "consciously and deliberately brought about"? Susan Brownmiller claims that rape is and long has been "nothing more or less than a conscious process of intimidation by which all men keep all women in a state of fear."[58] Susan Griffin maintains that "rape is a form of mass terrorism,"[59] which implies consciousness, deliberation, and strategy on the part of many, most, or all men. Susan Rae Peterson writes that "rape is not merely an accidental series of individual events, but is institutionalized. It is a Rawlsian kind of 'practice': a 'form of activity specified by a system of rules which define offices, roles, moves, penalties, defences, and so one, and which give the activity its structure.'"[60] I quote these passages not

to establish that fear of rape *is* deliberately created to serve male interests, a burden that I need *not* discharge here (and could not discharge by quotation anyway), but to suggest that it *might* be. And if it is, then even Hayekian critics must concede that it raises issues of distributive justice....

A third objection to my argument concerns the nature and extent of women's fear of crime, and in particular their fear of rape. Studies consistently show that women are victimized at a lesser rate than men, and yet women's fear of crime is greater and more widespread than that of men. In the case of rape, while "55 percent of American women are afraid of being raped ... the number of declared victims is very low (0.06 percent)."[61] These empirical findings suggest to some researchers that women's fear of crime is partly or wholly irrational — that it is without basis in fact. But the state, the objection goes, has no obligation rooted in justice to alleviate irrational fears. So justice does not require that steps be taken to reduce or eliminate women's fear of crime.

This objection confuses at least three points that ought to be kept separate: the first is women's greater fear vis-à-vis men; the second is the alleged disparity between women's fear of rape and their *own estimate* of the risk of rape; the third is the disparity between women's fear of rape (or of crime generally) and the *actual risk* of rape (crime). As for the first point, unless we take men's level of fear to be the norm of rationality, there is no reason to view women's greater fear as irrational. But even if men as a class *were* less fearful than women as a class, it would still be an open question which sex, if any, is irrational. If irrationality consists in a disproportion between fear and risk, then perhaps men rather than women are irrational; men, we might conclude, have too *little* fear. This much is clear: the mere fact that men and women have different levels of fear says nothing about who, if either of them, is irrational.

The second point, that women's fear of rape is disproportionate to their own estimate of the likelihood of being raped, and is on that account irrational, would be damaging if true, but lacks empirical support. In an extensive study of women's fear, researchers Gordon and Riger discovered that "women's fear [of rape] is proportionate to their own estimates of their own risks."[62] In other words, *given* a typical woman's perception of risk, however acquired, her level of fear is appropriate. Her fear tracks reality as she sees it. Therefore, if irrationality consists in disproportion between one's estimate of a given risk and the level of fear one experiences, women's fear of rape is not irrational.

Let us focus, then, on the third point. Let us suppose that women's fear of crime generally, and of rape in particular, *is* disproportionate to the actual risk. Does that alone undermine the state's obligation to reduce or eliminate fear? It seems not. If anything, it imposes a new and additional obligation: to educate women as to the real likelihood of being raped or otherwise victimized. The state's obligation to reduce fear, such as it is, is based on the burdensomeness of fear, and the burden exists whether the underlying fear is realistic or not. What constrains women, physically, psychologically, and socially, is their fear, not the risk to which they are exposed. Moreover, if the state's obligation is tied to risk rather than to fear, then those individuals (men, for example) who have less fear than is warranted by the risk would be entitled to greater resources than even they would view as necessary, which is puzzling if not absurd.

I believe that this is an adequate reply to the objection, but an even more powerful reply can be made. *Is* women's fear of rape irrational? That depends, of course, on how one conceives of rationality in this context. Warr has found that "age and sex differences in fear are largely a function of differential sensitivity to risk, meaning that the relation between fear and perceived risk varies among males and females, young and old."[63] For present purposes the important finding is that women are more sensitive than men to risk. This means that for a given level of perceived risk, women experience greater fear. Why? In studying differential sensitivity to risk, Warr discovered that it is a function of two variables: first, the perceived seriousness of the offense; and second, the presence of what he calls "perceptually contemporaneous offenses." Women as a class assign greater seriousness to the various criminal offenses,

including rape, than do men. As we saw in Part I, a significant percentage of women view rape and murder as equally serious. Women are also more likely than men to see rape as part of a cluster of offenses to which they are exposed.

Suppose Warr is right about this — that women are more sensitive than men to the risk of victimization. Can it be said that women's greater fear is irrational? Only if one is prepared to say that, of two evaluations of the seriousness of rape, one is rational and the other not. But this is to adopt a substantive conception of rationality that is dubious at best and incoherent at worst. Ordinarily we say that a particular attitude, belief, or response is rational *given* certain values. Given the high value I attach to my health, for example, my vegetarianism is rational; given the low value I attach to religion, my scorn for preachers and proselytizers is rational. Rationality is a relation between values (which are taken as given) and a particular response. The objection under considerations urges us to evaluate the values themselves. We are asked to say that women attach *too great* a value to their safety, bodily integrity, and lives — that the effects of rape and other crimes are not all *that* bad.[64] But it could just as easily be said, as I suggested above, that men attach too little value to these things.[65]

I conclude that women's fear of crime is not irrational in any sense that undermines the state's obligation to redistribute fear. That women fear crimes such as rape to a degree beyond what would be strictly necessary to protect them from harm suggests that women attach significant value to their lives, health, and well-being. This greater value manifests itself in a greater sensitivity to risk, which in turn manifests itself in greater fear of victimization. But I maintain that even if women's fear of crime *were* irrational (in the sense of unfounded), it would not follow that the state lacks an obligation to reduce or eliminate it. The objection is without merit.

A fourth and a final objection to my argument is that rectifying the injustice of women's disproportionate fear is the first step on a logical slippery slope to dystopia. There are two versions of this objection. One is that if, as I have argued, it is unjust for women to be disproportionately fearful, then, by parity of reasoning, it is unjust for the elderly, the poor, nonwhites, and urban residents to be disproportionately fearful — because these groups, too, as studies show, have greater fear than their counterparts. But it is absurd (says the objector) to think that there is so much injustice in society. Therefore, the state of affairs in which women are disproportionately fearful is not unjust. Put differently, either no fear differentials are unjust or all fear differentials are unjust, but not all fear differentials are unjust (for the reason given); therefore, none is.

This version of the objection is easily dismissed. Why, a priori, must there be only a certain amount of injustice in society? Can't a particular society be unjust through and through — to its core? Suppose a particular group of individuals, say middle-class white males, decides to oppress the poor, nonwhites, and females — and does so. Would we say that this is *impossible*, because too extensive? Surely not. What we would say is that the injustice has a common source, many faces, and must be combated on many fronts. Far from being an embarrassment to my argument, the fact that other groups in society (such as the elderly) are disproportionately fearful shows the power of the argument. It shows that the argument is not ad hoc, that it rests on a moral principle of broad application. Admittedly, this essay concerns only the fear that women experience, but I could just as easily have focused on the fear of the elderly, the poor, or the comparatively uneducated. The state, I would maintain, has an obligation to redistribute fear in those cases as well, and for the same reasons.

The second version of the objection differs from the first in that it *concedes* the injustice of women's disproportionate fear of crime — and also that of other groups, such as the elderly. But it claims that rectifying those injustices would be too costly in terms of liberty and other values. It says, in effect, that either all injustices must be rectified or no injustices need be rectified, but rectification of all injustices is too costly; therefore, no rectification is necessary. This is reminiscent of (although not identical to) Nozick's[66] and Hayek's[67] claims that

redistribution of wealth requires constant and unjust infringements of liberty. Since these thinkers assign great (one is tempted to say "absolute") value to liberty, and since in most cases of redistribution the aim is not to compensate for harm done, which would justify it, the redistribution (they say) is unjustified.

One need not deny the value of liberty to respond to this objection. All one needs to show is that the liberty in question results in significant harm to others, for even liberals such as Nozick concede that harm to others is a good reason to limit liberty.[68] I have argued in this essay that fear is a burden — a real harm — to individuals. Admittedly, it is difficult in most cases to identify the person causing the harm; but why is that a necessary condition of redistribution? If liberty may, consistently with justice, be infringed to protect others from significant harm, and if those being harmed and those creating the harm can be identified through group membership, as they are in the case of fear, it is at most a strategic matter how one goes about redistributing fear. It should be done at least cost to other values, of course, but it should be done. Justice requires it. Indeed, justice would not be the first virtue of social institutions, as Rawls maintains, if it could be easily overridden or outweighed by other considerations....[69]

Author's Note

This essay began life as an informal talk to an informal gathering sponsored by the Philosophy Club of the University of Texas at Arlington. The brainstorming that took place on that occasion was useful to me in developing my thoughts and ultimately in formulating my arguments. Steve Hiltz asked particularly good questions. The written version of that talk was presented, by invitation, to the Society for Philosophy and Public Affairs at the 1994 Pacific Division meeting of the American Philosophical Association in Los Angeles, California. The topic, on a panel chaired by Sally Haslanger, was "Justice and Sexual Violence." I thank Stanley French, Lois Pineau, Sally Haslanger, and several members of the audience for useful comments and criticism on that occasion. I also thank my partner, Lora Schmid-

Dolan, for encouragement, insight, and for bringing home to me the heretofore unacknowledged privilege I have, qua male, of walking the streets without fear — or with less fear than I might otherwise have.

NOTES

1. Kurt Weis and Sandra S. Borges, "Victimology and Rape: The Case of the Legitimate Victim," *Issues in Criminology* 8 (Fall 1973):94. See also Margaret T. Gordon and Stephanie Riger, *The Female Fear: The Social Cost of Rape* (Urbana and Chicago: University of Illinois Press, 1991), 118: "Feminist analyses of the effect of the threat of rape on women assert that it operates as an instrument of social control, encouraging women to restrict their behavior and keeping them in a state of continuous stress."

2. Stanley I. Benn, "Justice," *The Encyclopedia of Philosophy*, ed. Paul Edwards (New York: Macmillan, 1967; reprint ed. 1972), vol. 4, 298.

3. Here I borrow from Tom Campbell, *Justice* (Atlantic Highlands, NJ: Humanities Press International, 1988), 19; who writes: "With all these reservations, it remains illuminating to say that justice has to do with the distribution amongst persons of benefits and burdens, these being loosely defined so as to cover any desirable or undesirable thing or experience."

4. I do not imply that if it *were* distributed randomly, it would be morally acceptable — although, in that case, at least one ground of moral unacceptability would be absent.

5. See Mark Warr, "Fear of Victimization: Why Are Women and the Elderly More Afraid?," *Social Science Quarterly* 65 (September 1984):681.

6. See Terry L. Baumer, "Research on Fear of Crime in the United States," *Victimology: An International Journal* 3 (1978):256, 257; Stephanie Riger, Margaret T. Gordon, and Robert LeBailly, "Women's Fear of Crime: From Blaming to Restricting the Victim," *Victimology: An International Journal* 3 (1978):277; Allen E. Liska, Andrew Sanchirico, and Mark D. Reed, "Fear of Crime and Constrained Behavior Specifying and Estimating a Reciprocal Effects Model," *Social Forces* 66 (March 1988):828; Gordon and Riger, *The Female Fear*; 118; Yvonne Bernard, "North American and European Research on Fear of Crime," *Applied Psychology: An International Review* 41 (January 1992):70.

7. Baumer, "Research on Fear of Crime in the United States," 255; see also *ibid.*, 260; Margaret T. Gordon et al., "Crime, Women, and the Quality of Urban Life," *Signs: Journal of Women in Culture and Society* 5 (Spring 1980); S144.

8. Warr, "Fear of Victimization," 687.

9. *Ibid.*, 685.

10. Riger, Gordon, and LeBailly, "Women's Fear of Crime," 276.

11. *Ibid.*, see also Gordon *et al.*, "Crime, Women, and the Quality of Urban Life," 147.

12. Gordon *et al.*, "Crime, Women, and the Quality of Urban Life," 147.

13. Baumer, "Research on Fear of Crime in the United States." 255.

14. Many ordinary expressions reflect this. Fear is said to be misplaced, unnecessary, exaggerated, excessive, foolish, groundless, unjustified, baseless, unreasonable, unwarranted, and irrational. A phobia, popularly, is "a lasting abnormal fear or great dislike of something" Eugene Eherlich *et al.*, *Oxford American Dictionary* (New York: Oxford University Press, 1980), 501.

15. Warr, "Fear of Victimization," 698.

16. *Ibid.*, 696.

17. Baumer, "Research on Fear of Crime in the United States," 255; see also Warr "Fear of Victimization," 682. It is interesting that Rodney King, the victim of a brutal beating by police officers that captured the attention of the nation, chose rape as his phenomenological model. He testified that after the beating "I felt like I had been raped ... I felt like I was going to die." Quoted in *The Dallas Morning News*, 29 March 1994, 5A.

18. Warr, "Fear of Victimization," 695.

19. *Ibid.*, 700.

20. *Ibid.*, 698; but compare Riger, Gordon, and LeBailly, "Women's Fear of Crime," 278: "Among women, the fear of rape ranks second only to murder" (citations omitted).

21. See Warr, "Fear of Victimization," 698.

22. Martha R. Burt and Rhoda E. Estep, "Apprehension and Fear: Learning a Sense of Sexual Vulnerability," *Sex Roles* 7 (May 1981):512.

23. *Ibid.*, 520.

24. Warr, "Fear of Victimization," 698, 700.

25. *Ibid.*, 700 (italics in original).

26. Mark Warr, "Fear of Rape Among Urban Women," *Social Problems* 32 (February 1985):248.

27. *Ibid.*, 249.

28. Ehrlich *et al.*, *Oxford American Dictionary*, 81.

29. *Ibid.*, 235: Fear is "an unpleasant emotion caused by the nearness of danger or expectation of pain etc." I refer here to the phenomenological aspect of fear (the way it feels "from the inside") rather than to its intentional aspect (what it is about). Even so-called cognitive theories of emotion, in which emotions involve or are caused by beliefs, allow room for this aspect. See, for example, Ronald Alan Nash, "Cognitive Theories of Emotion," *Noûs* 23 (September 1989):481-504; John Morreall, "Fear Without Belief," *The Journal of Philosophy* 90 (July 1993):359-366. Nothing in my essay hinges on accepting or rejecting a particular theory of the notion of fear, let alone a theory of the nature of emotion.

30. Gordon *et al.*, "Crime, Women, and the Quality of Urban Life," 157-158; see also Warr, "Fear of Rape Among Urban Women," 248.

31. See Riger, Gordon, and LeBailly, "Women's Fear of Crime," 281.

32. Gordon *et al.*, "Crime, Women, and the Quality of Urban Life," S158.

33. See Gordon and Riger, *The Female Fear*, 14, 15-18, 113-14, 121, 122; Warr, "Fear of Rape Among Urban Women," 247-249.

34. Pauline B. Bart, review of *Intimate Violence: A Study of Injustice*, by Julie Blackman; *The Female Fear: The Social Cost of Rape*, by Margaret T. Gordon and Stephanie Riger; *Battered Women as Survivors*, by Lee Ann Hoff; *Women and Rape*, by Cathy Roberts; and *Fraternity Gang Rape: Sex, Brotherhood, and Privilege on Campus*, by Peggy Reeves Sanday, in *Signs: Journal of Women in Culture and Society* 19 (Winter 1994):530.

35. See Catharine A MacKinnon, *Toward a Feminist Theory of the State* (Cambridge, MA: Harvard University Press, 1989), 149, 151.

36. See Andra Medea and Kathleen Thompson, *Against Rape* (New York: Farrar, Straus and Giroux, 1974), 146.

37. Susan Sontag, "The Third World of Women," *Partisan Review* 40 (1973):184; see also, in this connection, Sarah Lucia Hoagland "A Note on the Logic of Protection and Predation," *American Philosophical Association Newsletter on Feminism and Philosophy* 88 (November 1988):7-8.

38. Gordon and Riger, *The Female Fear*, 121. See also Medea and Thompson, *Against Rape*, 5: "For women the luxury of going out for a walk alone, of getting away for a few minutes, is almost impossible. Every day of their lives, women learn to accept the fact that their freedom is limited in a way that a man's is not. There is a curfew on women in this country and it is enforced by rapists."

39. Cf. Benn, "Justice," 299: "It is not for a judge to decide the respects in which men are equal but to decide whether the respects in which they are unequal are relevant to the issues in the case."

40. Here I employ the principle that "Where no good ground can be shown for treating people differently, they ... ought to be treated alike." *Ibid.*, 301. By the way, I am not implying that sex is sometimes morally relevant, nor am I implying that it is never morally relevant. I concern myself only with the irrelevance of sex for the distribution of *fear.*

41. John Rawls, *A Theory of Justice* (Cambridge: Harvard University Press, 1971), 3.

42. *Ibid.*

43. According to Richard Posner, research conducted by Isaac Ehrlich "shows that rapists, like other criminals, respond to increases in the severity as well as probability of punishment." Richard A. Posner, *Sex and Reason* (Cambridge, MA: Harvard University Press, 1992), 394 (citation omitted).

44. *Ibid.*, 394. "The heavier the punishment for a particular crime is known to be, the more inclined a jury may be to resolve doubts in the defendants' favor." See also *ibid.*, 401: "[A]n increase in the severity of punishment may be offset by a reduction in the probability of conviction, leaving expected punishment costs (the product of the probability and the severity of punishment) unchanged or even lower."

45. For a discussion and illustration of such techniques, see Medea and Thompson, *Against Rape*, chap. 7, 73-96.

46. Gordon and Riger, *The Female Fear*, 54 (citation omitted). See also ibid., 52, 115, 129, 135, 136. This is not to say that women will eagerly enroll in such courses. As Medea and Thompson point out, "Few people would object to a little boy's learning to defend himself, but in a group of women who had gathered together to work against rape, one woman worried about encouraging women to learn self-defense because, she said, it would be a 'brutalizing' experience. Most women have encountered that attitude before and have been affected by it." Medea and Thompson, *Against Rape*, 54. The authors trace this attitude to "the feminine ideal," which (they say) teaches that "Women are not supposed to take care of themselves, to be independent. They are taught that it is appealing to be weak, that it is attractive to be helpless." *Ibid.*

47. Weis and Borges, "Victimology and Rape," 83. See also Medea and Thompson, *Against Rape*, 22.

48. Weis and Borges, "Victimology and Rape," 81

49. Gordon and Riger write that "Perhaps more than anything else, the women who shared their stories [of rape] suggest that egalitarian views of women's roles and education are related to less fear, less isolation, and less restricted behavior." Gordon and Riger, *The Female Fear*, 123. This would suggest an obligation on the part of the state to undermine traditional sex roles rather than remain neutral with respect to them.

50 *Ibid.*, 135.

51. Bernard, "North American and European Research on Fear of Crime," 69.

52. See Gordon and Riger, *The Female Fear*, xiv. The Center suffered massive budget cuts and significant personnel turnover during the Reagan administration. See *ibid.*, 127.

53. See Gordon and Riger, *The Female Fear*, 112.

54. See F.A. Hayek, *Law, Legislation and Liberty: A New Statement of the Liberal Principles of Justice and Political Economy*, vol. 2: *The Mirage of Social Justice* (Chicago: The University of Chicago Press, 1976), chap. 9, 62-100.

55. Hayek says that "only human conduct can be called just or unjust. If we apply the terms to a state of affairs, they have meaning only in so far as we hold someone responsible for bringing it about or allowing it to come about. A bare fact, or a state of affairs which nobody can change, may be good or bad, but not just or unjust." *Ibid.*, 31.

56. Campbell, *Justice*, 15-16 (italics in original).

57. Hayek engages in persuasive definition when he insists that "only situations which have been created by human will can be called just or unjust." Hayek, *The Mirage of Social Justice*, 33. In fact, he admits as much. According to Hayek, "the manner in which the benefits and burdens are apportioned by the market mechanism would in many instances have to be regarded as very unjust *if* it were the result of a deliberate allocation to particular people." *Ibid.*, 64 (emphasis in original). So it is only Hayek's *decision* not to use the word "unjust" for these instances that prevents such a distribution from being unjust. And Hayek's decision not to use the word rests on his ideological commitment to a laissez-faire economy.

58. Susan Brownmiller, *Against Our Will: Men, Women and Rape* (New York: Simon and Schuster, 1975), 15; see also *ibid.*, 209, 254, 309, 398-403.

59. Susan Griffin, "Rape: The All-American Crime," in *Feminism and Philosophy*, ed. Mary Vetterling-Braggin, Frederick A. Elliston, and Jane English (Totowa, NJ: Littlefield, Adams, 1977), 331. See also Robin Morgan, "Theory and Practice: Pornography and Rape," in *Take Back the Night: Women on Pornography*, ed. Laura Lederer (New York: William Morrow and Company, 1980), 135 ("Knowing our place is the message of rape — as it was for blacks the message of lynchings. Neither is an act of spontaneity or sexuality — they are both acts of political terrorism, designed consciously *and* unconsciously to keep an entire people in its place by continual reminders" (emphasis in original)); Claudia Card, "Rape As a Terrorist Institution," in *Violence, Terrorism, and Justice*, ed. R.G. Frey and Christopher W. Morris (Cambridge: Cambridge University Press, 1991), 296-319.

60. Susan Rae Peterson, "Coercion and Rape: The State as a Male Protection Racket," in Vetterling-Braggin, Elliston, and English, eds., *Feminism and Philosophy*, 360-361.

61. Bernard, "North American and European Research on Fear of Crime," 70.

62. Gordon and Riger, *The Female Fear*, 121 (emphasis in original).

63. Warr, "Fear of Victimization," 681.

64. Gordon and Riger give the following explanation of women's evaluation of the seriousness of rape: "Since women know the devastating emotional consequences of rape and know they are held responsible for preventing it, their heightened fear is a rational response." Gordon and Riger, *The Female Fear*, 47. It may be that men make lower estimates of, or ignore, these costs.

65. Warr concludes his essay as follows: "[D]ifferences in fear among individuals or groups must ultimately come down to normative differences (judgments about the value of one's person or property), and surely there is no universal metric by which such judgments can be deemed 'correct' or 'incorrect.'" Warr, "Fear of Victimization," 701. Perhaps women's fear of rape is viewed as irrational because (1) men determine what is rational and irrational, (2) men attach comparatively little value to women's lives and bodily integrity, and (3) men assume that women share their (men's) low evaluation of them (women).

66. See Robert Nozick, *Anarchy, State, and Utopia* (New York: Basic books, 1974), 160-164.

67. See Hayek, *The Mirage of Social Justice*, 82-85.

68. See, e.g., Joel Feinberg, *The Moral Limits of the Criminal Law*, vol. 1: *Harm to Others* (New York: Oxford University Press, 1984). Feinberg, a liberal (see *ibid.*, 15), defends what he calls "the harm principle," which states that "It is always a good reason in support of penal legislation that it would probably be effective in preventing (eliminating, reducing) harm to persons other than the actor (the one prohibited from acting) *and* there is probably no other means that is equally effective at no greater cost to other values." *Ibid.*, 26 (emphasis in original). Feinberg's concern in this and the other volumes of the tetralogy is the criminal law, but presumably he would be concerned to reduce or eliminate harm in noncriminal contexts as well. At any rate, that is *my* concern.

69. A slightly altered version of this essay will form a chapter of my book *Rape: A Philosophical Investigation* (Dartmouth Publishing, 1996).

GENDER INEQUALITY AND CULTURAL DIFFERENCES

Susan Moller Okin

Susan Moller Okin was the Martha Sutton Weeks Professor of Ethics in Society at Stanford University. She is the author of Women in Western Political Thought *(1979) and* Justice, Gender, and the Family *(1989) as well as of numerous articles in feminist theory and political theory more generally. Okin died in 2004.*

Okin concedes the force of objections from within feminism that what are often presented as accounts of experiences shared by all women have excluded women whose experiences reflect the effects of race, class, ethnicity, and other differences. Okin worries, however, that an emphasis on differences undermines attempts to formulate a theory of justice that can address injustices, particularly those suffered by women in developing countries. She defends the idea that there is a "generalizable, identifiable and collectively shared experience of womanhood" and sets out to describe it by criticizing current theories of justice and of development that fail to consider gender altogether. Okin argues that Western feminist accounts of justice can be applied to the situations of poor women in many poor countries and that their experiences are "similar to ours but more so."

Theories of justice are undergoing something of an identity crisis. How can they be universal, principled, founded on good reasons that all can accept, and yet take account of the many differences there are among persons and social groups? Feminists have been among the first to point out that large numbers of persons have typically been excluded from consideration in purportedly universalist theories. And some feminists have gone on to point out that many feminist theories, while taking account of sexist bias or omission, have neglected racist, heterosexist, class, religious, and other biases. Yet, joining our voices with those of others, some of us discern problems with going in the direction of formulating a theory of justice entirely by listening to every concrete individual's or group's point of view and expression of its needs. Is it possible, by taking this route, to come up with any principles at all? Is it a reliable route, given the possibility of "false consciousness"? Doesn't stressing differences, especially cultural differences, lead to a slide toward relativism? The problem that is being grappled with is an important one. There can no longer be any doubt that many voices have not been heard when most theories of justice were being shaped. But how can all the different voices express themselves and be heard and still yield a coherent and workable theory of justice? This question is one I shall (eventually) return to in this essay.

Feminism, Difference and Essentialism

Feminists have recently had much to say about difference. One aspect of the debate has been a continuation of an old argument — about how different women are from men, what such differences may be due to, and whether they require that laws and other aspects of public policy should treat women any differently from men.[1] Another, newer, aspect of the debate is about differences among women. It is "essentialist," some say, to talk about women, the problems of women, and especially the problems of women "as such."[2] White middle- and upper-class feminists, it is alleged, have

excluded or been insensitive to not only the problems of women of other races, cultures, and religions but even those of women of other classes
than their own. "Gender" is therefore a problematic category, those opposed to such essentialism
say, unless always qualified by and seen in the
context of race, class, ethnicity, religion, and other
such differences (Childers and hooks 1990; Harris
1990; hooks 1984; Lorde 1984; Minow and
Spelman 1990; Spelman 1988.)

The general allegation of feminist essentialism
certainly has validity when applied to some work.
Feminists with such pedigrees as Harriet Taylor,
Charlotte Perkins Gilman, Virginia Woolf, Simone
de Beauvoir, and Betty Friedan (in *The Feminine
Mystique*) all seem to have assumed, for example,
that the women they were liberating would have
recourse to servants. With the partial exception of
Woolf, who remarks briefly on the difficult lot of
maids, they did not pay attention to the servants,
the vast majority of whom were also, of course,
women. The tendency of many white middle- and
upper-class feminists in the mid-nineteenth
century to think only of women of their own class
and race (some were explicitly racist) is what
makes so poignant and compelling Sojourner
Truth's words in her famous "Ain't I a woman?"
speech.[3] However, I think, and will argue, that this
problem is far less present in the works of most
recent feminists. But the charges of "essentialism"
seem to grow ever louder. They are summed up in
Elizabeth Spelman's (1988) recent claim that "the
focus on women 'as women' has addressed only
one group of women — namely, white middle-
class women of Western industrialized countries"
(p.4). This has come to be accepted in some circles
as virtually a truism.

The claim that much recent feminist theory is
essentialist comes primarily from three (to some
extent, overlapping) sources — European-influ-
enced postmodernist thought; the work of African-
American and other minority feminist women in
the United States and Britain; and, in particular,
Spelman's recent book, *Inessential Woman* (hereafter *IW*). Postmodernism is skeptical of all universal or generalizable claims, including those of
feminism. It finds concepts central to feminist

thinking, such as "gender" and "woman," as illegitimate as any other category or generalization
that does not stop to take account of every difference. As Julia Kristeva, for example, says,

> The belief that "one is a woman" is almost as
> absurd and obscurantist as the belief that "one is
> a man..." [W]e must use "we are women" as an
> advertisement or slogan for our demands. On a
> deeper level, however, a woman cannot "be"; it
> is something which does not even belong in the
> order of *being*. (Quoted in Marks and de
> Courtivron 1981, 137)

In the same interview, she also says that, because
of the very different history of Chinese women, "it
is absurd to question their lack of 'sexual liberation'" (in Marks and de Courtivron 1981, 140).
Clearly, she thinks we could have no cross-cultural
explanations of or objections to gender inequality.

Spelman argues that "the phrase 'as a woman' is
the Trojan horse of feminist ethnocentrism" (*I.W.*,
13). The great mistakes of white middle-class feminists have been to exclude women different from
themselves from their critiques or, even when they
are included, to assume that, whatever their differences, their experience of sexism is the same. At
best, she says, what is presented is "[a]n additive
analysis [which] treats the oppression of a black
woman in a society that is racist as well as sexist as
if it were a further burden when in fact it is a *different burden*" (*IW*, 123; emphasis added).

These antiessentialist arguments, however, are
often long on theory and very short on empirical
evidence. A large proportion of Spelman's examples of how women's experiences of oppression
are different are taken from periods of slavery in
ancient Greece and, especially, in the pre-Civil
War South. It is not clear, though, how relevant is
the obvious contrast between the experience of
white slaveholders' wives and black female slaves
to most issues involving the sameness or difference
of forms of gender oppression today.

Apart from the paucity of relevant evidence
(which I shall return to), there seem to me to be
two other related problems with Spelman's general
antiessentialist argument. One is the claim that

unless a feminist theorist perceives gender identity as intrinsically bound up with class, race, or other aspects of identity she ignores the effects of these other differences altogether. Spelman writes, "If gender were isolatable from other forms of identity, if sexism were isolatable from other forms of oppression, then what would be true about the relation between any man and any woman would be true about the relation between any other man and any other woman" (*IW*, 81). But this does not follow at all. One can argue that sexism is an identifiable form of oppression, many of whose effects are felt by women regardless of race or class, without at all subscribing to the view that race and class oppression are insignificant. One can still insist, for example, on the significant difference between the relation of a poor black woman to a wealthy white man and that of a wealthy white woman to a poor black man.

The second problem is that Spelman misplaces the burden of proof, which presumably affects her perception of the need for her to produce evidence for her claims. She says, "Precisely insofar as a discussion of gender and gender relations is really, even if obscurely, about a particular group of women and their relation to a particular group of men, it is unlikely to be applicable to any other group of women" (*IW*, 114). But why? Surely the burden of proof is on the critic. To be convincing, she needs to show that and how the theory accused of essentialism omits or distorts the experience of persons other than those few the theorist allegedly does take account of. This, after all, is the burden that many of the feminists Spelman considers "essentialist" have themselves taken on in critiquing "malestream" theories. One of the problems of antiessentialist feminism (shared, I think, with much of postmodernist critique) is that it tends to substitute the cry "we're all different" for both argument and evidence.

There are, however, exceptions, and they tend to come from feminists who belong to racial minorities. One of the best critiques of feminist essentialism that I know of is that by Angela Harris (1990), in which she shows how ignorance of the specifics of a culture mars even thoroughly well-intentioned feminist analyses of women's experiences of oppression within that culture. She argues, for example, that in some respects, black women in the United States have had a qualitatively rather than simply quantitatively different experience of rape than that of white women (see esp. 594, 598-601). Even here, though, I think the antiessentialist critique is only partly convincing. Although more concerned with evidence for the salience of differences than most antiessentialists seem to be, Harris raises far more empirical questions than she provides answers. She provides just one example to support her assertion that black women's experience of rape is, even now, radically different from that of white women — that it is "an experience as deeply rooted in color as in gender" (p. 598).[4] Yet she, like Spelman, is as much disturbed by white feminists' saying that black women are "just like us only more so" as she is by their marginalizing black women or ignoring them altogether. As I shall argue, this "insult[ing]" conclusion — that the problems of other women are "similar to ours but more so" — is exactly the one I reach when I apply some Western feminist ideas about justice to the situations of poor women in many poor countries.

In this essay, I put antiessentialist feminism to what I think is a reasonably tough test. In doing this, I am taking up the gauntlet that Spelman throws down. She says, referring to the body of new work about women that has appeared in many fields,

> Rather than assuming that women have something in common as women, these researchers should help us look to see whether they do.... Rather than first finding out what is true of some women as women and then inferring that this is true of all women ... we have to investigate different women's lives and see what they have in common. (*IW*, 137)

Trained as a philosopher, she does not seem to consider it appropriate to take up the challenge of actually looking at some of this empirical evidence. Having said the above, she turns back to discussing Plato. Trained as a political scientist, I shall attempt to look at some comparative evidence. I'll put some Western feminist ideas about justice and inequality to the test (drawing on my recent book and the many feminist sources I use to support some of its arguments) by seeing how well these theories — developed in the context of women in well-off Western industrialized countries — work when used to look at the very different situations of some of the poorest women in poor countries. How do our accounts and our explanations of gender inequality stand up in the face of considerable cultural and socioeconomic difference?

Differences and Similarities in Gender Oppression: Poor Women in Poor Countries

Does the assumption "that there is a generalizable, identifiable and collectively share experience of womanhood" (Benhabib and Cornell 1987, 13) *have* any validity, or is it indeed an essentialist myth, rightly challenged by Third World women and their spokesfeminists? Do the theories devised by First World feminists, particularly our critiques of nonfeminist theories of justice, have anything to say, in particular, to the poorest women in poor countries, or to those policymakers with the potential to affect their lives for better or for worse?

In trying to answer these questions, I shall address, in turn, four sets of issues, which have been addressed both by recent feminist critics of Anglo-American social and political theory and by those development scholars who have in recent years concerned themselves with the neglect or distortions of the situation of women in the countries they study. First, why and how has the issue of the inequality between the sexes been ignored or obscured for so long and addressed only so recently? Second, why is it so important that it be addressed? Third, what do we find, when we subject households or families to standards of justice — when we look at the largely hidden inequalities between the sexes? And finally, what are the policy implications of these findings?

Why Attention to Gender Is Comparatively New

In both development studies and theories of justice, there has, until recently, been a marked lack of attention to gender — and in particular to systematic inequalities between the sexes. This point has been made about theories of justice throughout the 1980s (e.g., Kearns 1983; Okin 1989b; Crosswaite 1989). In the development literature, it was first made earlier, in pioneering work by Ester Boserup, but has lately been heard loud and strong from a number of other prominent development theorists (Chen 1983; Dasgupta 1993; Sen 1990b; Jelin 1990). In both contexts, the neglect of women and gender seems to be due primarily to two factors. The first is the assumption that the household (usually assumed to be male-headed) is the appropriate unit of analysis. The dichotomy between the public (political and economic) and the private (domestic and personal) is assumed valid, and only the former has been taken to be the appropriate sphere for development studies and theories of justice, respectively, to attend to. In ethical and political theories, the family is often regarded as an inappropriate context for justice, since love, altruism, or shared interests are assumed to hold sway within it. Alternatively, it is sometimes taken for granted that it is a realm of hierarchy and injustice. (Occasional theorists, like Rousseau, have said both!) In economics, development and other, households until recently have simply been taken for granted as the appropriate unit of analysis on such questions as income distribution. The public/private dichotomy and the assumption of the male-headed household have many serious implications for women as well as for children that are discussed below (Dasgupta 1993; Jacquette 1982, 283; Okin 1989b, 10-14, 124-33; Olsen 1983; Pateman 1983).

The second factor is the closely related failure to disaggregate data or arguments by sex. In the development literature it seems to appear simply in this form (Chen, Huq, and D'souza 1981, 68; Jaquette 1982, 283-84). In the justice literature, this used to be obscured by the use of male pronouns and other referents. Of late, the (rather more insidious) practice that I have called "false gender neutrality" has appeared. This consists in the use of gender-neutral terms ("he or she," "persons," and so on), when the point being made is simply invalid or otherwise false if one actually applies it to women (Okin 1989b, esp. 10-13, 45). But the effect is the same in both literatures; women are not taken into account, so the inequalities between the sexes are obscured.

The public/domestic dichotomy has serious implications for women. It not only obscures intrahousehold inequalities of resources and power, as I discuss below, but it also results in the failure to count a great deal of the work done by women as work, since all that is considered "work" is what is done for pay in the "public" sphere. All of the work that women do in bearing and rearing children, cleaning and maintaining households, caring for the old and sick, and contributing in various ways to men's work does not count as work. This is clearly one of those instances in which the situation of poor women in poor countries is not qualitatively *different* from that of most women in rich countries but, rather, "similar but worse," for even more, in some cases far more, of the work done by women (and children) in poor countries is rendered invisible, not counted, or "subsumed under men's work." The work of subsistence farming, tending to animals, domestic crafts (if not for the market) and the often arduous fetching of water and fuel are all added to the category of unrecognized work of women that already exists in richer countries.[5] Chen notes that women who do all these things "are listed [by policymakers] as housewives," even though "their tasks are as critical to the well-being of their families and to national production as are the men's" (Chen 1983, 220; see also Dasgupta 1993; Drèze and Sen 1989, chap. 4; Jaquette 1982, citing Bourgue and Warren 1979; Waring 1989).

Why Does it Matter?

This may seem like a silly question. Indeed, I hope it will soon be unnecessary, but it isn't — yet. I therefore argue, at the outset of *Justice, Gender, and the Family*, that the omission from theories of justice of gender, and of much of women's lives, is significant for three major reasons. Each of these reasons applies at least as much to the neglect of gender in theories of development. The first is obvious: women matter (at least they do to femi-

nists), and their well-being matters at least as much as that of men. As scholars of development have recently been making clear, the inequalities between the sexes in a number of poor countries have not only highly detrimental but *fatal* consequences for millions of women. Sen (1990a) has recently argued that as may as one hundred million fewer women exist than might normally be expected on the basis of male/female mortality rates in societies less devaluing of women — not only the Western industrialized world but much of sub-Saharan Africa, too (see also Dasgupta 1993; Drèze and Sen 1989, chap 4; Drèze and Sen 1990, Introduction, 11-14; but cf. Harriss 1990; Wheeler and Abdullah 1988). So here too we can reasonably say that the issue of the neglect of women is "similar but *much* worse."

The second reason I have raised (in the U.S. context) for the necessity for feminist critique of theories of social justice is that equality of opportunity — for women and girls — but also for increasing numbers of boys — is much affected by the failure of theories of justice to address gender inequality. This is in part due to the greater extent of economic distress in female-headed households. In the United States, nearly 25 percent of children are being raised in single female-headed households, and three-fifths of all chronically poor households with children are among those supported by single women. It has been recently estimated that throughout the world one-third of house-holds are headed by single females, with the percentage much higher in regions with significant male out-migration (Chen 1983, 221; Jaquette 1982, 271). Many millions of children are affected by the higher rate of poverty among such families.[6] Theories of justice or of economic development that fail to pay attention to gender ignore this, too.

In addition, the gendered division of labor has a serious and direct impact on the opportunities of girls and women, which crosses the lines of economic class. The opportunities of females are significantly affected by the structures and practices of family life, particularly by the fact that women are almost invariably primary caretakers, which has much impact on their availability for full-time wage work. It also results in their frequently being *over*worked and renders them less likely than men to be considered economically valuable. This factor, too, operates "similarly but more so" within poor families in many poor countries. There, too, adult women suffer — often more severely — many of the same effects of the division of labor as do women in richer countries. But, in addition, their daughters are likely to be put to work for the household at a very young age, are much less likely to be educated and to attain literacy than are sons of the same households and, worst of all — less valued than their brothers — they have less chance of staying alive because they are more likely to be deprived of food or of health care (Dasgupta 1993; Drèze and Sen 1990, chap. 4; Sen 1990a; Papanek 1990).

Third, I have argued that the failure to address the issue of just distribution within households is significant because the family is the first, and arguably the most influential, school of moral development (Okin 1989b, esp. 17-23). It is the first environment in which we experience how persons treat each other, in which we have the potential to learn how to be just or unjust. If children see that sex difference is the occasion for obviously differential treatment, they are surely likely to be affected in their personal and moral development. They are likely to learn injustice by absorbing the messages, if male, that they have some kind of "natural" enhanced entitlement and, if female, that they are *not* equals and had better get used to being subordinated if not actually abused. So far as I know, this point was first made in the Western context by John Stuart Mill, who wrote of the "perverting influence" of the typical English family of his time — which he termed "a school of despotism" (Mill [1869] 1988, 88). I have argued that the still remaining unequal distribution of benefits and burdens between most parents in two-parent heterosexual families is likely to affect their children's developing sense of justice (Okin 1989b, e.g., 21-23, 97-101). In the context of poor countries, as Papanek (1990) notes, "Domestic groups in which age and gender difference confer power on some over others are poor environments in which to unlearn the norms of

inequality" (pp. 163-65). She also notes that "given the persistence of gender-based inequalities in power, authority, and access to resources, one must conclude that socialization for gender inequality is by and large very successful" (p. 170). When such basic goods as food and health care are unequally distributed to young children according to sex, a very strong signal about the acceptability of injustice is surely conferred. The comparison of most families in rich countries with poor families in poor countries — where distinctions between the sexes often start earlier and are much more blatant and more harmful to girls — yields, here too, the conclusion that, in the latter case, things are not so much different as "similar but more so." Many Third World families, it seems, are even worse schools of justice and more successful inculcators of the inequality of the sexes as natural and appropriate than are their developed world equivalents. Thus there is even more need for attention to be paid to gender inequality in the former context than in the latter.

Justice in the Family

What do we find when we compare some of Anglo-American feminists' findings about justice within households in their societies with recent discoveries about distributions of benefits and burdens in poor households in poor countries? Again, in many respects, the injustices of gender are quite similar.

In both situations, women's access to paid work is constrained both by discrimination and sex segregation in the workplace and by the assumption that women are "naturally" responsible for all or most of the unpaid work of the household (Bergmann 1986; Fuchs 1988; Gerson 1985; Okin 1989b, 147-52, 155-56; Sanday 1974). In both situations, women typically work longer total hours than men:

Time-use statistics considering all work (paid and unpaid economic activity and unpaid housework) reveal that women spend more of their time working than men in all developed and developing regions except northern America and

Australia, where the hours are almost equal. (United Nations Report 1991, 81 and chap. 6 passim; see also Bergmann 1986; Hochschild 1989)

In both situations, developed and less developed, vastly more of women's work is not paid and is not considered "productive."[7] Thus there is a wide gap between men's and women's *recorded* economic participation. The perception that women's work is of less worth (despite the fact that in most places they do more, and it is crucial to the survival of household members) contributes to women's being devalued and having less power both within the family and outside the household (Blumstein and Schwartz 1983; Dasgupta 1993; Drèze and Sen 1990, chap. 4; Okin 1989b, chap. 7; Sanday 1974; Sen 1990a, 1990b). This in turn adversely affects their capacity to become economically less dependent on men. Thus they become involved in "a cycle of socially caused and distinctly asymmetric vulnerability" (Okin 1989b, 138; Drèze and Sen 1989, 56-59). The devaluation of women's work, as well as their lesser physical strength and economic dependence on men, allows them to be subject to physical, sexual, and/or psychological abuse by men they live with (Gordon 1988; United Nations Report 1991, 19-20). However, in many poor countries, as I have mentioned, this power differential extends beyond the abuse and overwork of women to deprivation in terms of the feeding, health care, and education of female children — and even to their being born or not: "of 8,000 abortions in Bombay after parents learned the sex of the foetus through amniocentesis, only one would have been a boy." (United Nations Report 1991; see also Dasgupta 1993; Drèze and Sen 1989, chap. 4; Sen 1990a.)

In cross-regional analyses, both Sen and Dasgupta have found correlations between the life expectancies of females relative to males and the extent to which women's work is perceived as having economic value. Thus in both rich and poor countries, women's participation in work outside the household can improve their status within the family, but this is not necessarily assured. It is interesting to compare Barbara Bergmann's (1986)

analysis of the situation of "drudge wives" in the United States, who work full-time for pay and who also perform virtually all of the household's unpaid labor, with Peggy Sanday's earlier finding that, in some Third World contexts, women who do little of the work that is considered "productive" have low status, whereas many who do a great deal of it become "virtual slaves" (Sanday 1974, p. 201; Bergmann 1986, pp. 260-73).[8]

This leads us to the issue of women's economic dependence (actual and perceived). Although most poor women in poor countries work long hours each day, throughout the world they are often economically dependent on men. This, too, is "similar to but worse than" the situation of many women in richer countries. It results from so much of their work being unpaid work, so much of their paid work being poorly paid work, and, in some cases, from men's laying claim to the wages their wives and daughters earn. Feminist critics since Ester Boserup (1970) have argued that women's economic dependency on men was in many cases exacerbated by changes that development theory and development policy makers saw only as "progressive." All too ready to perceive women as dependents, mainstream theorists did not notice that technology, geographical mobility, and the conversion from subsistence to market economies were not, from the female point of view, "unalloyed benefits, but ... processes that cut women out from their traditional economic and social roles and thrust them into the modern sector where they are discriminated against and exploited, often receiving cash incomes below the subsistence level, ... in turn increas(ing) female dependency" (Jaquette 1982; see also Boserup 1970; Rogers, in Jaquette).[9]

In both rich and poor countries, women who are the sole economic support of families often face particular hardship. However, whereas some are, not all of the reasons for this are the same. Discrimination against women in access to jobs, pay, retention, and promotion are common to most countries, with obviously deleterious effects on female-supported families. In the United States, the average full-time working woman earns a little more than two-thirds of the pay of a full-time male worker, and three-fifths of the families with children who live in chronic poverty are single female-parent families. Many such women in both rich and poor countries also suffer from severe "time poverty."

But the situation of some poor women in poor countries is different from — as well as distinctly worse than — that of most Western women today. It is more like the situation of the latter in the nineteenth century: even when they have no other means of support, they are actually *prohibited* (by religiously based laws or oppressive cultural norms) from engaging in paid labor. Martha Chen (forthcoming) has studied closely the situation of such women in the Indian subcontinent. Deprived of the traditional economic support of a male, they are prevented from taking paid employment by rules of caste, or *purdah*. For such women, it can indeed be liberating to be helped (as they have been by outsiders like Chen) to resist the sanctions invoked against them by family elders, neighbors, or powerful social leaders. Although many forms of wage work, especially those available to women, are hardly "liberating," except in the most basic sense, women are surely distinctly less free if they are *not* allowed to engage in it, especially if they have no other means of support. Many employed women in Western industrialized countries still face quite serious disapproval if they are mothers of young children or if the family's need for their wages is not perceived as great. But at least, except in the most oppressive of families or subcultures, they are *allowed* to go out to work. By contrast, as Chen's work makes clear, the basic right to be allowed to make a much needed living for themselves and their children is still one that many women in the poorest of situations in other cultures are denied.

Here, then, is a real difference — an oppressive situation that most Western women no longer face. But to return to similarities: another that I discovered, while comparing some of our Western feminist ideas about justice with work on poor women in poor countries, has to do with the dynamics of power within the family. The differential exit potential theory that I adopt from Albert Hirschman's work to explain power within the family has

recently been applied to the situation of women in poor countries (cf. Okin 1989b, chap. 7 with Dasgupta 1993 and Sen 1990b). Partha Dasgupta (1993) also uses exit theory in explaining the "not uncommon" desertion by men of their families during famines. He writes, "The man deserts [his wife] because *his* outside option in these circumstances emerges higher in his ranking than any feasible allocation within the household" (p. 329). He regards the "hardware" he employs — John Nash's game-theoretic program — as "needed if we are to make any progress in what is a profoundly complex matter, the understanding of household decisions" (p. 329). But the conclusion he reaches is very similar to the one that I reach, drawing on Hirschman's theory of power and the effects of persons' differential exit potential: any factor that improves the husband's exit option or detracts from the wife's exit option thereby gives him additional voice, or bargaining power in the relationship. Likewise, anything that improves the wife's exit option — her acquisition of human or physical capital, for example — will increase her autonomy and place her in a better bargaining position in the relationship (Dasgupta 1993, 331-33; Okin 1989b, chap.7)[10]

In the United States, recent research has shown that women's and children's economic status (taking need into account) typically deteriorates after separation or divorce, whereas the average divorcing man's economic status actually improves (McLindon 1987; Weitzman 1985; Wishik 1986). This, taken in conjunction with the exit/voice theory, implies less bargaining power for wives within marriage. In poor countries, where circumstances of severe poverty combine with a lack of paid employment opportunities for women, increasing women's dependency on men, men's power within the family — already in most cases legitimized by highly patriarchal cultural norms — seems very likely to be enhanced. Although, as Dasgupta (1993) points out, Nash's formula was not intended as a normative theory, employed in this context, the theory not only *explains* (much as does my employment of Hirschman's theory) the cyclical nature of women's lack of power within the family. It also points to the injustice of a situation in which the assumption of women's responsibility for children, their disadvantaged position in the paid workforce, and their physical vulnerability to male violence all contribute to giving them little bargaining room when their (or their children's) interests conflict with those of the men they live with, thereby in turn worsening their position relative to that of men. The whole theory, then, whether in its more or its less mathematical form, seems just as applicable to the situations of very poor women in poor countries as it is to women in quite well-off households in rich countries. Indeed, one must surely say, in this case, too, "similar but *much* worse," for the stakes are undeniably higher — no less than life or death for more than a hundred million women, as has recently been shown (Drèze and Sen 1990, chap. 4; Sen 1990a).

Policy Implications

Some of the *solutions* to all these problems, which have been suggested recently by scholars addressing the situation of poor women in poor countries, closely resemble solutions proposed by Western feminists primarily concentrating on their own societies. (By "solutions to problems" I mean to refer to both what theorists and social scientists need to do to rectify their analyses and what policymakers need to do to solve the social problems themselves.) First, the dichotomization of public and domestic spheres must be strongly challenged. As Chen (1983) writes, in the context of poor rural regions, "So long as policy-makers make the artificial distinction between the farm and the household, between paid work and unpaid work, between productive and domestic work, women will continue to be overlooked" (p. 220). Challenging the dichotomy will also point attention to the inequities that occur within households — various forms of abuse, including the inequitable distribution of food and health care. As Papanek (1990) argues, "given a focus on socialization for inequality, power relations within the household — as a central theme in examining the dynamics of households — deserve special attention" (p. 170).

Second, and following from the above, the unit of analysis both for studies and for much policy-

making must be the individual, not the household.[11] Noting that, given the greater political voice of men, public decisions affecting the poor in poor countries are often "guided by male preferences, not [frequently conflicting] female needs," Dasgupta (1993) concludes that

the maximization of well-being as a model for explaining household behaviour must be rejected.... Even though it is often difficult to design and effect it, the target of public policy should be persons, not households.... Governments need to be conscious of the household as a resource allocation mechanism. (Pp. 335-36)

Especially as women are even more likely in poor countries than in richer ones to be providing the sole or principal support for their households, as Chen (1983) points out, they require as much access as men to credit, skills training, labor markets, and technologies (and, I would add, equal pay for their work) (p. 221). Policies prompting women's full economic participation and productivity are needed increasingly for the survival of their households, for women's overall socioeconomic status, and for their bargaining position within their families. As Drèze and Sen (1989) say, "important policy implications" follow from the "considerable evidence that greater involvement with outside work and paid employment does tend to go with less anti-female bias in intra-family distribution" (p. 58). Because of the quite pervasive unequal treatment of female children in some poor countries, the need for equal treatment of women by policymakers is often far more urgent than the need of most women in richer countries — but again, the issue is not so much different as "similar but more so."

Implications for Thinking about Justice

Finally, I shall speculate briefly about two different ways of thinking about justice between the sexes, in cultures very different from ours. I have tried to show that, for feminists thinking about justice, John Rawls's theory, if revised so as to include women and the family, has a great deal to be said for it, and the veil of ignorance is particularly important (Rawls 1971; Okin 1989a, 1989b). If everyone were to speak only from his or her own point of view, it is unclear that we would come up with any principles at all. But the very presence of the veil, which hides from those in the original position any particular knowledge of the personal characteristics or social position they will have in the society for which they are designing principles of justice, forces them to take into account as many voices as possible and especially to be concerned with those of the least well-off. It enables us to reconcile the requirement that a theory of justice be universalizable with the seemingly conflicting requirement that it take account of the multiple differences among human beings.

In a recent paper, Ruth Anna Putnam (forthcoming), arguing a strongly antiessentialist line, and accusing Rawls and myself of varying degrees of exclusionary essentialism, considers instead an "interactive" (some might call it "dialogic" feminism: "that we listen to the voices of women of color and women of a different class, and that we appropriate what we hear" (p. 21).[12] Listening and discussing have much to recommend them; they are fundamental to democracy in the best sense of the word. And *sometimes* when especially oppressed women are heard, their cry for justice is clear — as in the case of the women Martha Chen worked with, who became quite clear that being allowed to leave the domestic sphere in order to earn wages would help to liberate them. But we are not always enlightened about what is just by asking persons who seem to be suffering injustices what they want. Oppressed people have often internalized their oppression so well that they *have* no sense of what they are justly entitled to as human beings. This is certainly the case with gender inequalities. As Papanek (1990) writes, "The clear perception of disadvantages ... requires conscious rejection of the social norms and cultural ideal that perpetuate inequalities and the use of different criteria — perhaps from another actual or idealized society — in order to assess inequality as a prelude for action" (pp. 164-65). People in seriously deprived conditions are sometimes not only accepting of them but relatively cheerful —

the "small mercies" situation. Deprivations sometimes become gagged and muffled for reasons of deeply rooted ideology, among others. But it would surely be ethically deeply mistaken to attach a correspondingly small value to the loss of well-being of such people because of their survival strategy.

Coming to terms with very little is no recipe for social justice. Thus it is, I believe, quite justifiable for those not thoroughly imbued with the in-egalitarian norms of a culture to come forth as its constructive critics. Critical distance, after all, does not have to bring with it detachment: *committed* outsiders can often be better analysts and critics of social injustice than those who live within the relevant culture. This is why a concept such as the original position, which aims to approximate an Archimedean point, is so valuable, at least in addition to some form of dialogue. Let us think for a moment about some of the cruelest or most oppressive institutions and practices that are or have been used to "brand" women — foot binding, clitoridectomy, and purdah. As Papanek shows, "well socialized" women in cultures with such practices internalize them as necessary to successful female development. Even though, in the case of the former two practices, these women may retain vivid memories of their own intense pain, they perpetuate the cruelties, inflicting them or at least allowing them to be inflicted on their own daughters.

Now, clearly, a theory of human flourishing, such as Nussbaum and Sen have been developing, would have no trouble delegitimizing such practices (Nussbaum1992). But given the choice between a revised Rawlsian outlook or an "interactive feminist" one, as defined by Putnam, I'd choose the former any day, for in the latter, well-socialized members of the oppressed group are all too likely to rationalize the cruelties, whereas the men who perceive themselves as benefiting from them are unlikely to object. But behind the veil of ignorance, is it not much more likely that both the oppressors and the oppressed would have second thoughts? What Moslem man is likely to take that chance of spending his life in seclusion and dependency, sweltering in head-to-toe solid black clothing? What pre-revolutionary Chinese man would cast his vote for the breaking of toes and hobbling through life, if he well might be the one with the toes and the crippled life? What man would endorse gross genital mutilation, not knowing *whose* genitals? And the women in these cultures, required to think of such practices from a male as well as a female perspective, might thereby, with a little distance, gain more notion of just how, rather than perfecting femininity, they perpetuate the subordination of women to men.

Martha Nussbaum (1992) has recently written of what happens when outsiders, instead of trying to maintain some critical distance, turn to what amounts to the worship of difference. Citing some examples of sophisticated Western scholars who, in their reverence for the integrity of cultures, defend such practices as the isolation of menstruating women and criticize Western "intrusions" into other cultures, such as the provision of typhoid vaccine, Nussbaum finds a strange and disturbing phenomenon:

> Highly intelligent people, people deeply committed to the good of women and men in developing countries, people who think of themselves as progressive and feminist and antiracist, ... are taking up positions that converge ... with the positions of reaction, oppression, and sexism. Under the banner of their radically and politically correct "antiessentialism" march ancient religious taboos, the luxury of the pampered husband, ill health, ignorance, and death. (p. 204)

As Nussbaum later concludes, "Identification need not ignore concrete local differences: in fact, at its best, it demands a searching analysis of differences, in order that the general good be appropriately realized in the concrete case. But the learning about and from the other is motivated ... by the conviction that the other is one of us" (p. 241).

As the work of some feminist scholars of development shows, using the concept of gender and refusing to let differences gag us or fragment our analyses does not mean that we should overgeneralize or try to apply "standardized" solutions to the problems of women in different circumstances. Chen argues for the value of a situation-by-situation

analysis of women's roles and constraints before plans can be made and programs designed. And Papanek, too, shows how helping to educate women to awareness of their oppression requires quite deep and specific knowledge of the relevant culture.

Thus I conclude that gender itself is an extremely important category of analysis and that we ought not be paralyzed by the facts that there are differences among women. So long as we are careful and develop our judgments in the light of empirical evidence, it is possible to generalize about many aspects of inequality between the sexes. Theories developed in Western contexts can clearly apply, at least in large part, to women in very different cultural contexts. From place to place, form class to class, from race to race, and from culture to culture, we find similarities in the specifics of these inequalities, in their causes and their effects, although often not in their extent or severity.

Author's Note

I am grateful to Elisabeth Friedman, Elisabeth Hansot, Robert O. Keohane, Martha Nussbaum, and Louise Tilly for helpful comments on an earlier draft of this article.

NOTES

1. This debate has been conducted mostly among feminist legal and political theorists. The legal literature is already so vast that it is difficult to summarize, and it is not relevant to this essay. For some references, see Okin (1991), ns. 1-3.

2. "Essentialism," employed in the context of feminist theory, seems to have two principal meanings. The other refers to the tendency to regard certain characteristics or capacities as "essentially" female, in the sense that they are unalterably associated with being female. Used in this second way, essentialism is very close to, if not always identical with, biological determinism. I am not concerned with this aspect of the term here.

3. In 1851, at an almost entirely white women's rights convention, Truth said,

    That man over there says women need to be helped into carriages and lifted over ditches, and to have the best place everywhere. Nobody ever helps me into carriages, or over mud puddles, or gives me any best place. And ain't I a woman? Look at me! Look at my arm! I have ploughed, and planted, and gathered into barns, and no man could head me! And ain't I a woman? I could work as much and eat as much as a man — when I could get it — and bear the lash as well! And ain't I a woman? I have borne thirteen children, and seen most all sold off to slavery, and when I cried out with my mother's grief, none but Jesus heard me! And ain't I a woman?

4. The example is that of the many black women (and few white women) who answered Joann Little's appeal on behalf of Delbert Tibbs, a black man who had been falsely accused of raping a white woman and sentenced to death. I do not think the example clearly supports Harris's assertion that black women have "a unique ambivalence" about rape, any more than it supports the assertion she claims to refute — that their experience is similar, but different in magnitude. Black women's present experience of rape is surely similar to that of white women in several important respects: many are raped (by acquaintances as well as by strangers), they fear being raped, they sometimes modify their behavior because of this fear, and they are victimized as witnesses at the trials of their rapists. But their experience is probably also worse because, in addition to all of this, they have to live with the knowledge and experience of black men's being victimized by false accusations, harsher sentences, and, at worst, lynchings. Only empirical research that involved asking them could show more certainly whether the oppression of black men as alleged rapists (or the history of master/slave rape, which Harris also discusses) makes black women's entire contemporary experience of rape different from that of white women.

5. However, the detailed division of labor between the sexes varies considerably from culture to culture. As Jane Mansbridge (1993) has recently written, in a discussion of "gratuitous gendering":

Among the Aleut of North America, for example, only women are allowed to butcher animals. But among the Ingalik of North America, only men are allowed to butcher animals. Among the Suku of Africa, only the women can plant crops and only the men can make baskets. But among the Kaffa of the Circum-Mediterranean, only the men can plant crops and only the women can make baskets. (p. 345).

Her analysis is derived from data in George P. Murdoch and Caterina Provost. "Factors in the Division of Labor by Sex: A Cross-Cultural Analysis." *Ethnology* 12 (1973): 203-25. However, the work done by women is less likely to be "outside" work and to be paid or valued.

6. Poverty is both a relative and an absolute term. The poorest households in poor countries are absolutely as well as relatively poor and can be easily pushed below subsistence by any number of natural, social, or personal catastrophes. Poverty in rich countries is more often relative poverty (although there is serious malnutrition currently in the United States for example and drug abuse with all its related ills, is highly correlated with poverty). Relative poverty, although not directly life-threatening, can however be very painful, especially for children living in societies that are not only highly consumer-oriented but in which many opportunities — for good health care, decent education, the development of talents, pursuit of interests, and so on — are seriously limited for those from poor families. Single parents also often experience severe "time poverty," which can have a serious impact on their children's well-being.

7. See Dasgupta (1993) on members' perceived "usefulness" affecting the allocation of goods within poor households in poor families. Western studies as well as non-Western ones show us that women's work is already likely to be regarded as less useful — even when it is just as necessary to family well-being. So when women are really made less useful (by convention or lack of employment opportunities), this problem is compounded. Dasgupta questions simple measures of usefulness, such as paid employment, in the case of girls (1993). Where young poor women are not entitled to parental assets and their outside employment opportunities are severely restricted, the only significant "employment" for then is as childbearers and

housekeepers — so marriage becomes especially valued (even though its conditions may be highly oppressive).

8. There seems to be some conflicting evidence on this matter. See Papanek (1990, 166-68).

9. This seems similar to changes in the work and socioeconomic status of women in Western Europe in the sixteenth to eighteenth centuries.

10. I do not mean to imply here that most women, whether in developed or less developed societies, think about improving their exit options when making decisions about wage work and related issues. Indeed, in some cultures, women relinquish wage work as soon as their families' financial situation enable them to do so. But their exit option is nevertheless reduced, and their partner's enhanced, thereby in all likelihood altering the distribution of power within the family.

11. This point seems to have been first explicitly made in the context of policy by George Bernard Shaw, who argues in *The Intelligent Woman's Guide to Socialism and Capitalism* (New Brunswick, NJ: Transaction books, 1984) that the state should require all adults to work and should allocate an equal portion of income to each — man, woman, and child.

12. As Joan Tronto has pointed out to me, the use of "appropriate" here is noteworthy, given Putnam's professed desire to treat these other women as her equals.

REFERENCES

Benhabib, Seyla and Drucilla Cornell. 1987. Introduction: Beyond the politics of gender. In *Feminism as critique*. Minneapolis: University of Minnesota Press.

Bergmann, Barbara R. 1986. *The economic emergence of women.* New York: Basic Books.

Blumstein, Philip, and Pepper Schwartz. 1983. *American couples.* New York: Morrow

Boserup, Ester. 1970. *Women's role in economic development.* London: Allen & Unwin.

Chen, Lincoln C., Emdadul Huq, and Stan D'Souza. 1981. Sex bias in the family allocation of food and health care in rural Bangladesh. *Population and Development Review* 7:55-70.

Chen, Martha Alter. 1983. *A quiet revolution: Women in transition in rural Bangladesh.* Cambridge, MA: Schenkma.

— . [1995]. A matter of survival: Women's right to work in India and Bangladesh. In [*Women, Culture and Development*], edited by Nussbaum and Glover. Oxford: Oxford University Press.

Childers, Mary, and bell hooks. 1990. A conversation about race and class. In *Conflicts in feminism*, edited by Marianne Hirsch and Evelyn Fox Keller. New York: Routledge, Chapman & Hall.

Crosswaite, Jan. 1989. Sex in the original position. Unpublished manuscript, Department of Philosophy, University of Auckland.

Dasgupta, Partha. 1993. *An inquiry into well-being and destitution.* Oxford: Clarendon.

Drèze, Jean, and Amartya Sen. 1989. *Hunger and public action.* Oxford: Clarendon.

— , eds. 1990. *The political economy of hunger: Vol. 1. Entitlement and well-being.* Oxford: Clarendon.

Fuchs, Victor. 1988. *Women's quest for economic equality.* Cambridge, MA: Harvard University Press.

Gerson, Kathleen. 1985. *Hard choices: How women decide about work, career, and motherhood.* Berkeley: University of California Press.

Gordon, Linda. 1988. *Heroes of their own lives.* New York: Viking.

Harris, Angela P. 1990. Race and essentialism in feminist legal theory. *Stanford Law Review* 42:581-616

Harriss, Barbara. 1990. The intrafamilial distribution of hunger in south Asia. In *The political economy of hunger: Vol. 1. Entitlement and well-being,* edited by Jean Drèze and Amartya Sen. Oxford: Clarendon.

Hochschild, Arlie. 1989. *The second shift: Working parents and the revolution at home.* New York: Viking.

hooks, bell. 1984. *Feminist theory: From margin to center.* Boston: south End Press.

Jaquette, Jane S. 1982. Women and modernization: A decade of feminist criticism. *World Politics* 34:267-84.

Jelin, Elizabeth, ed. 1990. *Women and social change in Latin America.* London: Zed Books.

Kearns, Deborah. 1983. A theory of justice and love: Rawls on the family. *Politics (Journal of the Australasian Political Studies Association)* 18 (2): 35-42.

Lorde, Audre. 1984. An open letter to Mary Daly. In *Sister outsider*, edited by Audre Lorde. Trumansburg, NY: Crossing Press.

Mansbridge, Jane. 1993. Feminism and democratic community. In *Democratic community*, edited by John Chapman and Ian Shapiro. New York: New York University Press.

Marks, Elaine, and Isabelle de Courtivron, eds. 1981. *New French feminisms: an anthology*. New York: Schocken.

McLindon, James B. 1987. Separate but unequal: the economic disaster of divorce for women and children. *Family Law Quarterly* 12:3.

Mill, John Stuart. [1860] 1988. *The subjection of women*. Reprint. Indianapolis: Hackett.

Minow, Martha, and Elizabeth V. Spelman.1990. In context. *Southern California Law Review* 63 (6): 1597-1652.

Nussbaum, Martha. 1992. Human functioning and social justice: In defense of Aristotelian essentialism. *Political theory* 20: 202-46.

Okin, Susan Moller. 1989a. Reason and feeling in thinking about justice. *Ethics* 99 (2): 229-49.

— . 1989b. *Justice, gender, and the family*, New York: Basic Books.

— . 1991. Sexual difference, feminism and the law. *Law and Social Inquiry*.

Olsen, Frances. 1983. The family and the market: A study of ideology and legal reform. *Harvard Law Review* 96 (7).

Papanek, Hanna. 1990. To each less than she needs, from each more than she can do: Allocations, entitlements, and value. In Irene Tinker, ed., *Women and world development*. New York and London: Oxford University Press.

Pateman, Carole. 1983. Feminist critiques of the public/private dichotomy. In *Public and private in social life,* edited by Stanley Benn and Gerald Gaus. London: Croom Helm. Also in Pateman, *The disorder of women*. Stanford, CA: Stanford University Press, 1989.

Putnam, Ruth Anna. [1995] Why not a feminist theory of justice? in [*Women, Culture, and Development*], ed. Nussbaum and Glover.

Rawls, John. 1971. *A theory of justice*. Cambridge, MA: Harvard University Press.

Sanday, Peggy R. 1974. Female status in the public domain. In Michelle Zimbalist Rosaldo and Louise Lamphere, eds., *Woman, culture, and society*. Stanford, CA: Stanford University Press.

Sen, Amartya. 1990a. More than 100 million women are missing. *New York Review of Books*, December 20.

— . 1990b. Gender and co-operative conflicts. In Irene Tinker, ed., *Women and world development*. New York and London: Oxford University Press.

Spelman, Elizabeth V. 1988. In essential woman: *Problems of exclusion in feminist thought*. Boston: Beacon.

United Nations Report. 1991. *The world's women: Trends and statistics*, 1970-1990. New York: United Nations Publication.

Waring, Marilyn. 1989. *If women counted: A new feminist economics*. San Francisco: Harper & Row.

Weitzman, Lenore. 1985. *The Divorce Revolution: The unexpected social and economic consequences for women and children*. New York: Free Press.

Wheeler, E.F., and M. Abdullah. 1988. Food allocation within the family: Response to fluctuating food supply and food needs. In I. De Garine and G.A. Harrison, *Coping with uncertainty in food supply*. Oxford: Clarendon.

Wishik, Heather Ruth. 1986. Economics of divorce: an exploratory study. *Family Law Quarterly* 20:1.

UNDER WESTERN EYES:
FEMINIST SCHOLARSHIP AND COLONIAL DISCOURSES

Chandra Talpade Mohanty

Chandra Mohanty is Associate Professor of Women's Studies at Hamilton College, Clinton, New York. She is author of Feminism Without Borders: Decolonizing Theory, Practicing Solidarity *(2003) and co-editor of* Third World Women and the Politics of Feminism *(1991, with Lourdes Torres and Ann Russo) and of* Feminist Genealogies, Colonial Legacies, and Democratic Futures *(1997, with M. Jacqui Alexander).*

Mohanty is critical of the tendency in some Western feminist scholarship to understand women in non-Western countries as a monolithic group having similar identities, experiencing similar kinds of oppression and disadvantage, and needing similar strategies for addressing injustices. She provides examples of the diverse experiences, beliefs, practices, and values in different social and political contexts to challenge this tendency. Mohanty argues that failing to recognize the diversity amongst women has resulted in Western feminists advocating policies that are actually detrimental to the lives of women in particular non-Western countries.

It ought to be of some political significance at least that the term "colonization" has come to denote a variety of phenomena in recent feminist and left writings in general. From its analytic value as a category of exploitative economic exchange in both traditional and contemporary Marxisms (cf. particularly such contemporary scholars as Baran, Amin and Gunder-Frank) to its use by feminist women of colour in the US, to describe the appropriation of their experiences and struggles by hegemonic white women's movements,[1] the term "colonization" has been used to characterize everything from the most evident economic and political hierarchies to the production of particular cultural discourse about what is called the "Third World."[2] However sophisticated or problematical its use as an explanatory construct, colonization almost invariably implies a relation of structural domination, and a discursive or political suppression of the heterogeneity of the subject(s) in question. What I wish to analyse here specifically is the production of the "Third World Woman" as a sin-gular monolithic subject in some recent (western) feminist texts. The definition of colonization I invoke is a predominantly *discursive* one, focusing on a certain mode of appropriation and codification of "scholarship" and "knowledge" about women in the third world by particular analytic categories employed in writings on the subject which take as their primary point of reference feminist interests as they have been articulated in the US and western Europe.

My concern about such writings derives from my own implication and investment in contemporary debates in feminist theory, and the urgent political necessity of forming strategic coalitions across class, race and national boundaries. Clearly, western feminist discourse and political practice is neither singular nor homogenous in its goals, interests or analyses. However, it is possible to trace a coherence of *effects* resulting from the implicit assumption of "the west" (in all its complexities and contradictions) as the primary referent in theory and praxis. Thus, rather than claim simplistically that "western Feminism" is a mono-lith, I would like to draw attention to the remark-ably similar effects of various analytical cate-gories and even strategies which codify their relationship to the Other in implicitly hierarchical terms. It is in this sense that I use the term "western feminist." Similar arguments pertaining to questions of methods of analysis can be made in terms of middle-class, urban African and Asian scholars producing scholarship on or about their rural or working-class sisters which assumes their own middle-class culture as the norm, and codi-fies peasant and working-class histories and cul-tures as Other. Thus, while this article focuses specifically on western feminist discourse on women in the third world, the critiques I offer also pertain to identical analytical principles employed by third-world scholars writing about their own cultures.

Moreover, the analytical principles discussed below serve to distort western feminist political practices, and limit the possibility of coalitions among (usually white) western feminists and working-class and feminist women of colour around the world. These limitations are evident in the construction of the (implicitly consensual) pri-ority of issues around which apparently *all* women are expected to organize. The necessary and inte-gral connection between feminist scholarship and feminist political practice and organizing deter-mines the significance and status of western femi-nist writings on women in the third world, for fem-inist scholarship, like most other kinds of scholarship, does not comprise merely "objective" knowledge about a certain subject. It is also a directly political and discursive *practice* insofar as it is purposeful and ideological. It is best seen as a mode of intervention into particular hegemonic discourses (for example, traditional anthropology, sociology, literary criticism, etc.), and as a political praxis which counters and resists the totalizing imperative of age-old "legitimate" and "scientific" bodies of knowledge. Thus, feminist scholarly practices exist within relations of power — rela-tions which they counter, redefine, or even implic-itly support. There can, of course, be no apolitical scholarship.

The relationship between Woman — a cultural and ideological composite Other constructed through diverse representational discourse (scien-tific, literary, juridical, linguistic, cinematic, etc.) — and women — real, material subjects of their collective histories — is one of the central ques-tions the practice of feminist scholarship seeks to address. This connection between women as his-torical subjects and the representation of Woman produced by hegemonic discourses is not a relation of direct identity, or a relation of correspondence or simple implication.[3] It is an arbitrary relation set up in particular cultural and historical contexts. I would like to suggest that the feminist writings I analyse here discursively colonize the material and historical heterogeneities of the lives of women in the third world, thereby producing/representing a composite, singular "third-world woman" — an image which appears arbitrarily constructed but nevertheless carries with it the authorizing signa-ture of western humanist discourse.[4] I argue that assumptions of privilege and ethnocentric univer-sality on the one hand and inadequate self-con-sciousness about the effect of western scholarship on the "third world" in the context of a world system dominated by the west on the other, char-acterize a sizable extent of western feminist work on women in the third world. An analysis of "sexual difference" in the form of a cross-cultur-ally singular, monolithic notion of patriarchy or male dominance leads to the construction of a sim-ilarly reductive and homogeneous notion of what I shall call the "third-world difference" — that stable, ahistorical something that apparently oppresses most if not all the women in these coun-tries. It is in the production of this "third-world dif-ference" that western feminisms appropriate and colonize the constitutive complexities which char-acterize the lives of women in these countries. It is in this process of discursive homogenization and systematization of the oppression of women in the third world that power is exercised in much of recent western feminist writing, and this power needs to be defined and named....

Western feminist scholarship cannot avoid the challenge of situating itself and examining its role in such a global economic and political framework.

To do any less would be to ignore the complex interconnections between first — and third-world economies and the profound effect of this on the lives of women in *all* countries. I do not question the descriptive and informative value of most western feminist writings on women in the third world. I also do not question the existence of excellent work which does not fall into the analytic traps I am concerned with. In fact I deal with an example of such work later on. In the context of an overwhelming silence about the experiences of women in these countries, as well as the need to forge international links between women's political struggles, such work is both pathbreaking and absolutely essential. However, it is both to the *explanatory potential* of particular analytical strategies employed by such writing, and to their *political effect* in the context of the hegemony of western scholarship, that I want to draw attention here. While feminist writing in the US is still marginalized (except perhaps from the point of view of women of colour addressing privileged white women), western feminist writing on women in the third world must be considered in the context of the global hegemony of western scholarship — i.e., the production, publication, distribution and consumption of information and ideas. Marginal or not, this writing has political effects and implications beyond the immediate feminist or disciplinary audience. One such significant effect of the dominant "representations" of western feminism is its conflation with imperialism in the eyes of particular third-world women.[5] Hence the urgent need to examine the *political* implications of our *analytic* strategies and principles.

My critique is directed at three basic analytical presuppositions which are present in (western) feminist discourse on women in the third world. Since I focus primarily on the Zed Press "Women in the Third World" series, my comments on western feminist discourse are circumscribed by my analysis of the texts in this series.[6] This is a way of focusing my critique. However, even though I am dealing with feminists who identify themselves as culturally or geographically from the "west," as mentioned earlier, what I say about these presuppositions or implicit principles holds

for anyone who uses these analytical strategies, whether third-world women in the west, or third-world women in the third world writing on these issues and publishing in the west. Thus, I am not making a culturalist argument about ethnocentrism; rather, I am trying to uncover how ethnocentric universalism is produced in certain analyses. As a matter of fact, my argument holds for any discourse that sets up its own authorial subjects as the implicit referent, i.e., the yardstick by which to encode and represent cultural Others. It is in this move that power is exercised in discourse.

The first analytical presupposition I focus on is involved in the strategic location or situation of the category "women" *vis-à-vis* the context of analysis. The assumption of women as an already constituted and coherent group with identical interests and desires, regardless of class, ethnic or racial location, implies a notion of gender or sexual difference or even patriarchy which can be applied universally and cross-culturally. (The context of analysis can be anything from kinship structures and the organization of labour to media representations.) The second analytical presupposition is evident on the methodological level, in the uncritical way "proof" of universality and cross-cultural validity are provided. The third is a more specifically political presupposition, underlying the methodologies and the analytic strategies, i.e., the model of power and struggle they imply and suggest. I argue that as a result of the two modes — or, rather, frames — of analysis described above, a homogeneous notion of the oppression of women as a group is assumed, which, in turn, produces the image of an "average third-world woman." This average third-world woman leads an essentially truncated life based on her feminine gender (read: sexually constrained) and being "third world" (read: ignorant, poor, uneducated, tradition-bound, religious, domesticated, family-oriented, victimized, etc.). This, I suggest, is in contrast to the (implicit) self-representation of western women as educated, modern, as having control over their own bodies and sexualities, and the "freedom" to make their own decisions. The distinction between western feminist representation of women in the third world, and western feminist self-presentation is a distinction of the same order as that made by some Marxists between the "maintenance" function of the house-wife and the real "productive" role of wage-labour, or the characterization by developmental-ists of the third world as being engaged in the lesser production of "raw materials" in contrast to the "real" productive activity of the first world. These distinctions are made on the basis of the privileging of a particular group as the norm or referent. Men involved in wage-labour, first-world producers, and, I suggest, western feminists who sometimes cast third-world women in terms of "ourselves undressed" (Michelle Rosaldo's term; Rosaldo, 1980: 389-412, especially 392), all con-struct themselves as the normative referent in such a binary analytic.

"Women" as Category of Analysis, or: We are All Sisters in Struggle

By women as a category of analysis, I am referring to the crucial presupposition that all of us of the same gender, across classes and cultures, are somehow socially constituted as a homogeneous group identifiable prior to the process of analysis. The homogeneity of women as a group is produced not on the basis of biological essentials, but rather on the basis of secondary sociological and anthro-pological universals. Thus, for instance, in any given piece of feminist analysis, women are char-acterized as a singular group on the basis of a shared oppression. What binds women together is a sociological notion of the "sameness" of their oppression. It is at this point that an elision takes place between "women" as a discursively con-structed group and "women" as material subjects of their own history.[7] Thus, the discursively con-sensual homogeneity of "women" as a group is mistaken for the historically specific material reality of groups of women. This results in an assumption of women as an always-already consti-tuted group, one which has been labelled "power-less," "exploited," "sexually harassed," etc., by feminist scientific, economic, legal and sociologi-cal discourses. (Notice that this is quite similar to sexist discourse labelling women as weak, emo-tional, having math anxiety, etc.) The focus is not on uncovering the material and ideological speci-ficities that constitute a group of women as "pow-erless" in a particular context. It is rather on finding a variety of cases of "powerless" groups of women to prove the general point that women as a group are powerless.[8]

In this section I focus on five specific ways in which "women" as a category of analysis is used in western feminist discourse on women in the third world to construct "third-world women" as a homogeneous "powerless" group often located as implicit *victims* of particular cultural and socio-economic systems. I have chosen to deal with a variety of writers — from Fran Hosken, who writes primarily about female genital mutilation, to writers from the Women in International Develop-ment school who write about the effect of develop-ment policies on third-world women for both western and third-world audiences. I do not intend to equate all the texts that I analyse, nor ignore their respective strengths and weaknesses. The authors I deal with write with varying degrees of care and complexity; however, the *effect* of the rep-resentation of third-world women in these texts is a coherent one. In these texts women are variously defined as victims of male violence (Fran Hosken); victims of the colonial process (M. Cutrufelli); victims of the Arab familial system (Juliette Minces); victims of the economic development process (B. Lindsay and the — Liberal — WID school); and finally, victims of the economic basis of *the* Islamic code (P. Jeffery). This mode of defining women primarily in terms of the *object status* (the way in which they are affected or not affected by certain institutions and systems) is what characterizes this particular form of the use of "women" as a category of analysis. In the context of western women writing about and studying women in the third world, such objectifi-cation (however benevolently motivated) needs to be both named and challenged. As Valerie Amos and Pratibha Parmar argue quite eloquently, "Fem-inist theories which examine our cultural practices as 'feudal residues' or label us 'traditional,' also portray us as politically immature women who need to be versed and schooled in the ethos of western feminism. They need to be continually challenged" (1984: 7).

Women as Victims of Male Violence

Fran Hosken, in writing about the relationship between human rights and female genital mutilation in Africa and the Middle East, bases her whole discussion and condemnation of genital mutilation on one privileged premise: the goal of genital mutilation is "to mutilate the sexual pleasure and satisfaction of woman" (1981: 3-24, especially 11).[9] This in turn, leads her to claim that woman's sexuality is controlled, as is her reproductive potential. According to Hosken, "male sexual politics" in Africa and around the world "share the same political goal: to assure female dependence and subservience by any and all means." Physical violence against women (rape, sexual assault, excision, infibulation, etc.) is thus carried out "with astonishing consensus among men in the world" (14). Here, women are defined systematically as the *victims* of male control — the "sexually oppressed." Although it is true that the potential of male violence against women circumscribes and elucidates their social position to a certain extent, defining women as archetypal victims freezes them into "objects-who-defend-themselves," men into "subjects-who-perpetrate-violence," and (every) society into a simple opposition between the powerless (read: women) and the powerful (read: men) groups of people. Male violence (if that indeed is the appropriate label) must be theorized and interpreted *within* specific societies, both in order to understand it better, as well as in order to effectively organize to change it.[10] Sisterhood cannot be assumed on the basis of gender; it must be forged in concrete historical and political praxis.

Women as Universal Dependants

Beverley Lindsay's conclusion to the book, *Comparative Perspectives on Third World Women: The Impact of Race, Class and Sex* states: "Dependency relationships, based upon race, sex and class, are being perpetuated through social, educa-

tional, and economic institutions. These are the linkages among Third World Women" (1983: especially 298, 306). Here, as in other places, Lindsay implies that third-world women constitute an identifiable group purely on the basis of shared dependencies. If shared dependencies were all that was needed to bind us together as a group, third-world women would always be seen as an apolitical group with no subject status! Instead, if anything, it is the *common context* of political struggle against class, race, gender and imperialist hierarchies that may constitute third-world women as a strategic group at this historical juncture. Lindsay also states that linguistic and cultural differences exist between Vietnamese and Black American women, but "both groups are victims of race, sex and class" Again, Black and Vietnamese women are characterized and defined simply in terms of their victim status.

Similarly, examine statements like: "My analysis will start by stating that all African women are politically and economically dependent" (Cutrufelli, 1983: especially 13). Or: "Nevertheless, either overtly or covertly, prostitution is still the main if not the only source of work for African women" (Cutrufelli, 1983: 33). *All* African women are dependent. Prostitution is the only work option for African women as a *group*. Both statements are illustrative of generalizations sprinkled liberally through a recent Zed Press publication, *Women of Africa: Roots of Oppression,* by Maria Rosa Cutrufelli, who is described on the cover as an "Italian Writer, Sociologist, Marxist and Feminist." In the 1980s is it possible to imagine writing a book entitled "Women of Europe: Roots of Oppression?" I am not objecting to the use of universal groupings for descriptive purposes. Women from the continent of Africa can be descriptively characterized as "Women of Africa." It is when "women of Africa" becomes a homogeneous sociological grouping characterized by common dependencies or powerlessness (or even strengths) that problems arise — we say too little and too much at the same time.

This is because descriptive gender differences are transformed into the division between men and women. Women are constituted as a group via dependency relationships *vis à vis* men, who are implicitly held responsible for these relationships. When "women of Africa" (versus "men of Africa" as a group?) are seen as a group precisely because they are generally dependent and oppressed, the analysis of specific historical differences becomes impossible, because reality is always apparently structured by divisions between two mutually exclusive and jointly exhaustive groups, the victims and the oppressors. Here the sociological is substituted for the biological in order, however, to create the same — a unity of women. Thus, it is not the descriptive potential of gender difference but the privileged positioning and explanatory potential of gender difference as the *origin* of the oppression that I question. In using "women of Africa" (as an already constituted group of oppressed peoples) as a category of analysis, Cutrufelli denies any historical specificity to the location of women as subordinate, powerful, marginal, central or otherwise, *vis à vis* particular social and power networks. Women are taken as a unified "powerless" group prior to the historical and political analysis in question. Thus, it is then merely a matter of specifying the context *after the fact*. "Women" are now placed in the context of the family, or in the workplace, or within religious networks, almost as if these systems existed outside the relations of women with other women, and women with men.

The problem with this analytical strategy is, let me repeat, that it assumes men and women are already constituted as sexual-political subjects prior to their entry into the arena of social relations. Only if we subscribe to this assumption is it possible to undertake analysis which looks at the "effects" of kinship structures, colonialism, organization of labour, etc., on women, who are defined in advance as a group. The crucial point that is forgotten is that women are produced through these very relations as well as being implicated in forming these relations. As Michelle Rosaldo argues, "woman's place in human social life is not in any direct sense a product of the things she does (or even less, a function of what, biologically, she is) but the meaning her activities acquire through concrete social interactions" (1980: 400). That

women mother in a variety of societies is not as significant as the value attached to mothering in these societies. The distinction between the act of mothering and the status attached to it is a very important one — one that needs to be stated and analysed contextually.

Married Women as Victims of the Colonial Process

In Levi-Strauss's theory of kinship structures as a system of the exchange of women, what is significant is that exchange itself is not constitutive of the subordination of women; women are not subordinate because of the *fact* of exchange, but because of the *modes* of exchange instituted, and the values attached to these modes. However, in discussing the marriage ritual of the Bemba, a Zambian matrilocal, matrilineal people, Cutrufelli in *Women of Africa* focuses on the fact of the marital exchange of women before and after western colonization, rather than the value attached to this exchange in this particular context. This leads to her definition of Bemba women as a coherent group affected in a particular way by colonization. Here again, Bemba women are constituted rather unilaterally as the victims of western colonization. Cutrufelli cites the marriage ritual of the Bemba as a multi-stage event "whereby a young man becomes incorporated into his wife's family group as he takes up residence with them and gives his services in return for food and maintenance" (1983: 43). This ritual extends over many years, and the sexual relationship varies according to the degree of the girl's physical maturity. It is only after the girl undergoes an initiation ceremony at puberty that intercourse is sanctioned, and the man acquires legal rights over the woman. This initiation ceremony is the most important act of the consecration of women's reproductive power, so that the abduction of an uninitiated girl is of no consequence, while heavy penalty is levied for the seduction of an initiated girl. Cutrufelli asserts that the effect of European colonization has changed the whole marriage system. Now the young man is entitled to take his wife away from her people in return for money. The implication is that Bemba women have now lost the protection of tribal laws. However, while it is possible to see how the structure of the traditional marriage contract (as opposed to the post-colonial marriage contract) offered women a certain amount of control over their marital relations, only an analysis of the political significance of the actual practice which privileges an initiated girl over an uninitiated one, indicating a shift in female power relations as a result of this ceremony, can provide an accurate account of whether Bemba women were indeed protected by tribal laws *at all times.*

However, it is not possible to talk about Bemba women as a homogeneous group within the traditional marriage structure. Bemba women *before* the initiation are constituted within a different set of social relations compared to Bemba women *after* initiation. To treat them as a unified group, characterized by the fact of their "exchange" between male kin, is to deny the specificities of their daily existence, and the differential *value* attached to their exchange before and after their initiation. It is to treat the initiation ceremony as a ritual with no political implications or effects. It is also to assume that in merely describing the *structure* of the marriage contract, the situation of women is exposed. Women as a group are positioned within a given structure, but there is no attempt made to trace the effect of the marriage practice in constituting women within an obviously changing network of power relations. Thus, women are assumed to be sexual-political subjects prior to entry into kinship structures.

Women and Familial Systems

Elizabeth Cowie, in another context (1978: 49-63), points out the implications of this sort of analysis when she emphasizes the specifically political nature of kinship structures which must be analysed as ideological practices which designate men and women as father, husband, wife, mother, sister, etc. Thus, Cowie suggests, women as women are not simply *located* within the family. Rather, it is in the family, as an effect of kinship structures, that women as women are *constructed,* defined within and by the group. Thus, for

instance, when Juliette Minces (1980: especially 23) cites *the* patriarchal family as the basis for "an almost identical vision of women" that Arab and Muslim societies have, she falls into this very trap. Not only is it problematical to speak of a vision of women shared by Arab and Muslim societies, without addressing the particular historical and ideological power structures that construct such images, but to speak of the patriarchal family or the tribal kinship structure as the origin of the socio-economic status of women is again to assume that women are sexual-political subjects prior to their entry into the family. So while on the one hand women attain value or status within the family, the assumption of a singular patriarchal kinship system (common to all Arab and Muslim societies, i.e., over twenty different countries) is what apparently structures women as an oppressed group in these societies! This singular, coherent kinship system presumably influences another separate and given entity, "women." Thus all women, regardless of class and cultural differences, are seen as being similarly affected by this system. Not only are *all* Arab and Muslim women seen to constitute a homogeneous oppressed group, but there is no discussion of the specific *practices* within the families which constitute women as mothers, wives, sisters, etc. Arabs and Muslims, it appears, don't change at all. Their patriarchal families carried over from the times of the Prophet Muhammad. They exist, as it were, outside history.

Women and Religious Ideologies

A further example of the use of "women" as a category of analysis is found in cross-cultural analyses which subscribe to a certain economic reductionism in describing the relationship between the economy and factors such as politics and ideology. Here, in reducing the level of comparison to the economic relations between "developed" and "developing" countries, the question of women is denied any specificity. Mina Modares, in a careful analysis of women and Shi'ism in Iran, focuses on this very problem when she criticizes feminist writings which treat Islam as an ideology separate from and outside social relations and practices, rather than a discourse which includes rules for economic, social and power relations within society (Modares 1981: 62-82.) Patricia Jeffery's otherwise informative work on Pirzada women in purdah (1979) considers Islamic ideology as a partial explanation for the purdah. Here, Islamic ideology is reduced to a set of ideas whose internalization by Pirzada women contributes to the stability of the system. The primary explanation for purdah is located in the control that Pirzada men have over economic resources, and the personal security purdah gives to Pirzada women. By taking a specific version of Islam as *the* Islam, Jeffery attributes a singularity and coherence to it. Modares notes, "'Islamic Theology' then becomes imposed on a separate and given entity called 'women.' A further unification is reached: Women (meaning *all women*), regardless of their differing positions within societies, come to be affected or not affected by Islam. These conceptions provide the right ingredients for an unproblematic possibility of a cross-cultural study of women." (1981: 63)....

Women and the Development Process

The best examples of universalization on the basis of economic reductionism can be found in the liberal "Women in Development" literature. Proponents of this school seek to examine the effect of development on third-world women, sometimes from self-designated feminist perspectives. At the very least, there is an evident interest in and commitment to improving the lives of women in "developing" countries. Scholars like Irene Tinker, Ester Boserup, and Perdita Huston[11] have all written about the effect of development policies on women in the third world. All three women assume that "development" is synonymous with "economic development" or "economic progress." As in the case of Minces' patriarchal family, Hosken's male sexual control, and Cutrufelli's western colonization, "development" here becomes the all-time equalizer. Women are seen as being affected positively or negatively by economic development policies, and this is the basis for cross-cultural comparison.

For instance, Perdita Huston states that the purpose of her study is to describe the effect of the development process on the "family unit and its individual" in Egypt, Kenya, Sudan, Tunisia, Sri Lanka and Mexico. She states that the "problems" and "needs" expressed by rural and urban women in these countries all centre around education and training, work and wages, access to health and other services, political participation and legal rights. Huston relates all these "needs" to the lack of sensitive development policies which exclude women as a group. For her, the solution is simple: improved development policies which emphasize training for women fieldworkers, use women trainees and women rural development officers, encourage women's cooperatives, etc. Here, again women are assumed to be a coherent group or category prior to their entry into "the development process." Huston assumes that all third-world women have similar problems and needs. Thus, they must have similar interests and goals. However, the interests of urban, middle-class, educated Egyptian housewives, to take only one instance, could surely not be seen as being the same as those of their uneducated, poor maids. Development policies do not affect both groups of women in the same way. Practices which characterize women's status and roles vary according to class. Women are constituted as women through the complex interaction between class, culture, religion and other ideological institutions and frameworks. They are not "women" — a coherent group — solely on the basis of a particular economic system or policy. Such reductive cross-cultural comparisons result in the colonization of the specifics of daily existence and the complexities of political interests which women of different social classes and cultures represent and mobilize.

Thus it is revealing that for Perdita Huston women in the third-world countries she writes about have "needs" and "problems," but few if any have "choices" or the freedom to act. This is an interesting representation of women in the third world, one which is significant in suggesting a latent self-presentation of western women which bears looking at. She writes, "What surprised and moved me most as I listened to women in such very different cultural settings was the striking commonality — whether they were educated or illiterate, urban or rural — of their most basic values: the importance they assign to family, dignity, and service to others" (Huston, 1979: 115). Would Huston consider such values unusual for women in the west?

What is problematical, then, about this kind of use of "women" as a group, as a stable category of analysis, is that it assumes an ahistorical, universal unity among women based on a generalized notion of their subordination. Instead of analytically *demonstrating* the production of women as socio-economic political groups within particular local contexts, this analytical move — and the presuppositions it is based on — limits the definition of the female subject to gender identity, completely bypassing social class and ethnic identities. What characterizes women as a group is their gender (sociologically not necessarily biologically defined) over and above everything else, indicating a monolithic notion of sexual difference. Because women are thus constituted as a coherent group, sexual difference becomes coterminous with female subordination, and power is automatically defined in binary terms: people who have it (read: men), and people who do not (read: women). Men exploit, women are exploited. Such simplistic formulations are both historically reductive; they are also ineffectual in designing strategies to combat oppressions. All they do is reinforce binary divisions between men and women.

What would an analysis which did not do this look like? Maria Mies's work is one such example. It is an example which illustrates the strength of western feminist work on women in the third world and which, does not fall into the traps discussed above. Maria Mies's study of the lace-makers of Narsapur, India (1982), attempts to analyse carefully a substantial household industry in which "housewives" produce lace doilies for consumption in the world market. Through a detailed analysis of the structure of the lace industry, production and reproduction relations, the sexual division of labour, profits and exploitation, and the overall consequences of defining women

as "non-working housewives" and their work as "leisure-time activity," Mies demonstrates the levels of exploitation in this industry and the impact of this production system on the work and living conditions of the women involved in it. In addition, she is able to analyse the "ideology of the housewife," the notion of a woman sitting in the house, as providing the necessary subjective and socio-cultural element for the creation and the maintenance of a production system that contributes to the increasing pauperization of women, and keeps them totally atomized and disorganized as workers. Mies's analyses show the effect of a certain historically and culturally specific mode of patriarchal organization, an organization constructed on the basis of the definition of the lace-makers as "non-working housewives" at familial, local, regional, statewide and international levels. The intricacies and the effects of particular power networks are not only emphasized; they also form the basis of Mies's analysis of how this particular group of women is situated at the centre of a hegemonic, exploitative world market.

This is a good example of what careful, politically focused, local analyses can accomplish. It illustrates how the category of woman is constructed in a variety of political contexts that often exist simultaneously and overlaid on top of one another. There is no easy generalization in the direction of "women" in India, or "women in the third world"; nor is there a reduction of the political construction of the exploitation of the lace-makers to cultural explanations about the passivity or obedience that might characterize these women and their situation. Finally, this mode of local, political analysis which generates theoretical categories from within the situation and context being analysed, also suggests corresponding effective strategies for organizing against the exploitations faced by the lace-makers. Here Narsapur women are not mere victims of the production process, because they resist, challenge, and subvert the process at various junctures....It is only by understanding the *contradictions* inherent in women's location within various structures that effective political action and challenges can be devised. Mies's study goes a long way towards offering such an analysis. While there are now an increasing number of western feminist writings in this tradition,[12] there is also unfortunately a large block of writing which succumbs to the cultural reductionism discussed earlier.

Methodological Universalisms, or: Women's Oppression is a Global Phenomenon

Western feminist writings on women in the third world subscribe to a variety of methodologies to demonstrate the universal cross-cultural operation of male dominance and female exploitation. I summarize and critique three such methods below, moving from the most simple to the most complex methodologies.

First, proof of universalism is provided through the use of an arithmetic method. The argument goes like this: the more the number of women who wear the veil, the more universal is the sexual segregation and control of women (Deardon, 1975: 4-5). Similarly, a large number of different, fragmented examples from a variety of countries also apparently add up to a universal fact. For instance, Muslim women in Saudi Arabia, Iran, Pakistan, India and Egypt all wear some sort of a veil. Hence, this indicates that the sexual control of women is a universal fact in those countries in which the women are veiled (Deardon, 1975: 7, 10). Fran Hosken writes: "Rape, forced prostitution, polygamy, genital mutilation, pornography, the beating of girls and women, purdah (segregation of women) are all violations of basic human rights" (1981: 15). By equating purdah with rape, domestic violence, and forced prostitution, Hosken asserts its "sexual control" function as the primary explanation for purdah, whatever the context. Institutions of purdah are thus denied any cultural and historical specificity and contradictions and subversive aspects are totally ruled out. In both these examples, the problem is not in asserting that the practice of wearing a veil is widespread. This assertion can be made on the basis of numbers. It is a descriptive generalization. However, it is the analytic leap from the practice of veiling to an assertion of its general significance in controlling women that must be questioned. While there may be a physical similarity in the veils worn by women in Saudi Arabia and Iran, the specific meaning attached to this practice varies according to the cultural and ideological context. In addition, the symbolic space occupied by the practice of purdah may be similar in certain contexts, but this does not automatically indicate that the practices themselves have identical significance in the social realm. For example, as is well known, Iranian middle-class women veiled themselves during the 1979 revolution to indicate solidarity with their veiled working-class sisters, while in contemporary Iran mandatory Islamic laws dictate that all Iranian women wear veils. While in both these instances similar reasons might be offered for the veil (opposition to the Shah and western cultural colonization in the first case, and the true Islamicization of Iran in the second), the concrete *meanings* attached to Iranian women wearing the veil are clearly different in the two historical contexts. In the first case, wearing the veil is both an oppositional and revolutionary gesture on the part of Iranian middle-class women; in the second case it is a coercive, institutional mandate.[13] It is on the basis of such context-specific differentiated analysis that effective political strategies can be generated. To assume that the mere practice of veiling women in a number of Muslim countries indicates the universal oppression of women through sexual segregation is not only analytically reductive, but also proves to be quite useless when it comes to the elaboration of oppositional political strategy.

Second, concepts like reproduction, the sexual division of labour, the family, marriage, household, patriarchy, etc., are often used without their specification in local cultural and historical contexts. These concepts are used by feminists in providing explanations for women's subordination, apparently assuming their universal applicability. For instance, how is it possible to refer to "the" sexual division of labour when the *content* of this division changes radically from one environment to the next, and from one historical juncture to another? At its most abstract level, it is the fact of the differential assignation of the tasks according to sex that is significant; however, this is quite different from the *meaning* or *value* that the content of this sexual division of labour assumes in different contexts. In most cases the assigning of tasks on the basis of sex has an ideological origin. There is no question that a claim such as "women are concentrated in service-oriented occupations in a large number of countries around the world" is descriptively valid. Descriptively, then, perhaps the existence of a similar sexual division of labour (where women work in service occupations like nursing, social work, etc., and men in other kinds of occupations) in a number of different countries can be asserted. However, the concept of the "sexual division of labour" is more than just a descriptive category. It indicates the differential *value* placed on "men's work" versus "women's work."

Often the mere existence of a sexual division of labour is taken to be proof of the oppression of women in various societies. This results from a confusion between and collapsing together of the descriptive and explanatory potential of the concept of the sexual division of labour. Superficially similar situations may have radically different, historically specific explanations, and cannot be treated as identical. For instance, the rise of female-headed households in middle-class America might be construed as indicating women's independence and progress, whereby women are considered to have *chosen* to be single parents, there are increasing numbers of lesbian mothers, etc. However, the recent increase in female-headed households in Latin America,[14] where women might be seen to have more decision-making power, is concentrated among the poorest strata, where life choices are the most constrained economically. A similar argument can be made for the rise of female-headed families among Black and Chicana women in the US. The positive correlation between this and the level of poverty among women of colour and white working-class women in the US has now even acquired a name: the feminization of poverty. Thus, while it is possible to state that there is a rise in female-headed households in the US and in Latin America, this rise cannot be discussed as a universal indicator of women's independence, nor can it be discussed as

a universal indicator of women's impoverishment. The *meaning* and *explanation* for the rise must obviously be specified according to the socio-historical context.

Similarly, the existence of sexual division of labour in most contexts cannot be sufficient explanation for the universal subjugation of women in the workforce. That the sexual division of labour does indicate a devaluation of women's work must be shown through analysis of particular local contexts. In addition, devaluation of *women* must also be shown through careful analysis. In other words, the "sexual division of labour" and "women" are not commensurate analytical categories. Concepts like the sexual division of labour can be useful only if they are generated through local, contextual analyses.[15] If such concepts are assumed to be universally applicable, the resultant homogenization of class, race, religious, and daily material practices of women in the third world can create a false sense of the commonality of oppressions, interests and struggles between and amongst women globally. Beyond sisterhood there is still racism, colonialism and imperialism!...

To summarize: I have discussed three methodological moves identifiable in feminist (and other academic) cross-cultural work which seeks to uncover a universality in women's subordinate position in society. The next and final section pulls together the previous sections attempting to outline the political effects of the analytical strategies in the context of western feminist writing on women in the third world. These arguments are not against generalization as much as they are for careful, historically specific generalizations responsive to complex realities. Nor do these arguments deny the necessity of forming strategic political identities and affinities. Thus, while Indian women of different backgrounds might forge a political unity on the basis of organizing against police brutality towards women,[16] an *analysis* of police brutality must be contextual. Strategic coalitions which construct oppositional political identities for themselves are based on generalization and provisional unities, but the analysis of these group identities cannot be based on universalistic, ahistorical categories.

The Subject(s) of Power

This last section returns to an earlier point about the inherently political nature of feminist scholarship, and attempts to clarify my point about the possibility of detecting a colonialist move in the case of structurally unequal first/third-world relation in scholarship.... Power relations are structured in terms of a unilateral and undifferentiated source of power and a cumulative reaction to power. Opposition is a generalized phenomenon created as a response to power — which, in turn, is possessed by certain groups of people. The major problem with such a definition of power is that it locks all revolutionary struggles into binary structures — possessing power versus being powerless. Women are powerless, unified groups....

What happens when this assumption of "women as an oppressed group" is situated in the context of western feminist writing about third-world women? It is here that I locate the colonialist move. By contrasting the representation of women in the third world with what I referred to earlier as western feminisms' self-presentation in the same context, we see how western feminists alone become the true "subjects" of this counter-history. Third-world women, on the other hand, never rise above the debilitating generality of their "object" status.

While radical and liberal feminist assumptions of women as a sex class might elucidate (however inadequately) the autonomy of particular women's struggles in the west, the application of the notion of women as a homogeneous category to women in the third world colonizes and appropriates the pluralities of the simultaneous location of different groups of women in social class and ethnic frameworks; in doing so it ultimately robs them of their historical and political *agency*. Similarly, many Zed Press authors, who ground themselves in the basic analytic strategies of traditional Marxism, also implicitly create a "unity" of women by substituting "women's activity" for "labour" as the primary theoretical determinant of women's situation. Here again, women are constituted as a coherent group not on the basis of "natural" qualities or needs, but on the basis of the

sociological "unity" of their role in domestic production and wage labour.[17] In other words, western feminist discourse, by assuming women as a coherent, already constituted group which is placed in kinship, legal and other structures, defines third-world women as subjects *outside* of social relations, instead of looking at the way women are constituted as women *through* these very structures. Legal, economic, religious and familial structures are treated as phenomena to be judged by western standards. It is here that ethnocentric universality comes into play. When these structures are defined as "underdeveloped" or "developing" and the women are placed within these structures, an implicit image of the "average third-world women" is produced. This is the transformation of the (implicitly western) "oppressed woman" into the "oppressed third-world woman." While the category of "oppressed woman" is generated through an exclusive focus on gender difference "the oppressed third-world woman" category has an additional attribute — the "third-world difference"! The "third world difference" includes a paternalistic attitude towards women in the third world.[18] Since discussions of the various themes I identified earlier (e.g., kinship, education, religion, etc.) are conducted in the context of the relative "underdevelopment" of the third world (which is nothing less than unjustifiably confusing development with the separate path taken by the west in its development, as well as ignoring the unidirectionality of the first/third-world power relationship), third-world women as a group or category are automatically and necessarily defined as religious (read "not progressive"), family oriented (read "traditional"), legal minors (read "they-are-still-not-conscious-of-their-rights"), illiterate (read "ignorant"), domestic (read "backward") and sometimes revolutionary (read "their-country-is-in-a-state-of-war; they-must-fight!"). This is how the "third-world difference" is produced.

When the category of "sexually oppressed women" is located within particular systems in the third world which are defined on a scale which is normed through Eurocentric assumptions, not only are third-world women defined in a particular way prior to their entry into social relations, but since no connections are made between first- and third-world power shifts, it reinforces the assumption that people in the third world just have not evolved to the extent that the west has. This mode of feminist analysis, by homogenizing and systematizing the experiences of different groups of women, erases all marginal and resistant modes of experiences.[19] It is significant that none of the texts I reviewed in the Zed Press series focuses on lesbian politics or the politics of ethnic and religious marginal organizations in third-world women's groups. Resistance can thus only be defined as cumulatively reactive, not as something inherent in the operation of power. If power, as Michel Foucault has argued recently, can really be understood only in the context of resistance,[20] this misconceptualization of power is both analytically as well as strategically problematical. It limits theoretical analysis as well as reinforcing western cultural imperialism. For in the context of a first/third-world balance of power, feminist analyses which perpetrate and sustain the hegemony of the idea of the superiority of the west produce a corresponding set of universal images of the "third-world woman" images like the veiled woman, the powerful mother, the chaste virgin, the obedient wife, etc. These images exist in universal ahistorical splendour, setting in motion a colonialist discourse which exercises a very specific power in defining, coding and maintaining existing first/third-world connection.

To conclude, then, let me suggest some disconcerting similarities between the typically authorizing signature of such western feminist writings on women in the third world, and the authorizing signature of the project of humanism in general-humanism as a western ideological and political project which involves the necessary recuperation of the "East" and "Woman" as Others....[I]t is only in so far as "Woman/Women" and "the East" are defined as Others, or as peripheral, that (western) Man/Humanism can represent him/itself as the centre. It is not the centre that determines the periphery, but the periphery that, in its boundedness, determines the centre. Just as feminists like Kristeva, Cixous, Irigaray and others deconstruct

the latent anthropomorphism in western discourse, I have suggested a parallel strategy in this article in uncovering a latent ethnocentrism in particular feminist writings on women in the third world.[21]

As discussed earlier, a comparison between western feminist self-presentation and western feminist representation of women in the third world yields significant results. Universal images of "the third-world woman" (the veiled woman, chaste virgin, etc.), images constructed from adding the "third-world difference" to "sexual difference," are predicated on (and hence obviously bring into sharper focus) assumptions about western women as secular, liberated, and having control over their own lives. This is not to suggest that western women *are* secular and liberated and have control over their own lives. I am referring to a *discursive* self-presentation, not necessarily to material reality. If this were a material reality there would be no need for feminist political struggle in the west. Similarly, only from the vantage point of the west is it possible to define the "third world" as under-developed and economically dependent. Without the overdetermined discourse that creates the *third* world, there would be no (singular and privileged) first world. Without the "third-world woman," the particular self-presentation of western women mentioned above would be problematical. I am suggesting, in effect, that the one enables and sustains the other. This is not to say that the signature of western feminist writings on the third world has the same authority as the project of western humanism. However, in the context of the hegemony of the western scholarly establishment in the production and dissemination of texts, and in the context of the legitimating imperative of humanistic and scientific discourse, the definition of "the third-world woman" as monolith might well tie into the larger economic and ideological praxis of "disinterested" scientific inquiry and pluralism which are the surface manifestations of a latent economic and cultural colonization of the "non-western" world. It is time to move beyond the ideological framework in which even Marx found it possible to say: They cannot represent themselves; they must be represented.

Author's Note

This paper would not have been possible without S.P. Mohanty's challenging and careful critical reading. I would also like to thank Biddy Martin for our numerous discussions about feminist theory and politics. They both helped me think through and sharpen some of the arguments in this paper.

NOTES

1. See especially the essays in Moraga and Anzaldua (1983); Smith (1983); Joseph and Lewis (1981) and Moraga (1984).

2. Terms like "third" and "first" world are very problematical both in suggesting over-simplified similarities between and amongst countries labelled "third" or "first" world, as well as implicitly reinforcing existing economic, cultural, and ideological hierarchies. I use the term "third world" with full awareness of its problems, only because this is the terminology available to us at this moment. The use of quotation marks is meant to suggest a continuous questioning of the designation "third world." Even when I do not use the quotation marks, I mean to use the term critically.

3. I am indebted to Teresa de Lauretis for this particular formulation of the project of feminist theorizing. See especially her introduction to de Lauretis (1984); see also Sylvia Wynter, "The Politics of Domination," unpublished manuscript.

4. This argument is similar to Homi Bhabha's (1983) definition of colonial discourse as strategically creating a space for a subject peoples through the production of knowledge and the exercise of power.

5. A number of documents and reports on the UN International Conferences on Women, Mexico City 1975, and Copenhagen 1980, as well as the 1976 Wellesley Conference on Women and Development attest to this. Nawal el Saadawi, Fatima Mernissi and Mallica Vajarathon in "A Critical Look At The Wellesley Conference" (*Quest*, IV:2, Winter 1978, 101-7), characterize this conference as "America-planned and organized," situating third world participants as passive audiences. They focus espe-

cially on the lack of self-consciousness of western women's implication in the effects of imperialism and racism in their assumption of an "international sisterhood." Amos and Parmar (1984) characterize Euro-American Feminism which seeks to establish itself as the only legitimate feminism as "imperial."

6. The Zed Press "Women in the Third World" series is unique in its conception. I choose to focus on it because it is the only contemporary series of books I have found which assumes that "women in the Third World" is a legitimate and separate subject of study and research. Since 1985, when this essay was first written, numerous new titles have appeared in the Zed "Women in the Third World" series. Thus, I suspect that Zed has come to occupy a rather privileged position in the dissemination and construction of discourses by and about third-world women. A number of the books in this series are excellent, especially those which deal directly with women's resistance struggles. In addition, Zed Press consistently publishes progressive, feminist, anti-racist and anti-imperialist texts. However, a number of texts written by feminist sociologists, anthropologists, and journalists are symptomatic of the kind of western feminist work on women in the third world that concerns me. Thus, an analysis of a few of these particular texts in this series can serve as a representative point of entry into the discourse I am attempting to locate and define. My focus on these texts is therefore an attempt at an internal critique: I simply expect and demand more from this series. Needless to say, progressive publishing houses also carry their own authorizing signatures.

7. Elsewhere I have discussed this particular point in detail in a critique of Robin Morgan's construction of "women's herstory" in her introduction to *Sisterhood is Global: The International Women's Movement Anthology* (1984) (see Mohanty) "Feminist Encounters" (pp. 30-44, especially pp. 35-7).

8. My analysis in this section of the paper has been influenced by Felicity Eldhom, Olivia Harris and Kate Young's excellent discussions (Eldhom, Harris and Young, 1977). They examine the use of the concepts of "reproduction" and the "sexual division of labour" in anthropological work on women, suggesting the inevitable pull towards uni-

versals inherent in the use of these categories to determine "women's position."

9. Another example of this kind of analysis in Mary Daly's *Gyn/Ecology*. Daly's assumption in this text, that women as a group are sexually victimized, leads to her very problematic comparison between the attitudes towards women witches and healers in the west, Chinese footbinding, and the genital mutilation of women in Africa. According to Daly, women in Europe, China, and Africa constitute a homogeneous group as victims of male power. Not only does this label (sexual victims) eradicate the specific historical realities which lead to and perpetuate practices like witch-hunting and genital mutilation, but it also obliterates the differences, complexities and heterogeneities of the lives of, for example, women of different classes, religions and nations in Africa. As Audre Lorde pointed out, women in Africa share a long tradition of healers and goddesses that perhaps binds them together more appropriately then their victim status. However, both Daly and Lorde fall prey to universalistic assumptions about "African women" (both negative and positive). What matters is the complex, historical range of power differences, commonalities and resistances that exist among women in Africa which construct African women as "subjects" of their own politics. See Daly (1978: 107-312) Lorde in Moraga and Anzaldua (1983).

10. See Eldhom, Harris and Young (1977) for a good discussion of the necessity to theorize male violence within specific societal frameworks, rather than to assume it as a universal fact.

11. These views can also be found in differing degrees in collections like: Wellesley Editorial Committee, ed., *Women and National Development: The Complexities of Change* Chicago: University of Chicago Press 1977, and *Signs*, Special Issue, "Development and the Sexual Division of Labor," 7.2, (Winter 1981). For an excellent introduction to WID issues see ISIS, *Women in Development: A Resource Guide for Organization and Action* Philadelphia: New Society Publishers, 1984. For a politically focused discussion of feminism and development and the stakes for poor third-world women, see Sen and Grown, (1987).

12. See essays by Vanessa Maher, Diane Elson and Ruth Pearson, and Maila Stevens in Youn, Walkowitz and McCullagh (1981); and essays by Vivian Mota and Michelle Mattelart in Nash and Safa (1980). For examples of excellent self-concious work by feminists writing about women in their own historical and geographical locations, see Lazreg (1988) on Algerian women; Gayatri Chakravorty Spivak's "A literary Representation of the Subaltern: A Woman's Text from the Third World," in Spivak (1987), and Lata Mani's essay, "Contentious Traditions: The Debate on SATI in Colonial India," *Cultural Critique* No. 7, Fall 1987, pp. 119-56.

13. See Tabari (1980) for a detailed discussion of these instances.

14. Olivia Harris in Harris (1983: 4-7). Other MRG reports include Deardon (1975) and Jahan (1980).

15. See Eldhom, Harris and Young (1977) for an excellent discussion of this.

16. See Kishwar and Vanita (1984) for a discussion of this aspect of Indian women's struggles.

17. See Haraway (1985: 65-108, especially 76).

18. Amos and Parmar (1984: 9) describe the cultural stereotypes present in Euro-American feminist thought "The image is of the passive Asian women subject to oppressive practices within the Asian family, with an emphasis on wanting to 'help' Asian women liberate themselves from their role. Or there is the strong, dominant Afro-Caribbean woman, who despite her 'strength' is exploited by the 'sexism' which is seen as being a strong feature in relationships between Afro-Caribbean men and women." These images illustrate the extent to which *paternalism* is an essential element of feminist thinking which incorporates the above stereotypes, a paternalism which can lead to the definition of priorities for women of colour by Euro-American feminists.

19. I discuss the question of theorizing experience in my "Feminist Encounters" (1987), and in an essay co-authored with Biddy Martin in de Lauretis (1986).

20. This is one of Foucault's central points in his reconceptualization of the strategies and workings of power networks. See Foucault (1978 and 1980).

21. For an argument which demands a *new* conception of humanism in work on third-world women, see Lazreg (1988).

REFERENCES

Abdel-Malek, Anouar (1981) *Social Dialectics: Nation and Revolution.* Albany: State University of New York Press.

Amin, Samir (1977) *Imperialism and Unequal Development.* New York: Monthly Review Press.

Amos, Valerie and Parmar, Pratibha (1984) "Challenging Imperial Feminism." *Feminist Review* No. 17.

Baran, Paul A. (1962) *The Political Economy of Growth.* New York: Monthly Review Press.

Berg, Elizabeth (1982) "The Third Woman." *Diacritics.* Summer.

Bhabha, Homi "The Other Question — The Stereotype and Colonial Discourse." *Screen* 24:6, p. 23.

Boserup, Ester (1970) *Women's Role in Economic Development.* New York: St. Martin's Press; London: Allen & Unwin.

Brown, Beverly (1983) "Displacing the Difference — Review, Nature, Culture and Gender." *m/f* No. 8.

Cixous, Hélène (1981) "The Laugh of the Medusa" in Marks and de Courtivron (1981).

Cowie, Elizabeth (1978) "Woman as Sign." *m/f* No.1.

Cutrufelli, Maria Rosa (1983) *Women of Africa: Roots of Oppression.* London: Zed Press.

Daly, Mary (1978) *Gyn/Ecology: The Metaethics of Radical Feminism* Boston: Beacon Press.

De Lauretis, Teresa (1984) *Alice Doesn't: Feminism, Semiotics, Cinema.* Bloomington: Indiana University Press.

— . (1986) ed. *Feminist Studies/Critical Studies.* Bloomington: Indiana University Press.

Deardon, Ann (1975) ed. *Arab Women.* London: Minority Rights Group Report No.27.

Deleuze, Giles and Guattari, Felix (1977) *Anti-Oedipus: Capitalism and Schizophrenia.* New York: Viking.

Derrida, Jacques (1974) *Of Grammatology.* Baltimore: Johns Hopkins University Press.

Eisenstein, Hester (1983) *Contemporary Feminist Thought.* Boston: G.K. Hall & Co.

Eisenstein, Zillah (1981) *The Radical Future of Liberal Feminism.* New York: Longman.

Eldhom, Felicity, Harris, Olivia and Young, Kate (1977) "Conceptualising Women." Critique of Anthropology "Women's Issue" No. 3.

Foucault, Michel (1978) *History of Sexuality Volume One.* New York: Random House.

— . (1980) *Power/Knowledge.* New York: Pantheon.

Gunder-Frank, Andre (1967) *Capitalism and Underdevelopment in Latin America.* New York: Monthly Review Press.

Haraway, Donna (1985) "A Manifest for Cyborgs: Science, Technology and Socialist Feminism in the 1980's." *Socialist Review* No. 80.

Harris, Olivia (1983a) "Latin American Women — An Overview." in Harris (1983b).

Harris, Olivia (1983b) editor *Latin American Women* London: Minority Rights. Group Report No. 57.

Hosken, Fran (1981) "Female Genital Mutilation and Human Rights." *Feminist Issues* 1:3.

Huston, Perdita (1979) *Third World Women Speak Out.* New York: Praeger.

Irigaray, Luce (1981) "This Sex Which Is Not One" and "When the Goods Get Together" in Marks and de Courtivron (1981).

Jahan, Rounaq (1980) editor. *Women in Asia.* London: Minority Rights Group Report No. 45.

Jeffery, Patricia (1979) *Frogs in a Well: Indian Women in Purdah.* London: Zed Press.

Joseph, Gloria and Lewis, Jill (1981) *Common Differences: Conflicts in Black and White Feminist Perspectives.* Boston: Beacon Press.

Kishwar, Madhy and Vanita, Ruth (1984) *In Search of Answers: Indian Women's Voices from Manushi.* London: Zed Press.

Kristeva, Julia (1980) *Desire in Language.* New York: Columbia University Press.

Lazreg, Marnia (1988) "Feminism and Difference: the Perils of Writing as a Woman on Women in Algeria." *Feminist Issues* 14:1

Lindsay, Beverley (1983) editor *Comparative Perspectives of Third World Women: The Impact of Race, Sex and Class.* New York: Praeger.

Lorde, Audre (1983) "An Open Letter to Mary Daly," in Moraga and Anzaldua (1983).

Marks, Elaine and De Courtivron, Isobel (1981) editors *New French Feminisms.* New York: Schoken Books.

Mies, Maria (1982) *The Lace Makers of Narsapur: Indian Housewives Produce for the World Market.* London: Zed Press.

Minces, Julliette (1980) *The House of Obedience: Women in Arab Society.* London: Zed Press.

Modares, Mina (1981) "Women and Shi'ism in Iran." *m/f* Nos. 5 and 6.

Mohanty, Chandra and Martin, Biddy (1986) "Feminist Politics: What's Home Got to Do With It?" in De Lauretis (1986)

Mohanty Chandra (1987) "Feminist Encounters: Locating the Politics of Experience." *Copyright* 1, Fin de Siècle 2000.

Moraga, Cherrie and Anzaldua, Gloria (1983) editors *This Bridge Called My Back: Writings by Radical Women of Color.* New York: Kitchen Table Press

Moraga, Cherrie (1984) *Loving in the War Years.* Boston: South End Press.

Morgan, Robin (1984) editor *Sisterhood is Global: the International Women's Movement Anthology.* New York: Anchor Press/Doubleday; Harmondsworth: Penguin.

Nash, June and Safa, Helen I.(1980) editors *Sex and Class in Latin America: Women's Perspectives on Politics, Economics and the Family in the Third World.* Massachusetts: Bergin & Garvey.

Rozaido, M.Z. (1980) "The Use and Abuse of Anthropology: Reflections on Feminism and Cross-Cultural Understanding." *Signs* 5:3.

Said, Edward (1978) *Orientalism.* New York: Random House.

Sen, Sita and Grown, Caren (1987) *Development Crises and Alternative Visions: Third World Women's Perspectives.* New York: Monthly Review Press.

Smith, Barbara (1983) editor *Home Girls: a Black Feminist Anthology.* New York: Kitchen Table Press.

Spanos, William V. (1984) "Boundary 2 and the Polity of Interest: Humanism, the 'Center Elsewhere,' and Power." *Boundary 2* Vol. X11, No.3 /Vol XIII, NO. 1 Spring/Fall.

Spivak, Gayatri Chakravorty (1987) *In Other Worlds: Essays in Cultural Politics.* London and New York: Methuen.

Strathern, Marilyn and McCormack, Carol (1980) editors *Nature, Culture and Gender.* Cambridge: Cambridge University Press.

Tabari, Azar (1980) "The Enigma of the Veiled Iranian Women." *Feminist Review* No. 5.

Tinker, Irene and Bramsen, Michelle Bo (1972) editors. *Women and World Development.* Washington DC: Overseas Development Council.

Young, Kate, Walkowitz, Carol and McCullagh, Roslyn (1981) editors *Of Marriage and the Market: Women's Subordination in International Perspective.* London: CSE Books.

THE GOOD TERRORIST: DOMESTICITY AND THE POLITICAL SPACE FOR CHANGE

Janice Newberry

Janice Newberry teaches Anthropology at the University of Lethbridge in Alberta. Her area study is Indonesia, and her areas of research include the intersections of gender, the home, and political structures. She is the author of Backdoor Java *(forthcoming, 2006).*

Newberry uses the metaphor of the good terrorist to explore how the daily domestic practices of urban working-class women in a Javanese neighborhood illustrate that the state-mandated domesticity of PKK has practical uses in the lives of local women. Despite the poor fit between women's working lives and the imagined role of housewives as shaped by colonialism, independence movements, and the state in Indonesia, working-class women reproduce their own version of the housewife in the very processes of accomplishing the mundane tasks demanded by the state. Consequently, the denigrated national housewives' organization takes on new meaning, and state rule and moral order is reproduced even as it is reformed.

Something was clearly afoot. Neighborhood women leaned longer at the fence, talking to one another. Glances were cast at the house of Pak Wayang, the puppet-maker, and then heads came together. Slower to understand neighborhood gossip than others, I did not know at first what the trouble was. In fact, it wasn't until the drama was over that I came to hear the story of the trouble at our end of the street. The only hint I had that something had changed in the neighborhood's view of Pak Wayang[1] and his family was when Bu Sae sniffed dismissively that Bu Wayang didn't keep good house and worst of all did not cook for herself. Indexed in her disdain for Bu Wayang's housekeeping skills was an accusation about the family's moral standing. Her failure as an *ibu rumah tangga* (housewife) was surely a sign that theirs was not a good home.

This incident, detailed from my ethnographic work in a working-class Javanese neighborhood or *kampung*[2] came late in my fieldwork and confirmed what I had come to suspect already. That is, the disparaged government program known as

PKK (from *Pembinaan Kesejahateraan Keluarga*, or Support for the Prosperous Family) was more meaningful for local Javanese women than was generally acknowledged. While it was true that this national housewives' organization, a quasi-public structure that includes all adult[3] women in Indonesia, was denigrated in local conversation, its central feature — a mother/wife who takes care of her family and hence her community — had become a resource in the local value system that was invoked when Bu Sae categorized Bu Wayang as a bad housewife. That is, although PKK was often called *Perempuan Kurang Kerja*, or Women without Enough Work to Do, the gender values at its very center were actually used by local women to manage their own communities. And this is so despite the fact that the category of housewife is a relatively recent one in Indonesia (Tiwon 1996).

My research shows that what might be considered the retrograde social role of housewife, which has been fostered by the Indonesian government at least since it institutionalized PKK in 1973, has come to be used by residents as a resource for shaping local and, simultaneously, national politics. In this paper I examine the structure and practice of PKK to show how the social category of housewife, commonly perceived as conservative, has the potential for generating social change and, moreover, how the quotidian use of the category in working-class women's lives illustrates the cultural process of state formation. That is, the political order that is the state and its social reproduction are related to the daily practices of citizens, and further, the formation of the state may properly and profitably be understood as the negotiation of state structures in everyday life. From this perspective then, the state is less a set of elite institutions, legal codes, and political instrumentalities than it is the accretion of myriad daily acts of conformation and contestation that constitute a particular moral order.

After reviewing the sources of the various inflections of women's domestic roles and spaces in Java, I will consider how the resources provided by PKK are used by women to render credible accounts of themselves as housewives to meet and manage social obligations on a local level. These daily negotiations and investments are what animate and make real the social category of housewife, despite its ambivalent fit in women's lives. In this way, I hope to show that the formation of a moral state order is comprised in part in the everyday practice of female subject-citizens, and the power associated with reproduction in an expanded sense has volatile political potential when wielded by these *good terrorists*.

PKK: State-Sponsored Domesticity

The government will support PKK which we hope will be a spearhead for the development of society from below, "motored" by women. I ask that the various activities programmed at the national level be channeled through PKK. We can have many programs for women to enhance the role of women in development. But it should not be forgotten that these programs are aimed and to be implemented by women in the villages, whether in the urban or rural areas. If there are too many organizations, it is not in accordance with their simple desires and way of thinking, and will only serve to confuse them. (Presidential meeting on the occasion of the National Working Meeting of P2W-KSS, 2 March 1981, cited in Suryakusuma 1991: 57)

The structure of the Indonesian government is a pyramid that reaches from the office of the president in an unbroken hierarchy that reaches at its lowest level to the unpaid, popularly selected representatives of blocks of 10-20 households. This smallest division is known as the *RT* for *Rukun Tetangga* or Harmonious Neighbors. Six of these small units are comprised within a single *RW, Rukun Warga* or Harmonious Citizens. These lowest two levels of governance are unpaid positions, and all levels above are considered civil service. The leadership structure of PKK is a mirror image of the predominantly male administrative structure; that is, the titular head of PKK is the wife of the President of Indonesia, and the local head of PKK is the wife of the Bapak RT. Thus, the Pak RT and Bu RT are the married couple who represent the government's regulation of local community and who mediate local residents' relationship to the state apparatus (as do the Pak and Bu RW for the larger neighborhood grouping at the next level up). The base membership of PKK, however, is every adult woman in Indonesia.

The activities of PKK are synopsized in the 10 important programs of PKK (*10 Program Pokok PKK*), which appear in the form of plaques and signs at the entrance to most villages and *kampung* in Java. These programs include support for the government's ideology of *Pancasila*,[4] mutual self-help, clothing and food, skills training, health, developing cooperation, preservation of the neighborhood, and health planning. In their administration, these programs translate into, among other things, monthly baby weighings to monitor their health, literacy programs for older women, and mosquito reduction as well as cooking demonstrations and fashion shows.

In essence, the Indonesian government uses PKK to mobilize women as unpaid community development workers, whose efforts improve the standards of living of their families and communities. On the face of it, such a program seems an efficient way for a lower income country to provide necessary social services in a low cost manner. Most of the community projects are self-funded or receive very small amounts of government cash. Yet, the basis for this program is the nuclear family organized around a single couple, with the woman staying at home, a description that arguably does not fit the majority of Indonesian families. In fact, in my own small sample, only two out of 47 families conform to this ideal.

The use of state-sponsored domesticity to organize social welfare by the Indonesian government is related to its promotion of a specific form of community organization and governance. Despite a complicated history of pre-colonial, Dutch colonial, Japanese occupational, and nationalist influences, the ideal community is presented rhetorically as that essential rural *Javanese* social form — the cooperative peasant village.[5] The discursive work of (re)instantiating these forms of community and cooperation is accomplished in part through PKK, and the connections made between women, the ideal family, and community are quite clear in government publications:

The objective of the PKK movement is to materialize family welfare, which covers mental, spiritual, and physical wellbeing. The target of the programmes is the family. Since the mother performs the central role in the family the programmes are mostly focused on her. In this context the woman is viewed as an individual, a mother, a wife, often co-breadwinner, and a fellow citizen... (Ministry of Home Affairs 1983)

Or, as another government publication puts it, PKK is "aimed at establishing a healthy prospering family in order to create a welfaring community" (Department of Information 1984: 31). Indeed, women's participation is built into the very structure of community administration, and women are positioned as the point of articulation between the family and the state, and between the family and the community.

Yet, the rhetoric of PKK not only tries to persuade women to stay at home, raise good citizens, and keep good house and community, it also encourages them to search for supplemental income. That is, women are encouraged to begin cottage-type industries in their homes and neighborhoods so that they may work for extra cash without entering the formal waged economy. Such efforts are supported in various ways by the government, which offers loans, classes, and various incentives to women to begin such businesses. Enterprises include sewing for others, cooking for sale, and handicraft industries such as making shoes, handbags, and other small-scale work. Home-based or community-based small-scale enterprises and multiple occupations have long been used by families to supplement general income; the difference is now the government officially supports these efforts.

As a consequence, Indonesia's low-cost labor is reproduced, chronic male under-employment is masked and subsidized, and the bottleneck of educated, unemployed youths who spend a long period finding employment is ameliorated. That is to say, the simultaneous increase in state intervention in the agricultural sector which led to the dis-employment of female labor through changing technological and social relations along with the appearance of PKK programs aimed at encouraging women to stay home and support their families appears more than coincidental.[6] The scale of PKK, once it was nationalized in the early 1970s, suggests its importance to the government: "when one considers that there is a PKK in each one of the nearly 700,000 villages in Indonesia, and that two-thirds of government funds for women in Indonesia are allotted to PKK, the implications are great" (Suryakusuma 1991: 55). It could be argued that the government's desire for national development of human and productive resources could logically have led to structural unemployment as well as the emergence of PKK, and, indeed, no hypothesis of a governmental conspiracy is offered here. Instead, the near simultaneity of the release of female labor and the institution of programs aimed at domesticity likely has many causes along with multiple effects.

Still, the benefits of PKK for the Indonesian government seem indisputable. In a situation of surplus labor, the informal sector and family labor of women serves to keep households afloat while it removes women from competition for jobs with the male unemployed. While the official stance towards women in formal sector employment appears pro-active, the practices of the government work to encourage women to stay home and work in the informal sector. And up to this point, the informal sector appears to be infinitely absorptive. The work of women not only supports the young and educated in the period before they attain employment, it also serves to support the family in the face of low male employment. Thus, the institution and continuation of PKK is overdetermined by the various needs of the Indonesian state — crucially, the reproduction of a large reserve army of labor and willing low-wage workers. Working-class women are not only encouraged to reproduce and support this army of reserve labor, but to do so under the guise of correct moral guidance and service to the Republic of Indonesia as good managers of homes and communities.

What is of concern to me here is the effect of these programs on the everyday lives of Javanese women and how the domestic and political space that is created through PKK and its programs can be used to contest, affirm, and sometimes change the social formation of the state. As the preceding discussion suggests, reproduction has several aspects, and women's roles must be considered in terms of all three: the biological reproduction of humans, the reproduction of socialized humans, and the reproduction of the social relations that sustain the state structure, that is, state formation (cf. Moore 1994). It is the centrality of women's roles in this expanded sense of reproduction — the very thing that makes them so useful to the state — that makes them ideally suited to be *good terrorists*.[7]

Good Terrorists

The "Good Terrorist" is a reference to a book of the same name by Doris Lessing (1985). I use the idea of the Good Terrorist to challenge the position of housewives in official Indonesian rhetoric and in popular Western culture alike, because, although the idea of resistance has come to stand for the limited political space of the down-trodden (and is too often understood as discourse alone), in fact, the housewife and her domestic space offer the opportunity for room for movement.

Lessing's novel concerns a half-baked group of would-be terrorists who call themselves the Communist Centre Union, and it charts their development from a bunch of unemployed marginal "radicals" to their eventual, almost accidental, bombing of a crowded street in London. At the center of the novel is Alice Mellings, who works assiduously not only to be a good radical but to create a comfortable house for the radicals. Alice "is strong, emotionally intuitive, and sympathetic, brave, warmhearted, hard-working, and generous — the sort of woman whose domestic skills and maternal sympathy have traditionally held the world together..." *(New York Times Book Review,* December 19, 1985). Alice is also a committed radical, working with a cell of nascent terrorists who squat in an abandoned house while they lay plans. It is Alice who cleans, paints, finds furniture, and persuades local authorities to restore utility services, and it is Alice who comforts the other squatters and cooks healthy soups and stews for them. It is Alice who confronts her bourgeois parents and demands money to pay for the politics of her little band — made necessary by her parent's middle-class life — and it is Alice who recreates the comforts of home for her compatriots. As one review noted, it is "one of the most disturbing ironies of this disturbing novel that Alice's best qualities, her domestic genius, her generosity and sympathy and energy, are ultimately responsible for the transformation of a collection of dissatisfied radicals into a terrorist gang" *(New York Times Book Review,* December 19, 1985).

The appeal of the Good Terrorist is that it puts together the idea of maintaining a social order, in Alice's case the bourgeois refinements of home, with the idea of subversion and social change. Alice's character illustrates nicely two issues significant in a consideration of domesticity: that the work of cooking and cleaning must always be done — even for disenfranchised radicals — and that the figure of the housewife, often taken to be one associated with conservatism, can actually be an

agent of change. These two features follow necessarily from the centrality of reproductive work to
human life. Yet, this very centrality entails room
for significant contradictions, and hence the
paradox of the "Good Terrorist." How can housekeeping, its second term implying "keeping"
things as they are, have anything to do with subversion and transformation? How can conservation
and change occupy the same political space?

As the next sections of this paper will show, the
critical importance of reproduction has prompted
governments, colonial and nationalist, to try and
control women and the moral power of domestic
space. Yet, the contradictions implied in the emergence of the housewife as a key social figure from
the colonial and nationalist eras shows that the
contents of such social categories are volatile, and
the uses of such categories and resources may
differ from their official conceptions. In contemporary Indonesia, for example, the "cult of domesticity" with its ideal housewife and mother/citizen
figures prominently in developmentalist ideology
and government programs to raise standards of
living and improve local infrastructure. Paradoxically, this emphasis on the good mother and housewife has worked to provide working-class women
with the resources needed to challenge and change
local conditions. Although the creation of the home
and the housewife can be said to be inherently
oppressive to women — this is after all, the site of
Engels's world historic defeat of women
(1942[1902]) — it is also the case, as my own
work suggests, that new political spaces are
created that have the potential to help women
improve and expand their lives.

Domestic Angels or Cult Followers

Social historians now observe as commonplaces
(1) that the emergence of a developed "domestic
domain" — associated with women, unwaged
housework, and child raising, and the "private"
— was a corollary of industrial capitalism ...;
(2) that "domesticity" was integral to the cult of
"modernity" at the core of bourgeois ideology;
and (3) that, far from being a natural or universal social institution, it grew to maturity with the

rise of the factory system, which entailed the
reconstruction of relations of production, of personhood and value, of class and gender.
(Comaroff and Comaroff 1992 : 38)

The literature on the emergence of the ideology of
home as the domestic haven, seat of filial piety, of
sentiment, of family values, and the habitat of the
domestic angel, has been analyzed predominantly
by social historians and feminist historians as the
peculiar result of the emergence of the bourgeois
nation-state in England and parts of Europe.

During the age of empire in nineteenth-century
Victorian Europe, evolutionary histories, Social
Darwinism, and laissez-faire capitalism were at
their height. The "Victorian debate on women"
ramified in the lives of both European women and
Indigenous, colonized women. In the metropole,
middle- and upper-class women were being consigned to the domestic sphere as distinct from the
public, a feat made possible by the contemporaneous consignment of lower-class women to the
domestic sphere of elite women's kitchens, not to
mention the very public industrial labor force.
Although it was the experience of middle- and
upper-class women that would inform bourgeois
ideology, as Maria Mies, who coined the term
housewifization (1986), suggests, it resulted in all
women being socially defined as housewives,
dependent on their husbands, whether they were or
not. In this way, the class specific outlines of the
domestic sphere were extended to all women, and
inequality was masked. Others have noted the
equivalence of the process of domestication or
"housewifization" as a protracted historical
process "comparable with and closely related to
proletarianization" (Bennholdt-Thomsen 1988:
159).

A suite of meanings associated with the Victorian ideal of private home life emerged alongside
the transformation of social relations that accompanied the deepening of industrial capitalism.[8] The
separation of women away from the world created
the moral space of the home as the dominant model
for domestic life, even for those women who
earned their wage inside the domestic haven of
others. The moral dimensions of the Victorian

home are clear in its descriptions, such as that offered by Ruskin:

"It is a place of Peace; the shelter, not only from all injury, but from all terror, doubt, and division ... a sacred place." He concludes the romantic image of the domestic angel with a telling profile of her qualities: "she must be enduringly, incorruptibly good; instinctively, infallibly, wise — wise, not for self-development, but for self renunciation." (cited in Callaway 1987: 33)

The creature at the center of the Victorian home, the domestic angel, has turned out to be remarkably resilient across cultures in every succeeding generation, despite the fact that she was the product of a very particular phase of industrial capitalism in one part of the world. Part of the resiliency of the "housewife" and "good mother" is her association with what appear to be essentially feminine qualities such as nurturing of the young, care, and loving sacrifice, all of which were understood to be the surface manifestations of her biologically determined role as mother. And as Olivia Harris notes, "since the human body is ideologically presented as a natural given, outside of history ..., it is easy to slide into treating domestic labour as a natural activity, also outside the scope of historical analysis" (Harris 1984: 148).

Morality and Domestic Space in the Colonies

The persistence of the dual spheres of male and female endlessly reiterated through the distinctions public/private, culture/nature, and material/spiritual and their apparent "naturalness" provided the motive force behind the effective extension of this signifying system and its attendant social forms to the colonies and subsequently its use by post-colonial nationalist and revolutionary movements. The physical enclosure of middle-class women within the single family home was accompanied by their capture within an ideological space that served to exclude not only the dirty world of money and manufacture but the poor, the racially degenerate, and, by extension to the colonies, the native. The physical space of the home became wedded with

the moral space associated with appropriate sexuality, proper child rearing, and correct social behavior.

Purity of race and questions of racial degeneracy, when combined with presumptions of appropriate home life, marriage, sex, and family, were a powerful means to control social hierarchy in the colonies. In the early stages of colonialism in the Dutch East Indies, for example, reproductive work, including sexual intercourse, was performed by the native *nyai*, who served as a housekeeper and bedmate to the lonely Dutch man. The VOC (East Indies Company) would not allow Dutch women to join their husbands without special dispensation (Stoler 1985; Gouda 1995; Taylor 1983), although after 1652, "men above the ranks of soldier and assistant in the civilian hierarchy" were allowed to bring out their families (Taylor 1983: 29). In the early years of colonialism, social and sexual relationships were relatively fluid: children born of Dutch-Javanese unions were recognized as Dutch, and Dutch Indies society included many Eurasians. Over time, as the colonial presence deepened, Dutch women were allowed to emigrate, and what had previously been a situation of fluid social arrangements between colonials and the Indigenes became rigid.

The policing of this social distance often fell to women, whose position as reproducers of empire's children and culture obscured their commonalities with other subordinate classes. Colonial discourse on both race and gender concealed the issues of stratification within the empire, both at home and in the colonies. *Nyais* were replaced by proper Dutch wives whose children may have been raised by native *baboes*, but whose parents were purely Dutch.

The arrival of white women in colonies as diverse as Sumatra, Fiji, Nigeria, and the Solomon Islands[9] corresponded to the fixing of social and physical space within the colony in imitation of the metropole. Remarkably, despite their place on lower rungs of civilization's evolutionary ladder, European women were thought to exemplify both the best and worst of the national identity of the European metropoles, engendering a civilized response from their European men while exciting native men almost beyond control and inscribing social distance so effectively that they were accused of being bigots worse than the imperially dispatched patriarch of the household. Frances Gouda describes how "incorporated" European wives were the "foot soldiers — either willingly or with moral qualms — who were in charge of defending an elaborate colonial pecking order that placed indigenous women at the bottom and classified white men at the top." In their daily domestic routines, Dutch women gave concrete expression to a male-defined imperial agenda and knowingly contributed to "the ideological work of gender" (Gouda 1995: 162-63).

The literature on European women in the colonies suggests that they were the bearers of a metropolitan moral tradition, based on nineteenth-century scientific racism and laissez-faire economics, rather than any primordial female character. Subsequently, during reactions to colonialism, women again provided the moral symbol and force to be manipulated by a male, nationalist leadership to rally opposition to the empire.

Neutralizing Popular and Sexual Power

Caught between the desire to modernize their countries along the lines of European technologic and economic excellence and the desire to assert independence, nationalist discourses in many parts of the Third World made use of an invented tradition that privileged women as a sign of a distant and glorious pre-colonial past.[10] Thus, the very logic of separate spheres that had emerged in the metropole and been used to secure colonial dominance through racial and sexual purity and separation was used in reverse to justify a nationalist independence that preserved what was taken to be *authentic* culture — embodied in women. Paradoxically then, nationalist movements often served to conserve the Western division of male and female spheres, using women again to defend a particular moral order and frequently domesticating Third World women in all too familiar ways. For nationalist Indonesia, the power of an early radical women's movement led to its subsequent capture by the new Indonesian state within pro-

grams such as PKK. This appropriation of the momentum to change women's roles by the state illustrates not only the potential volatility of women's moral power, but also how it may be secured by the state.

During the nationalist period in what would become Indonesia, the domestic needs of women became a rallying cry for GERWANI (*Gerakan Wanita*, Women's Movement), one of many vigorous women's organizations that emerged during the early 1900s. As Saskia Wieringa suggests, PKK and GERWANI were initially nearly identical in many of their goals. The activities of GERWANI included "credit groups, kindergartens, consumer cooperatives, literacy courses, assistance to women with marriage problems, handicraft courses, campaigns to lower the prices of staple foodstuffs" (Wieringa 1993: 20). GERWANI, however, offered assistance to leftist organizations like the Indonesian Communist Party (PKI, *Parti Komunis Indonesia*), although it addressed "a group of women the PKI never paid any attention to: housewives" (Wieringa 1993). The difference between GERWANI and PKK was the political connotation of each, as should be clear from the reference to the Indonesian Communist Party above. It was during the crackdowns after the alleged attempted Communist coup of 1965 that GERWANI was banned while PKK became the focus of the government's goals regarding women. This shift was part of a larger attempt to de-politicize the successful grassroots organizations associated with the Indonesian nationalist revolution while capturing their momentum for change.

One explanation for how this was accomplished is offered by Wieringa (1993; see also Wieringa 1988), who discusses the persistent story that members of GERWANI were involved in the genital mutilation and torture deaths of the generals associated with the alleged coup attempt in 1965 that led to the New Order regime of Suharto. Despite evidence that this did not in fact occur (Anderson 1987), the myth continues, presumably because of its power to discourage women's active participation in politics. Campaigns to construct "an image of GERWANI members as whores and sexually perverted women" were orchestrated, while PKK members were "extolled as good ibus [mothers] and dutiful and respectable citizens" (Wieringa 1993: 17). In the early years of the new republic following the revolution, Indonesian women engaged in a genuine suffrage movement, but with the coming of the New Order all of that changed. After the coup of 1965, the government "opted pragmatically simply to co-opt women in the organization structure of their husbands" (Suryakusuma 1996: 100). The new developmentalist regime used programs such as PKK to specify women's roles in the developmental process, but this was accomplished by structuring women's participation as part of a "non-political women's movement," while still using elements of older women's associations and groups (Gerke 1992: 30, n.17).

The difference between PKK and GERWANI was not just who controlled their structure but in their apparent potential for radical social change. GERWANI was an independent women's organization; PKK is an arm of the government. It is significant that the rhetoric used to discredit GERWANI was overtly sexual; that is, not only were its members communists, but they were whores and prostitutes as well. Here we have the good terrorist in another guise. Women were to remain important "motors" for social change but through a structure thoroughly de-politicized by the Indonesian state. The transmogrification of organizations such as GERWANI from a group of sexually perverse and dangerous subversives working to topple the government to good terrorists working for social change at the behest of the government — and importantly without the taint of unrestrained sexuality — resonates with the earlier colonial obsession with proper sexual conduct and right culture. The successful depoliticization of PKK in the government's eyes is clear since currently "PKK is the only organization allowed to work at the village grass-roots level" (Wieringa 1993: 24).

The gutting of the nationalist-era women's movement and the retention of the general form of these organizations to be used in state development is only one of the many contradictions embedded within the organization of PKK. There is, more critically perhaps, an inherent contradiction in the linking of the maintenance of healthy families and communities to the work of stay-at-home mothers. Javanese women, particularly rural Javanese women, have long been economically active and engaged in a variety of income-generating activities that take them out of their homes. If indeed the model of rural community is embraced as a national ideal, as the Indonesian government declares, then it would immediately contradict the PKK ideal of women at home. In fact, the PKK stay-at-home mom is an artifact of the particular history of change in the Javanese countryside matched with Dutch notions of middle-class women and their place (Carey and Houbens 1987; Gouda 1995; Taylor 1983). This is not to say that women in Java have not been involved in the management and support of communities and families, but that this was done in addition to work outside the home.

Power and Morality's Mother

The association of women with right morals, whether those of the colonial metropole or those of the nationalist revolution, persists in modern politics in ways that continue the linked association of domestic and moral space. Indeed, women's roles in producing good citizens has proved (and continues to prove) to be a particularly powerful way for women to affect public policy. The "mother" as somehow outside or beyond political guile has great symbolic and practical political power. The protests by the mothers of the disappeared in Argentina, the so-called *Plaza de Mayo Madres*, proved to be such a powerful protest to the ruling junta as they marched day after day holding the pictures of their disappeared children and wearing embroidered diapers on their heads to signify their domestic roles *because* they were *just mothers* (Schirmer 1994; Perelli 1994). Other women have used the role of mother to win political office, offering the differing politics of the domestic as an alternative to politics as usual; for example, Violetta Chamorro ran successfully for the presidency of Nicaragua on the basis of her experience as a *mother*. Yet, the symbolic power of the mother and her practical work may be captured for less happy causes. Claudia Koonz (1987) documents the role of Nazi women in a fascist regime that sought to end women's electoral privileges as it sanctified their roles as reproducers of the master race (see also De Grazia 1992 on Italian fascism and its effects for women). Nazi women reproduced a pleasant home place for their families even while they worked to forbid that haven to those who were racially unworthy.

The political power of the Mother, or the *Ibu*, is also evident in Indonesia. Djajadiningrat-Nieuwenhuis coined the term *ibuism* to refer to the combination of elite *priyayi*[11] values with those of the Dutch petit-bourgeois that produces an ideology that sanctions any action taken by a mother on the part of family, class, or country without asking for anything in return (1987: 44). *State ibuism* has been used subsequently by Suryakusuma to suggest the New Order government's role in promoting such self-sacrifice for state goals. PKK is a prime example of this state-sponsored domestic cult. The moral power of the role of mother, devolving from colonial, nationalist, and developmentalist histories, has been fully captured within the rhetoric of the Indonesian state. For example, *Hari Ibu* (Mother's Day)[12] was inaugurated officially in 1953 along with the Mother's Day Banner.

> The banner shows the Melati flower as the symbol of pure motherhood, while its buds symbolize the natural unity and relation between the Mother as the source of love and her children. The five petals of the stylised Melati flower stand for Pancasila, the Five Principles of the state philosophy. The slogan on the banner reads "Merdeka melaksanakan Dharma," meaning "Free to do one's social duties." (Department of Information 1984: 10-11)

During my fieldwork, the mutual ideological constitution of good mothers, wives, and citizens was made abundantly clear in a banner promoting breast feeding: *Aku Sayang Ibu, Aku Sayang Istri, Aku Sayang Indonesia*, or I love my mother, I love my wife, I love Indonesia.

Women's roles as defenders of the moral order, whether colonial or nationalist, has granted them some political space and authority such that the Indonesian government has tried to control it. Yet the political space opened for women as mothers can be used to mobilize for local change in homes and communities. Once appropriated, the moral power of the good mother provides room for acts of terrorism.

Kampung Space

The movement from the cult of domestic angels, to the colonial architecture of proper domestic life, to the construction of the nationalist home as site of authentic culture describes an arc that is general enough to capture the experience in many different parts of the world. Yet, the specific curvature in any particular place requires some adjustment. To understand the particular effects of PKK, current, local practice of morality must be considered. The daily dramas of *kampung* life that I observed and in which I participated illustrate not only the value and salience of community for *kampung* inhabitants, but the key role of women in its functioning. More importantly here, the programs, practices, and propaganda of PKK have now become resources to be used in the negotiation of community and morality by *kampung* dwellers.

In taking seriously the daily use of PKK in *kampung* women's lives, their roles as managers of household accounts become significant. The women I worked and lived among in the *kampung* managed not only the financial and domestic accounts of their households, but their social and moral accounts as well. Ethnomethodologists make use of the concept of *accountability* in a similar way; for example, Harold Garfinkel (1967: 1) speaks of situated practices of "looking-and-telling" that allow members of a group or community to be held accountable. Behaviors that are "observable-and-reportable" to other community members necessitate attempts to render credible accounts of oneself as a good neighbor, citizen, or, in this instance, housewife. This idea of accountability not only dovetails nicely with the ethnomethodologist's "theme of tacit or 'taken for granted' understandings" (Giddens 1995: 237), but it also offers a micro-level tool for understanding the connection between state structure and everyday action. To suggest that PKK is an ideological instrument of the Indonesian state is not a sufficient explanation for how it becomes real in the lives of Javanese housewives. My ethnographic fieldwork in a working-class *kampung* showed that women used PKK as a resource to render credible accounts of themselves in their daily lives, thus reproducing a particular state and moral order even while opening up room for change.

Raising good children and keeping good house are used as barometers of social character not only in the macrocosm of colonial society and nationalist rhetoric but in the microcosm of the *kampung*, and so it was with the family of the puppet-maker from my earlier example. Pak Wayang appeared to be a good addition to the neighborhood at first, at least to the nearby Cipto family who never turned down a good time. Not only did his puppet-making industry provide job opportunities, but at night the men would gather in the open area that earlier had been filled with workers to play *keroncong* music (the Javanese equivalent to country-western music that is derived from Portuguese songs; Ferzacca 1997). The men would typically sit up until late in the night drinking *jamu*, a traditional health tonic, in this case bolstered with beer or wine. These late night gatherings often led to card games.

Over time, in a fashion so subtle that I almost missed it, local *kampung* sentiment began to shift against Pak Wayang and his family. What began as whispered conversations among women as they swept their front steps and the narrow street or *gang* in front of their houses each day in the *sore* (early evening), soon became a full-fledged lobbying effort on the part of women to do something about the situation at Pak Wayang's. Apparently, the gambling had become a problem. Bu Apik's ne'er-do-well husband was taking money from her purse to gamble and was losing. Other men were losing money too. Since women typically control family finances, neighborhood wives were immediately aware of the peril posed by this new gambling problem. To make matters worse for Bu Sae, who lived practically next

door, her youngest son had taken to spending his nights there as well.

I began to hear stories about the troubles at Pak Wayang's. As already mentioned, his wife, who was never much involved in *kampung* affairs anyway, was described as being a poor housekeeper. This whispered campaign centered around Bu Sae and Bu Apik, the two women most unhappy about what was happening. In *kampung* cases such as this, the plaintiffs typically seek out the Pak RT, who as the most local representative of the government is charged with keeping order, to ask for his counsel and intervention in what is perceived as a threat to *kampung* security. Unfortunately, the Pak RT had become one of the cohort of regular gamblers at Pak Wayang's. As a result, the women sought the help of one of the local neighborhood's other moral bulwarks, Pak Hormat. While the impetus for change was the product of the lobbying of women who felt the threat first, they looked to a male patron to take direct action. In the case of Pak Wayang's deviance from *kampung* norms, Pak Hormat was apparently asked to approach him. Not long after, the gambling stopped.

This example of moral control in the *kampung* illustrates the role of women in keeping accounts and monitoring one another's behavior, particularly that of other women. After all, the first reports I heard were about Bu Wayang's poor housekeeping skills. It also illustrates the indirect power of women in mobilizing support, while leaving direct action to a male. The moral force of good housekeeping and good community is also evident. After all, Bu Sae and Bu Apik were just keeping good house and good community. Elizabeth Fox-Genovese noted this extension of women's domestic roles to community politics in Anglo-American history: "women presented many of their most impressive accomplishments as 'social housekeeping' and justified them in the name of prescribed domestic responsibilities" (Fox-Genovese 1991: 37).

Yet another example of community morality mobilized for what might conventionally be considered a private concern actually happened a year or so before we arrived in the *kampung*, although based on what residents said, it remained fresh in people's memories. The fullest telling of the incident came from Bu Apik herself, who was at the center of the story. According to Bu Apik, her husband was bewitched by a woman who lived at the other end of our street, in the far eastern section of the adjoining RT. Her magic had led him to begin an affair with her. It had to be bewitchment, according to Bu Apik, because the woman in question was not blessed in looks or temperament. This affair between a man and a woman at opposite ends of the narrow street that stretched between the two extreme ends of the adjoining RT apparently became a cause for public scandal, because a community meeting was convened in an attempt to solve the problems. At the meeting, Bu Apik's husband was asked to choose between the two women — publicly. This meeting was a painful event in Bu Apik's life, because her handsome, troublesome husband chose to stay with his lover at that time. When we arrived in the *kampung*, Bu and Pak Apik had been reunited, and although I never heard how that happened, I heard repeatedly about their earlier troubles.

It is perhaps inconceivable to an American audience that a neighborhood meeting would be called to settle an instance of marital infidelity, but different codes of behavior and community conduct were at play in the *kampung*. The tacit agreement to play by the rules is part of the responsibility of living in such a close and closed community. This agreement is made clear daily in the *kampung*, especially as new challenges to its logic arise.

Bu Apik and her continuing troubles provide a counterpart to Bu Sae's life and her role in the family and *kampung*. Bu Sae was a lightning rod for *kampung* morality. She represented not only the generation of working-class families whose children were doing better, she personally was an example of a successful PKK ibu. In her income-generating activities, Bu Sae fit the PKK ideal. Not only had she and the other women of the PKK shop where she worked pursued government funds to open it, she further added to her family's income by cooking peanuts to order and selling the ice from her refrigerator. Her husband was gainfully employed as were her two oldest children. Bu Sae

was an active member of PKK, and she and her husband had served a long tenure as Bapak and Ibu RT. The back room of her house had a large cupboard that was still filled with the plates, cutlery, and glasses necessary for hosting the various meetings associated with serving as Bu RT. Yet, Bu Sae was a problematic figure in the *kampung*. Despite her successful identification with the goals and roles of PKK, she was perceived by her neighbors to be haughty, withholding of resources, and condescending to those who couldn't match her high moral standards. She lived within a dense network of kin, not all of whom were on good terms with her. Nonetheless, Bu Sae used PKK to better herself and her family, and she did serve as a moral arbiter for the community.

Bu Apik and Bu Sae provide an interesting contrast in terms both of their use of PKK as a resource and of its effects on their standing in the community. Bu Sae was not well liked by many of her close neighbors and family because they believed she had gotten above herself (a clear *kampung* taboo). Still Bu Sae and her family were considered to be very respectable, and her active involvement in PKK enhanced that reputation. On the other hand, Bu Apik, despite involvement in several levels of community governance and PKK work (she was the local birth control officer, for example), could not redeem her disreputable family. More popular than Bu Sae, Bu Apik nonetheless struggled to improve her family's reputation. The experiences of these two women illustrate both the power of PKK and its local limitations.

Kampung morality is not disconnected from the state-sponsored forms of appropriate domesticity and citizenry. Although *kampung* morality hinges on more than the behavior of women, women are — just as the PKK cant would have it — a critical point of articulation between individual households and the community. Javanese housewives, in their roles as mediators in community and national development, in effect mirror social relations to the state apparatus but also serve to refract state directives to the local community. These two levels of experience are related in ways that light up the connection between the personal and the public. *Kampung* dwellers use the sentiments of harmonious community and of proper domestic conduct on a daily basis. This is not to say that everyone subscribes to these beliefs wholeheartedly. As already demonstrated, many women and *kampung* folk have a very developed sense of irony about some of the contortions required in state rhetoric. Still, every time an official transgression is noted and acted upon and every time a woman or family seeks status through official service, they are indexing these ethics and making them real. Moreover, whether women agree with PKK or not, it is often true that to give a credible account of oneself within a *kampung* community may mean making use of the resources of PKK. Those women unable to give credible accounts of themselves as household managers, as well as PKK workers, suffered not just the sting of gossip but the very real cut of not receiving mutual aid and community support.

Still, PKK offers more than a way for women to police other women and their own communities. In my time in the *kampung*, I saw women using PKK as a different kind of resource. Many of the women in the two RTs where I did most of my fieldwork work for wages, both inside and outside of the home, and, as a consequence, they often experienced the monthly PKK meetings as an onerous demand on their time. Even those not involved in the higher levels of PKK administration needed to attend as many as four regular meetings a month, plus help with the specific activities of PKK, such as the baby weighings, hospital visits, and other neighborhood obligations. It is not surprising that *kampung* women view PKK with some ambivalence; not only does the very idea of stay-at-home mother contradict their working lives in many cases, it also poses yet another demand on their limited time. It is all the more interesting then that PKK is now being used by these women to accomplish community social reproduction in ways that lighten their loads. A good example of this are the activities of the PKK group in my RT associated with Ramadan, the Muslim month of fasting.

Before the month of fasting begins, each family is obligated to send a meal to neighbors, relatives, and close friends. This meal typically includes *apem*, a rice flour griddle cake, as well as a sweet cassava dish. In the past, each family fulfilled this obligation on its own, requiring large amounts of labor on the part of the women of the family. What has happened in recent years is that the women of PKK organize a communal cooking session to produce a single boxed meal for everyone in the neighborhood, thereby greatly reducing the labor for the individual women. The use of the PKK organization to solve a community responsibility results not from government planning but from the redirection of government structure for local practice. The effects for community maintenance are contradictory. While community obligations are met and women's workloads are decreased, individual family responsibility for social obligations is also attenuated.

The use of PKK and its offices to meet community-wide social obligations suggests several things. First, it shows that community obligation still has valence, and this is reinforced by the community support that goes on within *and without* government administrative units. The use of PKK to solve local problems reveals not only the continuing importance of community cooperation, it also suggests the importance of women in this work. It is women who visit hospitals, who collect social funds, who cook communally, and who make certain that family obligations to community are met. Moreover, the adaptation of PKK to meet these needs indexes not only women's increased workloads but shows that the structure provided by the government may be used for different ends. Thus, the organization founded around the ideal of the stay-at-home mom actually serves to help women who work outside the home meet *kampung* obligations.

Political Space for Change

Drawing on past legacies, contemporary black women can begin to reconceptualize ideas of homeplace, once again considering the primacy of domesticity as a site for subversion and resistance. (hooks 1990: 48)

Taking the ethnomethodologist's emphasis on accountability, on giving credible accounts through daily practices of living and telling, and using it to understand *kampung* morality returns our gaze to reproduction. Passing as a good PKK housewife means, necessarily, the reproduction of a particular gendered experience. The contortions of *kampung* women as they fit themselves around PKK womanhood are the micro-technology of adjustment to an international division of labor, a national developmentalist regime, and a local culture of common sense. Henrietta Moore notes that in reproducing a set of social relations, the experience of these social relations is also reproduced: "These conventional understandings can be seen as local theories of entitlement, and such theories are always bound up with ideologies and with unequal power relations" (Moore 1994: 104). Simultaneously, the introduction of new resources and the changes in use of old resources offers a means to change. And, as Moore suggests, shifts in meaning can often follow from a "reordering of practical activities.... such as putting something in the wrong place or placing it in relation to something else from which it is normally kept separate" (Moore 1994: 83).

When Bu Sae and Bu Apik approached Pak Hormat to put an end to the gambling threatening their families and community, they might be said to have engaged a long-standing set of ideas about appropriate community conduct, but these ideas coincide with a governmental view of women as the upholders of community morality. When Bu Apik takes on more and more roles within PKK, she may be responding to personal family problems, but she is also activating the power of state-sponsored domesticity to improve her own status as well as that of her community. By calling on the resources of the PKK ideal of womanhood in their own lives, women make the policy manifest. And when women feel compelled to acknowledge this discourse or to gesture to it by acknowledging its credibility in their daily accounts, it enters the realm of common sense and the daily life of culture (Goffman 1959). That is, PKK becomes real in everyday life when *kampung* women feel embarrassed about their non-attendance or non-conformity to the extent that they maintain their reputation by apologizing, temporizing, or avoiding the behavior in the first place. Most importantly, when women take the resources intended to bolster

women's roles within the family and community and use them to make short work of these duties, the original intent of the program can be said to have been misplaced, consequently changing PKK, its relationship to women, and their relationship to the state, however subtly. It matters less here whether *kampung* dwellers are imagining that they are involved in "traditional" patterns of *gotong-royong* (mutual self-help) or that the state perpetuates imagined ideals of community and motherhood. The effect is the same. Women and community are reproduced through the local-level use of state resources, and state rule is reproduced through the action of women in giving credible accounts of themselves. The result of this zig-zag between the state and the local is what constitutes state formation, and it is an eminently *cultural* process that belies the "non-political" character of PKK in the government's eyes.

I am arguing here that my Javanese neighbors are good terrorists. They comply with government directives on appropriate homes and domesticity only insofar as it serves their own ends. And they often "misplace" these directives, ideas, and programs by using them to suit other local *kampung* needs. In so doing, *kampung* members subvert — at least partially — the government's attempts to structure lives in a particular way and instead make the programs their own. This might be understood as resistance to the degree that *kampung* dwellers fail to comply with government programs in the strict sense they were intended, but it is more profitable to see that by accepting and reforming these programs within their own lives, *kampung* dwellers not only live the state but change it.

So the Javanese women with whom I worked were placed in the role of housewives as a consequence of a long history of colonial intervention and by a nationalist, developmentalist government seeking to deal with unemployment and other structural issues in the economy, but these women took up PKK when it served their own ends. They are quite capable of cynicism about their roles in the organization known as "women without enough work to do," while effectively fulfilling their positions in the organization, thereby reproducing the category of community-oriented house-wife, and, as I have suggested, producing a new type of gendered subject position in modernizing Indonesia: the underemployed female as mother of the country. Yet, by using the goals and rhetoric of PKK within their families and communities as justification and moral code, they make this government program real within their lives. And when they misplace the rhetoric of PKK to deal with their own community issues, they open up a space for change. They are good women insofar as they work to support their families and communities, but they are terrorists as they reform government directives to suit their own ends.

Author's Note

This paper is based on doctoral fieldwork supported by grants from the Southeast Asia Council (SEAC) and the University of Arizona Graduate School. I would like to thank the *Lembaga Ilmu Pengetahuan Indonesia* (LIPI) for permission to conduct this research, and the American-Indonesian Exchange Foundation (AMINEF) for all their support. I would also like to thank Steve Ferzacca and Mei Sugiarti for their research assistance.

NOTES

1. Pak is the shortened form of the male honorific *Bapak*, or father, which is used for all of equal or higher status than the speaker. *Bu* is the shortened form of the female honorific *Ibu*. All the names provided here are pseudonyms.

2. *Kampung* refers to a specific type of community, circumscribed both spatially and socially. The term has meant variously ethnic enclave, guild neighborhood, and urban or rural village community. Current meanings for *kampung* vary by social position. From within, *kampung* are described as home community with a sense of cohesion, cooperation, and intimate social relations; from without, *kampung* are frequently described as urban slums (cf. Sullivan 1992).

3. Adult is defined here as being married or having children or being the sole or main breadwinner of a household.

4. Pancasila comprises the five basic principles of the Republic of Indonesia: belief in one God, a just and civilized humanity, the unity of all of Indonesia, a democracy guided by wise and representative deliberation, and social justice for all Indonesians.

5. Any implied isomorphism between the small island of Java, where the largest percentage of population resides, and the Republic of Indonesia, which comprises many different islands and ethnic groups, is problematic. Still, the experience of Java, which is the focus of this paper, has likewise been central to definitions of what is Indonesia, as programs such as PKK illustrate.

6. Drastic changes in the Indonesian economy took place in the years between 1965-85 with the introduction of Green Revolution technologies and related economic restructuring. The introduction of high yielding varieties (HYV) of rice and related technology to the countryside eventually moved Indonesia to being a net exporter of rice. In the process, there was rapid release of labor, especially female labor, in the agricultural sector. For example, the replacement of the small hand knife, or *ani-ani*, used by female rice harvesters, with the sickle, used by men, reduced labor requirements in harvesting by up to 60 per cent (Wolf 1992; Collier *et al.* 1973; Hart 1986), and the introduction of the mechanized rice huller meant estimated job losses "as high as 1.2 million in Java alone and as high as 7.7 million in all of Indonesia" (Cain 1981: 134).

7. I use the term "terrorist" here to be provocative. Its use is not intended to minimize the reality and violence of terrorist acts nor their effects on the lives of those who have experienced it, nor does it imply a sustained discussion of what constitutes terrorism — a worthy goal beyond the scope of this paper. I use it here, particularly in contrast with the adjective "good," to challenge the conventional and essentialized characteristics of women as housewives.

8. See, for example, Boris and Bardaglio 1983; Corrigan and Sayer 1985; Davidoff and Hall 1987; Oakley 1974; Scott and Tilly 1975; Williams 1961.

9. See Boutilier 1982; Callaway 1987; Knapman 1986; Stoler 1989a, 1989b, 1996. See also Chatterjee 1989; Strobel 1993; and White 1990.

10. Jayawardena's discussion of Third World feminisms (1986), like Chatterjee's classic piece (1989) on Indian nationalism, highlight the gendered effects of nationalist revolutions (see also Rowbotham 1972). Such revolutions are not just confined to the so-called Third World. The American Revolution saw similar effects on women's roles (see Matthews 1987; Cott 1977).

11. *Priyayi* refers to the bureaucratic elites made up of old court retainers and the bureaucrats who worked for the Dutch.

12. In Indonesia, Mother's Day is actually *Hari Ibu Kartini* or *Mother Kartini Day*. Princess Kartini is known in Indonesia for her advocacy of girl's education in domestic skills. In a famous series of letters to her Dutch benefactor, Kartini described how she longed for the life of a young Dutch girl and the freedom to pursue her education (Kartini 1920). Although associated with Mother's Day, Kartini did not long for the role of mother. She died in childbirth at the age of 25 after an arranged marriage she resisted.

REFERENCES

Anderson, Benedict. 1987. How did the Generals die? *Indonesia* 43: 109-13.

Bennholdt-Thomsen, Veronika. 1988. Why do housewives continue to be created in the third world too? In *Women: The last colony*, ed. Maria Mies, Veronika Bennholdt-Thomsen, and Claudia von Werlhof. London: Zed Books.

Boris, Eileen, and Peter Bardaglio. 1983. The transformation of patriarchy: The historic role of the state. In *Families, politics, and public policy*, ed. Irene Diamond. New York, NY: Longman.

Boutilier, James. 1982. European women in the Solomon Islands, 1900-1942: Accommodation and change on the Pacific frontier. In *Rethinking women's roles: Perspectives on the Pacific*, ed. Denise O'Brien and Sharon Tiffany. Berkeley, CA: University of California Press.

Cain, Melinda. 1981. Java, Indonesia: The introduction of rice processing technology. In *Women and tech-nological change in developing countries*, ed. R. Dauber and M. Cain. Boulder, CO: Westview.

Callaway, Helen. 1987. *Gender, culture and empire: European women in colonial Nigeria*. Oxford, UK: Macmillan Press.

Carey, Peter, and Vincent Houben. 1987. Spirited Srikandhis and sly Sumbadras: The social, political and economic role of women at the central Javanese courts in the 18th and early 19th centuries. In *Indonesian woman in focus: Past and present notions*, ed. Elsbeth Locher-Scholten and Anke Neihof. Dordrecht, Holland: Foris Publications.

Chatterjee, Partha. 1989. Colonialism, nationalism and colonised women: The contest in India. *American ethnologist* 16(4): 622-33.

Collier, W., Gunawan Wiradi, and Soetono. 1973. Recent changes in rice harvesting methods. *Bulletin of Indonesian economic studies* 9(2): 36-45.

Comaroff, Jean, and John Comaroff. 1992. Home-made hegemony: Modernity, domesticity, and colonialism in South Africa. In *African encounters with domesticity*, ed. Karen Tranberg Hansen. New Brunswick, NJ: Rutgers University Press.

Corrigan, Philip, and Derek Sayer. 1985. *The great arch: English state formation as cultural revolution*. Oxford, UK: Basil Blackwell.

Cott, Nancy. 1977. *The bonds of womanhood: "Woman's sphere" in New England, 1780-1835*. New Haven, CT: Yale University Press.

Davidoff, Leonore, and Catherine Hall. 1987. *Family fortunes: Men and women of the English middle class*. Chicago, IL: University of Chicago Press.

de Grazia, Victoria. 1992. *How fascism ruled women: Italy, 1922-1945*. Berkeley, CA: University of California Press.

Department of Information. 1984. *The women of Indonesia*. Second printing. Republic of Indonesia.

Djajadiningrat-Nieuwenhuis, Madelon. 1987. Ibuism and priyayization: Path to power? In *Indonesian woman in focus: Past and present notions*, ed. Elsbeth Locher-Scholten and Anke Neihof. Dordrecht, Holland: Foris Publications.

Engels, Friedrich. 1942[1902]. *The origin of the family, private property and the state, in the light of the researches of Lewis H. Morgan*. New York, NY: International Publishers.

Ferzacca, Steve. 1997. Keroncong music in a Javanese

neighborhood: Rehearsals with spirits of the popular. Paper given to Society for Ethnomusicology, Forty-Second Annual Meeting, Pittsburgh, PA, October 24.

Fox-Genovese, Elizabeth. 1991. *Feminism without illusions: A critique of individualism.* Chapel Hill, NC: University of North Carolina Press.

Garfinkel, Harold. 1967. *Studies in ethnomethodology.* Englewood Cliffs, NJ: Prentice-Hall.

Gerke, Solvay. 1992. *Social change and life planning for rural Javanese women.* Saarbrucken: Verlag Breitenbach Publishers.

Giddens, Anthony. 1995. *Politics, sociology and social theory: Encounters with classical and contemporary social thought.* Stanford, CA: Stanford University Press.

Goffman, Erving. 1959. *The presentation of self in everyday life.* Garden City, NY: Doubleday.

Gouda, Frances. 1995. *Dutch culture overseas: Colonial practice in the Netherlands Indies, 1900-1942.* Amsterdam: Amsterdam University Press.

Harris, Olivia. 1984. Households as natural units. In *Of marriage and the market: Women's subordination internationally and its lessons,* ed. by K. Young, C. Wolkowitz, and R. McCullagh. London: Routledge, Kegan Paul.

Hart, Gillian. 1986. *Power, labor, and livelihood: Processes of change in rural Java.* Berkeley, CA: University of California Press.

hooks, bell.1990. *Yearning: Race, gender, and cultural politics.* Boston, MA: South End Press.

Jayawardena, Kumari. 1986. *Feminism and nationalism in the third world.* London: Zed Books.

Kartini, Raden Adjeng. 1920. *Letters of a Javanese princess.* Translated by Agnes Louise Symmers. New York, NY: Alfred Knopf.

Knapman, Claudia. 1986. *White women in Fiji, 1985-1930: The ruin of empire?* Sydney: Allen and Unwin.

Koonz, Claudia. 1987. *Mothers in the fatherland: Women, the family and Nazi politics.* New York, NY: St. Martin's.

Lessing, Doris. 1985. *The good terrorist.* New York, NY: Knopf.

Matthews, Glenna. 1987. *"Just a housewife": The rise and fall of domesticity in America.* New York, NY: Oxford University Press.

Mies, Maria. 1986. *Patriarchy and accumulation on a world scale: Women in the international division of labour.* London: Zed Books.

Ministry of Home Affairs. 1983. The family welfare movement in Indonesia: PKK. Directorate General of Rural Development. Mimeograph.

Moore, Henrietta. 1994. *A passion for difference: essays in anthropology and gender.* Bloomington, IN: Indiana University Press.

New York Times Book Review. 1985. Bad housekeeping. December 19: 8-9.

Nugent, Daniel. 1993. *Spent cartridges of revolution: An anthropological history of Namiquipa, Chihuahua.* Chicago, IL: University of Chicago Press.

Oakley, Ann. 1974. *Woman's work: The housewife, past and present.* New York, NY: Pantheon.

Perelli, Carina. 1994. *Memoria de sangre*: Fear, hope, and disenchantment in Argentina. In *Remapping memory: The politics of TimeSpace,* ed. Jonathon Boyarin. Minneapolis, MN: University of Minnesota Press.

Rowbotham, Sheila. 1972. *Women, resistance, and revolution; a history of women and revolution in the modern world.* New York, NY: Pantheon Books.

Schirmer, Jennifer. 1994. The claiming of space and the body politic within national-security states: The Plaza de Mayo madres and the Greenham Common women. In *Remapping memory: The politics of TimeSpace,* ed. Jonathon Boyarin. Minneapolis, MN: University of Minnesota Press.

Scott, Joan, and Louis Tilly. 1975. Woman's work and the family in nineteenth-century Europe. In *The family in history,* ed. Charles Rosenberg. Philadelphia, PA: University of Pennsylvania Press.

Stoler, Ann Laura. 1985. *Capitalism and confrontation in Sumatra's plantation belt, 1870-1979.* New Haven, CT: Yale University Press.

— . 1989a. Making empire respectable: The politics of race and sexual morality in 20th-century colonial cultures. *American ethnologist* 16(4): 643-60.

— . 1989b. Rethinking colonial categories: European communities and the boundaries of rule. *Comparative studies in society and history* 31:134-61.

— . 1996. A sentimental education: Native servants and the cultivation of European children in the Netherlands Indies. In *Fantasizing the feminine in Indonesia,* ed. Laurie Sears. Durham, SC: Duke University Press.

Strobel, Margaret. 1993. Gender, sex, and empire. In *Islamic and European expansion: The forging of a global order*, ed. Michael Adas. Philadelphia, PA: Temple University Press.

Sullivan, John. 1992. *Local government and community in Java: An urban case-study*. Singapore: Oxford University Press.

Suryakusuma, Julia. 1991. State Ibuism: The social construction of womanhood in the Indonesian New Order. *New Asian visions* 6(2): 46-71.

— . 1996. The state and sexuality in New Order Indonesia. In *Fantasizing the feminine in Indonesia*, ed. Laurie Sears. Durham, NC: Duke University Press.

Taylor, Jean Gelman. 1983. *The social world of Batavia: European and Eurasian in Dutch Asia*. Madison, WI: University of Wisconsin Press.

Tiwon, Sylvia. 1996. Models and maniacs: Articulating the female in Indonesia. In *Fantasizing the feminine in Indonesia*, ed. by Laurie Sears. Durham, NC: Duke University Press.

White, Luise. 1990. *The comforts of home: Prostitution in Colonial Nairobi*. Chicago, IL: University of Chicago Press.

Wieringa, Saskia. 1988. Aborted feminism in Indonesia: A history of Indonesian socialist feminism. In *Women's struggles and strategies*, ed. S. Wieringa. Aldershot, UK: Gower.

— . 1993. Two Indonesian women's organizations: Gerwani and the PKK. *Bulletin of concerned Asian scholars* 25(2).

Williams, Raymond. 1961. *The long revolution*. New York, NY: Columbia University Press.

Wolf, Diane. 1992. *Factory daughters: Gender, household dynamics, and rural industrialization in Java*. Berkeley, CA: University of California Press.

STUDY QUESTIONS

1 According to Elayne Saltzberg and Joan Chrisler, what are the differences in perceptions and self-perceptions of women's bodies that mark them as different from men's bodies? Do you agree that these differences exist? Is there an idea of the perfect female body? Defend your answers.

2 Describe what Saltzberg and Chrisler identify as some of the physical and psychological consequences for women of trying to achieve the ideal of the perfect female body. Is this true for all women? Do you think these consequences identify ways in which women are oppressed? Defend your answers.

3 Has learning about some of the effects of trying to achieve the ideal of the perfect female body made any difference with respect to your behavior or attitudes about yourself or women more generally?

4 Keith Burgess-Jackson argues that the difference between men and women with respect to levels of fear is one that ought to concern us. Is Burgess-Jackson correct to suggest that an unequal distribution of fear needs to be addressed in theories of distributive justice? Is the fact that fear is a burden rather than a benefit problematic for an account of the distribution of fear? Provide reasons for your answers.

5 What evidence does Burgess-Jackson provide for the claim that women bear a much greater burden of fear than do men? How does he answer possible objections to this claim?

6 What are the consequences for women of being more fearful than men? Who should bear the cost of easing this burden and why? Do you think that the suggestions Burgess-Jackson makes for redistributing fear are good ones? Provide reasons for your answers.

7 Why is Susan Moller Okin concerned about addressing charges from within feminism that essentialist accounts of women need to be avoided? Do you agree with her claim that anti-essentialist feminists lack empirical evidence to support their claims that there are no experiences shared by all women? Defend your answer.

8 Do you agree with Okin that the debate about differences amongst women in various parts of the world undermines attempts to address issues of injustice? Do you think that Okin provides a convincing case for her argument that the experiences of oppression by poor women in poor countries are similar to those of white middle-class women in Western countries "only more so"? Why or why not?

9 Chandra Mohanty argues that there is a tendency in Western feminist writing to present "third world woman" as a "monolithic subject." In your view, does Okin's account of gender fall prey to these charges? Why or why not?

10 What evidence does Mohanty provide that might cast doubt on Okin's defense of a "generalizable, identifiable, and collectively shared experience of womanhood"? Formulate your answer to this question by discussing at least one example from each of the Okin and Mohanty readings.

11 According to Mohanty, Western feminist assumptions and methodologies contribute to the misrepresentation of the lives and experiences of women in developing countries and to the creation of policies that have a detrimental effect on their lives. Evaluate this claim by explaining what Mohanty means by Western feminist assumptions and methodologies.

12 What does Janice Newberry mean by the term "state-sponsored domesticity"? What does she mean by the term "good terrorist"? Does the particular situation of women in Indonesia afford a good opportunity for exploring the notion of the good terrorist? Why or why not?

13 Newberry argues that the role of reproduction in the extended sense of reproducing children, socializing them into citizens, and reproducing social relations are used by women in Indonesia not only to create and sustain society, but also to subvert and change the restricted aspects of state-sponsored domesticity. Is the case she presents convincing? Can these insights about the subversive aspects of roles of reproduction be applied to women in general? Provide reasons for your answers.

14 From what you have learned about women in Indonesia, do you think that these women lead lives
    that are subversive and conducive to social and political change in ways that can eliminate the oppres-
    sive aspects of their state-sponsored roles? Give reasons for your answer.

SUGGESTED READINGS

Accad, Evelyne. "Sexuality and Sexual Politics: Conflicts and Contradictions for Contemporary Women
    in the Middle East." In *Third World Women and the Politics of Feminism*, edited by Chandra
    Mohanty, Ann Russo, Lourdes Torres. Bloomington, IN: Indiana University Press, 1991.

Archard, David. *Sexual Consent*. Boulder, CO: Westview Press, 1998.

Brison, Susan J. "Surviving Sexual Violence: A Philosophical Perspective." *Journal of Social Philoso-
    phy*, v. 24 (1993): 5-22.

Burgess-Jackson, Keith. "On the Coerciveness of Sexist Socialization." *Public Affairs Quarterly*, v. 9,
    no. 1 (January 1995): 15-27.

—. "Statutory Rape: A Philosophical Analysis." *The Canadian Journal of Law and Jurisprudence*, v. 8,
    no. 1 (1995): 139-58.

Burgess-Jackson, Keith (editor). *A Most Detestable Crime: New Philosophical Essays on Rape*. New
    York, NY: Oxford University Press, 1999.

Calhoun, Laurie. "On Rape: A Crime Against Humanity." *Journal of Social Philosophy*, v. 28 (1997):
    101-09.

Card, Claudia. "Rape as a Weapon of War." *Hypatia*, v. 11 (1996): 5-18.

Cindoglu, Dilek. "Virginity Tests and Artificial Virginity in Modern Turkish Medicine." *Women's Studies
    International Forum*, v. 20, no. 2 (1997): 253-61.

Clatterbaugh, Kenneth. "Are Men Oppressed?" In *Rethinking Masculinity: Philosophical Explorations
    in Light of Feminism*, 2nd edition, edited by Larry May, Robert Strikwerda, and Patrick D. Hopkins.
    Lanham, MD: Rowman & Littlefield, 1996.

Cudd, Ann E. "Oppression by Choice." *Journal of Social Philosophy*, 25th Anniversary Special Issue
    (1994): 22-44.

Cuomo, Chris J. "War is Not Just an Event: Reflections on the Significance of Everyday Violence."
    Hypatia, v. 11 (1996): 30-45.

Davion, Victoria. "Rape, Group Responsibility and Trust." *Hypatia*, v. 10 (1995): 153-56.

Davis, Kathy. "The Rhetoric of Cosmetic Surgery: Luxury of Welfare?" In *Enhancing Human Traits:
    Ethical and Social Implications*, edited by Erik Parens. Washington, DC: Georgetown University
    Press, 1998.

Davis, Angela Y. "Radical Perspectives on the Empowerment of Afro-American Women: Lessons for the
    1980s." *Harvard Educational Review*, v. 58, no. 3 (August 1988): 348-53.

Foley, Rebecca. "Muslim Women's Challenges to Islamic Law: The Case of Malaysia." *International
    Feminist Journal of Politics*, v. 6, no. 1 (March 2004): 53-84.

Francis, Leslie (editor). *Date Rape: Feminism, Philosophy, and the Law*. University Park, PA: Penn State
    Press, 1996.

Fraser, Nancy. "Multiculturalism and Gender Equity: The U.S. 'Difference' Debates Revisited." *Con-
    stellations*, v. 3, no. 1 (1996): 61-72.

Friedman, Marilyn. "Multicultural Education and Feminist Ethics." *Hypatia*, v. 10, no. 2 (Spring 1995):
    56-68.

Frye, Marilyn. "Sexism." In *The Politics of Reality*. Freedom, CA: Crossing Press, 1982.

Gilligan, Carol. *In a Different Voice: Psychological Theory and Women's Development*. Cambridge, MA:
    Harvard University Press, 1982.

Holmstrom, Nancy. "Do Women Have a Distinct Nature?" *Philosophical Forum (Boston)*, v. 14, no. 1 (Fall 1982): 25-42.

Jaggar, Alison. "Sexual Difference and Sexual Equality." In *Theoretical Perspectives on Sexual Difference*, edited by Deborah L. Rhode. New Haven, CT: Yale University Press,1990.

LeMoncheck, Linda. *Dehumanizing Women: Treating Persons as Sex Objects*. Lanham, MD: Rowman & Littlefield, 1985.

Li, Xiaorong. "Gender Inequality in China and Cultural Relativism." In *Women, Culture and Development: A Study of Human Capabilities*, edited by Martha Nussbaum and Jonathan Glover. Oxford: Clarendon Press, 1995.

Little, Margaret. "Cosmetic Surgery, Suspect Norms, and the Ethics of Complicity." In *Enhancing Human Traits: Ethical and Social Implications*, edited by Erik Parens. Washington, DC: Georgetown University Press, 1998.

Lucas, J.R. "Because You Are a Woman." *Philosophy*, v. 48 (1973): 161-71.

MacKinnon, Catharine. *Sexual Harassment of Working Women*. New Haven, CT: Yale University Press, 1979.

May, Larry, and Robert Strikwerda. "Men in Groups: Collective Responsibility for Rape." *Hypatia*, v. 9, no. 2 (Spring 1994): 134-51.

— . "Reply to Victoria Davion's Comments on May and Strikwerda." *Hypatia*, v. 10 (1995): 157-58.

Minow, Martha, and Mary Lyndon Shanley. "Relational Rights and Responsibilities: Revisioning the Family in Liberal Political Theory and Law." *Hypatia*, v. 11, no. 1 (Winter 1996): 4-29.

Moyo, Otrude N., and Saliwe M. Kawewe. "The Dynamics of Racialized, Gendered, Ethnicized, and Economically Stratified Society: Understanding the Socio-Economic Status of Women in Zimbabwe." *Feminist Economics*, v. 8, no. 2 (2002): 163-81.

Narayan, Uma. "Male-Order Brides: Immigrant Women, Domestic Violence and Immigration Law." *Hypatia*, v. 10, no. 1 (Winter 1995): 104-19.

Nussbaum, Martha. "Human Capabilities, Female Human Beings." In *Women, Culture and Development: A Study of Human Capabilities*, edited by Martha Nussbaum and Jonathan Glover. Oxford: Clarendon Press, 1995.

— . *Women and Human Development: The Capabilities Approach*. Cambridge: Cambridge University Press, 2000.

Nzegwu, Nkira. "Recovering Igbo Traditions: A Case for Indigenous Women's Organizations in Development." In *Women, Culture and Development: A Study of Human Capabilities*, edited by Martha Nussbaum and Jonathan Glover. Oxford: Clarendon Press, 1995.

Robeyns, Ingrid. "Sen's Capability Approach and Gender Inequality: Selecting Relevant Capabilities." *Feminist Economics*, v. 9, nos. 2-3 (2003): 61-92.

Sen, Amartya. "Gender Inequality and Theories of Justice." In *Women, Culture and Development: A Study of Human Capabilities*, edited by Martha Nussbaum and Jonathan Glover. Oxford: Clarendon Press, 1995.

Sumner, L.W. "Positive Sexism." *Social Philosophy and Policy*, v. 5, no. 1 (1987): 204-22.

Valdés, Margarita, M. "Inequality in Capabilities Between Men and Women in Mexico." In *Women, Culture and Development: A Study of Human Capabilities*, edited by Martha Nussbaum and Jonathan Glover. Oxford: Clarendon Press, 1995.

Whitbeck, Caroline. "Theories of Sex Differences." *Philosophical Forum*, v. 5 (1973): 54-80.

Williams, Joan C. "Dissolving the Sameness/Difference Debate: A Post-Modern Path Beyond Essentialism in Feminist and Critical Race Theory." *Duke Law Journal* (1991): 296-323.

CHAPTER FOUR: SEXUAL ORIENTATION

INTRODUCTION

In the final reading of the previous chapter, Janice Newberry directed our attention to a global context in which European colonization gave prominence to the model of women's proper domain in a private sphere as mother, housewife, and caretaker. This chapter connects this model to sexual orientation: the caretaker in the private sphere is a woman married to, having sexual relations with, and bearing the children of a man who is the breadwinner, public actor, and political decision-maker. Issues of sexual orientation bring to the fore the question of proper sexual relations and the values and behavior considered appropriate to the people in them. Yet, while there are similarities between discrimination on the basis of gender and of sexual orientation, there are also differences. In the diversity of views on gender in the previous chapter, there seemed to be a consensus about what makes gender a moral issue. Gender is or becomes a moral issue when the roles assigned on the basis of being male or female result in the devaluation of and inequalities in women's lives. In this chapter, we will examine similarities and differences in the inequalities and injustices associated with discrimination on the basis of sexual orientation. We shall also explore the relevance of the social construction of identities and self-identities in the context of sexuality and sexual practices.

The chapter opens with a reading by Jeffrey Jordan, who explores a set of questions he poses at the beginning of the reading. Is homosexual sex on a moral par with heterosexual sex? Is it wrong to discriminate against homosexuals by treating them in less favorable ways than one treats heterosexuals? Jordan sets out to answer these questions by outlining two sets of arguments: the "parity thesis" holds that there are no morally relevant differences between heterosexuality and homosexuality that justify a difference in treatment, and the "difference thesis" holds that there are morally relevant

differences that permit different treatment. Jordan defends the difference thesis in the case of same-sex marriage by developing an account of the moral impasse and public dilemma generated by homosexuality.

Moral impasses arise out of disputes in which there are conflicting beliefs regarding the moral status of a particular issue or act. When many people hold the conflicting views, the moral impasse can have policy implications that bring it into the public domain. Public dilemmas are moral impasses that have public policy ramifications. Jordan turns to religious views to show that a deeply entrenched position on the immorality of homosexual acts supports the difference thesis, at least for acts in the public domain such as same-sex marriage. He argues that the state should be, as far as possible, neutral with regard to the disputing parties in a public dilemma. Otherwise, the state risks forcing people to live under a government that tolerates and promotes activities that many find immoral. If the state were to sanction same-sex marriage, it would be taking sides in the impasse and sanctioning that which religion-based opponents find seriously immoral. Jordan argues that accommodation can be made by allowing homosexual activity to be personal choices in a private realm, but not by sanctioning same-sex marriage in the public realm.

In the second reading, Christine Overall can be said to challenge a premise foundational to Jordan's argument — his claim that "it is clear that heterosexual unions merit the state recognition known as marriage, along with all the attendant advantages." Overall describes heterosexuality as a pervasive characteristic of the human condition, so much a part of human relationships as to be invisible and yet appear natural and unquestionable. Heterosexuality, argues Overall, is an institution of contemporary Western cultures that embodies a set of social standards, customs, and expected practices that regulate relationships in ways that enforce heterosexuality. She then provides a feminist critique of the differential impact of the institution of heterosexuality on men and women, one that highlights the unequal power relations between men and women that are perpetuated and endorsed by heterosexuality.

Radical feminists argue that heterosexuality is enforced through social practices, religion, education, culture, and the law in ways that benefit men and present costs for women in the violence, degradation, and exploitation that it condones and in the separation of women from each other that it promotes. Overall argues, however, that this analysis raises two questions. First, if social pressure to be heterosexual is enforced and failure to conform is punished, can a woman be said to choose heterosexuality? Second, if talk about choice is meaningful here, *should* a woman choose non-heterosexuality as a way of undermining the institution of heterosexuality? Overall rejects the portrayal of women as victims of false consciousness that is implied by the argument that women do not choose heterosexuality. While the institution of heterosexuality is oppressive, not all heterosexual relationships are. By *choosing* heterosexuality, a woman can be said to be rejecting the view that male sexuality is inevitably and innately violent and exploitative and to be engaged in the project of understanding the power and limits of the heterosexual institution so as to challenge and change it.

Cheshire Calhoun is skeptical that we can arrive at an adequate understanding of discrimination on the basis of sexual orientation through an analysis of race and gender discrimination. To understand gender injustice, for example, is to understand the place of women in socioeconomic structures and practices, the disadvantages of occupying those places, and the factors that keep women in those places. Here socialization, the structure of the family, the devalued status of domestic-reproductive labor, the distinction between public and private spheres, and the normalization of violence toward women are relevant. Calhoun argues that there are substantial differences in form between

sexuality injustice and gender and racial injustice. Gay men and lesbians do not constitute a social group in the same way that women do because homosexuals are not readily distinguishable from heterosexuals, homosexuality can be deliberately concealed, and the presumption that persons are heterosexual allows homosexuals to be treated as members of the social group "heterosexuals." Gay men and lesbians evade statistical concentration because they are everywhere and are not located in the structural places of the private sphere, urban ghettoes, menial jobs, the sex industry, poverty zones, or "pink collar" jobs that racial minorities and women are. Sexual orientation does not make the kind of difference to one's material conditions that gender or race does.

Calhoun identifies the particularities of sexuality injustice through an examination of the history of laws, policies, and practices in the Western tradition that enforce and support heterosexuality and displace gays and lesbians to the outside of civil society. This displacement is central to her analysis of sexuality injustice, which is apparent in the requirement that all citizens either have a heterosexual identity or adopt a pseudonymous one as a condition of access to the public sphere. Laws may entitle individuals to be lesbian or gay in public spaces, but not to represent themselves as lesbian or gay in the public sphere. Policies intervene in restricting gay and lesbian parenting, employment in child care, and participation in early education and child service organizations. Cultural images and perceptions that mark homosexual activity as immoral and gay men and lesbians as criminals perpetuate stereotypes of them as untrustworthy and deny them equal standing to participate in legal, social, and moral debates about the place of gay and lesbian identity in the public and private spheres. All of these factors maintain the displacement of gay men and lesbians to the outside of civil society and comprise sexuality injustice.

Calhoun does not advocate strategies or recommend policies for alleviating the injustice experienced by gay men and lesbians, but her analysis of displacement implies policies of inclusion in civil society. In the reading that follows, Claudia Card raises questions about whether equal rights strategies in liberal societies in areas such as same-sex marriage are appropriate or adequate for addressing sexuality injustice. She argues that those who identify as lesbian or gay should be reluctant to campaign for legal equality with heterosexuals in marriage and in parenting because these institutions are deeply flawed as they currently exist and should be neither emulated nor reproduced. Card is not opposed to long-term relationships or to forming bonds between adults and children or to guiding, educating, and caring for children, but she wonders if the interests and needs of people in these important relationships are best met by the institutions of marriage and motherhood.

Benefits such as affordable health and dental insurance, social securities, inheritance and visitation rights, and workers' compensation pressure people into marrying. The financial burdens of divorce and the lack of state protection against violent spouses act as disincentives for leaving bad marriages. While marriage may seem to provide an important environment for rearing children, the model of parenting evident in laws that grant the status of parent to only two persons at a time is not the only or best model and is being challenged by gay and lesbian parenting and by communities where there is collective responsibility for childrearing and many people have roles as caretakers for many children. Every society, argues Card, would benefit from attending to the experiences of children, the relationships of children to adults, and the conditions under which children grow into adulthood. Such attentiveness should undermine the model of mothers as primary caretakers and the institution of marriage within which mothering takes place. Like other feminist and lesbian theorists, Card advances the notion that gay men and lesbians have relationships and live lives that not only challenge a status quo of heterosexuality, but present new ways of being with others and of caring for others.

In the final reading, Bruce Dunne has us consider the specificity of conceptions of sexual relations in North America by explaining how homosexuality is and has been understood and practiced in the Middle East. Historically, sexual relations in Middle Eastern societies have been about social hierarchies of dominant and subordinate social positions: adult men on top and women, boys, and slaves below. For men in positions of power, to have sexual relations is to have them with those in subordinate positions. Dunne argues that the distinction between sexuality and gender identity made in modern Western understandings of "sexuality" — between *kinds* of sexual predilections and *degrees* of masculinity and femininity — has had, until quite recently, little resonance in the Middle East. Relationships of dominant/subordinate and heterosexual/homosexual reflect structures of power and position social actors as powerful or powerless, "normal" or "deviant." Dunne ends by claiming that the concept of "queerness," evident in contemporary practices in the Middle East, plays on the contradictions in the traditional understandings of homosexuality there by recognizing and displaying the complex realities of multiple and shifting positions of sexuality, identity, and power.

"IS IT WRONG TO DISCRIMINATE ON THE BASIS OF HOMOSEXUALITY?"

Jeffrey Jordan

Jeffrey Jordan teaches philosophy at the University of Delaware, Newark, Delaware. He specializes in metaphysics and the philosophy of religion and has interests in the area of individual rights.

Jordan argues that there is a moral impasse in the U.S. about whether it is wrong to discriminate against homosexuals. He defends the principle that the state ought to be neutral as far as possible about moral impasses that constitute public dilemmas and uses this principle to justify discriminating against homosexuals in certain public matters such as marriage. He argues that state sanctioning of same-sex marriage is not a neutral policy for those who have religious objections to homosexuality. Jordan leaves open the possibility that discriminating against homosexuals in contexts that affect private matters is not justified.

Much like the issue of abortion in the early 1970s, the issue of homosexuality has exploded to the forefront of social discussion. Is homosexual sex on a moral par with heterosexual sex? Or is homosexuality in some way morally inferior? Is it wrong to discriminate against homosexuals — to treat homosexuals in less favorable ways than one does heterosexuals? Or is some discrimination against homosexuals morally justified? These questions are the focus of this essay.

In what follows, I argue that there are situations in which it is morally permissible to discriminate against homosexuals because of their homosexuality. That is, there are some morally relevant differences between heterosexuality and homosexuality which, in some instances, permit a difference in treatment. The issue of marriage provides a good example. While it is clear that heterosexual unions merit the state recognition known as marriage, along with all the attendant advantages — spousal insurance coverage, inheritance rights, ready eligibility of adoption — it is far from clear that homosexual couples ought to be accorded that state recognition.

The argument of this essay makes no claim about the moral status of homosexuality per se.

Briefly put, it is the argument of this essay that the moral impasse generated by conflicting views concerning homosexuality, and the public policy ramifications of those conflicting views justify the claim that it is morally permissible, in certain circumstances, to discriminate against homosexuals.[1]

1. The Issue

The relevant issue is this: does homosexuality have the same moral status as heterosexuality? Put differently, since there are no occasions in which it is morally permissible to treat heterosexuals unfavorably, whether because they are heterosexual or because of heterosexual acts, are there occasions in which it is morally permissible to treat homosexuals unfavorably, whether because they are homosexuals or because of homosexual acts?

A negative answer to the above can be termed the "parity theses." The parity thesis contends that homosexuality has the same moral status as heterosexuality. If the parity thesis is correct, then it would be immoral to discriminate against homosexuals because of their homosexuality. An affirmative answer can be termed the "difference thesis" and contends that there are morally relevant differences between heterosexuality and homosexuality which justify a difference in moral status and treatment between homosexuals and heterosexuals. The difference thesis entails that there are situations in which it is morally permissible to discriminate against homosexuals.

It is perhaps needless to point out that the difference thesis follows as long as there is at least one occasion in which it is morally permissible to discriminate against homosexuals. If the parity thesis were true, then on no occasion would a difference in treatment between heterosexuals and homosexuals ever be justified. The difference thesis does not, even if true, justify discriminatory actions on every occasion. Nonetheless, even thought the scope of the difference thesis is relatively modest, it is, if true, a significant principle which has not only theoretical import but important practical consequences as well.[2]

A word should be said about the notion of discrimination. To discriminate against X means treating X in an unfavorable way. The word "discrimination" is not a synonym for "morally unjustifiable treatment." Some discrimination is morally unjustifiable; some is not. For example, we discriminate against convicted felons in that they are disenfranchised. This legal discrimination is morally permissible even though it involves treating one person unfavorably different from how other persons are treated. The difference thesis entails that there are circumstances in which it is morally permissible to discriminate against homosexuals.

2. An Argument for the Parity Thesis

One might suppose that an appeal to a moral right, the right to privacy, perhaps, or the right to liberty, would provide the strongest grounds for the parity thesis. Rights talk, though sometimes helpful, is not very helpful here. If there is reason to think that the right to privacy or the right to liberty encompasses sexuality (which seems plausible enough), it would do so only with regard to private acts and not public acts. Sexual acts performed in public (whether heterosexual or homo-

sexual) are properly suppressible. It does not take too much imagination to see that the right to be free from offense would soon be offered as a counter consideration by those who find homosexuality morally problematic. Furthermore, how one adjudicates between the competing rights claims is far from clear. Hence, the bald appeal to a right will not, in this case anyway, take one very far.

Perhaps the strongest reason to hold that the parity thesis is true is something like the following:

1. Homosexual acts between consenting adults harm no one. And,
2. respecting persons' privacy and choices in harmless sexual matters maximizes individual freedom. And,
3. individual freedom should be maximized. But,
4. discrimination against homosexuals, because of their homosexuality, diminishes individual freedom since it ignores personal choice and privacy. So,
5. the toleration of homosexuality rather than discriminating against homosexuals is the preferable option since it would maximize individual freedom. Therefore,
6. the parity thesis is more plausible than the difference thesis.

Premise (2) is unimpeachable: if an act is harmless and if there are persons who want to do it and who choose to do it, then it seems clear that respecting the choices of those people would tend to maximize their freedom.[3] Step (3) is also beyond reproach: since freedom is arguably a great good and since there does not appear to be any ceiling on the amount of individual freedom — no "too much of a good thing" — (3) appears to be true.

At first glance, premise (1) seems true enough as long as we recognize that if there is any harm involved in the homosexual acts of consenting adults, it would be harm absorbed by the freely consenting participants. This is true, however, only if the acts in question are done in private. Public acts may involve more than just the willing participants. Persons who have no desire to participate, even if only as spectators, may have no choice if the acts are done in public. A real probability of there being unwilling participants is indicative of the public realm and not the private. However, where one draws the line between private acts and public acts is not always easy to discern; it is clear that different moral standards apply to public acts than to private acts.[4]

If premise (1) is understood to apply only to acts done in private, then it would appear to be true. The same goes for (4): discrimination against homosexuals for acts done in private would result in a diminishing of freedom. So (1)-(4) would lend support to (5) only if we understand (1)-(4) to refer to acts done in private. Hence, (5) must be understood as referring to private acts; and, as a consequence, (6) also must be read as referring only to acts done in private.

With regard to acts which involve only willing adult participants, there may be no morally relevant difference between homosexuality and heterosexuality. In other words, acts done in private. However, acts done in public add a new ingredient to the mix; an ingredient which has moral consequence. Consequently, the argument (1)-(6) fails in supporting the parity thesis. The argument (1)-(6) may show that there are some circumstances in which the moral status of homosexuality and heterosexuality are the same, but it gives us no reason for thinking that this result holds for all circumstances.[5]

3. Moral Impasses and Public Dilemmas

Suppose one person believes that X is morally wrong, whole another believes that X is morally permissible. The two people, let's stipulate, are not involved in a semantic quibble; they hold genuinely conflicting beliefs regarding the moral status of X. If the first person is correct, then the second person is wrong; and, of course, if the second person is right, then the first must be wrong. This situation of conflicting claims is what we will call an "impasse." Impasses arise out of moral disputes. Since the conflicting parties in an impasse take contrary views, the conflicting views cannot all be true, nor can they all be false.[6] Moral

impasses may concern matters only of a personal nature, but moral impasses can involve public policy. An impasse is likely to have public policy ramifications if large numbers of people hold the conflicting views, and the conflict involves matters which are fundamental to a person's moral identity (and, hence, from a practical point of view, are probably irresolvable) and it involves acts done in public. Since not every impasse has public policy ramifications, one can mark off "public dilemma" as a special case of moral impasses: those moral impasses that have public policy consequences. Public dilemmas, then, are impasses located in the public square. Since they have public policy ramifications and since they arise from impasses, one side or another of the dispute will have its views implemented as public policy. Because of the public policy ramifications, and also because social order is sometimes threatened by the volatile parties involved in the impasse, the state has a role to play in resolving a public dilemma.

A public dilemma can be actively resolved in two ways.[7] The first is when the government allies itself with one side of the impasse and, by state coercion and sanction, declares that side of the impasse the correct side. The American Civil War was an example of this: the federal government forcibly ended slavery by aligning itself with the Abolitionist side of the impasse.[8] Prohibition is another example. The Eighteenth Amendment and the Volstead Act allied the state with the Temperance side of the impasse. State mandated affirmative action programs provide a modern example of this. This kind of resolution of a public dilemma we can call a "resolution by declaration." The first of the examples cited above indicates that declarations can be morally proper, the right thing to do. The second example, however, indicates that declarations are not always morally proper. The state does not always take the side of the morally correct; nor is it always clear which side is the correct one.

The second way of actively resolving a public dilemma is that of accommodation. An accommodation in this context means resolving the public dilemma in a way that gives as much as possible to all sides of the impasse. A resolution by accommodation involves staking out some middle ground in a dispute and placing public policy in that location. The middle ground location of a resolution via accommodation is a virtue since it entails that there are no absolute victors and no absolute losers. The middle ground is reached in order to resolve the public dilemma in a way which respects the relevant views of the conflicting parties and which maintains social order. The Federal Fair Housing Act and, perhaps, the current status of abortion (legal but with restrictions) provide examples of actual resolutions via accommodation.[9]

In general, governments should be, at least as far as possible, neutral with regard to the disputing parties in a public dilemma. Unless there is some overriding reason why the state should take sides in a public dilemma — the protection of innocent life, or abolishing slavery, for instance — the state should be neutral, because no matter which side of the public dilemma the state takes, the other side will be the recipient of unequal treatment by the state. A state which is partial and takes sides in moral disputes via declaration, when there is no overriding reason why it should, is tyrannical. Overriding reasons involve, typically, the protection of generally recognized rights.[10] In the case of slavery, the right to liberty; in the case of protecting innocent life, the right involved is the negative right to life. If a public dilemma must be actively resolved, the state should do so (in the absence of an overriding reason) via accommodation and not declaration since the latter entails that a sizable number of people would be forced to live under a government which "legitimizes" and does not just tolerate activities which they find immoral. Resolution via declaration is appropriate only if there is an overriding reason for the state to throw its weight behind one side in a public dilemma.

Is moral rightness an overriding reason for a resolution via declaration? What better reason might there be for a resolution by declaration than that it is the right thing to do? Unless one is prepared to endorse a view that is called "legal moralism" — that immorality alone is a sufficient reason for the state to curtail individual liberty — then one had best hold that moral rightness alone is not an overriding reason. Since some immoral acts neither harm nor offend nor violate another's rights, it seems clear enough that too much liberty would be lost if legal moralism were adopted as public policy.[11]

Though we do not have a definite rule for determining a priori which moral impasses genuinely constitute public dilemmas, we can proceed via a case by case method. For example, many people hold that cigarette smoking is harmful and, on that basis, is properly suppressible. Others disagree. Is this a public dilemma? Probably not. Whether someone engages in an imprudent action is, as long as it involves no unwilling participants, a private matter and does not, on that account, constitute a public dilemma.[12] What about abortion? Is abortion a public dilemma? Unlike cigarette smoking, abortion is a public dilemma. This is clear from the adamant and even violent contrary positions involved in the impasse. Abortion is an issue which forces itself into the public square. So, it is clear that, even thought we lack a rule which filters through moral impasses designating some as public dilemmas, not every impasse constitutes a public dilemma.

4. Conflicting Claims on Homosexuality

The theistic tradition, Judaism and Christianity and Islam, has a clear and deeply entrenched position on homosexual acts: they are prohibited. Now it seems clear enough that if one is going to take seriously the authoritative texts of the respective religions, then one will have to adopt the views of those texts, unless one wishes to engage in a demythologizing of them with the result that one ends up being only a nominal adherent of that tradition.[13] As a consequence, many contemporary theistic adherents of the theistic tradition, in no small part because they can read, hold that homosexual behavior is sinful. Though God loves the homosexual, these folk say, God hates the sinful behavior. To say that act X is a sin entails that X is morally wrong, not necessarily because it is harmful or offensive, but because X violates God's will. So, the claim that homosexuality is sinful entails the claim that it is also morally wrong. And, it is clear, many people adopt the difference thesis just because of their religious views: because the

Bible or the Koran holds that homosexuality is wrong, they too hold that view.

Well, what should we make of these observations? We do not, for one thing, have to base our moral conclusions on those views, if for no other reason than not everyone is a theist. If one does not adopt the religion-based moral view, one must still respect those who do; they cannot just be dismissed out of hand.[14] And, significantly, this situation yields a reason for thinking that the difference thesis is probably true. Because many religious people sincerely believe homosexual acts to be morally wrong and many others believe that homosexual acts are not morally wrong, there results a public dilemma.[15]

The existence of this public dilemma gives us reason for thinking that the difference thesis is true. It is only via the difference thesis and not the parity thesis, that an accommodation can be reached. Here again, the private/public distinction will come into play.

To see this, take as an example the issue of homosexual marriages. A same-sex marriage would be a public matter. For the government to sanction same-sex marriage to grant the recognition and reciprocal benefits which attach to marriage would ally the government with one side of the public dilemma and against the adherents of religion-based moralities. This is especially true given that, historically, no government has sanctioned same-sex marriages. The status quo has been no same-sex marriages. If the state were to change its practice now, it would be clear that the state has taken sides in the impasse. Given the history, for a state to sanction a same-sex marriage now would not be a neutral act.

Of course, some would respond here that by not sanctioning same-sex marriages the state is, and historically has been, taking sides to the detriment of homosexuals. There is some truth in this claim. But one must be careful here. The respective resolutions of this issue whether the state should recognize and sanction same-sex marriages do not have symmetrical implications. The asymmetry of this issue is a function of the private/public distinction and the fact that marriage is a public matter. If the state sanctions

same-sex marriages, then there is no accommodation available. In that event, the religion-based morality proponents are faced with a public, state-sanctioned matter which they find seriously immoral. This would be an example of a resolution via declaration. On the other hand, if the state does not sanction same-sex marriages, there is an accommodation available: in the public realm the state sides with the religion-based moral view, but the state can tolerate private homosexual acts. That is, since homosexual acts are not essentially public acts; they can be, and historically have been, performed in private. The state, by not sanctioning same-sex marriages is acting in the public realm, but it can leave the private realm to personal choice.[16]

5. The Argument from Conflicting Claims

It was suggested in the previous section that the public dilemma concerning homosexuality, and in particular whether states would sanction same-sex marriages, generates an argument in support of the difference thesis. The argument, again using same-sex marriages as the particular case, is as follows:

7. There are conflicting claims regarding whether the state should sanction same-sex marriages. And,
8. this controversy constitutes a public dilemma. And,
9. there is an accommodation possible if the state does not recognize same-sex marriages. And,
10. there is no accommodation possible if the state does sanction same-sex marriages. And,
11. there is no overriding reason for a resolution via declaration. Hence,
12. the state ought not sanction same-sex marriages. And,
13. the state ought to sanction heterosexual marriages. So,
14. there is at least one morally relevant case in which discrimination against homosexuals, because of their homosexuality, is morally permissible. Therefore,
15. the difference thesis is true.

Since proposition (14) is logically equivalent to the difference thesis, then, if (7)-(14) are sound, proposition (15) certainly follows.

Premises (7) and (8) are uncontroversial. Premises (9) and (10) are based on the asymmetry that results from the public nature of marriage. Proposition (11) is based on our earlier analysis of the argument (1)-(6). Since the strongest argument in support of the parity thesis fails, we have reason to think that there is no overriding reason why the state ought to resolve the public dilemma via declaration in favor of same-sex marriages. We have reason, in other words, to think that (11) is true.

Proposition (12) is based on the conjunction of (7)-(11) and the principle that, in the absence of an overriding reason for state intervention via declaration, resolution by accommodation is the preferable route. Proposition (13) is just trivially true. So, given the moral difference mentioned in (12) and (13), proposition (14) logically follows.

6. Two Objections Considered

The first objection to the argument from conflicting claims would contend that it is unsound because a similar sort of argument would permit discrimination against some practice which, though perhaps controversial at some earlier time, is now widely thought to be morally permissible. Take mixed-raced marriages, for example. The opponent of the argument from conflicting claims could argue that a similar argument would warrant prohibition against mixed-race marriages. If it does, we would have good reason to reject (7)-(14) as unsound.

There are three responses to this objection. The first response denies that the issue of mixed-race marriages is in fact a public dilemma. It may have been so at one time, but it does not seem to generate much, if any, controversy today. Hence, the objection is based upon a faulty analogy.

The second response grants for the sake of the argument that the issue of mixed-race marriages generates a public dilemma. But the second response points out that there is a relevant difference between mixed-race marriages and same-sex marriages that allows for a resolution by declara-

tion in the one case but not the other. As evident from the earlier analysis of the argument in support of (1)-(6), there is reason to think that there is no overriding reason for a resolution by declaration is support of the parity thesis. On the other hand, it is a settled matter that state protection from racial discrimination is a reason sufficient for a resolution via declaration. Hence, the two cases are only apparently similar, and, in reality, they are crucially different. They are quite different because, clearly enough, if mixed-race marriages do generate a public dilemma, the state should use resolution by declaration in support of such marriages. The same cannot be said for same-sex marriages.

One should note that the second response to the objection does not beg the question against the proponent of the parity thesis. Though the second response denies that race and sexuality are strict analogues, it does so for a defensible and independent reason: it is a settled matter that race is not a sufficient reason of disparate treatment; but, as we have seen from the analysis of (1)-(6), there is no overriding reason to think the same about sexuality.[17]

The third response to the first objection is that the grounds of objection differ in the respective cases: one concerns racial identity; the other concerns behavior thought to be morally problematic. A same-sex marriage would involve behavior which many people find morally objectionable; a mixed-race marriage is objectionable to some, not because of the participants' behavior, but because of the racial identity of the participants. It is the race of the marriage partners which some find of primary complaint concerning mixed-race marriage. With same-sex marriage, however, it is the behavior which is primarily objectionable. To see this latter point, one should note that, though promiscuously Puritan in tone, the kind of sexual acts that are likely involved in a same-sex marriage are objectionable to some, regardless of whether done by homosexuals or heterosexuals.[18] So again, there is reason to reject the analogy between same-sex marriages and mixed-race marriages. Racial identity is an immutable trait and a complaint about mixed-race marriages necessarily involves, then, a complaint about an immutable trait. Sexual behavior is not an immutable trait and it is possible to object to object to same-sex marriages based on the behavior which would be involved in such marriages. Put succinctly, the third response could be formulated as follows; objections to mixed-race marriages necessarily involve objections over status, while objections to same-sex marriages could involve objections over behavior. Therefore, the two cases are not strict analogues since there is a significant modal difference in the ground of the objection.

The second objection to the argument from conflicting claims can be stated so: if homosexuality is biologically based — if it is inborn[19] — then how can discrimination ever be justified? If it is not a matter of choice, homosexuality is an immutable trait which is, as a consequence, morally permissible. Just as it would be absurd to hold someone morally culpable for being of a certain race, likewise it would be absurd to hold someone morally culpable for being a homosexual. Consequently, according to this objection, the argument from conflicting claims "legitimizes" unjustifiable discrimination.

But this second objection is not cogent, primarily because it ignores an important distinction. No one could plausibly hold that homosexuals act by some sort of biological compulsion. If there is a biological component involved in sexual identity, it would incline but it would not compel. Just because one naturally (without any choice) has certain dispositions, is not in itself a morally cogent reason for acting upon that disposition. Most people are naturally selfish, but it clearly does not follow that selfishness is in any way permissible on that account. Even if it is true that one has a predisposition to do X as a matter of biology and not as a matter of choice, it does not follow that doing X is morally permissible. For example, suppose that pyromania is an inborn predisposition. Just because one has an inborn and, in that sense, natural desire to set fires, one still has to decide whether or not to act on that desire.[20] The reason that the appeal to biology is specious is that it ignores the important distinction between being a homosexual and homosexual acts. One is status; the other is behavior. Even if one has the status

naturally, it does not follow that the behavior is morally permissible, nor that others have a duty to tolerate the behavior.[21]

But, whole moral permissibility does not necessarily follow if homosexuality should turn out to be biologically based, what does follow is this: in the absence of a good reason to discriminate between homosexuals and heterosexuals, then, assuming that homosexuality is inborn, one ought not discriminate between them. If a certain phenomenon X is natural in the sense of being involuntary and nonpathological, and if there is no good reason to hold that X is morally problematic, then that is reason enough to think that X is morally permissible. In the absence of a good reason to repress X, one should tolerate it since, as per supposition, it is involuntary. The argument from conflicting claims, however, provides a good reason which overrides this presumption.

7. A Second Argument for the Difference Thesis

A second argument of the difference thesis, similar to the argument from conflicting claims, is what might be called the "no-exit argument." This argument is based on the principle that:

A. no just government can coerce a citizen into violating a deeply held moral belief or religious belief.

Is (A) plausible? It seems to be since the prospect of a citizen being coerced by the state into a practice which she finds profoundly immoral appears to be a clear example of an injustice. Principle (A), conjoined with there being a public dilemma arising over the issue of same-sex marriages, leads to the observation that if the state were to sanction same-sex marriages, then persons who have profound religious or moral objections to such unions would be legally mandated to violate their beliefs since there does not appear to be any feasible "exit right" possible with regard to state sanctioned marriage. An exit right is an exemption from some legally mandated practice, granted to a person or group, the purpose of which is to protect the religious or moral integrity of that person or group. Prominent examples of exit rights include conscientious objection and military service, home-schooling of the young because of some religious concern, and property used for religious purposes being free from taxation.

It is important to note that marriage is a public matter in the sense that, for instance, of one is an employer who provides health care benefits to the spouses of employees, one must provide those benefits to any employee who is married. Since there is not exit right possible in this case, one would be coerced, by force of law, into subsidizing a practice one finds morally or religiously objectionable.[22]

In the absence of an exit right, and if (A) is plausible, then the state cannot morally force persons to violate deeply held beliefs that are moral or religious in nature. In particular, the state morally could not sanction same-sex marriages since this would result in coercing some into violating a deeply held religious conviction.

8. A Conclusion

It is important to note that neither the argument from conflicting claims nor the no-exit argument licenses wholesale discrimination against homosexuals. What they do show is that some discrimination against homosexuals, in this case the refusal to sanction same-sex marriages, is not only legally permissible but also morally permissible. The discrimination is a way of resolving a public policy dilemma that accommodates, to an extent, each side of the impasse and, further, protects the religious and moral integrity of a good number of people. In short, the arguments show us that there are occasions in which it is morally permissible to discriminate on the basis of homosexuality.[23]

NOTES

1. The terms "homosexuality" and "heterosexuality" are defined as follows. The former is defined as sexual feelings or behavior directed toward individuals of the same sex. The latter, naturally enough, is defined as sexual feelings or behavior directed toward individuals of the opposite sex.

Sometimes the term "gay" is offered as an alternative to "homosexual." Ordinary use of "gay" has it as a synonym of a male homosexual (hence, the common expression, "gays and lesbians"). Given this ordinary usage, the substitution would lead to a confusing equivocation. Since there are female homosexuals, it is best to use "homosexual" to refer to both male and female homosexuals and reserve "gay" to signify male homosexuals, and "lesbian" for female homosexuals in order to avoid the equivocation.

2. Perhaps we should distinguish the weak difference thesis (permissible discrimination on some occasions) from the strong difference thesis (given the relevant moral differences, discrimination on any occasion is permissible).

3. This would be true even if the act in question is immoral.

4. The standard answer is, of course, that the line between public and private is based on the notion of harm. Acts which carry a real probability of harming third parties are public acts.

5. For other arguments supporting the moral parity of homosexuality and heterosexuality, see Richard Mohr *Gays/Justice: A Study of Ethics, Society and Law* (NY: Columbia, 1988); and see Michael Ruse, "The Morality of Homosexuality" in *Philosophy and Sex*, eds. R. Baker and F. Elliston (Buffalo, NY: Prometheus Books, 1984), pp. 370-390.

6. Perhaps it would be better to term the disputing positions "contradictory" views rather than "contrary" views.

7. Resolutions can also be passive in the sense of the state doing nothing. If the state does nothing to resolve the public dilemma, it stands pat with the status quo, and the public dilemma is resolved gradually by sociological changes (changes in mores and in beliefs).

8. Assuming, plausibly enough, that the disputes over the sovereignty of the Union and concerning states' rights were at bottom disputes about slavery.

9. The Federal Fair Housing Act prohibits discrimination in housing on the basis of race, religion, and sex. But it does not apply to the rental of rooms in single-family houses, or to a building of five units or less if the owner lives in one of the units. See 42 U.S.C. Section 3603.

10. Note that overriding reasons involve generally recognized rights. If a right is not widely recognized and the state nonetheless uses coercion to enforce it, there is a considerable risk that the state will be seen by many or even most people as tyrannical.

11. This claim is, perhaps, controversial. For a contrary view see Richard George, *Making Men Moral* (Oxford: Clarendon Press, 1993).

12. This claim holds only for smoking which does not affect other persons — smoking done in private. Smoking which affects others, second-hand smoke, is a different matter, of course, and may well constitute a public dilemma.

13. See, for example, Leviticus 18:22, 21:3; and Romans 1:22-32; and Koran IV:13.

14. For an argument that religiously-based moral views should not be dismissed out of hand, see Stephen Carter, *The Culture of Disbelief: How American Law and Politics Trivialize Religious Devotion* (NY: Basic Books, 1993).

15. Two assumptions are these: that the prohibitions against homosexuality activity are part of the religious doctrine and not just an extraneous addition; second, that if X is part of one's religious belief or religious doctrine, then it is morally permissible to hold X. Though this latter principle is vague, it is, I think, clear enough for our purposes here (I ignore here any points concerning the rationality of religious belief in general, or in particular cases).

16. This point has implications for the moral legitimacy of sodomy laws. One implication would be this: the private acts of consenting adults should not be criminalized.

17. An *ad hominem* point: If this response begs the question against the proponent of the parity thesis, it does not beg the question any more than the original objection does by presupposing that sexuality is analogous with race.

18. Think of the sodomy laws found in some states which criminalize certain sexual acts, whether performed by heterosexuals or homosexuals.

19. There is some interesting recent research which, though still tentative, strongly suggests that homosexuality is, at least in part, biologically based. See Simon LeVay, *The Sexual Brain* (Cambridge, MA: MIT Press, 1993), pp. 120-122; and J.M. Bailey and R.C. Pillard. "A Genetic Study of Male Sexual Orientation," *Archives of General Psychiatry* 48 (1991) 1089-1096; and C. Burr, "Homosexuality and Biology," *The Atlantic* 271/3 (March 1993) 64; and D. Hamer, S. Hy, V. Magnuson, N. Hu, A. Pattatucci, "A Linkage Between DNA Markers on the X Chromosome and Male Sexual Orientation," *Science* 261 (16 July 1993) 321-327; and see the summary of this article by Robert Pool, "Evidence for Homosexuality Gene," *Science* 261 (16 July 1993) 291-292.

20. I do not mean to suggest that homosexuality is morally equivalent or even comparable to pyromania.

21. Even if one were biologically or innately impelled to do X, it clearly does not follow that one is thereby impelled to do X *in public*. Again, the public/private distinction is morally relevant.

22. Is the use of subsidy here inappropriate? It does not seem so since providing health care to spouses, in a society where this is not legally mandatory, seems to be more than part of a salary and is a case of providing supporting funds for a certain end.

23. I thank David Haslett, Kate Rogers, Louis Pojman, and Jim Fieser for helpful and critical comments.

HETEROSEXUALITY AND FEMINIST THEORY

Christine Overall

Christine Overall is Professor of Philosophy and Associate Dean, Faculty of Arts and Science, at Queen's University, Kingston. She is the author of a number of books including Aging, Death, and Human Longevity: A Philosophical Inquiry *(2003),* Thinking Like a Woman: Personal Life and Political Ideas *(2001),* A Feminist I: Reflections From Academia *(1998), and* Human Reproduction: Principles, Practices, Policies *(1991). She also writes a weekly feminist column, "In Other Words," for the* Kingston Whig-Standard.

Overall examines the phenomenon of heterosexuality as an institution of contemporary Western culture, one that reflects the systematized set of social standards, customs, and expected practices that both regulate and restrict romantic and sexual relationships between men and women. She argues that the tremendous social pressure toward heterosexuality has differential impacts on men and women in the areas of benefits, reproduction, law, education, and levels of violence. Overall raises questions about the possibility of a feminist heterosexuality and uses the notion of a continuum to argue that feminists can choose to be heterosexual and at the same time undermine the institution of heterosexuality by being aware of its effects and working to change its oppressive nature for women.

Heterosexuality, which I define as a romantic and sexual orientation toward persons not of one's own sex, is apparently a very general, though not entirely universal, characteristic of the human condition. In fact, it is so ubiquitous a part of human interactions and relations as to be almost invisible, and so natural-seeming as to appear unquestionable, indeed, the 1970 editions of *The Shorter Oxford English Dictionary* defines "heterosexual" as "pertaining to or characterized by the *normal* relation of the sexes."[1]

In this respect heterosexuality is strikingly different from the romantic and sexual orientation toward persons of one's own sex, or what I shall call, for the sake of brevity, non-heterosexuality.[2] I caution that the use of the term "non-heterosexuality" could be misleading, since it falsely suggests a uniformity among other sexual orientations comparable to that of heterosexuality. There are many significant differences among lesbianism, male homosexuality, and both male and female bisexuality. But what I am concerned with is not those differences, significant and far-ranging as they are, but rather the general contrast they collectively provide to heterosexuality.

Historically, for example, there has been a tendency to investigate the causes of forms of non-heterosexuality, but not of heterosexuality; to consider whether non-heterosexuality, but not heterosexuality, can be spread through as sort of contagion effect;[3] to ask whether non-heterosexuality is unnatural, but not to contemplate whether heterosexuality in any sense could be. If we make any assumption about a person's sexual orientation, it is almost always the assumption that the person is heterosexual. Ordinarily most parents seldom wonder whether their offspring will grow up to be heterosexual, and, compared to the ubiquitous depictions of heterosexual relations, there are very few widely available cultural images of non-heterosexuality. If one is not heterosexual, one may have the choice to pass as heterosexual; one may, that is, attempt for purposes of self-protection to assimilate into the dominant culture. But except within the context of the very specific non-heterosexual culture, we would not usually speak of someone as passing as non-heterosexual. To be a sexual being, in our culture, is just to be heterosexual. Moreover, heterosexual expression is defined as *real* sex by reference to which all other sexual stages and activities — e.g., "virginity," "foreplay," etc. — are defined.

This is, then, the first of what I shall refer to as the paradoxes of heterosexuality: As an expected, supposedly normal characteristic of adult and even pre-adult life, it is so pervasive that it melts into our individual lives; its invisibility as a social condition makes it seem to be just a matter of what is personal private, and inevitable. Heterosexuality is simultaneously the only "real" form of sexuality, and yet (for that very reason) very difficult to perceive. Heterosexuality is transparent, in the way that a piece of plastic wrap is transparent. Yet, like plastic wrap, it has the ability to hold things in place, to keep things down, and to provide a barrier to prevent other things from coming in contact with that which it seems to be protecting.

I The Institution of Heterosexuality

It is this transparent, virtually invisible, yet very powerful condition that I wish to subject to examination. But I am not primarily concerned with *individual* heterosexual relationships: who loves whom, who is attracted to or turned on by whom, or who does what to whom. Although, of course, what happens in those individual heterosexual relationships is not at all irrelevant to the understanding of heterosexuality, nevertheless it is not individual practices in and of themselves which interest me here. Instead, it is heterosexuality as an *institution* of contemporary western culture which is the focus of my examination. Although this institution is not the only cultural influence upon human sexuality, it is one of the most significant. By the institution of heterosexuality, or what I shall call for short the heterosexual institution, what I mean is the systematized set of social standards, customs, and expected practices which both regu-

late and restrict romantic and sexual relationships between persons of different sexes in late twentieth-century western culture.

The heterosexual institution by definition involves both men and women. But, given the constraints imposed by patriarchal society, in which oppression for the fact of being female is often both accepted and promoted, it cannot be expected that the heterosexual institution will say and do the same things to women as it does to men, or that it will be experienced in the same way by women and by men. As Marilyn Frye points out, "institutions *are* humanly designed patterns of access — access to persons and their services."[4] It is important to be aware of the ways in which access is patterned differently for women and for men. As a feminist, what I therefore want to discuss is the reality of the heterosexual institution *for women:* that is, its effects on women, its meanings for women, what it says to and about women. I shall first describe some main features of the heterosexual institution, and then turn to a discussion of the place of heterosexuality in women's lives and its interpretation by feminist theory. I cannot accomplish any of this without saying a fair amount about men, but I think that an examination of the heterosexual institution as it is experienced by men would be an endeavour quite different from this one.[5]

In referring to heterosexuality as an institution, I am rejecting an essentialist or reified view of sexual orientations. Human sexuality is culturally constructed, that is, it is "a social, not [only] a biological phenomenon."[6] There is no reason to suppose that sexual activity and expression are more immune to the effects of enculturation than are other apparently "natural" human activities such as caring for children, or eating. Of course, the fact that sexuality is culturally constructed does not entirely preclude the possibility that some form of sexual expression is innate or "natural," or that we have "biological inclinations" toward some form of sexual activity. But it does imply both that the evidence for such a natural sexuality will be virtually impossible to detect, and that the stronger hypothesis is that there is no such natural sexuality. One cannot even refer to primordial feelings or irresistible passions as natural, since enculturation processes, including the heterosexuality institution, help to define what feelings we do and do not, or ought and ought not to have.

I shall therefore assume that there is no "fixed sexual, 'essence' or 'nature' that lies buried beneath layers of social ordering"[7] in any of us. In particular, I deny that most human beings are "naturally" or innately heterosexual; if sexual desire and activity are socially constructed, then one sort of orientation is no more natural, innate, or inevitable than another. Nor do I make the somewhat more fashionable (these days) assumption that human beings are "naturally" bisexual. Bisexual is no more what we *really* are than is heterosexual.[8] In other words, if the heterosexual institution somehow did not exist, I see no more (and no less) reason to suppose that individuals would therefore be romantically and sexually oriented to persons of both sexes than to suppose that individuals would be romantically and sexually oriented to persons of only one sex or the other. Neither of these seems to be more natural or inevitable than the other. In fact, the only useful interpretation of the claim some have made that we are "really" bisexual is just that we all have the physical capacity for sexual interactions with members of both sexes. And no one would dispute that, for the reason that it is not a very interesting or controversial claim; and it certainly tells us nothing whatsoever about a person's "real" or "natural" sexual orientation.

But, for the purposes of this paper, nothing much depends upon the assertion that no sexual orientation is innate. For, whatever our inherent proclivities may or may not be, there is undeniably tremendous social pressure toward heterosexuality. This pressure is a part of the heterosexual institution. Indeed, I wonder why, if heterosexuality is innate, there are so many social voices telling us, ad nauseam, that is what we should be. These voices include the ideology that surrounds heterosexual romance, "dating," and marriage; the mythology of falling in (and out of) heterosexual love, of flings, crushes, affairs, passions, and helpless attractions; the cultural apparatus that purports to assist women to be heterosexually attractive, to

be coy, alluring, "sexy," and flirtatious, in order to "find true love" or to "catch a man," and then to maintain his interest once he's caught; the psychotherapies and medical treatments, together with literature ranging from self-help manuals to scholarly treatises, that claim to prescribe the nature and forms of and adjustment to healthy female heterosexuality and the cures of panaceas for its disfunctions; the cultural images, in popular music, paintings, dance crazes, novel, stories, advice columns, films, videos, plays, and advertising, that interpret human sexuality and love exclusively in terms of two by two heterosexual pairing; and the predominant instruments of western social life — the bars, dances, parties, clubs — that recognize only the heterosexual couple. Why is there so much insistence, via these intensive socialization mechanisms, that all women *be* heterosexual and *learn* to be heterosexual, if that is what we are all naturally inclined to be anyway? So the presence of that strong social insistence upon heterosexuality is, to my mind, one very large piece of evidence that heterosexuality is not innate. But, whether it is or it is not, it is the heterosexual institution that is the subject of discussion in this paper.

II The Politics of Heterosexuality

To examine the heterosexual institution is to raise questions not only about sex but about the nature of love, passion, loyalty, and trust between men and women. These are, at least at first glance, moral questions, about human responsibility, obligation, and commitment. But, since the heterosexual institution involves connections between unequals, they are also political questions, concerned with the uneven distribution of power between members of two groups which have been socially constructed to be very different. Hence, a feminist discussion of heterosexuality requires the consideration of questions about allegiances and affiliations, about separatism, and about political choices and strategies.

To arrive at a better understanding of the political nature of the heterosexual institution, it is helpful to consider one aspect of the dictionary definition of "institution." The *Shorter Oxford English Dictionary* defines "institution" as "an establishment, organization, or association instituted for the *promotion of some object*, especially one of public utility, religious, charitable, educational, etc."[9] This definition raises the question, what object is promoted by the heterosexual institution?

In asking about the object of the heterosexual institution, I am not of course assuming that there is any consciously chosen goal of heterosexuality. No person or power, no god or father nature, created the heterosexual institution, and I am not asking a theological question here. The easy answer, that the object of the heterosexual institution is the facilitation of human reproduction, seems not to be the whole story, for it overlooks the institution's historically variant features. Although there is undeniably some connection between heterosexual behaviour and reproduction, that connection is becoming more tenuous, with the availability of contraception on the one hand and new reproductive technologies on the other.

In fact, a number of observations count against the claim that the object of the heterosexual institution is reproduction. First, not all heterosexual activity, even when unconstrained by deliberate use of contraception and abortion, results in procreation — consider the case of heterosexually active individuals who are too young or too old to reproduce, or who are, for other reasons, infertile, or who engage in non-reproductive sexual behaviour. Such persons may be just as interested in heterosexual activity as those who do wish to reproduce, and that interest is fostered by the heterosexual institution quite independently of their willingness or ability to reproduce. Second, it is remarkable that women who are celibate, whether by choice or through force of circumstance, are usually still thought of as being heterosexual; the presumption of heterosexuality operates in the absence of reproductive activity. Third, heterosexual desire is not at all the same as the desire to reproduce; one may have either one without the other[10] and there is no longer much pressure in western culture to promote or to evaluate heterosexual desire by reference to reproductive goals. Fourth, the heterosexual institution continues to operate at full force even in places where, one would think, the needs of reproduction are already amply or even excessively filled. Finally, seeing

reproduction as the object of the heterosexual institution simply "portrays men and women as the dupes of their own physiology and considers eroticism as a mere cover-up for Nature's reproductive aims."[11] Hence, although heterosexual activity and reproduction are sometimes causally connected, the latter is not the object, or at least not the only object, of the former. The heterosexual institution does not exist merely to further procreation; it has some other important function or functions.

My question about the object of the heterosexual institution is akin to questions about the object of other institutions such as the state, the family, the educational systems, or religion. And one way of starting to answer such questions is by looking to see what individuals or groups of individuals benefit from the institution, what the benefits are, how those benefits are created and distributed, and at whose cost the benefits are acquired.

For the past two decades, radical feminists have offered disturbing answers to these questions. They have argued, first, that the heterosexual institution primarily benefits men, not women; and that it affords men easy sexual gratification and material possession of women, as well as reproduction of themselves and their offspring. Second, these benefits are created and distributed through what Adrienne Rich and others have described as the compulsory nature of heterosexuality; female heterosexual desire and activity must be enforced and coerced, through a myriad of social practices in the family, in culture, in religion, education, and law.[12] This process has been described as the deliberate recruitment of women into active participation in heterosexuality.[13] Mariana Valverde states,

[G]iven the enormous social weight of heterosexism, one cannot accurately describe heterosexuality as merely a personal preference, as though there were not countless social forces pushing one to be heterosexual. People do not generally choose heterosexuality out of a number of equally valid, equally respected lifestyles.

... As long as certain choices are punished while others are presented as natural, as the norm, it is naive to describe the complicated process of the construction of conformity and/or deviance by reference to a consumer-type notion of personal preference.[14]

Third, whatever its rewards may be (and they are more than amply celebrated in romantic fiction, films, songs, and everyday mythology) the costs for women of providing the benefits of female heterosexuality for men are of two types: First, violence, degradation, and exploitation of women's bodies and women's sexuality, through such practices as prostitution, rape and other forms of sexual assault, woman battering, pornography, and incest; and second, the deliberately cultivated separation of women from their allies, each other. The operation of the heterosexual institution is a very successful demonstration of the political maxim that to keep a subject group down, it is important to keep its members divided, to prevent them from developing loyalties to each other, and to direct their trust and commitment to members of the oppressor group. In short, the heterosexual institution is the strongest arm and most powerful manifestation of patriarchy; and therefore one of its most important objects is the oppression of women.

As an agent of patriarchal oppression, the heterosexual institution generates a second paradox in heterosexuality: the conjunction of heterosexual privilege and heterosexism. On the one hand, the heterosexual institution grants a certain privilege to heterosexual women that is not possessed by non-heterosexual women. A heterosexual woman is validated for having (or at least wanting) men in her life: the presence of a boyfriend or husband — or even the search for a male partner — confirms that the woman is a "real woman"; that (some) men (sometimes) find her attractive; that, whatever else she might be or feel or think, she is not (so the assumption goes) a "manhater" and therefore beyond the moral pale (even though woman hating is considered a fairly normal part of human civilization). A woman's heterosexuality, visibly demonstrated, shields her from the vicious attacks reserved for non-heterosexual women.

At the same time, heterosexual privilege is coupled with heterosexism, that is, discrimination

on grounds of non-heterosexual orientation. Hence, heterosexual privilege has its price: strict conformity to the standards and requirements of heterosexual behaviour and appearance. On the one hand, deviations, even apparent ones are usually noticed and punished, through verbal and even physical violence, ostracism, and the threatened loss of employment, reputation, peace and safety, home, children, or financial security. In many instances to be a feminist (regardless of one's sexual activities) is to invite heterosexist vituperation; many people, including some feminists as well as non-feminists, are inclined to regard the work "lesbian" as a dangerous term whose application to oneself undermines one's credibility and acceptability. Yet on the other hand, successful conformity to heterosexual standards of behaviour and appearance may also be painful, and necessitate contortions, self-abasement, and continual self observation or order to regulate one's feelings, speech and behaviour to fit the image of the heterosexual woman. Hence, not only are there tremendous costs for the person who is non-heterosexual, but also the heterosexual woman is in a classic double-bind situation: to avoid the damages of non-conformity, she must incur the damages of conformity.

III Heterosexuality and Choice

In one of my favourite cartoons, a young woman asks her tough and savvy feminist mother, "Ma, can I be a feminist and still like men?" "Sure," replies the mother, "Just like you can be a vegetarian and like fried chicken." When I recounted this joke in an introduction to feminism course, my young female students were disturbed rather than amused. And this is not surprising. To some, the mother's reply may seem to be a *reductio ad absurdum* of combining feminism and heterosexuality. A good vegetarian, one might think, just does not like fried chicken; or she certainly *ought* not to like it. And if, in a moment of weakness, she does consume fried chicken, then she is either not a good, moral, consistent vegetarian, or, worse still, she is not a vegetarian at all. So also with the feminist. While many of my students hoped that it would be both logically and empirically possible to be a feminist and still like men, or even to love them, they also saw considerable tension in being both heterosexual and feminist. Some feminists who love men have expressed both doubt and guilt about the legitimacy of their lives, and some non-heterosexual feminists have encouraged those feelings. For some women, for example,

> feminism has made them sharply aware of how male power is used, abused and reproduced In personal relationships, to the point where they despair of ever achieving equality. They begin to question their attachment to men and wonder if it is really men's bodies they desire, or if they are merely addicted to their power ... [To be heterosexual seems like a weakness, like a] chink in [one's] feminist armour.[15]

Is, then, a "feminist heterosexuality" possible?[16] To answer that question, it is necessary first to consider the nature of choice. If, as some feminists have argued, heterosexuality in women is coerced, it would seem that no woman chooses to be heterosexual. When there are not several recognized and legitimate options, when there are so many pressures to be heterosexual, and when failure to conform is so heavily punished, it is difficult to regard heterosexuality as the genuine expression of a preference. In fact, as one (heterosexual) woman remarked to me, given the damning indictment of heterosexuality which has been presented by some feminists, it might seem that any woman would be heterosexual only if it were *not* a choice.

But this is not all that can be said about the possibility of choosing heterosexuality. For, first, a single-minded focus on the coercive aspects of the heterosexual institution absolves heterosexual women of any responsibility for their sexual practice in a way that seems inappropriate, at least in the case of feminist women, who have had some opportunities to reflect upon the role of heterosexuality in patriarchal oppression. The idea that all heterosexual women (unlike non-heterosexual women) just can't help themselves and are somehow doomed to love and be attracted to men gives too much weight to the view of women as

victims, and too little credit to the idea that women can act and make decisions on their own behalf. Moreover, it implicitly imputes to all heterosexual women a sort of false consciousness. Most such women will not see themselves as victims of coercion. Although they may not think of heterosexual practice as a choice they have made, they also do not necessarily feel like helpless victims of the heterosexual institution. But if no woman can choose to be heterosexual, then all heterosexual women either fail to correctly understand their own sexuality, or they can correctly understand their sexuality only be seeing themselves as helpless victims.

On the contrary, I would argue, it is a mistake to summarily dismiss all heterosexual women's experience as a failure to understand their own sexuality. Indeed, it is possible that some such women may

> have actively chosen, rather than fallen into, a life of heterosexual marriage and children ... and that in their heterosexual relationships, they have control over their own sexuality and share equally in the enjoyment of and participation in their sexual relationships.[17]

I am not saying here only that some heterosexual women may lead exceptional lives in the sense that their relationship with their man (or men) is experienced as egalitarian and uncoercive; I am saying that there is an important sense in which a woman can genuinely and even sanely choose to be heterosexual, although the conditions and opportunities for that choice may be fairly rare. Beyond the claim that heterosexuality is innate (which seems to be an insufficiently grounded essentialist claim) and the claim that heterosexuality is coerced (which seems true in regard to the heterosexual institutions as a whole) there is a third possibility: that heterosexuality is or can be chosen, even — or especially! — by feminists.

If it is possible to choose *not* to be heterosexual — and most radical feminists have argued that it is — then it is possible to actively choose to be heterosexual. To some degree, each of us is able to make ourselves into the kinds of sexual beings we are, through a process of interpretation and reinterpretation of our past and present experiences and of our feelings and emotions, and through active interaction with other persons, not just passive receptivity to their influence. By choosing one's heterosexuality I mean not merely acquiescing in it, or benefiting from heterosexual privilege, but actively taking responsibility for being heterosexual. Admittedly, most apparently heterosexual women never make, and never have an opportunity to make, such an active conscious choice. In what cases, then, might it be correct to say that a woman has genuinely chosen her heterosexuality? The following remark by Charlotte Bunch provides a crucial insight into the paradoxical answer to that question:

> Basically, heterosexuality means men first. That's what it's all about. It assumes that every woman is heterosexual; that every woman is defined by and is the property of men. Her body, her services, her children belong to men. If you don't accept that definition, you're a queer — no matter who you sleep with. ...[18]

For a heterosexual woman, to start to understand the institution of heterosexuality and the ideology of heterosexism is already to start to leave standard heterosexuality behind. For part of what is customarily meant by the ascription of heterosexuality is its unconscious "perfectly natural" character. Persons who are non-heterosexual never have the luxury of accepting their sexuality in this way. As Mariana Valverde has pointed out, even those non-heterosexuals who feel driven by their sexual needs and desires, and compelled to seek sexual partners of the same sex,

> are forced at some point to define themselves, and ask how and why they have come to such desires ... Since we all "naturally" grow up to be heterosexual, it is only the deviations that call out for an explanation; the norm appears as natural, and few heterosexual people ever wonder whatever caused them to be heterosexual.[19]

Anne Wilson Schaef claims that in general, women do not view the world in sexual terms:

First, we do not categorize individuals and situations according to their sexuality. Second, we do not assume that each and every relationship must be sexual, nor do we view everything we do and everyone we meet as having some sexual significance. In fact, women do not define the world in sexual terms.[20]

Sometimes, however, instead of being enlightened, as Schaef seems to assume, this refusal or inability to categorize in sexual terms may be a form of blindness. Marilyn Frye has pointed out that in discussions of sexual prejudice and discrimination one may often hear a statement such as "I don't think of myself as heterosexual" presumably said by a person who engages in heterosexual activity.[21] Heterosexuals ordinarily extend to others the somewhat dubious privilege of assuming that everyone is like them; since to be sexual is to be *hetero*sexual, "[t]he question often must be *made* to arise, blatantly and explicitly, before the heterosexual person will consider the thought that one is lesbian or homosexual."[22] On the other hand, such persons often perceive non-heterosexuals as being unnecessarily preoccupied with their sexuality, unable to stop talking about it and "flaunting" it to the world. But, Frye suggests,

> Heterosexual critics of queers' "role-playing" ought to look at themselves in the mirror on their way out for a night on the town to see who's in drag. The answer is, everybody is. Perhaps the main difference between heterosexuals and queers is that when queers go forth in drag, they know they are engaged in theater — they are playing and they know they are playing. Heterosexuals usually are taking it all perfectly seriously, thinking they are in the real world, thinking they *are* the real world. [23]

The person whose sexual practice is heterosexual and who honestly and innocently states that she does not think of herself as heterosexual shows herself most clearly to be heterosexual in the standard sense. Paradoxically, then, for a woman to firmly and unambiguously affirm her heterosexuality may already be to begin to leave it behind, that is, to cease to be heterosexual in the unthinking unconscious way she once was: She ceases to participate wholeheartedly in the heterosexual institution, and begins the process of disaffiliation from it.[24] When that sort of reflection takes place, I believe, the woman is beginning genuinely to choose her heterosexuality; and she is choosing heterosexual practice without a concomitant endorsement of the heterosexual institution.

Of course, for such a woman, heterosexuality is still something which is enforced, in Rich's sense; that is, persistent cultural pressures strive to ensure her conformity, and deviance from heterosexuality is penalized, often severely. No amount of awareness of the heterosexual institution can, by itself, change the compulsory nature of heterosexuality, and disaffiliation by one woman will not rock the institution.

Nevertheless, that awareness can make a difference, for the previously unawarely heterosexual woman, in the dimensions of her own sexuality: she can begin the process of shaping her own sexuality, by making decisions and choices based upon an understanding of the power and the limits of the heterosexual institution. For she can explore her own personal history and determine how and when her sense of the erotic became separated from women and connected to men.[25] In so doing, she can no longer regard her heterosexual orientation as something over which she has no power or control, as something which just dominates her sexual feelings and practices. Instead, she can distinguish between sexual passion and attraction, on the one hand, and dependence, need, fear, and insecurity on the other. She can become aware of her feelings about women's and men's bodies, and discover whether and/or to what degree she has internalized a socially validated revulsion toward the female body. She can genuinely ask herself whether sexual activity with men is something she wants, or merely something in which she engages. (For, of course, we cannot assume that all women whose sexual practice is heterosexual also enjoy their sexual activities.)

If the answer is no, it is not something she wants, she then has the prospect of choosing to be non-heterosexual. On the other hand, if the answer is yes, she can, in a way, begin to come out as a heterosexual: not in the heterosexist fashion by which almost all heterosexuals, male and female, ordinarily mark their heterosexuality, but rather in terms of an informed and self-aware feminist evaluation of her life as a heterosexual,[26] renouncing as far as possible the privilege accorded by heterosexuality,[27] and recognizing both the different varieties of oppression non-heterosexuals undergo and also the affinities she shares with non-heterosexual women. She can support non-heterosexual women, validate their relationships, and refuse any longer to be complicitous in the erasures they often undergo. She thereby chooses to be heterosexual as a matter of sexual practice, but not as a matter of the exclusive heterosexist alignment or orientation of her life.

Nevertheless, although it may now seem that heterosexuality can be genuinely chosen by women, for some feminists the question may still remain whether it *ought* to be chosen, whether it is ever a good choice, a choice a feminist could responsibly make. Although some heterosexual feminists pride themselves on their "exceptional" heterosexual relationships, relationships which are, apparently, non-oppressive and egalitarian, still, whatever the particular relationship is like, it nonetheless remains *possible* for the man to take advantage of his potential power. All that stands in his way of his using that power is his own good will, while he is not similarly dependent on the woman's good will. And he still benefits, however indirectly, from male hegemony, and "even the advantages that he is in a position to refuse are waiting for him if he changes his mind."[28]

[C]hanging our expectations will [not] by itself change the unequal power relationship. It does not, for instance, change the expectations and behaviour of the man. Neither does it remove the institutional power vested in the male in heterosexual relationships.[29]

Moreover, the woman in such a relationship is still giving her energies very largely to a man, consorting intimately with a member of an oppressor group, and hence, indirectly withholding her energies from a woman. For any woman, heterosexual orientation seems to mean putting men, or at least a man, first. And even while rejecting the heterosexual institution, such a woman also still benefits from heterosexual privilege. Thus, no matter how idyllic her relationship, it seems to fail of its very nature to challenge the status quo, and to reinforce the apparent exclusive loyalty of a woman to her man. Together, the two persons in the relationship still appear to participate in and contribute to the perpetuation of an institution which is oppressive of women, particularly of non-heterosexual women and unattached women of any orientation, as well as of heterosexual women in abusive relationships.[30] And of course having an exceptional relationship does not in any way spare a woman from the worst excesses of the heterosexual institution as they may be visited upon her by men other than her immediate sexual partner(s).

The foregoing observations appear to call into question the *legitimacy* of a woman's deliberately deciding to be heterosexual, and I have only very tentative responses to them. The first involves taking seriously the distinction between the institution of heterosexuality on the one hand, and on the other hand, specific heterosexual relations and the persons who become involved in them. This is the same sort of distinction made by Adrienne Rich in her discussion of motherhood. Rich has urged us to recognize that while motherhood itself is an oppressive institution, mothering particular children may be a delightful, worthwhile, valuable human activity.[31] Similarly, while heterosexuality is an oppressive institution, not all heterosexual relationships are valueless as a result. Glimpsing this possibility might also encourage feminists to make a distinction between what could be called the *institution* of manhood, on the one hand, and individual men on the other. It must have been some such distinction that I had implicitly in mind years ago when I complained to a male friend at some length about masculine behaviour. After he mildly pointed out that he was a man (and therefore, presumably, a counterexample to some of the generalizations I was inclined to make), I spontaneously patted his hand and replied, "But Bob, I don't think of you as a man!"

In regard to this distinction between being male and being "a man," or masculine, Marilyn Frye writes,

I have enjoined males of my acquaintance to set themselves against masculinity. I have asked them to think about how they can stop being men, and I was not recommending a sex change operation.[32]

This answer, by itself, has of course all the weaknesses of any "individual solution" to problems of oppression. For it depends upon a commitment of the man in the relationship not to avail himself of the power of his position. And so, it must be said, for a woman to actively choose to be heterosexual is an act of faith — faith first of all in the fundamental humanity of the men whom she chooses to love. By actively choosing to be heterosexual, a feminist woman is rejecting the view that male sexuality is inevitably and innately violent and exploitive, and that men are hopelessly fated to engage only in aggressive and oppressive relationships. Although members of the two sexes acquire very different roles, men just as much as women learn to participate in the heterosexual institution. And it is a lesson which men can reject. The heterosexual institution is a social artifact that can be changed, and men themselves may be the allies of women in changing it.

A woman who deliberately chooses to be heterosexual is also expressing her faith in her own individual power and strengths, her belief that a woman in a heterosexual relationship can be something far more than a helpless victim. She is rejecting the invidious all-or-nothing fallacies that restrict what she is and can be. She is recognizing that she is not, or need not be, only a sexual being; that she is not, or need not be, only heterosexual. Joanna Russ points out that in the late nineteenth century the new focus on sexuality as an indicator of the "health" of one's personality led to the invention of a new kind of person: "The Homosexual."[33] Similarly, I think, some recent feminist theory has resulted in the invention of "The Heterosexual," seen as a woman entirely defined by her sexual orientation to men. Both moves, though they originate from very different sources and agendas, hypothesize the existence of an entire personality and political affiliation on the basis of a species of sexual activity. But while we can easily recognize the power and ubiquity of the heterosexual institution, we need not thereby conclude that that institution subsumes entire personalities. To describe a woman as heterosexual (or as not heterosexual) in no way provides an exhaustive description of that woman's activities, beliefs, values, attitudes, or temperament.

There are, moreover, degrees of heterosexuality. Heterosexual orientation need not mean the exclusion of loyalty to, attraction toward, and love for women. Women who are heterosexual can develop intimate relationships with women, and value them at least as much as they value their relationships with men. Adrienne Rich has spoken movingly of what she calls "the lesbian continuum." She defines it as

> [the full] range — through each woman's life and throughout history — of women identified experience; not simply the fact that a woman has had or consciously desired genital sexual experience with another woman. [The lesbian continuum] embrace[s] many more forms of primary intensity between and among women, including the sharing of a rich inner life, the bonding against male tyranny, [and] the giving and receiving of practical and political support...[34]

Sometimes, unfortunately, the concept of the lesbian continuum is appealed to by some feminists rather prematurely as a way of foreclosing on confrontation and acrimony between heterosexual and non-heterosexual women. Nevertheless, provided the differences between heterosexual and non-heterosexual woman in culture, experience, oppression, and privilege are not glossed over, the concept of the lesbian continuum is a powerful source of insight for women who have chosen to be heterosexual, and a reminder that they are not or need not be only heterosexual. So far, under patriarchal conditions, what women's sexuality is and can be has scarcely been explored; but in a non-patriarchal society there would be no limitations on life-promoting human relationships.

Author's Note

An earlier version of this paper was first presented at the Queen's University Philosophy Department Colloquium, and I am grateful for the suggestions which I received. I am particularly indebted to Michael Fox for his detailed and thoughtful commentary.

NOTES

1. *Shorter Oxford English Dictionary,* Addenda (1970), my emphasis.
2. Frances Giberson has pointed out to me that celibacy could also be thought of as a type of non-heterosexuality, indeed, a rejection of the heterosexual institution. In men, the absence of heterosexual behaviour is usually taken as prima facie evidence of homosexuality; whereas in women, the absence of heterosexual behaviour is often taken to mean the woman is celibate. Unfortunately, there is not space in this paper to explore further the important issues connected with celibacy.
3. See Christine Overall, "Sexuality, Parenting, and Reproductive Choices," *Resources For Feminist Research/Documentation sur la recherche féministe* 16 (September 1987) 44.
4. Marilyn Frye, "Some Reflections on Separatism and Power," in her *The Politics of Reality: Essays in Feminist Theory* (Trumansburg, NY: The Crossing Press 1983) 106-7, Frye's emphasis.
5. And it has been done. See, for example, Howard Buchbinder's "Male Heterosexuality: The Socialized Penis Revisited," in Howard Buchbinder et al., eds., *Who's On Top? The Politics of Heterosexuality* (Toronto: Garamond Press 1987) 63-82.
6. Carole S. Vance and Ann Barr Snitow, "Toward a Conversation About Sex in Feminism: A Modest Proposal," *Signs* 10 (1984) 127.
7. Ruth Bleier, *Science and Gender: A Critique of Biology and Its Theories on Women* (New York: Pergamon Press 1984) 166.
8. Mariana Valverde, *Sex, Power and Pleasure* (Toronto: Women's Press 1985) 113-14.
9. *Shorter Oxford English Dictionary,* my emphasis.
10. Alan Soble, "Preface: Changing Conceptions of Human Sexuality," in Earl E. Shelp, ed., *Sexuality*

and Medicine: Conceptual Roots (Boston: D. Reidel 1987) xiii.

11. Valverde, 50.

12. Adrienne Rich, "Compulsory Heterosexuality and Lesbian Existence," in Catharine R. Stimpson and Ethel Spector Person, eds., *Women: Sex and Sexuality* (Chicago: University of Chicago Press 1980) 62-91.

13. Beatrix Campbell, "A Feminist Sexual Politics: Now You See It, Now You Don't" in The Feminist Review, ed., *Sexuality: A Reader* (London: Virago Press 1987) 23.

14. Valverde, 114.

15. *Ibid.*, 62-3.

16. The question is taken from the title of Angela Hamblin's article, "Is a Feminist Heterosexual Possible?," in Sue Cartledge and Joanna Ryan, eds., *Sex and Love: New Thoughts on Old Contradictions* (London: The Women's Press 1983) 105-23.

17. Bleier, 182-3. Cf. Ann Ferguson, "Patriarchy, Sexual Identity, and the Sexual Revolution," in Nannerl O. Keohane, Michelle Z. Rosaldo, and Barbara C. Gelpi, eds., *Feminist Theory: A Critique of Ideology* (Chicago: University of Chicago Press 1982) 159.

18. Charlotte Bunch, "Not For Lesbians Only," In Charlotte Bunch et al., Eds., *Building Feminist Theory: Essays From Quest* (New York: Longman 1981) 69.

19. Valverde, 114-15.

20. Anne Wilson Schaef, *Women's Reality: An Emerging Female System in a White Male Society* (Minneapolis: Winston Press 1985) 47.

21. Marilyn Frye, "Lesbian Feminism and the Gay Rights Movement: Another View of Male Supremacy, Another Separatism," In the *Politics of Reality*, 147. Michael Ramberg has pointed out to me that to say "I don't think of myself as heterosexual" could also mean "I am not *only* heterosex-

ual" or "I will not always be heterosexual."

22. Marilyn Frye, "On Being White: Toward A Feminist Understanding of Race and Race Supremacy," in *The Politics of Reality*, 116, her emphasis.

23. Marilyn Frye, "Sexism," in *The Politics of Reality*, 29, her emphasis.

24. Frye, "On Being White," 127.

25. Marilyn Frye, "A Lesbian Perspective on Women's Studies," in Margaret Cruikshank, ed., *Lesbian Studies: Present and Future* (Old Westbury, NY: The Feminist Press 1982) 197.

26. See Katherine Arnup, "Lesbian Feminist Theory," *Resources for Feminist Research/Documentation sur la recherche feministe* (12 March 1983) 55.

27. Amy Gottlieb, "Mothers, Sisters, Lovers, Listen," in Maureen Fitzgerald, Connie Guberman, and Margie Wolfe, eds., *Still Ain't Satisfied! Canadian Feminism Today* (Toronto: Women's Press 1982) 238-9.

28. Sara Ann Ketchum and Christine Pierce, "Separatism and Sexual Relationships," in Sharon Bishop and Marjorie Weinzweig, eds., *Philosophy and Women* (Belmont, CA: Wadsworth 1979) 167-168.

29. Hamblin, 117.

30. See Lees Revolutionary Feminist Group, "Political Lesbianism: The Case Against Heterosexuality," in *Love Your Enemy? the Debate Between Heterosexual Feminism and Political Lesbianism* (London: Only Women Press 1981) 5-10.

31. Adrienne Rich, *Of Woman Born: Motherhood as Experience and Institution* (New York: Bantam Books 1976).

32. Frye, "On Being White," 127.

33. Joanna Russ, *Magic Mommas, Trembling Sisters, Puritans and Perverts* (Trumansburg, NY: The Crossing Press 1985) 67.

34. Rich, "Compulsory Heterosexuality and Lesbian Existence," 81.

SEXUALITY INJUSTICE

Cheshire Calhoun

Cheshire Calhoun is Professor of Philosophy at Colby College, Waterville, Maine. She is the author of numerous articles as well as of Feminism, the Family, and the Politics of the Closet: Lesbian and Gay Displacement *(2000) and* Leaving Home: Reflections on Lesbianism and Feminism, *in Chinese only, translated by Chuanfen Chang (1997).*

Calhoun differentiates sexuality injustice from racial and gender injustice. Because persons who are gay or lesbian can evade being publicly identified, sexuality injustice, unlike racial and gender injustice, does not consist in their disproportionate occupation of disadvantaged places in the socioeconomic structure. Instead, sexuality injustice consists in the displacement of homosexuality and lesbianism to the outside of society. Calhoun examines this displacement through phenomena such as the requirement that all citizens adopt a real or pseudonymous heterosexual identity as a condition of access to the public sphere; the reproduction of heterosexual society through legal, psychiatric, educational, and familial practices whose aim is to prevent future generations of lesbian and gay people; and the legitimation of heterosexual society through the construction of criminalizing stereotypes of gay and lesbian identity.

It was while reading Susan Okin's *Justice, Gender, and the Family* that it occurred to me to wonder if there was a *sexuality* injustice comparable to the gender injustice that has been the target of feminist critique.

The language of "gay and lesbian rights," following as it does on the heels of the civil rights and women's rights movements, suggests that there is indeed an analogy, between the political position of gay men and lesbians on the one hand and of women and racial minorities on the other. At first glance, affinities are not hard to find. Lesbians and gays face a formidable array of discriminatory policies and practices that limit their liberty and opportunity. Legally, we are in much the same position as racial minorities and women were prior to the civil rights act — unprotected against informal discrimination, and subject to differential treatment under the law.

But the feminist notion of gender injustice goes well beyond the thought that women confront legal inequities. Over the past several decades, feminists have carefully developed the idea that gender injustice is a matter of oppression, not just legal inequities.[1] That is, the devaluation of women is systematically built into the ways that we, as a society, live and think. The consequence *and evidence* of this systematic devaluation is that women are disproportionately clustered in opportunity-limiting and highly exploitable places. So for instance, the private sphere, pink collar jobs, domestic labor, the sex industry, the roster of welfare clients, and the poverty zone are all places disproportionately inhabited by women. To understand gender injustice is to understand the *places* that women occupy in socio-economic structures and practices, the disadvantaging *effects* of occupying those places, and the factors (including the law) that systematically keep women *in place*.

What I want to understand is the presumably analogous injustice to which gay men and lesbians are subject. What content can be given to the idea of a *sexuality* injustice comparable gender injustice?[2] A central difficulty in developing this notion of sexuality injustice is that lesbians and gay men, unlike women, do not appear to be located in any particular social structural places. This is largely because, unlike women or racial minorities, gays and lesbians often can evade having their sexual orientation recognized. The social presumption that persons are heterosexual unless there is clear evidence to the contrary helps to conceal gay men and lesbians. Moreover, like criminal identity, sexual identity can be deliberately concealed by adopting, in James Woods's term, a counterfeit heterosexual identity. As a result, persons who *are* lesbian or gay are often treated *as* heterosexuals. Thus anti-gay ideology and discriminatory policies and practices do not have the necessary consequence of *systematically* undermining gays' and lesbians' material conditions or access to opportunities. Consider, for example, the substantially different impact of the military policy barring women from combat and its policy of barring gay men and lesbians from military service. The former effectively bars all women from combat. The latter does not effectively bar gays and lesbians from service; it only bars the *identifiably* gay or lesbian. So long as they pass as heterosexual, gays and lesbians will occupy virtually the same location in the opportunity structure as heterosexuals.

Thus it seems that sexuality injustice is *not* closely analogous to gender or racial injustice. In particular, sexuality injustice does not materialize in a disadvantaging *place* in which gays and lesbians are disproportionately concentrated. Organizations on the religious right, such as Lou Sheldon's Traditional Values Coalition have capitalized on this fact, coming to the conclusion that there is no such thing as sexuality injustice and thus that gay and lesbian rights must be special rights.

What I want to suggest instead is that sexuality injustice consists in the systematic *dis*-placement of gays and lesbians to the outside of civil society so that lesbians and gays have no legitimized place — not even a disadvantaged one. One mechanism for displacing lesbians and gays is the requirement that all citizens have an apparent heterosexual identity as a condition of access to the public sphere. This means that gays and lesbians must

adopt a pseudonymous heterosexual identity in order to gain full access to the public sphere. As a result, gay and lesbian *identities* are effectively displaced from the public sphere. A second mechanism for displacing lesbians and gays is the institutionalization of legal, psychiatric, educational, and familial practices whose aim is to prevent future generations of lesbian and gay people. So for example, both anti-gay child custody decisions and anti-gay educational policies are aimed at reproducing heterosexuality and thus displacing homosexuality and lesbianism from our social future. This heterosexualization of society is then legitimized through the social construction of criminalizing stereotypes of lesbian and gay identity that undermines the claim of lesbians and gays to full civic status. I will consider both mechanisms of displacements in turn, concluding with some comments about the criminalization of lesbian and gay identity.

I. Displacing Gay and Lesbian Identities from the Public Sphere

In discussing the displacement of gay and lesbian identities from the public sphere, I will begin with some brief observations about the legal construction of same-sex sexuality as the publicly *unmentionable* crime. I will then turn to a discussion of the way that military policy, employment practice, and Court decisions work to displace gay and lesbian *identities*, though not the persons themselves, from the public sphere. I will conclude this first part with some reasons why I think that the First Amendment does not adequately secure lesbians' and gays' entitlement to represent their identities publicly.

Sodomy has a long, distinctive history, as the unmentionable crime. Prior to the secularization of sodomy prohibitions in the 1500s, "sodomy had been defined in strictly ecclesiastical terms as one of the gravest sins against divine law whose name alone proved such an affront to God that it was often named only as the unnamable." Throughout the 1600s, sodomy continued to be referred to within British law as the crime that among Christians is not to be mentioned, and a century later,

William Blackstone uses this same (non)description in his *Commentaries on the Laws of England*. He remarks,

> I will not act so disagreeable a part, to my readers as well as myself, as to dwell any longer upon a subject, the very mention of which is a disgrace to human nature. It will be more eligible to imitate in this respect the delicacy of our English law, which treats it, in its very indictments, as a crime not fit to be named.

In the United States, some state statutes still refuse to name what they prohibit, instead referring with vague decency to "crimes against nature."[3] And in his concurring opinion in *Bowers v. Hardwick*, Justice Burger recalled the words of Blackstone, pronouncing sodomy "a heinous act 'the very mention of which is a disgrace to human nature,' and 'a crime not fit to be named.'"[4]

The history of laws prohibiting sodomy and acts of gross indecency between men is thus simultaneously a history of the linguistic taboo on publicly naming and describing same-sex sexuality. It is the history of laws that not only render privately performed sex a matter of public concern but that *also* privatize public acts of linguistic representation. That dual history ultimately has the dual effect of undercutting the claim of gays and lesbians to have a private sphere where their sexual, affiliational, and familial relations are protected from public intrusion *and* of denying them any entitlement to represent themselves in the public sphere as lesbians and gays. The unmentionability of homosexuality and lesbianism in the *public* sphere effectively displaces gay and lesbian identities to the outside of civil society.

By contrast, unlike this love that dare not speak its name, heterosexuality is the love whose name is continually spoken in the everyday routines and institutions of public social life. Heterosexuals move about in the public sphere as heterosexuals, and that identity is by no means a private matter. Public social interaction and the structure of public institutions are pervaded with the assumption that public actors are heterosexual and with opportunities to represent themselves as such. Humor,

formal and informal dress codes, corporate benefits policies, "scripts" for everyday conversation about personal life, public display of family pictures, and so on presuppose that public persons *are* heterosexual. They also enable individuals to publicly represent themselves *as* heterosexuals.[5]

This double standard for heterosexual versus homosexual self-representation is based on the assumption that heterosexuality is and ought to be constitutive of what it means to be a public actor, a citizen. The equation of 'public actor' with 'heterosexual actor' is in part sustained by regarding homosexual identity as a private, behind-closed-doors matter. It is also sustained by requiring that lesbians and gays adopt a pseudonymous heterosexual identity as a condition of access to the public sphere, and by instituting a set of discriminatory practices and policies that penalize individuals for publicly representing themselves as gay or lesbian. Military policy is a case in point.

Military policy has in the past implicitly invoked,[6] and now explicitly invokes, a distinction between status and conduct. Supposedly, that distinction is critical to framing a policy that does not discriminate on the basis of who one *is* yet still grants the military authority to regulate what its members *do*. In reality, the distinction is critical to controlling the identities that are allowed to appear in the military's public space.

Prior to 1994, military policy prohibited not only sexual activity between persons of the same sex, it also prohibited making one's homosexuality known.[7] Publicly stating "I am a lesbian" warranted discharge no less than did private lesbian sexual acts. In discussing the proposed new policy, revealingly dubbed "don't ask, don't tell," Sam Nunn, affirmed that avowing one's homosexuality or lesbianism *is* conduct and ought to be prohibited.[8] Although the policy that actually went into effect in 1994 does not make self-identifying statements automatic grounds for dismissal, it does make them grounds for starting an investigation, "and once such an investigation is started, the service member would have to prove that he had not engaged in homosexual acts."[9] In controlling public identity, not just sexual acts, both old and new policies require that the persons who are to be exempted from status-discrimination adopt a pseudonymous heterosexual identity.[10]

Courts have also invoked the status-conduct distinction to the same end of controlling public identity. In *Singer v. United States Civil Service Commission*,[11] for example, the Court concluded that the Civil Service Commission had not acted improperly in firing John F. Singer. Singer was a clerk typist for the Seattle Office of (ironically) the EEOC. He had been fired by the Civil Service Commission for "flaunting" and "broadcasting" his homosexuality and for receiving "wide-spread publicity in this respect in at least two states."[12] The Commission noted that Singer had kissed a male in front of the building elevator and in the company cafeteria, had applied with another man for a marriage license, had "homosexual advertisements" on the windows of his car, was on the Board of Directors of the Seattle Gay Alliance, showed by his "dress and demeanor" that he intended to continue his homosexual activity, and he had received television, newspaper, radio, and magazine publicity.[13] The Commission denied that Singer was discharged because of his status. Instead, it claimed that Singer's "repeated flaunting and advocacy of a controversial lifestyle"[14] would undermine public confidence in, and thus the efficiency of, the Civil Service. The Court agreed, noting that this case differed from *Norton v. Macy*. In *Norton v. Macy*, the D.C. Circuit Court ruled that NASA could not discharge an employee for being gay. What made Singer's case different was that Singer had not attempted, as Norton had, to keep his homosexuality private.[15] In the eyes of both the EEOC and the Court, Singer brought discredit on his employer by publicly occupying a discredited identity.

What both the military in its new policy, and the Courts in *Norton* and *Singer*, acknowledge is that the presence of persons who *are* gay or lesbian need not "contaminate" the heteronormativity of public space. Public actors may *be* gay or lesbian. What they may not do is make those identities known by *representing* themselves as lesbian or gay. Instead, both military policy and government employment practice in effect require lesbians and gays to adopt pseudonymous heterosexual identities in their public lives.

Briefly considering what the gender analog to status-conduct distinguishing policies would look like brings the problem into sharper focus. Imagine, for example, a military service policy that, while claiming not to discriminate against persons who *are* women, proceeded to ban all "conduct" that made women publicly identifiable *as* women. Women would be subject to discharge both for engaging in womanly activities (say, joining the National Organization for Women or wearing women's clothing) and for making the self-identifying statement "I am a woman." Avowing their womanhood and flaunting or carelessly displaying their unorthodox gender in public would constitute a breach of acceptable military conduct.[16] While not discriminating on one level (one may *be* a woman), this fictional policy clearly discriminates on another. It would burden women with the task of managing their public identities so that they appear to be men. And it would prohibit women from doing what men may do, namely, represent themselves as having the identities that they do have.[17]

It is tempting to argue that these restrictions on public self-representation violate First Amendment rights to freedom of speech and association. This is exactly what Judge Edwards and later Justice Brennan did argue in dissenting opinions concerning *Rowland v. Mad River Local School District*. Marjorie Rowland was a high school counselor. She disclosed her bisexuality to several fellow school employees, and was subsequently asked to resign. When she refused, she was suspended, then transferred to a position with no student contact, and then not rehired after her contract expired. The Sixth Circuit Court deemed Rowland's disclosure merely personal, not the public speech of a citizen speaking on a matter of public concern and debate. It thus refused to grant first amendment protections to her disclosure.

Both Judge Edwards and Justice Brennan took issue with this classification of Rowland's identity-statement as merely personal. The Circuit Court had argued that "[t]here was absolutely no evidence of any public concern in the community or at Stebbins High with the issue of bisexuality among school personnel when [Rowland] began speaking to others about her own sexual preference."[18] Taking a larger view of the public, both Judge Edwards[19] and Justice Brennan[20] argued that public debate about the rights of homosexuals was in fact currently ongoing (even if not at Stebbins High), and thus "[t]he fact of petitioner's bisexuality, once spoken, necessarily and ineluctably involved her in that debate."[21]

However tempting invoking first amendment protections in this way may be, there is something odd about classifying representations of one's identity as *either* public or private speech. Consider, first, the fictional gender policy. Is discharging a person for stating "I am a woman" best criticized as a violation of rights to speech, expression, and association? Is one's gender, like one's political views, simply a possible subject of speech or basis of association? Or is it instead constitutive of being a speaker? In our social world, gender is such a fundamental social category that it is the first thing people want to know about the persons with whom they interact. Furthermore, in our social world the psychological process of becoming gendered is part of the process of becoming a self, a subject, an 'I'. In short, speakers enter into the world of speech and expression as gendered subjects. Thus gender is better viewed as a feature of being a speaker rather than simply something one might wish to express to others. To prohibit a particular gendered self-representation in the public world is, then, to do much more than restrict what a speaker may say or with whom she may associate. It is to deny that a particular subject may speak at all. Under the fictional gender policy, women may not speak. Only men, real and pseudonymous, may.

Like gender, sexuality is a fundamentally constitutive feature of our social world and of the persons who inhabit it. For better or worse, we have inherited a view of sexuality as something that, like gender, pervades the entire personality and orients persons in the social world. Persons enter the adult world of speech and expression as sexual subjects. Unlike gender, however, the pressure to know others' and make clear one's own sexuality is relieved, for heterosexuals at least, by the presumption of universal heterosexuality. That presumed heterosexuality, however, is better viewed as a presumption about what it means to be a speaker rather than a presumption about what speakers might wish to express. As in the case of gender, prohibiting a particular sexual self-representation in the public world not only restricts the content of speech, but more importantly denies that lesbian, gay, or bisexual subjects may speak at all. Only heterosexuals, real and pseudonymous, may.

The upshot of the Court's decision in *Rowland* was precisely to deny that a bisexual subject may speak. Although denying that Rowland could be penalized simply for her status as a bisexual, it affirmed that it was permissible for the school to discipline her for making statements about her sexual preference.[22] In a social context like ours, where speakers' heterosexuality is presumed, this amounts to ruling that employers may penalize their employees for refusing to speak as (presumed) heterosexual subjects.

In sum, neither status-based anti-discrimination policies nor first amendment protections of speech adequately guarantee lesbians and gays that they may dare speak their names. First, status-based policies — like the military's or the EEOC's — may simply entitle individuals to *be* lesbian or gay in public space, but not to *represent* themselves as lesbian or gay in public space. Second, the first amendment protects speech, guaranteeing that some things *may be said*. It does not protect speakers, guaranteeing that some sorts of speakers *may do the saying*. When Marjorie Rowland announced "I am a bisexual," she specified who was doing the saying.

II. Preventing Future Generations of Gay and Lesbian Persons

I turn now to the displacement of lesbians and gays from our social future. I will begin with some historical remarks about the psychiatric distinction between true and situational homosexuality. Then I will turn to considering how this distinction has affected psychiatric, legal, educational, and familial practices whose aim is to prevent future generations of lesbians and gays.

From the first emergence of "sexual inversion" in psychiatric taxonomies of the late 1800s, the distinctions between congenital and acquired conditions, between personality type and behavior, and between cross-genderization and same-sex conduct were central to understandings of the forms that homosexuality and lesbianism could take. For turn of the century sexologists, Havelock Ellis and Richard von Krafft-Ebing, both of whom played a central role in establishing sexual inversion as a psychiatric condition — "true" inverts came by their homosexuality congenitally; and their distinguishing feature was not the orientation of their desire, but their cross-genderization, that is, their apparent constitution as a unique personality type — the "third sex."[23] True, congenital inversion was contrasted with acquired, situational inversion. Situational factors were thought to be capable of turning "true" heterosexuals into persons who, though not significantly cross-gendered, sexually desired others of the same sex. Those situational factors included childhood masturbation, confinement to same-sex environments in prisons, convents, and boarding schools, participation in the women's movement, and the seductive advances of true inverts. While congenital inversion was, perhaps, incorrigible, acquired inversion was, on this view, both curable and preventable by manipulating situational factors and inculcating proper sexual habits.

The "true" versus "acquired" distinction affected and continues to affect policy concerning gay men and lesbians in this century. During World War II, for example, motivated partly by psychiatric insistence on the difference between true homosexuality and mere homosexual conduct, and partly by the practical need to retain military personnel, the military attempted to distinguish "true" from "salvageable" homosexuals.[24] Current military policy continues to distinguish between true and situational homosexuals, with the burden of proof falling on those charged with homosexual conduct to demonstrate that they are "truly" heterosexuals.[25]

In the 1990s, the search for a gay gene continues the tradition of equating true homosexuality with a congenital condition. Arguments for gay-tolerant policies based on the claim that gays and lesbians are "born that way" fall squarely in line with turn of the century arguments for social acceptance of the congenital invert.[26] However, given a pervasive cultural distinction between true and situational homosexuals, such arguments are doomed from the outset to be ineffective against a broad band of social policies whose aim is not so much the differential treatment of truly and incorrigibly gay or lesbian as the prevention of new gay and lesbian persons.

In an essay ironically titled "How to Bring Your Kids up Gay," Eve Sedgwick argues that increasing tolerance of adult gay persons has gone hand in hand with the attempt to prevent new gay persons from coming into being.[27] She notes that in the same year that the American Psychiatric Association depathologized homosexuality, it added a new category — Gender Identity Disorder of Childhood — to its Diagnostic and Statistical Manual's roster of pathological conditions.[28] Boys become susceptible to this diagnosis if, in addition to expressing distress about being a boy, they display a "preoccupation with female stereotypical activities as manifested by a preference for either cross-dressing or simulating female attire, or by a compelling desire to participate in the games and pastimes of girls."[29] The revised edition, DSM-III-R, adds, "... and rejection of male stereotypical toys, games, and activities."[30] Similarly, girls become susceptible to this diagnosis if, in addition to expressing distress about being a girl, they show a "persistent marked aversion to normative feminine clothing and insistence on wearing stereotypical masculine clothing, e.g., boys' underwear and other accessories."[31] Harkening back to sexologists' equation of true inversion with cross-genderization, this new disorder appears to be as much about the early detection and prevention of lesbianism and homosexuality as about control of gender deviance. The message of DSM-III, in Sedgwick's view, is that while *existing adult* homosexuals deserve dignified treatment at the hands of psychiatric professionals, psychiatrists may intervene in the lives of proto-gay *children* to prevent new lesbian and gay persons from coming into being.[32]

Gay preventative measures have been framed not only as matters of gender health, but matters also of parental rights and duties. One of the psychiatrists Sedgwick critiques, for example, invokes the theory of parental dominion to justify parental intervention in proto-gay children's lives. He remarks: "the rights of parents to oversee the development of children is a long-established principle. Who is to dictate that parents may not try to raise their children in a manner that maximizes the possibility of a heterosexual outcome?"[33] Others construe intervention as obligatory. For example, in her article advocating gay access to surrogacy, Sharon Elizabeth Rush, moves swiftly from sanctioning adult homosexuality to condemning the creation of new gay persons. She says,

Many heterosexual parents may be quite tolerant and accepting of homosexuality, and many homosexual parents may be quite proud to be homosexual. Nevertheless, given the social reprobation that at present attaches to being homosexual in the United States, and given the love and affection that most parents feel toward their children, I find it unbelievable that any parents — heterosexual or homosexual — would teach their children to be homosexual.[34]

However legitimated — whether on grounds of psychological health, parental rights, or parental obligation — the goal of preventing kids from turning out gay underlies policy that restricts gay and lesbian parenting, gay and lesbian employment in child care, early education, and child service organizations (such as the Boy Scouts), as well as the sexual content of school curricula.

For instance, one of the University of Missouri's principal reasons for refusing to recognize the student group Gay Lib was that "[w]hat happens to a latent or potential homosexual from the standpoint of his environment can cause him to become or not to become a homosexual."[35] In the University's and dissenting Judge Regan's view, the University had a responsibility to protect potential homosexuals from becoming overt homosexuals.[36] And that, in their view, meant protecting them from being influenced by their fellow (overtly) gay and lesbian students.

This goal of preventing new gay and lesbian persons also figured centrally in the court ruling on

the New Hampshire adoption law that "prohibits any person who is homosexual from adopting any person, from being licensed as a member of a foster family, and from running day care centers."[37] When asked for a judicial opinion on the constitutionality of this law, the New Hampshire Supreme Court ignored any criteria of fitness to parent other than capacity to raise children to be heterosexual. In its view, "the legislature can rationally act on the theory that a role model can influence the child's developing sexual identity,"[38] and thus can legitimately regard gay and lesbian persons as unfit for adoptive and foster parenting.

Gay prevention also underlies attempts to outlaw the so-called "promotion" of homosexuality. In 1988, Britain passed Clause 28 of the Local Government Act which stipulated that "A local authority shall not — (a) intentionally promote homosexuality or publish material with the intention of promoting homosexuality; (b) promote the teaching in any maintained school of the acceptability of homosexuality as a pretended family relationship."[39] In a similar vein, a 1992 Oregon ballot measure would have amended the state constitution to prohibit the use of state facilities to "promote, encourage, or facilitate homosexuality." It would also have required that the Oregon Department of Higher Education and the public schools, "assist in setting a standard for Oregon's youth that recognizes homosexuality....as abnormal, wrong, unnatural and perverse and that these behaviors are to be discouraged and avoided."[40] Both "no promo homo" policies, as legal theorist Nan Hunter calls them, were antedated by the (failed) 1978 California Briggs Initiative under which any school employee could be fired for "advocating, soliciting, imposing, encouraging or promoting of private or public homosexual activity directed at, or likely to come to the attention of schoolchildren and/or other employees."[41]

Heterosexual control over standards of child mental health, over blood, adoptive, and foster parenting, and over the socialization of children in public institutions facilitates the reproduction of heterosexual society. It ensures that adult gay men and lesbians will have little say in what kinds of persons future generations will be. And even if it is not possible to make proto-gay children turn out heterosexual, gay preventative socialization practices can go some way toward ensuring that the next generation of lesbians and gays will accept as reasonable both the requirement of adopting a pseudonymous heterosexual identity as a condition of access to the public sphere and their exclusion from any socially legitimated, "nonpretended" private sphere of marriage, parenting, and the family.

It is tempting to respond to these various gay preventative strategies by arguing that pathologizing gender deviance in childhood makes little sense in a psychiatric scheme that depathologizes homosexuality; that in point of fact the children of lesbians and gays are just as likely to grow up heterosexual as are the children of heterosexuals; and that "no promo homo" policies involve censorship and the legal underwriting of one set of moral values. Though having a place, such arguments miss the deeper issue. That deeper issue concerns whether heterosexuals as a social group may legitimately claim for themselves exclusive entitlement to determine the character of future generations.

III. Constructing Gay and Lesbian Persons as Unnatural Criminals

I turn now to the stereotype of lesbians and gays as criminals which legitimizes the displacement of gays and lesbians from civil society. Again, I will begin with some historical comments about the social construction of this criminalizing identity. I will then turn to considering the effects that it has had on gays and lesbian civic status.

The moral prohibition on sodomy, understood as a crime against nature and sin against God, dates from the Middle Ages when it was part of a more general prohibition on nonreproductive sexual acts.[42] Prior to the late 1800s the prohibition on sodomy did not presuppose a special sort of actor (the homosexual), nor was sexual object choice the determinant of who counted as a sinner.[43] But with the social construction in the late 1800s of a special sort of sexual actor — the homosexual — sodomy shifts from being simply a forbidden act, like abortion or adultery, to being one among many indica-

tors of an underlying psycho-sexual personality structure. The invention of the homosexual — the pervert, the degenerate, the sexual psychopath — opened the doors for the invention of the person for whom moral depravity and criminality were constitutive of his or her nature. Criminality and immorality come to reside less in *what* one does than in *who* one is.

In *Morrison v. State Board of Education*, judicial discussion of Morrison's same-sex activity was mediated by assumptions about who Morrison was.[44] When Marc Morrison's week-long sexual relationship with a fellow teacher, Fred Schneringer, came to light, the California State Board of Education charged Morrison with immoral and unprofessional conduct, and revoked his licenses to teach secondary school and exceptional children. The court argued that the Board's interpretation of "immoral conduct" was overly broad, unconnected to considerations of employees' fitness to teach, and threatened "arbitrarily [to] impair the right of the individual to live his private life, apart from his job, as he deems fit."[45] Moreover, there was no evidence that Morrison had sought improper relations with students, had failed to convey to them correct principles of morality, or that his relationship with co-workers had been affected by the incident; in short, there was no evidence of his unfitness to teach.[46] However, the particular facts that the court chose to highlight in *Morrison* do not support this line of reasoning. Instead those facts suggest that Morrison was not really a homosexual, even if he had engaged in same-sex sex. The court repeatedly stressed the "limited" nature of Morrison's homosexual relationship and observed that Morrison and Schneringer were suffering severe emotional stress at the time, that Morrison had suggested women whom Schneringer might date, that with the exception of the Schneringer incident Morrison had not had any "homosexual urges" in a dozen years, and that there was no evidence of "abnormal activities or desires" since that incident.[47] Here the court seems less interested in ascertaining whether Morrison's private conduct affected his public work performance than in ascertaining *who* Morrison really is. Is he really a homosexual, that is, a morally suspect kind of person, whose fitness to teach might reasonably be doubted? Or is he more innocently just a heterosexual performer of homosexual acts?

The image of lesbians and gays as morally depraved and prone to criminal conduct fully flowered in the McCarthy era's programs to purge the military and civil service of all "sexual perverts." Gay men and lesbians were, by their very nature, a threat to national security, an inherently subversive element in society, and "generally unsuitable" for government employment.[48] They were declared to be so by an executive order, which commanded their dismissal from all branches of government service.[49] And in 1952, Congress officially closed the national borders to immigrants with "psychopathic personalities," i.e., gays and lesbians.[50]

Because of this equation, consolidated in the 1950s, of *being* gay or lesbian with criminality and immorality, the normative status of the identities 'gay' and 'lesbian' ends up *preceding* and infecting the normative status of their acts. What makes same-sex touching, kissing, hand holding, knee-squeezing, cohabitation, and marriage wrong is neither so much their same-sexedness nor their likely eventuation in sodomy. Rather, it is their being done by a kind of person, that is, their being *homosexual* or *lesbian* acts — not just their same-sexedness. This is perhaps nowhere more clearly evident than in military policy itself. Army Regulations exempt from automatic discharge soldiers who have engaged in same-sex sex but who can prove that same-sex sexuality was a departure from customary behavior, is unlikely to recur, and is undesired.[51] As Judge Norris nicely summarizes Army policy in *Watkins v. U.S. Army,*

> If a straight soldier and a gay soldier of the same sex engage in homosexual acts because they are drunk, immature or curious, the straight soldier may remain in the Army while the gay soldier is automatically terminated. In short, the regulations do not penalize soldiers for engaging in [same-sex] acts; they penalize soldiers who have engaged in [same-sex] acts only when the Army decides that those soldiers are actually gay.[52]

The distinction between an act of same-sex sex (which can be done by either heterosexuals or non-heterosexuals) and a specifically *homosexual* act (which can only be done by homosexuals) is here out in the open. It is also out in the open in New Hampshire's statute against gay and lesbian adoption, which distinguishes between "true" homosexuals and those who have engaged in same-sex sex but can claim a heterosexual identity.[53]

The combined effect of equating homosexuality with criminality but *only* statutorily forbidding sodomy is the production a novel civic status: the citizen-criminal. Almost everything that lesbians and gays might consider constitutive of or connected to their being lesbian or gay is legal: non-sodomitical sex practices, kissing, holding hands, membership in gay organizations, going to gay bars, holding a marriage ceremony, providing AIDS and safe sex education, publishing books about being lesbian or gay, lobbying for AIDS research funding and against anti-gay initiatives, and so on. Given the legality not just of *being* gay (viewed as some inner "tendency") but also of conducting one's life as a lesbian or gay man, anyone who is gay or lesbian might naturally conclude that they have the same citizenship status that any heterosexual has. However, because all things gay or lesbian are routinely coupled, in legal and lay imaginations, with sodomy (or child abuse, or solicitation, or some other category of illegality), nothing one does *as* a gay or lesbian person is untainted by the specter of criminality. Everything one does becomes an act of promoting criminality or immorality. And every gay-positive statement metamorphoses into an endorsement of crime or immorality.

Constructed as citizen-criminals, gay men and lesbians occupy a shadowy territory neither fully outside nor fully inside civil society. Unlike the criminally insane, whose inability to tell right from wrong disqualifies them from civic status, gays and lesbians formally possess civic status. But unlike heterosexual citizens, whose relation to crime is presumed to be merely contingent (they might or might not violate the law), gays and lesbians are presumed to be inherently implicated in criminal activity.

This citizen-criminal status gives discriminatory policies against gays and lesbians a distinctive flavor. While racial and gender discrimination are largely predicated on *inferiorizing* stereotypes, sexuality discrimination is largely predicated on *criminalizing* stereotypes whose ultimate suggestion is not that gays and lesbians are *incompetent*, but that they are *untrustworthy* members of civil society. Socially constituted as beings whose very nature it is to commit crimes against nature, God, and state, lesbians and gays, insofar as they publicly claim those identities, speak under a pall of guilt. Unlike their presumed "innocent" and civic-minded heterosexual counterparts, they cannot represent themselves as lesbian or gay without undermining their standing in the public sphere. That includes their standing to challenge conventional moral and legal norms. Heterosexuals have, for example, been extremely successful in decriminalizing heterosexual "crimes against nature," which include use of birth control, abortion, adultery, heterosexual sodomy. Heterosexuals have also been reasonably successful in pluralizing acceptable family arrangements — divorce, single-parenting, egalitarian gender arrangements, separate husband and wife domiciles. As presumed trustworthy members of civil society, heterosexuals have the standing to claim that they simply have different moral opinions about the permissibility of "alternative" sexual and familial practices and thus have the standing to request that law and social practices recognize differences of opinion. As presumed untrustworthy members, lesbians' and gays' expression of different, disagreeing moral opinions is continuously vulnerable to being reconstituted as promotion of immorality, if not also criminality.

IV. Conclusion

To conclude: Sexuality injustice is not best understood as a matter of confining persons who are gay or lesbian to subordinate, disadvantaging, exploitable places within sexuality-structured public and private hierarchies. Thus specific measures, such as extending privacy rights and anti-discrimination protection to gay men and lesbians,

should not be seen as primarily aimed at remedying systematic inequities in their material condition and access to opportunities.

Instead, sexuality injustice is, I think, better understood as a matter of displacing gays and lesbians to the "outside" of civil society, and thus denying a place for gays and lesbians within both public and private spheres. First, gay and lesbian *identities* are displaced from workplaces, streets, the military, markets, schools, and other public spaces by requiring lesbians and gays to adopt pseudonymous heterosexual identities as a condition of access to those public spaces. Displacing gay and lesbian identities from the public sphere in this way amounts to reserving the public sphere for heterosexuals only. Second, homosexuality and lesbianism are displaced from our social future via legal, educational, psychiatric, and familial practices that are aimed at insuring the heterosexuality of future generations. This institutionalization of gay preventative and heterosexual productive measures amounts to reserving for heterosexuals only exclusive entitlement to determine the character of future generations. Finally, the displacement of lesbians and gays from civil society is legitimized by equating being gay or lesbian with criminality, immorality, and untrustworthiness as a citizen. Defined as citizen-criminals, gays and lesbians are denied equal standing to participate in legal, social, and moral debates, including most importantly debates over the place of gays and lesbians in the public and private spheres.

NOTES

1. Marilyn Frye gives a classic definition of oppression: "The experience of oppressed people is that the living of one's life is confined and shaped by forces and barriers which are not accidental or occasional and hence avoidable, but are systematically related to each other in such a way as to catch one between and among them and restrict or penalize motion in any direction." *The Politics of Reality* 4 (1983).

2. I have made up the term "sexuality injustice." I would have preferred the less cumbersome term "sexual injustice," but this has long been used

synonymously with "gender injustice." The only other available terms — "homophobia" and "heterosexism" — bear, like "gynophobia" and "sexism," overly strong attitudinal connotations and thus are ill-suited for describing social, structural, and conceptual features.

3. Massachusetts (Mass. Gen. L. ch. 272 §34 (1986)), Tennessee (Ten. Code Ann. §39-2-612 (1980)), Florida (Fla. Stat. §800.02 (1987)), Mississippi (Section 97-29-59, Mississippi Code of 1972]

4. 478 US at 194.

5. James D. Woods & Jay H. Lucas, *The Corporate Closet: The Professional Lives of Gay Men in America*, generally, gives a thorough account of the heterosexualization of corporate life.

6. The Army at least *claimed* in *Watson* that it discriminated only on the basis of conduct not status. Judge Norris argued that Army policy could not reasonably be interpreted as drawing a conduct-status distinction (infra pp. 40-41).

7. One of the bases for separation was the fact that "[t]he member has stated that he or she is a homosexual or bisexual...." 32 *Code of Federal Regulations* Pt. 41, App. A, part 1, H.1.c.2 (1992).

8. Pat Towell, "Nunn Offers a Compromise: 'Don't Ask/Don't Tell'," *Cong. Q. Weekly Rep.*, May 15, 1993, at 1240.

9. Michael R. Gordon, "Pentagon spells out rules for ousting homosexuals" *New York Times* Dec. 23, 1993, at A14.

10. Revealingly, General Norman Schwarzkopf testified that "homosexuals have served in the past and done a great job serving their country, and I feel they can in the future" but "it's *open* homosexuality in a unit that causes this breakdown in unit cohesion." Quoted in Anne B. Goldstein, "Reasoning about Homosexuality: A Commentary on Janet Halley's 'Reasoning about Sodomy: Act and Identity In and After *Bowers v. Hardwick*'," 79 *Virginia Law Review* 1781, 1803, my italics (1993).

11. 530 F. 2d 247 (1976).

12. Ibid. at 250 (quoting Civil Service Commission letter to Singer).

13. Ibid. at 249 (summarizing Commission letter to Singer).

14. Ibid. at 251.

15. Ibid. at 255.

16. Although some women would find it easier than others to conceal their gender and adopt a pseudonymously male identity (just as some gay men and lesbians find it easier than others to adopt a pseudonymous heterosexual identity), the status-conduct distinction would permit the military or any other institution that adopted such a policy to claim that it was not discriminating against persons who *are* women, but only against womanly conduct.

17. The example is not entirely fictional. While claiming not to discriminate against persons because they are women or black, employers may penalize employees for not exhibiting sufficiently masculine or white traits. The disanalogy between gay men and lesbians on the one hand and women and blacks on the other is perhaps best understood as one of degree.

18. *Rowland* 730 F.2d at 449.

19. Ibid. at 452-453.

20. *Rowland* 470 U.S. at 1012.

21. Ibid.

22. *Rowland*, 730 F.2d at 450.

23. Havelock Ellis, *Studies in the Psychology of Sex, Vol. II: Sexual Inversion* (1928). Richard von Krafft-Ebing, *Psychopathia Sexualis: A Medico-Forensic Study* (1947).

24. Allan Bérubé, *Coming Out Under Fire: A History of Gay Men and Women in World War II* 136-138 (1990) [hereafter Bérubé].

25. 32 *Code of Federal Regulations* Pt. 41, App. A, part 1, H.1.c.1 (1992).

26. John Lauritsen and David Thorstad, *The Early Homosexual Rights Movement, 1864-1935* (1974) [hereafter Lauritsen].

27. Eve Kosofsky Sedgwick, "How to Bring Your Kids up Gay," in *Fear of a Queer Planet: Queer Politics and Social Theory*. 69 (Michael Warner ed. 1993).

28. American Psychiatric Association, *Diagnostic and Statistical Manual of Mental Disorders*, (3rd ed., 1980) (DSM-III). The American Psychiatric Association de-pathologized homosexuality in 1973, although DSM-III was not published until 1980.

29. Ibid. at 266.

30. American Psychiatric Association, *Diagnostic and Statistical Manual*, 73 (3rd revised ed., 1987), (DSM-III-R).

31. Ibid.
32. Dignified treatment of gay men and lesbians within psychiatry has not, of course, always been the norm. Efforts to "cure" gay men and lesbians reached their peak during the 1950s and 1960s. For an autobiographical account, see Martin Duberman, *Cures: A Gay Man's Odyssey* (1992).
33. Sedgwick supra note 27, at 78.
34. Sharon Elizabeth Rush, "Breaking with Tradition: Surrogacy and Gay Fathers," in *Kindred Matters: Rethinking the Philosophy of the Family* 102, 119 (Diana Tietjens Meyers, Kenneth Kipnis, and Cornelius F. Murphy eds., 1993).
35. *Gay Lib v. University of Missouri* 558 F.2d 848, 852 (1977) (summarizing the Board of Curators of the University of Missouri's resolution).
36. Ibid. at 859.
37. Quoted in *Opinion of the Justices*, Supreme Court of New Hampshire, 530 A.2d 21, 23 (N.H. 1987).
38. Ibid. at 25.
39. Quoted in Jeffrey Weeks, "Pretended Family Relationships," in *Against Nature: Essays on History, Sexuality, and Identity* 134, 137 (1991). Weeks also provides a socio-historical analysis of why the family became a focus of British legal attention.
40. Timothy Egan, "Oregon Measure Asks State to Repress Homosexuality," *New York Times*, August 16, 1992, at A34.
41. Cal. Proposition 6, §3(b)(2) (1978). Quoted in Nan D. Hunter, "Identity, Speech, and Equality," 79 *Virginia Law Review* 1695 (1993) at 1703. She gives a detailed account of the full range of no promo homo policies.
42. John Boswell, "Categories, Experience and Sexuality," in *Forms of Desire: Sexual Orientation and the Social Constructionist Controversy* 157-158 (Edward Stein ed., 1990).
43. Ibid. at 159.
44. 461 P .2d 375 (Cal. 1969).
45. Ibid. at 394.
46. Ibid. at 392.
47. Ibid. at 377-378.
48. Employment of Homosexuals and Other Sex Perverts in Government, Interim Report by the Subcomm. for Comm. on Expenditure in the Exec. Dep'ts, S. Doc. 24, 81st Cong., 2d Sess. (1950), 3.
49 Order 10,450. 18 Fed. Reg. 2489 (1953).
50. Immigration and Nationality Act, Pub. L. No. 82-414, 66 Stat. 163 (1952). For an historical account of the McCarthy era purge of homosexuals, see Bérubé supra note 24.
51. Lauritsen supra note 26.
52. 875 F.2d 699, 715 (1989) (Judge Norris, concurring). For clarity, I have substituted "same-sex" for "homosexual" in the original text.
53. *Opinion of the Justices* 530 A.2d at 24.

AGAINST MARRIAGE AND MOTHERHOOD

Claudia Card

Claudia Card teaches in the Philosophy Department as well as in Women's Studies and Environmental Studies at the University of Wisconsin, Madison. She is the author of The Unnatural Lottery: Character and Moral Luck *(1996),* On Feminist Ethics and Politics *(1999), and* The Atrocity Paradigm: A Theory of Evil *(2002), and is the editor of* Adventures in Lesbian Philosophy *(1994) and* Feminist Ethics at the Turn of the Millennium *(1999).*

Card argues that advocating lesbian and gay rights to legal marriage and parenthood insufficiently criticizes both marriage and motherhood as they are currently practiced and structured by Western legal institutions. Instead, she claims, we would do better not to let the state define our intimate unions, and parenting would be improved if the power presently concentrated in the hands of one or two guardians were diluted and distributed through an appropriately concerned community.

The title of this essay is deliberately provocative, because I fear that radical feminist perspectives on marriage and motherhood are in danger of being lost in the quest for equal rights. My concerns, however, are specific. I am skeptical of using the institution of motherhood as a source of paradigms for ethical theory. And I am skeptical of legal marriage as a way to gain a better life for lesbian and gay lovers or as a way to provide a supportive environment of lesbian and gay parents and their children. Of course, some are happy with marriage and motherhood as they now exist. My concern is with the price of that joy being borne by those trapped by marriage or motherhood and deeply unlucky in the company they find there. Nevertheless, nothing that I say is intended to disparage the characters of many magnificent women who have struggled in and around these institutions to make the best of a trying set of options.

Backgrounds

My perspective on marriage is influenced not only by other's written reports and analyses but also by my own history of being raised in a lower-middle-class white village family by parents married (to each other) for more than three decades, by my firsthand experiences of urban same-sex domestic partnerships lasting from two and one half to nearly seven years (good ones and bad, some racially mixed, some white, generally mixed, in class and religious backgrounds), and by my more recent experience as a lesbianfeminist whose partner of the past decade is not a domestic partner. My perspective on child rearing is influenced not by my experience as a mother, but by my experience as a daughter reared by a full-time mother-housewife, by having participated heavily in the raising of my younger siblings, and by having grown to adulthood in a community in which many of the working-class and farming families exemplified aspects of what bell hooks calls "revolutionary parenting" (hooks 1984, 133-46).

bell hooks writes, "Childrearing is a responsibility that can be shared with other childrearers, with people who do not live with children. This form of parenting is revolutionary in this society because it takes place in opposition to the idea that parents, especially mothers, should be the only childrearers. Many people raised in black communities experienced this type of community-based child care" (hooks 1984, 144). This form of child rearing may be more common than is generally acknowledged in a society in which those whose caretaking does not take place in a nuclear family are judged by those with the power to set standards as unfortunate and deprived. Although bell hooks continues to use the language of "mothering" to some extent in elaborating "revolutionary parenting," I see this revolution as offering an alternative to mothering as a social institution.

Because it appears unlikely that the legal rights of marriage and motherhood in the European American models of those institutions currently at issue in our courts will disappear or even be seriously eroded during my lifetime, my opposition to them here takes the form of skepticism primarily in the two areas mentioned above: ethical theorizing and lesbian/gay activism. I believe that women who identify as lesbian or gay should be reluctant to put our activist energy into attaining legal equity with heterosexuals in marriage and motherhood — not because the existing discrimination against us is in any way justifiable but because these institutions are so deeply flawed that they seem to me unworthy of emulation and reproduction.

For more than a decade, feminist philosophers and lesbian/gay activists have been optimistic about the potentialities of legal marriage and legitimated motherhood. This should be surprising, considering the dismal political genealogies of those institutions, which have been generally admitted and widely publicized by feminist thinkers. Yet, in the project of claiming historically characteristic life experiences of women as significant data for moral theory, many are turning to women's experiences as mothers for ethical insight. Not all focus on marriage and motherhood. Feminist philosophers are taking as valuable theoretical paradigms for ethics many kinds of caring relationships that have been salient in women's lives. Marilyn Friedman, for example, has explored female friendship in *What Are Friends For?* (1993). Sarah Hoagland (1988) offers value inquiry based on experiences of lesbian bonding in many forms. *Mothering*, edited by Joyce Trebilcot (1983), includes essays repre-

senting critical as well as supportive stances regarding motherhood. These works, however, are exceptions to a wider trend of theorizing that draws mainly positive inspiration from the experiences of women as mothers. Thus, Sara Ruddick's *Maternal Thinking* (1989), which acknowledges the need for caution, is devoted to developing ethical ideas based on experiences of mother-child relationships. Nel Noddings's *Caring* (1984) and Virginia Held's *Feminist Morality* (1993) likewise take inspiration from the experience of "mothering persons" and other caregivers, and to some extent, Annette Baier does likewise in *Moral Prejudices* (1994). These last four philosophers urge an extension of mothering values to more public realms of activity.

In *Black Feminist Thought* Patricia Hill Collins also speaks of "a more generalized ethic of caring and personal accountability among African-American women who often feel accountable to all the Black community's children" (1991, chap.6). Her models for an "ethic of caring and personal accountability," however, differ significantly from the models characteristic of the work of so many white feminists in that her models already involve a wider community that includes "othermothers" as well as "bloodmothers," models elaborated by bell hooks as instances of "revolutionary parenting" (hooks 1984, 133-46). My skepticism is not aimed at such "revolutionary parenting" which I find has much to recommend it. Yet "parenting" by a wider community is a form of child care not currently enshrined in Northern legal systems. It is not the model guiding lesbian and gay activists currently agitating for equal rights before the law. For more communal child care, the language of "mothering" and even "parenting" is somewhat misleading in that these practices are not particularly "mother-centered" or even "parent-centered" but are centered on the needs of children and of the community.

Audre Lorde, who wrote about her relationship with her son (1984, 72-80), has left us with reflections on yet another model of parenting, that of a lesbian relationship struggling against the models of heterosexual marriage and patriarchal motherhood in her social environment. Nevertheless, she does not attempt to generalize from her experience or to treat it as a source of inspiration for ethical theory.

When confronted with my negative attitudes toward marriage and motherhood, some recoil as though I were proposing that we learn to do without water and oxygen on the ground that both are polluted (even killing us). Often, I believe, this reaction comes from certain assumptions that the reader or hearer may be inclined to make, which I here note in order to set aside at the outset.

First, my opposition to marriage is not an opposition to intimacy, nor to long-term relationships of intimacy, nor to durable partnerships of many sorts.[1] I understand marriage as a relationship to which the State is an essential third party. Also, like the practices of footbinding and suttee, which, according to the researches of Mary Daly (1978, 113-52) originated among the powerful classes, marriage in Europe was once available only to those with substantial social power. Previously available only to members of propertied classes, the marriage relation has come to be available in modern Northern democracies to any adult heterosexual couple neither of whom is already married to someone else. This is what lesbian and gay agitation for the legal right to marry is about. This is what I find calls for extreme caution.

Second, my opposition to motherhood is neither an opposition to the guidance, education, and caretaking of children nor an opposition to the formation of many kinds of bonds between children and adults.[2] Nor am I opposed to the existence of homes as places of long-term residence with others of a variety of ages with whom one has deeply committed relationships. When "the family" is credited with being a bulwark against a hostile world, as in the case of many families in the African and Jewish disaporas, the bulwark that is meant often consists of a variety of deeply committed personal (as opposed to legal) relationships and the stability of caring that they represent, or home as a site of these things. The bulwark is not the legitimation (often precarious or nonexistent) of such relationships through institutions of the State. The State was often one of the things that these relationships formed a bulwark against.

Marriage and motherhood in the history of modern patriarchies have been mandatory for and oppressive to women, and they have been criticized by feminists on those grounds. My concerns, however, are as much for the children as for the women that some of these children become and for the goal of avoiding the reproduction of patriarchy. Virginia Held, one optimist about the potentialities of marriage and motherhood, finds motherhood to be part of a larger conception of family, which she takes to be constructed of noncontractual relationships. She notes that although Marxists and recent communitarians might agree with her focus on noncontractual relationships, their views remain uninformed by feminist critiques of patriarchal families. The family from which she would have society and ethical theorists learn, ultimately, is a postpatriarchal family. But what is a "postpatriarchal family"? Is it a coherent concept?

"Family" is itself a family resemblance concept. Many contemporary lesbian and gay partnerships, households, and friendship networks fit not patriarchal stereotypes and are not sanctified by legal marriage, although their members still regard themselves as "family."[3] But should they? Many social institutions, such as insurance companies, do not honor such conceptions of "family." Family, as understood in contexts where material benefits tend to be at stake, is not constituted totally by noncontractual relationships. At its core is to be found one or more marriage contracts. For those who work to enlarge the concept of family to include groupings that are currently totally noncontractual, in retaining patriarchal vocabulary there is a danger of importing patriarchal ideals and of inviting treatment as deviant or "second class" at best.

"Family," our students learn in Women's Studies 101, comes from the Latin *familia,* meaning "household," which in turn came from *families,* which according to the *OED*, meant "servant." The ancient Roman *paterfamilias* was the head of a household of servants and slave, including his wife or wives, concubines, and children. He had the power of life and death over them. The ability of contemporary male heads of households to get away with battering, incest, and murder suggests to many feminists that the family has not evolved into anything acceptable yet. Would a household of persons whose relationships with each other transcended (as those families do) sojourns under one roof continue to be rightly called "family" if no members had significant social support for treating other members abusively? Perhaps the postpatriarchal relationships envisioned by Virginia Held and by so many lesbians and gay men should be called something else, to mark that radical departure from family history. But it is not just a matter of a word. It is difficult to imagine what such relationships would be.

In what follows, I say more about marriage than about motherhood, because it is legal marriage that sets the contexts in which and the background against which motherhood has been legitimated, and it defines contexts in which mothering easily becomes disastrous for children.

Lesbian (or Gay) Marriage?

A special vantage point is offered by the experience of lesbians and gay men, among whom there is currently no consensus (although much strong feeling on both sides) on whether to pursue the legal right to marry a same-sex lover (Blumenfeld, Wolfson, and Brownworth, all 1996). When heterosexual partners think about marriage, they usually consider the more limited question whether they (as individuals) should marry (each other) and if they did not marry, what the consequences would be for children they might have or raise. They consider this in the context of a State that gives them the legal option of marriage. Lesbians and gay men are currently in the position of having to consider the larger question whether the legal option of marriage is a good idea, as we do not presently have it in relation to our lovers. We have it, of course, in relation to the other sex, and many have exercised it as a cover, as insurance, for resident alien status, and so forth. If it is because we already have rights to marry heterosexually that right-wing attackers of lesbian or gay rights complain of our wanting "special rights," we should reply that, of course, any legalization of same-sex marriage should extend that "privilege" to heterosexuals as well.

The question whether lesbians and gay men should pursue the right to marry is not the same as the question whether the law is wrong in its refusal to honor same-sex marriages. Richard Mohr (1994, 31-53) defends gay marriages from that point of view as well as I have seen it done. Evan Wolfson develops powerfully an analogy between the denial of marriage to same-sex couples and the antimiscegenation laws that were overturned in the United States just little more than a quarter century ago (Wolfson 1996). What I have to say should apply to relationships between lovers (or parents) of different races as well as to those of same-sex lovers (or parents). The ways we have been treated are abominable. But it does not follow that we should seek legal marriage.

It is one thing to argue that others are wrong to deny us something and another to argue that what they would deny us is something we should fight for the right to have. I do not deny that others are wrong to exclude same-sex lovers and lovers of different races from the rights of marriage. I question only whether we should fight for those rights, even if we do not intend to exercise them. Suppose that slave-owning in some mythical society were denied to otherwise free women, on the ground that such women as slave-owners would pervert the institution of slavery. Women (both free and unfree) could (unfortunately) document empirically the falsity of beliefs underlying such grounds. It would not follow that women should fight for the right to own slaves, or even for the rights of other women to own slaves. Likewise, if marriage is a deeply flawed institution, even though it is a special injustice to exclude lesbians and gay men arbitrarily from participating in it, it would not necessarily advance the cause of justice on the whole to remove the special injustice of discrimination.

About same-sex marriage I feel something like the way I feel about prostitution. Let us, by all means, *decriminalize* sodomy and so forth. Although marriage rights would be *sufficient* to enable lovers to have sex legally, such rights should not be necessary for that purpose. Where they *are* legally necessary and also available for protection against the social oppression of same-sex lovers, as for lovers of different races, there will be enormous pressure to marry. Let us not pretend that marriage is basically a good thing on the ground that durable intimate relationships are. Let us not be eager to have the State regulate our unions. Let us work to remove barriers to our enjoying some of the privileges presently available only to heterosexual married couples. But in doing so, we should also be careful not to support discrimination against those who choose not to marry and not to support continued state definition of the legitimacy of intimate relationships. I would rather see the state *de*regulate heterosexual marriage than see it begin to regulate same-sex marriage.

As the child of parents married to each other for thirty-two years, I once thought I knew what marriage meant, even though laws vary from one jurisdiction to another and the dictionary, as Mohr notes, sends us around in a circle, referring us to "husband" and "wife," in turn defined by "marriage." Mohr argues convincingly that "marriage" need not presuppose the gendered concepts of "husband" and "wife" (1994, 31-53). I will not rehearse that ground here. History seems to support him. After reading cover to cover and with great interest John Boswell's *Same-Sex Unions in Premodern Europe* (1994), however, I no longer feel so confident that I know when a "union" counts as a "marriage." Boswell, who discusses many kinds of unions, refrains from using the term "marriage" to describe the same-sex unions he researched, even though they were sanctified by religious ceremonies. Some understandings of such unions, apparently, did not presuppose that the partners were not at the same time married to someone of the other sex.

Mohr, in his suggestions for improving marriage law by attending to the experience of gay men, proposes that sexual fidelity not be a requirement (1994, 49-50). What would remain without such a requirement, from a legal point of view, sounds to me like mutual *adoption*, or guardianship. Adoption, like marriage, is a way to become next-of-kin. This could have substantial economic consequences. But is there any good reason to restrict mutual adoption to two parties at a time? If mutual adoption is what we want, perhaps the law of adop-

tion is what we should use, or suitably amend. And yet the law of adoption is not without its problematic aspects, some similar to those of the law of marriage. For it does not specify precisely a guardian's rights and responsibilities. Perhaps those who want legal contracts with each other would do better to enter into contracts the contents of which and duration of which they specifically define.

As noted above, my partner of the past decade is not a domestic partner. She and I form some kind of fairly common social unit which, so far as I know, remains nameless. Along with such namelessness goes a certain invisibility, a mixed blessing to which I will return. We do not share a domicile (she has her house; I have mine). Nor do we form an economic unit (she pays her bills; I pay mine). Although we certainly have fun together, our relationship is not based simply on fun. We share the sorts of mundane details of daily living that Mohr finds constitutive of marriage (often in her house, often in mine). We know a whole lot about each other's lives that the neighbors and our other friends will never know. In times of trouble, we are each other's first line of defense, and in times of need, we are each other's main support. Still, we are not married. Nor do we yearn to marry. Yet if marrying became an option that would legitimate behavior otherwise illegitimate and make available to us social securities that will no doubt become even more important to us as we age, we and many others like us might be pushed into marriage. Marrying under such conditions is not a totally free choice.

Because of this unfreedom, I find at least four interconnected kinds of problems with marriage. Three may be somewhat remediable in principle, although if they were remedied, many might no longer have strong motives to marry. I doubt that the fourth problem, which I also find most important, is fixable.

The first problem, perhaps easiest to remedy in principle (if not in practice) is that employers and others (such as units of government) often make available only to legally married couples benefits that anyone could be presumed to want, married or not, such as affordable health and dental insurance, the right to live in attractive residential areas, visitation rights in relation to significant others, and so forth. Spousal benefits for employees are a significant portion of many workers' compensation. Thus married workers are often, in effect, paid more for the same labor than unmarried workers (Berzon 1988, 266; Pierce 1995, 5). This is one way in which people who do not have independent access to an income often find themselves economically pressured into marrying. Historically, women have been in this position oftener than men, including, of course, most pre-twentieth century lesbians, many of whom married men for economic security.

The second problem is that even though divorce by mutual consent is now generally permitted in the United States, the consequences of divorce can be so difficult that many who should divorce do not. This to some extent is a continuation of the benefits problem. But also, if one partner can sue the other for support or receive a share of the other's assets to which they would not otherwise have been legally entitled, there are new economic motives to preserve emotionally disastrous unions.

The third issue, which would be seriously troublesome for many lesbians, is that legal marriage as currently understood in Northern democracies is monogamous in the sense of one *spouse* at a time, even though the law in many states no longer treats "adultery" (literally "pollution") as criminal. Yet many of us have more than one long-term intimate relationship during the same time period. Any attempt to change the current understanding of marriage so as to allow plural marriage partners (with plural contracts) would have economic implications that I have yet to see anyone explore.

Finally, the fourth problem, the one that I doubt is fixable (depending on what "marriage" means) is that the legal rights of access that married partners have to each other's persons, property, and lives makes it all but impossible for a spouse to defend herself (or himself), or to be protected against torture, rape, battery, stalking, mayhem, or murder by the other spouse. Spousal murder accounts for a substantial number of murders each year. This factor is made worse by the presence of the second problem mentioned above (difficulties for divorce that lead many to remain married when they should not), which provide motives to violence within marriages. Legal marriage thus enlists state support for conditions conductive to murder and mayhem.

The point is not that all marriages are violent. It is not about the frequency of violence, although the frequency appears high. The points are, rather, that the institution places obstacles in the way of protecting spouses (however many) who need it and is conducive to violence in relationships that go bad. Battery is, of course, not confined to spouses. Lesbian and gay battery is real (see Renzetti 1992; Lobel 1986; Island and Letellier 1991). But the law does not protect unmarried batterers or tend to preserve the relationships of unmarried lovers in the way that it protects husbands and tends to preserve marriages.

Why, then, would anyone marry? Because it is a tradition, glorified and romanticized. It grants status. It is a significant (social) mark of adulthood for women in patriarchy. It is a way to avoid certain hassles from one's family of origin and from society at large — hassles to oneself, to one's lover (if there is only one), and to children with whom one may live or whom one may bring into being. We need better traditions. And women have long needed other social marks of adulthood and ways to escape families of origin.

Under our present exclusion from the glories of legal matrimony, the usual reason why lesbians or gay men form partnerships and stay together is because we care for each other. We may break up for other kinds or reasons (such as one of us being assigned by an employer to another part of the country and neither of us being able to afford to give up our jobs). But when we stay together, that is usually because of how we feel about each other and about our life together. Consider how this basic taken-for-granted fact might change if we could marry with the State's blessings. There are many material benefits to tempt those who can into marrying, not to mention the improvement in one's social reputation as a reliable citizen (and for those of us who are not reliable citizens, the protection against having a spouse forced to testify against us in court).

Let us consider each of these four problems further. The first was that of economic and other benefits, such as insurance that employers often make available only to marrieds, the right of successorship to an apartment, inheritance rights, and the right to purchase a home in whatever residential neighborhood one can afford. The attachment of such benefits to marital status is a problem in two respects. First, because the benefits are substantial, not trivial, they offer an ulterior motive for turning a lover relationship into a marriage — even for pretending to care for someone, deceiving oneself as well as others. As Emma Goldman argued in the early twentieth century, when marriage becomes an insurance policy, it may no longer be compatible with love (1969). Second, the practice of making such benefits available only to marrieds discriminates against those who, for whatever reason, do not marry. Because of the first factor, many heterosexuals who do not fundamentally approve of legal marriage give in and marry anyhow. Because of the second factor, many heterosexual feminists, however, refuse legal marriage (although the State may regard their relationship as common law marriages)

Now add to the spousal benefits problem the second difficulty, that of the consequences of getting a divorce (for example, consequences pertaining to shared property, alimony, or child support payments and difficulties in terms of access to children), especially if the divorce is not friendly. Intimate partnerships beginning from sexual or erotic attraction tend to be of limited viability, even under favorable circumstances. About half of all married couples in the United States at present get divorced, and probably most of the other half should. But the foreseeable consequences of divorce provide motives to stay married for many spouses who no longer love each other (if they ever did) and have even grown to hate each other. Staying married ordinarily hampers one's ability to develop a satisfying lover relationship with someone new. As long as marriage is monogamous in the sense of one *spouse* at a time, it interferes with one's ability to obtain spousal benefits for a new lover. When spouses grow to hate each other, the access that was a joy as lovers turns into

something highly dangerous. I will return to this.

Third, the fact of multiple relationships is a problem even for relatively good marriages. Mohr, as noted, argues in favor of reforming marriage so as not to require sexual exclusiveness rather than officially permitting only monogamy. Yet he was thinking not of multiple *spouses* but of a monogamous marriage in which neither partner expects sexual exclusiveness of the other. Yet, one spouse per person is monogamy, however promiscuous the spouses may be. The advantages that Mohr enumerates as among the perks of marriage apply only to spouses, not to relationships with additional significant others who are not one's spouses. Yet the same reasons that lead one to want those benefits for a spouse can lead one to want them for additional significant others. If lesbian and gay marriages were acknowledged in Northern democracies today, they would be legally as monogamous as heterosexual marriage, regardless of the number of one's actual sexual partners. This does not reflect the relationships that many lesbians and gay men have or want.

Boswell wrote about same-sex unions that did not preclude simultaneous heterosexual marriages (1994). The parties were not permitted to formalize unions with more than one person of the same sex at a time, however. Nor were they permitted to have children with a person of the other sex to whom they were not married. Thus, in a certain restricted sense, each formal union was monogamous, even though one could have both kinds at once.

Christine Pierce argues, in support of the option to legalize lesbian and gay marriages, that lesbian and gay images have been cast too much in terms of individuals — *The Well Of Loneliness* (Hall 1950), for example — and not enough in terms of relationships, especially serious relationships involving long-term commitments (Pierce 1995, 13). Marriage gives visibility to people "as couples, partners, family, and kin," a visibility that lesbians and gay men have lacked and that could be important to dispelling negative stereotypes and assumptions that our relationships do not embody many of the same ideals as those of many heterosexual couples, partners, family, and kin (Pierce 1996). This is both true and important.

It is not clear, however, that legal marriage would offer visibility to our relationships as they presently exist. It might well change our relationships so that they became more like heterosexual marriages, loveless after the first few years but hopelessly bogged down with financial entanglements or children (adopted or products of turkey-baster insemination or previous marriages), making separation or divorce (at least in the near future) too difficult to contemplate, giving rise to new motives for mayhem and murder. Those who never previously felt pressure to marry a lover might confront not just new options but new pressures and traps.

My views on marriage may surprise those familiar with my work on the military ban (Card 1995). For I have argued against the ban and in favor of lesbian and gay access to military service, and I argued that even those who disapprove of the military should object to wrongful exclusions of lesbians and gay men. In the world in which we live, military institutions may well be less dispensable than marriage, however in need of restraint military institutions are. But for those who find legal marriage and legitimate motherhood objectionable, should I be moved here by what moved me there — that it is one thing not to exercise an option and another to be denied the option, that denying us the option for no good reason conveys that there is something wrong with us, thereby contributing to our public disfigurement and defamation, and that these considerations give us good reasons to protest being denied the option even if we never intend to exercise it? I am somewhat but not greatly moved by such arguments in this case. The case of marriage seems to me more like the case of slavery than like that of the military.

Marriage and military service are in many ways relevantly different. Ordinarily, marriage (like slavery) is much worse, if only because its impact on our lives is usually greater. Marriage is supposed to be a lifetime commitment. It is at least open-ended. When available, it is not simply an option but tends to be coercive, especially for women in a misogynist society. For those who choose it, it threatens to be a dangerous trap. Military service is ordinarily neither a lifetime nor open-ended commitment; one signs up for a certain number of years. During war, one may be drafted (also for a limited time) and, of course, even killed, but the issue has not been whether to draft lesbians and gay men. Past experience shows that gay men will be drafted in war, even if barred from enlistment in peace. When enlistment is an option, it does not threaten to trap one in a relationship from which it will be extremely difficult to extricate oneself in the future. There is some analogy with the economically coercive aspect for the marriage "option." Because those who have never served are ineligible for substantial educational and health benefits, many from low- (or no-) income families enlist to obtain such things as college educations and even health and dental insurance. However, the service one has to give for such benefits as an enlistee is limited compared to spousal service. Being killed is a risk in either case.

In such a context, pointing out that many marriages are very loving, not at all violent, and proclaim to the world two people's honorable commitment to each other, seems to me analogous to pointing out, as many slave-owners did, that many slave-owners were truly emotionally bonded with their slaves, that they did not whip them, and that even the slaves were proud and honored to be the slaves of such masters.

Some of the most moving stories I hear in discussions of gay marriage point out that the care rendered the ill by families is a great service to society and that the chosen families of gay AIDS patients deserve to be honored in the same way as a family based on a heterosexual union. The same, of course, applies to those who care for lesbian or gay cancer patients of for those with sever disabilities or other illnesses. But is this a service to society? Or to the State? The State has a history of depending on families to provide care that no human being should be without in infancy, illness, and old age. Lesbians and gay men certainly have demonstrated our ability to serve the State in this capacity as well as heterosexuals. But where does this practice leave those who are not members of families? Or those who object on principle to being members of these unions as sanctified by the State?

To remedy the injustices of discrimination against lesbians, gay men, and unmarried heterosexual couples, many municipalities are experimenting with domestic partnership legislation. This may be a step in the right direction, insofar as it is a much more voluntary relationship, more specific, more easily dissolved. Yet, partners who are legally married need not share a domicile unless one of them so chooses; in this respect, eligibility for the benefits of domestic partnership may be more restrictive than marriage. And the only domestic partnership legislation that I have seen requires that one claim only one domestic partner at a time, which does not distinguish it from monogamous marriage (see Berzon 1988, 163-82).

Whatever social unions the State may sanction, it is important to realize that they become State-defined, however they may have originated. One's rights and privileges as a spouse can change dramatically with one's residence, as Betty Mahmoody discovered when she went with her husband to Iran for what he had promised would be a temporary visit (Mahmoody with Hoffer 1987). She found after arriving in Iran that she had no legal right to leave without her husband's consent, which he then denied her, leaving as her only option for returning to the United States to escape illegally (which she did). Even if a couple would not be legally recognized as married in a particular jurisdiction, if they move from another jurisdiction in which they *were* legally recognized as married, they are generally legally recognized as married in the new jurisdiction, and they are held to whatever responsibilities the new jurisdiction enforces. The case of Betty Mahmoody is especially interesting because it involves her husband's rights of access. Spousal rights of access do not have the same sort of contingency in relation to marriage as, say, a right to family rates for airline tickets.

Marriage is a legal institution the obligations of which tend to be highly informal — i.e., loosely defined, unspecific, and inexplicit about exactly what one is to do and about the consequences of failing. In this regard, a marriage contract differs from the contract of a bank loan. In a legal loan contract, the parties' reciprocal obligations become highly formalized. In discharging the obligations

of a loan, one dissolves the obligation. In living up to marriage obligations, however, one does not dissolve the marriage or its obligations; if anything, one strengthens them. As I have argued elsewhere, the obligations of marriage and those of loan contracts exhibit different paradigms (Card 1988, 1990). The debtor paradigm is highly formal, whereas the obligations of spouses tend to be relatively informal and fit better a paradigm that I have called the trustee paradigm. The obligations of a trustee, or guardian, are relatively abstractly defined. A trustee or guardian is expected to exercise judgment and discretion in carrying out the obligations to care, protect, or maintain. The trustee *status* may be relatively formal — precisely defined regarding dates on which it takes effect, compensation for continuing in good standing, and the consequences of losing the status. But consequences of failing to do this or that specific thing may not be specified or specifiable, because what is required to fulfill duties of caring, safekeeping, protection, or maintenance can be expected to vary with circumstances, changes in which may not be readily foreseeable. A large element of discretion seems ineliminable. This makes it difficult *to hold a trustee accountable for abuses* while the status of trustee is retained, and it also means that it is difficult to prove that the status should be terminated. Yet the only significant sanction against a trustee may be withdrawal of that status. Spousal status and parental status fit the trustee model, rather than the debtor model, of obligation. This means that it is difficult to hold a spouse or a parent accountable for abuse.

Central to the idea of marriage, historically, has been intimate access to the persons, belongings, activities, even histories of one another. More important than sexual access, marriage gives spouses physical access to each other's residences and belongings, and it gives access to information about each other, including financial status, that other friends and certainly the neighbors do not ordinarily have. For all that has been said about the privacy that marriage protects, what astonishes me is how much privacy one gives up in marrying.

This mutual access appears to be a central point of marrying. Is it wise to abdicate legally one's privacy to that extent? What interests does it serve? Anyone who in fact cohabits with another may seem to give up similar privacy. Yet, without marriage, it is possible to take one's life back without encountering the law as an obstacle. One may even be able to enlist legal help in getting it back. In this regard, uncloseted lesbians and gay men presently have a certain advantage — which, by the way, "palimony" suits threaten to undermine by applying the idea of "common law" marriage to same-sex couples (see, e.g., Faulkner with Nelson 1993).

Boswell argued that, historically, what has been important to marriage is consent, not sexual relations. But, consent to what? What is the point of marrying? Historically, for the propertied classes, he notes, the point of heterosexual marriage was either dynastic or property concerns or both. Dynastic concerns do not usually figure in arguments for lesbian or gay marriage. Although property concerns do, they are among the kinds of concerns often better detached from marriage. That leaves as a central point of marriage the legal right of cohabitation and the access to each other's lives that this entails.

It might still be marriage if sexual exclusivity, or even sex, were not part of it, but would it still be marriage if rights of cohabitation were not part of it? Even marrieds who voluntarily live apart retain the *right* of cohabitation. Many rights and privileges available to marrieds today might exist in a real relationship that did not involve cohabitation rights (for example, insurance rights, access to loved ones in hospitals, rights to inherit, and many other rights presently possessed by kin who do not live with each other). If the right of cohabitation is central to the concept of legal marriage, it deserves more critical attention that philosophers have given it.

Among the trappings of marriage that have received attention and become controversial, ceremonies and rituals are much discussed. I have no firm opinions about ceremonies or rituals. A far more important issue seems to me to be the marriage *license*, which receives hardly any attention at all. Ceremonies affirming a relationship can take place at any point in the relationship. But a license is what one needs to initiate a legal marriage. To marry legally, one applies to the state for a license,

and marriage, once entered into, licenses spouses to certain kinds of access to each other's person and lives. It is a mistake to think of a license as simply enhancing everyone's freedom. One person's license, in this case, can be another's prison. Prerequisites for marriage licenses are astonishingly lax. Anyone of a certain age, not presently married to someone else, and free of certain communicable diseases automatically qualifies. A criminal record for violent crimes is, to my knowledge, no bar. Compare this with other licenses, such as a driver's license. In Wisconsin, to retain a driver's license, we submit periodically to eye exams. Some states have more stringent requirements. To obtain a driver's license, all drivers have to pass a written and a behind-the wheel test to demonstrate knowledge and skill. In Madison, Wisconsin, even to adopt a cat from the humane society, we have to fill out a form demonstrating knowledge of relevant ordinances for pet-guardian. Yet to marry, applicants need demonstrate no knowledge of the laws pertaining to marriage nor any relationship skills nor even the modicum of self-control required to respect another human being. And once the marriage exists, the burden of proof is always on those who would dissolve it, never on those who would continue it in perpetuity.

Further disanalogies between drivers' and marriage licenses confirm that in our society there is greater concern for victims of bad driving than for those of bad marriages. You cannot legally drive without a license, whereas it is now in many jurisdictions not illegal for unmarried adults of whatever sex to cohabit. One can acquire the status of spousehood simply by cohabiting heterosexually for several years, whereas one does not acquire a driver's license simply by driving for years without one. Driving without the requisite skills and scruples is recognized as a great danger to others and treated accordingly. No comparable recognition is given the dangers of legally sanctioning the access of one person to the person and life of another without evidence of the relevant knowledge and scruples of those so licensed. The consequence is that married victims of partner battering and rape have less protection than anyone except children. What is at stake are permanently disabling and life-threatening injuries, for those who survive. I do not, at present, see how this vulnerability can be acceptably removed from the institution of legal marriage. Measures could be taken to render its disastrous consequences less likely than they are presently but at the cost of considerable state intrusion into our lives.

The right of cohabitation seems to me central to the question whether legal marriage can be made an acceptable institution, especially to the question whether marriage can be envisaged in such a way that its partners could protect themselves, or be protected, adequately against spousal rape and battery. Although many states now recognize on paper the crimes of marital rape and stalking and are better educated than before about marital battering, the progress has been mostly on paper. Wives continue to die daily at a dizzying rate.

Thus I conclude that legalizing lesbian and gay marriage, turning a personal commitment into a license regulable and enforceable by the state, is probably a very bad idea and that lesbians and gay men are probably better off, all things considered, without the "option" (and its consequent pressures) to obtain and act on such a license, despite some of the immediate material and spiritual gains to some of being able to do so. Had we any chance of success, we might do better to agitate for the abolition of legal marriage altogether.

Nevertheless, many will object that marriage provides an important environment for the rearing of children. An appreciation of the conduciveness of marriage to murder and mayhem challenges that assumption. Historically, marriage and motherhood have gone hand in hand — ideologically, although often enough not in fact. That marriage can provide a valuable context for motherhood — even if it is unlikely to do so — as an argument in favor of marriage seems to presuppose that motherhood is a good thing. So let us consider next whether that is so.

Why Motherhood?

The term "mother" is ambiguous between a woman who gives birth and a female who parents, that is, rears a child — often but not necessarily the same

woman. The term "motherhood" is ambiguous between the experience of mothers (in either sense, usually the second) and a social practice the rules of which structure child rearing. It is the latter that interests me here. Just as some today would stretch the concept of "family" to cover any committed partnership, household, or close and enduring network of friends, others would stretch the concept of "motherhood" to cover any mode of child rearing. That is not how I understand "motherhood." Just as not every durable intimate partnership is a marriage, not every mode of child rearing exemplifies motherhood. Historically, motherhood has been a core element of patriarchy. Within the institution of motherhood, mother's primary commitments have been to father and only secondarily to his children. Unmarried women have been held responsible by the State for the primary care of children they birth, unless a man wished to claim them. In fact, of course, children are raised by grandparents, single parents (heterosexual, lesbian, gay, asexual, and so on), and extended families, all in the midst of patriarchies. But those have been regarded as deviant parenting, with nothing like the prestige or social and legal support available to patriarchal mothers, as evidenced in the description of the relevant "families" in many cases as providing at best "broken homes."

Apart from the institution of marriage and historical ideals of the family, it is uncertain what characteristics mother-child relationships would have, for many alternatives are possible. In the good ones, mother-child relationships would not be as characterized as they have been by involuntary uncompensated caretaking. Even today, an ever-increasing amount of caretaking is being done contractually in day-care centers, with the result that a legitimate mother's relationship to her child is often much less a caretaking relationship than her mother's relationship to her was. Nor are paid day-care workers "mothers" (even though they may engage briefly in some "mothering activities"), because they are free to walk away from their jobs. Their relationships with a child may be no more permanent or special to the child than those of a babysitter. Boswell's history *The Kindness of Strangers* (1988) describes centuries of children being taken in by those at whose doorsteps babies were deposited, often anonymously. Not all such children had anyone to call "Mother." Children have been raised in convents, orphanages, or boarding schools rather than in households. Many raised in households are cared for by hired help, rather than by anyone they call "Mother." Many children today commute between separated or divorced parents, spending less time in a single household than many children of lesbian parent, some of whom, like Lesléa Newman's Heather, have two people to call "Mother" (Newman 1989). Many children are raised by older siblings, even in households in which someone else is called "Mother."

My point is not to support Newt Gingrich by glorifying orphanages or other hired caretakers but to put in perspective rhetoric about children's needs and about the ideal relationships of children to mothers. Much ink has been spilled debunking what passes for "love" in marriage. It is time to consider how much of the "love" that children are said to need is no more love that spousal attachments have been. Children do need stable intimate bonds with adults. But they also need supervision, education, health care, and a variety of relationships with people of a variety of ages. What the State tends to enforce in motherhood is the child's access to its mother, which guarantees none of these things, and the mother's answerability for her child's waywardness, which gives her a motive for constant supervision, thereby removing certain burdens from others but easily also endangering the well-being of her child if she is ill supplied with resources. Lacking adequate social or material resources, many a parent resorts to violent discipline in such situations, which the State has been reluctant to prevent or even acknowledge. This is what it has meant, legally, for a child to be a mother's "own": her own is the child who has legal rights of access to her and for whose waywardness she becomes answerable, although she is largely left to her own devices for carrying out the entailed responsibilities.

By contrast, children raised by lesbian or gay parents today are much more likely to be in relationships carefully chosen and affirmed by their caretakers.[4] Even though that would no doubt con-

tinue to be true oftener of the children of lesbian and gay parents in same-sex marriages that of the children of heterosexual parents, marriage would involve the State in defining who really had the status of "parent." The State has been willing to grant that status to at most two people at a time, per child. It gives the child legal rights of access to at most those two parties. And it imposes legal accountability for the child's waywardness on at most those two parties. Under the present system that deprives lesbian and gay parents of spousal status, many lesbian and gay couples do their best anyway to emulate heterosexual models, which usually means assuming the responsibilities without the privileges.[5] Others I have know, however, attempt to undermine the assumption that parental responsibility should be concentrated in one or two people who have the power of a child's happiness and unhappiness in their hands for nearly two decades. Children raised without such models of the concentration of power may be less likely to reproduce patriarchal and other oppressive social relationships.

The "revolutionary parenting" that bell hooks describes (1984) dilutes the power of individual parents. Although children retain special affectional ties to their "bloodmothers," accountability for children's waywardness is more widely distributed. With many caretakers (such as "othermothers"), there is less pressure to make any one of them constantly accessible to a child and more pressure to make everyone somewhat accessible. With many caretakers, it is less likely that any of them will get away with prolonged abuse, or even be tempted to perpetrate it.

In my childhood, many adults looked out for the children of my village. I had, in a way, a combination of both kinds of worlds. My parents, married to each other, had the legal rights and the legal responsibilities of patriarchal parents. Yet, some of those responsibilities were in fact assumed by "othermothers," including women (and men) who never married anyone. Because it could always be assumed that wherever I roamed in the village, I would never be among strangers, my parents did not think they always needed to supervise me, although they were also ambivalent about that, as they would be legally answerable for any trouble I caused. I used to dread the thought that we might move to a city, where my freedom would probably have been severely curtailed, as it was when we lived in a large, white middle-class urban environment during World War II. In the village, because everyone assumed (reasonably) that someone was watching us, we children often escaped the intensity of physical discipline that I experienced alone with my mother amid the far larger urban population.

There are both worse and better environments that can be imagined for children than stereotypical patriarchal families. Urban environments in which parents must work away from home but can neither bring their children nor assume that their children are being watched by anyone are no doubt worse. Children who have never had effective caretakers do not make good caretakers of each other, either. Feminism today has been in something of a bind with respect to the so-called postpatriarchal family. If both women and men are to be actively involved in markets and governments and free to become active members of all occupations and professions, when, where, and how is child care going to be done? The solution of many feminists has been, in practice, for two parents to take turns spending with the children. There is an increasing tendency today for parents who divide responsibilities for the children to pay others to do the child care, if they can afford it, when their turn comes. To the extent that this works, it is evidence that "mothering" is not necessary for child care. Children who have had effective caretakers may be better at taking care of themselves and each other, with minimal supervision to protect them against hazards to life and health, than is commonly supposed. Charlotte Perkins Gilman's solutions in *Women and Economics* (1966) and Herland (1992) was twofold. On one hand, she would turn child care into one of the professions that everyone with the requisite talents and motivations is free to enter. At the same time, she would *make the public safe* even for children, by an ethic that incorporated aspects of good caretaking. Virginia Held's *Feminist Morality* also suggests the latter strategy. A danger of this strategy, of course, is instituting paternalism among adults but spelled with an *m* instead of a *p*. Still, the idea of improving the safety of the public environ-ment is compelling. If it were improved enough, there might be no need for motherhood — which is not to say that children would not need to bond with and be supervised by adults.

In *Feminist Morality* Virginia Held maintains that the mother-child relationship is the fundamen-tal social relationship, not in a reductive sense but in the sense that so much else depends on one's relationships to primary caretakers (Held 1994, 70). This idea, also urged by Annette Baier (1994), seems to me in a certain sense incontrovertible and its general appreciation by philosophers long overdue. The sense in which it seems to me incon-trovertible is that when one does in fact have a primary caretaker who has, if not the power of life and death, then the power of one's happiness and unhappiness in their hands for many years in the early stages of one's life, the influence of that expe-rience on the rest of one's life is profound. It seems, for example, to affect one's ability to form good relationships with others in ways that are extremely difficult to change, if they are changeable at all. Yet, there is another sense in which the observation that the mother-child relationship is fundamental may be misleading. It may be misleading if it suggests that everyone really needs a single primary care-taker (or even two primary caretakers) who has the power of one's happiness and unhappiness in their hands for many years during the early stages of one's life. Perhaps people need that only in a society that refuses to take and share responsibility collectively for its own consciously and thought-fully affirmed reproduction. In such a society, con-scientious mothers are often the best protection a child has. But if so, it is misleading to say that such a relationship as the mother-child relationship is the, or even a, fundamental social relationship. It has been even less fundamental for may people, historically, than one might think, given how many children have been raised in institutions other than households or raised by a variety of paid caretakers with limited responsibilities.

Because mothers in a society that generally refuses to take collective responsibility for repro-duction are often the best or even the only protec-tion that children have, in the short run it is worth fighting for the right to adopt and raise children within lesbian and gay households. This is emergency care for young people, many of whom are already here and desperately in need of care. There is little that heterosexual couples can do to rebel as individual couples in a society in which their relationship is turned into a common law relationship after some years by the State and in which they are given the responsibilities and right of parents over any children they may raise. Communal action is what is required to implement new models of parenting. In the long run, it seems best to keep open the option of making parenting more "revolutionary" along the lines of communal practices such as those described by bell hooks. Instead of encouraging such a revolution, legal marriage interferes with it in a state that glorifies marriage and takes the marriage relationship to be the only truly healthy contest in which to raise children. Lesbian and gay unions have great potentiality to further the revolution, in part because we *cannot* marry.

If motherhood is transcended, the importance of attending to the experiences and environments of children remains. The "children" if not the "mothers" in society are all of us. Not each of us will choose motherhood under present conditions. But each of us has been a child, and each future human survivor will have childhood to survive. Among the most engaging aspects of a major feminist treatise on the institution of motherhood, Adrienne Rich's *Of Woman Born*, are that it is written from the perspective of a daughter who was mothered and that it is addressed to daughters as well as to mothers. This work, like that of Annette Baier, Virginia Held, bell hooks, Patricia Hill Collins, and Sara Ruddick, has the potential to focus our attention not entirely or even especially on mothers but on those who have been (or have not been) mothered, ultimately, on the experience of children in general. Instead of finding that the mother-child relationship provides a valuable paradigm for moral theorizing, even one who has mothered might find, reflecting on both her experience as a mother and her experience of having been mothered, that mothering should not be necessary, or that it should be less necessary than has been thought, and that it has more potential to do harm than good. The power of mothers over children may have been historically far more detrimental to daughters than to sons, at least in societies where daughters have been more controlled, more excluded from well-rewarded careers, and more compelled to engage in family service than sons. Such a finding would be in keeping with the project of drawing on the usually unacknowledged historically characteristic experiences of women.

In suggesting that the experience of being mothered has great potential for harm to children, I do not have in mind the kinds of concerns recently expressed by political conservatives about mothers who abuse drugs or are sexually promiscuous. Even these mothers are often the best protection their children have. I have in mind the environments by mothers who in fact do live up to contemporary norms of ideal motherhood or even exceed the demands of such norms in the degree of attention and concern they manifest for their children in providing a child-centered home as fully constructed as their resources allow.

Everyone would benefit from a society that was more attentive to the experiences of children, to the relationships of children with adults and with each other, and to the conditions under which children make the transition to adulthood. Moral philosophy might also be transformed by greater attention to the fact that adult experience and its potentialities are significantly conditioned by the childhoods of adults and of those children's relationships to (yet earlier) adults. Whether or not one agrees with the idea that motherhood offers a valuable paradigm for moral theorizing, in getting us to take seriously the significance of the child's experience of childhood and to take up the standpoint of the "child" in all of us, philosophical work exploring the significance of mother-child relationships is doing feminism and moral philosophy a great service.

Author's Note

Thanks to Harry Brighouse, Vicky Davion, Virginia Held, Sara Ruddick, anonymous reviewers for *Hypatia,* and especially to Lynne Tirrell for helpful comments and suggestions and to audiences who heard ancestors of this essay at the Pacific and

Central Divisions of the American Philosophical Association in 1995.

NOTES

1. Betty Berzon claims that her book *Permanent Partners* is about "reinventing our gay and lesbian relationships" and "learning to imbue them with all the solemnity of marriage without necessarily imitating the heterosexual model" (1988, 7), and yet by the end of the book it is difficult to think of anything in legal ideals of the heterosexual nuclear family that she has not urged us to imitate.

2. Thus I am not an advocate of the equal legal rights for children movement as that movement is presented and criticized by Purdy (1992), namely, as a movement advocating that children have exactly the same legal rights as adults, including the legal right not to attend school.

3. See, for example, Weston (1991), Burke (1993), and Slater (1995). In contrast, Berzon (1988) uses the language of partnership, reserving "family" for social structures based on heterosexual unions, as in chap. 12, subtitled "Integrating Your Families into Your Life as a Couple."

4. An outstanding anthology on the many varieties of lesbian parenting is Arnup (1995). Also interesting is the anthropological study of lesbian mothers by Lowing (1993). Both are rich in references to many resources on both lesbian and gay parenting.

5. Lewin (1993) finds, for example, that lesbian mothers tend to assume all caretaking responsibilities themselves, or in some cases share them with a partner turning to their families of origin, rather than to a friendship network of peers, for additionally needed support.

REFERENCES

Arnup, Katherine, ed. 1995. *Lesbian parenting: Living with pride and prejudice.* Charlottetown, P.E.I.: Cynergy Books.

Baier, Annette C. 1994. *Moral prejudices: Essays on ethics.* Cambridge: Harvard University Press.

Berzon, Betty. 1988. *Permanent partnerships: Building lesbian and gay relationships that last.* New York: Penguin.

Blumenfeld, Warren J. 1996. Same-sex marriage: Introducing the discussion. *Journal of Gay, Lesbian and Bisexual Identity* 1 (1): 77.

Boswell, John. 1988. *The kindness of strangers: the abandonment of children in Western Europe from late antiquity to the Renaissance.* New York Pantheon.

— . 1994. *Same-sex unions in premodern Europe.* New York: Villard.

Brownworth, Victoria A. 1996. Tying the knot or the hangman's noose: The case against marriage. *Journal of Gay, Lesbian, and Bisexual Identity* 1(1): 91-98.

Burke, Phyllis. 1993. *Family values: Two moms and their son.* New York: Random House.

Card, Claudia. 1988. Gratitude and Obligation. *American Philosophical Quarterly* 25 (2): 115-27.

— . 1990. Gender and Moral Luck. In *Identity, character, and morality: Essays in moral psychology*, ed. Owen Flanagan and Amelie Oksenberg Rorty, Cambridge: MIT Press

— . 1995. *Lesbian choices.* New York: Columbia University Press.

Collins, Patricia Hill. 1991. *Black feminist thought: Knowledge, consciousness, and the politics of empowerment.* New York: Routlege.

Daly, Mary. 1978. *Gyn/Ecology: The metaethics of radical feminism.* Boston: Beacon.

Faulkner, Sandra, with Judy Nelson. 1993. *Love match: Nelson vs. Navratilova.* New York: Birch Lane Press.

Gilman, Charlotte Perkins. 1966. *Women and economics: The economic factor between men and women as a factor in social evolution*, ed. Carl Degler. New York: Harper.

— . 1992. *Herland.* In *Herland and selected stories by Charlotte Perkins Gilman,* ed. Barbara H. Solomon. New York: Signet.

Goldman, Emma. 1969. Marriage and Love. In *Anarchism and other essays.* New York: Dover.

Hall, Radclyffe. 1950. *The well of loneliness.* New York: Pocket Books. (Many editions; first published 1928).

Held, Virginia. 1993. *Feminist morality: Transforming culture, society, and politics.* Chicago: University of Chicago Press.

Hoagland, Sarah Lucia. 1988. *Lesbian ethics: Toward*

new value. Palo Alto, CA: Institute of Lesbian Studies.

hooks, bell. 1984. *Feminist theory from margin to center*. Boston: South End Press.

Island, David, and Patrick Letellier. 1991. *Men who beat the men who love them: Battered gay men and domestic violence*. New York: Harrington Park Press.

Lewin, Ellen. 1993. *Lesbian mothers*. Ithaca: Cornell University Press.

Lobel, Kerry, ed. 1986. *Naming the violence: Speaking out about lesbian battering*. Seattle: Seal Press.

Lorde, Audre. 1984. *Sister outsider: Essays and speeches*. Trumansburg: Crossing Press.

Mahmoody, Betty, with William Hoffer. 1987. *Not without my daughter*. New York: St. Martin's.

Mohr, Richard D. 1994. *A more perfect union: Why straight America must stand up for gay rights*. Boston: Beacon.

Newman, Leslea. 1989. *Esther has two mommies*. Northampton, MA: In Other Words Publishing.

Pierce, Christine. 1995. *Gay marriage*. Journal of Social Philosophy 28 (2): 5-16.

Purdy, Laura M. 1992. *In their best interest! The case against equal right for children*. Ithaca: Cornell University Press.

Renzetti, Clair M. 1992. *Violent betrayal: Partner abuse in lesbian relationships*. Newbury Park, CA: Sage Publications.

Rich, Adrienne. 1976. *Of woman born: Motherhood as experience and as institution*. New York: Norton.

Ruddick, Sara. 1989. *Maternal thinking: Toward a politics as peace*. Boston: Beacon.

Slater, Suzanne. 1995. *The lesbian family life cycle*. New York: Free Press.

Trebilcot, Joyce, ed. 1983. *Mothering: Essays in feminist theory*. Totowa, N.J.: Rowman and Allanheld.

Weston, Kath. 1991. *Families we choose*. New York: Columbia University Press.

Wolfson, Evan. 1996. Why we should fight for the freedom to marry: The challenges and opportunities that will follow a win in Hawaii. *Journal of Lesbian, Gay, and Bisexual Identity* 1 (1): 79-89.

POWER AND SEXUALITY IN THE MIDDLE EAST

Bruce Dunne

Bruce Dunne teaches Middle East history at Georgetown University in Washington, DC. He is the editor of the journal Middle East Report, *in which this article appears.*

Dunne explains that the conceptualization of sexual relations in North America is different from how homosexuality is understood and practiced in the Middle East. Historically, sexual relations in Middle Eastern societies have been about social hierarchies of dominant and subordinate social positions. Dunne argues that the distinction made in modern Western societies between sexuality and gender identity — between kinds *of sexual predilections and* degrees *of masculinity and femininity — has had little resonance in the Middle East until quite recently. Relationships of both dominant/subordinate and heterosexual/homosexual reflect structures of power and position social actors as powerful or powerless, "normal" or "deviant." Dunne claims that the contemporary concept of "queerness" displays the contradictions in the traditional understandings of homosexuality in the Middle East by recognizing the complex realities of multiple and shifting positions of sexuality, identity, and power.*

In early 1993, news of President Clinton's proposal to end the US military's ban on service by homosexuals prompted a young Egyptian man in Cairo, eager to practice his English, to ask me why the president wanted "to ruin the American army" by admitting "those who are not men or women." When asked if "those" would include a married man who also liked to have sex with adolescent boys, he unhesitatingly answered "no." For this Egyptian, a Western "homosexual" was not readily comprehensible as a man or a woman, while a man who had sex with both women and boys was simply doing what men do. It is not the existence of same-sex sexual relations that is new but their association with essentialist sexual identities rather than hierarchies of age, class or status.

A recent study of family and urban politics in Cairo suggests that social taboos and silences relating to sexual behavior provide a space of negotiability.[1] They accommodate discreet incidents of otherwise publicly condemned illicit sexual behavior — adultery, homosexuality, premarital sex — provided that paramount values of family mainte-

nance and reproduction and supporting social networks are not threatened. Such silences, however, leave normative constructions of licit and illicit sexual behavior unchallenged, sustain patriarchal family values, and legitimize patterns of sexual violence such as honor crimes, female circumcision and gay bashing.[2]

Also in 1993, an Egyptian physician affiliated with Cairo's Qasr al-'Aini Hospital informed me that AIDS and venereal diseases were not problems in Egypt because neither prostitution nor homosexuality exist in an Islamic country. While this statement may express conventions deemed appropriate for conversations with foreigners, it is profoundly ahistorical. Over the centuries, Islamic societies have accorded prostitution much the same levels of intermittent toleration, regulation and repression as their Christian counterparts and, until recently, have been more tolerant of same-sex sexual practices.[3] Denying the existence of transgressive sexual practices helps obscure the ideological nature of "transgression," making it difficult, for example, to see prostitutes as workers who support themselves or their families by performing services for which there is a social demand. Such denials also legitimize failures to respond effectively to public health concerns such as AIDS.[4]

Representations of Power and Sexuality

Western notions of sexual identity offer little insight into our contemporary young Egyptian's apparent understanding that sexual behavior conforms to a particular concept of gender. His view, informed by a sexual ethos with antecedents in Greek and late Roman antiquity, is characterized by the "general importance of male dominance, the centrality of penetration to conceptions of sex [and] the radical disjunction of active and passive roles in male homosexuality."[5] Everett Rowson has found this sexual ethos "broadly representative of Middle Eastern societies from the 9th century to the present." This is not to suggest that there has been an unchanging or homogeneous historical experience for the Arabo-Muslim world but rather to acknowledge both the remarkable continuity reflected in the sources and the need for research that would further map historical variations.[6]

Islam recognizes both men and women as having sexual drives and rights to sexual fulfillment and affirms heterosexual relations within marriage and lawful concubinage. All other sexual behavior is illicit. Whether the 7th century message of the Qur'an undermined or improved the position of women is much debated. There is more agreement that in subsequent centuries Muslim male elites, adopting the cultural practices of conquered Byzantine and Sasanian lands, construed that message to promote the segregation and seclusion of women and to reserve public and political life for men. Social segregation was legitimized in part by constructing "male" and "female" as opposites: men as rational and capable of self-control; women as emotional and lacking self-control, particularly of sexual drives. Female sexuality, if unsatisfied or uncontrolled, could result in social chaos (*fitna*) and social order thus required male control of women's bodies.[7] The domain of licit sexuality was placed in service

to the patriarchal order. The patriarchal family served as paramount social institution and the proper locus of sex, thus ensuring legitimate filiation. Its honor required supervision of women by male family members, while marital alliances among families of equal rank maintained social hierarchies.

Where men rule, sexes are segregated, male and family honor is linked to premarital female virginity and sex is licit only within marriage or concubinage. Those denied access to licit sexuality for whatever reasons — youth, poverty, occupation (e.g., soldiers), demographic sexual imbalances — require other sexual outlets. Such contradictions between normative morality and social realities supported both male and female prostitution and same-sex practices in Middle Eastern societies from the medieval to the modern period. Ruling authorities saw prostitution as a socially useful alternative to potential male sexual violence (e.g., against respectable women) and a welcome source of tax revenues, even as some religious scholars vigorously objected. According to Abdelwahab Bouhdiba, "institutional prostitution forms part of the secret equilibrium of Arabo-Muslim societies," necessary to their social reproduction.[8]

In medieval Islamic societies, understood through their (male-authored) literature of morals, manners, medicine and dream interpretation, sexual relations were organized in conformity to principles of social and political hierarchy. "[S]exuality was defined according to the domination by or reception of the penis in the sex act; moreover, one's position in the social hierarchy also localized her or him in a predetermined sexual role."[9] Sex, that is, penetration, took place between dominant, free adult men and subordinate social inferiors: wives, concubines, boys, prostitutes (male and female) and slaves (male and female). What was at stake was not mutuality between partners but the adult male's achievement of pleasure through domination. Women were viewed as naturally submissive; male prostitutes were understood to submit to penetration for gain rather than pleasure; and boys, "being not yet men, could be penetrated without losing their potential manliness." That an adult male might take pleasure in a subordinate sexual role, in sub-mitting to penetration, was deemed "inexplicable, and could only be attributed to pathology."[10]

Rowson explains the relation between gender roles and sexual roles in medieval Muslim soci-eties by locating them in, respectively, distinct public and private realms. Adult men, who domi-nated their wives and slaves in private, controlled the public realm. Sex with boys or male prostitutes made men "sinners," but did not undermine their public position as men or threaten the important social values of female virginity or family honor. Women, who could not penetrate and were con-fined to the private realm, were largely irrelevant to conceptions of gender; female homoeroticism received little attention. Effeminate men who vol-untarily and publicly behaved as women (*mukhan-naths*) gave up their claims to membership in the dominant male order. They "lost their respectabil-ity [as men] but could be tolerated and even valued as entertainers" — poets, musicians, dancers, singers. Men who maintained a dominant public persona but were privately submissive threatened presumptions of male dominance and were vulner-able to challenge.[11]

The articulation of sexual relations in conformity to social hierarchies represents an ideological framework within which individuals negotiated varied lives under changing historical conditions. Adult male egalitarian homosexual relations may have been publicly unacceptable, but there is evi-dence that, in the medieval period, men of equal rank could negotiate such relations by alternating active and passive sexual roles.[12] In Mamluk Egypt, lower-class women could not afford to observe ideals of seclusion and secluded upper-class women found ways to participate in social and economic life and even used the threat of withhold-ing sex to negotiate concessions from their hus-bands. Women in the Ottoman period went to court to assert their rights to sexual fulfillment (e.g., to divorce an absent or impotent husband).[13] State efforts to repress illicit sexual conduct or promote social-sexual norms (e.g., by closing brothels or ordering women indoors) were sporadic, short-lived and typically occasioned by political circum-stances and the need to bolster regime legitimacy.[14]

Ideological Reproduction

Reproduction of ideological Islamic sexual roles in the modern period has accompanied dramatic transformations, including the rise of modern state systems, Western colonial intervention, and various reform and nationalist movements. These complex processes have not significantly chal-lenged the patriarchal values that undergird the sexual order or impaired the capacity of states, elites and political groups to deploy both secular and Islamic discourses in their support. Colonial authorities left existing gender relations largely intact, as did middle-class reform and nationalist movements. While secular legal codes have been adopted in many countries, they have generally deferred to religious authority in matters of family or personal status laws. Both nationalist and Islamist discourses have invoked ideals of Islamic morality and cultural authenticity to control and channel change.[15]

Increased economic and educational opportuni-ties for women and the rise of nuclear family resi-dential patterns have eroded patriarchal family structures, with, for example, older forms of arranged marriages giving way to elements of romantic attachment. Nonetheless, as Walter Arm-brust and Garay Menicucci suggest in their film discussions in this issue, the popular media con-stantly reaffirm that family interests and normative sexual behavior take precedence over individual romantic aspirations. Moreover, because regimes link their legitimacy to the defense of morality and the licit sexual order, opposition groups and ordi-nary people draw attention to the existence of sex-ually transgressive behavior to criticize a range of government policies.[16] Thus, premarital and homosexual relations among Moroccan youth, in the context of AIDS prevention debates discussed in this issue by Abdessamad Dialmy, are attributed to the government's failure to provide employment and, hence, access to marriage and licit sexual rela-tions. Both official and oppositional discourses affirm sexual norms.

Sexual relations, whether heterosexual or homo-sexual, continue to be understood as relations of power linked to rigid gender roles. In Turkey,

Egypt and the Maghrib, men who are "active" in sexual relations with other men are not considered homosexual; the sexual domination of other men may even confer a status of hyper-masculinity.[17] The anthropologist Malek Chebel, describing the Maghrib as marked by an "exaggerated machismo," claims that most men who engage in homosexual acts are functional bisexuals; they use other men as substitutes for women — and have great contempt for them. He adds that most Maghribis would consider far worse than participation in homosexual acts the presence of love, affection or equality among participants.[18] Equality in sexual relations, whether heterosexual or homosexual, threatens the "hyper-masculine" order.

Gender norms are deeply internalized. A recent study of sexual attitudes among rural Egyptian women found that they viewed female circumcision as a form not of violence but of beautification, a means of enhancing their physical differentiation from men and thus female identity.[19] An informal study of men in Egypt found that aspirations to "hegemonic notions of masculinity" informed a continuous process of negotiating the nature of masculinity — the ability to provide for families or exercise control over women — in response to declining economic conditions.[20] The persistent notion that women lack sexual control affords broad scope and social sanction to aggressive male sexuality. Women alone bear the blame — and the often brutal consequences evidenced by honor crimes — for even the suggestion of their involvement in illicit sexual activities. Suzanne Ruggi notes in this issue that honor crimes may account for 70 percent of murder cases involving Palestinian women. Honor crimes are also common in Egypt, Jordan and Morocco.

Violence directed against male homosexuals appears to be on the rise. Effeminate male dancers known as *khawals* were popular public performers in 19th-century Egypt; today that term is an insult, equivalent to "faggot."[21] The 19th-century *khawals* may not have enjoyed respect as "men," but there is little evidence that they were subjected to violence. Hostility to homosexual practices has been part of the political and cultural legacy of European colonialism. Today, global culture's images of diverse sexualities and human sexual rights have encouraged the formation of small "gay" subcultures in large cosmopolitan cities such as Cairo, Beirut and Istanbul and a degree of political activism, particularly in Turkey. Although homosexuality is not a crime in Turkey, Turkish gays, lesbians, bisexuals, transvestites and transsexuals have been harassed and assaulted by police and sometimes "outed" to families and employers. Turkish gay activists have specifically been targeted. Effeminate male prostitutes in contemporary Morocco are described as a marginal group, ostracized and rejected by their families, living in fear of police and gay-bashers (*casseurs de pédés*). For some, as for Turkish transsexuals, prostitution serves as one of the few ways in which they can live their sexuality.[22] Many homosexuals in Middle Eastern countries have sought asylum in the West as refugees from official persecution.[23]

"Queering" the Middle East

In noting the threat posed to the dominant sexual order by egalitarian sexual relationships, Malek Chebel acknowledges the great silence that surrounds the fact that widespread active male homosexual relations in Middle Eastern societies presuppose the widespread availability of passive partners.[24] Demet Demir, a political activist and spokesperson for Turkish transsexuals, touches upon the same contradiction when she states, with reference to the popularity as prostitutes of Istanbul's transsexuals: "These people who curse us during the day give money to lie with us at night."[25] Is this the "functional" — and misogynist – "bisexuality" described by Chebel above the mere substitution by men of other, available men for unavailable women? That view, which hardly explains the choice of a male or transsexual over a female prostitute, is entirely consistent with and sustains the ideology that positions public or visible or audible men as sexually dominant.

Little attention has been given to the nature of these expressions of male sexual desire which, as Deniz Kandiyoti has noted, seem to "combine a whole range of masculinities and femininities."[26]

There are, she suggests, generational and institutional dimensions to the production of masculine identities. Thus, men who are expected to be "dominant" in one context may experience subordination, powerlessness and humiliation in others, for example in relation to their fathers and to superiors at school or during military service. How does "masculinity" change meaning in these different domains? The complexity of questions of sexuality, identity and power are explored in this issue by Yael Ben-zvi who finds herself, in Israel, simultaneously privileged as an Ashkenazi Jew and marginalized as a lesbian. The aim of "queerness," therefore, is to recognize identity as "permanently open as to its meaning and political use [and to] encourage the public surfacing of differences or a culture where multiple voices and interests are heard."[27]

NOTES

1. Diane Singerman, *Avenues of Participation: Family, Politics, and Networks in Urban Quarters of Cairo* (Cairo: American University in Cairo Press, 1997), pp. 92 and 100.

2. See Latefa Imane, "Un programme de sensibilisation et de soutien auprès de prostitués masculins," *Le Journal du SIDA* 92-93 (December 1996-January 1997), p. 55.

3. See As'ad AbuKhalil, "A Note on the Study of Homosexuality in the Arab/Islamic Civilization," *Arab Studies Journal* 1/2 (Fall, 1993), pp. 32-34.

4. See Malek Chebel, "La séparation des sexes engendre un masculin maghrébin," *Le Journal du SIDA* 92-93 (December 1996-January 1997), p. 27.

5. Everett K. Rowson, "The Categorization of Gender and Sexual Irregularity in Medieval Arabic Vice Lists," in Julia Epstein and Kristina Straub, eds., *Body Guards: The Cultural Politics of Ambiguity* (New York and London: Routledge, 1991), p. 73.

6. Ibid., pp. 72-73.

7. See Judith Tucker, *Gender and Islamic History* (Washington, DC: American Historical Association, 1993), pp. 3-13; Steven M. Oberhelman, "Hierarchies of Gender, Ideology, and Power in Ancient and Medieval Greek and Arabic Dream Literature," in J.W. Wright Jr. and Everett K. Rowson, eds.

Homoeroticism in Classical Arabic Literature (New York: Columbia University Press, 1997), p. 66.

8. Hassanein Rabie, *The Financial System of Egypt: A.H. 564-641/A.D. 1169-1341* (London: Oxford University Press, 1972), p. 119; André Raymond, *Artisans et commerçants au Caire au XVIIIe siècle* (Damascus, 1973), pp. 508-09 and 527; Abdelwahab Bouhdiba, *Sexuality in Islam* (London: Routledge & Kegan Paul, 1985), p. 193.

9. Oberhelman, op. cit., pp. 67-68.

10. Rowson, op. cit., pp. 66-67.

11. Ibid., pp. 66 and 72-73.

12. Ibid., p. 66.

13. Huda Lutfi, "Manners and Customs of Fourteenth-Century Cairene Women: Female Anarchy versus Male Shar'i Order in Muslim Prescriptive Treatises," in Nikki R. Keddie and Beth Baron, eds. *Women in Middle Eastern History* (New Haven: Yale University Press, 1991), pp. 101 and 109-18; Tucker, op. cit., pp. 18-19.

14. Rabie, op. cit., p. 119; Raymond, op. cit., pp. 604-09.

15. See Tucker, op. cit., pp. 19-33.

16. Singerman, op. cit., pp. 93-94 and 100.

17. Huseyin Tapinc, "Masculinity, Femininity, and Turkish Male Homosexuality," in Kenneth Plummer, ed., *Modern Homosexualities: Fragments of Lesbian and Gay Experiences* (London and New York: Routledge, 1992), p. 46; Singerman, op. cit., p. 99; Chebel, op. cit., p. 27.

18. Chebel, op. cit., p. 27.

19. Hind Khattab, *Women's Perceptions of Sexuality in Rural Giza* (Giza, Egypt: The Population Council: Monographs in Reproductive Health 1, 1996), p. 20.

20. Kamran Asdar Ali, "Notes on Rethinking Masculinities: An Egyptian Case," *Learning about Sexuality: A Practical Beginning* (The Population Council and the International Women's Health Coalition, 1995), pp. 106-07.

21. Singerman, op. cit., p. 100.

22. Imane, op. cit., p. 55; *Turkish Daily News*, August 22, 1997; Amnesty International, *Breaking the Silence: Human Rights Violations Based on Sexual Orientation* (London: Amnesty International UK, 1997), pp. 26-27, 52.

23. Information provided to MERIP courtesy of the International Gay and Lesbian Human Rights Commission Asylum Project, San Francisco.

24. Chebel, op. cit., p. 27.

25. *Turkish Daily News*, August 22, 1997.

26. Deniz Kandiyoti, "The Paradoxes of Masculinity," in Andrea Cornwall and Nancy Lindisfarne, eds., *Dislocating Masculinities: Comparative Ethnographies* (London and New York: Routledge, 1994), p. 212.

27. Steven Seidman, "Introduction," in Steven Seidman, ed., *Queer Theory/Sociology*, (Cambridge, Mass.: Blackwell, 1996), p. 12.

STUDY QUESTIONS

1 What does Jeffrey Jordan mean by moral impasses? What does he mean by public dilemmas? What is it about homosexuality that has Jordan conclude that this is a case of a moral impasse that constitutes a public dilemma about which the state can only remain neutral if it does not sanction same-sex marriage? Do you agree? Why or why not?

2 While Jordan argues that discrimination against homosexuals in the case of allowing them to marry is justified, he leaves open the possibility that discrimination against homosexuals is impermissible in other cases. What might these cases be? Would it include allowing homosexuals to adopt children or enter the army? Make use of Jordan's account of the "parity thesis" to answer these questions.

3 Is the state being neutral by not allowing same-sex marriage? Is Jordan right to suggest that legislation regarding same-sex marriage is different from that of mixed-race marriage? Provide reasons for your answers.

4 Does Christine Overall's analysis of heterosexuality as an institution that is "transparent, virtually invisible, yet very powerful" undermine Jordan's argument that the state can only remain neutral if it does not sanction same-sex marriage? Why or why not?

5 What evidence does Overall provide to support her argument that women and men are differentially affected by the institution of heterosexuality and the social pressures to be heterosexual?

6 If heterosexuality is enforced in the ways described by Overall, can women *choose* heterosexuality? Can a feminist be heterosexual? Does Overall's use of the notion of a "lesbian continuum" help to answer these questions? According to Overall, what sorts of feminist strategies would challenge or undermine the institution of heterosexuality?

7 Cheshire Calhoun differentiates the sorts of inequality and oppression experienced by gays and lesbians from that experienced by racial minorities and women. What are the main differences she outlines as constituting what she refers to as "sexuality injustice"? Does her account challenge Overall's feminist analysis of heterosexuality? Why or why not?

8 What does Calhoun mean when she claims that sexuality injustice consists in the displacement of homosexuality and lesbianism to the outside of society? Outline and evaluate the three main arguments she uses to support this claim.

9 Claudia Card gives reasons very different from those given by Jordan for questioning the legitimacy of institutionalizing same-sex marriage. What are they? Whose account do you favor and why?

10 Why does Card also raise doubts about the institution of motherhood and how are these doubts connected to her skepticism about supporting same-sex marriage?

11 According to Bruce Dunne, how is the conceptualization of sexual relations in the Middle East different from that in North America? If sexual relations in the Middle East are about power and relations of domination and subordination, does this have you think differently about your understanding of sexual orientation? Provide reasons for your answer.

12 According to Dunne, how does the concept of "queerness" challenge traditional understandings of sexual relations and practices in the Middle East? Do you think this is a viable and effective strategy for change? Provide reasons for your answer.

SUGGESTED READINGS

Abelove, Henry, *et al.* (editors). *The Lesbian and Gay Studies Reader.* New York, NY: Routledge, 1993.

Allison, Dorothy. *Skin: Talking about Sex, Class, & Literature.* Ithaca, NY: Firebrand Books, 1994.

Almaguer, Tomás. "Chicano Men: A Cartography of Homosexual Identity and Behavior." *differences: A Journal of Feminist Cultural Studies*, v. 3, no. 2 (1991): 75-100.

Austin, Andrea, and Adrian Alex Wellington. "Outing: The Supposed Justifications." *The Canadian Journal of Law and Jurisprudence*, v. 8, no. 1 (1995): 83-105.

Bedecarré, Corrinne. "Swear by the Moon." *Hypatia*, v. 12, no. 3 (Summer 1997): 189-97.

Bolte, Angela. "Do Wedding Dresses Come in Lavender? The Prospects and Implications of Same-Sex Marriage." *Social Theory and Practice*, v. 24, no. 1 (Spring 1998): 111-31.

Butler, Judith. "Imitation and Gender Insubordination." In *Inside/Out: Lesbian Theories, Gay Theories*, edited by Diana Fuss. New York, NY: Routledge, 1991.

Beyer, Jason A. "Public Dilemmas and Gay Marriage: Contra Jordan." *Journal of Social Philosophy*, v. 33, no. 1 (Spring 2002): 9-16.

Calhoun, Cheshire. *Feminism, the Family, and the Politics of the Closet: Lesbian and Gay Displacement.* Oxford: Oxford University Press, 2000.

Card, Claudia. *Lesbian Choices.* New York, NY: Columbia University Press, 1995.

Clarke, Cheryl. "Lesbianism: An Act of Resistance." In *This Bridge Called My Back: Writings by Radical Women of Color*, edited by Cherrie Moraga, Gloria Anzaldua. New York, NY: Kitchen Table, Women of Color Press, 1983: 128-37.

Däumer, Elisabeth D. "Queer Politics: Or, The Challenges of Bisexuality to Lesbian Ethics." *Hypatia*, v. 7, no. 4 (Fall 1992): 91-105.

Eskridge, William N. Jr. "Beyond Lesbian and Gay 'Families We Choose.'" In *Sex, Preference, and Family: Essays on Law and Nature*, edited by David M. Estlund and Martha Nussbaum. Oxford: Oxford University Press, 1996.

Frye, Marilyn. *Willful Virgin: Essays in Feminism.* Freedom, CA: The Crossing Press, 1992.

Hale, Jacob. "Are Lesbians Women?" *Hypatia*, v. 11, no. 2 (Spring 1996): 94-121.

Halperin, David. "Is There a History of Sexuality?" *History and Theory*, v. 28 (1989): 257-74.

Heldke, Lisa. "In Praise of Unreliability." *Hypatia*, v. 12, no. 3 (Summer 1997): 174-82.

Hoagland, Sarah. *Lesbian Ethics: Toward New Value.* Palo Alto, CA: Institute of Lesbian Studies, 1988.

Ilkkaracan, Pinar. "Women, Sexuality, and Social Change in the Middle East and the Maghreb." *Social Research*, v. 69, no. 3 (Fall 2002): 753-79.

O'Connor, Peg. "Warning! Contents Under Heterosexual Pressure." *Hypatia*, v. 12, no. 3 (Summer 1997): 184-88.

Rich, Adrienne. "Compulsory Heterosexuality and Lesbian Existence." *Signs: Journal of Women in Culture and Society*, v. 5, no. 4 (1980): 631-60.

Rubin, Gayle. "Thinking Sex: Notes for a Radical Theory of the Politics of Sexuality." In *Pleasure and Danger: Exploring Female Sexuality*, edited by Carole Vance. New York, NY: Routledge, 1984.

Ruse, Michael. "Is Homosexuality Bad Sexuality?" In *Homosexuality.* Oxford: Blackwell, 1988.

Wellington, Adrian Alex. "Why Liberals Should Support Same Sex Marriage." *Journal of Social Philosophy*, v. 26, no. 3 (Winter 1995): 5-32.

CHAPTER FIVE: DISABILITY

INTRODUCTION

By now a clear story should have started to take shape to help us in thinking about issues of diversity and equality, a story of the highly complex nature of kinds of discrimination that are now taken to be morally wrong. Many of the chapters in this volume highlight the role that stereotypes play in forming perceptions and self-perceptions of members of disadvantaged groups in ways that shape their lives and affect their life prospects. For example, stereotypes of racial minorities and women as intellectually inferior have resulted in their underrepresentation in institutions of higher education and positions of power. One result of stereotypes of gay men and lesbians is their exclusion from debates about policies regarding sexuality, marriage, parenting, childcare, and education. While there are similarities in the ways in which forms of discrimination are manifested and in the inequalities that result, there are also significant differences as well as places where intersections result in the creation of new issues and problems for a particular form of discrimination. As we move to questions about the difference that disability makes to a person's life prospects, it is a good idea to keep this complexity in mind.

The World Health Organization (WHO) distinguishes three concepts related to disability. *Impairments* are physiological, psychological, or anatomical abnormalities or losses as described by biomedical scientists. *Disabilities* are restrictions or lack of ability to perform an activity in the manner or range considered normal. Disabilities can be the result of impairments, but not all impairments result in disabilities. *Handicaps* are disadvantages created by how the disabilities or impairments are perceived by others and received by society as a whole. If I am an amputee in a wheelchair, my impairment is the loss of my legs and my disability means that I cannot walk, but I am handicapped by a social environment that does not provide ramps to let me into buildings. The conceptual clarification is meant to capture the idea that disadvantages experienced by persons with disabilities arise from the interaction of their impairments with the social environment and not from biology or social practices alone. We will come to appreciate the complexity and difficulty with the very project of categorizing and defining in the final reading in this chapter, where Shelley Tremain takes issue with the discourse of "impairment" and "disability" in the social model promoted in the WHO definitions just outlined.

The importance of conceptual understandings of disability is central to the discussion by David Wasserman in the first reading. Wasserman explores changes to perceptions of and policies with respect to disability by examining the *Americans with Disabilities Act* (ADA) enacted by the U.S. Congress in 1990. The ADA acknowledges that people with disabilities were bypassed by early civil rights movements and that individuals experiencing discrimination on the basis of disability had no legal recourse to address such discrimination. Wasserman argues that the ADA's anti-discrimination framework attempts to change the lack of understanding of discrimination on the basis of disability by emphasizing similarities between the treatment of people with disabilities and the treatment of other minorities, thus encouraging society to find the source of disadvantages in its own attitudes and practices rather than in the disabilities themselves and supporting the notion that accommodating people with disabilities is a matter of justice and not charity.

The ADA supports a "reasonable accommodation" requirement, one that defends a conception of equality that demands more than the removal of legal barriers to opportunities in its recommendations for reconstructing the social world itself to accommodate the full range of human abilities.

The requirement serves functions similar to forced busing and affirmative action measures in that it compensates for the effects of past and ongoing injustice and it undermines stereotypes that have kept people with disabilities out of the workforce and mainstream society more generally. Wasserman supports the framework of the ADA and its policies, but argues that it offers little guidance on how much accommodation justice requires in the face of limited resources and severe disabilities.

Anita Silvers also examines the ADA and in the process raises a few questions about Wasserman's analysis. She agrees with Wasserman that the ADA reconceptualizes disability as an issue that is not to be located in the physical or mental state of a minority of society's members, but in the way society is organized and structured so as to disadvantage this minority. She argues, however, that Wasserman does not fully grasp the conceptual shift advanced by the ADA and thereby implicitly accepts the devaluing stereotypes that the ADA opposes and attempts to dislodge. At the bottom of these devaluing stereotypes of persons with disabilities as deviant, disgusting, beyond cure by modern science, and in need of caregivers is the standard medical model that treats persons with disabilities as biologically inferior and incapable of moral agency. Silvers holds that the assumptions underlying the standard medical model can also be found in a model of care. Care, she argues, promotes dependency and undermines agency by assuming that a "normal" able-bodied person can understand what it is like to be in a disabled person's place. The goal of the ADA, argues Silvers, is not the medical model one of making the disabled whole or of caring for them, but of eliminating social practices that implicitly or explicitly favor the non-disabled. The ADA requires that persons with disabilities be treated as fully equal, and this goes much further than does the medical model and theories of care that emerge from it.

In the third reading, G. Goggin and C. Newell situate their analysis of disability in the context of Australia and, more specifically, in the current and controversial debates regarding embryonic stem cell research. They examine media representations of disability as a way of understanding how disability is constructed in discourses of nationhood and biotechnology. Media representations that present disability as catastrophe, for example, are crucial to promoting policies that allow access to a variety of biotechnologies, such as embryonic stem cell research. Goggin and Newell analyze such media representations to show the structure of privilege that exists in debates regarding disability and biotechnology — the media selects the views of those praising the advantages of biotechnology for disabled people and excludes the views of those who are critical or wary. They argue that the diversity of voices on disability in the Australian community is not represented and that people with disabilities are not quoted as experts on disability. An awareness of the media's construction of disability will not only allow a better understanding of disability, they argue, but will better meet the requirements of the international disability rights movement motto of "nothing about us without us," recently emphasized in the Disabled Peoples' International Europe 2000 statement on biotechnology.

The final reading in this chapter provides a critique of prevailing models and theories of disability, ones that have been surveyed in the readings thus far in discussions of the social, medical, and care models of disability. Shelley Tremain rejects the realist position, evident in both the medical and social models of disability, that impairments are objective, transhistorical, and transcultural. She borrows from Foucault's work to argue that impairments, the supposedly timeless and objective physical manifestations of disability, are historically specific effects of systems of knowledge and power. "Bio-power" captures the idea that medical and scientific authorities rationalize problems that a group of human beings with specific characteristics pose in order to manage and control health care and medical practices. Under this scheme, the body is treated as a thing that can be categorized, manipulated, and governed.

Tremain uses the concept of "bio-power" to argue that both the medical and social models of disability are deficient. The social model distinguishes impairments taken to be physical and "real" from disabilities that reflect the social disadvantages resulting from the perception and reception of impairments. But in forcing a separation of these categories, impairment is accepted, left untheorized, and put back in the hands of medical interpretation and practice. Tremain argues that impairments are themselves subject to regimes of truth and power, historical contexts, and circumstances.

According to Tremain, the concept of "natural impairment" is like that of "natural sex" in that they both emerge from certain historical conditions and contingent relations of social power and are not categories reflecting biological facts. Sexual anatomy is not fixed or unambiguous, but is made so by medical surgery that "corrects" intersexed infants at birth. The social model of disability allows a discourse in which only those who have or are presumed to have an "impairment" get to count as "disabled." These people are then dealt with in ways that naturalize impairments as essential to identities. Tremain ends by advocating that the disabled people's movement develop strategies for challenging and rejecting the identities that thereby structure their oppression. Challenging the dominant discourse can help to reveal how disability has been naturalized as impairment and how mechanisms of truth and knowledge in science, policy, and medical and legal practices regulate and govern disabled people's lives.

DISABILITY, DISCRIMINATION, AND FAIRNESS

David Wasserman

David Wasserman is a Research Scholar at the Institute for Philosophy and Public Policy at the University of Maryland, College Park. In addition to numerous articles and book chapters, he has written A Sword for the Convicted: Representing Indigent Defendants on Appeal *(1990), co-edited* Genetics and Criminal Behavior: Methods, Meanings, and Morals *(1998, with Robert Wachbroit), and co-authored* Disability, Difference, Discrimination: Perspectives on Justice in Bioethics and Public Policy *(1998, with Anita Silvers and Mary Mahowald).*

Wasserman provides a critical examination of the Americans with Disabilities Act (ADA) enacted by the U.S. Congress in 1990. He argues that the ADA serves the important functions of emphasizing similarities between the treatment of people with disabilities and the treatment of other disadvantaged groups, encouraging society to find the source of the disadvantages in its own attitudes and practices rather than in the disabilities, and defending the view that accommodating persons with disabilities is a matter of justice. Yet, Wasserman argues, the ADA's injunction against discrimination and its requirement of equal opportunity to benefit offer little practical guidance about what justice requires when society is faced with limited resources and severe disabilities.

It is widely agreed that people with disabilities are treated unfairly in our society: that they are the victims of pervasive discrimination, and that they have been denied adequate accommodation in areas ranging from housing construction to hiring practices to public transportation. As Congress declared in enacting the Americans with Disabilities Act (ADA) in 1990:

[I]ndividuals with disabilities are a discrete and insular minority who have been faced with restrictions and limitation, *subjected to a history of purposeful unequal treatment,* and relegated to a position of political powerlessness in our society. ...[emphasis added]

Yet people with disabilities were largely bypassed by the civil rights revolution of the past generation. Congress found that "unlike individuals who have experienced discrimination on the basis of age, color, sex, national origin, religion, or age, individuals who have experienced discrimination on the basis of disability have often had no legal recourse to redress such discrimination."

The ADA is intended to provide that legal recourse. It requires employers, transit systems and public facilities to modify their operations, procedures, and physical structures so as to make reasonable accommodation for people with disabilities. The ADA recognizes broad exceptions in cases where these modifications would result in "undue hardship" or pose risks to third parties. But in principle, the statute treats the failure to ensure that people with disabilities have an "equal opportunity to benefit" from a wide range of activities and services as a form of discrimination.

The ADA's anti-discrimination framework serves several important functions. It emphasizes similarities between the treatment of people with disabilities and the treatment of other minorities. It encourages society to find the source of the disadvantages experienced by people with disabilities in its own attitudes and practices, rather than in the disabilities themselves, and it supports the proposition that accommodating people with disabilities is a matter of justice, not charity.

But the anti-discrimination model offers little guidance on how much accommodation justice requires in the face of limited resources and severe disabilities. Its requirement of equal opportunity to benefit is ambiguous, and its emphasis on remedial action by private individuals and organizations overlooks our collective responsibility for constructing a more accommodating environment. The difficult problems of social justice raised by disabilities cannot be resolved by a simple injunction against discrimination.

The Civil Rights Analogy

The ADA has obvious similarities with recent civil rights legislation. It is designed to protect members of a group long subject to exclusion and prejudice, and it does this by removing barriers to the employment and accommodation of that group. The ADA recognizes that people with disabilities have suffered from false beliefs about their capacities, just as blacks and women have, and that their exclusion has been insidiously self-perpetuating, denying them the experience needed to overcome such biases.

The tendency to devalue those with "visible differences" goes beyond overt prejudice. A recent study of the impact of disability on neo-natal treatment decisions found that doctors and parents were both more likely to decline treatment for premature infants in cases involving a disability, while denying that the disability played any role in their decisions. The researchers saw this as "testimony to the insidious depths to which social stigmas associated with disability can embed themselves in individual consciousness."

Like earlier civil rights law, the ADA recognizes that such deeply embedded prejudice will work its way into the design of social structures and practices, and that stringent measures may be necessary to root it out. The enduring and pervasive impact of prejudice has long prompted the courts to give close scrutiny to "facially neutral" policies with an adverse impact on mistreated and disfavored groups. If public officials, for example, decide that children should attend schools in their own neighborhoods, this may appear to be a neutral basis for school assignment, but in fact it perpetuates the effects of residential covenants and other discriminatory practices that have kept minority families out of affluent suburban communities. Forced busing is not intended to achieve racially diverse schools *per se*, but to undo the enduring effects of those practices. Similarly, affirmative action is not designed to achieve demographic representativeness so much as to surmount the barriers to employment left by generations of exclusion.

The ADA's requirement of "reasonable accommodation" serves many of the same remedial functions, helping to overcome the enduring effects of conscious and unconscious discrimination. As Gregory Kavka notes, the rationales for affirmative action under earlier civil rights law are equally applicable to reasonable accommodation under the ADA: to establish the kinds of role models and "old-boy" networks that dominant groups now enjoy; to correct for the systematic errors in evaluation that result from stereotyping and over-generalization; and to compensate for the effects of past and ongoing injustice, such as exclusion from relevant training.

On the other hand, the assumption that any adverse impact can be traced to prejudice, hatred, contempt, or devaluation — to what Ronald Dworkin has called "invidious discrimination" — is clearly less tenable for disability than for race or ethnicity. The ADA itself recognizes that the physical endowment of people with disabilities contributes to their disadvantage: the statute defines disability as "physical or mental impairment" that "substantially limits [the impaired person's] pursuit of major life activities." Thus, while the ADA rightly holds the attitudes and practices of the larger society responsible for much of the limitation experienced by people with disabilities, it also recognizes an objective category of biological impairment; a person whose major life activities were limited *only* by other people's attitudes or practices would be "disabled" only in a derivative sense. The disadvantages experienced by people with disabilities arise from the interaction of their physical conditions and their social environment; those disadvantages can rarely be attributed to biology *or* social practice alone.

But this understanding of disability raises a critical question about the meaning of "equal opportunity to benefit" under the ADA. In one obvious sense, we assure equal opportunity by removing *legal* barriers to entry or access. (Keep in mind that legal barriers have, in the not-too-distant past, been oppressive and pervasive; in an era when one of the great liberal Supreme Court justices could declare that "three generations of imbeciles is enough," people with disabilities were often forbidden to work, to marry, to have children, or even to be seen in public.) Yet equal opportunity conceived as freedom from legal restriction is clearly inadequate to encompass the kind of accommodations to which people with disabilities seem entitled. A more demanding notion of equal opportunity would require us to undo the effects of invidious discrimination, past and present, de jure and de facto. But even this would fail to address the severely constricted opportunities available to many people with disabilities.

A much stronger sense of equal opportunity is suggested by the ADA's mandate to eliminate "architectural barriers" and other structural impediments to access and mobility. In order to provide equal opportunity in this sense, we must remove not only barriers imposed intentionally by law and prejudice, but also barriers imposed incidentally by designs and structures that ignore the needs of people with disabilities. We must reconstruct the social world to better accommodate the range of abilities of those who inhabit it.

Structural Accommodation and Equal Opportunity

This stronger conception of equal opportunity emerges from the feminist critique of earlier civil rights laws, with their focus on invidious discrimination. Many feminists argue that the design of physical structures and social practices to accommodate one group — able-bodied males — denies equal opportunity to everyone else. The structures and practices of our society embody a dominant

norm of healthy functioning, just as they embody a dominant norm of male functioning. As Susan Wendell argues:

In North America at least, life and work have been structured as though no one of any importance in the public world ... has to breast-feed a baby or look after a sick child .... Much of the world is also structured as though everyone is physically strong ... as though everyone can walk, hear and see well....

The public world provides stairs to the able-bodied so that they can overcome the force of gravity; it is less consistent about providing ramps so that paraplegics can do the same. To build stairs for the one group without building ramps for the second denies the latter equal opportunity to benefit.

This position was anticipated a generation ago by Jacobus tenBroek, who argued that the right of people with disabilities "to live in the world" required comprehensive changes in our physical and social order: not just in the design of buildings and public spaces, but in the duties of care owed by "abled" pedestrians, drivers, common carriers, and property owners to people with disabilities as they travel in public spaces. The refusal to make these changes denies people with disabilities their right to live in the world — the same right that was denied to blacks and women when they were excluded from public facilities.

However, providing equal opportunity for people with disabilities involves a more ambiguous and problematic commitment than the example of stairs and ramps might suggest. Ramps cost little more than stairs and are useful for people of widely varying abilities. The same is true for most of the design standards mandated by the ADA. These standards were developed more than 30 years ago, when tenBroek was writing, and their prompt implementation at that time would have probably brought about dramatic improvements in mobility and access at very slight cost.

But other opportunities to benefit do not come so cheaply. Technology sometimes offers considerable benefits, but only at enormous cost: one thinks of the devices that allow Stephen Hawking to "speak." More often, perhaps, the benefits of costly technology are slight or uncertain. Does the failure to provide quadriplegics with the latest advances in robotics deny them equal opportunity? We could spend indefinitely more on robotic research and equipment, but no matter how much we spent, the opportunities of some quadriplegics would remain severely constricted.

More broadly, we cannot reasonably expect to raise all people with disabilities to a level of functioning where they can receive the same benefit from facilities and services as able-bodied people. There are many areas of employment, transit, and public accommodation where it would be impossible to achieve absolute equality in the opportunity to benefit, and where significantly reducing inequalities in the opportunity to benefit would exhaust the resources of those charged with the task of equalization.

In addressing the issue of how much a decent society should spend to improve the opportunities of people with disabilities, an equal opportunity standard is either hopelessly ambiguous or impossibly demanding. Within the ADA, moreover, there is an unresolved tension between the equal opportunity standard it affirms and the degree of inequality that will remain acceptable under its regulatory guidelines. For example, although the public transit provisions of the statute speak of equal opportunity, the accompanying regulations will leave most people with disabilities with a far greater burden of mobility than most able-bodied people. Perhaps the regulations should require more. But however much they required, they would fall short of assuring equal mobility.

The fact of biological impairment, recognized by the ADA in its definition of disability, makes the notion of "equal opportunity to benefit" problematic. This is a serious defect in a statute that treats the denial of such opportunity as a form of discrimination.

Disability and Biological Misfortune

Recognizing impairments as biological disadvantages raises the question of the extent to which a decent society must accommodate natural misfor-

tune. Such misfortune matters greatly in determining fair treatment within the smaller unit of the family. Consider, for instance, the father's dilemma presented by Thomas Nagel:

Suppose I have two children, one of which is quite normal and quite happy, and the other of which suffers from a painful handicap ... Suppose I must decide between moving to an expensive city where the second child can receive special medical treatment and schooling, but where the family's standard of living will be lower and the neighbourhood will be unpleasant and dangerous for the first child — or else moving to a pleasant semi-rural suburb where the first child ... can have a free and agreeable life ... [Suppose] the gain to the first child of moving to the suburb is substantially greater than the gain to the second child of moving to the city. After all, the second child will also suffer from the family's reduced standard of living and the disagreeable environment. And the educational and therapeutic benefits will not make [the second child] happy but only less miserable. For the first child, on the other hand, the choice is between a happy life and a disagreeable one.

Because the second child is worse off, his interests have a greater urgency than those of the first child. Moving to the city would be the more egalitarian decision, and, if the difference in benefit to the two children is only slight, the fairer decision. But the urgency of the second child's interests does not give them absolute priority; we would think it unfair to the first child to reduce him to the same level of misery as the second for very slight gains in the second child's well-being.

This dilemma is writ large in the allocation of educational resources for children with learning disabilities. Special education is very expensive, and many financially strapped school systems find that providing more than minimal benefit to severely disabled children would require drastic cutbacks in other programs, such as honors classes for gifted students. Yet the Education for All Handicapped Children Act of 1975 (EHA) mandates "free appropriate education" for all children, regardless of ability. This mandate has been variously interpreted to mean that children with disabilities must receive "some educational benefit," that they must receive benefit "commensurate" with that accorded to normal children, or that they must receive the "maximum possible" benefit.

William Galston makes a powerful argument for a commensurate benefit standard:

In spite of profound differences among individuals, the full development of each individual — however great or limited his or her natural capacities — is equal in moral weight to that of every other ... [A] policy that neglects the educable retarded so that they do not learn how to care for themselves and must be institutionalized is, considered in itself, as bad as one that deprives extraordinary gifts of their chance to flower.

But technology makes "natural capacity" and "full development" very elastic notions, and this raises serious problems for a standard of equal opportunity that requires a comparison of actual and potential development.

If a society were a family, some loss of educational benefit to the most gifted students might seem justified in a school system intent upon enhancing opportunity for students with disabilities. But even in that case, an allocation that left the most gifted at the same low level of educational development as the most grievously disabled would seem grossly unfair. And it is not clear that even the modest sacrifices that would be appropriate within a family would be appropriate for the larger society; perhaps one feature that distinguishes families from larger, impersonal social units is a greater concern for the welfare of each member than for each one's share of external resources.

Clearly, biological misfortune raises issues about the meaning of fair treatment that the ADA's anti-discrimination framework gives us little guidance in resolving. That framework also limits the social response to disabilities by imposing the costs of accommodation primarily on individuals.

As we saw in the case of special education, the larger society may not always be able to bear such costs. But in other cases, burdens that would be excessive for an individual or agency may well be reasonable for a city or state. An individual should not have to plead undue hardship in order to avoid costs properly imposed on the community; a person with disabilities should not be denied accommodation because it imposes an undue hardship on an individual employer.

A recent analysis of the employment provisions of the ADA predicted that its anti-discrimination framework would have the effect of confining its benefits to a "disability elite" — those workers "who have the least serious disabilities and the strongest education, training, and job skills." Because employers have to bear the costs of accommodation, they will "skim the 'cream' of the population with disabilities," bypassing those with more severe and debilitating conditions. In order to help those with the most serious and pervasive disabilities, the government must significantly increase its investments in welfare, employer subsidies, and job training. But such measures are matters of distributive justice, and the fact that they are not among the remedies mandated by the ADA suggests the limitations of the anti-discrimination model upon which the current law rests.

Nevertheless, the specific provisions of the ADA on employment, transit, and public accommodation reflect, in Chief Justice Earl Warren's famous phrase, "the evolving standards of decency that mark the progress of a maturing society." To say that the question of fair treatment for people with disabilities does not have an obvious or final answer is not to say that we cannot reach a consensus on what fairness requires at our level of affluence and technological development. The ADA represents a major step towards achieving such a consensus.

SOURCES

Amundson, Ron. "Disability, Handicap, and the Environment," *Journal of Social Philoso*phy, vol. 23, no.1 (1992).

Burkhauser, Richard V. "Beyond Stereotypes: Public Policy and the Doubly Disabled," *The American Enterprise* (September/October 1992).

Dworkin, Ronald. *Taking Rights Seriously* (Harvard University Press, 1977).

Evans, Daryl. "The Psychological Impact of Disability and Illness on Medical Treatment Decisionmaking," *Issues in Law and Medicine,* vol. 5, No. 3 (1989).

Galston, William. *Liberal Purposes: Goods, Virtues, and Diversity in the Liberal State* (Cambridge University Press, 1991).

Kavka, Gregory S. "Disability and the Right to Work," *Social Philosophy & Policy*, vol. 9, No. 1 (1992).

Nagel, Thomas. "Equality," in *Readings in Social and Political Philosophy*, edited by Robert M. Stewart (Oxford University Press, 1986)

Rebell, Michael A. "Structural Discrimination and the Disabled," *Georgetown Law Journal*, vol. 74 (1986).

tenBroek, Jacobus. "The Right to Live in the World: The Disabled in the Law of Torts," *California Law Review*, vol. 54 (1966).

Trouwers-Crowley, S. *ADA Primer: A Concise Guide to The Americans With Disabilities Act of 1990* (Prentice Hall, 1990).

Wendell, Susan. "Toward a Feminist Theory of Disability," *Hypatia*, vol. 4, no. 2 (1989).

(IN)EQUALITY, (AB)NORMALITY,
AND THE AMERICANS WITH DISABILITIES ACT

Anita Silvers

Anita Silvers teaches philosophy at San Francisco State University. She is co-author of Disability, Difference, Discrimination: Perspectives on Justice in Bioethics and Public Policy *(1998) and co-editor of* Medicine and Social Justice: Essays on the Distribution of Health Care *(2002),* Americans with Disabilities: Exploring Implications of the Law for Individuals and Institutions *(2000), and* Physician Assisted Suicide: Expanding the Debate *(1998).*

Silvers argues that the 1990 Americans with Disabilities Act *enacted a conceptual shift in the meaning of "disability." Rather than defining "disability" as a disadvantageous physical or mental deficit of persons, it codified the understanding of "disability" as a defective state of society which disadvantages these persons. Silvers criticizes the standard medical model for conceptualizing disabled persons as biologically inferior and so confining them to the role of recipients of benevolence or care. She then claims that turning to an ethic of caring yields counter-intuitive results that conflict with the conceptual apparatus of the ADA. Silvers argues that in order to liberate social thought from the medical model, the ADA's conceptual framework must be adopted so that current practice is re-conceptualized.*

I. The Americans with Disabilities Act

The United States Constitution's Fourteenth Amendment codifies the protection that no State shall "deny any person within its jurisdiction the equal protection of the laws." In 1990, Congress enacted the Americans with Disabilities Act (ADA), public law 101-336, which extends equal protection to individuals whose physical or mental impairments substantially limit one or more life functions. Congress cited a history of isolation and discrimination to explain the need for this law.

Historically, society has tended to isolate and segregate individuals with disabilities, and despite some improvements, such forms of discrimination ... continue to be a serious problem.... Individuals with disabilities are a discrete and insular minority who have been faced with restrictions and limitation, subjected to a history of purposeful unequal treatment, and relegated to a position of political powerlessness in our society based on characteristics that are beyond the control of such individuals and resulting from stereotypic assumptions not truly indicative of the individual ability of such individuals to participate in, and contribute to society (ADA, 1990).

While the ADA contains no explicit references to health care delivery, its requirements reach to the core of medical thought because through it Congress legislates a reconceptualization of the meaning of "disability." The ADA codifies into law the understanding that a disabling condition is a state of society itself, not a physical or mental state of a minority of society's members, and that it is the way society is organized rather than personal deficits which disadvantages this minority.

In striking contrast, the standard medical model[1] conceptualizes the disabled as biologically inferior, and in so conceiving confines such individuals to the role of recipients of benevolence rather than as persons with social and moral agency. This model assumes that uncompromised and unimpaired physical and mental status is the standard of "normalcy" for both medical practice and social policy.

In this paper I will argue that shifting the locus of disability from immutable personal shortcoming to remediable public failure liberates disabled individuals from the encroachment of the medical model. The ADA reformulates disabled persons' moral status, casting them in positive roles as responsible agents. Concomitantly, the ADA liberates society from having any special charitable duties to the disabled. I will begin the argument by laying out some of the conceptual history of the medical model which informs the attitudes of many physicians and other health care workers. My argument will proceed then in three parts. First, I will argue that the medical model pervasively infects typical medical rationing schemes, such as the Oregon Plan. Second, to its detriment, much philosophical discussion assumes the medical model. Third, turning to an ethic of caring has counter-intuitive results and conflicts with the ADA's conceptual framework. In sum, perceiving individuals with impairments as needing care subordinates them to care givers; when viewed as perpetual patients rather than as persons, their equality is limited.

II. A Conceptual History

To fully grasp the impact of the ADA, one must comprehend the ingrained historical categories of repression to which the disabled have been subjected. It is but a short slippery slide from thinking of a disability as a misfortune or a shame to considering it to be shameful. When we see a disabled person it is our practice to look away. This "etiquette" is an example of that which Charles Taylor terms the oppressive withholding of recognition (1992, p. 36). Until relatively recently the invisibility of disabled people even had legal sanction. For example, testimony supporting the passage of the ADA referenced a Chicago municipal ordinance that barred maimed, mutilated or otherwise deformed individuals from public ways or other public places. And the Wisconsin Supreme Court

upheld the exclusion of a boy with cerebral palsy from school because he "produce(d) a depressing and nauseating effect on the teachers and school children." Personal testimony to the Congress was filled with narratives about how disabled citizens were expelled from public events because they were "disgusting to look at," from theaters because the manager did "not want her in here," from a zoo because an official believed the disabled individual would "upset the chimpanzees," and from being an account holder in a bank because the disabled customer "did not fit the image the bank wished to project" (ADA, 1989).

That we withhold social recognition from individuals with disabilities by not even looking at, let alone seeing, them has a long social history. In the thirteenth and fourteenth centuries the disabled began to be treated as a deviant social group. With the breakdown of the feudal system, laborers gained geographical mobility, however the need for place bound laborers remained pressing. Consequently, laws were enacted which forbade able-bodied workers from traveling between towns without special authorization. Disabled individuals, on the other hand, were encouraged to travel among towns to afford the able-bodied relief from their protracted presence. This mechanism effectively expelled the disabled from the ranks of the laboring class.

Persons with disabilities were grouped into a single inferior social class. It is this institutionalizing process from which sprang the concept of the disabled as a minority of persons whose physical and mental impairments disadvantage them in society. By the seventeenth century, the virtue of according charitable benevolence to those in need clashed outright with the fear of creating a class of drones. To combat this fear there emerged the concept of the deserving poor, a class which was reserved for those who would have worked if it were not for their unfortunate impairments.

Members of the deserving poor were carefully distinguished from the undeserving, willfully malfunctioning poor. However, careful attention to appropriate character was necessary if a disabled person was to avoid slipping into the undeserving class. With the advent of the medical model of disability, those with impairments were urged to submit themselves regularly to curative processes as proof of their dissatisfaction with their defective state. Because these often failed, the medical model rendered disability a state not only involuntary but immutable, one beyond redemption by modern science.

As a social class, the disabled were required, by definition, to be non-productive, and thus were considered incapable of responsible use of the goods which charity bestowed. Thus there emerged the social class of care-givers whose profession it was to channel and administer charity for the disabled. The role assigned to the disabled in this scheme magnified mere malfunctioning into an incapacity to shoulder responsibility and make a contribution. It is against this historical backdrop that the ADA would make its first decisive stand against the medical model.

III. The ADA's First Test: The Oregon Plan

In 1992, the Oregon Plan's rationing system for health care included language which legislated existing or potential disabilities as reasons for disallowing or diminishing medical treatment.[2] The Plan denied persons with existing or potential disabilities equal treatment under the law, and thus federal legal assessment concluded that the proposal violated the civil rights of the disabled.

Oregon's policies grew out of a telephone survey in which nondisabled individuals were asked to rank a variety of treatments and health care levels in various life circumstances. Physical or mental impairment of a kind which defied medical restoration was ranked lower than able-bodiness and thus Medicaid coverage for individuals with certain types of impairments was ranked lower than other types of coverage. The rankings assumed a conceptual framework in which to be physically or mentally impaired meant to live a life of an inferior quality. For instance, the Oregon commission ranked liver transplants for alcoholics much lower than liver transplants for persons without this debilitating condition. This ranking reflects the stereotypical belief that liver transplants must have poorer outcomes in alcoholic

patients. No such data exist (Forman, 1993). The commission failed to dis-ambiguate between alcoholics who continue to imbibe large quantities of alcohol and those who have ceased. Only those who continue to drink have an increased chance of recurring liver disease.

Taken as a group, alcoholics may have a greater probability of recurring liver disease. Nevertheless, it is a fallacy to conclude that the higher probability attributable to the group as a whole applies equally to each member of the group. If such a mistake is made in association with withholding medical treatments for persons with disabilities, the ADA classifies it as a violation of the law. Thus, in so far as alcoholism can be classified as a disability, the ADA considers it a violation to bar a recovered alcoholic, who no longer drinks alcohol, from life saving treatment available to non-alcoholics. Assigning a lower priority for health care to persons in virtue of some debilitating condition is in direct conflict with the ADA's representation of a disability as a condition that does not diminish an individual's right to be recognized and cared for as a fully equal person.

In part the Oregon Plan's problems arose through the use of quality adjusted life year (QALY) calculations. The Oregon Health Services Commission designated that three factors — cost of the treatment, years of life saved, and amount of improvement in quality of life — be considered in rank-ordering a comprehensive list of medical services. Rationing based on QALY calculations incorporates the medical model; it assumes that an un-compromised, unimpaired physical and mental status is the desideratum which should guide the expenditure of health care dollars. QALY calculations cut across the conceptual distinctions of the ADA in that they generally assign a lower value to saving disabled persons with life threatening medical problems that to able-bodied persons with identical medical problems.

IV. The Persistence of Disability Discrimination

The medical model has intruded its influence into policy analyses. In a report on the ADA commissioned for the Report from the Institute for Philosophy and Public Policy, David Wasserman contended that nature makes persons with disabilities less equal than other persons (1993, pp. 7-12). He maintains that there are biological differences which constitute the definitive characteristics of the class protected by the ADA. Such properties, according to Wasserman, render the class's members irreparably inferior in respect to claims to fair or equitable treatment.

> ... [The ADA] also recognizes an objective category of biological impairment; a person whose major life activities were limited only by other people's attitudes or practices would be "disabled" only in a derivative sense (p. 9).

And later,

> [t]he fact of biological impairment, recognized by the ADA in its definition of disability, makes the notion of "equal opportunity to benefit" problematic. This is a serious defect in a statute that treats the denial of such opportunity as a form of discrimination (p.10).

However, the ADA neither mentions nor otherwise refers to biological impairment. While meticulously inclusive in its coverage of both physically and cognitively impaired persons, the ADA does not legislate that disability is biological in origin. In any case, although some impairments have a genetic or chemical origin, many are the result of traumatic injury, which is a mechanical rather than a biological process.

Conceiving of disability as essentially biological has the effect of explaining the social exclusion visited upon the disabled as "natural" or as ascribable to a non-social source. Policy makers who naturalize the isolation of the disabled have denied that society has any obligation to correct the social disadvantage which burdens individuals with disabilities. As Ron Amundson argues:

> (I)f handicaps are natural consequences (rather than social consequences) of disabilities, the victim's loss of opportunity can be thought of as beyond the resources, or at least beyond the

responsibility of society to remedy. Someone whose disadvantage comes from a natural disaster may be an object of pity, and perhaps of charity.... Someone whose disadvantage occurs as a result of social decision has a more obvious claim for social remediation (1991, p. 113).

Those who suffer disadvantage as a result of social oppression may be owed rectification, while those whose disadvantage is of natural origin may be due only pity or charity. Suggestions that a social explanation of the disabled's isolation and disadvantage is not as objective as a biological explanation are spurious. This line of argument only functions as an apology to absolve society from responsibility for remedying the adverse impact of socially sanctioned exclusionary practices.

Wasserman also fails to recognize the conceptual shift inherent in the ADA's understanding of disability. He argues that

> (t)he ADA itself recognizes that the physical endowment of people with disabilities contributes to their disadvantage: the statue defines disability as "physical or mental impairment" that "substantially limits (the impaired person's) pursuit of major life activities" (p. 8).

The ADA, however, does not cite any direct causal connection between physical or mental state and disadvantage. The term "disadvantage" occurs in its text only in Finding 6, which argues that empirical research demonstrates that people with disabilities "occupy an interior status in our society, and (are) severely disadvantaged socially, vocationally, economically, and educationally" (ADA, 1990). Thus, the law explicitly conjoins the disadvantaged state of disabled persons with the social status to which they have been consigned. This demonstrates the conceptual shift. "Disability" is not a physical or mental state of persons. Rather, the ADA codifies disability as a state of society which disadvantages persons. *As such, it is a problem which occurs as a result of social decision and is therefore subject to social correction.*

Moreover, while an impairment may not be an advantage, it does not logically follow that it must be a disadvantage. Disadvantages are heavily context dependent and relative to the ends or goals of an individual. In an age of corrective lenses and supermarkets, nearsightedness is not the disadvantage that it was to a Neanderthal hunter.

Informed by the historical perspective outlined above, and the medical model which grew out of it, Wasserman views the ADA as a mandate for charitable rather than equitable treatment. Without fully comprehending the conceptual shift, it is impossible to understand that *equal opportunity* rather than *exceptional treatment* is the ADA's legislative objective. For instance, the ADA's preface sets out the goal or remedying inequalities of opportunity which handicap citizens with disabilities.

> The continuing existence of unfair and unnecessary discrimination and prejudice denies people with disabilities the opportunity to compete on an equal basis ... (ADA, 1990).

Wasserman finds it impossible for individuals with disabilities to compete on an equal basis with the able-bodied. His report interprets the ADA's standard as guaranteeing equal outcomes, and argues that such a warrant is absurd.

> More broadly, we cannot reasonably expect to raise all people with disabilities to a level of functioning where they can receive the same benefits from facilities and services as able bodied people ... (p. 10).

This argument interposes a straw man.[3] Neither the ADA nor any disabled advocacy group proposes identity of outcomes as the test that people with disabilities are being treated equally. The goal is not to make the disabled whole, but rather to eliminate social practices which implicitly or explicitly favor the non-disabled. Benefiting equally from public transportation, for example, means having the opportunity to travel the same public routes with approximately the same time and expenditure as nondisabled individuals.

The ADA does not try to render mobility-impaired individuals fully mobile. Wasserman's

criticism that the regulation would still "leave most people with disabilities with a far greater burden of mobility than most able-bodied people" (p. 10) is at best irrelevant. It mistakenly imputes to the ADA the medical notion of the disabled as patients to be either made whole or cared for.

Wasserman confounds and obscures the distinction between two quite different questions. First, a medical question: whether a departure from normal physical or mental status is correctable. Second, a social question: whether society ought to ignore, repair, or adapt to a person's physical or mental impairment. To confound these two issues is tantamount to accepting the devaluing stereotypes which it is the ADA's avowed purpose to oppose. Thus Wasserman condemns the ADA by adopting the flawed social perspective it was designed to dislodge.

V. The Model of Caring

One philosophical response to Wasserman's criticisms is to turn to an ethics of care, in which moral relations are defined as taking place among unequals. In this type of moral framework being abnormal does not result in being morally marginalized. As Laurence Blum insists, it is not by reasoning about whether defective individuals are equal, but rather by feeling about their situations as they do themselves, that we can conduct ourselves morally towards them (1991).

Blum's diagnosis grows out of a conviction that logic driven judgments fail in situations where agents must behave ethically toward persons less advantaged than themselves. Rather than attempting to judge impartially or categorically, agents should respond so sensitively that their perception of the particularities of any situation match the perceptions of those with whom they are interacting.

Consider a case in which a worker debilitated by distress is treated callously by a supervisor, who refuses to adjust her standards to his impaired performance. Blum argues that it is natural to recognize the reality of another's pain, even if one cannot imagine one's self being in such pain. The pain of another is invisible only to the morally blind. Utilizing this moral schema, Blum argues that certain types of emotional responses impair moral vision in such a way that threatening aspects of reality are blocked out. Able-bodied persons dread beholding damaged persons out of a fear that they, themselves, might someday be impaired (1991, p. 718). Blum concludes that it is the supervisor's impaired moral perception which blocks her from accepting the pained person's estimation of the incapacitating impact of his pain, and his assessment of what the supervisor owes him with regard to it.

But Blum's assessment of this case is not accurate. To condemn the supervisor's moral proficiency in this manner has bizarre implications. A common experience among disabled individuals who have adapted to their impairments is to regret that there was an initial period of debilitating panic and self abdication. Regret of this sort is recounted again and again in anecdotal autobiographical material. On Blum's schema, though, persons who are now reconciled to their disabilities must be guilty of moral insensitivity toward their earlier despondent selves. This result is absurd. A disabled person does not owe it to his earlier self to regard prior self pity as credible. If such reasoning is absurd intra-personally, why should it be valid inter-personally? Concomitantly, there is a logical flaw in thinking that the supervisor owes a debilitated worker acceptance of the worker's own assessment of the quality of his life.

On the other hand, it is also not the case that a disabled individual ought necessarily to accept an able-bodied person's assessment of the disabled person's situation. Recognizing this point requires a rejection of the stereotypes stubbornly embedded in our social perceptions. As Amundson observes:

The "sick role" ... relieves a person of normal responsibilities, but carries other obligations with it. The sick person is expected to ... regard his or her condition as undesirable. These requirements resonate with the attitudes of society toward disabled people.... One interesting correlation is that able-bodied people are often offended by disabled people who appear satisfied or happy with their condition (1992, pp. 114,118).

Society expects its projected image of regret to be in evidence. It is this expectation which places the disabled into the role of the sick to whom care must be given.

Proponents of the ethics of caring argue that social intimacy, originating from the natural affection of parents for their young, is the foundation of moral interaction. Within a functional family, defects in persons cause them to be cared for rather than condemned; it is this model that proponents attempt to apply to all moral interaction. Notice that this model is potentially limited if tender feelings for familial dependents are not largely extendible to total strangers.[4]

Functionally, a dependent stance is advantageous only if genuine; that is, if the putative dependent truly requires dependency status. In social systems which erect social and physical barriers to the disabled, and in which caring-for is the primary manner in which the able bodied relate to the disabled, it becomes socially incumbent upon the latter to possess dependency status, even if they are more competent than the former.

Unfortunately, this type of moral framework lends itself to harming the putative dependent. It can lead to a requirement that the putative dependent accept lesser quality care than they would administer to themselves. There is no obligation that some individuals ought to allow themselves to be harmed simply to afford others with opportunities to be virtuous. Is it reasonable for a moral framework to make it virtuous to be poor simply so that the rich have the opportunity to act charitably? Analogously, this framework typecasts the disabled as subordinate, encouraging them to be vulnerable so that others may care for them.

To his credit, Blum recognizes that (dis)advantage and (mis)fortune are anchored to particular points of view. Consequently, his proposal to remediate inequality between the positions of moral agents assigns moral priority to the manner in which whomever is *disadvantaged* desires to be treated. Individuals with disabilities are allowed to designate appropriate conduct advanced toward themselves, and thus potentially equalize their relationship vis-à-vis the advantaged agent. Privileging the perspective of disabled individuals, however, is no improvement over disregarding their perspectives. *Such a framework merely assumes that it is the disabled which are subordinate and thus disadvantaged.* If forbearance for subordinates, rather than respect for equals, motivates moral conduct, then if disabled persons abandon the compliant behavior which mark them as subordinate, they dissolve the moral binds which link them to others. Thus, modeling morality on caring appears to make such self-sacrificing compliant behavior obligatory. This result is counter-intuitive in the extreme.

VI. Equality

What impedes persons with disabilities from commanding the respect due to equals? Why should a disabled person not count as fully in moral deliberation as someone unimpaired? The unreflective reaction to this question seems to be that being unable to perform some major life activity thoroughly devastates an individual's capacity for responsible performance and destroys the person's potential for all of life. Were this bleak depiction a fact instead of an over-reaction, no familiar moral criteria would afford individuals with disabilities equal moral weight. Amundson's critique of Amartya Sen's view of the disabled is worth repeating here to illustrate how the attribution of a physical or mental impairment may exclude an individual from the general application of consequentialist principles.[5]

Sen criticizes utilitarian moral theory on the grounds that it would distribute income unfairly, as for example in "a case where one person A derives exactly twice as much utility as person B from any given level of income, say, because B has some handicap, e.g., being a cripple" (Sen, 1973). Sen apparently sees the "incapacitation" of cripples to be so global as to affect even their capacity for enjoyment — or at least their capacity to experience increases in personal utility from increases in resources proportional to those experience by able-bodied people. This is a profoundly mistaken and destructive stereotype (1992, p. 114).

Similarly, Charles Taylor, commenting on the extent to which egalitarianism characterizes modern moral thought, exaggerates the impact of a disability and thus blocks equitable access to categorical moral principles affirming that humans generally deserve respect. Taylor identifies "the basis for our intuitions of equal dignity" as "an universal human potential, a capacity that all humans share." But, he continues, "our sense of the importance of potentiality reaches so far that we extend this protection even to people who through some circumstance that has befallen them are incapable of realizing their potential in the normal way — handicapped people ... for instance" (1992, pp. 42-42). This manner of explicating matters intimates that "handicapped" people are equal only by extension or derivation or fiction because they really do not possess the essentially human capacity to fulfill their potential "normality."

Yet reflection exposes the flaw in purporting to delineate normal from abnormal, or restricted, realization of human potential in this matter. Every person, equally, has potentials and whether these could have been fulfilled "in the normal way," and whether any loss accrues in not realizing them "in the normal way" is merely speculative. We would not dream of declaring that an athletically gifted person, who cannot realize his potential as a boxer because he wants to play the violin, is equal only in some extended sense. So, why place an artistically gifted person such as Itzhak Perlman, who for different reasons is not a boxer, in an inferior category?

Ethical thinking is obstructed because reasoning responds to the common, rather than the deviant. Modern moral thought has not construed disability as being like other particularities which differentiate moral agents from each other. While modern moral thought commonly dismisses differences between persons as contingent and external, and thus as inessential to a person's moral being, disability unmistakably has been embraced as *a morally essential attribute*; one which assigns the disabled to the borderline of moral worth. It is curious that modern thought, with its emphasis on inferiority and its disregard of external variation, fails to accept disability as inessential. But, as I have argued, the continuing influence of the medical model springs from social and historical prejudices which deny individuals with disabilities this acceptance.

The moral status of individuals with disabilities is impaired because society's stereotype defeats a condition imposed by most, perhaps all, rational moral systems, namely, that reasons for action must not be opaque to normal adults. For a moral reason to have motivating power, agents must at least understand the reason. However, a "normal" able-bodied individual is physically and socially blocked from accurately grasping what it is like to be in a "damaged" individual's place (as was evident in the Oregon health Plan's flawed telephone survey). Truths about how one would want to be treated if one were disabled are likely to be opaque to "normal" individuals and thus unable to motivate them morally. Far from extending protection so that it cloaks even individuals with disabilities, modern moral thought tends to magnify the influence of the medical model, with the result, inexorably, of excluding these individuals from normal moral recognition. The compulsion to dismiss them as abnormal — that is, as being in a state unthinkable for one's self — renders all appeals to what one would wish done, if one were to be in the other's place, ineffective.

Is inequality, cast as an intractable aspect of a person's experience, an essential human condition, or merely the artifact of an inequitable social arrangement? In the everyday life of persons mobilizing in wheelchairs, their experience of inequality, and their inequality in the eyes of others, manifests itself not only in the inability to walk but also in exclusion from bathrooms, from theaters, from transportation, from places of work, and from life-saving medical treatment. In keeping with this reality, it is the strategy of the ADA to require that whomever operates a facility or program must accommodate individuals with disabilities unless doing so would constitute an undue hardship, as measured against the overall financial resources of the facility or program. What informs this mandate is recognition that accessibility would be a commonplace, not a novelty, were the majority, not the minority, of the population disabled.

To conclude that physical or mental impairment, a contingent individual state, entails a moral deficit neglects the extent to which structural social arrangement permeates particular experience. Particularists like Blum, who legitimately focus on the experiential uniqueness of moral situations, tend to ground the possibility of interpersonal moral agreement in the existence of an "objective" moral reality, equally experientially accessible to all moral agents alike. They thereby discount the influence of the generalized social, political, and economic environment in composing experience, at most appealing to it to explain moral deviance, blockage, or blindness. In addition, they tend to discount the power of environmental reform to transfigure moral experience; including whether we can think of others, or ourselves, as equal. Likewise, essentialists who focus on universal human properties discount the extent to which social organization influences how we conceptualize or define ourselves.

Suppose that most persons used wheelchairs? Would we continue to build staircases rather than ramps? Suppose most were deaf? Closed-captioning would have been the standard for television manufacture long before July 1, 1993. By counterfactualizing about what society would do were persons with disabilities dominant rather than suppressed, it becomes evident that systematic exclusion of the disabled is a consequence not of their natural inferiority but of their minority social status.

VII. Conclusion

Very recently, it has become fashionable in philosophy, even commonplace, to challenge the theoretical transition from imagining one's self in others' places to accepting others as equivalent to one's self, which is the basis modern social thought has used since the enlightenment for assigning moral and social equality. It is argued that particularities of attachment, or of race or gender, exercise such substantial positive moral impact that to conceive of moral agents as fundamentally interchangeable strips away crucial moral features. In other words abstracting from the features which differentiate persons is no longer thought to be necessary —

indeed, is considered potentially counterproductive — to affording them equal moral recognition.

Heretofore, the particularities of disability have been impervious to this reform. And it remains to be seen whether particularizing, or, instead, universalizing, moral thinking better advances recognition of the moral agency of individuals with disabilities. I am inclined to have greater confidence in the latter approach, as my discussion in this essay makes manifest, but only if the social adjustments the ADA demands suffice to compel an understanding of equality which does not conflate being equal with being normal. On the other hand, were social practice to be reformed to expunge the influence of the medical model of disability, perhaps we could recognize how normal it is to be an individual with a disability and could accept such persons as fully rather than fictionally equal.

NOTES

1. In speaking of the "medical model" I refer to assumptions embedded deeply in current health care practice. I do not intend to stereotype all health care practitioners as accepting these assumptions. Nor do I contend that the relationships governed by these conceptions are injurious in every instance. Rather, my argument is that individuals with disabilities are confined to these relationships by the medical model.

2. Obtaining equitable health care is a widespread problem for individuals with disabilities (Evans, 1989).

3. In this part of his report, Wasserman appears to import Sen's metric of "capability" (Sen, 1980). However, Sen advances the goal of equality of capability as an alternative to equality of welfare, not as an alternative to equality of opportunity. Sen's concept of the responsibility of society to prefer individuals with disabilities as compensation for their deficits is not the ADA's assignment of responsibility not to discriminate against individual's with disabilities.

4. David Hume depicts these extended trust relationships as an "artificial contrivance for the convenience and advantage of society" and as requiring constant education and effort to maintain (1975).

5. Amundson somewhat misses Sen's point, which is that capability, not enjoyment, should be the metric of egalitarian distribution.

REFERENCES

Americans With Disabilities Act (ADA) 42 U.S.C., Sec 12101-12213 (Supp. II, 1990).

Americans With Disabilities Act (ADA) Record of Senate Hearing, 1989.

Amundson, R.: 1992, "Disability, handicaps, and the environment," *Journal of Social Philosophy*, Vol 23, no. 1, pp. 105-119.

Blum, L.: 1991, "Moral perception and particularity," *Ethics,* 101 (4), pp. 701-725.

Constitution of the United States, Fourteenth Amendment.

Evans, D.: 1989, "The psychological impact of disability and illness on medical treatment decision-making," *Issues in Law & Medicine*, Vol 5, no.3, pp. 295-6.

Forman, J.: 1993, "Defining basic benefits: Oregon and the challenge of health care reform," *Report from the Institute of Philosophy and Public Policy*, Winter/Spring, pp. 12-18.

Kolata, G.: 1992, "Ethical struggles with judgment of 'the value of life,'" *New York Times*, November 24, pp. B5, B7.

Mollat, M.: 1986, *The Poor in the Middle Ages: An Essay in Social History*, A. Goldhammer (trans.) New Haven: Yale University Press.

Sen, A.: 1973, *On Economic Inequality,* Oxford: Oxford University Press.

Sen, A.: 1980, "Equality of what?" *Tanner Lectures on Human Value*, S. McMurring (ed.), Cambridge: Cambridge University Press.

Silvers, A.: 1994, "'Defective' agents: Equality, difference and the tyranny of the normal," *The Journal of Social Philosophy*, June 1994.

Silvers, A.: 1995, "Damaged goods: Does disability disqualify people from just health care?" *The Mount Sinai Journal of Medicine*, Vol 62, No. 2, pp. 102-111.

Taylor, C. et al.: 1992, *Multiculturalism and 'The Politics of Recognition,'* Princeton: Princeton University Press.

Wasserman, D.: 1993, *Report for the Institute of Philosophy and Public Policy*, vol 13, No. 1/2, Winter/Spring.

UNITING THE NATION? DISABILITY, STEM CELLS, AND THE AUSTRALIAN MEDIA

G. Goggin and C. Newell

G. Goggin is in the Centre for Critical and Cultural Studies at the University of Queensland. C. Newell is in the School of Medicine at the University of Tasmania in Hobart, Tasmania. Goggin and Newell have co-authored Digital Disability: The Social Construction of Disability in New Media *(2003).*

   Goggin and Newell situate their analysis of disability in a discussion of the controversial debates regarding embryonic stem cell research in Australia. They examine media representations of disability as a way of understanding how disability is constructed in discourses of nationhood and biotechnology. Media representations reveal a structure of privilege with respect to the voicing of views regarding disability and biotechnology. Goggin and Newell argue that the diversity of voices on disability in the Australian community is not represented and that people with disabilities are not quoted as experts on disability. An awareness of the media's construction of disability will not only allow a better understanding of disability, they argue, but will better meet the requirements of the international disability rights movement motto of "nothing about us without us," recently emphasized in the Disabled Peoples' International Europe 2000 statement on biotechnology.

Mediating Disability

If we are to believe the dominant media representations, then salvation for those identified by society as having disability is just around the corner. In this article, we extend our existing area of research with regard to disability and media to look at biotechnology through the lens of several media moments. In particular, we examine the media representation of disability in the contemporary Australian debates regarding stem cells, including a case study in which one of the authors feature.

We understand disability not as a "deficit" or "lack," but as a cultural and political category and space. Disability, we suggest, operates as a crucial structuring cluster of concepts, figures and structures in discourses (Fulcher, 1989). Disability is a dynamic entity produced by social relations, as a range of theorists argue, particularly who those theorize the "social model" approach and those in

conversations around this important concept. Disability narratives structure our cultural texts and practices, something evident in media, as well as other cultural, literary and artistic forms (Mitchell and Snyder, 2001). Crucially, with respect to the media moments we examine in this article, it is through representations of and discourses on disability that the imaginary communities of nations are constructed.

While the study of media and the representation of disability remains fledgling, there are a number of helpful studies. In his important early work, Clogston categorized articles in terms of a taxonomy of different aspects of disability (Clogston, 1994), which fall into two basic groups, "traditional" attitudes to disability (including the "medical" and "social pathology" model) and "progressive" attitudes (such as the "minority/civil rights" and cultural pluralism model). To Clogson's categories, Haller adds three further models:

- the business model (people with disabilities as costly to society, especially economically);
- the legal model (people with disability as vested with legal rights);
- consumer (people with disability as an untapped market) (Haller, 1995, 2000).

Important as it has been in analysing the cultural scripts used to represent disability (a recent example is Gold and Auslander, 1999), content analysis tends to be based on such static models of disability. Meekosha and Dowse call, instead, for an "analysis sufficiently sophisticated to understand the interrelationship of gender, sexuality, race, class and disability as discourses of subordination and exclusion" (Meekosha and Dowse, 1997). Elsewhere, we have examined media and the representation of disability in Australia, with a case study of the 2000 Olympics and Paralympics, where we found that media representations of prestigious international sporting events reinforce the established power relations which oppress people with disability in society (Goggin and Newell, 2000).

There is a fundamental and difficult aspect to media and cultural representation of disability, which has not been well explored. There is a sense in which disability is both everywhere yet nowhere, common yet invisible. Mitchell and Snyder argue that the representation of disability differs from other categories of identity and subjectivity, because disability is actually present, not absent, in many cultural texts: "disabled people's marginalization has occurred in the midst of a perpetual circulation of their images" (Mitchell and Snyder, 2000, p. 6).

There is another dialectic between the visibility and invisibility of disability. There are dominant ways of "seeing" disability and making it "visible" to the social gaze, and dominant ways of making disability "invisible." While certain impairments are highly visible — physical impairments, leading to the most common signifier of disability, the wheelchair — other impairments are relatively invisible — including psychiatric or chronic conditions. There is a sense in which people can choose, in some circumstances and with some

impairments at least, whether or not to *pass* as a person with disabilities (Brueggeman, 1997).

An understanding of this unique "double bind" of disability is important for a consideration of how biotechnology is mediated, indeed how this and other technology is socially shaped (MacKenzie and Wacjman, 1999; Goggin and Newell, 2003). Indeed, we suggest that a critical disability perspective complements, and extends existing work on media, medical science and biotechnology (for instance, see early work such as Karpf, 1988, and later studies such as Marchessault and Sawchuk, 2000). There has been important work on the cultural representation of genetics (Nelkin and Lindee 1995; van Dijck, 1998; Conrad and Gabe, 1999), including analysis from a disability perspective (Shakespeare, 1999), we seek to make a contribution to such analysis by focusing on detailed analysis of media representations, drawing on concepts, theories and tools of contemporary media studies. In what follows, our focus is on media representations of debates on stem cell research in Australia in 2002. It is not our intention to focus on the moral or religious implications of such developments, but how biotechnology, and so too disability, is constituted within and by contemporary media.

"The Spirit of One Nation": Narrating the Nation

On April 5, 2002, Australian Prime Minister John Howard reached an agreement with Premiers of Australian states on guidelines for research into human embryo stem cells. At the press conference held to announce the decision, Howard declared that the Council of Australian Governments' agreement:

> balances the ethical considerations with the need for medical research. I thank my colleagues for the cooperative spirit that they've demonstrated through all of these discussions, the spirit of one nation, dare I say it, a united national approach. (Howard, 2002)

In what he acknowledged as his "rhetorical flourish" the Prime Minister effusively praised the leaders' efforts in uniting the Australian nation. The

Premier of the state of New South Wales, Bob Carr, also availed himself of the offer to share the glory:

> Premier Carr: This is very good news for researchers who are working to cure diseases and to save lives… It will be welcomed by people, by families who live with Alzheimers or with a child with type one diabetes. The people I've spoken to in wheelchairs will welcome the fact that research, cutting edge research dealing with embryonic stem cells can go ahead offering them as it does a chance of a breakthrough …it's good news for alleviating human suffering. (Howard, 2002)

The Prime Minister's "magnificent national outcome" was a good news story for most newspapers and many readers, with favourable headlines: "COAG reaches stem cell accord" (Lewis, 2002), "Cell research offers hope for the future" (Courier-Mail, 2002), and "No stemming the tide of hope" (Charlton, 2002).

This "stem cell accord" and "united nation" is one of the most highly publicized moments in which biotechnology circulated widely in mainstream Australian media, a phenomenon that forms part of international media flows and representations concerning disability and biotechnology. Media coverage of debate over stem cell research from late March to late May 2002 provides a fascinating case study of how disability is represented — and how such representation is a fulcrum for broader cultural, social, political and economic issues. Science and technology's centrality to national politics is evident in this piece of dramaturgy. It was front-page news that led bulletins on radio, television and the Internet. It was in the rhythms of news in which the nation was narrated, and thus imagined (Anderson, 1983; Bhabha, 1990; Mercer, 1992) — and disability represented and implicated.

The debate gathered momentum when Minister for Ageing, Kevin Andrews, put a plan to Federal Cabinet to ban research on spare *in vitro* fertilization (IVF) embryos on 25 February 2002. While his ministerial colleagues were apparently sympathetic, the Prime Minister decided personally to canvass the role of embryo stem cell research

before Cabinet approval and putting a submission to the Council of Australian Governments meeting. The Prime Minister's arrogation of the moral high ground ensured much attention from current affairs reporting and media generally over the next 6 weeks. "High" technology, and especially biotechnology plays an important symbolic role in political and economic discourses. With its prospect on a ban on research, the Andrews proposal drew responses from opponents with a mix of medical, scientific, and economic interests.

While scientists defended their right to conduct their research and make discoveries for the good of the common weal, others pointed to the hopes held to reap the industrial and economic benefits of such research. During the 1990s, industry policy in the old-fashioned Keynesian or Australian Labour party sense was thought to be no longer available as an serious option in the wake of the dominance of narrow neoclassical economics, competition and world trade rules.[1] So for Labour state premiers and chief ministers in 2002, touting for biotechnology became the next best thing. Not surprising then that these leaders leapt to defend biotechnology's prospects, forcing the Prime Minister to reconsider.

At the intersection of these political (the Prime Minister as statesman orchestrating ethical debate) and economic (anxieties of a small country in the face of globalization) discourses lies the paradoxical figure of disability. Nostalgic for the hubris of Margaret Thatcher's declaration that "there is no such thing as society" (Thatcher, 1987), enterprising leaders wish to vest their faith in the possessive individual. Yet, when it suits, leaders will espouse the national interest and recruit the social. Here, disability comes to hand, convenient and ready-made for connecting the economic to the social, the rational to the emotional — giving the ecstasy to economics (Morris, 1992).

The most evocative conscription of disability may be found not in the gestures of the Prime Minister, but in the NSW Premier Bob Carr's rhetorical flourish. Carr was in the van of outcry on possible banning of stem cell research. Former journalist Carr is noted for unremitting attention to his media image. In orchestrating state action,

Carr sought to rally public opinion by identifying himself with the depths of the tragedy of disability, the private catastrophe suffered by unfortunate individuals. He visited a spinal cord unit, and then wrote an apologia for embryo stem cell research:

> A 19-year-old woman lies paralysed from the neck down as a result of a car smash. I leave the spinal unit after meeting her, my mind racing. How many years before there is a cure? Before she can walk out of hospital? (Carr, 2002)

Carr's sally into the politics of pictures (Hartley, 1992) was, of course, received coolly by many — not least on the part of the national parliamentary press gallery:

> Carr … obviously believes the balance of opinion among the public is that if this research helps people who are suffering from debilitating illnesses, they'll be behind his more liberal approach. (Grattan, 2002)

Grattan's characterization of disability as a "debilitating illness," to be read in terms of the binary of liberal versus conservative, is worthy of further discussion, but here we merely observe that both she and Carr share, with most other journalists and parliamentary representations, a common epistemological and political framework.

When disability is given national news coverage, as in Bob Carr's and other media moments of the stem cell debate, the medical and social pathological model (Clogston), and business model (Haller) recur time and time again. The "catastrophe of disability" (Clapton, 2002) remains the dominant media representation of disability. In the coverage of stem cell and biotechnology — but as has been argued with respect to media representations of other quite different technologies also, such as cochlear implant and Deaf people (Goggin and Newell, 2003) — there is a consistent emplotment concerning the social tragedy of disability and delivery from the catastrophe for individuals. Underlying this narrative structure are some profoundly contentious assumptions:

- that disability is an individualized experience as opposed to being created and perpetuated by society;
- that people with disabilities are to be acted upon; that technology is paradoxically both value neutral and yet also inherently good for people with disabilities;
- that particular voices supportive of the technology and its tacit power relations are portrayed, magnified and appropriated;
- that the heroic delivery of us from disability is the moral trump card played in debates regarding biotechnology.

Schematically, we see this emplotment of disability sequenced in the following steps:

1. The tragic life of an individual or several devalued individuals is portrayed in a way designed to elicit maximum effect.
2. A technology is portrayed as delivering a person from disability, provided that society legalizes, funds, or embraces such a solution.
3. Securing the technology means that disability has then been "dealt with"; after deploying such rhetoric there is to be no more appeal to emotion, and the solution lies in the rational pursuit of the technology identified in step 2 (effectively there is only one, inexorable logical step);
4. Disability as a political issue goes away, until next time it is needed in the powerful politics of media representation.

We see these narrative elements of disability as forming a mythical structure in news and media (Bird and Dardenne, 1988). Media studies scholars such as John Hartley have suggested that news is constructed in terms of "us" and "them" (Hartley, 1996). Talking about "them" or "us" provides a way that media can address its audiences as a shared "we." What counts as "news" then is fundamentally structured by these categories of who does what to whom, and who is allowed to talk authoritatively about what counts (the news) to those interested (Hartley, 1996).

As a counter to such mythical structures and cultural scripting, there is an obvious starting-point. We suggest that, in Australia, similarly to many other countries (Cooke *et al.*, 2000), there has been a conspicuous lack of investigative journalism, as well as media and communications studies scholarship, exploring the nuances and marked differences within the disability community about biotechnology. Different formations of identity depend on how disabled subjectivity is experienced: for example, disability can take on different personal and social meanings, according to whether a person was born with a disability or acquired it early in life, compared with people with acquired disability. For those born with an impairment or condition, their lived experience and meaning of disability is an integral part of their life, whereas for many with acquired disability it becomes a tragedy. Our study confirms Shakespeare's observation that there is a "general absence of discussion of disability as the missing term in the debate around popular and scientific discourse of genetics" (Shakespeare, 1999, p. 171).

Our analysis of over 300 news and features items from print media in the period March–June 2002 indicate few alternative narratives and accounts of disability. People with disabilities were almost never quoted as authorities in news stories about stem cells. With rare exceptions they were not allowed to author opinion or commentary pieces on the debate (exceptions being Brock, 2002; Newell, 2002).When people with disabilities were quoted or reported upon, it was generally to give a first-hand testimonial to how biotechnology in the form of stem cell research could provide some sort of salvation, whether it be improved quality of life or escape from disability itself.

Superman Flies Again

If there is one image and voice that dominated the recent media portrayal of the Australian debate to do with cloning and stem cells, it was the figure of the broken superman, Christopher Reeve. Reeve is one of the very few international media stars who achieve and retain celebrity status because of, rather than despite their disability. A well-known actor before identifying as a person with disability,

Reeve is a representative figure for dominant media representations, as he provides a shorthand for a set of stubbornly engrained cultural assumptions about disability. Celebrity, fame and famous people is one of the ways that cultural consumption and media production operate (Turner *et al.*, 2000), and Reeve mediates disability for this system. Reeve was the signal exception to the "talked about, yet not yet allowed to talk" eclipse of people with disabilities in media representation of the stem cell debate.

The idea portrayed in many media accounts was that, with the use of embryonic stem cells, Christopher Reeve would be able to walk — and fly — again tomorrow. A man with quadriplegia, a hero known to many of us for his Superman role, Reeve held himself up to be, and was regarded by others, the ultimate argument for the use of embryonic stem cells for therapeutic and research purposes. Yet again, the tragedy of disability was the focal point for a policy debate. Of course, there was a difference in that Reeve is on record in the United States as also supporting the notion of therapeutic cloning. However, the way in which the debate transpired in Australia meant that the focus was on the use of embryonic stem cells. (There has been no substantial Australian media debate on so-called "therapeutic cloning" by the time of writing.)

Here is how the influential TV programme *Sixty Minutes* — an Australian version of its American parent show — framed the debate:

Presenter: Stem cell research is leading to perhaps the greatest medical breakthroughs of all time... Imagine a world where paraplegics could walk or the blind could see ... But it's a breakthrough some passionately oppose. A breakthrough that's caused a fierce personal debate between those like actor Christopher Reeve, who sees this technology as a miracle, and those who regard it as murder. (*Sixty Minutes*, 2002)

Sixty Minutes starkly portrays the debate in Manichean terms: lunatics standing in the way of technological progress versus Christopher Reeve flying again tomorrow:

Nick Tonti-Phillipini: The human embryo is the beginning of a human life. It may not be able to have all the functions of a human being yet but it has all the capacities.

Christopher Reeve: Well, there are the lunatic fringe all over the world. I know I'm being a little disrespectful but I have a hard time buying into that. I simply, you know, if they want to go that way and say that they don't want to be cured, then just step aside, because I am not happy spending my life in a wheelchair. It's unacceptable. (*Sixty Minutes*, 2002)

Reeve, however, shows no remorse in his self-opinionated disrespect for the views of another person with disability, with disagreeing thus with Tonti-Filippini's views:

I have a strong objection to whoever that gentleman is. I would love for this gentleman to spend a day in a wheelchair and then talk to me about this thing. (*Sixty Minutes*, 2002)

Reeve may not be aware, but he is speaking here of a fellow person with disability. Tonti-Filippini is a person with a chronic disabling condition. He has renal failure and dependence on haemodialysis, as a consequence of which he spends four 5-hour sessions in hospital each week. Tonti-Filippini knows too acutely the realities of disability and mobility impairment,[2] yet none of this context or information is presented by *Sixty Minutes*.

Further matters also not explored are also significant. In the broadcast *Sixty Minutes* interview, Reeve appears to be replicating an earlier account he gave to the American Congress (Reeve, 2002), where he also adopts an Utilitarian agenda:

Tara Brown: What would you urge the Australian government to do?

Christopher Reeve: The purpose of government, really in a free society, is to do the greatest good for the greatest number of people. And that question should always be in the forefront of legislators' minds. (*Sixty Minutes*, 2002)

Neither *Sixty Minutes* nor Reeve recognizes the adverse implications for himself individually and for all people with disabilities in adopting such a utilitarian stance. The notion of the "greatest good" might be seen to contradict the medical model and locating disability in the individual. Yet the utilitarian position poses other, more fundamental challenges. The greatest good for the greatest number inherently means that many of the public goods that people with disabilities claim would be avoided in such a social policy.

Muted Voices

As scientific and industrial industries lobbied heavily in the quest to secure embryonic stem cells, certain voices and figures were privileged ones, from which the media took its cue. Under the headline of "The Main Players," one journalist composed a prime that provided profiles of four politicians, one church leader and two scientists (Hope, 2002). This anatomy of power relations of the stem cell issue is quite accurate in terms of dominant media: people with disabilities do not rate a mention; they are simply off the map. They do not warrant having profiles devoted to them *qua* powerful "players" or having authority conferred upon them, as might leading Australian scientist Alan Trounson (for example, Smith, 2002b), or mainstream Roman Catholic or Anglican church leaders. A question and answer (Q&A) piece underlines this:

Q. Who is arguing against this embryonic stem cell research?

A. Right to life movement, religious leaders Catholic Archbishop George Pell and Anglican Archbishop Peter Jensen, some bioethicists. (Farr, 2002)

Scientists with a minority view, then, are marginalized, although not as radically as people with disabilities. A number of scientists, such as leading Australian scientist Sir Gustav Nossal, have suggested that many years of animal research would be needed before human applications would be possible. Other scientists overlooked by mainstream media have confirmed that any prospect of Christopher Reeve walking again many years after his injury was more science fiction than fact. There is evidence of long-term scientific benefit to be found in adult stem cells, but the contested ethics revolves around whether these are sufficient without the use of embryonic stem cells (for early discussion of embryo debates, see Mulkay, 1997). Yet the rush to secure embryonic stem cells precluded any form of inclusive or even rational conversation about how science policy should address the complex issues of disability.

The mainstream media did not feature such alternative voices, except in passing. One of the best sources of a broader science policy perspective was to be found in the Australian Broadcasting Corporation (ABC)'s website *Science On Line* (Salleh, 2002). It was difficult to find, in the media, a source that explicitly provided a recognition by the media of the reality that many of the voices that spoke trumpeting the salvation of society from disability tomorrow had vested commercial or professional interests. As well as ignoring the diversity of views in the scientific debates on biotechnology, there was scant attention paid to the multi-billion dollar nature of the biotech business (an exception being commentator Shanahan, 2002b).

With the 3 months of media coverage we studied, only very few dissenting voices on disability were allowed to convey different messages on stem cells. Apart from letters to the editor, we could find only one article written by a person who identified with disability, an article by Christopher Newell in the *Australian* (Newell, 2002). The Commissioner for Community Services in New South Wales, Robert Fitzgerald, in a letter to the editor also sought to raise public awareness about the appalling situation of Australians with disabilities, lamenting, "[i]f only people who have a disability were as loud and powerful as the US scientific and medical establishment — or for that matter, Superman" (Fitzgerald, 2002).[3]

One of the few dissenting voices of people with disabilities reported in the media was actually one of the authors of this article, Christopher Newell. Acknowledging our own implicated roles as media

activists, sources and shapers, we wish to turn to a brief but illustrative example of such coverage. Newell's views were also given prominence in a feature article by Simon Bevilacqua in the *Sunday Tasmanian*:

> Stem cell research promises the miracles of the travelling spiritual evangelist and Reeve will be first in line to walk into the tent and be blessed with the spirit of science. Disabled bio-ethics consultant Christopher Newell is not so fast to join the queue... You might think he and others with disabilities would unconditionally welcome the new cure-all. That, he says, is because most of us have not spoken to — or, more importantly, listened to — anyone with a disability. (Bevilacqua, 2002b)

Bevilacqua's short introduction to Newell as a person goes some way to challenging common stereotypes of disability and provides an accurate sense of his arguments. Yet Newell's quoted criticisms of Australian governments' stem cell decisions and the exclusion of people with disabilities from the wider debate about science and its uses may have been gainsayed by the article's headline: "Stemming the Research Rush."

A week later, Bevilacqua wrote a follow-up piece, this time profiling and giving coverage to Lee Stone, a person with disability, who disagreed with Newell's views:

> At age five, Lee ... was hit by a car ... Until 1994 he said the prospect of walking again was a dream, an unrealistic hope. But that all changed when Christopher Reeve, the actor who played Superman, became a quadriplegic after a fall from a horse... For that reason Lee is firmly in favour of stem cell research and the promise of leaping from his wheelchair. "I'll be a guinea pig, if they want. They can test it on me, I'd do anything to get out of this," he said, looking down at his wheelchair. "No one would choose to be in a wheelchair." (Bevilacqua, 2002b)

In our view Bevilacqua's article, which was entitled "I want to walk again, offer to be a guinea pig," draws upon the conventions of representing disability we have critiqued above. Here, the *Sunday Tasmanian* has used an old trick of journalism: constructing news by creating conflict by polarization — pitting Lee Stone, someone with quadriplegia, in a contest with Newell for who may speak in the name of people with disability.

As the controversy unfolded, several letters to the editor of the *Sunday Tasmanian* disputing the views of Newell as an ethicist with disability were printed. However, the debate framed in such a way that *ad hominem* attacks such as the following were encouraged, if not mandated (this letter was headed "Ethical Paralysis"):

> I know that Lee Stone, as a quadriplegic, and not Christopher Newell is the more representative of the disabled community. As a hemiplegic following a brain accident, I will gladly join the debate by supporting Lee's opinion…like Lee, I also am more than willing to offer myself as a human guinea pig for the benefit of disabled people…(Harmsen, 2002)

Such readers obviously found it difficult to think beyond the binaries of for or against biotechnology, with disability always being enlisted in the cause of the saviour science. They also did not attend to some of the nuance within Bevilacqua's piece, such as the final paragraphs noting common cause between Stone and Newell: "While Lee strongly disagreed with Dr Newell on the issue of stem cells and Christopher Reeve, he agreed with comments about the lack of services for disabled" (Bevilacqua, 2002a).

Whatever one's views about stem cells and cloning, it becomes clear that particular accounts of disability dominate, and that the voices of people with disability and others which are appropriated are overwhelmingly those supportive and uncritical of technology. Critical disability studies practitioners and activists have noted this elsewhere with respect to public debates on biotechnology more generally (Asch, 1989; Shakespeare, 1998; Newell, 2000a, b), but it takes peculiar and powerful forms in disabled media practices. Routine reporting of news has a deeply unequal

structure: excluded are those voices of people with disability who dare to critique the technology and its social relations.

Disability, Biotechnology and the Civil Society

A popular response to accounts of biotechnology is admiration that much attention is being given to disability by science. This popular response shaped by media representations revolves around a structure of privileged and excluded voices. The privileged voices predominantly are those which are supportive of dominant accounts of biotechnology as delivering us from disability, resting on the worldview that disability is a private catastrophe. Such accounts fail to address the fundamental problem of how disability fits into a comprehensive vision of a civil society. Indeed, in the voluminous literature on civil society, people with disabilities are routinely overlooked — perhaps as too uncivilized.

For example, in Australian celebrations of the nation's Centenary of Federation in 2001, disability rarely figured. A representative example is a collection of high-profile national lectures (Irving, 2002) in which commentators and scholars from diverse backgrounds celebrate Australian history, look at its diversity and explore civil society from a variety of perspectives. Disability is absent from this prominent series of talks, a fate people with disabilities continue to suffer in most other celebrations of national history, culture, society and politics — quite striking given that the Centenary of Federation marked the passage of 20 years after the 1981 International Year of Disabled People. Rarely, in national debates are important questions asked, such as how does disability figure in contemporary Australian society and conversations on how society should be, who do we count as members of our moral community and whom do we exclude? (Nelson, 2001).

This larger framework on the civil society and its various publics is an important context for media and biotechnology debates. Our claim to civil society and what civility it may offer is important to establish our specific argument here.

We are not neo-luddites: we are supportive of ethically appropriate stem cell research, genetic research and medical science in general.[4] Such knowledge and technology have much to offer people with disability and many of us are alive today because of medical developments. Yet, it is precisely because of the way in which disability is treated in biotechnology debates and because of the way in which our wider social situation is ignored, that Disabled Peoples' International Europe made a statement on biotechnology in 2000, the first demand of which is "Nothing about us without us" (DPI Europe, 2000).

In presenting disability in accordance with dominant notions of disability as tragedy and catastrophe, the media is generally failing to provide the diversity of cultural representations we need if people with disabilities are to be recognized and move from platitudes to ensuring civil rights enjoyed within a civil society become a reality in our everyday lives as people with disabilities. In Australia, the genetics and stem cell debate could have provided an opportunity to look at how Australia needs to incorporate the very plurality of our society in shaping science and health policy, and in addressing disability — not least to consider how to include people with disabilities, their families and careers at the highest level in social policy debates. If we are truly to embrace diversity then it must surely encompass all our social institutions including the media, science and the academy.

A starting point is to recognize the very existence of a structure of privileged and excluded voices in debates regarding disability and biotechnology, and their media coverage. The diversity of voices in the Australian community regarding disability is not being represented. Despite a reasonably diverse media in Australia, there are few people with disabilities who are quoted on disability as experts. The authorities on disability, relied upon by a surprising range of media in their construction of the "news" on disability, are almost invariably "experts" without the lived experience of disability. The corollary of this is that when people with disabilities are represented in the media — when they are selected as authoritative voices (what Hall *et al.*, 1978, famously defined in terms of "primary" and "secondary" definers), or when they make news, they are only permitted to speak in certain ways. Their speaking position is one in which they must speak according to the script, or risk unintelligibility or invisibility. Such media practices are "bad news," in the sense critiqued by the Glasgow Media Group more than two decades ago (Glasgow Media Group, 1976– 80).

The possibilities for humane biotechnology itself also rest on tackling these matters of media and cultural representation. We need to foster an ethics of listening that allows for media to represent disability in its complexity, to present the diversity of narratives about disability. There are obvious media strategies, such as guidelines on fair and accurate reporting (such as those developed by a number of media organizations around the world). There is also a need for the strategic use of media by people with disabilities and their organizations. Here, we embrace the issue of both of us being politically active with regard to disability. Indeed one of us is an actor in the media items we analyse in this paper. Rather than seeing this inherently as a disadvantage we would suggest that we need more "insider" insights into the way in which disability is constructed, and voices are privileged and excluded within the media moments that are about and, indeed, construct "biotechnology." Such diversity in representation is likely to provide a basis for greater dialogue and exchange across "medical" and "activist" discourses, promoting "listening and speaking carefully" (Shakespeare, 1999, p. 187) in the public sphere.

As well as providing "correctives" complexity of media and cultural representation, better interventions into the social relations and cultural representations of biotechnology could proceed from inclusive summits on media and disability, such as that conducted by Hartley and McKee on indigenous Australians and media (Hartley and McKee, 2000). We need to analyse and contest the mainstream media's construction of disability, intervening in the various sites of this struggle, in order to contribute to humane biotechnology and a truly civil society for people with disabilities.[5]

NOTES

1. In his biography of former Prime Minister Paul Keating, Don Watson writes of the horror that being suspected of being an advocate of "industry policy" would bring — not least the charge of being a "Creanite," so named after the ideas of then Labor Minister Simon Crean (Watson, 2002).

2. We have Dr Tonti-Filippini's permission to reveal this information directly, using the text he provided.

3. Fitzgerald's and other letters appearing in the *Sydney Morning Herald* on 6 April 2002, appeared under the headline of "The 'cells' that matter most are holding the disabled."

4. We say this plainly because of the will to misreading we have encountered in media debates. To give one example, Christopher was asked by a journalist from a state-based newspaper: "You're against stem cells, aren't you?." When Christopher replied: "We all have stem cells — they are vital for life. How could I be against them?," she replied: "Well, what are you against?"

5. We critically use ableist metaphors in this paper in a deconstructive way, mindful of their ableist history and meanings, but seeking to redeploy them otherwise.

REFERENCES

Anderson, B. (1983) *Imagined communities: reflections on the origin and spread of nationalism* (London, Verso).

Asch, A. (1989) Reproductive technology and disability, in: S. Cohen and N. Taub (Eds) *Reproductive Laws for the 1990s* (Clifton, NJ, Humana Press), 69-124.

Bevilacqua, S. (2002a) I want to walk again, offer to be a guinea pig, *Sunday Tasmanian*, 21 April, 3.

Bevilacqua, S. (2002b) Stemming the research rush, *Sunday Tasmanian*, 14 April.

Bhabha, H. (Ed.) (1990) *Nation and narration* (London, Routledge).

Bird, E. and Dardenne, R. (1988) Myth, chronicle and story: exploring the narrative qualities of news, in: J. Carey (Ed.) *Media, Myth and Narrative* (Beverly Hills, CA, Sage), 67-86.

Brock, P. (2002) Try telling the sufferers' families it's evil, *The Australian*, 1 April, 12.

Brueggeman, B. (1997) On (almost) passing, *College English*, 59, 647-660.

Carr, B. (2002) No time to waste in the search for embryonic stem cells secrets, *Sydney Morning Herald*, 4 April.

Charlton, P. (2002) No stemming the tide of hope, *Courier-Mail (Brisbane)*, 6 April, 27.

Clapton, J. (2002) Tragedy and catastrophe: contentious discourses of ethics and disability, *Ethics and Intellectual Disability*, 6(2), 1-3.

Clogston, J.S. (1994) Disability coverage in American newspapers, in: J.A. Nelson (Ed.) *The disabled, the media, and the information age* (Westport, CT, Greenwood Press), 45-58.

Conrad, P. and Gabe, J. (Eds) (1999) *Sociological Perspectives on the New Genetics* (Cambridge, Blackwell).

Cooke, C., Daone, L. and Morris, G. (2000) *Stop press!* (London, Scope).

Courier-Mail (2002) Cell research offers hope for the future, *Courier-Mail* (Brisbane), 6 April, 22.

Disabled Peoples' International, Europe (DPI Europe) (2000) *The right to live and be different*. Available online at: http://www.dpieurope.org/htm/bioethics/biodeclaration.htm (accessed 19 September 2002).

Farr, M. (2002) PM backs stem cells — but with conditions, *Daily Telegraph* (Sydney), 5 April, 2.

Fitzgerald, R. (2002) Letter to the Editor, *Sydney Morning Herald*, 6 April.

Fulcher, G. (1989) *Disabling policies?* (London, Falmer Press).

Glasgow Media Group (1976–80) *Bad News*, 2 vols (London, Routledge/Kegan Paul).

Goggin, G. and Newell, C. (2000) Crippling paralympics? Media, disability and Olympism, *Media International Australia*, 97, 71-84.

Goggin, G. and Newell, C. (2003) *Digital disability: the social construction of disability in new media* (Lanham, MD, Rowman & Littlefield).

Gold, N. and Auslander, G. (1999) Newspaper coverage of people with disabilities in Canada and Israel: an international comparison, *Disability & Society*, 14(6), 709-731.

Grant, F. (2002) Chasing stem cell miracle — "it could change my life," *Daily Telegraph* (Sydney), 4 April, 6.

Grattan, M. (2002) PM's shaky path on embryos, *Sydney Morning Herald*, 5 April 2002, p. 11.

Hall, S., Critcher, C., Jefferson, T., Clarke, J. and Robert, B. (1978) *Policing the crisis: mugging, the state, and law and order* (London, Macmillan).

Haller, B. (1995) Rethinking models of media representations of disability, *Disability Studies Quarterly*, 15, 26-30.

Haller, B. (2000) If they limp, they lead: news representations and the hierarchy of disability images, in: D. Braithwaite and T. Thompson (Eds) *Handbook of communication and people with disabilities: research and application* (Mahwah, NJ, Lawrence Erlbaum Associates), 273-288.

Harmsen, P. (2002) Ethical paralysis, letter to the Editor, *Sunday Tasmanian*, 28 April.

Hartley, J. (1992) *The politics of pictures: the creation of the public in the age of popular media* (London, Routledge).

Hartley, J. (1996) *Popular reality: journalism, modernity, popular culture* (London, Arnold/New York, St. Martin's Press).

Hartley, J. and McKee, A. (2000) *The indigenous public sphere: the reporting and reception of aboriginal issues in the Australian media* (Oxford, Oxford University Press).

Hope, D. (2002) The main players, *The Australian*, 1 April, 13.

Howard, J. (2002) Transcript of the Prime Minister the Hon John Howard MP, Joint Press Conference with Premiers and Chief Ministers (Canberra, Parliament House). Available online at:http://www.pm.gov.au /news/interviews/2002/interview1587.htm (accessed 15 June 2002).

Irving, H. (Ed.) (2002) *Unity and diversity: a national conversation* (Sydney, ABC Books).

Karpf, A. (1988) *Doctoring the media: the reporting of health and medicine* (London, Routledge).

Lewis, S. (2002) COAG reaches Stem Cell Accord, *Australian Financial Review*, 6 April, 3.

Mackenzie, D. and Wajcman, J. (Eds) (1999) *The Social Shaping of Technology* (2nd edn) (Buckingham, Open University Press).

Marchessault, J. and Sawchuk, K. (Eds) (2000) *Wild science: reading feminism, medicine, and the media* (London, Routledge).

Meekosha, H. and Dowse, L. (1997) Distorting images, invisible images: gender, disability and the media, *Media International Australia*, 84, 91-101.

Mercer, C. (1992) Regular imaginings: the newspaper and the nation, in: T. Bennett (Ed.) *Celebrating the nation* (Sydney, Allen & Unwin), 26-46.

Mitchell, D. and Snyder, S. (2000) *Narrative prosthesis: disability and the dependencies of discourse* (Ann Arbor, MI, University of Michigan Press).

Mitchell, D. and Snyder, S. (2001) Representation and its discontents: the uneasy home of disability in literature and film, in: G. Albrecht, K. Seelman and M. Bury (Eds) *Handbook of Disability Studies* (London, Sage), 195-218.

Morris, M. (1992) *Ecstasy and economics: American essays for John Forbes* (Sydney, Empress).

Mulkay, M. (1997) *The embryo research debate: science and the politics of reproduction* (New York, Cambridge University Press).

Nelkin, D. and Lindee, S. (1995) *The DNA mystique: the gene as a cultural icon* (New York, W. H. Freeman).

Nelson, H. (2001) *Damaged identities, narrative repair* (Ithaca, NY, Cornell University Press).

Newell, C. (2000a) Critical reflections on disability, difference and the new genetics, in: G. O'Sullivan, E. Sharman and S. Short (Eds) *Goodbye normal gene: confronting the genetic revolution* (Sydney, Pluto Press), 58-71.

Newell, C. (Ed.) (2000b) Special issue on bioethics and disability, *Interaction*, 13(3-4).

Newell, C. (2002) Superman's mission no miracle cure, *The Australian*, 28 March, 11.

Reeve, C. (2002) Testimony of Christopher Reeve to Senate Health, Education, Labor and Pensions Committee, United States Senate, Washington, 5 March 2002. Available online at: http://www.stemcellfunding.org/fastaction/news.asp?id=187 (accessed 15 June 2002).

Salleh, A. (2002) Scientists divided on stem cells, *News in Sciences*, Australian Broadcasting Corporation (ABC) Science Online. Available online at: http://www.abc.net.au/science/news/stories/s520 417.htm (accessed 15 June 2002).

Shakespeare, T. (1998) Choices and rights: eugenics, genetics and disability equality, *Disability & Society*, 13(5), 665-681.

Shakespeare, T. (1999) "Losing the plot"? Medical and activist discourses of the contemporary genetics and disability, in: P. Conrad and J. Gabe (Eds), *Sociological Perspectives on the New Genetics* (Cambridge, Blackwell), 171-190.

Shanahan, A. (2002a) Lobbyists' bogeyman a moral hero, *The Australian*, 5 March, 13.

Shanahan, A. (2002b) Profits chief lure for stem cell industry, *The Australian*, 21 May, 13.

Sixty Minutes (2002) Miracle or murder? *Sixty Minutes*, Channel 9, Australia, March 17. Available online at: http://news.ninemsn.com.au/sixtyminutes/stories/2002_03_17/story_532.asp (accessed 15 June 2002).

Smith, D. (2002a) The hard cell, *Sydney Morning Herald*, 30 March, 19.

Smith, D. (2002b) Pushing the boundary of cell research, *The Australian*, 1 April, 12.

Thatcher, M. (1987) AIDS, education and the year 2000, *Woman's Own*, 3 October, 10.

Turner, G., Bonner, F., and Marshall, D. (2000) *Fame games: the production of celebrity in Australia* (Cambridge, Cambridge University Press).

Van Dijck, J. (1998) *Imagination: popular images of genetics* (Basingstoke, Macmillan).

Watson, D. (2002) *Recollections of a bleeding heart: a portrait of Paul Keating PM* (Sydney, Random House).

ON THE GOVERNMENT OF DISABILITY

Shelley Tremain

Shelley Tremain teaches in the Philosophy Department at the University of Toronto, Mississauga. She is the editor of Foucault and the Government of Disability *(2005) and the author of a number of publications in journals and edited collections. Her current research is in the areas of disability and prenatal testing and screening, disability and the (bio)politics of stem cell research, and sexual ethics.*

Tremain uses the concept of "bio-power" to argue that both the medical and social models of disability are deficient. The social model distinguishes impairments as physical and "real" from disabilities that reflect the social disadvantages resulting from the perception and reception of impairments. Tremain argues that impairments are themselves subject to regimes of truth and power, historical contexts, and circumstances. The social model allows a discourse in which only those who have or are presumed to have an "impairment" get to count as "disabled." Impairments are then naturalized as essential to identities and used to explain medical and social practices that give different status and power to disabled people. Tremain ends by advocating that the disabled people's movement develop strategies for challenging the dominant discourse and thereby revealing how mechanisms of truth and knowledge in science, policy, and medical and legal practices regulate and govern disabled people's lives.

We believe that feelings are immutable, but every sentiment, particularly the noblest and most disinterested, has a history. We believe in the dull constancy of instinctual life and imagine that it continues to exert its force indiscriminately in the present as it did in the past ... We believe, in any event, that the body obeys the exclusive laws of physiology and that it escapes the influence of history, but this too is false.
— Foucault, "Nietzsche, Genealogy, History"[1]

Introduction: Bio-power and Its Objects

In the field of Disability Studies, the term "impairment" is generally taken to refer to an objective, transhistorical and transcultural entity of which modern bio-medicine has acquired knowledge and understanding and which it can accurately represent. Those in Disability Studies who assume this realist ontology are concerned to explain why social responses to "impairment" vary between historical periods and cultural contexts — that is, why people "with impairments" are included in social life in some places and periods and are excluded from social life in some places and periods.[2] Against these theorists, I will argue that this allegedly timeless entity (impairment) is an historically specific effect of knowledge/power. In order to advance this claim, I assume nominalism.[3]

Nominalists hold the view that there are no phenomena or states of affairs whose identities are independent of the concepts we use to understand them and the language with which we represent them. Some philosophers think this is a misguided stance. For these thinkers, objects such as photons, stars, and horses with which the natural sciences concern themselves *existed as* photons, stars, and horses long before any human being encountered them and presumed to categorize or classify them. Compelling arguments have been made, nevertheless, according to which not even the objects of the natural sciences (say, photons, stars, and Shetland ponies) have identities until someone names them.[4]

I want to set aside questions regarding the metaphysical status of these objects. In this paper, the only ontological commitments that interest me are those that pertain to elements of human history and culture. My aim is to show that impairment is an historical artifact of the regime of "bio-power"; therefore, I will restrict myself to claims that apply to objects of the human sciences.

Foucault's term "bio-power" (or "bio-politics") refers to the endeavor to rationalize the problems that the phenomena characteristic of a group of living human beings, when constituted as a population, pose to governmental practice: problems of health, sanitation, birthrate, longevity, and race. Since the late eighteenth century, these problems have occupied an expanding place in the government of individuals and populations. Bio-power is then the strategic movement of relatively recent forms of power/knowledge to work toward an increasingly comprehensive management of these problems in the life of individuals and the life of populations. These problems (and their management), Foucault thinks, are inextricable from the framework of political rationality within which they emerged and developed their urgency; namely, liberalism.[5]

The objectification of the body in eighteenth-century clinical discourse was one pole around which bio-power coalesced. As feminist historian Barbara Duden notes, in that historical context the modern body was created as the effect and object of medical examination, which could be used, abused, transformed, and subjugated. The doctor's patient had come to be treated in a way that had at one time been conceivable only with cadavers. This new clinical discourse about "the body" created and caused to emerge new objects of knowledge and information and introduced new, inescapable rituals into daily life, all of which became indispensable to the self-understandings, perceptions, and epistemologies of the participants in the new discourse. For the belief took hold that the descriptions that were elaborated in the course of these examinations truly grasped and reflected "reality."[6]

The dividing practices that were instituted in the spatial, temporal, and social compartmentalization of the nineteenth-century clinic worked in concert with the treatment of the body as a thing. Foucault introduced the term "dividing practices" to refer to modes of manipulation that combine a scientific discourse with practices of segregation and social exclusion in order to categorize, classify, distribute and manipulate subjects who are initially drawn from a rather undifferentiated mass of people. Through these practices, subjects become *objectivized* as (for instance) mad or sane, sick or healthy, criminal or good. Through these practices of division, classification, and ordering, furthermore, subjects become tied to an identity and come to understand themselves scientifically.[7] In short, this "subject" must not be confused with modern philosophy's *cogito*, autonomous self, or rational moral agent.

Technologies of normalization facilitate the systematic creation, identification, classification, and control of social anomalies by which some subjects can be divided from others. Foucault explains the rationale behind normalizing technologies in this way:

[A] power whose task is to take charge of life needs continuous regulatory and corrective mechanisms ... Such a power has to qualify, measure, appraise, and hierarchize, rather than display itself in its murderous splendor; it does not have to draw the line that separates the enemies of the sovereign from his obedient subjects; ... it effects distributions around the norm ... [T]he law operates more and more as a norm, and ... the juridical institution is increasingly incorporated into a continuum of apparatuses (medical, administrative, and so on) whose functions are for the most part regulatory.[8]

The power of the modern state to produce an ever-expanding and increasingly totalizing web of social control is inextricably intertwined with and dependent upon its capacity to generate an increasing specification of individuality in this way. As John Rajchman puts it, the "great complex idea of normality" has become the means through which to identify subjects and make them identify themselves in ways that make them governable.[9]

The approach to the "objects" of bio-medicine that I have outlined relies upon an anti-realism that conflicts with the ontological assumptions that condition dominant discourses of disability theory. In addition, this approach assumes a conception of power that runs counter to that which those discourses on disability take for granted.

Generally speaking, disability theorists and researchers (and activists) continue to construe the phenomena of disablement within what Foucault calls a "juridico-discursive" notion of power. In the terms of juridical conceptions, power is a fundamentally repressive thing possessed, and exercised over others, by an external authority such as a particular social group, a class, an institution, or the state. The "social model of disability," in whose framework a growing number of theorists and researchers conduct their work, is an example of the juridical conception of power that predominates in Disability Studies. Developed to oppose "individual" or "medical" models of disability, which represent that state of affairs as the detrimental consequences of an intrinsic deficit or personal flaw, the "social model" has two terms of reference, which are taken to be mutually exclusive. They are: *impairment and disability*.[10] As the formalized articulation of a set of principles generated by the Union for the Physically Impaired Against Segregation (UPIAS), the social model defines *impairment* as "the lack of a limb or part thereof or a defect of a limb, organ or mechanism of the body." By contrast, *disability* is defined as "a form of disadvantage which is imposed on top of one's impairment, that is, the disadvantage or restriction of activity caused by a contemporary social organization that takes little or no account of people with physical impairments."[11] Thus, Michael Oliver (one of the first proponents of the model) stresses that although "disablement *is* nothing to do with the body," impairment is "*nothing less than* a description of the physical body."[12]

Several interlocutors within Disability Studies have variously objected that insofar as proponents of the social model have forced a strict separation between the categories of impairment and disability, the former category has remained untheorized.[13] Bill Hughes and Kevin Paterson have remarked, for example, that although the impairment-disability distinction de-medicalizes disability, it renders the impaired body the exclusive jurisdiction of medical interpretation.[14] I contend that this amounts to a failure to analyze how the sort of bio-medical practices in whose analysis Foucault specialized have been complicit in the historical emergence of the category of impairment and contribute to its persistence.

Hughes and Paterson allow that the approach to disability that I recommend would be a worthwhile way to map the constitution of impairment and examine how regimes of truth about disabled bodies have been central to governance of them.[15] These authors claim nevertheless that the approach ultimately entails the "theoretical elimination of the material, sensate, palpable body."[16] This argument begs the question, however; for the materiality of the "(impaired) body" is precisely that which ought to be contested. In the words of Judith Butler, "there is no reference to a pure body which is not at the same time a further formation of that body."[17] Moreover, the historical approach to disability that I recommend does not deny the materiality of the body; rather, the approach assumes that the materiality of "the body" cannot be dissociated from the historically contingent practices that bring it into being, that is, bring it into being as that sort of thing. Indeed, it seems politically naive to suggest that the term "impairment" is value-neutral, that is, "merely descriptive," as if there could ever be a description that was not also a *prescription* for the formulation of the object (person, practice, or thing) to which it is claimed to innocently refer.[18] Truth-discourses that purport to describe phenomena contribute to the construction of their objects.

It is by now a truism that intentional action always takes place under a description. The possible courses of action from which people may choose, as well as their behavior, self-perceptions, habits, and so on are not independent of the descriptions available to them under which they may act; nor do the available descriptions occupy some vacuous discursive space. Rather, descriptions, ideas, and classifications work in a cultural matrix of institutions, practices, power relations, and material interactions between people and things. Consider, for example, the classification of "woman refugee." The classification of "woman refugee" not only signifies a person; it is in addition a legal entity, and a paralegal one to which immigration boards, schools, social workers, activists, and others classified in that way may refer. One's classification (or not) as a "woman refugee," moreover, may mean the difference between escaping from a war-torn country, obtaining safe shelter, and receiving social assistance and medical attention, or not having access to any of these.[19] In short, the ways in which concepts, classifications, and descriptions are imbricated in institutional practices, social policy, intersubjective relations, and medical discourses structure the field of possible action for humans.

This, then, is the place in which to make explicit the notion of power upon which my argument relies. Following Foucault, I assume that power is more a question of *government* than one of confrontation between adversaries. Foucault uses the term "government" in its broad, sixteenth-century sense, which encompasses any mode of action, more or less considered and calculated, that is bound to structure the field of possible action of others.[20] Discipline is the name that Foucault gives to forms of government that are designed to produce a "docile" body, that is, one that can be subjected, used, transformed, and improved.[21] Disciplinary practices enable subjects to act in order to constrain them.[22] For juridical power *is* power (as opposed to mere physical force or violence) only when it addresses individuals who are free to act in one way or another. Despite the fact that power appears to be repressive, the exercise of power consists in guiding the possibilities of conduct and putting in order the possible outcomes. The production of these practices, these *limits* of possible conduct, furthermore, is a concealing. Concealment of these practices allows the naturalization and legitimation of the discursive formation in which they circulate.[23] To put the point another way, the production of seeming acts of choice (*limits* of possible conduct) on the everyday level

of the subject makes possible hegemonic power structures.

In what follows, I will show that the allegedly real entity called "impairment" is an effect of the forms of power that Foucault identifies. I take what might seem a circuitous route to arrive at this thesis. For in order to indicate how bio-power naturalizes and materializes its objects, I trace a genealogy of practices in various disciplinary domains (clinical psychology, medico-surgical, and feminist) that produce two "natural" sexes. In turn, I draw upon these analyses in order to advance my argument that "impairment" (the foundational premise of the social model) is an historical artifact of this regime of knowledge/power.

Both "natural sex" and "natural impairment" have circulated in discursive and concrete practices as nonhistorical (biological) matter of the body, which is molded by time and class, is culturally shaped, or *on which* culture is imprinted. The matter of sex and of impairment itself has remained a prediscursive, that is, politically neutral, given. When we acknowledge that matter is an *effect* of certain historical conditions and contingent relations of social power, however, we can begin to identify and resist the ways in which these factors have material-*ized* it.

Governing Sex and Gender

In the first edition (1933) of the Oxford English Dictionary, there is no entry for "gender" that describes it as a counterpart to "sex" in the modern sense; instead, in the first edition of the OED, "gender" is described as a direct substitute for sex. In the second edition (1962) of the OED, a section appended to the main entry for "gender" reads: "in mod[ern]. (esp. feminist) use, a euphemism for the sex of a human being, often intended to emphasize the social and cultural, as opposed to biological, distinctions between the sexes." Examples cited to demonstrate this usage include ones taken from feminist scholarship in addition to ones drawn from earlier clinical literature on gender role and identity that developed out of research on intersexuality ("hermaphroditism") in the 1950s.[24]

In fact, it was in the context of research on intersex that Johns Hopkins psychologist John Money and his colleagues, the psychiatrists John and Joan Hampson, introduced the term "gender" to refer to the psycho-social aspects of sex identity. For Money and his colleagues, who at the time aimed to develop protocols for the treatment of intersexuality, required a theory of identity that would enable them to determine which of two "sexes" to assign to their clinical subjects. They deemed the concept of *gender* (construed as the psycho-social dimensions of "sex") as one that would enable them to make these designations.[25]

In 1972, Money and Anke Ehrhardt popularized this idea that sex and gender comprise two separate categories. The term "sex," they claimed, refers to physical attributes that are anatomically and physiologically determined; by contrast, the term "gender," they wrote, refers to the internal conviction that one is either male or female (gender identity) and the behavioral expressions of that conviction. As Money and Ehrhardt explained it, gender identity is "the sameness, unity, and persistence of one's individuality as male, female, or ambivalent."[26]

Money and Ehrhardt claimed that their theory of gender identity enabled medical authorities to understand the experience of a given subject who was manifestly one "sex," but who wished to be its ostensible other. Nevertheless, in the terms of their sex-gender paradigm, "normal development" was defined as congruence between one's "gender identity" and one's "sexual anatomy."[27] Although Money and his colleagues concluded from their studies with intersexed people that neither sexual behavior nor orientation as "male" or "female" have an innate, or instinctive, basis, they did not recant the foundational assumption of their theory, namely, there are only two sexes. To the contrary, they continued to maintain that intersexuality resulted from fundamentally *abnormal* processes; thus, they insisted that their patients required immediate treatment because they *ought* to have become either a male or a female.[28]

Despite the prescriptive residue of the sex-gender formation, it appealed to early "second-wave" feminists because of its motivational assumption that everyone has a "gender identity" that is detachable from each one's so-called "sex." Without questioning the realm of anatomical or biological sex, feminists took up the sex-gender paradigm in order to account for culturally specific forms of an allegedly universal oppression of women.

The distinction between sex and gender that Gayle Rubin articulated in 1975 through an appropriation of structuralist anthropology and Lacanian psychoanalysis has arguably been the most influential one in feminist discourse. By drawing on Claude Levi-Strauss's nature-culture distinction, Rubin cast *sex* as a natural (i.e., prediscursive) property (attribute) of bodies and *gender* as its culturally specific configuration. As Rubin explained it, "Every society has a sex-gender system — a set of arrangements by which the biological raw material of human sex and procreation is shaped by human, social intervention and satisfied in a conventional manner."[29] For Rubin, in other words, sex is a product of nature as gender is a product of culture.

The structuralist nature-culture distinction on which Rubin's sex-gender distinction relies was putatively invented to facilitate cross-cultural anthropological analyses; however, the universalizing framework of structuralism obscures the multiplicity of cultural configurations of "nature." Because structuralist analysis presupposes that nature is prediscursive (that is, prior to culture) and singular, it cannot interrogate what counts as "nature" within a given cultural and historical context, in accordance with what interests, whose interests, and for what purposes.[30] In fact, the theoretical device known as the nature-culture distinction is already circumscribed within a culturally-specific epistemological frame. As Sandra Harding remarks, the way in which contemporary western society distinguishes between nature and culture is both modern and culture-bound. In addition, the culture-nature distinction is interdependent on a field of other binary oppositions that have structured western modes of thought. Some of these others are: reason-emotion, mind-body, objectivity-subjectivity, and male-female. In the terms of this dichotomous thinking, the former term of each respective pair is privileged and assumed to provide the *form* for the latter term of the pair, whose very recognition is held to depend upon (that is, *require*) the transparent and stable existence of that former term.[31] In the terms of this dichotomous thinking, furthermore, any thing (person, object, or state of affairs) that threatens to undermine the stable existence of the former term, or to reveal its artifactual character (and hence the artifactual character of the opposition itself) must be obscured, excluded, or nullified.

To be sure, some feminists early criticized the nature-culture distinction and identified binary discourse as a dimension of the domination of those who inhabit "natural" categories (women, people of color, animals, and the non-human environment).[32] These early feminist critiques of the nature-culture distinction did not, however, extend to one of its derivatives: the sex-gender distinction. Donna Haraway asserts that feminists did not question the sex-gender distinction because it was too useful a tool with which to counter arguments for biological determinism in "sex difference" political struggles.[33] By ceding the territory of physical "sex," however, feminists actually encountered massive resistance and renewed attack on the grounds of biological difference from the domains of biology, medicine, and significant components of social science.[34]

The political and explanatory power of the category of gender depend precisely upon relativizing and historicizing the category of sex, as well as the categories of biology, race, body, and nature. Each of these categories has, in its own way, been regarded as foundational to gender; yet, none of them is an objective entity with a transhistorical and transcultural identity. In this regard, Nigerian anthropologist Oyeronke Oyewumi, for one, has criticized European and Euro-American feminists for their proposition according to which all cultures "organize their social world through a perception of human bodies as male or female." Oyewumi's criticism puts into relief how the imposition of a system of gender can alter how racial and ethnic differences are understood. In a detailed analysis, Oyewumi shows that in Yoruba culture, relative age is a far more significant social organ-

izer than sex. Yomba pronouns, for example, indicate who is older or younger than the speaker; they do not make reference to "sex."[35] In short, the category of sex (as well as the categories of biology, race, body, and nature) must be considered in the specific historical and cultural contexts in which it has emerged as salient.

Foucault makes remarks in another context that cast further suspicion on how the construct of an allegedly prediscursive "nature" operates within the terms of the sex-gender distinction. While the category of "sex" is generally taken to be a self-evident fact of nature and biology, Foucault contends that "sex is the most speculative, most ideal, and most internal element in a deployment of sexuality organized by power in its grip on bodies and their materiality, their forces, energies, sensations, and pleasures."[36] For Foucault, the materialization and naturalization of "sex" are integral to the operations of bio-power. In the final chapter of volume one of *The History of Sexuality*, Foucault explains that "the notion of `sex' made it possible to group together, in an artificial unity, anatomical elements, biological functions, conducts, sensations, and pleasures, and it enabled one to make use of this fictitious unity as a causal principle, an omnipresent meaning."[37] In other words, the category of "sex" is actually a phantasmatic *effect* of hegemonic power which comes to pass as the *cause* of a naturalized heterosexual human desire.

Butler refers to this alleged chain of events as the "heterosexual matrix."[38] The heterosexual matrix is the grid of cultural intelligibility in whose terms bodies and identities are understandable if they are tokens of an unambiguous male or female "sex" that is expressed through one's gender as "a man" or as "a woman," where these genders are defined in opposition to each other through the compulsory practice of heterosexuality. Currently the hegemonic conception of gender in Euro-American cultures, the heterosexual matrix presupposes a causal relation among sex, gender, and desire; in addition, this conception suggests that desire reflects, or expresses, gender and that gender reflects, or expresses, desire. With Butler, I contend, however, that this conception of sex, gender, and desire obscures the gender trouble that runs rampant within queer, bisexual, lesbian, gay, transgendered, and even heterosexual contexts, where in no way can gender be assumed to follow from so-called sex, nor can desire, sexual practice, or sexuality in general, be assumed to follow from gender.[39] Indeed, because the cultural visibility of (for instance) queers, cross-dressers, butch lesbians, drag queens and transgendered people threatens to betray the contingent and coercive status of this heterosexual hegemony, subjects of these social groups are routinely disciplined and punished through supposedly random and unrelated acts of public humiliation, bashing, intimidation, murder, and other forms of gender policing.

Now, it might seem counterintuitive to claim (as Foucault does) that there is no such thing as "sex" prior to its circulation in discourse, for "sex" is generally taken to be the most fundamental, most value-neutral aspect of an individual. Thus, one might wish to object that even a die-hard anti-realist must admit that there are certain sexually differentiated parts, functions, capacities, and hormonal and chromosomal differences that exist for human bodies. I should emphasize, therefore, that my argument does not entail the denial of material differences between bodies. Rather, my argument is that these differences are always already signified and formed by discursive and institutional practices. In short, what counts as "sex" is actually formed through a series of contestations over the criteria used to distinguish between two natural sexes, which are alleged to be mutually exclusive.[40] Because "sex" inhabits haunted terrain in this way, an army of scientific, medical, and social discourses must be continuously generated to refresh its purportedly definitive criteria. Of course, dominant beliefs about gender infect these discourses, conditioning what kinds of knowledge scientists endeavor to produce about sex in the first place. As the work on intersexuality of Fausto-Sterling and others shows, however, the regulatory force of knowledge/power about the category of sex is nevertheless jeopardized by the birth of infants whose bodies do not conform to normative ideals of sexual dimorphism, that is, infants who are both "male" and "female," or neither.

Recall that Money and his colleagues appraised intersexed bodies to be "abnormal" and in need of immediate medical treatment, despite concluding that sexed identity had no instinctual or innate basis. The clinical literature produced by those upon whom authority is conferred to make such pronouncements is in fact replete with references to the birth, or expected birth, of an intersexed infant as (for instance) "a medical emergency," "a neonatal surgical emergency," and "a devastating problem."[41] Since this is the almost universal reaction of medical practitioners to the birth (or expected birth) of an intersexual baby, substantial resources are mobilized to "correct" these so-called *unfortunate errors of nature*, including genetic "therapies" known to carry risks to the unborn, multiple surgeries that often result in genital insensitivity from repeated scarring, and life-long regimens of hormone treatments.[42] That these culturally condoned practices of genetic manipulation, surgical mutilation, and chemical control (these *technologies of normalization*) circulate as remedial measures performed on the basis of spurious projections about the future best interests of a given infant de-politicizes their disciplinary character; in addition, the role they play in naturalizing binary sex-gender and upholding heterosexual normativity remains disguised.

The argument according to which "sex" is an effect of contingent discursive practices is likely to encounter significant resistance from the domains of evolutionary and molecular biology (among others). I should underscore, therefore, that these disciplines do not stand apart from other discourses of knowledge/power about sex. On the contrary, social and political discourses on sex-gender have contributed to the production of evolutionary arguments and descriptions used in the physiology of reproduction, as well as to the identification of the objects of endocrinology (hormone science). From genitalia, to the anatomy of the gonads, and then to human chemistry, the signs of gender have been thoroughly integrated into human bodies. Fausto-Sterling points out, for example, that by defining as "sex hormones" groups of cells that are, in effect, multi-site chemical growth regulators, researchers *gendered* the chemistry of the body and rendered nearly invisible the far-reaching, non-sexual roles these regulators play in "male" and "female" development.

Fausto-Sterling remarks that the "discovery" of sex hormones early in the twentieth century heralded an extraordinary episode in the history of science. By 1940, scientists and researchers had identified, purified, and named these groups of cells. The scientists and researchers who investigated hormone science could make "hormones" intelligible, however, only in terms of the social and political struggles around gender and race that characterized the socio-cultural environments in which they worked. From the beginning, these research efforts both reflected and contributed to competing definitions of masculinity and femininity. As Fausto-Sterling explains it, with each choice these scientists and researchers made about how to measure and name the molecules they studied, they naturalized prevailing cultural ideas about gender.[43] In short, the emergence of scientific accounts about sex in particular and human beings in general can be understood only if scientific discourses and social discourses are seen as inextricable elements of a cultural matrix of ideas and practices.

Consider that if the category of sex is itself a *gendered* category (that is, politically invested and naturalized, but not natural), then there really is no *ontological* distinction between sex and gender. As Butler explains it, the category of "sex" cannot be thought as prior to gender as the sex-gender distinction assumes, since gender is required in order to think "sex" at all.[44] In other words, gender is not the product of culture and sex is not the product of nature, as Rubin's distinction implies. Instead, gender is the means through which "sexed nature" is produced and established as *natural*, as *prior to* culture, and as a politically neutral surface *on which* culture acts.[45] Rather than the manifestation of some residing essence or substrate, moreover, "gender identity" is the stylized *performance* of gender, that is, the sum total of acts believed to be produced as its "expression."

The claim that relations of power animate the production of sex as the naturalized foundation of gender draws upon Foucault's argument that juridical systems of power generate the subjects they subsequently come to represent. Recall that although juridical power appears to regulate political life in purely negative (repressive) terms by prohibiting and controlling subjects, it actually governs subjects by guiding, influencing, and limiting their actions in ways that seem to accord with the exercise of their freedom; that is, juridical power enables subjects to act in order to constrain them. By virtue of their subjection to such structures, subjects are in effect formed, defined, and reproduced in accordance with the requirements of them. That the practices of gender performance (construed as the cultural expression of a "natural sex") seem to be dictated by individual choice, therefore, conceals the fact that complicated networks of power have already limited the possible interpretations of that performance.[46] For only those genders that conform to highly regulated norms of cultural intelligibility may be lived without risk of reprisal.

The Subject of Impairment

Tom Shakespeare has claimed that the "achievement" of the U.K. disability movement (informed by the social model) has been to "break the causal link" between "our bodies" (impairment) and "our social situation" (disability).[47] Recall that the social model was intended to counter "individual" (or "medical") models of disability that conceptualized that state of affairs as the unfortunate consequences of a personal attribute or characteristic. In the terms of the social model, impairment neither equals, nor causes, disability; rather, disability is a form of social disadvantage that is imposed on top of one's impairment. In addition, impairment is represented as a real entity, with unique and characteristic properties, whose identity is distinguishable from, though may intersect with, the identities of an assortment of other bodily "attributes."

Proponents of the social model explicitly argue: (1) disablement is not a necessary consequence of impairment, and (2) impairment is not a sufficient condition for disability. Nevertheless, an unstated premise of the model is: (3) impairment is a necessary condition for disability. For proponents of the model do not argue that people who are excluded, or discriminated against, on the basis of (say) skin color are by virtue of that fact disabled, nor do they argue that racism is a form of disability. Equally, intersexed people who are socially stigmatized, and who may have been surgically "corrected" in infancy or childhood, do not seem to qualify as "disabled."[48] On the contrary, only people who *have* or are presumed to *have* an "impairment" get to count as "disabled." Thus, the strict division between the categories of impairment and disability that the social model is claimed to institute is in fact a chimera.

Notice that if we combine the foundational (i.e., necessary) premise of the social model (impairment) with Foucault's argument that modern relations of power produce the subjects they subsequently come to represent (that is, *form* and *define* them by putting in place the limits of their possible conduct), then, it seems that subjects are produced who "have" impairments because this identity meets certain requirements of contemporary political arrangements. My discussion below of the U.K. government's Disability Living Allowance policy shows, for example, that in order to make individuals productive and governable within the juridical constraints of that regime, the policy actually contributes to the production of the "subject of impairment" that it is claimed to merely recognize and represent. Indeed, it would seem that the identity of the subject of the social model ("people with impairments") is actually formed in large measure by the political arrangements that the model was designed to contest. Consider that if the identity of the subject of the social model is actually produced in accordance with those political arrangements, then a social movement that grounds its claims to entitlement in that identity will inadvertently *extend* those arrangements.

If the "impairments" alleged to underlie disability are actually constituted in order to sustain, and even augment, current social arrangements, they must no longer be theorized as essential, biological characteristics (attributes) of a "real" body upon which recognizably disabling conditions are imposed. Instead, those allegedly "real" impairments must now be identified as constructs of dis-

ciplinary knowledge/power that are incorporated into the self-understandings of some subjects. As *effects* of an historically specific political discourse (namely, bio-power), impairments are materialized as universal attributes (properties) of subjects through the iteration and reiteration of rather culturally specific regulatory norms and ideals about (for example) human function and structure, competency, intelligence, and ability. As universalized attributes of subjects, furthermore, impairments are naturalized as an interior identity or essence *on which* culture acts in order to camouflage the historically contingent power relations that materialized them as natural.[49]

In short, impairment has been disability all along. Disciplinary practices into which the subject is inducted and divided from others produce the illusion that they have a prediscursive, or natural, antecedent (impairment), one that in turn provides the justification for the multiplication and expansion of the regulatory effects of these practices. The testimonials, acts, and enactments of the disabled subject are *performative* insofar as the allegedly "natural" impairment that they are purported to disclose, or manifest, has no existence prior to or apart from those very constitutive performances. That the discursive object called *impairment* is claimed to be the embodiment of natural deficit or lack, furthermore, obscures the fact that the constitutive power relations that define and circumscribe "impairment" have already put in place broad outlines of the forms in which that discursive object will be materialized.

Thus, it would seem that insofar as proponents of the social model claim that disablement is not an inevitable consequence of impairment, they misunderstand the productive constraints of modern power. For it would seem that the category of impairment emerged and in part persists in order to legitimize the disciplinary practices that generated it in the first place.

The public and private administration and management (government) of impairment contribute to its objectivization. In one of the only detailed applications of Foucauldian analyses to disability, Margrit Shildrick and Janet Price demonstrate how impairment is naturalized and materialized in the context of a particular piece of welfare policy — the U.K.'s Disability Living Allowance (DLA) — that is designed to distribute resources to those who need assistance with "personal care" and "getting around." Shildrick and Price argue that although the official rationale for the policy is to ensure that the particularity of certain individuals does not cause them to experience undue hardship that the welfare state could ameliorate, the questionnaire that prospective recipients must administer to themselves abstracts from the heterogeneity of *their own* bodies to produce a regulatory category – impairment — that operates as a homogeneous entity in the *social* body.[50]

The definitional parameters of the questionnaire, and indeed the motivation behind the policy itself, posit an allegedly pre-existing and stable entity (impairment) on the basis of regulatory norms and ideals about (for example) function, utility, and independence. By virtue of responses to the questions posed on the form, moreover, a potential recipient/subject is enlisted to elaborate individuated specifications of this impairment. In order to do this (and to produce the full and transparent report that the government bureaucrats demand), the given potential recipient must document the most minute experiences of pain, disruptions of a menstrual cycle, lapses of fatigue, and difficulty in operating household appliances and associate these phenomena in some way with this abstraction. Thus, through a performance of textual confession ("the more you can tell us, the easier it is for us to get a clear picture of what you need"), the potential recipient is made a subject of impairment (in addition to being made a subject of the state), and is rendered "docile," that is, one to be used, enabled, subjugated, and improved.[51]

Despite the fact that the questions on the DLA form seem intended to extract very idiosyncratic detail from subject/recipients, the differences that they produce are actually highly coordinated and managed ones. Indeed, the innumerable questions and subdivisions of questions posed on the form establish a system of differentiation and individuation whose totalizing effect is to grossly restrict individuality.[52] For the more individualizing the nature of the state's identification of us, the farther

the reach of its normalizing disciplinary apparatus in the administration of our lives. This, Foucault believes, is a characteristic and troubling property of the development of the practice of government in western societies: the tendency toward a form of political sovereignty that is a government of "all and of each," one whose concerns are to totalize and to individualize.[53]

Because Foucault maintains that there is no outside of power, that power is everywhere, that it comes from everywhere,[54] some writers in Disability Studies have suggested that his approach is nihilistic, offering little incentive to the disabled people's movement.[55] Clearly, this conclusion ignores Foucault's dictum that "there is no power without potential refusal or revolt."[56] In fact, Foucault's governmentality approach holds that the disciplinary apparatus of the modern state that puts in place the limits of possible conduct by materializing discursive objects through the repetition of regulatory norms also, by virtue of that repetitive process, brings into discourse the very conditions for subverting that apparatus itself. The regime of bio-politics in particular has generated a new kind of counter-politics (one that Foucault calls "strategic reversibility"). For individuals and *juridically constituted* groups of individuals have responded to governmental practices directed in increasingly intimate and immediate ways to "life," by formulating needs and imperatives of that same "life" as the basis for political counter-demands.[57]

The disabled people's movement is a prime example of this sort of counter-discourse; that is, the disciplinary relations of power that produce subjects have also spawned a defiant movement whose organizing tool (the social model of disability) has motivated its subject to advance demands under the auspices of that subjectivity. The current state of disability politics could moreover be regarded as an historical effect of what Foucault describes as the "polymorphism" of liberal govern(-)mentality, which is its capacity to continually refashion itself in a practice of auto-critique.[58] Yet, insofar as the identity of that subject (people with impairments) is a naturalized construct of the relations of power that the model was designed to rebut, the subversive potential of claims that are grounded in it will actually be limited. As Wendy Brown argues, disciplinary power manages liberalism's production of politicized subjectivity by neutralizing (that is, re-*de*politicizing) identity through normalizing practices. For politicized identity both produces and potentially accelerates that aspect of disciplinary society that incessantly characterizes, classifies, and specializes through on-going surveillance, unremitting registration, and perpetual assessment.[59] Identities of the subject of the social model can therefore be expected to proliferate, splinter, and collide with increasing frequency as individualizing and totalizing diagnostic and juridical categories offer ever more finely tuned distinctions between and varieties of (for instance) congenital and acquired impairments, physical, sensory, cognitive, language, and speech impairments, mental illnesses, chronic illnesses, and environmental illnesses, aphasia, dysphasia, dysplasia, and dysarthria, immune deficiency syndromes, attention deficit disorders, attention deficit hyperactivity disorders, and autism.

This, then, is the paradox of contemporary identity politics, a paradox with which Disability Studies and the disabled people's movement must soon come to terms. Many feminists have long since realized that a political movement whose organizing tools are identity-based shall inevitably be contested as exclusionary and internally hierarchical. As I suggest elsewhere, a disabled people's movement that grounds its claims to entitlement in the identity of its subject ("people with impairments") can expect to face similar criticisms from an ever-increasing number of constituencies that feel excluded from and refuse to identify with those demands for rights and recognition; in addition, minorities internal to the movement will predictably pose challenges to it, the upshot of which are that those hegemonic descriptions eclipse their respective particularities.[60]

In short, my argument is that the disabled people's movement should develop strategies for advancing claims that make no appeal to the very identity upon which that subjection relies. Brown suggests, for example, that counter-insurgencies ought to supplant the language of "I am" ("with its

defensive closure on identity, its insistence on the fixity of position, and its equation of social with moral positioning") with the language of "I want this for us."[61] We should, in other words, formulate demands in terms of "what we want," not "who we are." In a rare prescriptive moment, Foucault too suggests that the target for insurgent movements in the present is to refuse subjecting individuality, not embrace it. As Foucault puts it, the political, ethical, social, philosophical problem of our day is not to liberate ourselves from the state and the state's institutions, but to liberate ourselves both from the state and the type of individualization that is linked to the state.[62]

The agenda for a critical Disability Studies movement, furthermore, should be to articulate the disciplinary character of that identity, that is, articulate the ways that disability has been naturalized *as* impairment by identifying the constitutive mechanisms of truth and knowledge within scientific and social discourses, policy, and medico-legal practice that have produced that contingent discursive object and continue to amplify its regulatory effects. Disability theorists and researchers ought to conceive of this form of inquiry as a "critical ontology of ourselves." A critical ontology of ourselves, Foucault writes, must not be considered as a theory, doctrine, or permanent body of knowledge; rather, this form of criticism must be conceived as a "limit-attitude," that is, an ethos, a philosophical life in which the critique of what we are is at the same time the historical analysis of the limits imposed on us.[63] In particular, the critical question that disability theorists engaged in an historical ontology would ask is this: Of what is given to us as universal, necessary, and obligatory, how much is occupied by the singular, the contingent, the product of arbitrary constraints? Lastly, a critical ontology of our current situation would be genealogical:

[I]t will not deduce from the form of what we are what it is impossible for us to do and to know; but it will separate out, from the contingency that has made us what we are, the possibility of no longer being, doing, or thinking what we are, do or think. It is not seeking to make possible a metaphysics that has finally become a science; it is seeking to give new impetus, as far and wide as possible, to the undefined work of freedom.[64]

Author's Note

I would like to thank Barry Allen and the guest editors of *Social Theory and Practice* for their comments and suggestions on earlier drafts of this paper, as well as Ron Amundson, with whom I discussed one of its arguments.

NOTES

1. Michel Foucault, "Nietzsche, Genealogy, History," in Donald F. Bouchard (ed.), *Language, Counter-Memory, Practice: Selected Essays and Interviews by Michel Foucault*, trans. Donald F. Bouchard and Sherry Simon (Ithaca, N.Y.: Cornell University Press, 1977), p. 153.

2. See, for instance, Colin Barnes, "Theories of Disability and the Origins of the Oppression of Disabled People in Western Society," in Len Barton (ed.), *Disability and Society: Emerging Issues and Insights* (Harlow: Longnum, 1996), pp. 43-60; Mark Priestley, "Constructions and Creations: Idealism, Materialism, and Disability Theory," *Disability & Society* 13 (1998): 75-94.

3. With an array of other diverse and even competing discourses, the nominalist approach to disability that I take in this paper has been identified as "idealist" and claimed to "lack ... explanatory power." See Priestley, "Constructions and Creations"; see also Carol Thomas, *Female Forms: Experiencing and Understanding Disability* (Buckingham: Open University Press, 1999). I contend, however, that these criticisms rely upon a misconstrual of those discourses in general and a misunderstanding of nominalism in particular.

4. See Ian Hacking, *The Social Construction of* What? (Cambridge, Mass.: Harvard University Press, 1999). See also Barry Allen, *Truth in Philosophy* (Cambridge, Mass.: Harvard University Press, 1993).

5 See Michel Foucault, "The Birth of Biopolitics," in *Ethics: Subjectivity and Truth*, ed. Paul Rabinow (New York: New Press, 1997), p. 73. See also

Barry Allen, "Foucault and Modern Political Philosophy," in Jeremy Moss (ed.), *The Later Foucault* (London: Sage Publications, 1998), pp. 293-352; and "Disabling Knowledge," in G. Madison and M. Fairbairn (eds.), *The Ethics of Postmodernity* (Evanston: Northwestern University Press, 1999), 89-103.

6. Barbara Duden, *The Woman Beneath the Skin: A Doctor's Patients in Eighteenth-Century Germany*, trans. Thomas Dunlap (Cambridge, Mass.: Harvard University Press, 1991), pp. 1-4.

7. Michel Foucault, "The Subject and Power," appended to Hubert Dreyfus and Paul Rabinow, *Michel Foucault: Beyond Structuralism and Hermeneutics* (Chicago: University of Chicago Press, 1983), pp. 208, 212.

8. Michel Foucault, *The History of Sexuality, Vol. 1: An Introduction,* trans. Robert Hurley (New York: Random House, 1978), p. 144.

9. See John Rajchman, *Truth and Eros: Foucault, Lacan, and the Question of Ethics* (New York: Routledge, 1991), p. 104.

10. Michael Oliver, *The Politics of Disablement* (London: Macmillan Education, 1990), pp. 4-11.

11. UPIAS, *The Fundamental Principles of Disability* (London: Union of the Physically Impaired Against Segregation, 1976). See Michael Oliver, *Understanding Disability: From Theory to Practice* (London: Macmillan, 1996), p. 22.

12. Oliver, *Understanding Disability*, p. 35; emphasis added.

13. See, for instance, Tom Shakespeare and Nicholas Watson, "Habeamus Corpus? Sociology of the Body and the Issue of Impairment," paper presented at Quincentennial Conference on the History of Medicine, Aberdeen, 1995; Bill Hughes and Kevin Paterson, "The Social Model of Disability and the Disappearing Body: Towards a Sociology of Impairment," *Disability & Society* 12 (1997): 325-40; Mairian Corker, "Differences, Conflations and Foundations: The Limits to the 'Accurate' Theoretical Representation of Disabled People's Experience," *Disability & Society* 14 (1999): 627-42.

14. Hughes and Paterson, "Social Model," p. 330.

15. Ibid., p. 332.

16. Ibid., pp. 333-34. See also Shakespeare and Watson, "Habeamus Corpus?"

17. Judith Butler, *Bodies that Matter: On the Discursive Limits of 'Sex'* (New York: Routledge, 1993), p. 10.

18. Cf. Corker, "Differences, Conflations and Foundations."

19. Hacking, *The Social Construction of* What? pp. 31, 103-4.

20. Foucault, "The Subject and Power," p. 221.

21. Michel Foucault, *Discipline and Punish: The Birth of the Prison*, trans. Alan Sheridan (New York: Pantheon Books, 1977), p. 136.

22. Cf. Hughes and Paterson, "Social Model," p. 334.

23. Judith Butler, *Gender Trouble: Feminism and the Subversion of Identity*, 10th anniversary ed. (New York: Routledge, 1999), p. 2.

24. Bernice L. Hausman, *Changing Sex: Transsexualism, Technology, and the Idea of Gender* (Durham: Duke University Press, 1995), p. 7.

25. Ibid., passim.

26. John Money and Anke Ehrhardt, *Man and Woman, Boy and Girl* (Baltimore: Johns Hopkins University Press, 1972), p. 257; quoted in Anne Fausto-Sterling, *Sexing the Body: Gender Politics and the Construction of Sexuality* (New York: Basic Books, 2000), p. 4.

27. Fausto-Sterling, *Sexing the Body*, p. 7.

28. Ibid., p. 46.

29. Gayle Rubin, "The Traffic in Women: Notes on the 'Political Economy' of Sex," in Rayna R. Reiter (ed.), *Toward an Anthropology of Women* (New York: Basic Books, 1975), p. 165.

30. See Butler, *Gender Trouble*, p. 48.

31. Sandra Harding, "The Instability of the Analytical Categories of Feminist Theory," in Micheline R. Malson, Jean F. O'Barr, Sarah Westphal-Wihl, and Mary Wyer (eds.), *Feminist Theory in Practice and Process* (Chicago: University of Chicago Press, 1989), p. 31.

32. See, for example, Sandra Harding, *The Science Question in Feminism* (Ithaca: Cornell University Press, 1986), pp. 163-96.

33. Donna Haraway, "'Gender' for a Marxist Dictionary: The Sexual Politics of a Word," in *Simians, Cyborgs, and Women: The Reinvention of Nature* (New York: Routledge, 1991), p. 134.

34. See Fausto-Sterling, *Sexing the Body*, p. 4.

35. Oyeronke Oyewumi, "De-confounding Gender: Feminist Theorizing and Western Culture, a Comment on Hawkesworth's 'Confounding Gender'," *Signs* 23 (1998): 1049-62, p. 1053; quoted in Fausto-Sterling, *Sexing the Body*, pp. 19-20.

36. Foucault, *The History of Sexuality*, Vol. I, p. 155.

37. Ibid.

38. Butler, *Gender Trouble*, pp. 45-100.

39. See ibid., p. 117.

40. See Butler, *Bodies that Matter*.

41. Fausto-Sterling, *Sexing the Body*, pp. 275-76 n. 1.

42. Fausto-Sterling, *Sexing the Body*. See also Cheryl Chase, "Affronting Reason," in Dawn Atkins (ed.), *Looking Queer: Body Image and Identity in Lesbian, Bisexual, Gay, and Transgender Communities* (New York: The Harrington Park Press, 1998); A.D. Dreger, *Hermaphrodites and the Medical Invention of Sex* (Cambridge, Mass.: Harvard University Press, 1998); Shelley Tremain, Review of Atkins (ed.), *Looking Queer: Body Image and Identity in Lesbian, Bisexual, Gay and Transgender Communities*, in *Disability Studies Quarterly* 18 (1998): 198-99; and Shelley Tremain, "Queering Disabled Sexuality Studies," *Journal of Sexuality and Disability* 18 (2000): 291-99.

43. Fausto-Sterling, *Sexing the Body*, pp. 147-59.

44. Butler, *Gender Trouble*, p. 143.

45. Ibid., pp. 10-11.

46. See Butler, *Gender Trouble*.

47. Tom Shakespeare, "A Response to Liz Crow," *Coalition* (September 1992), p. 40; quoted in Oliver, *Understanding Disability*, p. 39.

48. The analogical arguments that disability researchers and theorists make from "sex" not only reinstitute and contribute to the naturalization and materialization of binary sex — in addition, these arguments facilitate and contribute to the naturalization and materialization of impairment. To take one example, in order to argue that degrading cultural norms and values, exclusionary discursive and social practices, and biased representations produce disability, disability theorists have come to depend upon analogical arguments that illustrate how these phenomena operate in the service of sexism (e.g., Oliver, *The Politics of Disablement*). To take another example, the analogy from sexism is used

to identify inconsistencies and double standards between the treatment of sexual discrimination in public policy and law and the treatment in the same domains of disability discrimination (e.g., Anita Silvers, David Wasserman, and Mary B. Mahowald, *Disability, Difference, Discrimination: Perspectives on Justice in Bioethics and Public Policy* [Lanham: Rowman & Littlefield, 1998]). The analogical structure of these arguments requires that one appeal to clear distinctions between males and females, and men and women, as well as assume a stable and distinct notion of impairment. In the terms of these analogical arguments, furthermore, "sex" and "impairment" are represented as separate and real entities, each with unique properties, and each of whose identity can be distinguished from that of the other. The heterosexual assumptions that condition this manner of argumentation in Disability Studies preclude consideration of the implications for work in the discipline of the questions that intersexuality raises (see Tremain, "Queering Disabled Sexuality Studies"; and Shelley Tremain, Review of Thomas, *Female Forms: Experiencing and Understanding Disability*, in *Disability & Society*.

49. Cf. Paul Abberley, "The Concept of Oppression and the Development of a Social Theory of Disability," *Disability, Handicap & Society* 2 (1987): 5-19; and Carol Thomas, *Female Forms*.

50. Margrit Shildrick and Janet Price, "Breaking the Boundaries of the Broken Body," *Body & Society* 2 (1996): 93-113, p. 101.
51. Ibid., p. 102.
52. Ibid., pp. 101-2.
53. Foucault, "The Subject and Power"; Colin Gordon, "Governmental Rationality: An Introduction," in Graham Burchell, Colin Gordon, and Peter Miller (eds.), *The Foucault Effect: Studies in Governmentality* (Chicago: University of Chicago Press, 1991), p. 3.
54. Foucault, *The History of Sexuality*, Vol. 1, p. 93.
55. See, for example, Thomas, *Female Forms*, p. 137.
56. Michel Foucault, "Power and Sex," in *Politics, Philosophy, Culture: Interviews and Other Writings (1977-1984)*, ed. Lawrence D. Kritzman (London: Routledge, 1988), p. 84.
57. Gordon, "Governmental Rationality," p. 5.
58. Foucault, "The Birth of Biopolitics," pp. 74-77.
59. Wendy Brown, *States of Injury: Power and Freedom in Late Modernity* (Princeton: Princeton University Press, 1995), pp. 59, 65.
60. See Tremain, Review of Thomas, *Female Forms*.
61. Brown, *States of Injury*, p. 75.
62. Foucault, "The Subject and Power," p. 216.
63. Michel Foucault, "What is Enlightenment?" in *Ethics, Subjectivity and Truth*, p. 319.
64. Ibid., p. 315.

STUDY QUESTIONS

1 According to David Wasserman, what is the anti-discrimination framework adopted by the *Americans with Disabilities Act* (ADA) that allows us to understand it as a significant departure from previous conceptions of equal opportunity for persons with disabilities? Outline and evaluate the problems with and the limitations of the ADA as identified by Wasserman.

2 Anita Silvers agrees with Wasserman that the ADA represents a significant shift in policy with respect to persons with disabilities. She argues, however, that Wasserman does not fully grasp the conceptual shift it reflects. What objections does Silvers raise against Wasserman's analysis of disability and of his critique of the ADA's approach and policy?

3 Why does Silvers reject an ethic of care approach to issues of disability? From what you have learned about an ethic of care in readings from other chapters, is Silvers's account of an ethic of care and her application of it to issues of disability accurate or fair? Provide reasons for your answer.

4 Do you agree with Silvers that "a 'normal' able-bodied individual is physically and socially blocked from accurately grasping what it is like to be in a 'damaged' individual's place"? Why or why not? If true, what effect does this have on policies with respect to persons with disabilities?

5 G. Goggin and C. Newell argue that the diversity of voices on disability in the Australian community is not represented and that people with disabilities are not quoted as experts on disability. What difference do they think this makes with respect to the discourse on biotechnology and, in particular, on policies with respect to embryonic stem cell research?

6 Do you think that media representations of disability, biotechnology, and nationhood shape views regarding policy in these areas or do they merely reflect views that already exist and are entrenched? How do Goggin and Newell answer this question? How would you? Provide reasons for your answer.

7 Do you think that policies with respect to advances in biotechnology demand the voices and perspectives of those affected by these policies? How do we resolve differences in the views of persons with disabilities? Should policy be formulated at the international as well as national level?

8 Shelley Tremain is critical of the social model of disability assumed in many of the readings thus far. What is her critique of this model?

9 What is the concept of "bio-power" meant to capture? Do you think "impairments" in the medical sense are just as much the result of historical contexts and circumstances as are "disabilities" as understood in the social model of disability? Provide reasons for your answers.

10 According to Tremain, how is the concept of "natural impairments" similar to that of "natural sex"? Are you convinced by her arguments? Why or why not?

11 Tremain recommends that disabled people challenge the dominant discourse. What can this accomplish and is it effective for preventing the medical and legal regulation of disabled people's lives? Provide reasons for your answers.

12 In your view, are there similarities that allow us to attribute group identity to or endorse group politics for persons with disabilities? Formulate your answer by explaining how the authors in this chapter would answer these questions and by comparing discrimination based on disability with the kinds of discrimination examined in previous chapters.

SUGGESTED READINGS

Beresford, Peter. "Poverty and Disabled People: Challenging Dominant Debates and Policies." *Disability & Society*, v. 11, no. 4 (1996): 553-67.

Bickenbach, Jerome E. *Physical Disability and Social Policy*. Toronto, ON: University of Toronto Press, 1993.

Connors, Debra. "Disability, Sexism and the Social Order." In *With the Power of Each Breath: A Disabled Women's Anthology*, edited by Susan Browne, Debra Connors, and Nancy Stern. Pittsburgh, PA: Cleis Press, 1985.

Donoghue, Christopher. "Challenging the Authority of the Medical Definition of Disability: An Analysis of the Resistance to the Social Constructionist Paradigm." *Disability & Society*, v. 18, no. 2 (March 2003): 199-208.

Erevelles, Nirmala. "Disability and the Dialectics of Difference." *Disability & Society*, v. 11, no. 4 (1996): 519-37.

European Congress on People with Disabilities. *The Madrid Declaration: Non-Discrimination Plus Positive Action Results in Social Inclusion*. (March 2002).

Fine, Michelle, and A. Asch. (editors). *Women with Disabilities: Essays in Psychology, Culture and Politics*. Philadelphia, PA: Temple University Press, 1988.

Friesen, Bonita Janzen. "Bangladeshi Disabled Women Find Hope." In *Imprinting our Image: an International Anthology by Women with Disabilities*, edited by Diane Driedger and Susan Gray. Charlottetown, PEI: Gynergy Books, 1992.

Kopelman, Loretta M. "Ethical Assumptions and Ambiguities in the Americans with Disabilities Act." *Journal of Medicine and Philosophy*, v. 21 (1996): 187-208.

Lansdown, Gerison. *Disabled Children in Romania: Progress in Implementing the Convention on the Rights of the Child 2002: A Report*. Disability Awareness in Action, The International Disability and Human Rights Network, 2003.

McMahon, Jeff. "Cognitive Disability, Misfortune, and Justice." *Philosophy & Public Affairs*, v. 25, no. 1 (1996): 3-35.

Meekosha, Helen, and Leanne Dowse. "Enabling Citizenship: Gender, Disability and Citizenship in Australia." *Feminist Review*, v. 57 (Autumn 1997): 49-72.

Michailakis, Dimitris. "The Systems Theory Concept of Disability: One is not Born a Disabled Person, One is Observed to be One." *Disability & Society*, v. 18, no. 2 (2003): 209-29.

Oliver, Michael. *The Politics of Disablement*. London: Macmillan Education, 1990.

Silvers, Anita. "'Defective' Agents: Equality, Difference and the Tyranny of the Normal." *Journal of Social Philosophy*. 25th Anniversary Special Issue (1994): 154-74.

— . "Reconciling Equality to Difference: Caring (F)or Justice for People with Disabilities." *Hypatia*, v. 10, no. 1 (Winter 1995): 30-55.

Silvers, Anita, David Wasserman, and Mary B. Mahowald (editors). *Disability, Difference, Discrimination: Perspectives on Justice in Bioethics and Public Policy*. Lanham: Rowman & Littlefield, 1998.

Stummer, T. Christina F. "The ABCs of Disability." In *Imprinting our Image: an International Anthology by Women with Disabilities*, edited by Diane Driedger and Susan Gray. Charlottetown, PEI: Gynergy Books, 1992.

Thomas, Carol. *Female Forms: Experiencing and Understanding Disability*. Buckingham: Open University Press, 1999.

Tremain, Shelley. "Dworkin on Disablement and Resources." *Canadian Journal of Law and Jurisprudence*, v. IX, no. 2 (July 1996): 343-59.

Wendell, Susan. *The Rejected Body: Feminist Philosophical Reflections on Disability*. New York, NY: Routledge, 1996.

— . "Toward a Feminist Theory of Disability." *Hypatia*, v. 4, no. 2 (1989): 104-24.

CHAPTER SIX: POVERTY AND WELFARE

INTRODUCTION

Poverty is a moral issue because being poor affects life prospects; living conditions of health, safety, and longevity; and the sort of opportunities one has. Poverty is also a moral issue because of its effects on those who are already disadvantaged — statistics show that being poor tends to be linked to factors of race, ethnicity, gender, and disability. However, what poverty is and who is said to suffer from it is not as straightforward as may appear at first glance. Individual countries as well as international organizations such as the United Nations (UN) measure poverty in different ways, and these measurements produce different numbers and rankings. There are two standard definitions of poverty. *Absolute* poverty is the lack of basic necessities for life as measured by a specified level of income needed to purchase those basic goods. The absolute definition is taken as an objective measure and provides no account of individual, occupational, cultural, or ethnic differences. *Relative* poverty is the inability to live according to the customs and values of one's society. The relative definition takes income levels into account but ties an account of poverty to existing patterns of consumption and dominant customs, values, and patterns of living not shared or accepted by everyone.

As we will discover in the readings in this chapter, there are lots of data to show that gaps between those who are rich and those who are poor are increasing, both within countries and between countries. Moreover, there seems to be little progress in alleviating poverty even though there is international agreement, as articulated in the UN Millennium goals, that this needs to be a central goal. These statistics on growing gaps in wealth and high levels of poverty raise moral questions. Do rich countries have an obligation to alleviate poverty in poor countries? Can large gaps in wealth or high levels of poverty within a society be

justified and should they be tolerated? Within liberal societies, there are a number of different answers to the second question. Libertarians argue that rich people are either entitled to or deserve their wealth because they produced it themselves or it was transferred to them voluntarily. Other theorists defend the utilitarian argument that inequality in wealth is justified because it has the effect of expanding the gross national product and thereby increasing the sum of human happiness. Some argue that allowing people with talents and abilities to accumulate more wealth is an incentive for these people to produce more and thereby make those who are relatively poor better off than they would be if everyone had the same amount of wealth. Finally, egalitarians argue that gaps in wealth need to be avoided because they result in other sorts of inequalities not to be tolerated by a just society. The readings in this chapter will discuss these and other arguments on the issue of poverty and what should be done to alleviate it.

In many ways, then, the moral issues underlying poverty bring us full circle to the theoretical issues that opened Volume II. Poverty asks us to consider accounts of equality and what is needed to treat people with the dignity and respect they are owed. It asks whether people should be provided with the material resources to meet basic human needs. It also asks the more difficult question of how resources can be provided in a world with problems of overpopulation and starving populations. We have observed the important role that liberal theory has played in an understanding of equality, a role evident in the stated commitments to human rights in countries all over the world. We have also outlined the centrality of liberty in liberal accounts of human rights and examined the two conceptions of formal and substantive equality prominent in the liberal tradition. In this chapter, we begin our examination of poverty as it exists and is discussed in liberal societies and use this as a base for examining poverty in the global context.

In the first reading, Jeremy Waldron discusses the phenomenon of homelessness in the U.S. in order to uncover a tension between liberal accounts of the primacy of freedom and the strong liberal defense of private property. He distinguishes between private, collective, and common property rules to show how these rules determine who is allowed and not allowed to be in a given place. One way to describe homelessness is to say that there is no place governed by private property rules that the homeless are allowed to be unless they are invited in, in which case they are at the mercy of the owner and can be excluded. In an ideal libertarian society, where all land might be held as private property, there would be no place where a homeless person was allowed to be. But in the U.S., where some of its territory is held as collective property and made available for common use, the homeless are allowed to be in places such as streets, parks, and under bridges.

Waldron argues that the increasing interest in regulating streets, parks, and other public places and restricting the activities that can be performed in these places results in severe limitations to such basic freedoms as where the homeless can sleep, cook, eat, use bathroom facilities, and be. He argues that the liberal values of freedom of speech or of assembly are meaningless to a person who lacks the elementary necessities of life. The freedoms that matter are those that allow the homeless person to satisfy basic needs such as food, shelter, and clothing. Waldron argues that in a society with an economic system that allows homelessness, we need to ask ourselves whether we are willing to allow those in this predicament to have the freedom to look after their own needs in public spaces.

Waldron identifies and raises objections to various counter-arguments defending property rules and tolerating homelessness. One of these arguments is that the homeless are responsible for their condition and have the same opportunity as anyone else to change it. These beliefs are prevalent in the U.S., where there is an emphasis on negative rights that propound non-interference by the state in the affairs of citizens. The idea is that the removal of formal and legal barriers is both necessary and sufficient for satisfying the demands of justice. When no one is legally barred, everyone has an equal opportunity to obtain the goods needed to survive and thrive. In the second reading, Ingrid Robeyns turns our attention to contexts in which beliefs about what people are owed and what justice demands by way of equal treatment are different than they are in the U.S. Many Western European countries have histories and practices of positive rights that justify state welfare policies and provide income to those who are unemployed or unable to work as a matter of justice. Yet Europe is changing. Technological innovations and economic globalization have increased unemployment and European Union countries are being pressured to cut their welfare programs to reduce deficits. Robeyns takes this contemporary context of rapid change to be a reason for reexamining basic income as a viable policy for addressing poverty in Europe and the world as a whole.

Basic income is similar to universal health care in that it provides an income to everyone regardless of factors such as employment status and gender. The underlying view of most basic income advocates is that individuals have the right as citizens of a society to be provided with minimal financial means to acquire basic goods. Robeyns argues that a basic income is one of the material aspects of economic citizenship, just as the right to vote is one of the material aspects of political citizenship. She uses both practical and moral arguments to defend this idea. A basic income would result in lowering economic inequality. It could enable a society to eradicate unemployment and avoid the poverty traps of means-tested and workfare programs. It would give people real freedom so that they are not forced to take any kind of alienating, exploitative, or degrading job just to survive. A basic income would allow a worker to refuse a job that is unpleasant; to temporarily reduce hours of work to take care of children, ill relatives, or friends; or to take a break from work for personal reasons. Robeyns answers some of the objections raised against basic income. She explores ways in which it could be financed within a country and internationally, and she casts doubt on the argument that a basic income would further entrench gender roles by encouraging women to do long-term work such as caring for children or volunteering for community work.

Asuncion Lera St. Clair continues the discussion of strong welfare policies in European countries by describing the history and tradition of Norway. She argues that descriptions of how values and beliefs are shaped by a country's particular history can instruct us about what is needed to change attitudes, beliefs, and values about helping the poor, both within and outside a country's own borders. Norway's history shows the crucial role and participation of religious and social organizations in shaping a commitment that helping those who are less fortunate is a matter of justice and not charity. She argues that Norway extends this belief to helping those outside its borders and that this shows up in Norway being the leading country in foreign aid. Many theorists have explored the issue of whether rich countries have an obligation to provide aid to poor countries. St. Clair claims that learning about Norway's history shows how values of solidarity and justice originated in the initiatives and participation of both the poor and the non-poor in ways that influenced local, national, and international policies. She argues that the contextual analysis of how culture and history has shaped values in Norway can provide lessons for other donors, development agents, poor countries, international bodies, and development ethicists with respect to finding effective policies for reducing poverty.

In the readings so far, the authors might be said to assume an understanding of what constitutes poverty. In the fourth reading, Ashis Nandy casts some doubt on contemporary definitions of poverty and uses of them. Because numbers matter to politicians and economists, definitions of poverty are often used to either expand or reduce the number of people who count as poor, enabling people to believe poverty is being alleviated or to resign themselves to the idea that poverty will always be with us. Removing poverty

or mobilizing others to care about it becomes merely, then, a matter of manipulating numbers. Nandy argues for a move away from the ego defenses shaped by current definitions to clarity about poverty in the contemporary global context. He argues that there is a basic distinction to be made between poverty, which has always been with us, and destitution, which has become more pronounced only recently.

Processes of development, such as economic globalization, have resulted in the destruction of traditional communities and their life-support systems, forcing many people who lived off the land and without the need for income into over-populated urban centers. By international measures of levels of income those who live off the land count as poor even though they do not perceive themselves this way. By increasing destitution and focusing on providing jobs, globalization, argues Nandy, disguises both the declining political clout of the historically disadvantaged and an interest in poverty.

The final reading by Christine Koggel picks up on the theme of analyzing poverty in the contemporary context of economic globalization. Koggel uses relational insights from feminists and post-colonial theorists as a way to challenge the individualism in traditional liberal accounts of equality and to show the complexity of equality analysis when the focus is on relationships of all sorts. A relational approach allows us to attend to the details of the lives of those who are affected by unequal and oppressive relationships, ones that are in turn shaped by social practices in particular locations, by features of the global context, and by the intersections of the local and the global. She argues that these features of a relational approach are needed for an analysis of inequalities in the global context.

Globalization in the realm of economic relations has meant that markets and corporations in First World countries can extend their reach across borders, sometimes with devastating consequences for people in Third World countries. An account of how relationships of power at the global level intersect with, exploit, or interrupt relationships of power at the local level reveals inequalities that are otherwise easy to miss. Koggel argues that we obtain a more accurate account of various kinds of inequalities through the description and analysis of relationships of power and oppression in its diverse and interlocking forms at the global and local levels than we do when we examine individuals abstracted from contexts and the relationships they are in.

HOMELESSNESS AND THE ISSUE OF FREEDOM

Jeremy Waldron

Jeremy Waldron is in the School of Law at Columbia University. He is the author of The Right to Private Property *(1988),* Liberal Rights: Collected Papers 1981-1991 *(1993),* The Dignity of Legislation *(1999),* Law and Disagreement *(1999), and* God, Locke and Equality *(2002).*

　　Waldron examines liberal assumptions about the connection between property rights and freedom and the tension created between these in the case of homelessness. He explores the role of private property in Western societies in giving people the freedom to perform basic human functions such as sleeping and using a washroom and argues that these functions cannot be performed freely in the public spaces in which homeless people exist. He claims that moves to restrict even further what public spaces can be occupied and used by homeless people should be understood as placing severe limits on a person's freedom.

Introduction

There are many facets to the nightmare of homelessness. In this essay, I want to explore just one of them: the relation between homelessness, the rules of public and private property, and the underlying freedom of those who are condemned by poverty to walk the streets and sleep in the open. Unlike some recent discussions, my concern is not with the constitutionality of various restrictions on the homeless (though that, of course, is important).[1] I want to address a prior question — a more fundamental question — of legal and moral philosophy: how should we think about homelessness, how should we conceive of it, in relation to a value like freedom?

　　The discussion that follows is, in some ways, an abstract one. This is intentional. The aim is to refute the view that, on abstract liberal principles, there is no reason to be troubled by the plight of the homeless, and that one has to come down to the more concrete principles of a communitarian ethic in order to find a focus for that concern. Against this view, I shall argue that homelessness is a matter of the utmost concern in relation to some of the most fundamental and abstract principles of

liberal value. That an argument is abstract should not make us think of it as thin or watery. If homelessness raises questions even in regard to the most basic principles of liberty, it is an issue that ought to preoccupy liberal theorists every bit as much as more familiar worries about torture, the suppression of dissent, and other violations of human rights. That the partisans of liberty in our legal and philosophical culture have not always been willing to see this (or say it) should be taken as an indication of the consistency and good faith with which they espouse and proclaim their principles.

I. Location and Property

Some truisms to begin with. Everything that is done has to be done somewhere. No one is free to perform an action unless there is somewhere he is free to perform it. Since we are embodied beings, we always have a location. Moreover, though everyone has to be somewhere, a person cannot always choose any location he likes. Some locations are physically inaccessible. And, physical inaccessibility aside, there are some places one is simply not allowed to be.

One of the functions of property rules, particularly as far as land is concerned, is to provide a basis for determining who is allowed to be where. For the purposes of these rules, a country is divided up into spatially defined regions or, as we usually say, places. The rules of property give us a way of determining, in the case of each place, who is allowed to be in that place and who is not. For example, if a place is governed by a private property rule, then there is a way of identifying an individual whose determination is final on the question of who is and who is not allowed to be in that place. Sometimes that individual is the owner of the land in question, and sometimes (as in a landlord-tenant relationship) the owner gives another person the power to make that determination (indeed to make it, for the time being, even as against the owner). Either way, it is characteristic of a private ownership arrangement that some individual (or some other particular legal person) has this power to determine who is allowed to be on the property.

The actual rules of private property are, of course, much more complicated that this and they involve much besides this elementary power of decision.[2] However, to get the discussion going, it is enough to recognize that there is something like this individual power of decision in most systems of private ownership. Private ownership of land exists when an individual person may determine who is, and who is not, allowed to be in a certain place, without answering to anyone else for that decision. I say who is allowed to be in my house. He says who is to be allowed in his restaurant. And so on.

The concept of *being allowed* to be in a place is fairly straightforward. We can define it negatively. An individual who is in a place where he is not allowed to be may be removed, and he may be subject to civil or criminal sanctions for trespass or some other similar offense. No doubt people are sometimes physically removed from places where they *are* allowed to be. But if a person is in a place where he is not allowed to be, not only may he be physically removed, but there is a social rule to the effect that his removal may be facilitated and aided by the forces of the state. In short, the police may be called and he may be dragged away.

I said that one function of property rules is to indicate procedures for determining who is allowed and not allowed (in this sense) to be in a given place, and I gave the example of a private property rule. However, not all rules of property are like private property rules in this regard. We may use a familiar classification and say that, though many places in this country are governed by private property rules, some are governed by rules of collective property, which divide further into rules of state property, and rules of common property (though neither the labels nor the exact details of this second distinction matter much for the points I am going to make).[3]

If a place is governed by a *collective* property rule, then there is no private person in the position of owner. Instead, the use of collective property is determined by people, usually officials, acting in the name of the whole community.

Common property may be regarded as a subclass of collective property. A place is common property if part of the point of putting it under collective control is to allow anyone in the society to make use of it without having to secure the permission of anybody else. Not all collective property is like this: places like military firing ranges, nationalized factories, and government offices are off-limits to members of the general public unless they have special permission or a legitimate purpose for being there. They are held as collective property for purposes other than making them available for public use. However, examples of common property spring fairly readily to mind: they include streets, sidewalks, subways, city parks, national parks, and wilderness areas. These places are held in the name of the whole society in order to make them fairly accessible to everyone. As we shall see, they are by no means unregulated as to the nature or time of their use. Still, they are relatively open at most times to a fairly indeterminate range of uses by anyone. In the broadest terms, they are places where anyone may be.

Sometimes the state may insist that certain places owned by private individuals or corporations should be treated rather like common property if they fulfill the function of public places. For example, shopping malls in the United States are usually on privately owned land. However, because of the functions such places serve, the state imposes considerable restrictions on the owners' powers of exclusion (people may not be excluded from a shopping mall on racial grounds, for example) and on their power to limit the activities (such as political pamphleteering) that may take place there.[4] Though this is an important development, it does not alter the analysis I am developing in this Essay, and for simplicity I shall ignore it in what follows.

Property rules differ from society to society. Though we describe some societies (like the United States) as having systems of private property, and others (like the USSR — at least until recently) as having collectivist systems, clearly all societies have some places governed by private property rules, some places governed by state property rules, and some places governed by common property rules. Every society has private houses, military bases, and public parks. So if we want to categorize whole societies along these lines, we have to say it is a matter of balance and emphasis. For example, we say the USSR is (or used to be) a collectivist society and that the USA is not, not because there was no private property in the USSR, but because most industrial and agricultural land there was held collectively whereas most industrial and agricultural land in the United States is privately owned. The distinction is one of degree. Even as between two countries that pride themselves on having basically capitalist economies, for example, New Zealand and Britain, we may say that the former is "communist" to a greater extent (i.e., is more a system of common property) than the latter because more places (for example, all river banks) are held as common property in New Zealand than are held as common property in Britain. Of course, these propositions are as vague as they are useful. If we are measuring the "extent" to which a country is collectivist, that measure is ambiguous as between the quantitative proportion of land that is governed by rules of collective property and some more qualitative assessment of the importance of the places that are governed in this way.[5]

II. Homelessness

Estimates of the number of homeless people in the United States range from 250,000 to three million.[6] A person who is homeless is, obviously enough, a person who has no home. One way of describing the plight of a homeless individual might be to say that there is no place governed by a private property rule where he is allowed to be.

In fact, that is not quite correct. Any private proprietor may invite a homeless person into his house or onto his land, and if he does there *will* be some private place where the homeless person is allowed to be. A technically more accurate description of his plight is that there is no place governed by a private property rule where he is allowed to be whenever *he* chooses, no place governed by a private property rule from which he may not at any time be excluded as a result of someone else's say-so. As far as being on private property is concerned — in people's houses or gardens, on farms or in hotels, in offices or restaurants — the homeless person is utterly and at all times at the mercy of others. And we know enough about how this mercy is generally exercised to figure that the description in the previous paragraph is more or less accurate as a matter of fact, even if it is not strictly accurate as a matter of law.[7]

For the most part the homeless are excluded from *all* of the places governed by private property rules, whereas the rest of us are, in the same sense, excluded from *all but one* (or maybe all but a few) of those places. That is another way of saying that each of us has at least one place to be in a country composed of private places, whereas the homeless person has none.

Some libertarians fantasize about the possibility that *all* the land in a society might be held as private property ("Sell the streets!").[8] This would be catastrophic for the homeless. Since most private proprietors are already disposed to exclude him from their property, the homeless person might discover in such a libertarian paradise that there was literally *nowhere* he was allowed to be. Wherever he went he would be liable to penalties for trespass and he would be liable to eviction, to being thrown out by an owner or dragged away by the police. Moving from one place to another would involve nothing more liberating than moving from one trespass liability to another. Since land is finite in any society, there is only a limited number of places where a person can (physically) be, and such a person would find that he was legally excluded from all of them. (It would not be entirely mischievous to add that since, in order to exist, a person has to be *somewhere,* such a person would not be permitted to exit.)

Our society saves the homeless from this catastrophe only by the virtue of the fact that some of its territory is held as collective property and made available for common use. The homeless are allowed to *be* — provided they are on the streets, in the parks, or under the bridges. Some of them are allowed to crowd together into publicly provided "shelters" after dark (though these are dangerous places and there are not nearly enough shelters for all of them). But in the daytime, and for many of them, all through the night, wandering in public places is their only option. When all else is privately owned, the sidewalks are their salvation. They are allowed to *be* in our society only to the extent that our society is communist.

This is one of the reasons why most defenders of private property are uncomfortable with the libertarian proposal, and why that proposal remains sheer fantasy.[9] But there is a modified form of the libertarian catastrophe in prospect with which moderate and even liberal defenders of ownership seem much more comfortable. This is the increasing regulation of the streets, subways, parks, and other public places to restrict the activities that can be performed there. What is emerging — and it is not just a matter of fantasy — is a state of affairs in which a million or more citizens have no place to perform elementary human activities like urinating, washing, sleeping, cooking, eating, and standing around. Legislators voted for by people who own private places in which they can do all these things are increasingly deciding to make public places available only for activities other than these primal human tasks. The streets and subways, they say, are for commuting from home to office. They are not for sleeping; sleeping is something one does at home. The parks are for recreations like

walking and informal ball-games, things for which one's own yard is a little too confined. Parks are not for cooking or urinating; again, these are things one does at home. Since the public and the private are complementary, the activities performed in public are to be the complement of those appropriately performed in private. This complementarity works fine for those who have the benefit of both sorts of places. However, it is disastrous for those who must live their whole lives on common land. If I am right about this, it is one of the most callous and tyrannical exercises of power in modern times by a (comparatively) rich and complacent majority against a minority of their less fortunate fellow human beings.

III. Locations, Actions and Freedom

The points made so far can be restated in terms of freedom. Someone who is allowed to be in a place is, in a fairly straightforward sense, free to be there. A person who is not allowed to be in a place is unfree to be there. However, the concept of freedom usually applies to actions rather than locations: one is free or unfree to do X or to do Y. What is the connection, then, between freedom to be somewhere and freedom to do something?

At the outset I recited the truism that anything a person does has to be done somewhere. To that extent, all actions involve a spatial component (just as many actions involve, in addition, a material component like the use of tools, implements, or raw materials). It should be fairly obvious that, if one is not free to be in a certain place, one is not free to do anything at that place. If I am not allowed to be in your garden (because you have forbidden me) then I am not allowed to eat my lunch, make a speech, or turn a somersault in your garden. Though I may be free to do these things somewhere else, I am not free to do them there. It follows, strikingly, that a person who is not free to be in any place is not free to do anything; such a person is comprehensively unfree. In the libertarian paradise we imagined in the previous section, this would be the plight of the homeless. They would be simply without freedom (or, more accurately, any freedom they had would depend utterly on the forbearance of those who owned the places that made up the territory of the society in question).

Fortunately, our society is not such a libertarian paradise. There are places where the homeless may be and, by virtue of that, there are actions they may perform; they are free to perform actions on the streets, in the parks, and under the bridges. Their freedom depends on common property in a way that ours does not. Once again, the homeless have freedom in our society only to the extent that our society is communist.

That conclusion may sound glib and provocative. But it is meant as a reflection on the cold and awful reality of the experience of men, women, and children who are homeless in America. For them the rules of private property are a series of fences that stand between them and somewhere to be, somewhere to act. The only hope they have so far as freedom is concerned lies in the streets, parks, and public shelters, and in the fact that those are collectivized resources made available openly to all.

It is sometimes said that freedom means little or nothing to a cold and hungry person. We should focus on the material predicament of the homeless, it is said, not on this abstract liberal concern about freedom. That may be an appropriate response to someone who is talking high-mindedly and fatuously about securing freedom of speech or freedom of religion for people who lack the elementary necessities of human life.[10] But the contrast between liberty and the satisfaction of material needs must not be drawn too sharply, as though the latter had no relation at all to what one is free or unfree to do. I am focusing on freedoms that are intimately connected with food, shelter, clothing, and the satisfaction of basic needs. When a person is needy, he does not cease to be preoccupied with freedom; rather his preoccupation tends to focus on freedom to perform certain actions in particular. The freedom that means most to a person who is cold and wet is the freedom that consists in staying under whatever shelter he has found. The freedom that means most to someone who is exhausted is the freedom not to be prodded with a nightstick as he tries to catch a few hours sleep on a subway bench.

There is a general point here about the rather *passive* image of the poor held by those who say we should concern ourselves with their needs, not their freedom.[11] People remain agents, with ideas and initiatives of their own, even when they are poor. Indeed, since they are on their own, in a situation of danger, without any place of safety, they must often be more resourceful, spend more time working out how to live, thinking things through much more carefully, taking much less for granted, than the comfortable autonomous agent that we imagine in a family with a house and a job in an office or university. And — when they are allowed to — the poor do find ways of using their initiative to rise to these challenges. They have to; if they do not, they die.

Even the most desperately needy are not always paralyzed by want. There are certain things they are physically capable of doing for themselves. Sometimes they find shelter by occupying an empty house or sleeping in a sheltered spot. They gather food from various places, they light a fire to cook it, and they sit down in a park to eat. They may urinate behind bushes, and wash their clothes in a fountain. Their physical condition is certainly not comfortable, but they are *capable* of acting in ways that make things a little more bearable for themselves. Now one question we face as a society — a broad question of justice and social policy — is whether we are willing to tolerate an economic system in which large numbers of people are homeless. Since the answer is evidently, "Yes," the question that remains is whether we are willing to allow those who are in this predicament to act as free agents, looking after their own needs, in public places — the only space available to them. It is a deeply frightening fact about the modern United States that those who *have* homes and jobs are willing to answer "Yes" to the first question and "No" to the second.

A. Negative freedom

...To say — as I have insisted we should say — that property rules limit freedom, is not to say they are *eo ipso* wrong.[12] It is simply to say that they engage a concern about liberty, and that anyone who values liberty should put himself on alert when questions of property are being discussed. (The argument I have made about the homeless is a striking illustration of the importance of our not losing sight of that.)

Above all, by building the morality of a given property system (rights, duties, and the current distribution) into the concept of freedom, the moralizing approach precludes the use of that concept as a basis for arguing about property. If when we use the words, "free" and "unfree," we are already assuming that it is wrong for A to use something that belongs to B, we cannot appeal to "freedom" to explain why B's ownership of the resource is justified. We cannot even extol our property system as the bases of a "free" society, for such a boast would be nothing more than tautological. It is true that if we have independent grounds of justification for our private property system, then we *can* say that interfering with property rights is wrong without appealing to the idea of freedom. In that case, there is nothing question-begging about the claim that preventing someone from violating property rights does not count as a restriction on his freedom. But the price of this strategy is high. It not only transforms our conception of freedom into a moralized definition of positive liberty (so that the only freedom that is relevant is the freedom to do what is right), but it also excludes the concept of freedom altogether from the debate about the justification of property rights. Since most theorists of property do not want to deprive themselves of the concept of freedom as a resource in that argument, the insistence that the enforcement of property rules should not count as a restriction on freedom is, at the very least, a serious strategic mistake.

B. General prohibitions and particular freedoms

I think the account I have given is faithful to the tradition of negative liberty. One is free to do something only if one is not liable to be forcibly prevented from or penalized for doing it. However, the way I have applied this account may seem a little disconcerting. The issue has to do with the level of generality at which actions are described.

The laws we have usually mention general *types* of actions, rather than particular actions done by particular people at specific times and places. Statutes do not say, "Jane Smith is not to assault Sarah Jones on Friday, November 24, on the corner of College Avenue and Bancroft." They say, "Assault is prohibited," or some equivalent, and it is understood that the prohibition applies to all such actions performed by anyone anywhere. A prohibition on a general type of action is understood to be a prohibition on all tokens of that type. Jurists say we ought to value this generality in our laws; it is part of what is involved in the complex ideal of "The Rule of Law." It makes the laws more predictable and more learnable. It makes them a better guide for the ordinary citizen who needs to have a rough and ready understanding (rather than a copious technical knowledge) of what he is and is not allowed to do as he goes about his business. A quick checklist of prohibited acts, formulated in general terms, serves that purpose admirably.[13] It also serves moral ideals of universalizability and rationality: a reason for restraining any particular act of the same type, unless there is a relevant difference between them (which can be formulated also in general terms).[14]

All that is important. However, there is another aspect of "The Rule of Law" ideal that can lead one into difficulties if it is combined with this insistence on generality. Legal systems of the kind we have pride themselves on the following feature: "Everything which is not explicitly prohibited is permitted." If the law does not formulate any prohibition on singing or jogging, for example, that is an indication to the citizen that singing and jogging are permitted, that he is free to perform them. To gauge the extent of his freedom, all he needs to know are the prohibitions imposed by the law. His freedom is simply the complement of that.[15]

The difficulty arises if it is inferred from this that a person's freedom is the complement of the *general* prohibitions that apply to him. For although it is possible to infer particular prohibitions from prohibitions formulated at a general level ("All murder is wrong" implies "This murder by me today is wrong"), it is not possible to infer particular permissions from the absence of any general prohibition. In our society, there is no general prohibition on cycling, but one cannot infer from this that any particular act of riding a bicycle is permitted. It depends (among other things) on whether the person involved has the right to use the particular bicycle he is proposing to ride.

This does not affect the basic point about complementarity. Our freedoms *are* the complement of the prohibitions that apply to us. The mistake arises from thinking that the only prohibitions that apply to us are general prohibitions. For, in addition to the general prohibitions laid down (say) in the criminal law, there are also the prohibitions on using particular objects and places that are generated by the laws of property. Until we know how these latter laws apply, we do not know whether we are free to perform a particular action.

It is *not* a telling response to this point to say that the effect of the laws of property can be stated in terms of a general principle – "No one is to use the property of another without his permission." They *can* so be stated; but in order to apply that principle, we need particular knowledge, not just general knowledge.[16] A person needs to know that *this* bicycle belongs to him, whereas *those* bicycles belong to other people. He needs that particular knowledge about specific objects as well as his general knowledge about the types of actions that are and are not permitted.

At any rate, the conclusions about freedom that I have reached depend on taking the prohibitions relating to particular objects generated by property laws as seriously as we take the more general prohibitions imposed by the criminal law. No doubt these different types of prohibition are imposed for different reasons. But if freedom means simply the absence of deliberate interference with one's actions, we will not be in a position to say how free a person is until we know everything about the universe of legal restraints that may be applied to him. After all, it is not freedom in the abstract that people value, but freedom to perform particular actions. If the absence of a general prohibition tells us nothing about anyone's concrete freedom, then we should be wary of using only the checklist of general prohibitions to tell us how free or unfree a person or a society really is.

These points can readily be applied to the homeless. There are no general prohibitions in our society on actions like sleeping or washing. However, we cannot infer from this that anyone may sleep or wash wherever he chooses. In order to work out whether a particular person is free to sleep or wash, we must also ask whether there are any prohibitions *of place* that apply to his performance of actions of this type. As a matter of fact, all of us face a formidable battery of such prohibitions. Most private places, for example, are off-limits to us for these (or any other) activities. Though I am a well-paid professor, there are only a couple of private places where I am allowed to sleep or wash (without having someone's specific permission): my home, my office, and whatever restaurant I am patronizing. Most homeless people do not have jobs and few of them are allowed inside restaurants. ("Bathrooms for the use of customers only.") Above all, they have no homes. So there is literally no private place where they are free to sleep or wash.

For them, that is a desperately important fact about their freedom, one that must preoccupy much of every day. Unlike us, they have no private place where they can take it for granted that they will be allowed to sleep or wash. Since everyone needs to sleep and wash regularly, homeless people have to spend time searching for non-private places — like public restrooms (of which there are precious few in America, by the standards of most civilized countries) and shelters (available, if at all, only at night) — where these actions may be performed without fear of interference. If we regard freedom as simply the complement of the general prohibitions imposed by law, we are in danger of overlooking this fact about the freedom of the homeless. Most of us can afford to overlook it, because we have homes to go to. But without a home, a person's freedom is his freedom to act in public, in places governed by common property rules. That is the difference between our freedom and the freedom of the homeless.

C. Public places

What then are we to say about public places? If there is anywhere the homeless are free to act, it is in the streets, the subways and the parks. These regions are governed by common property rules. Since these are the only places they are allowed to be, these are the only places they are free to act.

However, a person is not allowed to do just whatever he likes in a public place. There are at least three types of prohibition that one faces in a place governed by rules of common property.

(1) If there are any general prohibitions on types of action in a society, like the prohibition on murder or the prohibition on selling narcotics, then they apply to all tokens of those types performed anywhere, public or private. And these prohibitions apply to everyone: though it is only the homeless who have no choice but to be in public places, the law forbids the rich as well as the poor from selling narcotics, and *a fortiori* from selling narcotics on the streets and in the parks.

(2) Typically, there are also prohibitions that are specific to public places and provide the basis of their commonality. Parks have curfews; streets and sidewalks have rules that govern the extent to which one person's use of these places may interfere with another's; there are rules about obstruction, jaywalking, and so on. Many of these rules can be characterized and justified as rules of fairness. If public places are to be available for everyone's use, then we must make sure that their use by some people does not preclude or obstruct their use by others.

(3) However, some of the rules that govern behaviour in public places are more substantive than that: they concern particular forms of behavior that are not to be performed in public whether there is an issue of fairness involved or not. For example, many states and municipalities forbid the use of parks for making love. It is not that there is any general constraint on lovemaking as a type of action (though some states still have laws against fornication). Although sexual intercourse between a husband and wife is permitted and even encouraged by the law, it is usually forbidden in public places. The place for that sort of activity, we say, is the privacy of the home.

Other examples spring to mind. There is no law against urinating — it is a necessary and desirable human activity. However, there is a law against urinating in public, except in the specially designated premises of public restrooms. In general, it is an activity which, if we are free to do it, we are free to do it mainly at home or in some other private place (a bathroom in a restaurant) where we have an independent right to be. There is also no law against sleeping — again a necessary and desirable human activity. To maintain their physical and mental health, people need to sleep for a substantial period every day. However, states and municipalities are increasingly passing ordinances to prohibit sleeping in public places like streets and parks.[17] The decision of the Transit Authority in New York to enforce prohibitions on sleeping in the subways attracted national attention a year or two ago.[18]

Such ordinances have and are known and even intended to have a specific effect on the homeless which is different from the effect they have on the rest of us. We are all familiar with the dictum of Anatole France: "[L]a majestueuse égalité des lois ... interdit au riche comme au pauvre de coucher sous les ponts. ..."[19] We might adapt it to the present point, noting that the new rules in the subway will prohibit anyone from sleeping or lying down in the cars and stations, whether they are rich or poor, homeless or housed. They will be phrased with majestic impartiality, and indeed their drafters know that they would be struck down immediately by the courts if they were formulated specifically to target those who have no homes. Still everyone is perfectly well aware of the point of passing these ordinances, and any attempt to defend them on the basis of their generality is quite disingenuous. Their point is to make sleeping in the subways off limits to those who have nowhere else to sleep.[20]

Four facts are telling in this regard. First, it is well known among those who press for these laws that the subway is such an unpleasant place to sleep that almost no one would do it if they had anywhere else to go. Secondly, the pressure for these laws comes as a response to what is well known to be "the problem of homelessness." It is not as though people suddenly became concerned about *sleeping* in the subway as such (as though that were a particularly dangerous activity to perform there, like smoking or jumping onto a moving train). When people write to the Transit Authority and say, "Just get them out. I don't care. Just get them out any way you can," we all know who the word "them" refers to.[21] People do not want to be confronted with the sight of the homeless — it is uncomfortable for the well-off to be reminded of the human price that is paid for a social structure like theirs — and they are willing to deprive those people of their last opportunity to sleep in order to protect themselves from this discomfort. Thirdly, the legislation is called for and promoted by people who are secure in the knowledge that they themselves have some place where they are permitted to sleep. Because *they* have some place to sleep which is not the subway, they infer that the subway is not a place for sleeping. The subway is a place where those who have some other place to sleep may do things besides sleeping.

Finally, and most strikingly, those who push for these laws will try to amend them or reformulate them if they turn out to have an unwelcome impact on people who are not homeless. For example, a city ordinance in Clearwater, Florida, prohibiting sleeping in public, was struck down as too broad because it would have applied even to a person sleeping in his car.[22] Most people who have cars also have homes, and we would not want a statute aimed at the homeless to prevent car owners from sleeping in public

Though we all know what the real object of these ordinances is, we may not have thought very hard about their cumulative effect. That effect is as follows.

For a person who has no home, and has no expectation of being allowed into something like a private office building or a restaurant, prohibitions on things like sleeping that apply particularly to public places pose a special problem. For although there is no *general* prohibition on acts of these types, still they are effectively ruled out altogether for anyone who is homeless and who has no shelter to go to. The prohibition is comprehensive in effect because of the cumulation, in the case of the homeless, of a number of different bans, differently imposed. The rules of property prohibit the homeless person from doing any of these acts in private, since there is no private place that he has a right to be. And the rules governing public places prohibit him from doing any of these acts in public, since that is how we have decided to regulate the use of public places. So what is the result? Since private places and public places between them exhaust all the places that there are, there is nowhere that these actions may be performed by the homeless person. And since freedom to perform a concrete action requires freedom to perform it at some place, it follows that the homeless person does not have the freedom to perform them. If sleeping is prohibited in public places, then sleeping is comprehensively prohibited to the homeless. If urinating is prohibited in public places (and if there are no public lavatories) then the homeless are simply unfree to urinate. These are not altogether comfortable conclusions, and they are certainly not comfortable for those who have to live with them....

V. Freedom and Important Freedoms

I have argued that a rule against performing an act in a public place amounts *in effect* to a *comprehensive* ban on that action so far as the homeless are concerned. If that argument is accepted, our next question should be: "How serious is this limitation on freedom?" Freedom in any society is limited in all sorts of ways: I have no freedom to pass through a red light nor to drive east on Bancroft Avenue. Any society involves a complicated array of freedoms and unfreedoms, and our assessment of *how* free a given society is (our assessment, for example, that the United States is a freer society than Albania) involves some assessment of the balance in that array.

Such assessments are characteristically qualitative as well as quantitative. We do not simply ask, "How many actions are people free or unfree to perform?" Indeed, such questions are very difficult to answer or even to formulate coherently.[23] Instead we often ask qualitative questions: "How important are the actions that people are prohibited from performing?" One of the tasks of a theory of human rights is to pick out a set of actions that it is thought particularly important from a moral point of view that people should have the freedom to perform, choices that it is thought particularly important that they should have the freedom to make, whatever other restrictions there are on their conduct.[24] For example, the Bill of Rights picks out things like religious worship, political speech, and the possession of firearms as actions or choices whose restriction we should be specially concerned about. A society that places restrictions on activities of these types is held to be worse, in point of freedom, than a society that merely restricts activities like drinking, smoking, or driving.

The reason for the concern has in part to do with the special significance of these actions. Religious worship is where we disclose and practice our deepest beliefs. Political speech is where we communicate with one another as citizens of a republic. Even bearing arms is held, by those who defend its status as a right, to be a special assertion of dignity, mature responsibility, civic participation, and freedom from the prospect of tyranny. And people occasionally disagree about the contents of these lists of important freedoms. Is it really important to have the right to bear arms, in a modern democratic society? Is commercial advertising as important as individual political discourse? These are disputes about which choices have this high ethical import, analogous to that attributed, say, to religious worship. They are disputes about which liberties should be given special protection in the name of human dignity or autonomy, and which attacks on freedom should be viewed as particularly inimical to the identity of a person as a citizen and as a moral agent.

On the whole, the actions specified by Bills of Rights are not what are at stake in the issue of homelessness. Certainly there would be an uproar if an ordinance was passed making it an offense to pray in the subway or to pass one's time there in political debate.[25] There has been some concern in America about the restriction of free speech in public and quasi-public places[26] (since it is arguable that the whole point of free speech is that it take place in the public realm). However, the actions that are being closed off to the homeless are, for the most part, not significant in this high-minded sense. They are significant in another way:

they are actions basic to the sustenance of a decent or healthy life, in some cases basic to the sustenance of life itself. There may not seem anything particularly autonomous or self-assertive or civically republican or ethically ennobling about sleeping or cooking or urinating. You will not find them listed in any Charter. However, that does not mean it is a matter of slight concern when people are prohibited from performing such actions, a concern analogous to that aroused by a traffic regulation or the introduction of a commercial standard.

For one thing, the regular performance of such actions is a precondition for all other aspects of life and activity. It is a precondition for the sort of autonomous life that is celebrated and affirmed when Bills of Rights are proclaimed. I am not making the crude mistake of saying that if we value autonomy, we must value its preconditions in exactly the same way. But if we value autonomy we should regard the satisfaction of its preconditions as a matter of importance; otherwise, our values simply ring hollow so far as real people are concerned.

Moreover, though we say there is nothing particularly dignified about sleeping or urinating, there is certainly something deeply and inherently *un*dignified about being prevented from doing so. Every torturer knows this: to break the human spirit, focus the mind of the victim through petty restrictions pitilessly imposed on the banal necessities of human life. We should be ashamed that we have allowed our laws of public and private property to reduce a million or more citizens to something approaching this level of degradation.

Increasingly, in the way we organize common property, we have done all we can to prevent people from taking care of these elementary needs themselves, quietly, with dignity, as ordinary human beings. If someone needs to urinate, what he needs above all as a dignified person is the *freedom* to do so in privacy and relative independence of the arbitrary will of anyone else. But we have set things up so that either the street person must *beg* for this opportunity, several times every day, as a favor from people who recoil from him in horror, or, if he wants to act independently on his own initiative, he must break the law and risk arrest. The generous provision of public lavatories would make an immense difference in this regard — and it would be a difference to freedom and dignity, not just a matter of welfare.

Finally we need to understand that any restriction on the performance of these basic acts has the feature of being not only uncomfortable and degrading, but more or less literally *unbearable* for the people concerned. People need sleep, for example, not just in the sense that sleep is necessary for health, but also in the sense that they will eventually fall asleep or drop from exhaustion if it is denied them. People simply cannot bear a lack of sleep, and they will do themselves a great deal of damage trying to bear it. The same, obviously, is true of bodily functions like urinating and defecating. These are things that people simply have to do; any attempt voluntarily to refrain from doing them is at once painful, dangerous, and finally impossible. That our social system might in effect deny them the right to do these things, by prohibiting their being done in each and every place, ought to be a matter of the gravest concern.[27]

It may seem sordid or in bad taste to make such a lot of these elementary physical points in a philosophical discussion of freedom. But if freedom is important, it is as freedom for human beings, that is, for the embodied and needy organisms that we are. The point about the activities I have mentioned is that they are both urgent and quotidian. They are urgent because they are basic to all other functions. They are actions that have to be performed, if one is to be free to do anything else without distraction and distress. And they are quotidian in the sense that they are actions that have to be done every day. They are not actions that a person can *wait* to perform until he acquires a home. Every day, he must eat and excrete and sleep. Every day, if he is homeless, he will face the overwhelming task of trying to find somewhere where he is allowed to do this.

VI. Homes and Opportunities

That last point is particularly important as an answer to a final objection that may be made. Someone might object that I have so far said nothing at all about the fact that our society gives everyone the *opportunity* to acquire a home, and that we are all — the homeless and the housed — equal in *this* regard even if we are unequal in our actual ownership of real estate.

There is something to this objection, but not much. Certainly a society that denied a caste of persons the right (or juridical power) to own or lease property would be even worse than ours. The opportunity to acquire a home (even if it is just the juridical power) is surely worth having. But, to put it crudely, one cannot pee in an opportunity. Since the homeless, like us, are real people, they need some real place to be....

In the final analysis, whether or not a person really has the *opportunity* to obtain somewhere to live is a matter of his position in a society; it is a matter of his ability to deal with the people around him and of there being an opening in social and economic structures so that his wants and abilities can be brought into relation with others.[28] That position, that ability, and that opening do not exist magically as a result of legal status. The juridical fact that a person is not legally barred from becoming a tenant or a proprietor does not mean that there is any realistic prospect of that happening. Whether it happens depends, among other things, on now he can present himself, how reliable and respectable he appears, what skills and abilities he can deploy, how much time, effort, and mobility he can invest in a search for housing, assistance, and employment, and so on.

Those are abstract formulations. We could say equally that it is hard to get a job when one appears filthy, that many of the benefits of social and economic interaction cannot be obtained without an address or without a way of receiving telephone calls, that a person cannot take *all* his possessions with him in a shopping cart when he goes for an interview but he may have nowhere to leave them, that those who have become homeless become so because they have run out of cash altogether and so of course do not have available the up-front fees and deposits that landlords require from potential tenants, and so on.

Everything we call a social or economic opportunity depends cruelly on a person's being able to *do* certain things — for example, his being able to wash, to sleep, and to base himself somewhere. When someone is homeless he is, as we have seen, effectively *banned* from doing these things; these are things he is *not allowed* to do. So long as that is the case, it is a contemptible mockery to reassure the victims of such coercion that they have the *opportunity* to play a full part in social and economic life, for the rules of property are such that they are *prohibited* from doing the minimum that would be necessary to take advantage of that opportunity.[29]

Conclusion

Lack of freedom is not all there is to the nightmare of homelessness. There is also the cold, the hunger, the disease and lack of medical treatment, the danger, the beatings, the loneliness, and the shame and despair that may come from being unable to care for oneself, one's child, or a friend. By focusing on freedom in this essay, I have not wanted to detract from any of that.

But there are good reasons to pay attention to the issue of freedom. They are not merely strategic, though in a society that prides itself as "the land of the free," this may be one way of shaming a people into action and concern. Homelessness is partly about property and law, and freedom provides the connecting term that makes those categories relevant. By considering not only what a person is allowed to do, but where he is allowed to do it, we can see a system of property for what it is: rules that provide freedom and prosperity for some by imposing restrictions on others. So long as everyone enjoys some of the benefits as well as some of the restrictions, that correlativity is bearable. It ceases to be so when there is a class of persons who bear *all* of the restrictions and nothing else, a class of persons for whom property is nothing but a way of limiting their freedom.

Perhaps the strongest argument for thinking about homelessness as an issue of freedom is that it forces us to see people in need as *agents*. Destitution is not necessarily passive; and public provision is not always a way of compounding passivity. By focusing on what we allow people to do to satisfy their own basic needs on their own initiative, and by scrutinizing the legal obstacles that we place in their way (the doors we lock, the ordinances we enforce, and the night-sticks we raise), we get a better sense that what we are dealing with here is not just "the problem of homelessness," but a million or more *persons* whose activity and dignity and freedom are at stake.

Author's Note

An earlier version of this essay was presented at faculty workshops at Cornell University and at Boalt Hall. I am grateful to all who participated in those discussions, but particularly to Gary Gleb, Carol Sanger, and Henry Shue for the very detailed suggestions they have offered.

NOTES

1. See, e.g., Siebert, "Homeless People: Establishing Rights to Shelter," 4 *Law & Inequality* 393 (1986) (no constitutional guarantee of adequate housing): Comment, "The Unconstitutionality of 'Antihomeless' Laws: Ordinances Prohibiting Sleeping in Outdoor Public Areas as a Violation of the Right to Travel," 77 *Calif. L. Re.* 595 (1989) (authored by Ades) (arguing that laws that proscribe sleeping in outdoor public areas violate the right to travel).

2. The best discussion remains Honoré, "Ownership," in *Oxford Essays in Jurisprudence* 107 (A.G. Guest ed. 1961); see also S. Munzer, *A Theory of Property* 21-61 (1990); J. Waldron, *The Right to Private Property* 15-36 (1988).

3. See J. Waldron, note 2 (above), at 40-42; Macpherson, "The Meaning of Property," in *Property: Mainstream and Critical Positions* 1, 4-6 (C. Macpherson ed. 1978).

4. In *Pruneyard Shopping Center v. Robins*, 447 U.S. 74 (1980), the United States Supreme Court held that the California courts may reasonably require the owners of a shopping mall to allow persons to exercise rights of free speech on their premises under the California Constitution, and that such a requirement does not constitute a taking for the purposes of the Fifth Amendment to the Constitution of the United States.

5. For a more complete discussion, see J. Waldron, note 2 (above), at 42-46.

6. Diluliu, "There But For Fortune," *New Republic*, June 24, 1991, at 27, 28.

7. But this ignores the fact that a large number of people with no home of their own are kept from having to wander the streets only by virtue of the fact that friends and relatives are willing to let them share their home, couches, and floors. If this generosity were less forthcoming, the number of "street people" would be much greater.

8. See, e.g., M. Rothbard, *For a New Liberty* 201-2 (1973).

9. Herbert Spencer was so disconcerted by the possibility that he thought it a good reason to prohibit the private ownership of land altogether. A. Reeve, *Property* 85 (1986) (quoting H. Spencer, *Social Statics* 114-15 (1851)).

10. For a useful discussion, see I. Berlin, "Introduction," in *Four Essays on Liberty* i, xlv-lv (1969).

11. See also Waldron, "Welfare and the Images of Charity," 36 *Phil. Q.* 463 (1986).

12. It is not even to deny that they may enlarge the amount of freedom overall. Isaiah Berlin put the point precisely: "Every law seems to me to curtail *some* liberty, although it may be a means to increasing another. Whether it increases the total sum of attainable liberty will of course depend on the particular situation." I. Berlin, note 10 (above), at xlix no. 1 (emphasis in original).

13. For the connection between generality, predictability, and the rule of law, see F. Hayek, *The Constitution of Liberty* 148-61 (1960).

14. See R. Hare, *Freedom and Reason* 10-21 (1963).

15. For example, Dicey puts forward the following as the first principle of "the rule of law": "no man is punishable or can be lawfully made to suffer in body or goods except for a distinct breach of law established in the ordinary legal manner before the ordinary courts of the land." A. Dicey, *Introduction to the Study of the Law of the Constitution* 188 (10th ed. 1959).

16. For a discussion of how a lay person applies the rules of property, see B. Ackerman, *Private Property and the Constitution* 116-18 (1977).

17. Here are some examples. The City Code of Phoenix, Arizona provides: "It shall be unlawful for any person to use a public street, highway, alley, lane, parkway, [or] sidewalk ... for lying [or] sleeping ... except in the case of a physical emergency or the administration of medical assistance." A St. Petersburg, Florida ordinance similarly provides that: "No person shall sleep upon or in any street, park, wharf or other public place." I am indebted to Paul Ades for these examples. *Comment*, note 1 (above), at 595 n. 5, 596 n. 7 (quoting Phoenix, Ariz., City Code § 23-48.01 (1981); St. Petersburg, Fla., Ordinance 25.57 (1973)).

18. And New Yorkers have grown tired of confronting homeless people every day on the subway, at the train station and at the entrances to supermarkets and apartment buildings.

"People are tired of stepping over bodies," the advocacy director for the Coalition for the Homeless, Keith Summa, said.

Lynette Thompson, a Transit Authority official who oversees the outreach program for the homeless in the subway, said there had been a marked change this year in letters from riders.

"At the beginning of last year, the tenor of those letters was, 'Please do something to help the homeless,'" Ms. Thompson said. "But since August and September, they've been saying: 'Just get them out. I don't care. Just get them out any way you can.' It got worse and people got fed up." ....

"Doors closing as Mood on the Homeless Sours," *N.Y. Times*, Nov. 18, 1989; at 1, col.2, 32, col.1, col.

19. A. France, *Le Lys Rouge* 117-18 (rev. ed. 1923) ("the law in its majestic equality forbids the rich as well as the poor to sleep under the bridges.").

20. See M. Davis, *City of Quartz: Excavating the Future in Los Angeles* 232-36 (1990) for an excellent account of similar devices designed to render public spaces in downtown Los Angeles "off-limits" to the homeless, as well as Davis's "Afterword — A Logic Like Hell's: Being Homeless in Los Angeles," 39 *UCLA L. Rev.* 325 (1991).

21. See note 18 (above).

22. Bracing for the annual influx of homeless people fleeing the Northern cold, the police here [in Miami, Florida] have proposed an emergency ordinance that would allow them to arrest some street people as a way of keeping them on the move.

The new measure would replace a century-old law against sleeping in public that was abandoned after a similar statute in Clearwater, Fla., was struck down by Federal courts in January. The courts said the statute was too broad and would have applied even to a person sleeping in his car. The new proposal seeks to get around the court's objection by being more specific. But it would also be more far-reaching than the original law, applying to such activities as cooking and the building of temporary shelters.

Terry Cunningham, a 23-year-old who lives on the steps of the Federal Courthouse, asked of the police, "Where do they expect me to sleep?"

City and county officials had no answer. "That's a good question," Sergeant Rivero of the Police Department said, "No one is willing to address the problem."

"Miami Police Want to Control Homeless by Arresting Them," *N.Y. Times*, Nov. 4, 1988, at A1, col.1. A16, col.4.

23. For a critique of the purely quantitative approach, see Taylor, "What's Wrong with Negative Liberty?" in *The Idea of Freedom* (A. Ryan, ed. 1979), at 183.

24. Cf. R. Dworkin, *Taking Rights Seriously* 270-72 (rev. ed. 1978) (discussion of the theory that a right to certain liberties can be derived from the "special character" of the liberties).

25. The failure of First Amendment challenges to restrictions on panhandling does not bode well for the survival of even these protections. *See* Young v. New York City Transit Auth., 903 F. 2d 146 (2d Cir.), *cert. denied,* 111 S. Ct. 516 (1990). *But see* Hershkoff and Cohen, "Begging to Differ: The First Amendment and the Right to Beg," 104 *Harv. L. Rev.* 896 (1991) (arguing that begging is protected speech).

26. See note 4 (above).

27. I hope it will not be regarded as an attempt at humor if I suggest that the Rawlsian doctrine of "the strains of commitment" is directly relevant here. J. Rawls, *A Theory of Justice* 175-76 (1971). If the effect of a principle would be literally unbearable to some of those to whom it applies, it must be rejected by the parties in Rawls's contractarian thought-experiment, known as the "original position."

28. This idea is sometimes expressed in terms of "social citizenship." See King and Waldron, "Citizenship, Social Citizenship, and the defense of Welfare Provision," 18 *Brit. J. Pol. Sci.* 415 (1988); see also R. Dahrendorf, *The Modern Social Conflict: An Essay on the Politics of Liberty* 29-47 (1988).

29. And this is to say nothing about the appalling deprivation of ordinary opportunity that will be experienced by those tens of thousands of *children* growing up homeless in America. To suggest that a child sleeping on the streets or in a dangerous crowded shelter, with no place to store toys or books, and no sense of hope or security, has an opportunity equal to that of anyone in our society is simply a mockery.

REFORMING THE WELFARE STATE:
THE CASE FOR BASIC INCOME

Ingrid Robeyns

Ingrid Robeyns is a post-doctoral researcher in the Department of Political Science at the University of Amsterdam. Her main areas of research are on Amartya Sen's capability approach and issues of social and distributive justice in welfare states. She is the author of a number of articles in journals such as Journal of Human Development, Feminist Economics, *and* Metaphilosophy.

Robeyns points out that in many Western European countries strong support for welfare policies is changing because of the impact of increased unemployment, economic globalization, and the European Union. She uses these changes as a reason to re-examine basic income as a viable policy. Basic income is similar to universal health care in that it provides an income to everyone regardless of factors such as employment status and gender. Robeyns argues that basic income has several practical and moral advantages: it would lower economic inequality; it could enable a society to eradicate unemployment and avoid the poverty traps of means-tested and workfare programs; and it would give people real freedom instead of being forced to take any kind of alienating, exploitative, or degrading job just to survive. Robeyns casts doubt on the argument that a basic income would further entrench gender roles by giving women the freedom to do long-term work such as caring for children or volunteering for community work.

The aim of a welfare state is to offer a safety net by providing social services and/or benefits for the unemployed, the poor, parents, children, the elderly and ill, or disabled people. In comparison with the U.S., most of the European welfare states are generous in terms of providing everyone with health care and other insurance against most social risks. As a consequence, the taxation levels needed to finance these welfare state provisions are often higher in Europe than in the U.S. Western European countries have lower average incomes than the U.S., but they do not necessarily have lower standards of living. In terms of life expectancy and educational achievement, West-European countries score slightly better than the U.S.[1]

In recent years, the European welfare states have come under pressure as governments try to reduce deficits and thereby diminish their role in the economy. The increased marketization of the economies, structural unemployment of the low-skilled, changes to family structures, the changing roles of women, and the priority that most governments have given to their monetary policies with the replacement of their national currencies with the Euro are some of the reasons for why changes to the European welfare state are needed. As a result, social policies are increasingly focused on people's individual responsibilities and on getting them into jobs, without sometimes paying sufficient attention to the quality of those jobs.[2]

However, not all social activists and scholars support the way in which Western European welfare states are developing. From a global perspective, Europe is perceived as affluent, yet there are still people excluded from society. Most big cities have homeless people, and others live in poor housing. Several million children and adults are living in relative poverty; while they are unlikely to die from hunger or illness, they are, nevertheless, excluded from playing a full part in society. Throughout the world, inequalities in income and wealth are on the rise, although inequality remains by far the largest in countries such as Britain and the U.S., which offer the least generous welfare state provisions.

One of the most pervasive social problems in Western Europe since the oil crisis of 1973 has been long-term structural unemployment, especially among the low-skilled. Due to technological innovations and processes of economic globalization, whole industries that once flourished in Western Europe — for example, textile manufacturing and mining — have virtually perished. Many jobs for low-skilled people have vanished. The wages paid to low-skilled employees in Europe were many times those now paid to workers doing similar work in emerging industries in Southern countries. Companies now reallocate to these countries where labor is cheaper and where labor laws are less stringent. For the low-skilled unemployed in Europe, the prospects of finding a job are slim. In turn, policies of welfare-to-work and means testing have become increasingly popular as ways of controlling and cutting welfare. This paper argues that these and other economic changes call for a re-examination of basic income as a viable policy for addressing poverty as it manifests itself in Europe and the world as a whole.

Problems with the Welfare State

Fortunately, the unemployed in Western Europe continue to be protected from extreme destitution by the welfare state. In most of these countries, poor people have a right to a guaranteed minimum income, and unemployed people have a right to unemployment benefits. However, these welfare states were designed after World War II in a time that was rather different from today. There were sufficient jobs for low-skilled people, and unemployment was low. Many jobs were secure for life; hence, job insecurity was not a real worry. Women and men conformed much more than they do now to the traditional gender division of labor, with husbands providing the income and wives caring

for children and managing the household. Families were much more stable than they are now, in the sense that divorce and separation were relatively rare and often disapproved of legally and socially.

Since these conditions have changed, governments in Western Europe widely acknowledge that welfare state reform is urgently needed. Most governments have reacted by subsidizing the wages of low-skilled employees or lowering social security contributions for the low-skilled. When employers of low-skilled workers pay lower financial contributions to the collective system of social security, the cost for these employers to hire such workers is lowered, which should result in more low-skilled workers being employed. At the same time, some governments have made the payment of unemployment benefits conditional upon people's willingness to retrain for another occupation and/or a willingness to accept any job they are offered, even when the job is far from where they live or the job hours are incompatible with their duties and responsibilities as parents. These shifts in welfare and social security policy are justified by arguments about the limitations of solidarity and about needing reciprocity to be the core value underlying the welfare state. In other words, only those who have contributed (or are willing to contribute) deserve help if they are in need. Finally, most of the welfare systems are not only job-oriented, but also means-tested: only people living in poverty who cannot fall back on the income of other household members and who are in material need are eligible for minimal income support. They receive a low minimum income from the state to protect them from absolute poverty. These so-called welfare-to-work and means-tested policies have already been in place in the U.S. for many years.

Basic Income: A Radical Counter-proposal

A radical alternative proposal with respect to welfare reform states that every person should receive a basic income, independent of her or his social and employment status, sex, level of need, work history, willingness to work, and so on. While no country has as yet implemented a full basic income for all, the proposal is not as idealistic as it sounds at first. Basic income would be an individual grant, with other household members' incomes not taken into account. When everyone is entitled to a basic income as a matter of citizenship rights, it would have a redistributive effect, as the more affluent people would contribute much more than the poor through measures such as taxation. Ideally, this basic income should be high enough to sustain a decent living for all, although concrete proposals allow for an introduction at a lower level, which is then gradually increased over time.[3] As will be discussed below, some countries have decent basic incomes for some groups (such as pensioners), while others have universal basic incomes but at very low levels.

One of the major arguments in favor of basic income over job-centered policies ("workfare") and means-tested welfare schemes is that it could enable a society to eradicate a number of unemployment and poverty traps. For example, if an unemployed person finds a job with a wage that is close to the level of unemployment or welfare benefits, she does not improve her financial situation significantly by taking the job and losing her benefits. Thus, she is "trapped" in her unemployment. Moreover, means-tested benefits are applied to the joint income of all members of the household, so that if one member of the household takes a job, another may lose her benefits. Schemes in several countries do not allow benefit-holders to enroll in a school, take up training courses, or sometimes even to engage in voluntary work. Hence, in some welfare states, poor or unemployed people are trapped in a passive situation where welfare state legislation discourages them from taking a job or engaging in other socially useful or productive activities.[4]

Basic income schemes could also reduce employment without worsening poverty by counteracting the poverty created by the current tendency to make labor markets more "flexible." In reality, "flexibility" means that more people are now working on short-term contracts and/or in temporary, unstable, or insecure jobs. Employers have argued that they need to be able to lay-off workers more easily if their firms want to compete and survive in the global market. However, individuals and their families suffer pressure from the uncertainty and unpredictability that this kind of flexibility creates. A basic income would help to secure workers' incomes and strengthen their power positions. Unconditional basic income would give employees more financial independence from employers, resulting in increased worker power to demand decent working conditions. It would also make it more feasible for employees to accept jobs when employers cannot pay higher wages due to global competition.

The ethical arguments in the basic income debate stress the importance of giving people more real freedom to live their lives in the way they wish, without being forced to take any kind of alienating, exploitative, or degrading job just to survive and without sacrificing their social and political autonomy in order to achieve economic security. A basic income would allow a worker to refuse a job that is unpleasant; to temporarily reduce hours of work to take care of children, ill relatives, or friends; or to take a sabbatical if she felt the need to stop rushing through life. A basic income would also give people more freedom to do long-term unpaid work, such as caring for children or volunteering for community work. These arguments support the view that people are empowered when their real freedom is enhanced, a view advocated forcefully by Amartya Sen.[5]

The underlying view of most basic income advocates is that one has the right as a citizen of a society to be provided with minimal financial means. A basic income is then one of the material aspects of economic citizenship, just as the right to vote is one of the material aspects of political citizenship. A basic income would result in lower economic inequality. It would require commitment and solidarity both from those who possess skills and capacities that are well-paid in the labor market and from those who have no constraints such as severe disabilities or care responsibilities that prevent them from holding down a job. As discussed later in this article, if a basic income is financed by taxation, the relatively affluent will pay more taxes that will then be redistributed to the poor, the unemployed, housewives, and others.

In these times of rampant anti-tax sentiments, one could ask why people would be willing to pay more taxes. In answer, it could be argued that the largest share of one's labor income is made possible only by stable and cooperative societal structures and institutions and by the talents that an individual does not deserve, but is simply lucky to possess. No citizen in Europe or North America can morally claim to own what they earn in the labor market, since they are born into well-organized societies that are the result of the collective efforts of others in both current and previous generations. In other words, most of the current wealth in Europe and North America exists because people have been cooperating for centuries and are still doing so. Moreover, the Western European countries' wealth has roots in colonial pasts, and that wealth is now protected in the post-colonial era by their position of relative power in the international political and economic system.[6] A good example of this power is the emissions of pollutants by consumers in Europe (and especially the U.S.), which contributes to global warming that primarily affects the livelihoods of the extreme poor in the South. Rich consumers perpetrate the majority of the environmental damage, while the poor bear the costs in terms of flooding and desertification and the increased risk of famines that this causes. While Europe, Japan, Australia, and Canada have recognized the urgency of the problem and committed themselves to reducing their emission of pollutants, the U.S. is unwilling to take responsibility for the damage that it causes directly to the global ecosystem and indirectly to the well-being of vulnerable people in the South.[7]

In addition to inequalities in wealth and income, there are other inequalities based on factors such as gender that raise ethical problems, ones that are rarely publicly addressed at local or global levels. However, if we pay attention to these inequalities and what to do to alleviate them, proposals that appear unrealistic at first sight, including basic income, start to make much more sense.

What Does Basic Income Mean for Gender Equality?

Where do gender issues fit into basic income proposals? In the 1990s, most of the publications on

basic income were gender-blind: it was simply assumed that basic income would be a good policy for women because they constituted the majority of the poor and because it would entail that housewives would get an income of their own. However, in public discussions it was often argued by feminists that a basic income might send women back home, leading to unintended negative consequences for their emancipation. A gender analysis of basic income proposals shows that the overall assessment is quite complicated.[8]

The current social security systems only protect the citizenship rights of people with access to formal paid employment. This generally excludes people who are primarily responsible for caring for children, the sick and frail, and the elderly. Caregivers are, in the majority of cases, women. Hence, a crucial advantage of basic income for women is the fact that it challenges the idea that the basis of citizenship is paid work and acknowledges instead that all citizens are entitled to the social and economic rights of citizenship.[9] However, it is unclear whether establishing a basic income would lead to a revaluation and recognition of unpaid work, since it would also be paid to people who do not make any social or economic contribution. From this perspective a "participation income," as proposed by Tony Atkinson, may be preferable to a basic income.[10] The difference between a participation income and a basic income is that the former is conditional upon being engaged in socially useful activities: working, looking for a job, doing voluntary work, undertaking some forms of training and education, and caring for children, the elderly, and disabled and ill people. The underlying ethos explicitly claims that all people who do socially valuable work or activities have a right to a minimum income. Because a basic income can allow someone to use it to lie on the beach, I agree with those who favor a participation income that requires citizens to do something useful by contributing to the well-being of others through paid or unpaid work or by working on their own personal development. Given that a basic income does not pose any requirements, it can lead to parasitic behavior. Since this literature tends not to distinguish between basic and participation income, I will stick to the terminology of basic income, but everything that follows can be applied to both proposals.

Some feminists have been skeptical about one aspect of basic income: its effect on the gender division of paid and unpaid labor. They have argued that a basic income would reinforce the traditional gender division of labor. The available evidence supports this worry.[11] Some recently implemented social policy measures, such as career interruption premia and "time credits" in Belgium that grant employees benefits for temporarily stepping (part-time) out of the labor market, are by a large majority taken up by women. Such schemes entitle workers to state-funded incomes for a maximum of three years if they leave their jobs for retraining, setting up a business, or caring for small children or terminally ill relatives. Women most often leave their jobs to raise small children, whereas men leave because they want to try to start an independent business or use the time as a transitional stage to early retirement. The available evidence thus suggests that if a basic income is implemented without other measures that try to redistribute unpaid work, it will probably strengthen the traditional gender division of labor, which, many argue, disadvantages women.[12]

Moreover, a gender analysis of basic income also points to the need to acknowledge women's diversity. For women who do not work outside the home and have no intention of doing so, a basic or participation income means an increase in their financial independence. However, if a woman lives with a man who strongly prefers that she stay at home, a basic income may work against her in the couple's decision-making process over the division of paid and unpaid work. For many other groups of women, the results are ambiguous and difficult to forecast. It seems that basic income would be especially supportive for those women who are most economically vulnerable, whereas better skilled women who have found lucrative formal employment might be disadvantaged if the basic income reinforces traditional gender roles.

Of course, ensuring a basic income in itself does not create restrictive and unequal roles for women. Nor is a basic income a magical formula that could

immediately end socioeconomic gender inequalities. As Martha MacDonald has argued, the challenge is to meet women's practical needs in their day-to-day responsibilities without undermining their strategic interest in changing unequal gender relations.[13] Most Western feminists want a revaluation and a redistribution of unpaid work. While a participation income will lead to a revaluation, evidence suggests it will not lead to redistribution. Therefore, a participation income should be part of a larger package that also tries to redistribute paid and unpaid work to make gender roles more equitable or to get rid of them altogether. Such a package could include an active policy to combat gender discrimination in the labor market. It could also work to change the culture of the labor market. This cultural change should take place in order to make normal a situation in which every worker is also assumed to be a caregiver and acknowledged as such, to challenge gender stereotypes in the media, and to introduce social policies enabling all men to experience the work of caring on a par with women.

The Feasibility of Funding a Basic Income

One of the main objections to the basic income proposal is that it would be financially unfeasible because financing it would mean raising income tax to such a high level that tax evasion would increase dramatically, people would be discouraged from working, and the whole system would break down. However, there is no need to think in terms of tax on labor or income only. We could also analyze the potential contributions of a carbon tax, which is a tax on the emission of carbon dioxide gases in production and consumption (car and airplane traffic, for example). Of course, a carbon tax makes a great deal of sense in itself, given the urgent need to cut greenhouse gas emissions to counter climate change and global warming. The main hurdle to imposing such taxes is not feasibility or economic efficiency, but the lack of political will of governments to tackle this problem. The U.S., for example, has about 4 per cent of the world population, but is causing 25 per cent of the carbon emissions. As Peter Singer and others point out, as long as Americans fail to grasp the urgency and gravity of the problem, there will not be any pressure on their government to join the global effort to reduce emissions.[14]

Another suggestion is to finance a basic income with the revenues of a tax on short-term international financial speculation — the so-called Tobin tax. Like the carbon tax, the Tobin tax has goals that are independent of generating revenue. These are to discourage financial speculation and to protect national economies from the effects that speculation can cause in consumer markets. A group of experts analyzing the idea of a Tobin tax has concluded that its feasibility is much more a political than a technical hurdle.[15] Financial and business interests with considerable political influence would surely lobby to oppose both of these taxes. However, if the political will were there, financing a basic income (at a low level) would certainly be feasible in rich countries and, if it were supplemented with a genuine commitment to global redistribution, perhaps even in all countries.

Obviously, the implementation of a basic income at a subsistence level is not a policy option for tomorrow. But there are some things to keep in mind when discussing the feasibility of basic income. A substantial basic income can be seen as the ultimate goal of basic income advocates, but this end can only be reached gradually by implementing partial measures. One such partial measure could be to give generous benefits to a select group of citizens who are not active in the labor market. Examples would be an unconditional basic pension for senior citizens, something which has existed in the Netherlands for decades and which is currently on the table in several other countries; paid parental leave for employees, which has recently been implemented in several European countries;[16] and the "voluntary ecological year" for young people in Germany.[17]

Alternatively, governments could introduce a universal benefit, pegged at a very low level. This is exactly what was done in the Dutch tax reform of 1 January 2001. All adult residents (except students, who are entitled to a study grant) are now given an annual individual refundable tax credit of 1507.[18] While the level is tiny in comparison to the costs of living in the Netherlands, it will allow

policy-makers and researchers to analyze how people respond to this tax credit and what its effects on poverty and inequality are. It might also pave the way for increasing the level of this tax credit in the future.

A real-world scheme that shares some features with basic income is the "Permanent Fund Dividend" in Alaska, an annual dividend of a state-managed fund which is based primarily on oil revenues. The dividend is given to all residents. Its value has ranged between about $1,000 and $1,900 over the last 10 years.[19]

Visions of Basic Income in the South

Basic income is not just an idea of interest to the richest countries. The goal of providing all citizens with the basic requirements of life has impelled Southern countries to develop social policies. For Southern countries that are in the middle-income range, constructing a welfare state and providing some sort of social safety net is seen as a desirable goal. However, people and governments in the South also recognize the problems of current welfare states in Europe. Some countries such as Brazil are, therefore, seeking a way to introduce a welfare state that combats poverty without increasing unemployment.

In 1991 the Brazilian senate passed legislation on a guaranteed minimum income first proposed by the Brazilian senator Eduardo Suplicy. In September 2000, 1,620 municipalities signed agreements to implement a guaranteed minimum income program. In some municipalities this program is targeted at poor families with children under 14, who receive support as long as they send their children to school. On February 1, 2003, Senator Suplicy proposed a bill to the Brazilian Senate to gradually establish an unconditional basic income for all Brazilian citizens. Starting in 2005, the basic income will be gradually introduced, starting with the poorest segments of the population and moving gradually toward full coverage of all citizens.[20] The bill was signed by Brazilian President Lula da Silva on January 8, 2004.

Brazil is not the only Southern country where basic income is taken seriously. Policies inspired by or related to basic income schemes are currently also being discussed in South Africa, where a group of researchers from the Economic Policy Research Institute have argued that a basic income might foster a virtuous circle in which growth and socioeconomic progress go hand in hand.[21] In this view, income support leads to lower poverty and increased productivity, which in turn generates higher growth, which they expect to result in further reductions of poverty.

Conclusion

Is a basic or participation income a crazy vision of an impossible ideal? It is certainly idealistic, but part of the aim of those who advocate it is to foster discussion of a long-term vision of how society can become fairer and better for all. Ultimately, whatever its degree of idealism, the idea of basic income forces us to think about work, jobs, and justice, and about what we owe to each other not only on a local, but also on a global scale.

A basic or participation income is not a socio-economic policy that can be implemented overnight. It requires a dramatic shift in our expectations of what we are entitled to and what society owes its citizens. The real feasibility problems of basic income and participation income are not so much financial or economic, but political or moral. Several analyses show that in the long run a basic income might be a better social policy than subsidized low-skilled work or a workfare policy. But in the short term, job creation by the government is more effective in reducing poverty and unemployment simultaneously. Given the pressure and political agenda created by the frequency of elections, it will be difficult to persuade governments to work on a long-term strategy of a basic income.

For women, basic income is definitely more promising than policies of workfare, where the goal is to do everything to get people into jobs, making them ineligible for benefits as soon as it is possible for them to have a job. Workfare focuses exclusively on getting women into formal employment, whereas basic or participation income schemes acknowledge the value of unpaid caring work and extend economic citizenship rights beyond participants in the formal labor market. A participation income policy would work even more strongly in women's interests than a basic income, since it could contribute to a genuine revaluation of unpaid work. At the same time, women would benefit most if such a policy could be implemented together with policy measures that combat gender inequalities and challenge gender roles.

Author's Note

An earlier version of this paper was published as "An income of one's own: a radical vision of welfare policies in Europe and beyond," in *Gender and Development* v. 9, no. 1 (2001): 82-89. I would like to thank Christine Koggel for suggestions on how to revise this paper.

NOTES

1. UNDP, *Human Development Report 2004* (New York, NY: Oxford University Press, 2004) 139.

2. For an overview of the contemporary challenges, see the various contributions in Gøsta Esping-Andersen *et al.*, *Why We Need a New Welfare State* (Oxford: Oxford University Press, 2002).

3. Some accessible introductions to basic income can be found in Philippe Van Parijs (editor), *Arguing for Basic Income* (London: Verso, 1992) and Robert van der Veen and Loek Groot (editors), *Basic Income on the Agenda: Policy Objectives and Political Chances*. (Amsterdam: Amsterdam University Press, 2000). For further reading, see also Keith Dowding, Jurgen De Wispelaere, and Stuart White (editors), *The Ethics of Stakeholding* (London: Palgrave/Macmillan, 2003).

4. Loek Groot and Robert van der Veen, "How attractive is a basic income for European Welfare States," in *Basic Income on the Agenda: Policy Objectives and Political Chances*, edited by Robert van der Veen and Loek Groot (Amsterdam: Amsterdam University Press, 2000).

5. Amartya Sen, *Development as Freedom* (New York, NY: Knopf, 1999).

6. For an account of how European countries benefited from abusing their colonies, see Adam Hochschild, *King Leopold's Ghost: A Story of*

Greed, Terror, and Heroism in Colonial Africa
(Boston, MA: Mariner Books, 1998). For an
account of how the global trade and financial struc-
tures benefit the rich countries, see Thomas Pogge,
World Poverty and Human Rights (Cambridge:
Polity Press, 2002).

7. Peter Singer, *One World: The Ethics of Globalization* (New Haven, CT: Yale University Press,
2002).

8. Ingrid Robeyns, "Hush money or emancipation
fee? A gender analysis of basic income," in *Basic
Income on the Agenda: Policy Objectives and
Political Chances*, edited by Robert van der Veen
and Loek Groot (Amsterdam: Amsterdam University Press, 2000).

9. Ailsa MacKay and Jo VanEvery, "Gender, family
and income maintenance: A feminist case for citizens' basic income," *Social Politics*, v. 7, no. 2
(2000): 266-84.

10. Tony Atkinson, "The case for a participation
income," *The Political Quarterly*, v. 67, no. 1
(1996): 67-70.

11. For more details, see the evidence presented in
Robeyns, "Hush money or emancipation fee?"

12. The claim that the traditional gender division of
labor is to the disadvantage of women is widespread in feminist research. See, for example,
Susan Moller Okin, *Justice, Gender and the Family*
(New York, NY: Basic Books, 1989). In the context
of basic income, see Ingrid Robeyns, "Will a basic
income do justice to women?," *Analyse und Kritik*,
v. 23, no. 1 (2001): 88-105.

13. Martha MacDonald, "Gender and social security
policy: pitfalls and possibilities," *Feminist Economics*, v. 4, no. 1 (1998): 1-25.

14. Singer, *One World*; and Verlyn Klinkenborg, "Be
afraid. Be very afraid," *The New York Times*,
Chronicle Environment (May 30, 2004).

15. Mahbub ul Haq, Inge Kaul, and Isabelle Grunberg
(editors) *The Tobin Tax: Coping with Financial
Volatility* (Oxford: Oxford University Press,
1996).

16. Jill Rubery, Mark Smith, and Colette Fagan,
Women's Employment in Europe (London: Routledge, 1999).

17. See <http://www.foej.de> (accessed October 8,
2004).

18. Loek Groot and Robert van der Veen, "Clues and
leads in the debate on basic income in the Netherlands," in *Basic Income on the Agenda: Policy
Objectives and Political Chances*, edited by Robert
van der Veen and Loek Groot (Amsterdam: Amsterdam University Press, 2000).

19. See <http://www.pfd.state.ak.us/> (accessed
October 8, 2004).

20. The full text of the proposed bill (in English) is
available at <http:// www.senado.gov.br/eduardosu-
plicy/Ingles/pls2662001ingles.htm> (accessed
October 8, 2004).

21. M. Samson, O. Babson, K. MacQuene, K. Van
Niekerk, and R. van Niekerk "The Macro-eco-
nomic implications of poverty-reducing income
transfers" (Cape Town: Economic Policy Research
Institute, 2000).

NORWAY: THE DEVELOPMENT ETHIC
OF A DONOR COUNTRY

Asuncion Lera St. Clair

Asuncion Lera St. Clair is Research Fellow in the Department of Sociology at the University of Bergen in Norway. Her work, supported by the Research Council of Norway, investigates the different roles of values on the conceptualizations of poverty and development and how these have changed over time in the United Nations Development Programme (UNDP) and the World Bank. She is the author of a number of articles on these topics.

  St. Clair argues that an account of the values and beliefs shaped by a country's particular history, in this case Norway, is instructive with respect to policies for alleviating poverty both within and outside a country's own borders. She states that learning about Norway's history shows how values of solidarity and justice originating in the initiatives and participation of both the poor and the non-poor influenced local, national, and international policies, making Norway the leading country in foreign aid. The contextual analysis of how culture and history shaped values in Norway can provide lessons for other donors, development agents, poor countries, international bodies, and development ethicists with respect to devising effective policies for reducing poverty.

---

1. Introduction

Of the developed countries, Norway gives the largest funding to international development proportional to its Gross Domestic Product (GDP). Its commitment to reducing global poverty is reflected in its latest plan for future Norwegian development policy, *Fighting Poverty: Norway's Action Plan 2015 for Combating Poverty in the South.*[1] Norway's policy-makers present the document as a tool for shifting development aid from a matter of charity to an issue of justice. The main goal of the *Action Plan* is to map the actions to be taken in order to accomplish the Millennium Development Goals (MDGs) set by the United Nations (UN), one of which calls for "halving the proportion of people living in extreme poverty, and so lifting more than 1 billion people out of it, by 2015".[2]

The claim that there is a moral obligation to help the poor has prefaced many speeches and policy documents by governments and international development agents in the past 50 years, but the claim has been used mostly rhetorically. An uncritical use of the language of moral obligation risks having it mainstreamed or made subservient to established and powerful self-interested goals and economic interests. Moreover, an uncritical use of ethical claims may end up raising the hopes of the poor for a more just social and economic global order without providing the necessary debate, the core tools, or the political will necessary to achieve such ends.

While it is clear that principles from development ethics have permeated Norwegian policy at a descriptive level, the ethical language used by Norway's document and by some of its current politicians has a much more forceful ethical meaning than is acknowledged by aid bureaucrats. This paper argues that Norway's factual level of economic aid, its involvement in the intellectual and political support of the UN, and the advocacy work it does to increase levels of aid by other donors by promoting open debates about human rights and just global international practices shape an *international* development ethic. This ethic can be tracked by examining the concrete role of solidarity (understood, of "mutuality") in shaping Norway's aid policy as one motivated by a system of values rather than a calculation of consequences. Norway's path from a pre-industrial to a welfare state to a welfare society shows how solidarity evolved through the participation of a number of groups and through discussion of and attention to value conflicts and class struggles.[3] We must look at the reasons for the wide consensus that such solidarity policies have had — and still have to a certain degree — among the whole spectrum of Norway's political parties and their constituencies. There is a symmetry between the development of a commitment to the *just* treatment of the poor at the national level and Norway's engagement in development policy in the global context.

This paper traces the historical evolution of Norway's policies to the participation of members from popular movements and voluntary organizations in the institutionalization of values of equity and solidarity and to the role that a relatively transparent relation between researchers and politicians had in the elaboration of universal social policies, particularly in the institutionalization of the principles of equality and universality. This role was crucial in three areas: 1) the role of Christian values and strategies in the formation of Norway during the early eighteenth and nineteenth centuries, specifically, the role of Haugianism; 2) the role of solidarity in the labor movement since the beginning of the twentieth century; and 3) the importance of social policy — the so-called "social question" — in the materialization of Norway's welfare state and welfare society after World War II and the wide political consensus of such policies since the 1960s. The paper concludes by attempting to construct the ethic that flows from this analysis of Norway.

2. Theoretical Framework: Value Analysis in Policy and Development Ethics

International development policies as well as aid policies of donor countries are value-laden.

Whether explicit or implicit, values underlie the recommendations that are brought about by policy. "Development" is itself a value-laden concept that entails judgments that certain types of economies and societies are better than others.[4] According to Des Gasper, development ethics

> looks at meanings given to societal change, at the types, distribution and significance of the costs and gains from major socio-economic change, and at value conscious ways of thinking about and choosing between alternative paths and destinations. It aims to help in identifying, considering and making ethical choices about societal "development," and in identifying and assessing the explicit and implicit ethical theories. (Gasper 2004: xi)[5]

Gasper emphasizes aspects similar to those that the pioneer of development ethics, Denis Goulet, pointed to when he claimed that development ethics "deals *ex professo* with the ethical judgments regarding the good life, the just society, and the quality of relations among people and with nature [which] always serve, explicitly or implicitly, as operational criteria for development planners and researchers" (Goulet 1997: 161). Development ethics can be carried out at a descriptive and/or normative level. Gasper defines descriptive ethics as "a wide ranging description and analysis of existing ethics, including practices as well as doctrines" and calls it a "sociology of ideas and practices" (Gasper 2001). I propose a genesis approach, an exercise in descriptive ethics that reconstructs the actual development ethic being practiced by a donor country, whose conscious evaluation and choice of alternative development paths forms an ethic at the national level. The goal of such a strategy is explanatory. It will unveil some of the ethical dilemmas and conflicts in poverty reduction and contribute to the discussion of how ethics can be practically included in development policy.

The approach distinguishes two levels of analysis with respect to the role of values in aid policies: in discourse and in practices. In discourse, values can operate as stated goals in policy documents and speeches by aid policy-makers and politicians and as justifications for policy, in the case of a donor country, to the public at home. The other level deals with the role of values in the actual practices of Norway as an international actor in aid policy. In order to trace Norway's development ethic, the analysis searches for the sources of the values, whether explicit or implicit, that are embedded in aid policy. The main assumption of this approach is that we must examine the content of development ethics not only in policy documents and policy practices, but also in the historical context and shared norms underpinning the political culture of policy making. A genesis approach not only allows us to unveil the actual values in discourse and practices, but to outline what type of ethic has been practiced over time by Norway. This analysis strengthens the hypothesis that the "real" ethic of development for a donor country must go beyond the mere explicit and rhetorical use of ethical concepts in policy documents. Actions and practice must go hand in hand: political will and policy implementations express the values that a development agent (in this case a donor country) cares about or is willing to promote and defend.[6]

3. Norwegian Development Aid[7]

Norway started giving foreign aid in 1952, during a period when the country was still in the process of reconstruction after the war and while itself being a recipient of foreign aid (mainly through the Marshall Plan). Since the early years, the main goal of Norwegian aid was and still is to reduce poverty through long-term improvements in economic, social, and political conditions for people in developing countries. The volume of Norwegian aid was initially modest, but by the 1970s it was significant enough to make aid a "national project" and one of the substantial characteristics defining Norway's relations outside Europe.[8] The volume of aid increased six-fold between 1973 and 1980, by which point Norwegian aid reached 1 per cent of GDP annually (Utenriksdepartementet 2002). Although the absolute volume has continued to increase (in 2001 it reached 12,103 million Nor-

wegian Crowns, or approximately US$1.5 billion), the overseas development aid (ODA) to GDP ratio has fallen to 0.83 per cent after it reached its peak of 1.1 per cent in 1990.[9] Nevertheless, Norway's volume of aid has been for a long time above the goal set for the Organization for Economic Cooperation and Development (OECD) countries (0.7 per cent of GDP) making Norway among the four most generous donors in terms of ODA/GDP for the last 20 years (the current average for the members of OECD's Development Assistance Committee is 0.24 per cent).

Another important feature of Norwegian foreign aid is the high proportion of bilateral aid channeled through non-governmental organizations (NGOs) — almost half of all bi-lateral aid, 80 per cent of which goes through Norwegian organizations. The geographical focus of Norwegian aid has traditionally been South Saharan Africa, the Horn of Africa, and to a lesser extent South Asia and Central America. Aid policies usually channel a large share of resources to a limited set of countries with which Norway has established long-term relationships. It is important to note that the selection of countries is neither related to prior colonial relationships (as is the case with ODA from the European Union (EU) and a series of individual EU countries)[10] nor to commercial interests nor to domestic security concerns (as is the case with much of the ODA from the U.S.). Rather, the recipient countries have been selected on the basis of a mix between observed poverty, a history of relations with Norwegian civil-society groups (primarily missionaries and solidarity organizations), and political leanings of the governments. For example, India and Tanzania were selected as main partners due to their respectively social- democratic and socialist policies at the time, and the strong focus on Africa was based on links established earlier by missionaries. Lately, Norwegian ODA has been tied increasingly to Norway's engagement as peace-negotiator in internal conflicts and its engagement in international peace operations. As a consequence of this engagement in peace efforts, a series of new countries with which Norway has not traditionally cooperated have been included as main recipients of aid.[11]

International cooperation related to peace processes has also been characterized by strong involvement of Norwegian NGOs.[12]

Norway is also a strong supporter of the multilateral system, channeling approximately 50 per cent of ODA through it. One-third of these funds go to the multilateral development banks (MDBs),[13] and the rest is distributed among different UN organizations.[14] Approximately one-third of the funds channeled through the multilateral organizations is actually bilateral aid administered by them. This is used primarily for co-financing of projects, technical assistance, and financing of Norwegian experts in areas particularly important on the Norwegian aid agenda. Unlike many other special funds administered by the multilateral organizations, the Norwegian Funds are directed to issues such as the environment, women in development, and social development. These special funding efforts are an attempt to influence policies of the MDBs in the direction of issues that Norway values. For example, environmental issues have long been a high priority for Norway, and it was under the leadership of Norway that the idea of "sustainable development" entered the conceptual arena in international development research.

Although Norway has refrained from any thorough critique of, for example, structural adjustment policies, it has attempted to shift the attention of the MDBs toward poverty reduction, social equity, and the environment. Thereby, Norway has continued to press other development actors to defend the social goals and principles put forward in the development studies literature during the 1970s and has defended some power structure changes proposed in the failed UN Conference on Trade and Development (UNCTAD) proposal for a New International Economic Order (NIEO). Norway was one of the few countries defending the NIEO. As I shall argue below, a substantial reason for the volume of aid and attempts to influence specific policies is the value content of Norway's policies.

When summarizing the experiences during 50 years of aid, the Norwegian Agency for International Development states: "Norwegian aid can be characterized as being driven by ethical motives in a stronger sense than many other countries" (Utenriksdepartementet 2002: 22). It adds: "This [ethical drive] explains much of the strong engagement found among individuals and the broad public support which is a distinguishing feature of the 50 years of Norwegian development cooperation" (Utenriksdepartementet 2002: 22). My analysis aims to explain that the direction of support for specific policies actually goes in a reverse way: it is the strong engagement by various actors within civil society and the particular traditions of state-society relationships existing within Norway that have made it a major donor country, one that has persistently based its policies in development ethics. In other words, the ethical content is a reflection of values in domestic policy and a consequence of the role of domestic constituencies in policy. Although ethical values are still used as a justification for aid domestically, at the international level it is the ethical content that makes Norwegian policy morally influential and relevant. Moreover, an ethical justification for aid also has consequences for the kind of aid policies that are pursued. When aid has few motives or justifications other than improving the lives of poor people, unethical behavior on the part of recipients is intolerable. For this reason, an ethical approach to development has had Norway become increasingly focused on corruption and the irresponsible use of funds on the part of the recipients.

4. Norway's Action Plan 2015

In the preface to the *Action Plan*, the Norwegian Prime Minister, Kjell Magne Bondevik, defines poverty as "the lack of freedom to meet one's basic needs and those of one's family." The policy document states that the first reason for combating poverty is a moral one. "Norway, as one of the richest countries in the world, has an obligation to take this challenge [reducing poverty] seriously. Poverty is an attack on human dignity. It is morally and politically intolerable that basic human rights are being violated in such a massive and constant way." In her opening at the official presentation of the plan, Hilde F. Johnson, the Norwegian minister of international development, declared that helping those living in poverty is a matter not of a people's or country's charity, but of justice.[15] In an explicit attempt to guarantee the moral content of the policy document, she added that it was the result of integrating Amartya Sen's conception of development as freedom with the background literature based on human rights approaches to development. Appropriately, the keynote speaker of the official presentation was Sen, who presented a brief outline of his latest work and established some connections between the findings of his account of development as freedom and of human rights in general, as well as to the Norwegian policy plan.

The *Action Plan* lists poverty's attack on human dignity as one of the main three reasons for bilateral aid (the second and third reasons are, respectively, the commitment made to accomplish the MDGs and the current level of knowledge and experience). Attacks on human dignity are violations of human rights, and accordingly, the *Action Plan* makes respect and promotion of human rights a necessary condition for the ends and means of development. "This is an ethical and altruistic project" the document states, and then adds, "[h]uman rights must be an inseparable part of the development process, because development is precisely about realizing the freedoms and possibilities implied in the concept of human rights."

In his keynote address, Sen outlined some of the views he defends in *Development as Freedom* as applied to poverty reduction. After distinguishing the normative sense entailed by the recognition that freedom is the primary objective of development — normative because it entails that development's achievements and goals must be seen in terms of what they contribute to the lives and freedoms of the people involved — Sen devoted most of his presentation to explaining the synergies and mutual support of different freedoms. Using empirical examples about the roles of democracy, of political and civil rights, and of social arrangements such as education, health care, and land reform, Sen illustrated the claim that "what a person has the actual capability to achieve is influenced by economic opportunities, political liberties, social facilities, and the enabling conditions of good health, basic educations, and the encourage-

ment and cultivation of initiatives" (Sen 2002: 3). As is usual in most of his writings and speeches, Sen emphasized the chain of good outcomes that comes from empowering women's lives. He used, for example, interesting new findings that strongly suggest a

causal pattern that goes from the nutritional neglect of women to maternal undernourishment, to fetal growth retardation and underweight babies, to greater incidence of cardiovascular afflictions much later in adult life (along with the phenomenon of undernourished children in the long run). (Sen 2002: 7)

It is this "world of interdependences" among different types of unfreedoms, Sen argued, that is relevant for poverty reduction policy and institutional reform. The different freedoms involved in poverty must be taken together if development efforts are to be effective, and in this regard, he praised the *Action Plan* for "taking an inclusive and integrative approach" (Sen 2002: 8).

The emphasis on the synergies among different freedoms — the instrumental interpretation of freedoms and their crucial role for poverty reduction — is the most characteristic use of Sen's views in the *Action Plan*, as Sen himself explicitly acknowledged. Within its own borders, Norway has been able to institutionalize a sense of solidarity with the poor and to transform such virtue into political action. The reasons must be found — as Sen rightly identified in his keynote address — in the "great Norwegian heritage of supportive cooperation across geography and wealth" (Sen 2002: 1). But this was first and primarily a domestic tradition, one that gave a central role to popular movements, to local governments across Norway's regions, and to the application of the Christian movement's ethical principles in the creation of a homogenously tied political, cultural, and economic life. "Cooperation" here refers to attacking inequalities and redistributing wealth. The next sections show that the reasons for Norway's development ethic are found *not* in the use or application of a particular theory from development ethics or in this country's participation in a consensus among a wide range of development agents on specific ethical approaches to development and poverty. Rather, these approaches to development ethics find a natural place in an already established ethical framework of social justice, one that has close similarities to Sen's own proposals.

5. Values in Norwegian International Development: From Domestic to International Solidarity[16]

5.1 Ethical Content of Aid Policy

According to a very detailed evaluation of Norwegian aid policy from its beginnings until the mid-1980s, a solidaristic approach to the needs of the poor has always been an important component of Norwegian development aid policy. Surveys of popular views show a high degree of support for development cooperation based on principles of solidarity. For example, solidarity with those in poor countries was part of the Labor party program of 1953, and an earlier assessment of Norwegian aid, the Engen Committee, claims that development cooperation in Norway is based on "the principle of equality of man and a feeling of solidarity with all countries and races" (Engen Committee 1962, quoted in Stokke 1989a).[17] To a significant degree, solidarity with those in need in other countries, specifically with the most poor and vulnerable, is a shared norm of Norwegian social, political, cultural, and economic life, particularly when we compare Norwegian politics and society to other non-Nordic Western countries (if we compare, for example, Norway with France or the U.S., these claims are strengthened). Even the Norwegian public school system curriculum explicitly includes the teaching of international solidarity and responsibility (Nordkvelle 1991).[18]

According to Olav Stokke, Norwegian aid policy has many determinants, one of the most important of which is the ethical values of the dominant socio-political norms of Norway. "Aid policy, like policies within other areas, will respond to the dominant socio-political norms and the overarching interests of the society" (Stokke

1989b: 159). According to Stokke's analysis, the determinants of Norwegian aid policy are:

1) Norway's dominant socio-political norms such as the welfare state ideology, Christian standards, and a humanistic tradition;
2) overarching systemic interests at the domestic level, such as Norway's participation in the North American Treaty Organization (NATO) or the promotion of Norwegian interests abroad;
3) private sector interests, such as exports promotion;
4) traditional relations with the Third World at the systemic and private-sector level;
5) the country's evolving economic situation;
6) Norway's participation with regional, international and multilateral groups, such as the Nordic countries, the Department of Army Civilians of the OECD, or the World Bank.

Stokke argues that even though these determinants of aid policy pull in different directions and aid policy is the result of a consensus among the different actors of these determinants, each can be distinguished as either altruistic or self-interested. Norway's aid policy, however, assumes a framework of *humane internationalism*, which entails "an acceptance of the principle that citizens of the industrial nations have moral obligations towards peoples and events; it implies sensitivity to cosmopolitan values" (Stokke 1989a: 10). Respect and promotion of economic, social, and political rights is given as much importance as the promotion of economic growth. Humane internationalism is not exclusively altruistic. Rather, morality is combined with and instrumental for the promotion of the interests and values of rich countries.[19] According to Stokke, Scandinavian countries have developed a particular type of internationalism — reform internationalism — that coincides with most of the objectives of humane internationalism. The difference is that reform internationalism goes further in asking for reform in the international political and economic system for the benefit of the South. An instance of such reform was the support of the Scandinavian countries to the claims of NIEO in the 1970s.

5.2. Norwegian Socio-Political Norms

In Stokke's view, the main origins of the Norwegian socio-political norms influencing development aid are: 1) the welfare state ideology, which, closely associated with social democracy (Labor Party), makes solidarity one of its core values, one that does not stop at geographical borders; 2) Christian standards, for which the universal brotherhood of man has also an international scope; and 3) a humanitarian tradition related to international relief with actors such as The Norwegian Red Cross Association. Stokke concludes that the main features of an aid policy emerging from these norms leads to aid policy

in which motives and objectives would be idealistic, oriented towards developmental objectives in the Third World (as opposed to self-centered objectives) and international common goods compatible with the norms identified. The general direction would be towards a large volume of aid on generous terms. The welfare state ideology would orient the policy towards international redistribution (poor countries) and economic and social justice at the national level (involving demands on the systems through which ODA is channeled), whereas humanitarian tradition would give emphasis to more immediate needs, including relief. Other norms would result in a policy aimed at strengthening independence, democracy in a broad sense and/or human rights (Stokke 1989b).

I agree with Stokke in the symmetries between domestic norms and values and international commitments. If fighting inequality and poverty were not a domestic concern, it would be unreasonable to expect consensus among different parties for a strong commitment to help the poor internationally, more so when one of the important drives of such aid is altruistic. Similarly, if social and economic rights were not a concern at home and their violation taken as a serious matter, it would be unreasonable to expect these same norms to guide foreign policy. Concerns for inequality and poverty and for the implementation of liberty rights as well as of social and economic rights prevail at the

domestic level and in Norwegian political debate today. During the 1990s inequalities that increased in Norway were debated in the media as well as in Parliament. During the last elections, the Conservative Party, currently in government, raised concerns for groups living under conditions of poverty, particularly children. Thus, a moral case for poverty reduction and equality still frames Norwegian political debate and political culture.[20] Even though Norway is being affected by neo-liberal free-market and consumerist tendencies, it is more than mere curiosity to notice that an excessive display of wealth is viewed as "tasteless."

Thus, an explanation of Norway's development ethic lies in domestic values, in the historical and contextual conditions that have given Norwegians, as citizens and as politicians, a certain internalized sense for being *morally averse to poverty and inequality*. At the domestic level, Stokke suggests that such conditions lie in the social democratic ideology of the welfare state and a longstanding Christian tradition of brotherhood. The role of Christian values is usually related to Norway's important tradition of missionary activities and strong NGOs working in the South. It is common as well to characterize Norwegian (and other Nordic countries') international development aid as an extension of the welfare state to other countries. But this characterization is misleading, because it entails that an ethical approach to development would require a *top-down* implementation of a specific socioeconomic and political structure to other countries, thereby opening the route for an easy critique of such policy as paternalistic. I suggest that the roots of Norway's conception of international solidarity can be found before the actual expansion of the welfare state after World War II and that this has important lessons for the role of ethical values in international development policy and for the promotion of policies that could, at least in principle, enhance the mechanisms that generate solidarity and concern for poverty reduction at many levels. After the 1960s, a relatively transparent relation between social scientists and policy-makers helped strengthen solidarity as mutuality through the implementation of universal and equity-based social policy. It is significant that researchers focused on conditions that could be agreed upon as "bad" for human life and that this research led to a more feasible social and political consensus.[21]

The ethical values underlying Norwegian aid, particularly a sense of "solidarity as mutuality" with the poor and the empowerment and respect of people's agency, are rooted in a longstanding tradition that has transformed equality and universality into the materialization of economic, social, and political rights.[22] This is a tradition of social and economic policy that moves from charity to justice, a tradition developed and reinforced by social democracy and the extension of the Scandinavian model of the welfare state after World War II. But the necessary conditions for the institutionalization of solidarity must be looked for in the social and economic structures of pre-industrial Norway in the eighteenth and nineteenth centuries.

These origins suggest that the "effective" participation of the most poor and vulnerable was one of the most important reasons for the wide consensus in Norwegian politics for helping the poor, first within the country itself and then in the rest of the world after the 1950s. Citizens such as peasants and fishermen in secular and religious voluntary organizations transformed their principles of solidarity and brotherhood into notions of equality and universality that were in turn translated first into local politics and later into state politics through poor people's participation in Norway's political parties. No matter what route one takes in examining the history and context, Norway is an instance where the institutionalization of solidarity is explained by the triumph of the interests of the poor as well as by the participation of self-reliant groups — the non-poor — in the resulting solidaristic policies (Baldwin 1990).

6. Roots of Domestic Solidarity: The Triumph of the Poor and the Consensus of the Non-Poor [23]

6.1. Sources for the Institutionalization of Solidarity

The Scandinavian welfare state dates back to the 1920s and the 1930s, prior to the social democracy

era. The main features of the Norwegian or Scandinavian model of the welfare state more generally, can be summarized as follows.

1) Social policy is comprehensive in its attempt to provide welfare. Policy embraces an extensive range of social needs. The principles of the welfare state are pushed further into civil society than is common in other non-Nordic countries. Governments pursue a holistic and integrated approach to social policy whose aim is to ensure a unified system of social protection.
2) Social entitlements are institutionalized. Scandinavian welfare states have vested citizens, as well as residents, with a series of rights and benefits intended to constitute a democratic right to a socially adequate standard of living.
3) Social legislation is universal and solidaristic. Welfare policies include the entire population. Social policy is actively employed in the pursuit of a more egalitarian society (Esping-Andersen and Korpi 1987: 40-41).

The three most important variables that indicate the degree of development of an institutional welfare state are de-commodification, solidarity, and the range of social policy. Welfare is then the responsibility of the social collective. The market, for example, has a subordinate role. Class and social status are subordinate as well; it is membership in the class of human beings that justifies the unconditional guarantee of rights and status, which leads, arguably, to giving equal legal weight to social *and* property rights.

The institutionalization of solidarity led to the institutionalization of economic, social, and political rights as well as to the redistribution of wealth by the state apparatus. This redistributive role is one of the most well-known characteristics of the Nordic welfare model. Yet, redistributive policies themselves are the result of another – crucial — characteristic of the specific historical context of the formation of the Nordic welfare states, which also originates in solidarity: the effective participation of and equal dialogue among members of different classes. There was neither a master "project" nor an overarching theory of social justice from which political arrangements were derived, "[r]ather, the significant feature in Norden political culture ... was the ability to establish durable compromises out of conflicting visions and plans" (Petersen and Christiansen 2001). The State became the *people's home*, a concept first developed in Sweden when policies for universal insurance were implemented in the 1890s. In Norway, there are two fundamental roots for such participatory democratic debate: the role of Christian (specifically Lutheran) religion in Norway's social and political life and the role of democratically based social movements in the institutionalization of universalistic and egalitarian social policy.

6.2 The Role of Religion: Christian Values

Christian values in general, and Lutheranism in particular, has been important in the creation of a just society based on principles of solidarity and brotherhood. Norwegian missionary work was based on such religious values. The historical evolution of the Hans Nielsen Hauge Movement in Norwegian Protestantism as the "people's religion" is particularly important for the understanding of widespread solidaristic attitudes and economic-based principles that have lasted until today. Hans Nielsen Hauge (1771-1824) created a practical religion that spoke the simple language of people, generating its own ethic and influencing the lifestyle of a crucial popular movement in Norwegian history. The movement's internal structure was guided by a Christian brotherhood ethic that extended to economic relationships. According to Hauge, the "friends" must concentrate on attaining economic independence, particularly as a means of strengthening the bargaining position of the poor (and Christian) against the more well-off. For members of the Haugian movement, good intentions were not enough: "the Haugian's friends should practice the idea of a Christian brotherhood. They should be socially responsible Christians. Those who had means at hand were duty bound to invest in new activities" (Gilje 1997: 264). Thus, Haugianism was instrumental in the creation of informal economic networks of people — ruled by

solidarity and trust — that would eventually become representatives within political parties. In short, members of the Haugian popular movement had not only spiritual kinship but also common social interests that "laid the foundation for a new type of political cooperation which distanced itself from traditional and local uprisings ... We can generally say that the Haugian revivalist movement created both the material and spiritual background for politically autonomous actors. The revival in this perspective was in part responsible for creating a modern democracy in Norway" (Gilje 1997: 256).

6.3 Voluntary Organization and Popular Movements

In the late nineteenth century there were six other important social movements in Norway: the farmers' movement, the labor movement, teetotalism, the laymen's movement, the language movement, and the sports movement (Khunle *et al.* 2002). All these movements were involved in the development of modern Norwegian society from the mid-1900s. According to research documenting these movements and the tradition and role of voluntary associations within them, "Norway and other Scandinavian countries were set early on a route leading to universal, citizen-based welfare institutions. The idea of the people's or universal social insurance was firmly on the political agenda from the 1880s, long before social democracy gained strength" (Kuhnle 1981; Seip 1984, in Kuhnle and Selle 1992: 76). This early route was traced by voluntary organizations and popular movements. The "people" of these groups were "welfare pioneers." These democratic and egalitarian groups were the first to challenge the poor laws of the time, to create organizations for the care of the sick and elderly, and to organize the work of women outside the house. And all these activities were the basis for the empowerment of the most vulnerable in the political arena and for the transition from charity to justice in regards to people's well-being. Their capacity for building relations of trust and for debating different views openly formed the basis for the creation of contemporary

Norwegian democratic institutions and for the acknowledgment and implementation of economic, social, and political rights. Norwegian and other Nordic countries' voluntary organizations of these early years were characterized as "institutional producers of welfare" (Kuhnle and Selle 1992; Baldwin 1990). Active participation of people through voluntary organizations led to a strong role for local politics. In Norway, the state relegated part of its authority to local councils "as early as 1837" (Bjørnson 2001: 198).

It is by looking into these groups' historical and contextual position during the pre-industrial era that we can grasp the levels of agreement among different sectors of society in the twentieth-century welfare state model in Scandinavia. Examples of the role of voluntary organizations as carriers of welfare abound in the health sector. For example, care for and prevention of tuberculosis, which was the biggest epidemic in Norway since the Black Death, started as charitable work from three main organizations, whose egalitarian structure and capacity to generate dialogue and understanding among different views, particularly the role of women in advocating for the rights of the sick, is partly responsible for the Norwegian national health care system (Blom 1998).

Legislation on tuberculosis and care for the ill "asserted a superior responsibility for the government and challenged traditional attitudes on the division between society and the individual citizen" (Kuhnle and Selle 1992: 79). Contemporary health experts characterize the system today in the following terms:

> There is a very strong public commitment to access to high quality health care for all and even the most right wing populist parties pay homage to this ideal....solidarity [related to health care] means devoting special consideration to the needs of the weakest, e.g., those who have less chance than others of making their voices heard or exercising their rights. (Holm *et al.* 1999:323)

The relationship of trust developed among members of voluntary organizations and popular movements was also one of the important ways of bridging disagreements among different social classes, a necessary requirement for the later institutionalization of egalitarian policies. This was true particularly in Norwegian women's associations, most of which were dedicated to care and social work. Asking how Norwegian women entered the public world, historian Anne Lise Seip shows that women's spirit of association and participation in the social charitable organizations during the nineteenth century led to the education of social workers in general and to the establishment of social issues in politics as a fundamental matter (Seip 1998).

What started as activities that gave women an opportunity to socialize with each other beyond the realm of the household ended as one of the crucial channels for the institutionalization of solidaristic and universal social policies. Women's charitable work was also instrumental in reconciling different class views: "Women were to build a bridge across the gap that distrust and class interests have created in our society by doing social work; they should act as bridge engineers" (Seip 1998: 57). Furthermore, a modification of gender roles and the recognition of women as agents of change were outcomes of such initial voluntary organizations based on what was considered at the time the natural space for women, social and care work.

6.4 Interdependence Theory in Practice

In Norway, social debate, the creation of democratic institutions, the institutionalization of all human rights, and the process of industrialization have parallel and integrated routes. "Voluntary organizations cooperated with government creating a mixed system that moved the role and values of social welfare increasingly from voluntary and charitable organizations to public responsibility" (Kuhnle and Selle 1992: 79). In contemporary Norway, although voluntary organizations still play an important role in society and politics, welfare as charity is an obsolete idea in politics because welfare is the domain of public responsibility. An important source of such a view is the level of participation and dialogue among different people through solidaristic voluntary organizations and popular movements and the permeation of their views and values (respect, participation, equality, care, and dialogue) into local politics, converging in the creation of state institutions and policies based on universality and equality. The role of civil society in influencing political culture in favor of welfare and democracy was possible in part because popular movement members and their organizations were *parties* or *peers* in the actual process of designing and implementing public policy as well as in the creation of institutions. They brought with their participation a strong notion of solidarity rather than the defense of their own individual or group interests. This process towards increasing public responsibility, which was rooted in personal responsibility and the struggle against inequality, made attitudes of charity toward the poor obsolete.

After World War II, the transparent debate among researchers and policy-makers about universal social policies and their normative underpinnings added strength and sustainability to the solidarity-as-mutuality tradition, a tradition that time has made stronger than welfare state critics want us to believe. Researchers had a very clear political and ethical mandate: to produce perspectives from below while keeping in mind the importance of social cohesion. For example, the most important study of Norwegian levels of living focused on *the individual as an actor endowed with human dignity* (NOU 1976). The study used *social equality* rather than poverty as its central concept. The choice of terms was very important: its goal was to avoid stigmatizing the poor and vulnerable while at the same time aiming to draw support from the powerful sectors of society. In addition, a focus on social equality is an instance of policy-making that integrates ethics with economic development.

Universality, equity, and solidarity are values that still support social policies, and the belief that globalization erodes or will erode them is mere speculation (Kuhnle and Hort 2003).[24] Far from paternalism, the consequences of having people's needs not in the hands of the market but mostly under collective responsibility is one of the most

fundamental reasons why Norway has ranked first in the annual *Human Development Report* from 2002 to 2004. Of course, Norway has had specific historical conditions that have favored this process, such as a lack of an aristocracy, a generalized distaste for such classes because of Norway's political dependence on Denmark, and a very homogenous population in terms of race, religion, and culture. But important lessons can still be drawn for other donor countries and for development agents in general about the role of ethics and the conditions for global solidarity.

The triumph of the poor and the consent of the non-poor was a result of constant bargaining and consensus, of power and class struggles, as well as many other self-interested reasons. We must ask what is left in contemporary Norway of the historical and contextual characteristics that have structured a society based on equality and the universality of human dignity. Left-wing critics today may disagree with the idea that the characterization drawn above still holds true in the Norwegian social and political scene. Solidarity is not a zero-sum game, and many argue that contemporary politics is being tilted too much toward market forces and particular interests, all to the detriment of the more vulnerable. Often it seems as if younger generations take for granted the achievements of social democracy without realizing that the benefits they enjoy are the result of a long "struggle for fairness." Yet, Norway is, in relation to many other non-Scandinavian donor countries, an example to study. Many lessons can be drawn from the above analysis for the application of ethical views in international development poverty reduction policies, as well as for the field of development ethics in general. This is of particular importance as globalization theorists and critics are increasingly proposing the globalization of social democracy or of human rights as needed alternatives to mere economic globalization.[25]

7. Lessons from History: What Type of Ethic Drives Poverty Reduction at Home and Abroad?

A look at the history and origins of the Norwegian welfare state teaches us that the values underlying

Norway's humanistic and solidaristic international development policies are rooted in the specific contextual and historical conditions of this country's evolution from a pre-industrial to a highly advanced and wealthy country. Norway and its Scandinavian neighbors grew to be among the richest countries in the world during the golden age of capitalism (the 1950s and the 1960s).[26] But we must remember that this occurred at the same time as the mature egalitarian and universal welfare state leading to today's welfare society was institutionalized. Solidaristic policy is the result of the empowerment and participation of the poor and vulnerable through their interaction, relations, and community life linked to voluntary organizations representing different popular movements. Yet the crucial step in the institutionalization of solidarity is the eventual participation in the shaping of local and state institutions over time. The construction of Norway's welfare society was a gradual and continual balancing act between stimulating economic development and promoting social justice.

In summary, Norway is an instance where an *ethic of development* is rooted in attitudes of solidarity that led to universal social policies and where the institutionalization of this attitude may be explained by the triumph of the interests of the poor as well as by the participation of self-reliant groups — the non-poor — in the resulting policies (Baldwin 1990). The recognition and actual participation of marginalized groups was as important as policies for redistributing wealth. The struggle for solidarity-as-mutuality in Norway entailed a blurring between the private and the public, between the individual and the social, and between the domains of the market and the non-market. Negotiating these domains seems to be, in part, a way toward a development ethic.

In conclusion, lessons for other donors, for other development agents such as multilaterals, for poor countries themselves, and for development ethicists include acknowledging that a contextual analysis of culture and values is crucial for understanding ways to motivate and implement poverty reduction policies. The path towards a welfare society is the result of conflict resolutions and combined work among state, business, and market institutions as well as trade unions and civil society. Promoting economic efficiency cannot be separated from improving the freedom of individuals to control their own lives. In this sense, democratic capitalism may be a good model for an ethic of development, given that it can promote economic growth without undermining welfare measures and vice versa. This view is similar to Sen's in that it treats democratic principles, social justice, equality, civil society participation, and the institutionalization of *all* human rights as coterminus with economic growth, employment issues, and economic development.

The case of Norway shows that an ethic of development and effective poverty reduction policies are rooted in values that originate in the initiatives of the poor as well as the non-poor through real participation in social and economic life and in ways that influence local and national politics. However, participation is not sufficient by itself. Current human rights approaches for poverty reduction and for development policy will remain weak unless they take into consideration and encourage, at least in parallel, the conditions for the solidarity consensus of different groups and classes in institutionalizing rights. Thus, a strong civil society needs to be complemented with political power if it is to lead to the institutionalization of all human rights. Economic, social, and political rights must be developed contemporaneously. The institutionalization of political rights without regard for social or economic matters has had no role in history in reducing poverty. This can be shown, for example, by a comparative analysis of the roles and histories of popular movements and voluntary organizations in Norway and in the U.S. The U.S. is a country with a strong tradition of voluntary organizations and charitable groups, yet such solidarity roles have not and still do not translate into public responsibility. Part of the reason is the emphasis on liberty rights and the neglect of social and economic ones in American society and political culture.

Finally, while the use of explicit ethical language or of views from development ethicists with respect to poverty reduction and development planning and projects may provide better descriptions of the problems to be tackled, it does not entail a development ethic. Development ethicists must go beyond explicit concern for the ends and means of development to search for the role of ethical and religious values in generating conditions for real "peer" participation in social and political life. And they must confront the conflicts that arise from promoting social justice side by side with economic efficiency. Development ethicists need to study the role of actual values in current societies and communities in generating solidarity or the lack thereof. Values and religious traditions that promote social cohesion and relations of trust, class consensus, democratic debate, and participation among its members should be defended ahead of other "norms" such as free market policies. The case of Norway indicates that before one can talk about social justice and of ethics and international development more generally, it is necessary to forge and maintain the roots of solidarity at the grass roots level and then to translate it into political will. Examining the sources of solidarity in religion and in a country's history and context provides development ethicists with the tools for undermining accounts of development in terms of artificial abstractions of human life, methodological individualism, and mere economic explanations of people's sufferings and needs.

Author's Note

I thank Benedicte Bull for suggestions and information on earlier drafts of this paper. Editorial suggestions and corrections by Christine Koggel have improved not only the writing but have also helped me clarify the opinions expressed here. All remaining mistakes are my own.

NOTES

1. Hereafter referred to as "Norway's Action Plan" or "Action Plan." The text in English and the original version in Norwegian can be found at the Ministry's web site: <http://www.odin.dep.no/ud/>.

2. <http://www.un.org/millenniumgoals/>

3. Today, even though Norway finances the Inter-American Development Bank initiative on "Social Capital, Ethics, and Development" (<http://www.iadb.org/etica/ingles/index-i.htm>), it could do more to promote debate about value conflicts.

4. There are many types of values, such as consumerism; moral justifications for self-interest; and cognitive values, such as measurability, testability, quantification, or simplicity. Cognitive values are pervasive in development policy and can be decisive in the spread or hindrance of particular ideas. For instance, "whether a concept is suitable to quantification and therefore easily measurable has been an important reason for the rapid or slow institutionalization of an idea" (St. Clair 2003).

5. For more information on development ethics, see <http://www.development-ethics.org>.

6. This does not solve the contradictory outcomes that policies from other ministries — for example, trade — may lead to. Yet such conflicts are at least being publicly raised by current policy-makers.

7. Help on this section from Benedicte Bull has broadened my analysis of Norway as a donor country.

8. This is the view of Norwegian historian Terje Tvedt (2002), who is also a strong critic of Norwegian aid because of what he views as a tendency towards self-righteousness in aid bureaucrats. In my view, it is precisely a transparent treatment of values and their source as motivators for aid that may lead to a more well-balanced development ethic. This entails that aid must be understood by looking at the North more often than aid scholars do. Furthermore, this may be the more feasible road towards establishing aid policies and projects as well as the knowledge that underpins them.

9. See OECD Aid and Debt Statistics: <http://www.oecd.org>.

10. Compare this with the statement of the European Union: "The origins of the EU's development policy can be traced to the association of certain overseas countries and territories for the European Community when it was created in 1957" (<http://www.europa.edu.int/scadplus/leg/en/lvb/r1 2000.htm>) or with the Spanish Law of international cooperation (article 6) stating that Spanish

aid primarily will be directed towards Ibero America, the Arab countries of North Africa, and the Middle East, or other countries with which Spain has particular historical or cultural connections (<http:///www.aeci.es/4-Legislacion/plan_director.htm>).

11. Examples of this include cooperation with Angola, Sudan, and Guatemala, but recently also with Afghanistan, Palestine, and the Federal Yugoslav republic (Serbia, including Kosovo and Montenegro).

12. As expressed by former deputy minister of foreign affairs, Jan Egeland: "We let the voluntary organizations be our operators, while we pay for it" (Vårt Land 08.11.93) <http://www.vartland.no/>.

13 The World Bank and the Regional Development Banks, of which the African Development Bank has received most support over the last five years.

14. The United Nations Development Program (UNDP) is the largest single recipient of funds, and the World Bank ranks second.

15. Symposium on Poverty and Development: Development as Freedom, Oslo, 4 March 2002.

16. The arguments and historical explanations in this section, although only related to Norway, can be applied to any Scandinavian or Nordic country.

17. Norwegian development cooperation was under the responsibility of the Ministry of Foreign Affairs since the early 1950s. During the early 1960s there was a small board administrating bilateral aid, and the Norwegian Agency for International Development was established in 1968. Since 1984, development has been under a specific Ministry for Development Cooperation, yet is still part of Foreign Affairs.

18. However, Nordkvelle goes on to argue that the contents of the textbooks used by social studies teachers are flawed because they offer a view of the poor that expresses pity and appeals to a mercenary spirit.

19. "Humane internationalism, accordingly, is associated with a set of objectives, viz. to promote economic and social growth and economic, social and political human rights in the third world and to alleviate human suffering. It is based on humanitar-

ian values and ethics, including respect for the dignity of man, and is motivated, in the first place, by compassion — the moral obligation to alleviate humane suffering and meet humane needs across national, political and cultural borders. However, self-interest is part of the motivation too; this includes both broader national interests related to objectives of mutual benefits across borders, and narrower interests related to, inter alia employment, or an expansion of trade and investment opportunities" (Stokke 1989a: 11).

20. I thank Stein Kuhnle for pointing out the relevance of this matter.

21. For an analysis of Norwegian social research traditions and their similarities to development ethics approaches such as the capabilities approach, see St. Clair and Waerness (forthcoming).

22. I thank Sigrun Mogedal, former State Secretary of the Norwegian Ministry for International Development, for pointing out that "mutuality" best captures the specific type of solidarity with the poor in Norway's culture.

23. I thank Ida Blom (historian), Nils Gilje (philosopher), Stein Khunle (political scientist), Gunnar Skirbekk (philosopher), and Olav Korsnes and Kari Waerness (sociologists) for conversations that have made this section better informed and more in tune with contemporary Norwegian research in each of their fields. The section also draws from an interview with Sigrun Møgedal.

24. For an excellent analysis of the lessons that the Scandinavian welfare state model may have for developing countries, see Khunle and Hort 2003.

25. See The World Commission on the Social Dimensions of Globalization <http://www.commissionon-globalization.org/> and David Held (2004).

26. Notice that strong economic growth is prior to the exploitation of oil in the North Sea, which did not start until the late 1970s. Today, the income from oil is saved in a trust fund for future generations. The oil business has changed Norway's relations with non-European countries and this may have changed the conditions for aid outlined in the earlier sections of the paper. However, Norway has created an ethics committee to oversee the investment of such revenue, and in December 1999 it set

up, together with Finland, The Trust Fund for Environmentally and Socially Sustainable Development (TFESSD). For research monitoring the TFESSD, see <http://www.sum.uio.no/research/global_governance/tfessd/index.html>.

REFERENCES

Baldwin, Peter. (1990). *The Politics of Social Solidarity: Class Bases of the European Welfare State (1875-1975)*. Cambridge: Cambridge University Press.

Bjørnson, Øyvind. (2001). "The Social Democrats and the Norwegian Welfare State: Some Perspectives," *Scandinavian Journal of History*, v. 26, no. 3: 192-223.

Blom, Ida. (1998). *Feberens Ville Rose: Tre Omsorgssystemer I Tuberkuloearbeidedt 1900-1960*. Bergen: Fagbokforlaget.

Esping-Andersen, Gosta, and Walter Kopi. (1987). "From Poor Relief to Institutional Welfare States: The Development of Scandinavian Social Policy." In *The Scandinavian Model: Welfare States and Welfare Research*, edited by R. Erikson, E.J. Hansen, S. Ringen, and H. Uusitalo. New York, NY: M.E. Sharpe

Gasper, Des. (2003). "Global Ethics and Global Strangers: Beyond the International Relations Framework: An Essay in Descriptive Ethics." *Parallax — The Journal of Ethics and Globalization*, <http://www.parallaxonline.org/eiglobalethicsp.html>, March 2003.

— . (2004). *The Ethics of Development*, Edinburgh: Edinburgh University Press.

Gilje, Nils. (1997). "Hans Nielsen Hauge and the Spirit of Capitalism." In *Philosophy Beyond Borders: An Anthology of Norwegian Philosophy*, edited by Ragnar Fjelland *et al*. Bergen: SVT Press, University of Bergen.

Goulet, Denis. (1997). "Development Ethics: A New Discipline." *International Journal of Social Economics*, v. 24, no. 11: 1160-71.

Held, David. (2004). *Global Covenant: The Social Democratic Alternative to the Washington Consensus*. London: Polity.

Holm, Soren, Per-Erik Liss, and Ole Frithjof Norheim. (1999). "Access to Health Care in the Scandinavian Countries: Ethical Aspects." *Health Care Analysis*, v. 7: 321-30.

Kuhnle, Stein. (1981). "The Growth of Social Insurance Programs in Scandinavia: Outside Influences and Internal Forces." In *The Development of Welfare States in Europe and America*, edited by Peter Flora and A. Heidenheimer. New Brunswick, NJ: Transaction Books.

Kuhnle, Stein, and Per Selle. (1992). "The Historical Precedent for Government-Nonprofit Cooperation in Norway." In *Government and the Third Sector: Emerging Relationships in Welfare States*, edited by B. Gidron, R.M. Kramer. and L.M. Salamon. San Francisco, CA: Jossey-Bass Publishers.

Kuhnle, Stein, *et al*. (2002). "Political Institutions, Democracy and Welfare: A Comparative Study of Norway and Korea." Background paper for the *World Development Report 2003*. World Bank.

Kuhnle, Stein, and Sven Hort. (2003). "The Developmental Welfare State in Scandinavia: Lessons to the Developing World." Background paper for *Social Policy in a Development Context*, United Nations Research Institute for Social Development (UNRISD).

Nordkvelle, Yngve. (1991). "Development Education in Norway: Context and Content for the Teaching of Solidarity." *International Journal of Educational Development*, vol. 11, no. 2: 161-71.

NOU (1976). Levekårundersøkelsen. no. 28. [Norway. "Level of Living Study"]

Petersen, Klaus, and Niels Finn Christiansen. (2001). "The Nordic Welfare States 1900-2000." *Scandinavian Journal of History*, v. 26, no. 3: 153-56.

Seip, Anne Lise. (1984). *Socialhilpstaten Blir Til*. Oslo: Glidental.

— . (1998). "Social Work — A Space for Women." In *Charitable Women: Philanthropic Welfare 1780-1930*, edited by Birgitta Jordansson and Tinne Vammen. Odense, Denmark: Odense University Press.

Sen, Amartya. (1999). *Development as Freedom*. New York, NY: Anchor Books.

— . (2002). "Development and the Foundation of Freedom." Keynote Speech Symposium on Poverty and Development, Oslo, 4 March 2002.

St. Clair, Asuncion Lera. (2003). "The Role of Ideas in the United Nations Development Programme." In *Framing the World: Ideas in the Multilateral System*, edited by Morten Boas Morten and Desmond McNeill. London: Routledge.

St. Clair, Asuncion Lera, and Kari Waerness. (Forth-coming). "Norwegian Social Research Traditions and International Development." *Sociologisk Tidskrift.*

Stokke, Olav. (1985). "Norwegian Development-Cooperation Policy: Altruism and International Solidarity." In *Norwegian Foreign Policy in the 1980s*, edited by Johan Jørgen Holst. Oslo: Norwegian University Press.

— . (1989a). "The Determinants of Aid Policies: General Introduction." In *Western Middle Powers and Global Poverty: The Determinants of the Aid Policies of Canada, Denmark, the Netherlands, Norway and Sweden*, edited by Olav Stokke. Uppsala and Oslo: The Scandinavian Institute of African Studies in cooperation with the Norwegian Institute of International Affairs.

— . (1989b). "The Determinants of Norwegian Aid Policy." In *Western Powers and Global Poverty: The Determinants of the Aid Policies of Canada, Denmark, the Netherlands, Norway and Sweden*, edited by Olav Stokke. Uppsala: The Scandinavian Institute of African Studies in cooperation with The Norwegian Institute of International Affairs

Tvedt, Terje. (2002). *Verdensbilder og selvbilder: en humanitær stormakts intellektuelle historie.* Oslo: Universitetsforl.

Utenriksdepartementet. (2002). *Norsk bistand i fokus. Utviklingspolitisk redegjørelse 2002.* Rapport om norks utviklingssamarbeid i 2001.

THE BEAUTIFUL, EXPANDING FUTURE OF POVERTY: POPULAR ECONOMICS AS A PSYCHOLOGICAL DEFENSE

Ashis Nandy

Ashis Nandy is Senior Fellow and Director of the Center for the Study of Developing Societies and Chairperson of the Committee for Cultural Choices and Global Futures, both located in Delhi. He is the author and editor of a number of books, some of the most recent of which include Time Warps: The Insistent Politics of Silent and Evasive Pasts *(2002),* Bonfire of Creeds: The Essential Ashis Nandy *(2004), and* Return from Exile: Alternative Sciences, Illegitimacy of Nationalism, the Savage Freud *(2004).*

Nandy casts some doubt on contemporary attempts to define poverty. Because numbers matter to politicians and economists, definitions of poverty are often used to either expand or reduce the number of people who count as poor, enabling people to believe poverty is being alleviated or to resign themselves to the idea that poverty will always be with us. Nandy calls for a move away from these psychological ego defenses to clarity about what poverty means in the contemporary global context. He argues that there is a basic distinction to be made between poverty, which has always been with us, and destitution, which has become more pronounced through processes of development, such as economic globalization. By increasing destitution and providing jobs where none existed before, globalization, argues Nandy, disguises the declining political clout of the historically disadvantaged and a genuine interest in alleviating poverty.

. . . panting in sweltering summers,
shivering in winter nights, drenched in
*   monsoon rains,*
I turned poorer.
But you were tireless; you came again.
"Poverty is a meaningless term ...
You have suffered deprivation all your life ..."

My suffering was endless ...
But you did not forget me;
This time, hand knotted into a fist, you said in
a rousing voice,
"Wake up, wake up, you the dispossessed of the
*   world..."*

... Many years passed, by now you were cleverer. ...
You brought a blackboard and carefully
*   chalked a neat, long line*
*   on it;*

Your strain showed; wiping sweat from your
*   forehead, you said,*
"This line you see, below it, much below it you
*   live."*

Fabulous!...
Thank you for my poverty, deprivation,
*   dispossession . . .*
Above all, thank you for the neat, long line,
*   that luminous gift.*
... My profound well wisher, thank you many
*   times over.*
— From Tarapada Roy, "The Poverty Line"

The undying myth of development, that it will remove all poverty forever from all corners of the world, now lies shattered. It is surprising that so many people believed it for so many years with such admirable innocence. For even societies that have witnessed unprecedented prosperity during the last five decades, such as the United States of America, have not been able to exile either poverty or destitution from within their borders. The world GNP has grown many times in the last fifty years; even more spectacular has been the growth of prosperity in the United States. Yet, consistently more than 11 percent of its citizens — the figure, according to some, rose to something like 18 percent a decade ago — have more or less consistently stayed in poverty throughout almost the entire period of American hyperprosperity.[1] We are told that in the current capital of world capitalism, New York, 25 percent of all children and 50 percent of African American children live in families with incomes below the official poverty line. Around 40,000 homeless adults live in the streets, subways, under bridges and in train tunnels of the city.[2] Cardinal Paulo Everisto Aras once said, "[T]here are 20 million abandoned and undernourished children in a country that not only has the means to feed all its own children but also hundreds of millions in other countries."[3]

I am not speaking here of sub-Saharan Africa, Afghanistan or South Asia. I am not speaking of countries that struggle to avoid famine or where millions go to bed hungry every night and where radical institutional changes are required to avoid hunger, malnutrition and high infant mortality. These countries can claim they do not have the capacity to remove poverty, at least in the short run. I am speaking of the richest country in the world, which has already spent, according to available estimates, between 5000 billion and four trillion dollars on only nuclear armament.[4] Given available data, I suspect that minor changes in the American economy, such as eliminating only the country's nuclear-powered navy, perhaps even the nuclear-armed submarines, can get rid of this poverty. For the gap between the system's expenditure on the poor, direct in the form of personal relief (food coupons, free medical service or dole) and indirect in the form of security against poverty-induced crimes and poverty-related violence, is not high. But those minor changes, I also suspect, will not be made.[5]

Does this mean that a particularly insensitive élite control the United States or is the American

philosophy of development flawed? Or should we argue that American poverty is not the same as sub-Saharan or South Asian poverty, forgetting that Americans, when they think of or ignore poverty, use their definition, not ours? Or can one stick out one's neck and claim that the dominant model of development, whatever else it can do, cannot abolish poverty, for it has two latent aims of a very different kind. It seeks to push a polity toward a stage when poverty, even if it persists as a nagging social problem, no longer remains salient in public consciousness; and, simultaneously and paradoxically, it seeks to continuously stretch the idea of poverty, to sustain the idea of pulling millions above an ever-shifting poverty line.[6]

As for the first aim, it is becoming more obvious that all large multi-ethnic societies, after attaining the beatific status of development, lose interest in removing poverty, especially when poverty is associated with ethnic and cultural groups that lack or lose political clout? Particularly in a democracy, numbers matter and, once the number of poor in a society dwindles to a proportion that can be ignored while forging democratic alliances, the political parties are left with no incentive to pursue the cause of the poor. Seen thus, the issue of poverty is a paradox of plural democracy when it is wedded to global capitalism. And the paradox is both political-economic and moral. The presently trendy slogan of globalization can be read as the newest effort to paper over that basic contradiction; globalization has built into it the open admission that removal of poverty is no longer even a central myth of our public agenda.

This also implies that the main means of removing poverty within the present global developmental regime is the one Sanjay Gandhi — the much-maligned, despotic, perhaps disturbed younger son of a troubled prime minister — intuitively grasped and crudely executed. During 1975-77, when civil rights were suspended in India, he tried to remove the poor in India's capital outside the angle of vision of proper citizens through police state methods. Normal politics, normal journalism and normal social sciences are now trying to do the same by making the concern with poverty somewhat *passé*. Perhaps, rightly so. Everyone knows what the problem is, and determined scrutiny only embarrasses one and disturbs normal life. The three richest persons in the world have wealth, the UN Human Development Report of 1998 tells us, that exceeds the combined gross domestic product of the forty-eight least developed countries. One of them is Indian and instead of grimly talking of poverty all the while, many Indians have diffidently begun to celebrate such national achievements. The UN report incidentally also tells us that the Americans and Europeans spend US $17 billion per year on pet food, four billion more than the additional funds needed to provide basic health and nutrition for everyone in the world.[7] These are not easy facts to live with; one has to spend enormous psychological resources to ensure that they do not interfere with our "normal" life by burdening us with a crippling sense of guilt.

"Normal" middle class citizens, particularly those belonging to the liberal-democratic tradition, are uncomfortable with these paradoxes. They usually push them under the carpet through various psychological subterfuges. Who wants to live in moral discomfort when easy escapes are available in the form of popular ideologies of development and easy, "radical" conspiracy theories that absolve one of all responsibility in the name of the inevitability of world historical forces? Who would not like to be on the right side of history if, in the long run, a cataclysmic revolution promises to remove cobwebs like global capitalism and class exploitation, despite our personal foibles, lifestyles or tastes? Indeed, these patterns of intellectualization, serving as powerful ego defenses, explain some of the more obscene instances of developmentalism, where the removal of poverty itself becomes a billion-dollar, multinational enterprise. Graham Hancock has told that part of the story in disturbing and occasionally hilarious detail in his book.[8]

In India, presently going through what conventional wisdom has begun to call early stages of "correct" development, the intellectual consequences of these moral paradoxes often become comically patent. How many Indians are poor? In the 1970s, V.M. Dandekar and Nilakantha Rath said

that around 35 percent lived below the poverty line in the country.[9] But it was then more radical — and intellectually *chic* — to estimate the number of the poor highly; others quickly objected to the figure. Some estimates went much higher. Indeed, the popular image of India then was that of a desperately poor country with pockets of obscene prosperity here and there. That fitted the dominant models of political analysis and social intervention.

Much has changed in India since then. After the unlamented demise of bureaucratic socialism, the Indian élite has now entered the brave new world of globalization. The image of India for them, too, has changed. Thus, by the middle of the 1990s, many were speaking of India as a sleeping giant, fettered not by poverty but by poor economics. Gurcharan Das, formerly of Proctor and Gamble and as enthusiastic a votary of conventional development as one can be, said that his acceptable ideal of a future India was a developed India with about 16 percent of the citizens living under the poverty line. Das talked as if that future was a distant one.[10] As if to please him, in January 1996 some columnists mentioned that the Planning Commission of the Government of India had data to show that, already by 1994 — that is, even before the economic reforms were fully in place — only 19 percent of Indians were living under the poverty line.[11] One set of figures, based on consumption data, now suggests that the poor in India could now be less than 17 percent.

True, there are occasional spoilsports. According to S.P. Gupta, between 1983 and 1990-91 when economic growth rate was about 5.6 percent, the proportion of Indians living below the poverty line had fallen by 3.1 percent per year. When between 1993-94 and 1997, the growth rate shot up to 6.9 percent per year, the figure went up from 35 to 37 percent.[12] A number of papers in a recent issue of a professional journal and at a conference on food security, too, have contested official figures and the claims of the protagonists of globalization.[13] In a detailed paper, Deepak Lai, Rakesh Mohan and I. Natarajan even suggest ways of reconciling the diverse findings on Indian poverty.[14] I do not want to enter that part of the story, for my interest is not in the measurement of poverty or development under globalization, but in the cultural-psychological constructions of poverty and how they enter public awareness. My argument is that, right or wrong, such data now have less and less impact on India's political culture. For the globally popular ego defense that there is a one-to-one relationship between growth rates and decline in poverty appears to have already become a part of the character armor of the development establishment and middle class consciousness.

I am suggesting that the idea of a decline in poverty, real or imaginary, may now defy the economists and acquire an autonomous life of its own.[15] It will also have, I suspect, predictable consequences in a competitive polity. Political regimes and parties will probably claim even sharper drops in the proportion of the poor, till we shall discover in a few years that, like bonded labor, poverty has "vanished" from the Indian scene, that Gurcharan Das's ideal is already there waiting to be celebrated. In the next few years, giving a low figure of the poor in India might become as fashionable among the Indian literati as giving a high figure was three decades ago. Meanwhile a majority of India's expanding middle class — including a majority of Indian politicians, economists and bureaucrats — will feel perfectly justified in getting on with the job of economic development and of building a powerful national-security state. In 1995, the same year Das wrote of his utopia, others claimed that roughly 200 million Indians did not have enough to eat. They also claim that during the same year, 5 million metric tons of food grains, including rice and wheat, worth nearly US $2 billion, were exported. There is no controversy over the fact that, with that money, we did not buy cheaper grains for the poor, but consumer goods and military hardware.[16] The suicide of farmers, which in recent years has reached almost epidemic proportions in India, almost never takes place in underdeveloped, ill-governed states like Bihar, but in India's most prosperous, economic-reforms-minded states. This is not an exception; 78 percent of the world's malnourished children come from countries that have food surpluses.

These are probably indicators of the changing culture of mainstream Indian and global politics

and the fact that we are trying to get socialized into a new style of poverty management — through blatant use of the ego defense of denial, of the kind the psychoanalysts and psychiatrists expect to confront only in a clinic. Rabi Ray, former Speaker of the Indian Parliament, seemed to have sensed this change. He recently pointed out that when, in Maharashtra, a relatively prosperous state in India, hundreds of tribal children died of starvation some months ago in the Amravati district, there was not even a ritual demand for the resignation of the chief minister. Likewise, when it was discovered that about Rs 840 million had been swindled from the public distribution system, that is, from funds meant to combat hunger and provide food security to the poor, newspapers only made passing references to it and concentrated on spicier but smaller scams.[17] It is unlikely that the political parties or the development community — or even the opponents of the World Bank — WTO regime — will spend sleepless nights over the fact that in India, "there is 36 percent diversion of wheat, 31 percent diversion of rice and 23 percent diversion of sugar from the system at national level."[18]

For those nasty, suspicious souls who distrust statistical gamesmanship, such examples pose a different set of problems. And this brings us to the second aim of the global developmental regime. Was India once really so underdeveloped that four-fifths of Indians lived under the poverty line? Is it now so developed that only one-fifth of its citizens can be considered poor? Is there something wrong with our concepts of poverty and prosperity? To answer these questions, we might need other kinds of social and political awareness and a different set of concepts. These concepts may have to come, however uncomfortable the possibility may look to us, from outside the conventional liberal ideas of democracy and psephocratic politics on the one hand and the standard format of globalized intellectual order on the other.

First a word on poverty. Poverty is not destitution. When some intellectuals and activists talk of poverty being degrading or reject any critique of development as romanticization of poverty, they actually have in mind destitution, not poverty, but are too clever by half to admit that. By collating or collapsing these two terms, apologists of development have redefined all low-consuming, environment-friendly lifestyles as poor and, thus, degrading and unfit for survival in the contemporary world. In fact, Anil Gupta points out that there is a high correlation between poverty and biodiversity.[19] This is understandable because modern economics "equates wealth creation with the conversion of national resources into cash. But cash is constantly depreciating. On the other hand ... what progressively increases in value, besides strengthening our economic foundations, are our finite and living natural resources."[20] Also, a modern political economy, with its maniacal emphasis on productivity, continues to reduce the range of diversity to serve the market.

Large parts of Africa, Latin America and Asia were poor by contemporary standards of income and consumption before colonial administrators and development planners began to identify them as poor. That does not mean that they had massive destitution or that the quality of life there was abysmally poor.[21] Destitution, or at least large-scale destitution, is a more recent phenomenon. It has been increasing among many traditionally poor communities over the last hundred years, partly as a direct result of urbanization and development. The most glaring instances of destitution are found not in traditional, isolated tribal communities, but among the poor communities that are uprooted and fragmented and move into cities as individuals or nuclear families. It is also found among landless agricultural laborers who for some reason lose their jobs in a situation where agriculture is industrialized or becomes nonprofitable. They are the ones who find themselves unable to cope with the demands of an impersonal market or the culture of a modern political economy. That is why poverty turned into a different kind of social problem when England began to see widespread enclosure movement and massive industrialization in the Victorian era. Indeed, when we talk of poverty, we usually have that other kind of created poverty in mind, but are too defensive to admit that. We suspect that our world-views, ideologies and lifestyles are in league with the creation of this new kind of modern poverty.

The reason is obvious. Poverty in societies unfortunately left outside the loving embrace of modernity did not necessarily mean starvation or total collapse of life-support systems. For lifestyles in such societies were not fully monetized and the global commons were relatively intact. Even with no income, one could hope to survive at a low, but perhaps not entirely meaningless level of subsistence. Community and nature partly took care of the needs of the poor, especially given that these needs in lush, tropical surroundings were not many. For the moment, I am ignoring the line of argument that supports the idea that "convivial poverty is a blessing, not a scourge" and that poverty, though it might not be the wealth of nations, can certainly be in many ways "the alternative wealth of the humankind."[22] That also is a powerful argument, even though it may not look so on the face of it. However, I cannot resist quoting the confession of a development expert from Guyana, who works for the United Nations, about the world's poorest region, sub-Saharan Africa:

For the last several years, my professional life has been focussed on answering a question that has troubled me for some time:... "how can you ask someone who is hungry now to care about the future generations."

In thinking about this, I stumbled over even more basic questions. Who are the poor? What does it mean to call people poor? ...

My first insight was a personal one. While I knew that I did not grow up in a "rich" family, I never knew that I was very poor until I learned the definitions of poverty put forth by economists such as the World Bank. I got the same reaction from many agropastoralists with whom I worked in Africa.... Local non-governmental organisations (NGOs) have said the same thing: many communities did not know that they were poor until development agencies told them so.

For more than 50 years, one of the main activities of the development enterprise has been to assess, analyse and make prescriptions to meet

the needs (basic or otherwise) of those considered "poor." It was an enterprise stimulated by
the Cold War.... Ever since US President
Truman announced in 1949 that non-aligned
countries were "underdeveloped," and that the
US would give them aid so that they can
become more like America ... , intense research
in the name of development has flourished.
Attention has been focussed on countries' deficiencies and needs; at the same time, the
strengths, gifts and successful strategies of the
"poor" diminished in importance.... These
semi-nomadic communities had tremendous but
non-monetary wealth; indigenous knowledge
cultivated over centuries of living in harmony
with the land, a rich cultural heritage and
highly-evolved adaptive strategies, which
enabled them to cope with shocks and stresses
to the systems that provided their livelihoods.[23]

Such arguments immediately provoke accusations of romanticizing of the past. Almost invariably by those complicit in the new slave trade of
our times — exporting living, contemporary communities and human beings to the past in the name
of progress and rationality. I have been for some
time speaking of a form of proletarianization new
to the modern world, but known to students of Hel-
lenic democracies. The proletariat in ancient
Greece were those who existed but were not
counted. In this century, we too have mastered the
art of looking at large sections of humanity as
obsolete and redundant. These sections seem to us
to be anachronistically sleepwalking through our
times, when they should be safely ensconced in the
pages of history. Such communities certainly
should not trouble us morally, we believe, by pretending to be a part of the contemporary world and
relevant to human futures. It is as an important part
of that belief that the idea of underdevelopment
has redefined many communities as *only* collections of the poor and the oppressed. We talk of
indigenous peoples, tribes or Dalits as if they had
no pasts, no myths, no legends and no transmit-
table systems of knowledge; as if their grandparents never told them any stories, nor did their
parents sing them any lullabies. We steal their pasts

paradoxically to push them into the past. To speak
on behalf of the poor and the oppressed has
become a major ego defense against hearing their
voices and taking into account their ideas about
their own suffering. But I am digressing. Let me
get back to my main argument.

Destitution usually means zero income in a fully
modern, contractual political economy. In an
impersonal situation where individualism reigns,
in the absence of money income, one can no longer
depend or fall back upon the global commons,
either because it is exhausted or depleted, or
because it has been taken over by the ubiquitous
global market. Neither can you live off the forest
and the land nor can you depend on the magna-
nimity of your relatives and neighbors. The neighbors are no longer neighbors; you discover that
they have become individualized fellow citizens,
who neither expect nor give quarter to any one,
often not even to their own families.

Simultaneously, the differences that traditionally
existed between lifestyles of the rich and the poor
begin to disappear. That distinction partly protected the poor from destitution and loss of dignity.
Till quite recently, in some traditional parts of
Africa and Asia, the rich lived in brick, stone or
concrete houses; the poor lived in mud houses. The
rich wore expensive clothes or Western dress; the
poor had two sets of traditional clothes. They wore
one when they washed the other, which suggests
that they probably could stay reasonably clean.
The rich ate well, the poor ate poorly, but they did
eat. In tropical surroundings, that meant that the
poor survived to constitute, in some cases, a politically important element in the society. Regimes at
least tried to give the impression of doing something for them and most political parties, in competitive democracies, vied for their support. In
India, for instance, the needs of the poor were an
important metaphor in politics until the beginning
of the 1980s.[24] That cultural difference between
the rich and the poor also probably ensured that
when some religious orders or movements spoke
of the beauties of voluntary poverty, it was not an
invitation to a life of indignity and constant hunger.
The Jaina or Buddhist *bhikshu* did live a meaningful social, not merely spiritual life.

In much of the world now, larger and larger proportions of the poor have everything the rich have, only they have its fourth-rate, down-market versions. The difference between the rich and the poor is becoming less cultural and more economic. The culture of poverty no longer protects the poor. In any North American slum one finds that they have the same range of things the rich have — perhaps a television set purchased for ten dollars in a garage sale, a pair of torn, unclean blue jeans made by low-brow clothiers, and even a sofa-set with springs coming out of the upholstery, discarded by the wealthy on a metropolitan footpath. Go to a poor Bangladeshi village or an East African tribe in a remote, less accessible part of the country, and you will find that the rich and the poor live differently. The poor can still survive by living a low-consuming, meaningful life at the edge of the monetized economy. Even today, villages in many Third World societies are not entirely the same as metropolitan cities in this respect. You do not usually find in villages, unless they are located near frontiers or on important trade routes, large-scale drug addictions or alcoholism, high crime rates, ethnic or religious violence, and pathetic dependence on means of mass communications for interpersonal linkages or entertainment.

That traditional safety net now increasingly lies in tatters. And increasingly a sizeable section of the world's poor are becoming destitute. In the cities, the very poor have been destitute for at least the past one hundred years, except to the extent that some cities, mainly slums, in the Southern world retain something of their older village ties and ambience. Development may have removed poverty in many societies, but it has done so by expanding the proportion and the absolute number of the destitute. There are only a few exceptions to this rule. All are due either to the inability to extract wealth through formal or informal colonialism, or through ruthless, authoritarian exploitation at home.[25]

It can be argued that other forms of social change also do not remove poverty, or remove it to a lesser extent than development does and hence we have no option but to live under a conventional developmental regime. But no system becomes morally acceptable only on the grounds that human

creativity or ingenuity has not yet found a better system. Nor does any system acquire an intrinsic moral stature or the right to snuff out alternative human possibilities by virtue of the fact that earlier systems were worse. For some reason, development has claimed such a stature and the rights that flow from it, and this claim is backed by development's alleged ability to remove poverty.

At the end, an autobiographical footnote. I have two brothers, both reasonably well-to-do by Indian standards. In interviews to newspapers and journals and in private they have said more than once that they come from a poor family. And I remember one enthusiastic interviewer who came close to discovering a "log cabin to white house" trajectory in our lives. Frankly, I have had the same upbringing as my brothers and I have never felt that we experienced poverty in our childhood. In my memory, our childhood was no different from the middle class upbringing many other Indians have experienced.

My brothers genuinely believe we were deprived because their standards have in the meanwhile changed. At one time, they seemed to have a different vision of prosperity and poverty. One of them, I remember, refused to refurnish his apartment after he joined a multinational corporation because he did not want his old friends to feel diffident when they visited him. Changing circles of friends, economic success, and growing exposure to the global middle class culture do change worldviews. The meaning of poverty itself expands to include many kinds of lifestyle that in another time would have qualified as a reasonably good life. As the idea of a "normal" life changes, so do the concepts of subnormality and abnormality. They begin to include things that were once a part of normality. It is a bit like modern concepts of mental illness, which now include many states of mind that once were considered part of normality and are still considered normal in many societies. Many problems of living have been medicalized and are now handled through elaborate psychopharmaceutical interventions.[26]

This is not spectacularly new. It is something like the changing concept of long life in a country where life expectancy is on the rise. Problems arise when the myths of permanent youth and immortality take over and we get busy keeping time at bay through cosmetics, tonics and fashionable technologies like cardiac bypass, designed mainly to bypass the fruits of overconsumption. I have now come to suspect that the shifting definition of poverty never allows one to remove destitution. It keeps people like us constantly busy pulling ourselves above an ever-shifting, mythic poverty line into a concept of "normal" life that should look less and less normal to socially sensitive psychologists, psychiatrists and psychoanalysts. Even though I might sound like a world-renouncing ascetic or a hard-boiled Gandhian, I cannot help echoing the Jaina philosopher and editor of *Resurgence*, Satish Kumar, and claim that poverty is not the problem, our idea of prosperity is.[27]

This is not a rehash of the nineteenth-century socialist rhetoric, which saw property as the original sin. That belief overlay the fantasy that in the end, natural resources being infinite, socialized property would make everyone prosperous; only in the short run did one have to pauperize the wealthy to ensure justice. Mine is an effort to capture the tacit faith of tens of thousands of social and political activists and environmentalists, who often include our own children. They constitute today a global underworld, a substratum of consciousness that defies at every step the mainstream culture of global economics. Frequently they go about their job foolishly, sometimes hypocritically, but occasionally with a degree of ideological commitment and moral passion, too. However woolly-headed they may look to us, we shall have to learn to live with that underworld in the new century. (The World Bank and the International Monetary Fund obviously understand this better than do many of their naïve supporters among journalists and corporate executives. Their spokespersons have had to repeatedly affirm, after the Seattle and Washington demonstrations during 1999-2000, that the Bank and the IMF shared the values of the demonstrators, who otherwise were misinformed or misguided.)

I seem to have come full circle. I now find that I have given you a strange, internally inconsistent set of arguments. On the one hand, I have argued that poverty cannot be eliminated through development because there seems to be an iron law of

democratic politics in large, multi-ethnic, diverse societies. This law ensures that once a sizeable majority of the population comes within the patronage structure of either the state or the modern political economy, the electoral fates of regimes and parties begin to be determined by issues other than poverty and poverty-induced human suffering. Indeed, development may or may not remove poverty in large, diverse, open societies, but it always tends to produce destitution. I have also suggested that the developmental regime can often serve as a psychological regime, and help us cultivate a social deafness and moral blindness toward parts of the living world around us.

On the other hand, I have argued that poverty cannot be eliminated because it is in many countries an ever-expanding concept and because true or absolute poverty, which I have called destitution, is usually a small part of it. Taking advantage of this psychological elasticity, the so-called mainstream culture of politics encourages you to work hard to remove your own poverty before bothering about the destitution of the others. For the latter you reserve the beauties of the trickle-down theories. However, the two propositions may not be as orthogonal as they look. I shall wait for my more knowledgeable economist friends and development experts to educate me on this score and help remove the anomaly. In the meanwhile, like M. K. Gandhi — the insane, subversive stepfather of the Indian nation-state — I recommend that we try to get rid of destitution and learn to live with poverty, at least ours.

Author's Note

Earlier versions of this paper were presented at the annual convention of the International Studies Association, Chicago, 22-25 February 2001 and as the Vincent Tucker Memorial Lecture given at the University of Cork, Ireland on 30 April 2001.

NOTES

1. Joint report of the Center for Budget and Policy Priorities and the American Foundation for Families, quoted in Majid Rahnema, "Global Poverty:

A Pauperising Myth,"*Intercultural* 14, No. 2 (Spring 1991), p. 21n. According to Michael Harrington, 5 million American children live in poverty. On poverty amidst plenty see Michael Harrington, *The American Poverty* (Harmondsworth, U.K.: Penguin, 1984).

2. Anna Lou De Havenon, "Globalisation and Increased Poverty in the United States Since 1970s: New York City as a Case Study," International Workshop on Poverty, Marginalisation and Development, New Delhi, 3-5 February 1996.

3. Cardinal Paulo Everisto Arns, "Sincerity Is Subversive," *Development*, No. 3 (1985), pp. 3-5, quoted in Rahnema, "Global Poverty," p. 31.

4. See, for instance, Stephen I. Schwartz, ed., *Atomic Audit: The Costs and Consequences of U.S. Nuclear Weapons Since 1940* (Washington, D.C.: Brookings Institution Press, 1998).

5. Two issues are especially relevant here, though they may look like digressions from the main concerns of this paper. First, even though students of political culture have not paid any attention to it, in the long run, the political cultures of countries that can but would not remove poverty cannot but be fundamentally different from that in countries that cannot remove poverty in the short run, even if they want to. All societies thrive on their distinctive structures of the ego defense of denial, but the first kind of societies have to structure this denial in a particular way, lest it collapses and that collapse begins to shape public consciousness. A certain mix of extraverted optimism and lonely consumerism is often an indirect by-product of this particular structure of denial. Second, do prosperous, diverse societies *need* poverty, in the sense that poverty plays an unrecognized, functional role in such societies? Many years ago, a structural-functionalist indeed argued this in the pages of a journal of sociology.

6. Majid Rahnema says, in "Global Poverty":
To what extent, if any, have various actions and interventions actually alleviated the sufferings caused by various forms of unwanted or unjust poverty? A first look at the state of the art seems to indicate that, despite the confluence of good intentions and many "campaigns," "wars" and "crusades" against poverty, the human sufferings

related to the concept are spreading. The claims of economic development to wipe out the causes of these sufferings have been far from being kept. In the meantime, only new, modernized forms of poverty have been added to the old list. Are the reasons for this inadequacy due to minor, managerial or temporary reasons, or do they raise more fundamental questions touching upon the very structures of the societies concerned? (p. 5).
See also Michael Chossudovsky, *The Globalisation of Poverty: Impacts of IMF and World Bank Reforms* (Goa, India: The Other India Press, 1997).

7. Quoted in Barbara Crossette, *New York Times*, September 27, 1998. Tariq Banuri warns me that such figures can often be untrustworthy and politically tinged. Once again, I remind the reader that I am not concerned here with the actual, empirically verifiable state of affairs, but the psychological "structures" with which the mainstream, global culture of politics lives.

8. Graham Hancock, *Lords of Poverty* (London: Mandarin, 1989). From Hancock's estimate it appears that, by the end of the 1980s, the development aid industry – only a small part of the global poverty alleviation bureaucracy — was already one of the world's largest multinational corporations (p. 45). The data on India are particularly disturbing in this respect. Antipoverty programmes spend Rs 200 billion annually. Of this only a fifth, roughly Rs 40 billion, reach the poor (Sunil Jain, "This One's for 'run Shourie'," *Indian Express*, April 29, 2000, p. 8). There is not much scope for debate on the subject. One Indian prime minister, Rajiv Gandhi, went to town with a similar set of data.

9. V.M. Dandekar and Nilakantha Rath, *Poverty in India* (Poona, India: Indian School of Political Economy, 1971), Ford Foundation Series.

10. Gurcharan Das, "Viewpoint," *The Times of India*, December 4, 1995; and "Our Second Independence," *The Times of India*, July 23, 1995.

11. "Gurcharan Das, "India Is Outpacing Poverty," *The Times of India*, March 24, 1996; and C. Rammanohar Reddy, "Poverty: Is the Decline Real?" *The Hindu*, January 19, 1996. Das also mentions that "spectacular" developmental success has brought down the percentage of people below the

poverty line from 58 to 17 during 1972-82 in Indonesia, 37 to 14 during 1973-87 in Malaysia, and from 49 to 26 during 1962-86 in Thailand. Yet he does not ask (1) why even in such small countries the success has not brought down the figures spectacularly below that of an unsuccessful country like India and (2) whether, even before the Southeast Asian economic crisis, removal of poverty went any further.

12. S.P. Gupta, "Trickle Down Theory Revisited: The Role of Employment and Poverty," Lecture at the Annual Conference of the Indian Society of Labour Economics, reported in "Has Poverty Worsened with Reforms," *The Hindu*, December 30, 1999.

13. *Economic and Political Weekly*, March 24, 2001; and Anna Panchayat, A Public Hearing on Hunger, Food Rights and Food Security, organized by the Research Foundation for Science, Technology and Ecology, New Delhi, India May 30-31, 2001.

14. Deepak Lai, Rakesh Mohan, and I. Natarajan, "Economic Reforms and Poverty Alleviation: A Tale of Two Surveys," *Economic and Political Weekly* March 24, 2001, pp. 1017-1028.

15. Not that the fate of the idea of poverty has been particularly dignified in economics and the other social sciences. I am reminded of the particularly insightful comment of Lakshman Yapa that "poverty does not reside exclusively in the external world independent of academic discourse that thinks about it; the discourse is deeply implicated in creating poverty insofar as it conceals the social origins of scarcity. Although the experience of hunger and malnutrition is immediately material, 'poverty' exists in a discursive materialist formation where ideas, matter, discourse, and power are intertwined in ways that virtually defy dissection." (p. 7 in "What Causes Poverty? A Postmodern View," *Annals of the Association of American Geographers* 86, No. 4 (1996), pp. 707-728.

16. Frances Moore Lappe, Joseph Collins, and Peter Rosset, *World Hunger: Twelve Myths* (New York: Grove Press, 1998), 2nd ed.

17. Rabi Ray, Inaugural address at Anna Panchayat, New Delhi, May 30-31, 2001.

18. Draft, Tenth Plan of the Planning Commission, Government of India, quoted in "PDS has Missed

Target: Planning Commission," *The Times of India*, June 7, 2001.

19. Anil Gupta, *Why Does Poverty Persist in Regions of High Biodiversity: A Case for Indigenous Property Right System*, Working Paper No. 938, mimeo (Ahmedabad, India: Indian Institute of Management, 1991).

20. Amrita Patel in her J.R.D. Tata Oration on Business Ethics, 1999, quoted in Rajni Bakshi, "Redefining Progress," *The Hindu*, December 12, 1999.

21. For a recent work that indirectly but powerfully argues this point, see *The Spirit of Regeneration: Andean Culture Confronting Western Notions of Development*, ed. Frédérique Apffel Marglin with PRATEC (Proyecto Andino de Tecnologias Campesinas, Peru) (London and New York: Zed Books, 1998). For an example of a work on precolonial India that takes this point of view see Dharampal, *Beautiful Tree: Indian Education in the Eighteenth Century* (New Delhi, India: Biblia Impex, 1983).

22. Rahnema, "Global Poverty," p. 44; Ivan Illich, *Celebration of Awareness* (London: Calder and Boyars, 1971); and *Toward a History of Needs* (New York: Pantheon Books, 1977). Also, A. Tevoedjre, *Poverty: Wealth of Mankind* (Oxford: Oxford University Press, 1979).

23. Naresh Singh, "The Wealth of the Poor," *Choices* 5, No. 2 (October 1996), pp. 12-13.

24. Rajni Kothari's *Growing Amnesia* (New Delhi, India: Penguin, 1996; London: Zed Books, 1996) supplies some clues to the political conditions under which the politics of poverty declines in importance in an open society. On the absence of economic democracy and its relationship with hunger, see Lappe, Collins, and Rosset, *World Hunger*.

25. Ashis Nandy, "Development and Violence," in Charles Strozier and Michael Flynn, eds., *Trauma and Community, Essays in Honour of Robert J. Lifton* (New York: Rowman and Littlefield, 1996), pp. 207-218.

26. I am reminded of the particularly insightful comment of Lakshman Yapa that "poverty does not reside exclusively in the external world independent of academic discourse that thinks about it;

discourse is deeply implicated in creating poverty insofar as it conceals the social origins of scarcity."

27. Satish Kumar, "Poverty and Progress," *Resurgence* 196 (September-October 1999), p. 6; and John Gray, "The Myth of Progress," Ibid., pp. 11-13, are only two of the more recent writers who have reemphasized this old formulation.

EQUALITY ANALYSIS:
LOCAL AND GLOBAL RELATIONS OF POWER

Christine M. Koggel

Christine Koggel teaches in and is currently Chair of the Department of Philosophy at Bryn Mawr College. She is the author of Perspectives on Equality: Constructing a Relational Theory *(1998), editor of* Moral Issues in Global Perspective *(first edition, 1999 and second edition, 2006), and co-editor with Wesley Cragg of* Contemporary Moral Issues *(fourth edition, 1997 and fifth edition, 2004).*

Koggel applies relational insights from feminist and postcolonial theory to economic globalization as a way of examining traditional liberal accounts of inequality. Focusing on relationships instead of individuals reveals that equality analysis needs to be much more complex than traditional liberalism would suggest. A relational approach allows us to attend to the details of the lives of those who are affected by unequal and oppressive relationships, ones that are in turn shaped by social practices in particular locations, by features of the global context, and by the intersections of the local and the global. Koggel argues that we obtain a more accurate analysis of inequalities when we take into account perspectives of people in relationships of power and oppression in their diverse and interlocking forms at the global and local levels than we do when we examine individuals abstracted from their contexts and relationships.

---

1. Introduction

Samantha Brennan writes that "the reshaping of moral concepts in light of feminist critiques of individualism and feminist development of relational alternatives represents significant progress in feminist ethics, indeed in ethics at large."[1] This appraisal of "progress in feminist ethics" serves as a starting point for applying a relational approach to inequalities in a global context in three ways. First, equality is a moral concept that has been and continues to be central to Western liberal theory, a theory that now dominates the world scene. Second, by using relationships, rather than individuals, as the focal point of analysis, a relational approach allows us to challenge the adequacy of individualist accounts in the global context. Third, relational insights from feminist ethicists and postcolonial feminists can be used to capture the complexity of equality analysis in the contemporary context of globalization.

An approach that focuses on relationships rather than individuals has several advantages. It is contextual rather than abstract. It allows us to attend to the details of the lives of those who are affected by unequal and oppressive relationships, ones that are in turn shaped by social practices in particular locations, by features of the global context, and by the intersections of the local and the global. Other moral theories such as utilitarianism and virtue ethics are also sensitive to context, but the relational account of equality that I defend has at least two distinctive features, both of which will be central to the analysis of equality in Sections 3, 4, and 5 below. By focusing on relationships of oppression and inequality and on how lives are shaped by them, a relational approach (1) uncovers the governing norms and practices that sustain inequalities of various sorts for those who are powerless and disadvantaged and (2) reveals the importance of the perspectives of those adversely affected by these relationships as resources for learning about various kinds of inequalities and the structures that sustain them. Other features important to the contextual, detailed, and perspectival nature of a relational approach emerge from these two central features.

A focus on relationships shows the interconnectedness of kinds of equality. It is not as simple as formulating a precise and abstract conception of equality as opportunity or wealth or resources or life prospects or results or well-being. A critical analysis of the network of relationships in which someone is situated can show how an account of resources or well-being, for example, is integrally connected with an account of the opportunities that people in relationships of inequality or oppression actually have. It can show that a person's opportunities are limited by oppressive relationships at the level of both the personal and political in ways that determine the resources one gets and even the perceptions of what one deserves or is capable of. For example, being disabled in our society affects how one is perceived by others, the job opportunities to which one has access, and the level of income one gets. The high costs of health care and transportation specific to kinds of disability along with a trend of cuts to welfare programs then work to entrench inequalities of well-being, self-respect, life prospects, and participation for those who are disabled.

A relational approach also has us pay attention to the ethos, the attitudes that reflect the set of norms within which relationships are embedded in particular contexts. This is important because working to change an ethos that upholds beliefs and sentiments that perpetuate inequalities will be part of what is needed to alleviate inequality.[2] These points about the relevance of an ethos support the argument that what justice demands is not limited to our interactions in a public sphere or to institutional structures: each of us in our day-to-day lives has a responsibility to learn about relationships of power and oppression and to change beliefs that perpetuate them. It should now be apparent that a focus on relationships highlights the complexity of the concept of equality, a feature that is needed when we move to an analysis of inequalities in the global context.

2. Globalization: Inequalities Within and Across Borders

International relations, markets, development, human rights, migration, nationhood, the environment, labor, technology, language and culture, tourism, population growth, education, health care, and poverty are just some of the phenomena being reshaped by globalization. In general terms, globalization represents increased flows of technology, trade, information, markets, capital, and people themselves. While current anti-globalization protests and movements have made people aware of many of the negative effects of globalization, it is fair to say that not everything that has emerged from a context of globalization has been or needs to be harmful or damaging. Technology has caused various environmental disasters, greatly reduced diversity in plant and animal species, and created weapons of mass destruction. But technology has also saved, prolonged, and improved human lives; made the fixing of (some) environmental problems possible; and created devices that increase leisure time and enhance human well-being. Information and communication networks have changed the way people organize, work, and live and have allowed us to learn about and interact with people from all parts of the world. But the Internet has also allowed a global traffic in arms, drugs, and the sex trade and made detection of these crimes much more difficult. Increased migration has threatened the continued existence of cultures once isolated from the world and exacerbated problems of health, unemployment, and overpopulation in greatly expanded urban areas. But migration has also enriched cultural and linguistic life in places that were once closed to difference and has pushed ethicists to develop accounts of human rights and development that are more sensitive to the richness of cultures and the diversity of values in them. Larger and more open markets have provided jobs for people where little opportunity existed before. But the corporate quest for profit has also resulted in the exploitation of workers in Third World countries and the destruction of families, communities, and the environment when corporations move to countries with even lower wage labor.

These brief descriptions show that we have to consider globalization piece by piece. They also suggest a feature of a relational approach already identified: the importance of a contextual analysis. Fair judgments about negative and positive effects need detailed descriptions of the places, people, factors, and time frame. Yet, there is one overarching factor in these descriptions: we live in a context of economic globalization, one where the dominance of markets, multinational corporations, international financial institutions and trade organizations, and neo-liberal policies structure major aspects of globalization that then shape relationships and their effects on people. While the hope was and continues to be that economic globalization may create opportunities, ease suffering, and reduce poverty, statistics show that there are ever-growing gaps between the rich and the poor both within and across borders.

The United Nations millennium report, *We the Peoples*, opens its chapter "Freedom from Want" with this description: "Nearly half the world's population still has to make do on less than $2 per day. Approximately 1.2 billion people — 500 million in South Asia and 300 million in Africa — struggle on less than $1 ... Of a total labour force of some 3 billion, 140 million workers are out of work altogether, and a quarter to a third are underemployed."[3] In a report by the Inter-American Development Bank, Nancy Birdsall writes that "the ratio of average income of the richest country in the world to that of the poorest has risen from about 9 to 1 at the end of the nineteenth century to at least 60 to 1 today. ... Today, 80 percent of the world's population lives in countries that generate only 20 percent of the world's total income."[4] The United Nations Development Program's (UNDP) *Human Development Report 1999* discloses that "people living in the highest-income countries had 86% of world GDP — the bottom fifth just 1%. ... The world's 200 richest people more than doubled their net worth in the four years to 1998, to more than $1 trillion. The assets of the top three billionaires are more than the combined GNP of all least developed countries and their 600 million people."[5] In its *Human Development Report 2003*, the UNDP assesses the UN millennium goals of ending

poverty and then declares that "despite these welcome commitments in principle to reducing poverty and advancing other areas of human development, in practice — as this Report makes very clear — the world is already falling short. ... More than 50 nations grew poorer over the past decade. Many are seeing life expectancy plummet due to HIV/AIDS. Some of the worst performers — often torn by conflict — are seeing school enrolments shrink and access to basic health care fall. And nearly everywhere the environment is deteriorating."[6]

Inequalities are not limited to huge gaps in wealth between rich and poor countries. It is well known that an ever-growing gap between the rich and the poor, increased levels of poverty, and high incidences of child poverty characterize some of the richest countries in the world. In its most recent report *Child Poverty in Rich Countries 2005*, UNICEF reports that "the proportion of children living in poverty in the developed world has risen in 17 out of the 24 OECD nations for which data are available." It then notes that Denmark and Finland rank high with the proportion of children in poverty at less than 3 per cent and that "at the bottom are the United States and Mexico where child poverty rates are higher than 20 per cent."[7] It would seem that learning about high rates of child poverty in the U.S. should translate into massive citizen protest and the political will to redistribute the vast wealth concentrated in the hands of an increasingly small percentage of Americans. Yet, this is not the effect on many who learn that more than one child out of five lives in poverty in the richest country in the world. In Section 3, I examine this phenomenon using G.A. Cohen's notion of an ethos, a concept that explains that a liberal egalitarian mindset has lost sway in many Western liberal societies and been replaced by complacency about high levels of poverty — a set of beliefs and attitudes, as Ashis Nandy tells us in his paper in this chapter, that requires "enormous psychological resources to ensure that they do not interfere with our 'normal' life by burdening us with a crippling sense of guilt."[8]

Most of the reports cited thus far concentrate on inequalities in wealth and income. These inequalities are emphasized in national reports and measured by numerous international and intergovernmental organizations. To get an idea of the real complexity of equality analysis and relational theory's ability to capture it, we also need to become aware of inequalities at the global level and in local contexts that are often missed in accounts that focus on inequalities in wealth. Some of these inequalities are mentioned in the *Human Development Report 2003* cited above: inequalities in health care, education, and environmental degradation. Others are inequalities based on factors such as gender, race, ethnicity, and disability and the various intersections of them. I discuss these inequalities in the sections that follow, but for now will briefly describe one of them, gender inequality as outlined in Chapter 5 of the 2000 report *The State of World Population.*[9] This United Nations Population Fund (UNPF) report lists gender inequalities in virtually all parts of the globe: rates of infant and maternal mortality; access to health care; incidences of violence and abuse; opportunities for education and literacy; representation at all levels of political and managerial workforce participation; employment and income; material resources such as land, homes, and credit; and decision-making power and leisure time in the home.[10]

These gender inequalities persist both in Western liberal democracies and Third World countries when factors such as race, class, ethnicity, and disability as well as the impact of features of globalization are taken into account. The UNPF lists some of the detrimental effects of gender inequality: it diverts resources from women's activities, often in favor of less productive investment in men; it obstructs social and economic participation and closes off numerous productive alternatives; and it "reduces women's effectiveness by failing to support them in meeting their responsibilities, challenges and burdens."[11] Two features of a relational approach noted in the introduction are worth repeating here.

First, these descriptions illuminate the interconnectedness of inequalities in opportunities, well-being, resources, participation, life prospects, and so on. Inequalities in one domain such as health care or education or workforce participation are connected with and have an impact on inequalities in the distribution of goods. Inequalities in the distribution of goods sustain inequalities in health care, education, reproductive choice, and participatory activity. Second, a contextual analysis shows that factors such as gender, race, ethnicity, disability, and class often determine who is disadvantaged and what inequalities they suffer. Not only do we need to identify inequalities in wealth and its effects on people, but we need to identify who is affected to understand how factors such as gender, race, disability, and so on work at both the local and global levels to create or sustain inequalities of various sorts. With its attention to relationships of power and oppression, a relational account is well positioned to identify the people disadvantaged by their membership in particular groups and the inequalities experienced by them. These inequalities are particularly pernicious in the context of multinational corporations and global capitalism.

While it is too quick to say that globalization as such has caused the kinds of inequalities described thus far, it is fair to say that multinational corporations, international financial institutions and trade organizations, and economically powerful countries do not have the reduction of inequalities as their main focus or motivation. It is also fair to say that relationships of interdependency and dependency characterize the global scene and that they are manifested in relationships of power between countries and peoples that are rich and poor, Western and non-Western, First and Third World, North and South. Examining these unequal relations and the inequalities that result from them will be the topic of Section 4 below.

I have taken some time to describe inequalities both within and across borders and at the local and global levels because we need to have them before us as we set out to show how an approach that scrutinizes relationships of power and oppression and those harmed by them can provide a needed corrective to abstract theories of equality and to oversimplified accounts of inequalities. To understand the global scene more clearly, I begin by applying a relational approach to inequalities in

our own context. As suggested above, liberal egalitarian ideals that advocate redistributive measures
to reduce inequalities in wealth seem to be losing
force in the contemporary global context. They
play a smaller role now in the mindset of many
Americans, for example, than when Rawls wrote *A
Theory of Justice*.[12] And as has just been shown, in
the current context of global markets and multinational corporations, the trend is in the opposite
direction: ever-greater gaps in wealth and persistent, increasing levels of poverty within the borders
of rich countries.

3. Inequalities in Wealth: Norms, Perspectives, and Ethos

Egalitarians occupy many parts of the political
spectrum, but what their accounts have in common
is attention to issues of distribution and specifically to the distribution and redistribution of
income and wealth. In *If You're an Egalitarian,
How Come You're So Rich?* Cohen distinguishes
two varieties of egalitarianism:

> One may distinguish, broadly, between egalitar-
> ian principles which locate value in equality
> properly so called, which is a relation between
> what different people get and which is strictly
> indifferent to how much they get, and egalitarian
> principles (like Rawls's difference principle)
> which affirm not, strictly speaking, equality
> itself, but a policy of rendering the worse off
> people as well off as possible. We can call the
> first sorts of egalitarians "relational egalitarians"
> and the second "prioritarians," since they assign
> priority to improving the condition of the worst
> off.[13]

Relational egalitarians, sometimes referred to as
radical, socialist, or Marxist egalitarians, argue that
the concept of equality is first and foremost a distributive ideal and that achieving an equal distribution of resources satisfies the principle of equality.
In other words, gaps in wealth matter to relational
egalitarians, who are sensitive to the connection
between those with wealth and those with power.
Prioritarians, or those referred to as liberal egali-

tarians, take equality to be primarily a social and
political ideal as captured in a substantive account
of equality of *opportunity*. For them, an account of
the fair distribution of goods emerges after the
basic institutional structures satisfying the principle of treating people with equal concern and
respect are in place. For liberal egalitarians such as
Rawls, treating people with equal concern and
respect (the first principle of justice) permits
inequalities in wealth (the second principle of
justice) as long as these inequalities benefit the
least well off.

An initial response is that both accounts fall
short of capturing the complexity of equality
analysis and the interconnectedness of kinds of
inequalities that I have defended so far. In agreement with relational egalitarians, I want to say that
equality is indeed a relational concept. To judge
inequalities is to compare the situations and conditions of particular people in relation to particular
others. But the relational approach to equality I
advocate will not want these comparisons to be
made in a general and abstract way or be limited to
issues of distribution. Relational and all other egalitarians pay attention to how people fare in relation
to others, but a relational approach is critical of
focusing on how some people fare compared to
others in terms of specified material goods. It will
thus be the case that the "relational" egalitarianism
Cohen identifies is distinct from my relational
approach to equality.

Equality involves more than equalizing distribution or bettering the situation of the worst off in
terms of material goods. Against prioritarians, we
need detailed and reliable information about the
situation of the worst off: who the people are; the
network of personal and public relationships they
are in; and what sorts of social practices create and
sustain inequalities in opportunities, life prospects,
resources, and so on for some members. Having
more money may improve the material conditions
of the worst off, but it may not advance other
equalities such as participation as a respected
member of society, being able to voice objections
to policies that affect one's livelihood and well-
being, or being treated with equal concern and
respect. Against relational egalitarianism, various

inequalities that it misses are highlighted when we attend to how people actually fare relative to others in terms of what they are able to do with the goods they have or are allotted. More equal amounts of income might not increase opportunities for those who cannot use public transportation or get into workplaces or benefit from employment training. And self-respect, which is vitally important to being treated with equal concern and respect, is not the kind of social good that can be obtained through a redistribution of income or material goods.

A relational approach to equality has us examine the details of concrete kinds of relationships and the shaping of them through particular social practices and in specific contexts, including the global context in which we now live. A central aspect of the relational approach I advance, one that differs from and builds on early accounts of the ethic of care, is to expand the network of relationships beyond those of dependency on which feminists, and care ethicists in particular, have tended to focus. "Relations of power, oppression, dominance, exploitation, authority, and justice form identities and self-concepts just as much as relations of dependency, benevolence, care, self-sacrifice, and friendship do."[14] Expanding the network of relationships under examination returns us to the features identified in the introduction as distinctive to a relational approach to equality. First is the importance of revealing the norms, standards, and practices that are in place and to which those who are in relationships of power and oppression need to respond. Second, the perspectives of those in relationships of oppression are important vantage points for understanding inequalities and what is needed to remove them. We can now apply these two features of my relational approach to an analysis of inequalities in our own society.

Beliefs that people living in poverty or on welfare are lazy and responsible for their state of affairs are prevalent in our society. An account that reveals the governing norms and accepted practices and that takes perspectives seriously holds that we cannot make general statements about responsibility, laziness, or even lack of contribution to a society until we know a lot more about the particularities of people's lives. For example, it is relevant to an analysis of equality to learn that statistics show a strong correlation between those who are living in poverty and those who are members of particular groups: women, disabled people, and people of color. Once we know this, it is difficult to justify their greater representation in the ranks of the poor by explaining that all members of these disadvantaged groups deserve less by way of material and social goods or that they just lack the abilities needed to compete for or obtain material and social goods. The attention to detail that a relational approach allows highlights poverty as, in large part, a feature of the systematic and systemic oppression of already disadvantaged group members.

Three examples will help to elucidate how a relational approach is important for revealing norms and challenging policies that support them. To qualify for welfare, the single mother who needs to prove that she cannot "work," when she considers child rearing to be valuable work, is forced to accept these norms about the meaning of work and to reject her own priorities and values regarding children. If the income she gets through welfare cannot cover the cost of childcare or job training, she often becomes trapped in a cycle of poverty: unable to get a job because she cannot afford childcare; without access to job training and thus dependent on the (often restricted) income from the state; or forced to find any job even if the pay cannot cover the cost of childcare or the childcare she gets is inferior to what she herself can provide. Disabled people can more easily "prove" that they cannot "work," but getting a fixed income determined as sufficient for meeting the basic needs of an able-bodied person will not address the specific needs of being unable to use public transportation or get into workplaces or pay for expensive medical devices and treatment above what an income for basic goods can provide. Lastly, the combination of low minimum wages and high costs of living make it virtually impossible for the working poor in the U.S. to pay for food and shelter even when they do double shifts of day and night work. These facts about the lives of the working poor are portrayed vividly in Barbara

Ehrenreich's *Nickel and Dimed*.[15] Ehrenreich temporarily gave up her life as a reporter to take minimum wage jobs in different parts of the U.S. only to learn that many people who work long and hard hours still live in poverty, unable to afford housing or basic needs such as food and clothing. The result in all three cases of knowing the details of actual lives and of kinds of people who are poor undermines stereotypes of the poor as lazy, taking easy handouts, or unknowledgeable about spending money.

Judgments made about inequalities already assume background structures and policies that in turn shape the relationships of power, inequality, and oppression that are central to the lives of those who are disadvantaged. We need to be aware of the relationships in which people who are judged to be worse off are embedded and by which their lives are then shaped. An examination of relationships can reveal the ways in which factors such as gender, race, and disability often determine who is in relationships of oppression and who suffers inequalities of various kinds and at various levels. It can also reveal the ways in which structures of power sustain and perpetuate particular sorts of inequalities. Finally, it can reveal the ways in which the opportunities, life prospects, well-being, and resources of people who are disadvantaged are often determined by those in power in ways that generate and entrench inequalities in these and other domains.

Not only do we need to attend to relationships in their multifarious forms and as they are shaped by particular practices and contexts, but we also need to ask who does the judging about the inequalities and who has the power to set policies for addressing them. This aspect of what it means to make judgments is obvious, but easily missed. When I judge someone to be worse off, I am likely to be comparing that person to someone who is better off. In other words, comparisons always take for granted a particular perspective from which judgments of inequality are made. When the perspectives assumed and reflected in norms, standards, and practices are those of the advantaged, various inequalities suffered by members of traditionally disadvantaged groups are missed or ignored. On

my account, the perspectives of those who are disadvantaged are taken to be valuable vantage points for revealing these inequalities.

Perspectives can reveal the entrenched attitudes, beliefs, and justifications that have the effect of maintaining the structures and policies that perpetuate conditions of inequality for many. Learning about these conditions from the perspectives of those whose lives are lived in relationships of inequality, oppression, and power is a key element in the relational approach I defend. Taking these perspectives seriously will not be easy. Prevailing stereotypes result in the kind of powerlessness that makes what those who are disadvantaged say about their conditions or about the structures that perpetuate them appear to be irrelevant, ungrateful, or even wrongheaded. When these stereotypes are internalized, self-respect is destroyed and the resulting self-doubt can have a silencing effect. Inequality is as much about issues of powerlessness, loss of dignity and respect, and exclusion from one's community and meaningful participation in it as it is about having less wealth. Giving voice to the powerless and disadvantaged means providing conditions that support attempts to be heard, to be considered, and to contribute to and participate in social and political institutions.[16] Taking perspectives seriously goes a long way to uncovering the norms, practices, beliefs, and structures that constitute the ethos, an ethos that in turn shapes the relationships in which people are embedded and the opportunities that individuals in them have.

Cohen defines the ethos of a society as "the set of sentiments and attitudes in virtue of which its normal practices, and informal pressures, are what they are."[17] As noted in the previous section, the contemporary context reflects an ethos that is even further removed from the liberal egalitarian ideals espoused by Rawls, ideals that endorsed minimal gaps in wealth. The American context can be said to be characterized by an ethos of citizens who seemingly accept high levels of poverty and great disparities in wealth, both within and across borders. Part of the reason for this, as Nandy explains in his paper in this chapter, is the context of globalization itself that has changed the face of poverty and our ability to care about it by focusing on and putting faith in the belief that economic processes can and will improve people's lives and the opportunities they have. The beliefs and sentiments that shape such an ethos are part of the relational context that needs to be considered, and changing this ethos will be part of what justice demands. Such an ethos is bound to have an effect on relationships by shaping and sustaining ones that limit opportunities and hinder prospects for the well-being of some people.

The dominant ethos in an increasing number of liberal societies shows entrenched beliefs about people on welfare as failing to measure up, not pulling their own weight, and taking easy handouts. More generally, those who are poor are not perceived as people who have managed to make it on their own by using their talents, working hard, managing their finances well, and contributing to the wealth of the country. In fact, they are often held to be responsible for the state in which they find themselves. Many people believe that welfare policies need provide only the bare minimum in income and should force welfare recipients to prove that they cannot work — because only these measures, they hold, will encourage people to get off welfare and take responsibility for removing themselves from the ranks of the poor.

This ethos begins to explain why having one child out of five living in poverty in the richest country in the world has elicited little by way of citizen protest or political action. It begins to explain why the question that is the title of Cohen's book is such an unpopular and difficult question in our times. It is all too easy to be complacent and accepting of conditions and economic trends that we feel powerless to change. After all, inequality in wealth is a global phenomenon, and it is what is supposed to produce greater wealth so that all can benefit. On my account, and on Cohen's, being able to ask the question, "how come you're so rich?" reveals the importance of challenging the prevailing ethos and of taking responsibility for the choices we make day to day and every day.

Revealing and analyzing power and oppression as it exists and operates in a network of both personal and public relationships extends the scope of justice beyond that of institutional structures and into the realm of individual lives and choices. A relational approach to equality holds people accountable for their beliefs, perceptions, and treatment of fellow citizens and for their moral choices in interaction with others. It points to the importance of perspectives by asking people to learn how policies and practices affect the opportunities, well-being, resources, and life prospects of people different from themselves. Responsible learning makes it more difficult to justify having more wealth relative to others based on unexamined beliefs about the necessity of monetary incentives or the inevitability of large disparities in wealth or the unavoidable advance of economic globalization, beliefs that are entrenched in many liberal societies today.

A relational approach both draws attention to the kinds of relationships that shape the ethos in particular contexts and permits an analysis of those relationships that are damaging to individuals, group members, and whole communities. It asks people to be accountable in their daily lives for having inaccurate beliefs: the stereotypes they have and the claims they make about people living lives very different from their own. It urges people to develop dispositions that can correct wrong beliefs and judgments and that can pick out details relevant to a proper analysis of inequalities. These dispositions cannot be developed on one's own or with like-minded people. They develop in interaction with others, particularly with those who can challenge prevalent beliefs and change the dominant ethos. A relational approach emphasizes the relevance of the perspectives of those in relationships of powerlessness and oppression for a full understanding of the prevailing ethos and of what is needed to change it.

This approach — namely, analyzing oppressive relationships in their multitudinous forms and the perspectives of those in them — is all the more powerful in an increasingly interdependent world that reflects the rise and effects of capitalism, multinational corporations, international financial institutions and trade organizations, and neoliberal policies. There are lessons to be learned from Asuncion Lera St. Clair's account that suggests that globalizing trends are beginning to threaten and undermine the ethos of solidarity that has shaped Norway's domestic and foreign policies as it becomes ever more situated in relationships of interdependency with other European Union countries, global financial institutions, and international bodies and agencies. There are also lessons to be learned from Ingrid Robeyns's account of how the greater interdependency of European Union countries encourages policies of cutting social welfare programs, even in those countries once committed to strong welfare programs. From these theorists, we learn about the strength and impact of factors of economic globalization. There are also lessons to be learned, however, about challenges to global trends in places such as Norway, Belgium, the Netherlands, and Brazil that are resisting pressures to cut social welfare programs. These challenges suggest that beliefs that are part of our dominant ethos can be changed and that we have a responsibility to remove our own complacency about high levels of poverty. These challenges also suggest that we can learn from countries whose ethos has been shaped by a history of paying attention to how inequality in the domain of wealth, for example, can generate inequalities in other domains of opportunities, well-being, agency, participation, self-respect, and so on.

In the introduction, I suggested that the contemporary context of the ascendance of neo-liberal policies and capitalist structures to the global scene calls for a critical reappraisal of concepts and values at the heart of liberal theory. I rejected the individual as the primary and isolatable unit for equality analysis because I view this approach as hindering a proper evaluation of the relationships of power and oppression in which individuals, group members, and whole states are embedded. We do not have a full account of inequalities experienced by individuals when we abstract them from their relationships and circumstances. Kinds of inequality experienced by the single mother on welfare, for example, become more apparent when we pay attention to the network of relationships, both personal and public, that shape her life and circumstances. In the contemporary context of globalization, relationships of

power are magnified, not only in terms of economic power but also in terms of vastly different cultures and values as reflected in relationships described in the dichotomies of developed/developing, Western/Non-Western, North/South, and First World/Third World. A relational approach is well equipped for illuminating the increasingly complex kinds of inequalities that are thereby generated.

4. Equality Analysis in a Global Context

In Section 2, I described the negative aspects of globalization as emerging from the dominance of markets and multinational corporations and the power they have to determine policy in areas such as trade, development, migration, the environment, labor, technology, language and culture, education, health care, and poverty. An analysis of equality in a global context needs to be informed about these economic features and processes of globalization. Globalization in the realm of economic relations has meant that markets and corporations in First World countries can extend their reach across borders, sometimes with devastating consequences for people in Third World countries. Commodities for consumption by people in rich countries can be manufactured by forced child labor or for starvation wages in poor countries where there are often no worker rights of health or safety protection and where union organizing is actively discouraged. Third World countries with little or no environmental protection legislation can have their resources degraded or depleted by multinational corporations that accumulate vast amounts of wealth of which corporate executives and investors are often the sole beneficiaries. If citizens of a country protest, multinational corporations can easily move to more politically stable investment zones, thereby putting pressure on governments of poor countries to squelch citizen protest within their own borders.

Feminist postcolonial theory is useful for telling us why an account of inequality needs to uncover the ways in which power at the global level of multinational corporations and financial institutions intersects with and utilizes power at the local level of beliefs, norms, practices, and traditions.[18]

In the process of providing this context specific and detailed analysis, we uncover the ways in which local understandings of gender, race, caste, and disability, for example, are often employed by multinational corporations in ways that perpetuate inequalities in some domains or create new ones in specific locations. This kind of analysis reveals how forces of power at the global level sometimes intersect with, sometimes utilize, sometimes desta-bilize, sometimes improve, and sometimes inten-sify relations of power at the local level and always in diverse and complicated ways. This information is needed if effective policies for addressing power imbalances created by ever-growing gaps in wealth within and between rich and poor countries are to be devised.

Chandra Mohanty's work exemplifies this strat-egy of emphasizing the importance of the overar-ching factor of economic globalization and paying attention to its specific manifestation at local levels where members of disadvantaged groups are affected in varied ways. Mohanty argues that we need to know about the ways in which factors of race, class, and ethnicity intersect with and also reflect, shape, and sustain relations of power in specific contexts. She borrows insights from femi-nist economists in her detailed descriptions of women's work to undermine ahistorical and uni-versal accounts of experiences shared by women,[19] whether Third World women or all women in the workforce. Commonalities then emerge from these detailed descriptions of the concrete realities of the lives of working women in specific contexts.[20] Importantly, a recognition of forces of power at the global level is never far away in the analysis of the local. This strategy of disclosing how relationships of power at the global level shape relationships of inequality and oppression at the local level can be further illustrated by examining Elisabeth Fussell's work on the female maquiladora labor force in Tijuana, Mexico.

Fussell shows how multinational corporations in Third World countries can keep production costs and wages lower than they can in First World countries, where labor laws specify minimum wages and conditions of work. She points out that since the 1970s, "when global trade began to inten-

sify, new production and labor-control technolo-gies and competition between low-wage produc-tion zones combined to make the cost of labor the most variable component of production."[21] To attract multinational corporations and under pres-sure through the North American Free Trade Agreement (NAFTA), the Mexico government implemented policies such as the dismantling of independent labor unions and the lowering of maquiladora wages to the "lowest of developing countries with strong export marketing sectors."[22]

In Tijuana, positioned at the northern border of Mexico and supplying textiles and electronics products for the U.S., Mexican women, who are already perceived and perceive themselves as sec-ondary wage earners supplementing men's wages, become ready suppliers of low-wage labor. More-over, multinational corporations have learned that labor costs can be kept even lower when they tap into the market of women who are the most disad-vantaged in the labor force: married women, women with children, and women and girls with little or no education. These women are perceived as and have proven to be docile and accepting of the challenges demanded by tedious assembly processes. They are less likely to risk losing their jobs through labor resistance than those who are more qualified and likely to demand higher wages and better working conditions. Fussell argues that if there was ever any potential to improve the lives of women in Mexico by providing them with jobs, it has been "lost to the search for low wages and a flexible labor force."[23]

Fussell's study shows that details matter for understanding the ways in which the lives of women maquiladora workers are affected by multi-national corporations and markets. Details matter for another reason too. In the short time since Fussell's study, conditions have changed yet again as men from rural communities are now being recruited to work in some maquiladoras and as other maquiladoras are closing down as markets in other countries with even lower wages open up.[24] Nonetheless, lessons from Mexico about exploita-tive working conditions and the disempowerment of workers subjected to them point us back to the overarching interests of global markets and multinational corporations in utilizing gendered and racialized meanings in specific locations so that wages are kept low and workers are deterred from organizing and protesting.

I need to clarify that I do not dispute the positive effects that multinational corporations have had on individual lives, in families, and for communities as a whole. They have provided job opportunities, increased household income and national wealth, and decreased unemployment rates. Rather, a relational approach warns that these distributional measures do not give us an adequate account of the inequalities that remain or are created by the changed conditions. A closer examination of how multinational corporations, with a vested interest in maximizing profits and minimizing costs, utilize entrenched meanings of gender and class in places such as Tijuana, highlights the importance of knowing these details for a full understanding of inequalities created and perpetuated in the global context.

Fussell's study undermines the idea that women necessarily benefit or benefit in all areas of their lives when they have jobs. There are many factors, both local and global, that are relevant to identifying inequalities, some that may be alleviated in particular locations or in specific domains of a person's life and others that are created or exacerbated in other locations and domains. Global corporate employers often utilize specific sectors and features of labor markets in Third World countries to the detriment of groups already disadvantaged. Changing local factors can generate further exploitation of workers when, for example, government policies are dictated by trade agreements, or a falling currency, or unemployment rates, or the exit of multinational corporations into more profitable locations. Other local factors such as discrimination of ethnic minorities or of members of particular groups can also determine who gets to work, what kind of work they get to do, and whether they can be active participants in the work place or society more generally. Providing details of places, practices, policies, and people is central to an adequate analysis of equality.

Earlier I said that a relational approach highlights the complexity of equality. Embracing the complexity also means that at the same time as inequalities are brought to light in particular places, through particular policies, and in the lives of particular people, attention can be paid to the positive changes that emerge, ones that can in turn shape policies that promote other changes. Examining the lives, relationships, and possibilities for change highlights the significance of an account of norms, perspectives, and ethos to an analysis of inequalities in a global context. This examination also underscores the difficult but vital importance of responsible learning in a global context in which relationships of power between rich and poor countries and between those holding Western and non-Western values prevail.

In a global context, responsible learning will be arduous and demanding at both the global and local levels and from the outside and on the inside. Detailed and contextual analyses will need to be revised in light of the constant, changing effects of economic globalization in international, national, and local contexts.[25] Possible negative effects of economic globalization in addition to those already mentioned will need to be taken into account. For example, how gender, race, class, ethnicity, and disability are understood most often reflects the Eurocentrism and ethnocentrism of rich Western countries, as is evident in many policies tied to aid and development projects and imposed on Third World countries. Furthermore, the imposition of these meanings of gender, race, and class on Third World countries contributes to and sustains inequalities at the local level. The meanings of gender, race, class, and ethnicity can also be redefined or reified by those in power at the local level in ways that structure the value of work and who gets to do it. These are but some places where an analysis of relationships of power and oppression can inform, complicate, and give substance to equality analysis at the global and local levels. We obtain a more accurate account of various kinds of inequalities through the description and analysis of relationships of power and oppression in its multifarious and interlocking forms at the global and local levels than we do when we examine individuals abstracted from contexts and the relationships they are in. An account of women's experiences as told in narratives and manifested in grassroots activities and sites of resistance needs to be central to shaping policy. Moreover, the enhanced understanding of inequality gained from taking perspectives seriously is vital for conceiving people as agents who in forming coalitions at local and global levels can devise effective policies for alleviating the specific effects of poverty in their own locations.

I began by providing descriptions of inequalities in wealth, both within and across borders. These are important starting points from which a relational interpretation of these facts reveals the importance of analyzing relationships of power and oppression at both the local and global levels. We do not have sufficient information about inequalities and how to eliminate them until we know about interpersonal relationships in particular locations where norms, practices, beliefs, and political and economic circumstances shape the lives of different citizens differently. A context of ever-greater levels and kinds of inequalities brought on by the increasing power and domination of multinational corporations, international financial institutions and trade organizations, and global capitalism makes feminist work on equality pressing and urgent. In the contemporary global context, the complexity of equality analysis steadily increases. An account of how relationships of power at the global level intersect with, exploit, or interrupt relationships of power at the local level reveals inequalities that are otherwise easy to miss. The global context requires that we challenge traditional liberal accounts of equality and what to do to promote it. An approach that has relationships as its focus of analysis is, I have argued, well equipped to provide this critique and to capture the complexity of the concept of equality and the effects of inequality on the lives of millions living in poverty.

Author's Note

An earlier and longer version of this paper appeared in the *Canadian Journal of Philosophy, Supplementary Volume: Feminism and Moral Philosophy*, v. 33, no. 2 (2003). I want to thank the editor of that volume, Samantha Brennan, whose interest in and critical comments on my relational approach to equality have been important to the development of it. I also want to thank Elisabeth Boetzkes, Sue Campbell, Steve Ferzacca, Virginia McGowan, Kai Nielsen, Christine Overall, Sally Scholz, Susan Sherwin, Bob Ware, and Karen Wendling. As always, I am grateful to Andrew Brook's unfailing support and keen critical eye.

NOTES

1. Samantha Brennan, "Recent Work in Feminist Ethics," *Ethics*, v. 109 (1999): 890.

2. In "Norway: The Development Ethic of a Donor Country" (in this chapter), Asuncion St. Clair describes the ethos that has shaped Norway's long history of social and political commitment to reducing inequalities within its own borders and to alleviating poverty in other countries. She argues that this strategy of describing historical contexts within which values are shaped can inform development ethics more generally by identifying what may be needed to change prevailing attitudes about poverty.

3. United Nations, *We the Peoples: The Role of the United Nations in the 21st Century* (New York, NY: Department of Public Information, 2000) 19. The UN millennium report then calls on the international community to "adopt the target of halving the proportion of people living in extreme poverty, so lifting more than 1 billion people out of it, by 2015" (20).

4. Nancy Birdsall, "Life is Unfair: Inequality in the World," in *Annual Editions, Developing World 01/02*, edited by R J. Griffiths (Guilford, CT: McGraw-Hill/Dushkin, 2001) 8.

5. United Nations Development Program, *Human Development Report 1999* (New York, NY: Oxford University Press, 1999) 3.

6. United Nations Development Program, *Human Development Report 2003* (New York, NY: Oxford University Press, 2003) v.

7. United Nations Children's Fund, *Child Poverty in Rich Countries 2005*. Report no. 6. (Florence: UNICEF, 2005) 3.

8. Ashis Nandy, "The Beautiful Expanding Future of Poverty: Popular Economics as a Psychological

Defense," *International Studies Review*, v. 4 (Summer 2002): 111 (reprinted in this chapter).

9. United Nations Population Fund, *The State of World Population 2000* (UNPF, 2000).

10. Amartya Sen has done extensive work on gender inequality. In *Development as Freedom*, he writes that the "extensive reach of women's agency is one of the more neglected areas of development studies, and most urgently in need of correction. Nothing, arguably, is as important today in the political economy of development as an adequate recognition of political, economic and social partic- ipation and leadership of women. This is indeed a crucial aspect of 'development as freedom,'" Amartya Sen, *Development as Freedom* (New York, NY: Anchor Books, 1999) 203.

11. United Nations Population Fund 1.

12. John Rawls, *A Theory of Justice* (Cambridge, MA: Harvard University Press, 1971).

13. Rawls 162.

14. Christine M. Koggel, *Perspectives on Equality: Constructing a Relational Theory* (Lanham, MD: Rowman & Littlefield, 1998) 163.

15. Barbara Ehrenreich, *Nickel and Dimed: On (Not) Getting By in America* (New York, NY: Henry Holt, 2001).

16. Jean Harvey provides a good, thorough account of speaking, protesting, being heard, and being con- sidered as relational rights owed to those who are powerless in her *Civilized Oppression* (Lanham, MD: Rowman & Littlefield, 2001).

17. Harvey 28.

18. Some examples of this work are in M. Jaqui Alexander, and Chandra Mohanty (editors), *Feminist Genealogies, Colonial Legacies, Democratic Futures* (New York, NY: Routledge, 1997); and Uma Narayan, and Sandra Harding (editors), *Decentering the Center: Philosophy for a Multicultural, Postcolonial, and Feminist World* (Bloomington, IN: Indiana University Press, 2000).

19. Chandra Mohanty, "Under Western Eyes: Feminist Scholarship and Colonial Discourses," *Feminist Review*, v. 30 (1988): 61-88.

20. Chandra Mohanty, "Women Workers and Capitalist Scripts: Ideologies of Domination, Common Inter- ests, and the Politics of Solidarity," in *Feminist Genealogies, Colonial Legacies, Democratic Futures*, edited by M.J. Alexander and C. Mohanty (New York, NY: Routledge, 1997) 7, her emphasis.

21. Elisabeth Fussell, "Making Labor Flexible: The Recomposition of Tijuana's Maquiladora Female Labor Force," *Feminist Economics*, v. 6 (2000): 60.

22. Fussell 64.

23. Fussell 60.

24. I thank Kai Nielsen and Verónica Vázquez Garcia for alerting me to these recent changes in the work- force composition of maquiladoras.

25. Christine M. Koggel, "Globalization and Women's Paid Work: Expanding Freedom?" *Feminist Eco- nomics, Special Issue: Amartya Sen's Work and Ideas*, v. 9, no. 2 (2003).

STUDY QUESTIONS

1 What are the distinctions between private, collective, and common property as outlined by Jeremy Waldron? What does Waldron mean when he claims that every society has private, collective, and common property and that property rules differ from society to society with respect to determining the balance and degree of each? How is this account of property relevant to his discussion of the issue of homelessness?

2 How does Waldron's examination of the plight of the homeless undermine liberal assumptions about the connection between property rights and freedom? What particular restrictions on freedom does he identify with respect to the homeless? What implications does his account have for policies with respect to the homeless?

3 How does Waldron answer the objection that "our society gives everyone the *opportunity* to acquire a home, and that we are all — the homeless and the housed — equal in *this* regard even if we are unequal in our actual ownership of real estate"? Are you convinced by Waldron's answer? Has Waldron changed your understanding of homelessness and your perceptions of homeless people? Why or why not?

4 Ingrid Robeyns contrasts beliefs about equality of opportunity prevalent in the U.S. (and evident in Waldron's depiction of those beliefs) with those in many Western European countries that support strong welfare measures. Would Waldron's account support the strengthening of welfare measures in the U.S.? Robeyns reports that there is a weakening of welfare measures in Western European countries. Why is this so?

5 What is "basic income" and why does Robeyns think that contemporary conditions call for the reexamination of basic income as a viable policy for addressing poverty in Europe and the world as a whole?

6 Do you agree with Robeyns that basic income should be treated as a right of economic citizenship in the same way as the right to vote is treated as a right of political citizenship? Why or why not? Should this right be universal? Does Robeyns view it as such? Defend your answers.

7 What are the practical and moral arguments that Robeyns uses to defend the idea of basic income? Do you find them convincing? Are some stronger than others? If so, which ones?

8 Do you think that basic income would further entrench gender roles? How does Robeyns answer this worry? Do you find her answer convincing? Why or why not?

9 Summarize Asuncion Lera St. Clair's account of the development of Norway's commitment to helping the poor, both inside and outside Norway. Do you agree with St. Clair that tracing this history is instructive with respect to understanding what might be needed to promote values of helping those in need? Provide reasons for your answer.

10 Why is it important for St. Clair to explain that Norway's continuing commitment to values of solidarity and justice was shaped by the participation of groups at all levels in Norway and throughout its history? Can you envision the possibility for such citizen initiative and involvement in countries where there hasn't been a commitment to helping the poor as a matter of justice?

11 What, if any, policies are suggested by St. Clair's account of the history and development of Norway as a leading country in foreign aid? Did learning about Norway influence your thinking about your own country and the obligations of rich countries to provide aid to poor countries?

12 Why is Ashis Nandy skeptical of defining poverty and providing numbers of those who count as poor? Why does he call these projects "psychological ego defenses"?

13 What is destitution and what causes it? Does Nandy's understanding of destitution challenge definitions of poverty? Does it challenge policies with respect to development?

14 Do you agree with Nandy that many people do not know they are poor until economists and politi-
    cians tell them they are? Is Nandy guilty of romanticizing poverty? Can standards change so that
    people who did not believe they were poor come to believe they were? Provide reasons for your
    answers.
15 What does Nandy mean when he says that he has provided "a strange, internally inconsistent set of
    arguments"? Do you agree? Why or why not?
16 How is Christine Koggel's analysis of the impact of globalization on understandings and levels of
    poverty different from Nandy's?
17 According to Koggel, how does a relational approach to equality challenge the individualist approach
    evident in traditional liberal theory? What are features of this approach that make it an appropriate
    tool for analyzing equality in the global context?
18 Are perspectives important to an understanding of poverty? How does taking them into account chal-
    lenge current definitions and understandings of poverty? Does it raise questions about poverty as dis-
    cussed by other authors in this chapter? Provide reasons for your answers.

SUGGESTED READINGS

Alkire, Sabina. *Valuing Freedoms: Sen's Capability Approach and Poverty Reduction*. Oxford: Oxford
    University Press, 2002.
Arthur, John. "Rights and the Duty to Bring Aid." In *World Hunger and Moral Obligation*, edited by
    William Aiken and Hugh LaFollette. Englewood Cliffs, NJ: Prentice Hall, 1977.
Barry, Brian. "Humanity and Justice in Global Perspective." In *Nomos XXIV: Ethics, Economics and the
    Law*, edited by J.R. Pennock and J.W. Chapman. New York, NY: New York University Press, 1982.
Belsey, Andrew. "World Poverty, Justice and Equality." In *International Justice and the Third World:
    Studies in the Philosophy of Development*, edited by Robin Attfield and Barry Wilkins. London:
    Routledge, 1992.
Cohen, G.A. "Incentives, Inequality, and Community." In *The Tanner Lectures on Human Values*, v. 13,
    edited by Grethe B Peterson. Salt Lake City, UT: The University of Utah Press, 1992: 261-329.
— . *If You're an Egalitarian How Come You're so Rich?* Cambridge, MA: Harvard University Press,
    2000.
Coole, Diana. "Is Class a Difference that Makes a Difference?" *Radical Philosophy*, v. 77 (May/June
    1996): 17-25.
Commoner, Barry. "Population and Poverty." In *Making Peace with the Planet*. New York, NY: Pantheon
    Books, 1990.
Ehrenreich, Barbara. *Nickel and Dimed: On (Not) Getting by in America*. New York, NY: Henry Holt.
    2001.
Fraser, Nancy. "Women, Welfare, and the Politics of Need Interpretation." In *Unruly Practices: Power,
    Discourse, and Gender in Contemporary Social Theory*. Minneapolis, MN: University of Minnesota
    Press, 1989.
Fraser, Nancy, and Linda Gordon. "'Dependency' Demystified: Inscriptions of Power in a Keyword of
    the Welfare State." *Social Politics*, v. 1 (1994): 4-31.
Galbraith, James K. "A Perfect Crime: Inequality in the Age of Globalization." *Daedalus*, v. 131, no. 1
    (Winter 2002): 11-35.
Gasper, Des. *The Ethics of Development: From Economism to Human Development*. Edinburgh: Edin-
    burgh University Press, 2004.
Govier, Trudy. "The Right to Eat and the Duty to Work." *Philosophy of the Social Sciences*, v. 5 (1975):
    125-43.

Hardin, Garrett. "Carrying Capacity as an Ethical Concept." *Soundings*, v. 59, no. 1(1976): 120-37.

Kahn, Herman. "The Confucian Ethic and Economic Growth." In *The Gap Between Rich and Poor*, edited by Mitchell A. Seligson. Boulder, CO: Westview Press, 1984.

LaPaglia, Nancy. "Working-Class Women as Academics: Seeing in Two Directions, Awkwardly." In *This Fine Place So Far From Home: Voices of Academics from the Working Class*, edited by C.L. Barney Dews and Carolyn Leste Law. Philadelphia, PA: Temple University Press, 1995.

Landes, David. *The Wealth and Poverty of Nations: Why Some Are So Rich and Some So Poor.* New York, NY: Norton, 1998.

Little, Daniel. *The Paradox of Wealth and Poverty: Mapping the Ethical Dilemmas of Global Development.* Boulder, CO: Westview Press, 2003.

Marin, Peter. "Helping and Hating the Homeless." *Harper's Magazine* (January 1987).

O'Neill, Onora. *Faces of Hunger: An Essay on Poverty, Justice, and Development.* London: Allen Unwin, 1986.

Peckham, Irvin. "Complicity in Class Codes: The Exclusionary Function of Education." In *This Fine Place So Far From Home: Voices of Academics from the Working Class*, edited by C.L. Barney Dews and Carolyn Leste Law. Philadelphia, PA: Temple University Press, 1995.

Piper, Deborah. "Psychology's Class Blindness: Investment in the Status Quo." In *This Fine Place So Far From Home: Voices of Academics from the Working Class*, edited by C.L. Barney Dews and Carolyn Leste Law. Philadelphia, PA: Temple University Press, 1995.

Pogge, Thomas W. *World Poverty and Human Rights: Cosmopolitan Responsibilities and Reforms.* Cambridge: Polity Press, 2002.

Sen, Amartya. "Population: Delusion and Reality." *The New York Review of Books* (22 September 1994): 62-71.

— . *Poverty and Famines.* Oxford: Oxford University Press, 1981.

— . "Poverty as Capability Deprivation." In *Development as Freedom*. New York, NY: Random House, 1999.

— . "Property and Hunger." *Economics and Philosophy*, v. 4 (1988): 57-68.

Shaffer, Paul. "Poverty Naturalized: Implications for Gender." *Feminist Economics*, v. 8, no. 3 (November 2002): 55-75.

Singer, Peter. "Famine, Affluence, and Morality." *Philosophy & Public Affairs*, v. 1, no. 3 (1972): 229-43.

— . *One World: The Ethics of Globalization.* New Haven, CT: Yale University Press, 2002.

ACKNOWLEDGEMENTS

"Human Functioning and Social Justice: In Defence of Aristotelian Essentialism" by Martha C. Nussbaum in *Political Theory*, v. 20, no. 2, 1992: 202-246. Reprinted with permission of the publisher.

"Insiders and Outsiders in International Development" by David A. Crocker in *Ethics & International Affairs*, v. 5, 1991:149-173. Copyright © Carnegie Council on Ethics and International Affairs. Reprinted with permission of the publisher.

"Cloning Cultures: The Social Injustices of Sameness" by Philomena Essed and David Goldberg in *Ethnic and Racial Studies*, v. 25, no. 6, November 2002: 1066-1082. Reprinted with permission of the publisher.

"The New Sovereignty" by Shelby Steele in *Harper's Magazine*, July 1992: 47-52. Copyright © 1992 Harper's Magazine, all rights reserved. Reprinted with special permission of the publisher.

"Social Movements and the Politics of Difference" by Iris Marion Young in *Justice and the Politics of Difference*. Princeton: Princeton University Press, © 1990: 156-173. Reprinted with permission of the publisher.

"Moral Deference" by Laurence Thomas in *The Philosophical Forum XXIV*, Fall-Spring 1992- 93: 233-250. Reprinted with permission of the publisher.

"Racisms" by Anthony Appiah in *Anatomy of Racism*. Edited by David Theo Goldberg, University of Minnesota Press, 1990: 3-17. Reprinted with permission of the publisher and Anthony Appiah.

"Future Genders? Future Races?" by Sally Haslanger. Published with permission of the author.

"White Women Feminist" by Marilyn Frye in *Overcoming Racism and Sexism*. Edited by Linda Bell and David Blumenfeld. Lanham: Rowman & Littlefield, 1995: 113-134.

"Reflections on the Meaning of White" by Victoria Davion in *Overcoming Racism and Sexism*. Edited by Linda Bell and David Blumenfeld. Lanham: Rowman & Littlefield, 1995: 135-139. Reprinted with permission of the publisher.

"Invisibility is an Unnatural Disaster: Reflections of an Asian American Woman" by Mitsuye Yamada in *This Bridge Called My Back: Writings by Radical Women of Color*. Edited by Cherrie Moraga and Gloria Anzaldua. New York: Kitchen Table, Women of Color Press, 1983: 35-40.

"Beauty is the Beast: Psychological Effects of the Pursuit of the Perfect Female Body" by Elayne A. Saltzberg and Joan C. Chrisler in *Women: A Feminist Perspective*. Edited by Jo Freeman. Fifth Edition. Mayfield Publishing, 1995: 306-315. Reprinted with permission of the author.

"Justice and the Distribution of Fear" by Keith Burgess-Jackson in *The Southern Journal of Philosophy*, v. XXXII, Winter 1994: 367-391. Reprinted with permission of the publisher.

"Gender Inequality and Cultural Differences" by Susan Moller Okin in *Political Theory*, v. 22, no.1, February 1994: 5-24. Reprinted with permission of the publisher.

"Under Western Eyes: Feminist Scholarship and Colonial Discourses" by Chandra Mohanty in *Feminist Review*, no. 30, Autumn 1988: 61-88. Reprinted with permission of the author.

"The Good Terrorist: Domesticity and the Political Space for Change" by Janice Newberry. Published with permission of the author.

"Is it Wrong to Discriminate on the Basis of Homosexuality?" by Jeffrey Jordan in *Journal of Social Philosophy*, v. 26, no. 1, Spring 1995: 39-52. Reprinted with permission of the publisher.

"Heterosexuality and Feminist Theory" by Christine Overall in *Canadian Journal of Philosophy*, v. 20, no. 1, March 1990: 1-18. Reprinted with permission of the publisher.

"Sexuality Injustice" by Cheshire Calhoun in *Notre Dame Journal of Law, Ethics & Public Policy*, v. 9, no. 1, 1995: 241-274. © 1995 Cheshire Calhoun. Reprinted with permission of the author.

"Against Marriage and Motherhood" by Claudia Card in *Hypathia*, v. 11, no. 3, Summer 1996: 1-23. © 1996 Claudia Card. Reprinted with permission of the publisher.

"Power and Sexuality in the Middle East" by Bruce Dunne in *Middle East Report*, no. 206, Spring 1998: 8-11 and 37. Reprinted with permission of MERIP, Middle East Research and Information.

"Disability, Discrimination, and Fairness" by David Wasserman in *Report from the Institute for Philosophy & Public Policy*, v. 13, no. 4, Fall 1993: 7-12. Reprinted with permission of the publisher and David Wasserman.

"(In)Equality, (Ab)normality, and the Americans With Disabilities Act" by Anita Silvers in *The Journal of Medicine and Philosophy*, v. 21, 1996: 209-224. © 1996 Swets & Zeitlinger Publishers. Reprinted with permission of the publisher.

"Uniting the Nation? Disability, Stem Cells, and the Australian Media" by G. Goggin & C. Newell in *Disability and Society*, v. 19, no. 1, January 2004: 47-60. Reprinted with permission of the publisher.

"On the Government of Disability" by Shelley Tremain in *Social Theory and Practice*, v. 27, no. 4, October 2001: 617-636. Reprinted with permission of the publisher.

"Homelessness and the Issue of Freedom" by Jeremy Waldron in *UCLA Law Review*, v. 39, 1991: 295-324. © 1991, The Regents of the University of California. All rights reserved. Reprinted with permission of the publisher and Jeremy Waldron.

"Reforming the Welfare State: The Case for Basic Income" by Ingrid Robeyns. Published with permission of the author.

"Norway: The Development Ethic of a Donor Country" by Asuncion Lera St. Clair. Published with permission of the author.

"The Beautiful, Expanding Future of Poverty: Popular Economics as a Psychological Defence" by Ashis Nandy in *International Studies Review,* v. 4, no. 2, Summer 2002: 107-121. Reprinted with permission of the publisher.

"Equality Analysis: Local and Global Relations of Power" by Christine M. Koggel. Published with permission of the author.

The editor of the book and the publisher have made every attempt to locate the authors of copyrighted material or their heirs and assigns, and would be grateful for any information that would allow them to correct any errors or omissions in a subsequent edition of the work.